CRESTWOOD HEIGHTS

A STUDY OF THE CULTURE OF SUBURBAN LIFE

CRESTWOOD HEIGHTS

A STUDY OF THE CULTURE OF SUBURBAN LIFE

John R. Seeley

R. Alexander Sim

Elizabeth W. Loosley

INTRODUCTION BY DAVID RIESMAN

UNIVERSITY OF TORONTO PRESS

WHEN I was in the middle of the manuscript of *Crestwood Heights*, I had the good luck to attend a meeting in Park Forest, a new-model suburb which is comparable to Crestwood Heights in the intensity with which it has been studied. The meeting was addressed by William H. Whyte, Jr. of *Fortune*, its imaginative, incisive, and not unsympathetic main surveyor. En route to the meeting Whyte observed that, when he had been interviewing in Park Forest, he had had the strange feeling of being virtually the only male in the place during the daytime; the men were all at work downtown or at various plants around Chicago, and there were some joking references to his being loose in a harem. Moreover, the problems to which he had addressed himself in his justly famous series of articles on Park Forest had frequently been those felt most keenly by the home-bound wives: problems of sociability and privacy in the rental courts; of the limits of idiosyncracy in décor; of how to put down roots while remaining, on behalf of their husbands' careers, potential transients. At the meeting where he was asked to speak, however, Whyte was surrounded—and kept at a distance from the mixed audience—by a panel composed entirely of men; these, and their friends in the first several rows of the audience, asked him questions largely of a technical "male" sort, e.g., concerning social science methodology or zoning regulations; only one woman managed to get in a word during the entire evening. Many of the questions were hostile, and appeared to spring from resentment of the possibility or claim that an outsider could learn anything that was not obvious to the local experts and founding fathers of 1947–48, the date of first settlement.

This volume by Seeley, Sim, and Loosley makes several important contributions to understanding such encounters. A brilliant chapter is devoted to the "triangle" between male experts and researchers, their female clients, and the latter's husbands. The husbands work all day in the city; they pride themselves on being practical, no-nonsense men— a pride partly maintained by polarizing themselves from their allegedly emotional, starry-eyed wives; they are willing to buy (and bury) social science in personnel and marketing departments(as one appurtenance, thanks in part to the corporation tax, of their being up-to-date), but not in affairs pertaining to their suburb and its schools. The wives have the leisure and education and energy to make a career out of suburbia— and to be anxious about themselves and their children. The social science experts, often marginal members of new professions, require lay co-operation in order to have subjects, financing, and the prestige some- times denied them in the scholarly world. These experts, much like artists, appear male vis-à-vis their female clients, counsellees, and de- votees, but not quite manly to the latter's spouses. The experts also have the advantage of being in the community in the daytime, and of having prestige in the eyes of subsidiary experts such as school teachers, social workers, and other semi-professionals of limited theoretical pretensions. It is understandable that the husbands, uneasy in any case because they are wedded to their work and only peripherally to their families, resent the experts with their psychological know-how, their intimate knowl- edge of the community, and their permissive notions of child-rearing (Whyte's notions were quite different, but this did not save him from triangulation).

The concern that Seeley, Sim, and Loosley have with this triangle and its dangers for all parties concerned—not least the expert, whose success with a lay public will divorce him still further from his academic colleagues—is part of a wider concern which runs through the book for the consequences of social research upon the communities (and other "objects") studied. Anthropologists have developed an ethical program to protect the tribes they visit from being unduly influenced by their presence, or that of other Westernized people; cultural relativ- ism is part of this program, with its now much qualified mandate of equal detachment from all cultures, a mandate as it were of attachment to the principle of culture as such. In their efforts to combat the paro- chialism and ethnocentrism of missionaries and administrators, they have until recently been able to aim their research reports entirely at their audience at home; by definition, "their" tribe would not read what was written about them, and would presumably be disturbed as little as possible by having an anthropologist living unassumingly among them, seeking to learn their language and sympathetically to under- stand their values. But today it gets harder and harder to find "uncontaminated" tribes and to assume one can leave them that way (Mrs. Bowen's *Return to Laughter* beautifully indicates the complexities and moral ambiguities involved), and anthropologists have become much more sensitive to their subjects as the world has shrunk. When the Lynds published their first *Middletown* book and when W. Lloyd Warner came back from an Australian tribe and started work on the "Yankee City Series," social science was directly plunged into the problem of reporting on its subjects to its subjects. Witness *Point of No Return*.

Seeley and his collaborators, like their predecessors in American community studies, have—unlike the *Fortune* articles—granted a kind of courtesy anonymity to their suburb, more as a sign of goodwill than in any hope that one can hide so distinctive a feature of the landscape as Crestwood Heights. But the authors collide, like Whyte, with a problem their predecessors only brushed against, for they are writing about *us*, about the professional upper middle class and its business man allies, not about a New England museum for the upper class, such as Yankee City, or a small and rather parochial town in the South or Midwest, such as Jonesville or Elmtown. They are writing, as they are almost too aware, about themselves, their friends, their "type" (I "type" the authors, of course, no doubt unjustly, by treating the trio as if they were one person). Moreover, the enterprise on which they report involved much more than simply a one-shot data-gathering expedition; this was "action research," with teams of clinicians for the school children, discussion leaders for the school teachers and parents (as implied above, only the mothers, by and large, took part), and leaders of Human Relations classes in the schools—classes in which the young people were encouraged, quite bravely, to bring up any problems of concern to them. In the High School, many of the suburban teen problems of parents, cars, sex, cliques arose, along with Crestwood Heights' exceptional sensitivity to inter-ethnic (mainly, Jewish-Gentile) amity; there also arose some very probing questions concerning the search for personal identity and integrity. So intertwined, in fact, is the research with the community that this book gives the impression that its authors are still stuck in the tar-baby; their moral intensity about their task and their responsibilities both as researchers and as reporters is, in all its humorlessness and intensity, rare and admirable.

I have occasionally asked novelists how they feel about using their friends and families, barely disguised, in an autobiographical book. Usually, if they have thought about the question at all, the immensely powerful ideology of *l'art pour l'art*, developed for use against the

Philistines, suffices to dismiss any scruples. Moreover, partly because of this ideology, writers have a vanity that researchers repress or seldom gain; as one, whose whole family garnishes a lurid novel, told me, "My book will be alive when all my family is dead"; his implication was they should be grateful for this immortality. To be sure, Randall Jarrell's *Pictures at an Institution* bursts with its tirade against a lady novelist who "heartlessly" cases a college community (the book in turn cruelly cases the lady). But Jarrell, as befits the author of *The Age of Criticism*, is unusually self-conscious about reflexivity for a literary man; most novelists so far as I can make out (Thomas Wolfe is a notable exception) take exploitation of their "material" for granted.

As I have implied, the consciences of the authors of *Crestwood Heights* are so involved with their research experience that I wish at times they had had the novelist's insouciance as well as the novelist's sensitivity to anxiety and other forms of mental suffering among the well-to-do. I myself often prefer, for reasons which I'm sure won't stand full examination, to suppose that social scientists exaggerate their power for weal or woe—hence in such cases as this their feelings of responsibility. Most social scientists, however, duck such moral issues by believing only in their subjects' subjectivity and not in their own, or by seeking to couch their findings in an opaque language which their subjects can presumably not decipher or which in any case is believed to be free from bias. Whatever discomfort is associated with the path chosen by Seeley, Sim, and Loosley, I will take it any day over the self-deceptions and ethical insensitivities of the majority. The authors of *Crestwood Heights* are not purse-proud about their professional training (and they lack the innocence of supposing that technical terms can long conceal one's values); one result is that there is not a line in this book with which I would suppose an educated non-professional reader will have any serious difficulty. In some measure, I rather regret this, for it means that the writing, for my taste, is not sufficiently dense and allusive; everything is painstakingly spelled out. And in one respect this prolixity is perplexing, for if one assumes that readers and subjects are, apart from accidents of residence, the same people, then one would not need all the ethnographic detail which overburdens this book. Though the authors have a keener eye for moral impasse and arabesque than for the material culture or for the merely sociable, they insist on telling us what the houses are like, or the orbits of time and season, and there is a long chapter on summer camps which seems to assume that the reader will neither have seen such a camp nor sent his children there. This chapter, incidentally, has a waspishness of tone—though not a penetration of idea—reminiscent of Mary McCarthy. And camps of course, with their pseudo-Indian lore, their parents who seek surrogates to toughen and discipline their children, their counsellors who "goof off," are easy targets for satire. Elsewhere in the book, one feels that the authors are trying not to be too severe on their own kind, not to join the current intellectual critique of liberal middle-class professional people, such as make up a considerable part of the population, as well as the leadership, of Crestwood Heights. But it is hard for description not to become parody when we are reading, not about strata or tribes remote from us, but about our own suburban (or in the case of the camps, in Spectorsky's phrase, "exurban") life. Compare the following, from the description of a presumably typical family:

Despite these separate rounds of activity, which intersect only occasionally (the husband states: "I am home so little, I only see the kids for an hour in the evening, that is if I'm not going off to a meeting"), the affection on the part of the children towards each other and their parents is demonstrative and this behavior is given high approval. . . . The giving of presents in this family is a highly regarded token of love and esteem. An equally strong norm, on the other hand, insists upon separate activities for each member of the family, with less frequent events in the nature of holiday or anniversary celebrations involving the whole group (the summer holiday together must be planned for a year or more in advance). Only a high degree of efficiency (faintly reminiscent of that of a well-run club or office) in operating the household makes this individualistic pattern of outside activities workable at all. The actual help given by the children can be symbolic only; more helpful, and unusual, is the presence of the same maid with this family over a six-year period.

Veblen knew that the apparently deadpan could be devastating, and part of Mary McCarthy's genius is to be able to say, for instance, that "the professor came into the room carrying his briefcase" so that the descriptive remark appears to undress him, to show him as he really ridiculously is, without pretence or illusion. But when I read such a passage as the one quoted above, and many like it, I wonder whether it is I who bring to the material a sardonic reaction or whether I find it there, in the use of the term "efficiency," in the comparison with the club or office, and in the awkwardness—neither quite jargon nor quite literature—of such phrases as "highly regarded token of love and esteem."

Readers will have to answer such questions for themselves, but it is part of the context that it is the very niceness of the Crestwood Heights people that lays them open to scrutiny either by the researchers or by the readers. The suburbanites (or at least the women and experts)

invited the research team in; they welcomed long and probing interviews and tests, in a way that less agreeable and perhaps less vulnerable
people would not have done. (It is perhaps an aspect of this ethos
which leads Crestwood Heights, if not always to welcome the influx of
Jews, at least not to tolerate any restrictions or quotas.) The same
defencelessness of Crestwood Heights appears in its devoutness, the
women's that is, towards each passing fad in child-rearing, and in the
social and psychological professions generally. The authors could not
help but be struck by the way in which mothers rejected their own
experience in favor of some formula—and if the researchers criticized
the formula they were themselves in danger of becoming the new priests,
only to be overthrown in turn. The anthropologist who goes into a culture that has successfully hardened against white contact does not face
this danger, nor does the industrial sociologist, whom the workers in a
factory regard as a tool or fool of management or of themselves. But
every perceptive teacher does have the experience of fearing a disciple-
ship which robs the student of independence, and might even prefer
students' disdain to their passivity. As I have already indicated, it is the
researchers' own niceness and defencelessness that makes them aware
of the ethical ambiguities of their invasion of Crestwood Heights; under
the circumstances, they could hardly be expected to possess the serene
confidence in science, in evidence, that a Martin Arrowsmith struggled
for. Moreover, Arrowsmith wanted to cure something obvious and concrete, something "outside," while the problems of Crestwood Heights
are on another level. Possibly the very existence of the suburb itself
(and the researchers studying themselves studying it) marks something
of a retreat from the intractable problems of society, though it would
seem fairer to say only that there is some loss of traditional forms of
venturesomeness as the echoing internal frontier replaces the vanishing
external one.

I have implied that the reader will not meet in this book people whom
he doesn't know, though he may know himself and his setting better—
I did—when he has gone through it. Reading, for instance, the extensive discussion of dating, it occurred to me that referring, as girls often
do, to one of their number as "boy-crazy" is, among other things, part
of an effort by the group to establish a norm to protect the skilfully
slow "producers" against the awkwardly fast rate-busters: boys are the
bosses, and a boy-crazy girl breaks down the oppressed group's effort
to train themselves to restrain their zeal and to train the bosses to expect
only limited and calculated returns from a series of graded incentives
(cf. *Lysistrata*). Throughout the book, in fact, the high school students

often seem to be more sophisticated and mature than their parents (they can also be contrasted with California and Massachusetts high school graduates who, as described in a report—still unpublished—by Professor A. J. Brodbeck, exhibit a fear of anything serious or "controversial" coming up in class, and value above all cautious good manners and the cool approach). Regrettably, the Crestwood Heights study didn't last long enough to see whether the teenagers became more stupid in later life and whether they became as sex-polarized concerning values as their parents are, with the father in charge of the department of realism (with sentiment his understudy), and the mother in charge of the department of utopianism (with practicality in reserve).

Or, to take another instance, never have I read a more searching account of why some reformers fear success and hence, as it were, plant the seeds of failure in their very attitude, finding in the hostility they arouse in others the alibi which will save them from recognizing their own volition in defeat (Chapter 12, pp. 402-3). Another gem is the discussion (Chapter 3) of the semantics of "house" and "home"— though the suburb is Canadian, Americans will recognize the shadings.

In fact, there is almost nothing in the book which strikes me as peculiarly Canadian, although when I visited Crestwood Heights during the course of this research I felt I was in the presence of three provincialisms: towards London, towards Hollywood-New York, and towards Tel Aviv (there were not enough French Canadians or other Catholics to add Rome to the list). Thus, I surmise that the reader from Scarsdale or Flossmoor or Belmont will feel that Crestwood Heights is not so very different from suburbs he has known; and one of the problems of the book as a research document is its lack of comparative material. For there are things about Crestwood Heights which may be somewhat differentiating. As a suburb of one of Canada's largest cities, it is within the orbit of one of the few remaining financial bonfires in North America outside of our own Southwest: the Province in which it lies is booming and its menfolk in business are more likely to be the last tycoons than are business men in the tamer parts of Wall Street or State Street, just as pukka sahib attitudes lingered in the British colonies long after dying in the Colonial Office. If I am right about this, then the authors' discovery that there were two cultures in Crestwood Heights, that of the men and that of the women-cum-experts—cultures far more distinct than the nominal differences of Jew and non-Jew, upper middle and lower middle, professional man and business man—would need qualification before being extended to the United States. Indeed, this sharp division of the sexes is reminiscent of an older America of tired business

men and *The Male Animal*, in which women hauled their menfolk, not
to the school psychologist or the PTA, but to the opera—an America
that still persists in the Midwest towns, cities, and elsewhere but which
is fast disappearing with what I have sometimes referred to as the growing homogenization of the sexes. This is the America in which I grew
up, in which, save among a few seaboard aristocrats and Jews, the intellectual *avant-garde* was almost entirely composed of women—leisured
housewives who read Joyce and Sherwood Anderson and Freud and
even Einstein; an America in which men flaunted their Babbittry and
women were Carol Kennicotts. Even in my own lifetime, this has dras-
tically changed: the *avant-garde* exurbanites are men (and not only
experts), and in many suburbs men as well as women read *The New
Yorker* and learn to laugh ironically at suburban life and values.

In Crestwood Heights, however, one is confronted by men who
apparently don't read anything and wives who will read this book and
have read others like it. Yet in its tolerance for Jews the community is
liberal and progressive for both sexes, and its large proportion of Jews
also makes for idiosyncratic elements which the book, not being comparative, cannot fully explore. For example, we do not know to what
extent the Jewish couples contribute to the general profile of very distinct male and female cultures, since no quantitative data controlled for
ethnicity are presented. It may be that the highly mobile Jewish business men, marrying somewhat more educated wives whom ethnicity
robs of a wider choice, help give Crestwood Heights men their aroma
of downtown "success" values as against the suburban "maturity"
values of their emancipated and pampered, if patronized, wives. Or it
may be, as I have already indicated, that this is the general Protestant
Canadian pattern as well, where the women are exposed through the
media to general North American currents against which the men are
defended by their Big City work and their British-style clubs. We might
get some clarification here if we knew how these Jewish and non-Jewish
families voted; I am not sure whether Canadian Jews, though on the
whole less organizationally differentiated than the immensely larger
American Jewish group, are as attached to the Liberal party by
historical factors as American Jews are to the party of Roosevelt and
Truman.

But of course it is absurd to expect the first full report on one suburb
to come up with comparisons with other suburbs. And it is a constitu-
tional vice of readers and reviewers, if not of introducers, to ask more
of a good book than it sets out to do—to ask, as it were, that it satisfy
the very stimuli it is its task to create. And perhaps in any case, I am

inclined to ask more than most readers would, because of some familiarity with Crestwood Heights itself and with research under way in other comparable places in Kansas City, Chicago, and elsewhere.

As already stated, Seeley and his colleagues have written out of their intense moral, pedagogic, and democratic preoccupations for the lay as well as the professional reader; in doing so, they have followed the model of the ethnographic report on a primitive tribe, with its chapters on time, space, and architecture, on the family and on the life cycle, on ceremonial and associational life, and on belief systems. The difficulty of this model is pointed out in Robert Redfield's recent *The Little Community*, namely that once one leaves the isolated, preferably island, tribe, it is hard to know how to bound one's unit of study—in this case, how to know where Crestwood Heights ends and where Big City, or Canada, or North America, or the Jewish subculture, or the Western world begins. Indeed, as we have seen, the evidence goes to show that only the women live in Crestwood Heights, along with the young people and the professionals servicing both, while the men are, so to speak, visiting husbands from the bush—from the "real world" of Canada's booming economy; and by the same token it is the women who are cosmopolitan and who bring new foods, new practices, and new beliefs into the suburb. Seeley, Sim, and Loosley are at their best in delineating the subtleties of this division of labor and ideology between the spouses, showing how each provides a requisite "countervailing power" for the other, with the wives' covert practicality saving the men from the consequences, in dealing with their children, of the fathers' sentimental toughness and realism, while the men's overt practicality saves their wives from the consequences of too wide swings of idealistic faddism in the schools and in the too-emancipated homes.

The authors also show, in several penetrating chapters, how both the parents look to the school, and to such auxiliary institutions as the summer camp, to mediate in their own struggles and to compensate for their own ambivalences. The school must teach co-operativeness and equality—yet prepare the children for competitive success. The school must treat each child as a unique individual—yet counter parental tendencies in this wealthy suburb to spoil the children. The school officials in this situation become accomplished diplomats, and their use of Home and School (PTA) meetings, where the parental pressures are nakedly revealed, is amazingly skilful. Yet here, too, there may be slight differences from comparable American settings, for educators seem to have a somewhat higher status and a surer intellectuality. And it would appear that there is a slightly greater tendency to send children away to

boarding school than would be the case in a Midwest American city—
an understandable tendency since in boarding school the dirty work of
discipline that mothers cannot and fathers and local public-school teachers dare not undertake can be accomplished behind the safe screen of
distance and of social status. Furthermore, the authors observe that the
teen-age children themselves cope with conflicting demands by organizing secret fraternities and sororities along ethnic lines—and then
cleverly traduce parental efforts at suppression by "Moscow Subway"
tactics: reminding the parents of their own country clubs, their own
unmixed marriages, their own duplicities generally. One suspects that
the maturity of the youngsters is in part the result of the conflict of cultures they must continuously reconcile at home and school. As already
implied, I hope Seeley & Co. can go back in another twenty years and
see what the youngsters of the 1950's have become.

In an introduction, my function is invitation rather than summary or
critique—invitation to browse in the interpretations and cogitations of
the later chapters as well as in the ethnographic review of the earlier
ones. Husbands and wives will enjoy reading it together, for it marshals
the arguments for a culturally produced sex difference in a way that
undercuts much of the rhetoric of masculinists and feminists—and that
raises profound questions concerning the identical education of boys
and girls for differential life experiences. In Crestwood Heights at present the semantics of tolerance and the liberal taboo on biological
("racist") explanations make it difficult to discuss seriously either male-
female or Jewish-Gentile differences—both are matters only for mutter-
ing in the clubs (or of vigilante tactics by the Canadian Jewish
Congress); by full yet gentle exploration, this book makes the topic
legitimate both in Crestwood Heights and in its analogues elsewhere.

Yet it is just this sort of reaction that Seeley and his collaborators,
preternaturally aware of lay over-simplifications of science, view with
foreboding; they want to better "their" community—yet leave it un-
harmed, its battle of the sexes unaffected. I understand this feeling all
too well. I have wished many times, no doubt naïvely, that books of
this sort could be read as the history of another time and place, or indeed another planet, curious and interesting but not a matter of the
life and death of one's day-to-day existence. The authors shrink from
the roles of prophet or practitioner—yet they know how an author's
unconscious needs may push him towards a lay audience whose all too
evident needs for rules of conduct press heavily upon him. No one of us
alone, of course, can solve so general a problem. For that, social scientists will have to come to terms more frequently than they now do with

their own temptations to grandiosity, to evasion of casuistical issues and of their own involvement in what they study. But the audience cannot wait for that, or trust to it: to defend itself without resort to the easy road (polemically favored by some humanists) of anti-science, it can become more skilful in the consumption of social science (in part by contributing to it through Mass Observation and other ways of recruiting amateur sociologists), more habituated to its inroads on privacy and opacity, and more lively in its curiosity about the methods and mores of the social scientist.

DAVID RIESMAN

Chicago, 1956

CONTENTS

Part One

STRUCTURE AND CONTEXT

1. THE STAGE

THIS BOOK attempts to depict, in part, the life of a community. North Americans may know its external features well, for some community like it is to be seen in and around almost any great city on this continent, from New York to San Francisco, from Halifax to Vancouver. In infinite variety, yet with an eternal sameness, it flashes on the movie screen, in one of those neat comedies about the upper middle class family which Hollywood delights to repeat again and again as nurture for the American Dream. It fills the pages of glossy magazines devoted to the current best in architecture, house decoration, food, dress, and social behavior. The innumerable service occupations bred of an urban culture will think anxiously about people in such a community in terms of what "they" will buy or use this year. Any authority in the field of art, literature, or science probably at some time has had, or will have, its name on a lecture itinerary. A teacher will consider it a privilege to serve in its schools. For those thousands of North Americans who struggle to translate the promise of America into a concrete reality for themselves, and, even more important, for their children, it is in some sense a Mecca.

The book attempts to pin down in time and space this thing of dreams for the many, and actual experience for the very few. One such community from among the many of its kind has been chosen. It will be called "Crestwood Heights."[1] It is "somewhere in central Canada"; the time falls in the years immediately following World War II.

Since the word "community" will be used throughout this study in reference to Crestwood Heights, it is important that the sense in which the term is apt be established in the very beginning. Although Crestwood Heights is officially a separate municipality within a greater metropolitan area, it is also something else. It exists *as a community* because of the relationships that exist between people—relationships revealed in the functioning of the institutions which they have created: family, school, church, community center, club, association, summer camp, and other more peripheral institutions and services. (Some of the many groups to which Crestwooders belong are to be found within the geographic boundaries of Crestwood Heights, though some are outside the area altogether.) These relationships develop within a material setting of brick, stone, wood, concrete, and steel—and of flowering gardens, shaded in several sections by trees which once arched over an earlier and a very different enterprise, the clearing of the forest by a more simple type of pioneer. Yet the Crestwood resident of the present day is also, in his way, a pioneer.

This complex network of human relationships which *is* the community exists from the viewpoint of the participants for a definite purpose. In Crestwood Heights the major institutional focus is upon child-rearing. How is a Crestwood Heights adult to be made? How will he grow and mature into manhood and womanhood? What ideals are to be placed before him? What are the pressures to be laid upon him for conformity? What are the obstacles to orderly, predictable growth? What are to be the stages of maturation? What is to be understood by "maturity" itself, and how is it finally to be achieved? Here are eminent local preoccupations.

These questions, which once primarily concerned poet, novelist, dramatist, and philosopher, now also supply data for scientific scrutiny. In this study, we as social scientists have attempted to look at some facts about child growth as it takes place in a comparatively homogeneous, prosperous, modern, urban and suburban environment.

Crestwood Heights exists both as a physical entity and as a psychological fact.

As the name suggests, it is built on a choice brow of land, overlooking a wide sweep of the metropolitan area. Yet, although it is literally a city built upon a hill, the closest investigation of the terrain from the air would fail to reveal definite boundaries. Should an intruder from outside wander through its streets, he would find little, except a slight difference in sign-posts, to distinguish Crestwood Heights from Big City —or from other suburbs near it.

There is, however, a subtle but decided line drawn between Crestwood Heights and Big City. The very name "Crestwood Heights" expresses to perfection the "total personality" of the community, particularly in its relation to the metropolis of which it is a part. That name suggests, as it is clearly meant to do, the sylvan, the natural, and the romantic, the lofty and serene, the distant but not withdrawn; the suburb that looks out upon, and over the city, not in it or of it, but at its border and on its crest. The name is a source of pride, a guide for differential conduct (to some degree at least), but first and foremost a symbol evoking deference. Crestwood Heights is bound inescapably to Big City by many ties, but the proximity of the heterogeneous metropolitan area provides chiefly a foil against which Crestwood Heights can measure its own superiority and exclusiveness, core of its communal identity. The psychological climate of Crestwood Heights is, otherwise, no easier to assess than are its physical contours.

Certain basic problems have always concerned all human groups. And upon the answers given, depend the particular flavor of a culture, the subtle qualities which differentiate it from all others. One anthropologist, Dr. C. Kluckhohn, lists as the fundamental questions, these:

What are assumed to be the *innate predispositions* of man?

What is the relation of man to *nature*?

What is the significant *time* dimension?

What is the dominant relationship of man to *other men*?[2]

To these might be added:

What is man's relationship to *space*?

One might attempt a general answer to these questions for Crestwood Heights. First, human nature is seen as a mixture of good and evil, which may rather readily be modified in the direction of greater good. This orientation is both like and unlike the traditional Christian belief that man is conceived in sin, but may be redeemed through God's grace. Under the growing influence of a newer, expert-mediated ideology, however, the child is seen rather as being endowed at birth with all the potentialities for good, potentialities which may be thwarted later by the environment (especially if it fails to provide maternal warmth and paternal support). Here, then, the shared view of human nature inclines towards "positive neutral."

The fundamental attitude towards nature and super-nature is definitely that of mastery: man is *over* nature. The Crestwooder tends to assume that little or nothing is beyond his control. Although he may cherish a somewhat sentimental reverence for nature, he is carefully screened by technology from its power. In the psychological and religious realms, he subscribes almost whole-heartedly to the proposition that he and he alone is the master of his fate—or ought to be.

As for time, Crestwooders live almost entirely *in* the present but *for* the near future (with the past largely obliterated). Its people fall almost

entirely into two generations: parents who have moved into Crestwood
Heights when adult, and their children who have been born or brought
up there. Closely associated with the Crestwood orientation towards
time, is the attitude to personality and human activity. Here, as in their
concept of human nature, Crestwooders are divided, but in this instance,
by sex. Men incline almost invariably towards "doing" in the present,
with a definite future reference; women tend more towards "being-in-
becoming" (as Dr. Kluckhohn calls it) though it is doubtful if their
active lives really allow for the joy of unfolding to be felt.

In their relationships with other human beings, Crestwooders are
highly individualistic.

Finally, in their orientation towards space, Crestwooders again experience a sense of mastery and fluidity. They are in a position to buy
privacy and sunlight, in spacious homes and gardens; and by their
possession of cars, in their freedom to travel, by plane, boat, train or
automobile, they have the sense of conquering both time and space.

Intertwined with these orientations is a deep allegiance to the great
North American dream, a dream of a material heaven in the here and
now, to be entered by the successful elect. The dream is, of course, not
confined to North America alone; it is perhaps as old as the world
itself. In other ages and in other lands it has occurred and recurred.
It led thousands of men and women from warring Europe to North
America. It was dreamed by starving Irish peasants in the peat bogs,
and by deposed Highland clans amid the northern heather. Without
it the waste lands of the North American continent would not today be
filled. The dreamers of Crestwood Heights are, in this sense, both
innovators and heirs of a long and strong tradition.

The dream has a specific content. Nothing in it suggests an age of
innocence and peace in the future, when "the wolf shall dwell with the
lamb" and "a little child shall lead them"; nor is the goal a "land flowing
with milk and honey," where men shall live without effort. What is
envisioned is rather a material abundance to be achieved and maintained only by unremitting struggle and constant sacrifice. No citizen
of Big City or its hinterland, casting a longing and covetous eye towards
Crestwood Heights, could easily envisage a life of leisure there. Should
he, by some stroke of fortune or through his own exertions, enter the
promised land, he will fully accept continuing work and increasing
anxiety as the price he must pay if he does not wish to be cast out of
his paradise. His character will have been so firmly structured by the
time he finally arrives in Crestwood Heights that leisure and inactivity
are now his greatest threats. Once there, the grandchild of Irish peasants,

propelled towards North America by the dream, could no more freely shed his cultural inheritance of thrift and industry, hoarding and frugality, than could the Jewish child of ghetto parentage cast off completely his age-old fear of segregation and persecution.

With material abundance social status is closely linked in the dream. Here, in North America, the possession of wealth confers prestige upon its holders. Because there are few strong ties of locality or kinship, a man is judged largely by the number and the quality of the things he owns. These objects must be seen, approved, and envied by other men—as they are in Crestwood Heights. In this sense, the community serves the psychological purpose of a super-marketplace, where status may be validated in the acquisition and exhibition of material and non-material "objects": houses, cars, clothes, jewellery, gadgets, furniture, works of art, stocks, bonds, membership in exclusive clubs, attendance at private schools.[3]

The accumulation of the latest and the best materially is paralleled by an urge to acquire the latest and the best in ideas, values, and "experiences." These are diligently "collected," often with little apparent reference to the person's own tastes or interests. A cult, a political party, a traditional religious denomination, or a university education may be "collected" and cherished in much the same fashion as a new car or a television set—and with much of the same desire to impress others.

Material abundance and social status are not, however, pursued openly and cynically for the direct and sole satisfaction of the competitors. The peculiar twist of the American dream is that the pursuit of the goal is not for oneself alone but for one's children (and, less importantly, less urgently, "for the community"). Other peoples have used this motivation, but it is particularly emphasized in North America, where the social structure is still sufficiently flexible to hold out some promise to the great majority of at least a measure of upward social mobility. The freedom from struggle which is deleted from the traditional version of the dream, is, in Crestwood Heights, somewhat wistfully and without too much hope, transferred to the children's future. "If there is to be a millennium of the more conventional utopian variety (which is doubtful) let it be for the children, since we, their parents, will stand forever without its gates."

In its main themes, then, the North American dream, as it looks to material abundance and social status, is also the dream of Crestwood Heights. But because Crestwood Heights is situated in Canada and not in the United States, its dream, interwoven with English threads, cannot be wholly "American." The *New Yorker*, correct reading for the smart

urban American, may be on the living-room table, but *Punch* is sometimes found beside it. For some Crestwooders, laughing spontaneously
at a Peter Arno cartoon, also feel that there *must* be something to *Punch*,
even if their enjoyment of its pages is sometimes strained or altogether
absent. Although the Crestwooder may consult *Home Beautiful* or *House
and Garden* as a guide to "interior decoration," he may also deal at
first hand with a firm importing textiles and furniture direct from
England. He makes his uneasy choice between American modern or
eighteenth- and nineteenth-century reproductions of English period
furniture, never quite certain in his own mind which is "right." He is as
likely to set his table with Spode or Minton as with Russel Wright. The
astute art dealers of Big City know very well that a dim, gilt-framed oil,
supposed once to have hung in some ducal gallery, will have a ready
sale in Crestwood Heights. And, where education is concerned, some
Crestwood residents select a private school taught by British "masters,"
in a pattern borrowed directly from the British Public Schools. Even the
vast majority of parents who send their children to the tax-supported
schools of the Heights proudly approve the word "Prep" which tags
each elementary school name. In the absence of a strong, indigenous
Canadian culture, the Crestwood Heighter, more so perhaps than his
American counterpart, is inclined to waver eternally under influences
from outside.

Once arrived in Crestwood Heights, the new resident finds himself
in an environment exceedingly well equipped to materialize, feed, and
cherish his particular version of the common dream. The real estate
companies of Big City vie with each other to offer him a selection of
houses, complete with garden, gadgets, space, sun, and privacy. The
municipality provides winding, tree-shaded streets, paved and well-kept,
and excellent protective services. But the necessity of continuous work,
if the dream is to be kept alive, is recognized in Crestwood's close
proximity to the heart of Big City where the office buildings, the financial
houses, the hospitals, the university, the big hotels are clustered. The
few stores in the Heights, mostly food purveyors, also understand the
dream. They provide delicacies from all parts of the world—side by side
with the common necessities to be found, nation-wide, in the chain
grocery stores. These fashionable accretions to the regular food outlets are skilfully geared towards guiding the uninitiated in the proper use
of unfamiliar foods, as well as towards the satisfying of an already
sophisticated taste. Beyond, in the outer wilderness of Big City, lies the
wealth of department stores and specialty shops where one may range at
will in the gratification of every imaginable material desire.

To feed the non-material aspects of the dream there are the schools.

Here the parent and the child alike may "acquire" ideas and values. These schools are more than locally famous for knowing their business exceedingly well. No longer need the newcomer feel uncertain and alone, wondering how he should conduct himself in Crestwood Heights. In the schools are men and women whose business it is to help him in this task. Here there are teachers and psychologists whose office doors are always open to the questioner. He has only to ask in order to receive. It is better, of course, if one does not have to ask too urgently, too obviously, or too often; but for the child or the adult who needs to find a way there are directions forthcoming, free and abundant. If the resources of the school prove insufficient, there are the summer camps, the private practitioners of psychology and psychiatry, the pediatricians of Big City and beyond. The churches too, on the fringes of Crestwood Heights, offer various forms of spiritual solace, from which one may make a selection. No longer need one feel compelled to attend a synagogue in the working class "Ward," Sabbath after Sabbath, or sit in the family pew of a half-empty downtown church. One may go to a beautiful new synagogue or "Temple," even, on occasion, with Gentile friends; one may try, if the more conventional denominations do not satisfy, the congregation of the Unitarians, where all are welcome, or enjoy a cosy "fireside" in the home of a Bahá'í.

Big City has further attractions which encourage the dream. Into Big City, beyond the tree-protected bounds of Crestwood Heights, one can sally forth with friends to cocktails at an exclusive club, to dinner, to concerts, plays, or movies. There is dancing in a variety of hotels, with the opportunity for adventures not to be had within Crestwood Heights itself. There are museums where one may pass an hour or two with wide-eyed children; art galleries, which one may attend in evening dress on opening night; a conservatory of music with its eurhythmics class for children and its ballet to help small girls towards a graceful manipulation of their bodies; a university where one may take a course or two during the serious winter months before the trip to Florida.

And, far beyond Big City, there is the North, into which one may penetrate in the summer time, the North of camps and cottages beside small wooded lakes or open sheets of rockbound water. It is as necessary to Crestwood Heights as is the South. Alternate retreats from a too strenuous pursuit of the dream, they mark the slowing phase in the rhythmically beating pulse: work and relaxation, leisure and renewed effort. In the South adults may escape from the children; or they may send them to the North to camp, secure in the knowledge that the dream will not let them go, while they forget it for a little while themselves. Indeed in the North child and adult can briefly pretend the dream does not exist, for here no elaborate technological screen divides one from the earth and rock, water, sun and rain. It is good to live by these alone —not too long, of course, for it is equally good to come back to the metered hot water in the colored tub, to the efficient sanitary toilet, to the oil-generated heat that comes at the flick of an automatic switch, to electric light, to all the amenities of the material and psychological environment which is Crestwood Heights.

Here then, is the raw material from which the dream may take on a form and shape. But, selecting and rejecting elements, each family or person builds a special version, a particular cultural pattern, like and yet unlike the neighbor's. The process is never fixed and final, for one learns to make new choices and new combinations endlessly. But although everyone, in some measure, has the power of choice, it is the adults, ultimately the controllers of the money which alone makes a choice a possibility, who have the greatest power. The sum total of all these choices creates the matrix in which the Crestwood Heights child is reared and in which his character is formed.

Crestwood Heights, at the local level, maintains a symbiotic relationship with the sprawling, variegated metropolitan area. As a separate municipality with a population of roughly 17,000[4] it does maintain some services: a council, municipal police and fire departments, schools. It has a voluntary community council, a community center, a very active Home and School Association, as well as some minor organizations. But, on the other hand, Crestwood Heights has no industry, no hospital, no large stores, no sewage disposal plant, no Community Chest or other social agencies; and virtually no slums, no service clubs, and only one church. Thus Crestwood Heights, together with other comparable upper middle class neighborhoods, is highly interdependent with the metropolitan area, however much it tries to hold itself aloof, for each offers services which make it attractive and necessary to the other. The institutional meshing between Crestwood Heights and Big City is well illustrated in the occupational pattern. Few of those employed in the institutions of Crestwood Heights live in the community. They commute there to work, leaving their families behind in some other, less expensive, section of the metropolis. Conversely, the institutions of Big City provide the incomes which maintain the homes of Crestwood Heights.[5]

In the highly organized industrial and commercial civilization into which this urban complex fits, there is a growing need for highly trained, highly specialized persons in management and professional positions. Their importance to that civilization is reflected in the favorable incomes which they receive, and by the relatively high standard of consumption enjoyed by them because of their status. These are the people who can afford the exclusive environment of Crestwood Heights, who, in very truth, *must* be able to afford it as part of their careers. The Crestwood resident proudly feels that he is outside the city—but by no means beyond the reach of urban amenities and conveniences. Although to the casual observer this distinction might seem tenuous, the Crestwooder jealously guards his privileged suburban status. Harder work, struggle, anxiety, and sacrifice are not considered too high a price to pay for a Crestwood Heights address, an address which symbolizes the screening out of the unpleasant features of urban existence, leaving only the rewards and joys.

It is not that Crestwood is merely a dormitory within the metropolis, though sleep is one common bond which brings family members with otherwise diverse interests together. The sharing of food and of many other forms of familial and communal activity and association, also play their part in making Crestwood the locus of a common life. While the Crestwood Heights father, and any other wage-earning members of the family, do carry on their occupations beyond the physical limits of Crestwood Heights, their removal is much less complete than it would be from a more distant commuting center. Frequent interchanges by telephone between downtown and Crestwood Heights, a member of the family picking up the car at the office, a luncheon rendezvous with friends or family at a Big City restaurant—all are easily arranged. Conversely, a series of services enters the back door as the wage-earning member takes his leave through the front. Cleaning women, deliveries of all kinds, repair services, stream into the community from the city. These are the men and women who help in multitudinous ways to sustain the prosperous but servantless[6] modern household of Crestwood Heights.

The fact that employment, golf clubs, symphonies, and like activities are almost all extra-communal tends to specialize, if not to deepen, those relations which are left exclusively local. These ties are institutionalized primarily in the family, secondarily in the school and its affiliated activities, and less powerfully, in the municipal services. The institutions of Crestwood Heights tend therefore to converge upon the family, existing as they do to regulate the life of a purely residential community devoted to child-rearing.

It is already evident that this community is not typical of the modern world in the sense that we can say of it "here is what modern Western life is generally like." Indeed, to those gazing from afar with ill- or well-judged envy, it may very well seem to be "out of this world." Here—except where the Heights is bifurcated by metropolitan arteries—is quiet to compensate for the modern world's clamor. Here is space where a man can live, a space which contrasts with both the crowdedness of the teeming city and the lost loneliness of the margins of the wilderness. Here is time where a man may take counsel of himself and others—time to discover what there is to discover, and to enjoy what there is to enjoy. Here are means in abundance for the satisfaction of the primary needs for food and shelter, and in super-abundance for the satisfaction of the secondary, "higher" or civilized desires. Not only are the means present in abundance and super-abundance, but the good ends for which men have so long and so desperately sought these means are incorporated to an unusual and striking degree in the institutions of the community and in the desires and the conversation of the men and women of good-will who seek to define policy for them. Indeed, it is in the very creation of such institutions that Crestwood Heights may look upon itself—as it does—as a pioneer community.

In a profound sense, therefore, Crestwood Heights represents far less what the world is like and far more what men say it should be like, or hope it will be like, if they share at all deeply in the dominant aspirations of the North American continent. Crestwood Heights does not quite actualize these aspirations; the reality cannot faithfully mirror the dream. But it provides, for at least some, a reasonable approximation.

THE STARTING-POINT

This, then, is the community. We turn now to say something of the origin and nature of the study which was carried out in Crestwood Heights.

It is customary in the introduction to a study to say what the study *is*. The study itself may take for granted the view that in order to understand its subject-matter we need to know not only what it is, but how it came to be—to understand genetically as well as analytically. But the authors rarely report the history of the study, which would help to make its characteristics, virtues (if any), and limitations comprehensible. We attempt in this introduction to make such a report for this particular study. Among other reasons for so doing is the fact that what the investigator *thinks* can and cannot be done reveals the assumptions he makes about the social situation before he begins to investigate; what he *finds* can and cannot be done demonstrates some of the discoveries he makes about that situation.[7] The conception, birth, and development of a study therefore inevitably tell something about the student as well as the society studied, and to this information, we feel, the reader should have access.

It is perhaps arbitrary to fix a point of conception for any social event—whatever may be true for biological ones—but fully recognizing that any starting-point is arbitrary, let us concede that a starting-point is convenient.

This study was "conceived," then, in that sense, in the period following upon the Second World War. The study was one of many outcomes of what was originally a grand—perhaps grandiose—design: "A National Mental Health Project." This "National Project," put forward by the National Committee for Mental Hygiene (Canada), called for a large increment in many on-going efforts to further mental health and it also called for a bold attack in the direction of "preventive psychiatry" or the "promotion of positive mental health." As the issue will show, the "National Project" was, under more conservative influence, gentled down from a proposed simultaneous attack on a great number of Canadian communities to a proposed pilot project to be conducted in two. One of these died a-borning, and the sole issue and residuary legatee was a complex experiment in one. The "National Project" became the "Crestwood Heights Project"—of which this study was one part. A detailed account of this history, of how Crestwood Heights was both chosen to be and chose itself as the experimental community, and of the eventual launching of the Crestwood Project by the National Committee and the University of Big City, may be consulted in the Appendix.

The Crestwood Heights Project was one whose planning was focused on the child and therefore on the public school through which he could most easily be reached. It was organized as an interaction of research, training, and service, to be carried on as a group effort by psychiatrists, psychologists, social workers, educators, and many others. *Service* was particularly the responsibility of the staff of the child guidance clinics; *training* was intended to provide a group of professionally specialized personnel, primarily educators (and called "Liaison officers"), who, for instance, might assist in recognizing serious problems in children and might handle trivial cases, and would thus relieve the general strain on clinic staff. Special personnel, in contrast, conducted discussions with ordinary school children on topics chosen by the children themselves; these came to be called Human Relations Classes. *Research*, to obtain from the experience of studying and working in Crestwood Heights the largest amount of information possible, was a major commitment. The present book is the result of one of the research projects.

The hope of amelioration and the context of action inevitably committed the study of Crestwood Heights to a scientific method—using that term in its widest sense—which is almost the polar opposite of the models of scientific attitude widely recommended today.[8]

Given the nature of the undertaking as a whole, it would have been difficult to enter the field with a set of exactly defined and, therefore, rigidly testable hypotheses; these would, in any case, probably have yielded information of interest to only a very limited number of participants in and contributors to the study. Neither, of course, did the researchers approach the data without *any* hypotheses. The researchers exposed themselves, rather, for as long as possible, and as sensitively and intensely as possible, to a wide variety of community activities, continuously examining and questioning these activities, from the viewpoint of any and all hypotheses in social scientific literature to date which would seem to illuminate any area of activity in the community under study.

It will be recognized from what has been said that the Project as a whole may be viewed as a species of attempted "social therapy"; the specific research methods used for this volume have marked analogies with psychotherapy—analogies which must be pressed.[9]

Just as the therapist has a "patient who comes to him for help" so we had a "community that came to us for help." Just as the therapist, at the outset, knows only in the vaguest way what it may be that is troubling his patient, so we of the research staff knew only in the vaguest way, at the outset, what was "troubling" the community in which we were to operate. Just as the therapist assumes that what his patient says has some relationship, but not necessarily a direct relationship, to the problem with which that patient is coping, so we assumed that what people in the community said and did could tell us something about that community and what was problematic in it, though, like the therapist, we would not assume that "the patient" knew what his problem was. Just as the therapist assumes that the patient will benefit by a clarification of what has actually happened in his life hitherto and is happening now, so we assumed that the community could benefit by a similar attempt at clarification. And lastly, we assumed, just as the therapist does, that a by-product of this activity would be a story of the patient's life as seen from the patient's viewpoint *and* corrected in the light of any objective evidence available. Like the therapist, we started with "what was on the patient's mind"—whatever people in the community wanted to tell us about, in the light of their definition of our interests; and, again, like him, we followed up these comments in relatively free association. Again like the therapist, we assumed that if the process of communication continued long enough, the pattern or structure for which we and they were looking together would emerge with greater clarity.

Perhaps the technique used was manifest in greatest clarity in the "Human Relations Classes" conducted with the children. Here, generally, in introducing the classes, nothing more was said than: "We talk about a lot of things in school every day, but perhaps these are not all the things that you are interested in talking about. If you like, we will set aside an hour, every week, for the rest of the school year to talk about all the things that *you* like. What we talk about, and how we talk about it, will be up to you. Would you like to try it?" From these Human Relations classes we obtained, as already stated, a great deal of material as to what child and adult life looked like to children at various age levels.

Not with the same crystalline purity, but with much of the same outlook we talked *in extenso* sometimes *to* but mostly *with* individual parents and groups of parents, particularly in the Home and School Association, over a five-year period. We talked, similarly, with school staff and school administration, with specialists and laymen. We did participant-observation in school conferences, and meetings, and in negotiations between other groups in Crestwood Heights. When we were permitted, we frequently only watched and listened. We had seminars on personality development with Crestwood Heights teachers which taught us at least as much about Crestwood Heights and its teachers as we taught them about the subject-matter in hand. Over the five-year period, we had a seminar of intense interaction with some thirty women of the Home and School Association. One part-time member of the research team had grown up and lived in Crestwood Heights, and another lived there during part of the time she was working on the study. Our clinic and our guidance teams were in continuous interaction with the parents and teachers of children who had problems, and with the children themselves.[10]

The major difference between our handling of children in Human Relations classes and in the clinic on one side, and our interaction with adults on the other side, was that in the latter case we felt free—having carefully warned our informants beforehand—to probe for information *we* wanted, and to serve our own interests as they had been defined (though these interests should not be thought of as necessarily in conflict with those of our informants). In adult groups, for instance, we felt free to direct attention to discrepancies in fact or outlook, to statements made and relatively rapidly shied away from, to the carefully avoided drawing of implications from premises recommended as valid. We sought to maintain with these adults the atmosphere of a common search for information and understanding in which they would benefit in one way while others, it was hoped, would through the research project benefit in another.

It was thus, at many points, probably impossible to distinguish whether people in Crestwood Heights, in a given role, were serving or being served. The same women who, over a period of months, were furnishing the research project with detailed documents covering the results of their probing into their own lives and those of their friends, families, and neighbors, were felt to be serving themselves also, by discovering further the nature of the world in which they lived. This atmosphere of a search with a common interest (which covered, but did not obscure, the possibility of separate interests) was maintained, as far as possible, throughout.

Perhaps the analogy between therapist and research staff should not be pushed too far—less because it will serve no further, and more because of existing misapprehensions of what it is that the therapist does; but it may serve to illuminate some other points. It is not properly a contrast with the operation of the therapist to say that we were as much interested in "what really happened" as in what people thought happened, though many will think it so; the therapist is also concerned in comparing and contrasting the account given him, as far as he can, with what happened "objectively," with the past *wie es eigentlich gewesen ist*, as it actually was. Neither is it a contrast with the operation of the therapist to say that at no point did we allow our operation to lose its investigative focus; we also took it for granted that, in the long run, there was a positive correlation between discovery of self and of others and improved psychological and social function. Beyond this, we faced the need of establishing rapport, at a sufficiently deep level to secure the kind of information we needed; of dealing with problems which are essentially the problems of "transference"; and of communicating our insights in non-traumatic ways to the community concerned, or, preferably, allowing members of the community to come to those insights for themselves.

It would not even be true to say that the analogy breaks down when the subject-matter of investigation is considered. It is true that we were not solely interested in intra-personal functioning, but also in inter-personal relations, and in the nature of the social structure which conditions both and is a function of them. But consciously or unconsciously this is true of the good therapist also; and we have not yet been able to discover how the one can be profitably examined without, by implication, examining the other.[11]

All the foregoing is not intended to suggest that we limited ourselves to therapy-like and problem-centered methods exclusively.[12] There was a great deal of participant-observation: in many cases we acted in situations with almost full involvement and derived some data—dangerous as this is—by introspective inquiry after the event. We sent people into the field, armed like good anthropologists with sensitive minds, open eyes, sharp pencils, and bulky notebooks. We examined and analyzed census material. We submitted the children—nearly two thousand of them—to extensive questionnaires dealing with many aspects of their lives, and seeking their opinions, among other things, about one another.[13] We secured existing diaries and intimate life-history data, and we asked people to keep diaries for us, sometimes with special reference to defined areas of their lives or those of others. We collected from the children at one time a systematic diary, for a sample week, of everything they did each day and whom (in the community) they did it with. We had access to medical records, to school achievement records, to data on land value and land use, etc. Wherever it seemed proper and profitable, in short, we used available data or we collected data in a systematic fashion; and, where neither seemed desirable or feasible, or where time lacked, or where the nature of the question precluded the use of these more systematic procedures, we conducted a continuing conversation with participants selected in terms of their availability and their suitability to the purpose in hand. We shall have to discuss below the difficult problem of "sampling" that is thus implied.[14]

Having pushed the analogy with therapy so far, it behooves us to emphasize that investigation and discovery, and not action and therapy, were our *primary* concern. If one might borrow the corresponding medical terms, we were much more interested in description, diagnosis, and etiology than in therapy. Given our outlook, the nature of the project, and what we now believe to be the nature of social research itself, we concluded that there might be much less difference than is commonly supposed between the methods of investigation we used and the methods becoming more generally used in psychotherapy. If one had to draw a distinction (which probably has no foundation in reality), one might say that the therapist pursues investigation for the sake of its effect on future action, whereas we attempted to facilitate the social process and communication for the sake of discovery (and, in the long run, therefore, again, for the sake of future social action). This may be a distinction without a difference; or it may represent merely a difference in subjective orientation. The activities pursued seem closely analogous, if not virtually identical.

This brings us to the problem of "sampling," and raises questions again parallel to those raised for the therapist when he uses his material to write about human nature or psychological process in general. He needs to know what his patient is a sample of; and he needs to know also concerning the material that his patient communicates to him, whether or not this is a random or in some other sense suitable sample of the universe of the patient's acts and thoughts; and, if the latter, representative or suitable in what respect. So also we need to know: (1) Of what is this community typical or representative? (2) In what sense can we say or not say that our informants typify or represent the community under study? (3) Is the material secured by us—whether through informants or otherwise—representative or typical of the sources from which it was drawn?

It is clear that in no one of the three respects have we a random sample, or, indeed, any reason to think that our sample even approaches a random character. The community was not picked in such a way as to be typical of a North American community of its size—whatever that may mean!—but was picked, or accepted when it picked itself (for the strategic grounds and the scientific reasons, see the Appendix), rather because it was felt to be a critical, in the sense of "crucial," community than a typical community. (It was perhaps atypical also in its ethnic composition, about a third of its population being Jewish.) Our informants were picked or welcomed, as already stated, in terms of "availability" as well as "suitability." This implies, particularly with respect to the last, that they were atypical at least in the sense that we believed them to be peculiarly well informed with respect to or interested in a given question. Lastly, we feel morally certain that we held a peculiar status in the community, were differentially defined, and that people, far from selecting at random from the universe of their thoughts and acts, exposed us to those thoughts and acts which they considered would be of interest to us, which they believed we could helpfully comment upon, or which would be helpful to the development and maintenance of the social relations between us. This does not mean, of course, that people were limited to making polite remarks to us in terms of their initial guesses as to our interests. Since we were able to ask questions, since we were able to define our interests as scientists concerned to know and eager to discover how things actually operated, and since we were able continuously to redefine in detail our role in the community, we were able, we think, both to penetrate below the surface of politeness which first met us, and to correct for initial errors in the original ascription to us of special interests. Nevertheless, and to guard against "errors of the second kind," we were forced, while defining ourselves ever more clearly, to retain a certain amount of studied ambiguity, corresponding to the "therapeutic anonymity" of the therapist. We did not wish to become defined in such detail, as persons or as scientists, that our informants would structure their spontaneous expressions and responses in terms of those detailed definitions. We think we avoided doing so by marking out clearly attitudes in general and areas of special interest, while still communicating the true posture of the investigator—*Humani nihil a me alienum puto.*

What we have, then, is a community which is typical of but few communities in North America. The amount of conscious attention devoted to the relation of Jew and Gentile may make it unique. It is, moreover, a community with a very high degree of self-consciousness, both individual and collective, and in this sense also it differs significantly, probably, from all but a handful of similarly situated suburbs.

That it is a "critical" community in many respects can hardly be doubted: critical for social action, and perhaps also for social theory.

From the viewpoint of action, it is likely that in the proximate future a disproportionate number of opinion-makers, professional leaders, and power figures in the worlds of commerce, finance, and politics will be drawn from communities like these, where there is a specially advantageous access to the means for preparing for such positions and to opportunities for getting into them. Whatever is done here, then, and however human nature is being shaped here, may well have a disproportionately important effect on fashion, opinion, and social policy in the next generation.

From the viewpoint of social theory, a community like this furnishes an excellent field for the testing of hypotheses in reference to social pathology, most of which have hitherto been based on the examination of areas in which pathology was either dramatically obvious or socially, economically, or politically inconvenient. The implications of such studies have widely run to the effect that, if poverty, ignorance, or moral misdirection could be corrected, the conditions in question would be sensibly affected for the better. Certainly the community under study lacks neither the means in money, time, or professional, highly trained people, nor a base in literacy and general information, nor—at least at a crude level of analysis—morale and morally laudable intentions. If, then, even here, problems, difficulties, and pathology are found, they might helpfully serve to raise questions about going hypotheses as to the causes of pathology—or at least as to the blithely and easily suggested remedies for it.

A third sense in which the community might be said to be "critical" rests only on the impression of the authors. We sense that it represents what life is *coming to be* more and more like in North America—at least in the middle classes—rather than what it already is. If this is true, the community *is* normative, or "typical," not in the sense of the average of an aggregate of such communities, but in the sense of representing the norm to which middle-class community life tends now to move.

What is true of the "critical" nature of the community, as against its statistically typical nature, is also (in an analogical fashion) true both for our informants and for their selection of the information passed on to us. We know, with certainty, that we had disproportionate communication with those most actively involved in the life of the community, and, in actuality, most effective in shaping its nature, especially with reference to the educational, child-rearing process in which we were interested. Our communication with "the people who live in marble mausoleums," whose children (if any) never attend the public school, and who are members of Crestwood Heights in a sense only geographical, was restricted indeed. At the other extreme, relatively restricted also was our communication with "the cliff-dwellers," particularly the inhabitants of small, select, expensive bachelor apartments, whose relation to Crestwood Heights is again almost wholly geographical, and wholly so from the viewpoint of child-rearing. The inhabitants of such apartments, though technically located in Crestwood Heights, are distributed along the main arteries of communication, which are themselves functions of metropolitan and not suburban life, and these people feel, indeed, that it is to that metropolitan life they belong. Our communication was most intense with those most active, most vocal, and most powerful in shaping the nature of life in Crestwood Heights as a community. This means, essentially, that the structure and weight of our communication paralleled the structure and weight of participation of persons in community life. The resultant bias is one which we feel it is proper to accept, since it was primarily this community life that we were interested in, and since the two relatively excluded categories, though substantial, furnish minorities whose effect upon the life of the community cannot be neglected, but who are, nevertheless, marginal to it.

Just so, also, are we confident that there is bias in the type of information which was offered to us, or which we were able to secure. The information would tend to be biased in its concentration on "problems"—or, at least, on what was sufficiently problematic to be *not* taken for granted—and probably also in its concentration on latent, as against manifest, meaning.

In the very nature of the enterprise, it seemed impossible to avoid the tendency in informants and reporters to take normal function for granted, and abnormal variation from it as interesting and worthy of report. Similarly, since manifest meaning was obvious and well known, it seemed impossible to avoid a disproportionate concentration on latent meaning—with a subsequent seeming implication that the latent meaning is somehow more "real" than the manifest meaning. We are not alone in confronting this problem, and readers of Freudian psychology or of sophisticated political analysis will recognize the same tendency in "probing below the surface," both to concentrate on what is less laudable and to treat latent meanings as though they had a higher degree of reality, or importance, than ostensible ones. This, we think, is a defect in the method, and a defect in the study, and one perhaps peculiarly to be regretted. The book does not convey adequately, at any point, the relative proportion of happy and productive functioning of individuals, groups, and institutions, nor, perhaps, does it give due weight to the degree to which manifest or charter functions are actually carried out, *as well as* latent or covert ends served. We can only take the reader into our confidence, ask him to bear this bias in mind, and allow for it throughout.

The possible bias of the observers themselves needs explicit examination. Quite apart from that which is involved in the selection of *any* scientific problem for investigation, there is, in the judgment of the writers, an inevitably significant element of bias in the interpretation of results.[15] The fact that the social research situation is indeed a social situation, and that the researcher is in it, as well as outside it, poses a subtle and difficult problem in all but the most superficial types of social science inquiry.[16]

Near the outset of the research, and with peculiar importance because of the team nature of the Project, the staff was forced to consider the whole matter of personal and social bias most carefully. The broader alternatives presented seemed to be to exclude from reporting those matters where bias would be most likely to show itself—practically all subtle, and certainly all important questions—and, thereby, to maximize objectivity and ensure triviality; or, to deal with all matters and risk bias and subjectivity. After careful consideration, it was decided to make mandatory for all members of the research team the recording of *all* impressions (as far as they could be recalled), no matter how uncertainly they seemed to be founded or how subjective they might be felt to be, provided that they were (within the capacity of each researcher) as clearly labelled in terms of their uncertainty and subjectivity as possible. One of the members of the research team put it in these words: "I have encouraged others to do what I do myself, namely, to let the petticoat of bias show." Bias shown and personal feelings expressed in the primary report could, it was felt, be used in the secondary and tertiary analysis to correct the data rather than to draw the report further in the direction of initial error; the latter might easily have happened if the peripheral impressions had been suppressed from consciousness and from the record. Moreover, the material produced was collected by twenty or thirty different people,[17] and editors, authors, and researchers discussed continuously and freely the discrepancies in their impressions; it therefore seems plausible to suppose that the tendency for personal biases to be cancelled out in the resulting agreed document would be very marked.

This would leave unexamined, and uncared for, however, such biases as might be common to the whole group of authors, editors, and researchers or such as might arise from mutual influence, from a common scientific outlook, from common preoccupation with certain problems once they were focused upon, or from common membership in the middle class. The same communality would not hold for national origin or experience, or residence (urban or rural), or age, or sex, or religious or philosophic outlook, since these differed widely in the various staff members.

Of the sources of like or common bias perhaps the tendency to concentrate exclusively on the aspects of a problem as first noted, might be the most dangerous. A conscientious attempt was made to correct for this, by examining a vast range of material which came to us from an enormous variety of sources, and by maintaining in our communications with one another a lively sense of the danger of seeing later only more of what we had first seen. It cannot be contended that all biases were thereby eliminated, but only that a conscientious and a conscious effort to minimize this kind of bias was made, and that this had a lively success, at least as far as is indicated by periodic corrections and restatements of what had at various stages been considered as relatively well established views.

Some attempt also was made to correct for the approximately common class position of the scientists involved, by conscious raising of the problem,[18] and a conscious attempt to use the different class origins and class experiences of the researchers—experiences which ranged all the way from lower-upper to lower-lower—to check the appearance and meaning of situations as they would appear in the different class perspectives of which the researchers had themselves experience and knowledge. The magnitude of the difficulty in this area should not, however, be underestimated. No matter what may be the other difficulties of investigating relatively "strange" cultures, it is highly unlikely that any discoveries about them will shake the inner security of the researcher concerned. The more nearly like to one's own culture, however, is the culture that one is examining scientifically, the closer does the research come to self-study, self-investigation, self-analysis, either in a directly personal way, or by way of the groups with which one is most intimately and vitally identified. In either case, the possibility of psychological threat is substantially increased, and greater strains are made on the determination and intellectual and emotional honesty of the persons concerned. It may be a trifling matter for a Western researcher to learn that some central institution of the Bantu is producing results quite different from those expected or claimed, but the same cannot be said for a similar discovery in reference to an institution in his own culture, to which the researcher, as a private person, has given credence and loyalty, and on which, therefore, part of his personal security-system depends.[19] The team nature of the operation was, again, probably an asset here, since it enabled members, not highly threatened by a given insight, to support those who were, turn in turn.

But more difficulties attend the publication of such a "sociographical" report than merely the elimination of biases. At least three deserve mention, the first of which has been touched upon, but needs emphasis: the very necessities of economical description must result in a mere sketch that sacrifices detail to a partly factitious simplicity and clarity. This is inevitable at any level of description, but the greater and more complex the unit the greater the evident violation of canons of adequacy.[20]

The second difficulty is inherent in the nature of the community. In so rapidly changing a situation, any fact except perhaps the fact of rapid change has a very limited life. Even in the short (five-year) period of the study, the last year had necessarily to be devoted to analysis and recording rather than continued observation. And, even in that short interval, with the "camera" no longer trained on the "object" the researchers were made again and again aware that the object had "moved" and that what was descriptively true in the third and fourth year required substantial revision to fit the state of affairs in the fifth. There is no visible logical or scientifically defensible termination date for this sort of study and, apart from economic considerations, any cut-off point is scientifically arbitrary and does violence to the sense of historic process. This also, on practical grounds, cannot be avoided.

The third difficulty has to do with the changes produced by the research as such. Quite apart from any effects on action consciously or unconsciously sought by the researchers in their capacities as persons, both the acts of inquiry and the partial reportings to the community of tentative findings acted to accelerate or decelerate on-going changes or to secure changes that would otherwise only improbably have occurred. In many cases, reporting was deeply disturbing, not to say shaking, to the "research-subjects"—now acting as research-consumers. For better or for worse, the community is different because an inquiry has been conducted within it, and for better or for worse it will be still more different after a report has been made upon it. Some of the changes attributed by residents to the research might have occurred anyway, but it is difficult to doubt the conscious emergence of new problems, new foci of concern, and even new vocabularies in the community paralleling those of the researchers. Even social structure and social relations were changed to some degree as the necessities of research led its directors either to bring together for convenience people who otherwise would improbably have "met," or, more frequently, to lead those who might *merely* have met into substantially more intimate relationship as research probes uncovered deeper and deeper layers of personality or more and more hidden attitudes behind appearances. This effect cannot be avoided either, but another research might attempt to take it more systematically and consciously into account.

It is frequently stated that scientific description is value-free or non-evaluative—in social science just as in physical science. This statement has been seriously questioned, and properly so. It can at best be only partially true. No extrication from a value-problem is possible for the scientist in deciding what aspects of a situation to study. And as long as social science uses the common language (instead of, say, a more neutral-seeming set of symbols) the very choice of words inevitably carries with it not the risk but the certainty of value-overtones if not value-judgments.

The bias of this report has already been touched upon. If it can be kept in mind by the reader, it ceases to operate as a bias. If many of the facts reported upon are seen (correctly) as quite general characteristics of human nature, or of Western culture, or of American life or of all middle-class behavior, what might otherwise seem invidious may be properly recognized for what it is: partial, but within its partiality, reasonably accurate characterization of a much more general situation than that of Crestwood Heights.

One potent source of seeming invidiousness is doubtless the fact that what is reported may be seen by the reader not against the background of other communities elsewhere, equally deeply probed, but against the background of whatever ideal constructs of "how things might be" his unfettered imagination has permitted him to build. Both views are useful, but one should not be mistaken for the other! The risk that this might occur calls perhaps for an explicit statement by the authors as to the "goodness" of the community they have studied, relative to other American communities known to them.

Against that background, Crestwood Heights emerges as a community of great generosities, immense and costly efforts, devoted and committed people ardently seeking intellectually and behaviorally a better world for themselves, their children, and men generally. To that end these people have elaborated institutions and activities which furnish the content of this book. That those institutions produce things less than and quite other than what had been hoped is not a distinctive characteristic, but a part of the fate of man everywhere, and nowhere more than of Western man at the present historical stage. What is intended is in no way an exposé of a hapless community, but an illumination of the dilemmas in which modern Western middle-class people find themselves.

2. SPACE

SPACE has perhaps much to tell us about Crestwood Heights and its people.

Part of that story—and the greater part of this chapter—tells how Crestwood came to be what it is, as a *place:* how the necessities of organization led to the selection of a site and a setting for that differentiated part of the urban way of life which is Crestwood.

But part of the story has to do more with people than with place. Since Crestwooders are largely free economically to choose where they will live, and, earlier, were free to impose to a large extent their will on the site selected, the story of the place is the story of its people. Thus the impress of the site on the people is a not unimportant theme, and what they have done with the space—building huge houses on small lots, for instance—suggests much. But a deeper and more important, though not wholly independent, theme is concerned with how Crestwooders view space itself, and how they view it in relation to time and money. These themes are interwoven with the principal theme of this chapter—the development of the site.

That "time is money" is a commonplace in our culture. But that space means time is familiar to every commuter, and that money means space (and place) is well known to every realtor and house-buyer. The relations among the three variables—with taste as a complicating fourth factor—call for subtle compromises, a complex balancing and regulating of competing considerations.

The house, for instance, must be large enough to ensure privacy and symbolize success—but not so large as to chill contact or to make maintenance crippling. Home and office must be far enough apart to connote exclusiveness and the power to annihilate distance—but not so far as to cause serious strain and inconvenience in the daily journey from the one world to the other. Some kind of balance between forces of concentration and of diffusion is found and established, even if only precariously, in matters of space, just as in matters of energy and emotion.

THE LAY OF THE LAND

Land is valuable in Crestwood Heights, no longer because it is fertile, but only because it is scarce. A great many people live there; many more would like to, but cannot. The wishes have something to do with space, and air, and height, with the lay of the land in the whole urban region, and with the way in which that region grew. To understand them one must examine the spatial organization of the metropolis, which eventually enveloped a square mile or more[1] of rural landscape and drew it into an urban complex to serve the special social purposes of Crestwood Heights.

The metropolis of which Crestwood Heights forms an integral part is situated on a great lake, and the downtown area is located on a rather flat region which recedes in a gentle slope from its waters. This flat land was once, in an earlier geological period, lake bottom; the upper levels of the metropolis, which are separated from downtown by a sharp crest, stood above the lake.[2] What is now the crest was then lake edge; and that old beachhead is today an urban heights. Once a barrier to the expansion of the city, it is now just a perilous ascent to motorists when the streets are icy. It provides an elevation with an accompanying view and—allegedly—cleaner air, a crisper, less humid cold in winter. It is a limited space for which realtors may bargain and the wealthy bid. Behind this first desirable ridge or crest, on a second slope which rises slowly from the ancient beach, lies Crestwood Heights.

The face of the first ridge itself, known today as "The Crest," is immediately to the south of Crestwood, and "below" it, then, in physical elevation. Nevertheless, the houses, except where obsolescence and decay are in command, are generally bigger, though less stylish, and they are not so often crowded onto small lots. The properties bestow more distinction than those of Crestwood Heights. In this older section, occupied a generation earlier by large Victorian structures, the streets were given names which today strike a note of genteel and prosperous respectability. Some of these streets of the Crest stretch northward into Crestwood. Though the value of the properties on them tends to diminish as they extend northward, yet the very names of the streets connote prestige to their end. Indeed, it is around these street names that the core of Crestwood's repute still revolves.

Actually, geology did very little to make Crestwood a splendid or dramatic site. Moreover, the "wood" which is an element in the town's name has largely disappeared. Some ancient trees still stand but there are no wooded lots, and in the few small parks the trees have been replanted.

Early photographs of the community do, however, give the impression of sylvan beauty. Yet within Crestwood Heights today, regardless of the size or cost of the houses, one is at once impressed by the scantiness of the land surrounding them and the absence of large wooded parks. This lack of spaciousness, except within the house, suggests that not much has been done to improve on the limited, yet by no means negligible contribution of nature to the site. Extensive sub-division with little provision for park space has thus diminished though it has not obliterated those qualities which give a measure of reality to the name "Crestwood Heights."

The topography was further moulded in contemporary times by the eroding force of several streams, flowing from the height of land to create small ravines. An earlier, major ravine traverses one corner of the municipality. Except for this, Crestwood has no natural boundaries which force the occupants in upon themselves and thus provide a physical basis of integration such as often characterizes a "natural area." Indeed, a large watercourse once cut across the area laterally, creating an effective barrier between the southern and northern parts of it—a barrier made more formidable later by a railway which followed the same gentle contour from east to west.

Historical factors in the growth of the larger urban area help explain why Crestwood Heights developed as it did. Long before Crestwood was conceived of, the metropolis had been developing as a center of population. By the middle of the seventeenth century a large Indian settlement was already located on the lake, the southern terminus of a fur trade route into the interior,[3] foreshadowing one eventual use of the land now occupied by Big City. In the later eighteenth and nineteenth centuries the early military roads of the white settlers began to radiate from this point. Ready access into the interior of the province, assisted by two rivers which here entered the lake, gave this land a peculiar advantage which attracted trade, commerce, industry to it and made it a suitable spot in which to locate modern transportation facilities: after the early canoe routes and military roads, the railways, lake shipping, limited access highways, and airways were to find their terminus at Big City. Thus more than one hundred years before the incorporation of Crestwood Heights in the 1920's, even before axe and plow had turned its area from forest to farm land, the foundations for the future metropolis were laid by a nucleus of tradesmen and entrepreneurs, who manoeuvred to defeat the mercantilist and aristocratic class which had previously exerted almost unlimited social and political control over the whole province.[4] These two groups shared the small pioneer lake front settlement, as they shared political power, in uneasy propinquity.[5]

The first surveys laid out the roads in grid pattern with intersections a mile and a quarter apart. Within each square there were five two-hundred acre lots. Along the roads, the wagon teams and stages carried a heavy traffic from the interior of the province to this bustling center, and to serve this traffic a series of cross-roads trading posts arose, with taverns to accommodate horses and travellers. At these points, small industries developed: tanneries, grist and flour mills, and brickyards. These semi-rural settlements grew quickly into small towns, largely dependent on the expanding center which was soon to envelop them, as it spread out from its pioneer nucleus.

In the area which was to become Crestwood Heights there was, however, no such early trading center, no mill; there is no record of a pioneer tavern. The presence of such facilities in adjacent areas, and their absence in what was then known only as "School Section # X," contributed to the prior urban development of the former, and thus made possible the eventual specialization and exclusiveness of the latter. Not until the second and third decades of the twentieth century did the metropolis reach that stage in its maturity when a separate municipality was required to serve the executive, entrepreneurial, and professional groups, which from the earliest days had helped to shape the destiny of city and province. The broad pattern of metropolitan development, therefore, along with the natural features of landscape and climate, established the conditions of growth for Crestwood Heights.[6]

The initial growth of the metropolis was bounded and contained by the lake front and two main rivers; these rivers, piercing the Crest, were later to give the railways access to the waterfront. The grid system of roads furnished the structure within which streets were interlaced, and divided the otherwise open space into two-hundred-acre lots out of which sub-divisions were subsequently to be carved. These were the physical facts, to which industry, commerce, and housing areas had to be fitted.

The resultant physical organization of space is shown by simplified representation in Figure 1: the safe harbor, the two rivers, with the Crest behind. The West River provided access to the northland; a trail for winter travel ran parallel to it. A fort was placed strategically nearby.

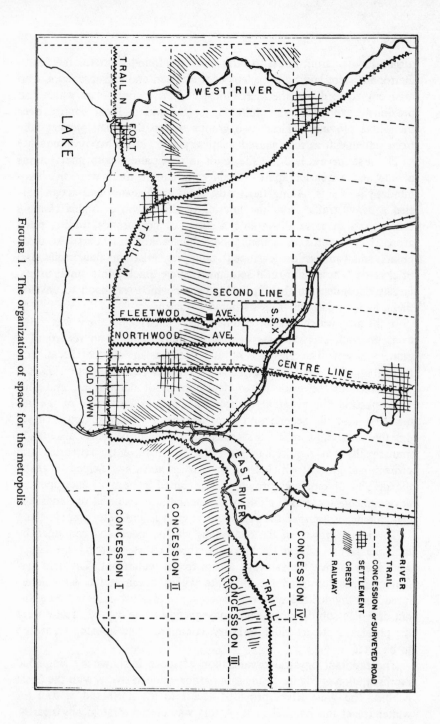

FIGURE 1. The organization of space for the metropolis

LAKE

WEST RIVER

TRAIL N

FORT

TRAIL M

SECOND LINE

S.S.X

FLEETWOD AVE.

NORTHWOOD AVE.

CENTRE LINE

OLD TOWN

EAST RIVER

CONCESSION I

CONCESSION II

CONCESSION III

CONCESSION IV

TRAIL L

RIVER
TRAIL
CONCESSION or SURVEYED ROAD
SETTLEMENT
CREST
RAILWAY

The first roads converged at the East River which served as a shipping depot and harbor. At the juncture of these roads and this river the center of population growth was located. Where river, or stream, and road intersected, mills were established. Hotels and taverns were spaced at frequent intervals to serve the slow-moving traffic which traversed the first primitive arteries of communication. Since the urban development tended to build upon and behind these arteries, the general pattern of the city, as shown in Figure 2, was that of an inverted T.[7]

Figure 1 also shows the grid system of roads. These, and the principal railway lines, tend to establish barriers to other types of transportation and to mark boundaries for developing urban areas. The sketch maps of Figure 2 show that, with urban growth, the inverted T shape has assumed more massive proportions. The letters A and B on these maps indicate the location of land which has not yet been converted to urban use. School Section # X, which was to become Crestwood Heights, is shown in the sketches by the characteristic shape of the municipality; it was located in space A. It will be seen that extension of Big City to the north and west tended to encircle and eventually envelop Crestwood Heights, and thus to impose upon it the implacable facts of urban growth.

THE CLASH OF INTERESTS

A. LAND USE

In 1871 (when the first Dominion census was taken), there was no metropolis, but a small city of 56,000 had spread out from the waterfront. In the townships surrounding it were to be found well-established farms and thriving rural villages. Today these townships are well within the metropolitan limits and the villages can be traced only in a street or neighborhood name; the farms have disappeared, though occasionally a discerning observer can still identify a former farm house occupying a narrow lot on a residential street. The landscape is now occupied by acres of houses, and great areas are filled with factories, stores, offices, and like evidences of maturity. A million people live within the metropolitan boundaries, while countless others commute into it and out of it to work, or seek in it entertainment and relaxation.

This massive transformation of the landscape was gradual. At first, virtually to the end of the nineteenth century, the Crestwood land, given to agriculture, was unaffected by the tide that would later inundate the high lands. Further down, below the Crest, wealthy people were moving to the then outskirts of the city to buy select sites for homes. Beyond this, wooded acreages were acquired for park-like estates where

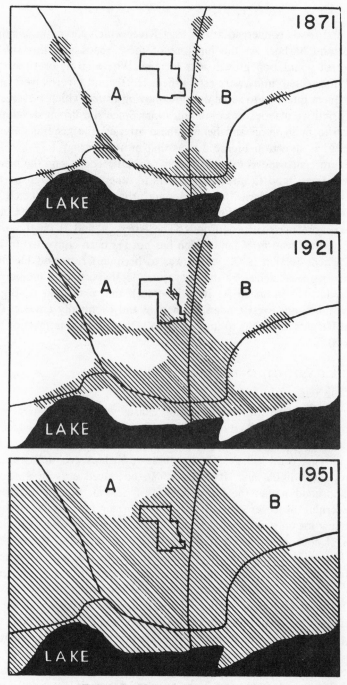

FIGURE 2. The extension of Big City

the life of the English gentry could be simulated. Soon, however, the city would press out even towards these holdings; and its sprawling, smoky industry, or unplanned groupings of inferior houses, would render this choice environment obsolescent.

Inevitably, the flood tide of urban growth began to lap upon the prehistoric beaches which were now known as the Crest. In summer, it was a favorite spot for a family picnic. In winter, snow-shoe parties would penetrate the Crest by following ravines inward. Then, after mounting the Crest by a circular movement, following the easy contours afforded by the old creek bed, they would approach the Crest from the rear and slide down its steep slopes while squatting on their snow-shoes.

Settlement first surmounted the Crest at Center Line, an historic highway northward; from this line it then began to move back in an easterly and westerly direction. The "Third Concession" provided a ready-made avenue for this development, running, as it did, westward immediately above the Crest, and joining traditional road M at the West River. When the community which is now Big City moved to annex this new territory, the inverted T had thickened to the extent that space A and School Section # X were virtually the same; the School Section thus became contiguous to Big City.

With further expansion, evidently the Crest was not sufficiently forbidding to limit north-south traffic to the Center Line. The "Second Line" now became a popular thoroughfare, and two other intermediary streets running north between these original country roads also probed the Crest. The one, Northwood Avenue, had found a means of relatively easy ascent over the Crest; the other, Fleetwood Avenue, beginning as a wide boulevard downtown, floundered at the base of the Crest, its way barred by the formidable elevation and by a "castle" erected on the summit by an entrepreneur with baronial tastes and aristocratic aspirations. Fleetwood finally resumes its way behind the castle, but the wayfarer must first search out tortuous and rather obscure alternative routes. Once the ascent is negotiated, however, Fleetwood Avenue proceeds directly through the center of Crestwood Heights till it terminates in a long-established Jewish cemetery.

These two roads might be described more fully since they symbolize, in a sense, the future destiny of Crestwood Heights. Northwood Avenue begins downtown near the financial district, passes around the provincial legislative buildings, and through the spacious university campus, presently to mount the Crest and to terminate, temporarily, at the gates of an exclusive boys' school. Just over the Crest, Northwood is flanked on either side by giant trees which protect large and imposing residences. Northwood is a Gentile street. The political, educational, and financial advantages of the Gentile upper class are, or were a generation ago, signalized by it. Significantly it did not touch Crestwood, but almost did so. Just west of the boys' school, and behind the big houses, stretched the land of S.S. # X.

Fleetwood Avenue also begins at the waterfront. As it enters the city, it becomes the headquarters of the Big City needle trades. Behind it on either side first settled Jewish and central European workers. As these groups increased numerically, as wealth was accumulated by their members, the more affluent began to move northward on Fleetwood towards the Crest.

In a society where entrepreneurial interests dominate, a city does not grow according to a neat, rational plan. The outcome of the struggle of competitive forces is seldom a clean-cut decision, and is often a deadlock. An area under development succumbs only partially to the blandishments of each interest bent on control, and the resulting compromises leave no clear definition of physical function; land often is neither completely commercial nor exclusively residential, and in the residential area there may be no enduring definition of use nor any permanent control of the type of housing.

Crestwood Heights is the product of just such a process. It was not to follow a single predestined path of development; the utilization of the land passed through several stages, sharp controversy and harsh political and economic bargaining marking the transitions. Each stage represents a compromise in these clashes of interest; simultaneously it provides a vivid reflection of the over-all development of metropolis and province.

In the clash between agricultural and urban interests the victor was unquestionably the burgeoning city. In this process, the wealthy city person, simulating a life of gentle rural leisure, usually allowed his love of capital gain to outbid his delight in pastoral calm. Even in advance of the realtor and the political manipulator, the infection of speculation had taken this land out of active agricultural use and assigned it to burdock and hawthorne in expectation of a capital return. Barns and fences fell into disrepair, orchards into blighted disuse. The land lay fallow for subdivision.

Somewhat as aquatic life supplants terrestrial when a river permanently inundates a flood-plain, so in Crestwood Heights a new way of life supplanted an old: a consumption economy displaced a production economy; dense settlement replaced open country. The individual lives of those who occupied the land as farm land may not have been too seriously disturbed, for the change was slow; a farm was sold here, and then another. For the realtor, the transfer of land to urban use, particularly as the site for fine large homes, is a symbol of the energy and promise of the urban way of life. For the farmer, who turned at this time to agrarian movements,[8] the same transaction was a warning that the city was a monster that devoured his farms; its abbatoirs, his livestock; its institutions, his children; and, equally sadly, its banks, mail order houses, and tax collectors, his money.

This emotional undertone to the incursion of steel, brick, mortar, and macadam up over the Crest is relevant because the triumph of the city in physical terms is so decisive and because within the values and institutions of the Crestwooder there continue to be uneasiness and indecision regarding growing things, the out-of-doors, and the physical work entailed in primary production. The Crestwooder in his key managerial position is a powerful but nostalgic instrument in the continuing rationalization and the systematic exploitation of the country's resources. In the clash of interests between the rural and agrarian on the one hand and the industrial and residential urban settlement on the other, the physical facts point to a clear-cut decision in favor of the latter. Yet Crestwood Heights is the locus of an active interest in industrial decentralization and town planning; its more successful citizens are bent on moving out to the country; several weeks of each year are spent by its residents at a summer (or winter) place. Time and again, its people express a keen delight in considering a quiet bucolic life, far from what is described as the hurry and insincerity of urban social relations. It cannot be said yet whether, for most, this is an expression merely of guilt, nostalgia, and the sense of having missed important experiences. For a known few, it is actual preparation for a step which will take them "beyond" Crestwood Heights (geographically and socially) when the time comes.

B. THE CHOICE OF DESTINY

As we have said, Crestwood Heights represents the outcome of a clash of interests in which no victor appears to be completely victorious, no loser completely lost. Each interest having a sometime stake in the community retains a residual holding in it.

It was inevitable that the landed estates should be pushed further into the hinterland as the metropolis grew. The area was too small and too near downtown, and the boundaries provided by nature and legislation too puny to reserve this area for privately owned parkland. Nevertheless, a few of the large houses remain. Their presence undoubtedly influenced the concentration of the most expensive properties in Crestwood's southeast quarter. That these large country dwellings should have been located here was also an accompaniment of the entire housing development on the Crest and on and near Northwood Avenue. A slum was the second feature to take form. The city boundaries had been extended to the margins of Crestwood. Across this boundary came a number of persons of very modest means who were partly dependent on urban employment, yet who wished to live in the open country. They were attracted by jobs on the estates, an opportunity for gardening and small-scale farming, by cheap land and low taxes. Not till later was it clear that their occupancy of two corners of the School Section was contrary to the utilization destined for the area as a whole. At these two separate points, small cottages and nondescript outbuildings were erected; and when Crestwood Heights was incorporated, these two neighborhoods were well-established, but embarrassing, small enclaves, in a reputedly exclusive residential area. They served a purpose in so far as they provided a source of labor for gardening, landscaping, and the building trades, but they are regarded as anomalous today by those in Crestwood Heights who are aware of their existence.[9]

Light industry has also made an ineffective bid to occupy Crestwood Heights, in association first with the Great Circle Railway, launched before the turn of the century. It was intended to run along the lake front, then northward following river valleys and low contours, and to complete the circle four or five miles from the downtown area in a great loop. Seeking an easy grade afforded by an old watercourse, the right-of-way cut across the northern part of School Section # X, separating about one-fifth of the area from the remainder. The railway was to connect, by a commuters' service, a series of existing or proposed suburban neighborhoods, but this scheme proved abortive when electric street railways and automobiles provided a more satisfactory service. The right-of-way was subsequently acquired by one of the major railway companies, and though it had the briefest use for passenger traffic, the growing congestion of railway lines along the lake front forced the company to make of this old right-of-way an artery for by-passing the city and for the pick-up and delivery of package freight from and to light industry.

The coming of the railway started the first real estate boom in the Crestwood area. Farms passed into the hands of speculators, and oat fields were surveyed for subdivision. But it was many years before the actual occupation of the area for residential purposes began. When it did, the railway was regarded as detracting from property values, and those who were selling land in the area promised that the railway would be removed. The railway, however, implacably withstood these organized pressures. There it stands today, to the resident a familiar but regretted feature of the landscape; to the sociologist a sign of conflict between the *region* of which the railway is a binding expression and the *locality* which it mars.

The persistence of a railway introduced a counter-pressure for a diversified development at the expense of the realtors' promise that this was to be an exclusive residential and exclusively a residential area. The small industries which tend to cluster around railway lines and which follow and support urban development were actively interested in zoning arrangements which would permit them to build and operate in this favored position. However, the structure of municipal government which gives each resident a vote, within a small unit like Crestwood Heights placed enough power in the hands of home-owners to enable them to secure zoning restrictions which effectively prevented the spread of light industry along the railway within the Heights, except for a number of enterprises allied to building and countenanced because of the vast program of residential expansion.

The railway was thus "contained," but the automobile has shown less respect for the expensive amenities which contribute to the prestige of Crestwood Heights. At the beginning of the organization of the municipality, neither of the "county roads" which intersect in Crestwood Heights was a main thoroughfare. A narrow wooden bridge on each, crossing one of the innumerable ravines, was adequate to carry the light burden of traffic contributed by Crestwood itself. But as the regions beyond the Heights were converted to urban uses, the need for traffic arteries to connect them with the downtown areas became more and more urgent, until it threatened the favored position of Crestwood Heights as a semi-rural place with urban advantages. The small wooden bridges, after prolonged and strenuous opposition from Crestwood Heights, were replaced by broad concrete viaducts, and as the volume of automobile traffic continued to increase, these streets became principal thoroughfares of the metropolis. It was as though great noisy canyons had been dug through the even quiet of the community. The absence of physical boundaries which might have excluded or delayed such a development, and lack of effective control over urban growth, led to a situation in which the space which was to have been the locus of a single integrated social entity with central shopping and cultural facilities was cut by highways which children must traverse and neighbors cross, if normal community interaction was to persist.

The character of Big City itself also influenced the use to which the land in the School Section was put, and, thus, the type of people who settled in it. Big City was not laid out on spacious lines. Minds such as those which fashioned Paris, Washington, or even some small cities of western Canada, quite obviously had not been at work here. The rapid growth of the city was met by makeshift and compromise rather than plan. No great boulevards connected the hinterland with the heart of the city, and no spacious parks in the center made life there amenable for those who could not afford to be selective. Lack of rapid transit or of railway commuting facilities made the center, until recently, moderately inaccessible. The local preference for detached single-family dwellings rather than apartment buildings contributed to the horizontal spread and conspired with topography to place a high premium on land occupying middle distance, if only it offered certain physical amenities. Such land was eagerly sought and strenuously bid for.

The Crestwood Heights area fell within this category. Less than three miles from downtown, with ready access to urban improvements, and adequate separation from inferior housing and from industry, it furnished suitable conditions for an elite dormitory.

The proximity to downtown, for one thing, ensures regular and prompt delivery of staples from the big stores to the Crestwood Heights resident; shopping facilities in the Heights itself offer what specialized and even exotic products are required. Accessibility to the services of the metropolis also includes access to two items most essential to urban life: a water supply and sewage disposal. These services, which are underground and therefore invisible, are "rented" by Crestwood Heights from the city. The school, police and fire protection, assessment, and the like, which are visible and from which a special type of performance can be secured, are, on the other hand, "owned" by Crestwood Heights. Each of these services is regarded, even outside the Heights, as exemplary. Visitors come to learn from Crestwood officials; and the officials take a special pride in their work and the recognition that it receives.

Crestwood Heights certainly represents compromise. It has elevation, but greater height lies beyond; the air is clearer than it is downtown, but it is much clearer in the Highlands to the north; there is a vista, but it is limited; there are some trees, but the streets are not wooded. There is privacy, but few houses are really screened from neighbors— any real privacy in Crestwood depends on the size of the house and is therefore rather the possibility of separation from the members of one's own family. (Even this privacy is only a possibility, not often actualized.) There is accessibility to downtown—"It only takes ten minutes except in the rush hour"—but the breadwinner almost invariably does travel in the rush hours and can seldom come home for lunch. The Crestwooder will argue that since privacy and accessibility in an urban world are contradictory, he gets as much as possible of each without losing too much of either. He will say that he has achieved, in the face of the many demands for a place to live, a balance that, *for the time being*, is satisfactory. This phrase—"for the time being"—pervades much thought and planning, and reflects the migratory habits and transitory values of a people: some, in a new land; most, in a new community; many, occupying new roles in a rapidly changing society.

C. POLITICAL

The emergence of an important suburb does not occur, of course, in a political vacuum. Formal and informal political forces were a part and a product of the conflict attendant on the changing patterns of land use and the growth in population of the territory. The moment the land passed from agriculture to speculative ownership, it became an area in which political interests developed and around which power was exercised in new ways.

When urban development first spilled over, out of the incorporated area into the unincorporated township to the north and west of the city, those with holdings in School Section # X and other parts of the township attempted to combine the entire area into a municipal organization with the status of a city. A general referendum was held, but the plan was defeated by the votes of the lower middle class residents in the area behind Crestwood Heights, who felt that big interests and real estate men were aiming to seize control of the entire area. The "planners" thereupon decided to carve out a smaller area in which they and others like them could agree on a policy and a method of development. As a result, those resident in School Section # X held a second referendum by which it was agreed that a municipal organization with the status of a village should be established. It was to render superior service to the superior residents of the newly incorporated territory. Aspirations which began with snow-ploughing[10] were later carried over into police and fire protection, the services of the municipal office, and the school system. An important early attraction in Crestwood Heights was that these services were to be provided while a low tax rate was maintained.[11]

The new municipality, at its inception, had on the total metropolitan area an influence which had little relation to its area. The political

structure of the metropolitan area was diffuse. There was no metropolitan council: transportation, sewage, water, police, and other services were arranged *ad hoc*. In some cases, the city rented services to
an infant municipality; in other cases, the latter established its own.
These numerous inter-municipal arrangements were under no metropolitan authority; whatever joint municipal undertakings there were
came under a County Council where urban and suburban interests met
once again with agricultural and rural ones in an uneasy compromise
of power. Here Crestwood Heights because of its prestige was able to
exert influence out of proportion to its size or economic importance. The
relations of Crestwood Heights with the city, with other suburban
municipalities, with the county and with the province were political
in fact but essentially social in form. Although the immediate end and
the immediate product were political, the ultimate end and the ultimate product had to do with social prestige and class position, and with
the preservation of the interests of those whom Crestwood Heights
served.

The outcome of these relationships and of this type of influence fell
far short, however, of the stereotyped expectation of unbridled power.
Indeed, since Crestwood Heights was occupied by aspirants to the
ruling class rather than by those who actually held power, by corporation managers rather than by corporation owners, indecision seemed
to enter more and more into the power relation in the period following
World War II. This became evident when a definite metropolitan
organization was mooted. There was still an official concern in Crestwood to express and maintain differences, and this concern implied a
policy of resistance to annexation. But the drive behind this resistance
was weakened by indecision, at a level just below the formal political
organization of Crestwood Heights, which did officially oppose amal-
gamation. The community appeared to lack the internal cohesion
and homogeneity necessary to bring about clear-cut action either for
or against such annexation. Political control of the area had long ago
slipped from the hands of the lower upper class into those of the upper
middle class — and the strata just below it — which did not have or
could not exercise blunt political force. The only result was that action
was delayed for many years. Finally (towards the end of this study),
an arrangement was made for the metropolitan area which unified
certain services but left others relatively intact. The official opposition
of its Council could delay, but could only partly deflect, a move which
threatened the very identity and separateness of Crestwood Heights.
The external pressures were aided by the ambivalence of the community
respecting its own destiny and self-definition.

ENTERPRISE : COMPROMISE

The compromises and ambivalences of Crestwood Heights have now
been sketched: compromises respecting use of land, respecting the
type and characteristics of the population, respecting the use and distribution of power. We have seen a system in which an idealized goal
is usually counterpoised by an opposed wish. The ideal of living in a
small-town, semi-rural atmosphere is met by a desire to be as near
the metropolis as possible. Desire to occupy an exclusive preserve is
matched by an ideal of inclusiveness and warmth. Desire to live in a
separate community with municipal appurtenances appropriate to the
atmosphere of the Heights is accompanied by guilt at the "selfishness"
of this desire; and both feelings are complicated by the fact that Crestwood taxes are getting to be as high as elsewhere in the metropolis.
In Crestwood Heights, unlike many other similar communities, such
guilt is largely assuaged by the fact that no restrictive covenant has
ever existed excluding any minority group. Well-to-do "non-Anglo-
Saxons" were allowed to buy property without hindrance and to live
in the community.[12] Political and social control, however, was not so
quickly shared.[13]

These various compromises[14] have been enumerated specifically in the
hope that they will be seen as a product of the social forces which have
shaped the metropolis and Canada. Indeed, the particular form of the
compromise and the result, which is contemporary Crestwood Heights,
should be seen not only as a generalized social product, but as a reflection of middle-class values and middle-class understandings of
proper and adequate social solutions. Such are the conclusions of the
social analyst. But, for the resident, for the upper middle class person,
for the executive, the professional, his wife and family, Crestwood
Heights is a niche in the sprawling metropolis which he can occupy
with satisfaction. For most of these, at least, and for others aspiring to
a place on the Crest, it offers space for living, space for growth.

FROM the territorial organization of space in the metropolis and in Crestwood Heights, from the two-dimensional layout of a city, we now turn to the three-dimensional organization of space within the house. This is the shelter which provides the physical setting for family life.

Wherever there are records of man's habitation, something has been said of shelter, of how he selects materials from his environment and fashions with skill and art a protection from wind and sun and cold or a haven for friends, a defence from enemies. Plains Indian tepee, Eskimo igloo, Iroquois longhouse, medieval moated castle, pioneer log cabin, or Crestwood house: each is an example of a solution to a problem of survival. It is also a reflection of family and community organization, of art, and of general belief.[1] Shelter, while it gives material protection to the body, also fortifies the spirit, develops taste, and creates a sensitivity to beauty. In a certain sense, occupants and house identify. Thus the study of shelter may reveal much about what influences the child's growth within his culture, since from it he gets his earliest ideas of space and distance and begins to understand things and substantial arrangements around him. Shelter in Crestwood Heights, as elsewhere, answers to physiological necessity, but also to psycho-cultural need.

WHAT THE HOUSE HOUSES

The Crestwood house, from one point of view, is little more than a repository of an exceedingly wide range of artifacts. It contains the traditional bed, stove, table and chairs, of course; but it also contains (among other things) freezers and furnaces, Mixmasters, medicines, bed-side lights, rugs, lamps, thermostats, letter boxes, radios, door bells, television sets, telephones, automobiles, foods of all kinds, lead pencils, address and engagement books, pots and pans, mousetraps, family treasures, pictures, contraceptives, bank books, fountain pens, and the most recent journalistic proliferations. All such objects are moveable personal possessions, kept in the house; they are the vestments which make habitable the bare shelter afforded by walls and roof. Within the house there is also the ephemeral and transient: yesterday's newspaper, the empty milk bottle, garbage, the echo of a radio program, a TV show with its momentary and flickering contact. Within the house are, again, other items precious beyond telling, delicate perhaps, but, unlike the house, immune to obsolescence: the wedding ring, the heirloom, the faded photograph, the symbolic trinket. This is the varied cargo which the human occupants and owners arrange to their taste.

The house is, of course, much more than a repository of artifacts; it is in its own right and *par excellence* an artifact to which deeply buried meanings are attached. It is the most massive, most costly, and most constantly utilized physical object possessed by the family in Crestwood Heights.[2] The school and the church are larger than any private home, as are the banks, factories, and stores downtown; but only the house is a private possession. In a sense it seems also to "possess" its occupants, because of the attention it requires and the monthly mortgage payments which it exacts from most owners.[3]

It is in the house, too, that persons related by blood or marriage make their voyage together through time. The house, its occupants, and movable things are the triad out of which the living experience of "home" develops. This is the setting for tenderness and laughter, bitter words, first steps, decisions, anxiety and hope. Here hospitality is practised, privacy is secured; here parent and child, husband and wife learn their roles and re-learn them as age and experience alter the conditions and expectations amid which the human drama is played.

But although it is undoubtedly important, the house is by no means the exclusive mode of shelter for the people of Crestwood Heights. Summer cottage, Florida hotel, office, summer camp, school, club, and even automobile serve as alternative abodes for members of the family over extended periods or at regular intervals during the year. Moreover, the functions regularly associated with a house—serving and consumption of food, sleep and relaxation, domicile, to mention only a few—are not exclusively limited to the house. Members of the family regularly eat, sleep, play, and "live" in places other than a house. Food is prepared commercially and brought to the house for serving. Laundry facilities, garbage disposal, water supply, the manufacture of textiles, the growing and storing of food products—which would in a simple society be the joint concern and occupation of members of the family— are services which the Crestwood family can and usually does share with other members of the community. The house here, then, is a center for consumption rather than production. Though it tends to exclude, with its closed door and curtained window, contact with all but the most intimate associates, yet it is locked in a ramification of social and economic relations, which make possible the highly specialized activities occurring within it.

PHYSIOLOGICAL AND PHYSICAL FUNCTIONS

The Crestwood Heights house is founded, as we have seen, on physiological fact: man, to survive, must be sheltered. Its people have the same need for such protection as the Mississauga Indians who once lived on this very crest. But the Crestwooder enjoys a continuously high level of comfort, of which the Indian could barely dream.

The Crestwood house is a complicated mechanical apparatus which stands between its inhabitants and a climate of severe extremes.[4] It is at the same time the primary locus of a family group and whatever adherents may have been added to it—domestic servants, dependent kin, and, more rarely, the covertly (and illegally) included boarder or tenant—all of whom make their peculiar demands upon the plant: for food, for relaxation, health, sanitation, and rest.

The need for nourishment is catered to from a kitchen equipped with electric (or more rarely, gas) stove, electric refrigerator, and numerous other mechanical gadgets, which facilitate the preparation of food. This equipment is considered essential by the Crestwood Heights woman who must, in most cases, prepare without the help of a maid such meals as the family eats at home. With the electric refrigerator and stove, cooking is changing in character. Refrigeration makes it possible to store large quantities of food and to save scraps. With "deep freeze" added, it permits major economies in food expenditure to be effected—possibly only to encourage extravagances in some other direction. It is no longer necessary to cook perishable food immediately, or to devise tasty recipes for left-overs. The Crestwood housewife seems now rather to serve in the capacity of household and dietary "manager," responsible for the buying of supplies; for the smooth functioning of complicated mechanical gadgets which assist her to put the finishing touches to processed and semi-processed foods; and, above all, for the maintenance of proper nutritional standards as laid down by dietitians. Rarely is she an artist in the preparation of food as the European woman of comparable status might be, for in the Crestwood culture food, while it must be wholesome in quality and dainty in appearance, must also serve strictly utilitarian ends. It is mandatory that food be— in repute at least—low in calories, and with a high protein, mineral, and vitamin content.

Procreation, nurture, and the private daily events of family life take place behind the screen provided by the second and third floors of the Crestwood house, the areas of greatest privacy. The needs for rest, relaxation, and family interaction are met by living-room, "den," recreation room, and home workshop, which form another area.

The house is also the scene of complex practices related to sanitation, personal cleanliness, and hygienic precaution. The struggle to ensure good health is not won by casual conformity to health rules, but by meticulous, costly, and constant vigilance.

The medicine cabinet contains few of the trusted patent medicines of an earlier generation, but it is nevertheless well stocked with astringents, deodorants, and antiseptic materials as well as with numerous half-finished bottles and tubes of costly physician-prescribed drugs, originally secured to combat an ailment of some family member. Much zealous trust is placed in the contents of the medicine cabinet.

Cleanliness is assured by an elaborate program. The laundry, sometimes adjoining the kitchen but more often located in the basement, contains the electric washing-machine and equipment for drying and pressing clothes. The family linen may or may not be washed and ironed at home, but personal laundry (with the frequent exception of men's shirts) is usually done there. The Crestwood Heights family, however, owns much clothing which is cleaned outside the home, but usually stored in the attic or bedroom cupboards.[5]

The Crestwood house is, obviously, not just a mere assemblage of brick, stone, steel, wood, and glass, built to protect its inhabitants against severe climatic conditions and to provide a shelter where they may procreate and nurture their young. Far less elaborate structures would serve these requirements, and do serve those of the majority of residents in Big City. The Crestwood house is an impressive and intricate material apparatus, the possession of which makes possible the Crestwood way of life, from a physical and, even more important, from a psychological point of view.[6]

PSYCHO-CULTURAL FUNCTIONS

The primary significance of the house from the viewpoint of child rearing, then, does not lie in its architecture, or in the artifacts with which it is furnished, or in its devices for the satisfaction of basic physiological needs. It is the body of attachments and meanings that are associated with the house which are in this connection important. In this role the house is a valuable means of ensuring privacy in a crowded city; a vehicle for enforcing family solidarity and conformity; a place to practise and perfect consumption skills; a major item of personal property, which, for the head of the family (and, to a less degree, for his wife and children), stands as a concrete symbol of his status and visible sign of his success. It is in terms like these that the significance of the house must be stated.

A. THE HOUSE AS PROPERTY

Property is an essential component of status in Crestwood Heights. The Crestwooder who owns an adequate house has become a substantial member of the community and, as such, is respected and admired by his peers. The house and its furnishings; the street and the street number; the location in Crestwood—all are acquired items which make up the total property complex of the house.

It is on these items, and other similar ones, that the competitive struggle of the Crestwooder for power focuses. These are the symbols around which he must center his efforts to realize the "good life," and organize the strivings which lend a meaning to his existence. Property does not, then, acquire its value directly from its intrinsic monetary worth, or from narrow utilitarian considerations, but from the public evaluations of things as they evolve in the markets of exchange and in the rialto of status.[7] It is the attributes imputed to broadloom, or a particular style of architecture, or the work of a fashionable artist, or a street and number, which give them an edge as weapons wielded in the battle for social position. Utility is secondary to social acceptability.

Typically, a Crestwood man announced at dinner, "Well, today I have satisfied a life-long ambition." After breathless inquiry from the family, he revealed the fact that he had purchased a new Cadillac. He had, he said, bought the automobile for personal gratification; but the spread of excitement to the whole family suggested that the aura of his success enveloped them also. Other articles—especially large and expensive ones—also evidently conferred status, for example, a new, deluxe model, electric stove and refrigerator, a television set, broadloom for the second floor. In another family, the husband would repeatedly suggest the purchase of a new refrigerator. Each time his wife would demur: she liked the one she had; she did not need a new one. Her reluctance was not motivated by economy, nor was his insistence based on technical need. His rationalization of the purchase was "I like pampering you." When he bought the refrigerator "as a surprise" she "loved it." If the wife wants something the husband does not wish to buy, the roles may be reversed, although the cajolery remains the same. The husband gives in; the wife is delighted; she likes being "spoiled"; he is endlessly pleased with the new gadget, the acquisition of which has, incidentally, raised the prestige of the home. Similarly the children receive or secure for distribution artifacts for general use or for individual consumption.

The new item is accepted into the family circle and incorporated into its life pattern. But it is not fully integrated until display has brought about its validation as property. The rug, or the painting, or the drapes are "shelter," not at the margin between bodily exposure and survival, but on the dividing line between discomfort and psychological well-being. The acclaim which the new article receives directly or indirectly spells out its value as "shelter" in the psychological sense; though a poised consumer who knows what will eventually be acclaimed needs less overt recognition, pleasant as well-modulated praise may be.

The owner tends to become deeply—but not irrevocably—identified with his house and its contents. This emotional tie is well known to real estate dealers and prospective buyers and is played upon in the course of all property transactions. One woman informant, who had lived away from home for many years, tells of the sale of the family house after her mother's death. In her account (as in the accounts of others) one may sense something close to an identification of the house with the body— somewhat the same fear of violation, somewhat the same defences against attack.

We had a beautiful house, one of the "show-places" of the district. Mother had wanted a house like that almost all her married life. When she had the chance to get it, she planned it down to the last detail with the architect. Of course, it wasn't the kind of architecture I would have chosen, pure Georgian, but it was very good of its type and Mother loved it. We moved into it just when I went away to college and I never really lived in it. Several times the house was broken into while we were away in the summer and, although nothing valuable was ever stolen, it upset Mother almost as much as if some accident had happened to one of us. She just couldn't bear "strangers" going through her belongings and treating them so roughly.

I was there with Dad when some people came to look over the house after Mother died. He was a Mr. X. who had just come from the States to take some important executive position in the T.W. plant. His wife came with him. She went over every inch of the house, running everything down: said the woodwork would all have to be bleached and that the place needed to be redecorated completely. Mr. X. tried to beat Dad down about the price, very rudely, as if money could buy everything. I had no idea I would feel it so much. After all, it was very much Mother's house and I hadn't ever lived there for any length of time. But I finally just had to go away and leave Dad to deal with them.

Into this world of things the child enters almost, it would seem, pre-natally. The nursery is equipped in advance of the first confinement, and is often refurnished before succeeding confinements. Many Crest-wood nurseries approach the streamlined efficiency of those appearing in the advertisements featured by women's journals. It is little wonder that some parents regard the sense of property as instinctive, for the child's earliest sensory experience may be, not at his mother's breast, but through contact with a set of lifeless objects: bottles, cloth, sides of the crib, and the like. Further indoctrination into the world of things follows: gift giving, the placing of bright objects in the crib and play pen for the child to manipulate. Finally, behavior is learned in which private possession and protective personal modesty are closely linked. The parents may play with the child, taking away a rattle, at the same time saying "mine," then returning it to its rightful "owner." It is not surprising that "mine" becomes a dominant word, not only in the games and quarrels of peer groups, but also in later life when the purchase of the largest house possible filled with the finest and most appropriate objects money can buy, betokens success in the struggle to acquire pres-tige and power.

Before this stage is reached, a lengthy series of subtle behavior pat-terns, centering around property, must be learned and practised, remi-niscent to some degree of the more primitive potlatch.[8] Never must this behavior become extreme or obvious, however. The young child likes, and is encouraged, to show off a new kiddie-car or article of clothing. Adults at first consider such behavior amusing because of its naïve enthusiasm. Later, the same tolerance is not forthcoming; for, in dis-play, the child must learn nonchalance, as well as delicacy.

Unlike the young child, the Crestwood adult automatically watches for the quick appraising glance which will tell him that the recently acquired property-item is acceptable and desirable. He knows that the artifact is ultimately valuable not in itself but only if it assures him of continued acceptance by his peers or prompts, what is even more esteemed, an invitation to join a group of higher status. Thus property, in which the house is all-important, is manipulated to confirm status and enforce prerogatives in Crestwood Heights.

B. THE HOUSE AS STAGE

The Crestwood house is adapted for the "staging" of "productions," and this characteristic is brought to the fore especially whenever formal hospitality is practised. On such occasions, the space which has been purchased at great price, lends itself to the gracious reception of guests. Indeed space is essential to permit the inclusion of a sufficiently impressive number of visitors. Space thus allows the ritual destruction of the privacy it has also created; for it is only as the symbols of status— acquired, presumably, for private enjoyment—are revealed to selected groups and individuals, that their ultimate cultural value can be determined.[9]

Since the guests play the role of audience, their attention and presence are concentrated upon the center of the stage, on those areas reserved for display and hospitality: the living-room, dining-room, and (a more recent accession) the recreation or "rumpus" room. In the wings, food and other symbols of hospitality are prepared, to be introduced as needed. The hall or reception room is unusually important. Here the opening scene is played, with its seldom remembered but inevitably significant opening verbal exchanges. Here also the finale is enacted, following which the family, with the curtain now drawn, resumes, sometimes with a little embarrassment, relationships at a less theatrical or "staged" level.

The Crestwood preparations for hospitality and the behavior appropriate to such occasions are noted in a statement submitted by a university student:

The entertainment of the middle middle-class is almost exclusively within the family residence. It is exceptional to find a guest being taken to the hotel for dinner, for example. It would be considered very poor taste, and suggest that the host and hostess did not consider their guest worthy of the trouble of entertaining him at home.

A person takes his "cue" from the individuals he is entertaining. When a woman has a tea or bridge party, how she patterns her behavior depends upon who is present. There are definite norms governing actions if members either of a lower or a higher class status have been invited because, in both cases, the hostess must use all her resources in an effort to impress her own position upon the guests. In such a case the best china is dusted and brought forth, the lace cloth and silver tea service come into use; even the topics of conversation are closely regulated by convention. Any controversial issues are carefully avoided; true inner feelings are repressed, else interaction among the individuals would be impossible. Conversation is maintained at a "sociable" level: talk for the sake of talking, being witty, amusing, amiable but never really saying anything. We may compare the house, in the situation, to a *stage*, and the people present to characters who are displaying the parts they play in the community at large.

The staging or "display" orientation is illustrated also in the use of "picture windows." They are most frequently located in the front of the house overlooking the street—rather than in the back where they would afford a view of the garden. The purpose seems less to give the occupants a view of the outside, for which a much smaller window would suffice, and more to extend an invitation to the outsider to look in. Through these windows, the mildly curious passing observer may identify, where the drapes permit, the owner of a grand piano, a valuable crystal chandelier, or a striking red brocade chair. There is an air here not only of display but of coquetry as well. The window is spacious, but it will not open; it is large, but it is often hooded by heavy drapes; it reveals an interesting room, but the revelation merely encourages the imagination to speculate on all the others.

The theatrical or staged appearance is not equally evident in all houses; some are more artless or conventional than others. Even children are aware of these differences and discuss them freely, especially after parties, when they comment with considerable candor on the homes they have visited. Said a five-year-old in a home known for its *avant-garde* taste, and very self-conscious about colorful display: "Mummie, aren't you afraid when people come to our house that they'll think they are coming to a furniture store?" One house may give a definite impression of "night club" décor, showing the pronounced influence of mass communication media, movies, and house decorating magazines. On the other hand, drabness in the decoration of some homes appeared to be quite as studied and self-conscious as the color in the examples cited above. In the former, however, the nonchalance of slip-covered furniture and the mute testimony of prestige-laden family heirlooms effectively indicate the status of the family which had arranged these props.

Entering one of the more patently theatrical abodes may produce an unusual effect upon the guest. Criticism may be hostile:

She uses pink a lot. That's her attempt to make the place warm and give it life, but she can't quite bring it off. Actually she doesn't live in that house at all, she's someplace else altogether; and when I visit her, I feel I'm in an empty house.

Or:

Everything is exceedingly studied in every detail. The décor is refined to the point where . . . well, the other day when I called there, I was afraid to lay down my green gloves because they clashed with everything. The walls and rugs are matching powder blue. This blends with the Wedgwood. The brass around the fireplace gives a dash of brightness, but the fire itself is seldom lit. When it is, the blaze is deeply shadowed. There is no thought of it giving warmth, but only an added, moving subdued light.

The Crestwood house seemed often oddly reminiscent of a series of department store windows, charmingly arranged, harmoniously matched in color, but rather cold and empty of life. On more than one occasion an interviewer had the experience of waiting while his hostess whisked the plastic covering off the furniture. In such a home one did not find children's toys on the living-room rug, or a piece of sewing dropped on the chesterfield or table, with the needle sticking in it and thread or thimble nearby. There was no homely litter to proclaim that family activity went on amidst the inanimate objects, chosen with such care. In some houses one was almost driven to ask, "But where do they *live?*" In others, the piled magazines and the evidences of hard use indicated that a room, though tidy at the moment, was indubitably a "living room." In still other cases, it was found that the so-called living-room, like the rural parlor, was spared daily wear—this is possible in a large house—while a small den or breakfast nook served the purpose.

For the outsider, the stage must always be set and ready. Intimates can be brought into a disordered house with the simple explanation: "This place is a shambles"; the wider circle of acquaintances cannot be received so casually. Certain articles are reserved for the most formal display only: in one house, a handsome silver tea service on an ornate Sheffield tray was enveloped in plastic, and the covering would not be removed for an outsider dining informally with the family.

The furnishing of this elaborate stage is an arduous undertaking. The people of Crestwood Heights appear to occupy a middle position, not only in the class structure, but also in the hierarchy of taste. The majority of them are not in a position to acquire the prestige-giving objects commonly found in upper-class homes. They lack the excess wealth, the judgment, the contacts, and, often, the desire, to secure them; yet they are compelled to collect material possessions from which they can derive pleasure and status. Rather than a Renoir, Crestwooders will buy an Emily Carr, a William Winter, an Arthur Lismer; or, at a lower economic level, good reproductions of modern artists. But these purchases pose nagging questions. Is the object still in style? Is it *passé?* Or is it already "coming back?" Crestwooders are not in a position to confer respectability upon an item simply because they have given it their patronage, since they themselves still hope to derive status from their purchase. Thus, in a changing, unstable society, there is, for those who are its most mobile members, a continuing need to revalidate the material objects with which the house has been "dressed."

Upon the stage of the Crestwood home the family plays out, then, several endless dramas, public and private, which include numerous characters, enacting many roles at different times and for different purposes. These dramas allow varying degrees of privacy and display. An area of privacy is never completely absent, even during a New Year's Eve party. Display is also never absent, even through the darkest hours of the night, for the family is solidly located in one particular street, in one particular section, and in one particular style of house. This backdrop of the house, is, in the minds of all those who are intimate with or know of its owners, as permanent a symbol of status as is the husband's position and income, or the wife's beauty, accent, and clothing. Thus the central theme of all the dramas the house supports becomes competition for social status; hope of success or chance of failure provide suspense, but the dénouement is never final, since in Crestwood Heights standards of style and taste shift and change in bewildering complexity.

C. THE HOUSE AS HOME

Although Crestwooders attach great importance to the house as a vehicle for competitive display, they also call it "home." The terms "house" and "home" point up the fundamental differentiation between the technological item and its emotional connotations.

The Crestwooder, like his contemporaries, builds or buys a house; but he "makes" a home. He sells a house, it burns down, or it is broken into; but a home is "broken up." Adjectives like "happy" and "harmonious" go with home. One hears of an unhappy home; but a house is empty, or bleak, or noisy, or dirty, or gaudy. Yet there is a great deal of ambiguity in Crestwood Heights about the "hominess" of the house. On the one hand, it is a quality which is taken for granted by many Crestwooders. One woman, in an interview, said:

I've never once thought about the house that way [an effect to be achieved]. I live here; I came here as a young married woman; I had my children here. They grew up and my husband and I have grown old here, so I just accept it.

On the other hand, this "old shoe" attitude towards the house is not universal; and, even when present, it often co-exists with anxiety about the acceptability of the house and with concern for the preservation of its contents, relieved perhaps by rather bitter remarks about neighbors who are over-ostentatious, and whose house "can never be a home because they are afraid of marring the theatrical arrangements prescribed by the decorator." With perhaps a trifle too much protestation, some residents repeatedly pointed to the fact that, in contrast to many others, their house *is* a home. Said one informant:

The whole neighborhood plays in this house. They are in and out all the time. We had a party here with girls. One boy said to my son, "Gee, you're lucky. My mother never allows me to take anyone home." One girl said to him, "Why, you live in a palace!" The boy said, "Yeah, I know; it's the best house I have even been in, but I have to take my shoes off before I go into my bedroom."

Another Crestwood mother reported that she liked having the house full of people; but when a researcher visited her, she seemed nervous, and she fussed about the furniture. In a routine psychological test given at school, this woman's child replied negatively to the question, "Do you like to have parties at your home?" When it is a question of the house being used as a home, in the sense that children, for example, might wish to use it, there is much evidence that parents are very protective of contents; and that they fear and resent boisterous behavior of their own or neighbors' children within the house. Yet the fiction is preserved that the home is one place where each member of the family may be himself, even though the house is designed by adults chiefly to suit their ambitions, comforts, and purposes. This is one point at which the focus on the child is blurred. The rumpus room and the children's rooms are, however, meticulously fitted to what decorators and the furniture trade consider the taste of a child.

Crestwooders make a definite distinction between behavior at home and the behavior appropriate to other forms of shelter, such as the club. While the club may afford the Crestwooder certain facilities and an atmosphere of privacy, which he may associate with the comforts of the ideal home, he still differentiates between the two. To him, club and home are not synonymous terms. And yet the hostess often finds the club more convenient than her own home as a place to entertain; perhaps because, as one woman revealed with some asperity, "if service is wrong or the food is off, you can blame the management of the club." The club, as this informant said, was not just more convenient; the anxious hostess felt more comfortable there than she did at home. The man in describing the joys of club life—"getting together with the boys," "putting your feet up"—seemed to be describing homey forms of relaxation.

The privacy which the house as home offers (or "should" offer) is highly prized by the Crestwooder. In a culture which, on the surface, has largely abandoned the Victorian concept of a carefully graded intimacy, free admittance to the home may still stand as one criterion of intimate friendship.[10] The home tends to become the only or primary means of guarding any inviolability of the private self. This self he may be forced increasingly to deny in the outside social, business, and professional contacts of his daily life, but the home can serve as psychological shelter for whatever fragment of it remains. The Crestwooder may not know of the abstract distinction, but his behavior with regard to admitting people to his home tends to make important its function as the citadel of the private self.

The behavior around doors, which control access from the outside world to all the areas of the house, is strongly differentiated. The back, or side door, exists for service deliveries. Honored guests are introduced into the house through a formal front entrance. Only a very intimate friend, usually a close neighbor, would think of entering through the side door, perhaps unannounced. Since Crestwood Heights is part of a large city, outside doors are customarily locked, and even children must learn very early to ring or knock for entrance at the appropriate door. In the case of the child, this may well mean the back, or side door, since the living and dining areas with their expensive furnishings must be well guarded from muddy feet and dirty hands. The Crestwood householder, therefore, recognizes that there are infinite gradations among people, and his judgments of these are manifested in their free or controlled entrance to the home.

The same screening process goes on within the home. In the second floor area (the most closely guarded, where outsiders are concerned), the cleansing of the body and the renewing of life in sleep or sexual intercourse take place. Here the human body is carefully groomed and clothed for public view; here the vestments of public life are removed, so that the body can shape itself to the contours of private existence.

Many parents boast of the freedom of movement permitted and encouraged at this upper level. "We don't care what we wear up here." "Our children know what the human body looks like." This decrease in intrafamilial "modesty" increases, in one sense, the private nature of the sleeping, toileting area of the second floor, since freedom is limited as yet only to the family of procreation. Because of this new intimacy, the first floor "powder room" becomes more necessary than ever. The child, too, must learn at an early age the bathroom behavior which is fitting for family members and for guests. The door that was usually left open or ajar is, in the presence of the guest, locked. Similarly, the spacious manner of allowing doors to remain open on the hall is altered. When strangers are about, they are shut, or almost shut—but not locked.[11]

Doors within the home should be clearly distinguishable. The guest venturing aloft, in a house where there is no ground floor powder room, will be escorted on his first trip, or carefully instructed, "It's the first door on the right." The visitor must be spared the embarrassment of either walking into a bedroom or having to knock on the bathroom door. He should be able to go directly into the bathroom without pause. The bedroom doors are so hung that they can be left ajar, for the tightly closed door in the emancipated home should not be necessary, but at the same time they should screen the bed and dressing table from the casual glance. Similarly the kitchen, basement, and laundry doors should be so placed that the guest will not enter these more private areas unwittingly.

While the house is an expensive device to permit and enforce privacy, it is also true that the superior purchasing power of the Crestwood resident is used to secure more and more mechanical devices that constantly invade this privacy: radio, television, and the telephone are almost universal. The telephone, which the more affluent place beside beds, and even occasionally in the bathroom, allows the invasion at any hour by a casual caller of the private areas that are regularly denied the nearest of kin and the dearest of friends. The automobile, which continues to grow sturdily in size and cost, seems to be only slightly less successful in gaining access to the home. The older houses in Crestwood Heights kept their garages (like the old coach house) discreetly out of sight. In the newer houses, however, the garage has entered into the essential design and rationale. The immense slab which serves as a single door for the two-car garage dominates the smaller, less pretentious door used by the human beings. The space devoted to the car is often greater than that occupied by the living-room.

The house not only serves as a means of separating the family from the outside world and even from its closest friends; it is also a device for separating members of the family from each other, thus preparing the child, and its parent, for ultimate separation when the child establishes his own home.

When interviewed about their houses, residents frequently give as their reason for moving to Crestwood Heights, the desire for more space. "The children were growing up, and needed separate bedrooms"; or "they needed a basement recreation room as a place to entertain their friends." Increased income always offers the possibility of buying more space. Privacy for each member of the family is the ideal—but not the isolation of anonymous shelter as offered by a hotel. The essence of the desired privacy is its very presence within the family unit.

One young matron, recently established in Crestwood, admitted quite frankly that, during the years she had lived in a small apartment, her dream had been to have a bedroom of her own, sacred to herself, which the children could not enter. After the long-contemplated move to Crestwood Heights, this woman with sincere delight planned the decoration of the master bedroom for her sole occupancy, stating that no one else, not even her husband, would use its bathroom.

The Crestwood home, must, ideally, provide ample space for separate sleeping and working quarters for each member of the family. There should be a desk or its equivalent in a well-demarcated area for each member of the family "old enough." These areas may be rooms, or merely corners, shelves, or drawers within a larger room; and little pressure is put on the individual to keep this area tidy. When occupying "his" space, the individual should not be disturbed; when absent, his possessions are not to be rearranged. A place for the mother may be the entire kitchen with a still more private corner where she keeps household bills, personal correspondence, recipes, receipts, and money; the boy may have a lab, or a dark-room, and a place for skates, skis, and other gear; the father will have a spot to keep his tobacco, pipes, golf clubs, bridge set, and he may possibly also have a workshop; the girl, similarly, will screen cherished items—letters, photos, diary, cosmetics —from the eyes of other family members. The bedroom is often the repository of most of these items of personal property around which the individual builds his own satisfactions, and which help to differentiate him from the other members of the inner circle of his life—indeed he will often reveal them more freely to a peer in age and sex than to a member of his own family.[12] If he leaves home, he will take these possessions with him.

One Crestwood mother, contrasting the difference between the contemporary house and the house of her girlhood, which was of comparable size, said:

When I was a girl, we all worked of an evening around the dining room table. We had a warm fire in the room and we all worked quietly or read in the same room. Now, we scatter throughout the house to follow our interests.

The hot stove and the oil lamp drew the family together; now, electric light and warmth, which are equally spread to all corners of the house, also disperse the members of the family. The description well underlines the difference between the activities of the Victorian family and the new individualistic pursuits of the family in Crestwood Heights, pursuits which the type of house encourages.

The material objects which fill the space bought at such a price illumine another important facet of the Crestwood house as home. The Crestwood house, in this context, is not the home celebrated even to recent times in folklore and song, the "home sweet home" which has a peasant meaning—a modest spot, fixed immovably in one locality through several generations, the only symbol of stability in a shifting, cruel world, an abode that is always "there" to "come back to." The dwelling-place does not have this traditional stability in Crestwood Heights, since the family takes for granted the fact that its members will live in a succession of houses. The Crestwooder, therefore, cannot cherish a single image of the home, fixed in time and rooted in space. Nevertheless it is important that the Crestwood resident have a current image of home, a spot to which he may return at the moment, and an object of which he may be proud. The home image may change in the course of time; and it is confidently expected that to those who fashion it this image will become increasingly satisfactory. In Crestwood Heights there is, for example, hardly a trace of looking back, of nostalgia for a "little grey home in the West"—but rather an anticipation of a bigger and better home for the future in some other environment altogether.

Yet the people of Crestwood Heights do not lack sentiment, and are far from nomadic. Although members of the family may belong to clubs, own a summer cottage in the North, patronize a ski lodge, or vacation in Florida during the winter, a relatively permanent deposit of material goods remains in that house which at any particular time they call "home." Indeed, the presence of these objects in a succession of houses is probably the most important factor in the Crestwood concept of the home. It is really the movables which create the air of homeliness, and which are psychologically immovable, rather than the physically rooted house, which is there to be moved into, grown into, moved out of and left behind—an outmoded shell to be reoccupied by another mobile family. The Crestwood house in this aspect impresses the observer again with the constant flux of paradox and compromise which characterizes life in the Heights. It serves as a vehicle for display in an atmosphere of uneasy aspiration; but, at the same time, it must also serve as a defence against the uncertainties created by rapid social change at this class level.

Different attitudes towards these material family possessions may be noted between ethnic groups, between old families and those with newly acquired wealth. The solid, well-established family, when it moves, will take its familiar relics with it; when a child marries, some of these objects are transferred by gift or loan to the new household. Others regard these treasures with bewilderment, and with a mixture of awe and disdain, as the following excerpt from an interview reveals:

There is no new furniture in the house and not a single piece less than forty-five years old. Everything is slipcovered and very genteel. The fireplace is the focal point in the house. It is used! It is a real living room. They keep fresh flowers in it even when they should be buying food with the money. Appearances are awfully important to them. Pictures on the walls are photographs of the children—one of F.R. himself in palmier days— and a very costly miniature of Junior. There must be at least a dozen pictures of Junior downstairs. He is "prince elect". . . . The house is full of inherited stuff. One piece of furniture will be from an aunt, another from a cousin, and so on. A lot of the furniture is sleazy maple and the rugs are threadbare broadloom. The dining room suite is very old; it was a gift and it's stunning. They eat every day with very old sterling; and they put their napkins in a ring. She bakes her own bread and does her own laundry— even his shirts—with an old electric washing machine and an ordinary electric iron. She has no new labor-saving gadgets. All their electric equipment is old. The furniture has an air of decadent gentility. They even say to us "We're not rich, like you! Our place is old. Everything is old, but we rather like it." The colors are faded greys. They had a couple of pictures— old paintings—but they belonged to someone else and the person who owned them borrowed them back.

This same informant also had comments to make on a home where these values did not obtain: "Every time they move, she has to have a new outfit: furniture, drapes, broadloom, and pictures." For such people, taste or selection of an interior decorator becomes all-important in the creation of a home. "They always have a beautiful place, but for them, *getting* the furnishings rather than maintaining and embellishing them, is the home-making adventure."

Thus, while each Crestwooder has different notions as to what collection of material objects constitutes a home, all are agreed that a home is necessary in their scheme of values: the indispensable screen for the functioning of the private selves which in interaction constitute the family unit. As home, the house must satisfy the personal emotional needs of parents and children, needs which are intensified by the varied, and sometimes conflicting, roles of family members.

To the father, the house as home may mean, not the material and visible sign of his success as bread-winner, but the one place he may be himself, relieved of pressing responsibilities, free of competition, sure of warmth and companionship. For the mother, the house as home tends to represent her major task, "the creation, for husband and children, of an environment in which security and understanding are paramount"—an effort, in turn, complicated by the obligation to oversee the complex mechanism for which she is frequently wholly responsible.

For the young child, the home acts, as it does for the woman, as the center and hub of this universe. This attitude gradually changes until the child, in his teens, may regard the home merely as a place to eat and to recuperate from a continuous round of activities outside its orbit; indeed, he may behave towards the parental home as if it were a well-run club, depending on its facilities to entertain his friends at no cost in money or in effort to himself.[13] The attitude changes again when the young adult prepares for marriage. The value of a home then again becomes paramount, since the individual's readiness to finance one of his own is the symbol that he is accepted as a full and functioning adult in his culture.

The house, then, as a focus for family life, becomes a most cherished possession. Male and female, at a certain stage of physical maturity, must acquire a house and in this process of proclaiming their social maturity, must further transform the house into a home. Within its walls, the wife plays her role as best she can, alternately maternal, seductive, efficient, but always sustaining husband and children. The house as home symbolizes the life-long social and biological union between a Crestwood man and woman, which must be maintained through and beyond the period of child-bearing and rearing. This requires sexual compatibility and a broad emotional adjustment—which are often mutually dependent; these, in large part, make possible and are made possible by the home, now no longer merely a house.

The attainment of these favorable conditions is made difficult both by the wife's interest in maintaining and exercising extra-familial interests (or even her former vocational skills) and in preserving her physical attractiveness, and by the high cost of child-rearing in Crestwood Heights. Even with a moderately high income, the Crestwooder is severely taxed to keep up a four-bedroom house and, at the same time, clothe, feed, and rear several children in an "appropriate" way. Yet a smaller house, if it is felt to be "over-crowded," cannot provide the space which is an essential aspect of the ideal home.[14] Should the tension for the family become too great, the only alternative might be to leave Crestwood Heights.

To meet the demands made on the home, the house is deliberately designed to be flexible. Even though certain members of the family may frequently be absent, and all are seldom in the house at the same time, the house must provide maximum service on demand. Indeed, as the children grow and leave home, the parents often maintain this large plant throughout the year, so that all the children may, if they choose, come home with their families on festive occasions. Although the husband may keep up club membership purely for the sake of entertaining, his house must, nevertheless, be designed and equipped to offer comparable hospitality.

To the Crestwooder, the term "home" conveys a special meaning. He does not expect his home to remain constant in time and space, but he does assume that, in whatever house he may occupy, he will be surrounded by his primary group and at least a minimum of familiar objects. In these expectations he does not differ too greatly from the Australian aborigine who, on his return from a field-trip with an American anthropologist, touched a stone on the edge of the desert, saying, with great emotion, "This—home."

D. THE HOUSE AS NURSERY

The Crestwood house and alternative forms of shelter have not been examined for a routine catalogue of items in a material culture. Our catalogue is not sufficiently detailed or exact; and moreover, such an undertaking hardly falls within the scope of this inquiry. Our concern, primarily, has been with the effect of this complex of artifacts upon the person, most especially the child; what are the ways in which this apparatus helps to define for him his world, his place in that world—in short, his self?

With growing consciouness of himself and his world, the child learns to recognize the house as his own. Unlike his parents, many of whom have known humbler surroundings, this place is *his* locale. He looks out on this locale and on other people from his play-pen and later from his picture window, or from the windows of the family's late-model car. Not only does the child first take for granted, and then accept the objects he sees, just as he does his mother, but they remain even more constantly within his vision, for his mother's community life does go on concurrently with child-rearing. He must learn to respect, to use, and, finally, to want such things enough to become the ambitious person idealized in the culture.

The Crestwood child, born into a world of fine houses and expensive gadgets, must learn, almost before he walks and talks, that some of the objects surrounding him are precious almost beyond telling. From word, facial expression, and gesture, he finally learns not to touch the fragile stemware, should it come within his reach; just as the farm child learns when beginning to walk, not to fall against the kitchen range; or as the

Manus child who lives on a pile-supported hut on a lagoon avoids drowning by learning to swim, with adult help and insistence, as soon as he learns to walk. Parental solicitude about things continues into the child's adolescence, culminating when he wishes to drive the automobile and to secure his own place of abode. In both cases, the parents express anxiety about the child's ability to use and to manage things.

Within the house, the child must learn the difference between utility and display, and the methods appropriate to each. The protective preoccupation of the adults with the broadloom (and with the equally svelte, almost equally sacred, lawn outside) helps him to differentiate between a useful floor covering, a pleasant tactile sensation, and a valuable item of property which could be ruined by unsteady bladder control in child or dog, if either were allowed upon this surface. Some Crestwood children are given unlimited access to the house, but many others are not. For them the spaciousness of the Crestwood house is somewhat illusory. In a similar way, the child learns that a fountain pen is something to write with, but that it is also an object precious beyond its function. Losing it, or breaking it, is "wrong." All this is doubly puzzling, because there are other things, cigarettes, for instance, which are bought simply to be destroyed. The display attributes of any item in the house are not at first appreciated by the child. To him, they "are," that is all. But the child does learn, very early, to follow his parents' lead, and a corresponding pattern of concern, pride, and display is built up around clothing and toys. Non-familial newness, shininess, and smells merely put a special edge on appreciation.

By its very nature, the Crestwood house with its separate areas for work and leisure is markedly different from the large, inclusive farm kitchen, for example; from the one-room dwelling in the slums; or from the crowded five-room bungalow of the lower middle classes; and it is by means of these differences that the impact of the type of house upon the structure of the family and the formation of personality must be assessed. The Crestwood child is never integrated into a kinship group to anything like the degree that children in these other environments are identified with their kinship groups. The Crestwood child sleeps alone; usually he has his own room. He may be left in the charge of various functionaries and experts for lengthy periods or, more casually, with "baby-sitters" for shorter periods. His mother is still his mother, but he shares her with the community and with his father's professional, business, and social activities.[15] He goes to camp and has experiences in which his family need not be included and from which they can be excluded. The personality norm held up in gradually increased detail before the Crestwood child is that of the individuated person who can and wants to separate himself from his kinship group and establish a new family unit. The child is prepared for this process of psychic separation in part by the very nature of the house in which he lives. The Crestwood house, where the child is concerned, may be responsible in great part for his later feeling of near-omnipotence as an adult, for his expectation that he should be able (or is able) to control and to plan his destiny in virtually every detail. Shelter, it has already been noted, is considerably above the subsistence level in Crestwood Heights. Life is sufficiently complex, sufficiently well engineered, that the periodic arrival of a truck to pump fuel oil into the basement furnace-tank is almost as automatic a phenomenon as the flow of water always available at the faucet, or of energy at the flick of an electric switch. The child may be well aware of hot and cold weather, but the vagaries of weather are not likely to do more than spoil his plans to play outside (just as rain might merely frustrate his father's intention to have a round of golf).

The weather, then, does not threaten the family livelihood in Crestwood Heights as it does that of the farmer; nor does it involve bodily survival, as it may in the case of the fisherman. The thermostat of the Crestwood house maintains an even temperature within the house, and the child is protected from the elements when he is outside by raincoat, snowsuit, station wagon coat, and the like—which are provided for him without effort on his part. The Crestwood child never experiences physical peril from the elements in the sense that the child of the prairie farm feels it when exposed to the terror of being lost with his family in a January blizzard. He must, it is true, learn the hazards of automobile traffic, but these are gadget-derived threats, and hence, to him, ultimately controllable. To this child, nature is seldom either beneficent or threatening. His milk comes out of a bottle; his fruit out of a basket. "Roughing it" is never a way of life for him, but a course offered at a summer camp with the implicit guarantee, in the parents' absence, not only of safety, but of benefit to character as well.

Crestwood Heights is only a few hours' drive from the frontier, and the ancestors of many of the residents knew actual physical peril in pioneer days. Consequently there is an often verbalized feeling of guilt that life is now too soft, and that everything is "too easy" for the children. Yet the Crestwood house represents a major preoccupation with protection of both children and adults, with shelter as lavish as family income will permit. It is an apparatus, which, when capably manipulated, secures the occupants against all the principal vagaries of existence— except only those stemming from the behavior of men themselves.

4. TIME

THE ANTHROPOLOGICAL LITERATURE on time, scanty though it is, indicates that the understanding of time varies widely among human
cultures, and that it is related closely to the technological arrangements
and cosmological beliefs in these cultures.[1]

Physical time has to do with the movements and rhythms of the
physical universe. Day and night, the lunar and the solar cycles are the
most immediate observable facts. Biological time is perceived in the
urgency of passion and birth, in the inevitability of death, and in the
human experiences that lie between these two events: here are the facts
of maturation and decay within the individual biological organism. But
only as man perceives and gives some order to these facts in language,
and accords them recognition in ritual, belief, and social organization,
are they in effect integrated in "social time."[2]

Social time, then, is derived from physical and biological time, in
the sense that the logic and symbolism of these two are the foundations
upon which a system of social time is built. Social time, however, provides its own definitions, meanings, and, if one likes, "distortions,"
which reflect the technological and symbolic necessities of the culture—
to turn night into day, for example, or to prolong through ritual emphasis a phase of the year, or of a life cycle.

In the measure of time in Crestwood Heights, a pendulum-like
swing occurs and recurs—between tension and relaxation, preparation
and realization, work and leisure, application and dalliance. The daily
round is dramatically segmented by nature into day and night: the
twenty-four hour cycle from dark to dawn, to full daylight, to dusk,
and again to dark, provides an existential pattern of sleep, awakening,
effort, fatigue, relaxation, and sleep again. Similar rhythms, observable
in the weekly and yearly cycles, will be described in due course.

TIME THE MASTER

In Crestwood Heights time seems almost the paramount dimension of existence, not only in the simple sense that all human events occur in sequence, and therefore in time, but rather because of the pervasiveness of time as a force in life and career patterns. There are constant demands for efficient work (that is to say, for the most economical use of time), for punctuality, for regularity, which call for an acute sense of timing. These are important factors in the estimation of success or failure.

An urban population with its ramifying interdependencies is almost compelled to adopt synchronized schedules. Work and even play are regulated, not only because life is determined in numerous ways by the exactitudes of machines, but also because so many social activities (meetings, luncheon engagements, and even weddings and funerals) must occur at a predetermined time in order that the day's events may run smoothly and the work of the city may be done.

The rewards for work are meted out in a quantitative medium— money. Work (in this sense only) is for the man; the child and the mother are less involved in and more loosely integrated into the time-values of a machine-dominated world. This difference is accentuated in the summer when the mother and children may live almost three months in a cottage in the Northland, to which the husband commutes for long weekends. The money which the father earns in a schedule-dominated life is used to purchase whatever is considered necessary — including leisure. His money rewards are a time equivalent. Time is saved by saving money—to buy "leisure."

Not all the leisure so bought is devoted to unscheduled loafing. By men, and to a less degree by women and children, loafing must be justified: "I needed this rest, I was fagged out" they will offer as apology, or boast. Most leisure is spent in scheduled events: watching the fights on TV, regular bridge club tournaments, curling on Saturdays, and the like. In many "play" activities there is a high degree of diligence, as the doctor knows who attempts to prescribe relaxed activity for a patient suffering from hypertension! Golf or gardening can be taken quite as seriously as business, and for many they *are* business.

Crestwooders nevertheless agree that the man works to have "time off," and that when he leaves his male environment of harsh exacting deadlines to return to his home and family, he expects and is expected to relax. Family life, however, is not entirely oriented around the father's work and leisure. His wife has her own activities outside the home which are carefully scheduled; and both have, as well, joint social engagements which bear on his career. The children have their school —which demands punctuality—scheduled appointments with dentist and dancing teacher, and numerous social activities. Home life is indeed often hectic, although there is for many a measure of quiet and relaxation in performing simple family duties and acts of mutual aid.

But the very nature of secondary group life beyond the primary, family circle can hardly permit too much of this simplicity, and the resultant schedules are so demanding that the parents feel themselves constantly impelled to inculcate the virtues of punctuality and regularity in themselves and the child, at meal hour, departures for picnics, and such occasions. Being on time for school becomes more important than eating breakfast. The intimacy of primary relations can be punctured easily: the flow of after-dinner conversations will often be broken clearly and sharply at nine by a vigilant host who has scheduled a television viewing as part of the hospitality of the evening; a chattering group of students will be divided neatly into two halves by an ongoing bus (four minutes late), half boarding the vehicle, the remainder continuing on foot; family dinner is interrupted by long-distance phone calls for father. The secondary institutions thus emphatically affect the rhythms and patterns of family life, and the family with its generalized function is hardly in a position to resist the outside institution with its specific function, which, within limits, permits it to demand the individual's participation. To take a perhaps extreme instance, if a televison program for children changes its schedule without warning, the family meal hour may have to be changed, unless the adult members are prepared to accept enforced silence and semi-darkness.

These secondary institutions are, of course, themselves bound to a time cycle: school is from nine to four, five days a week; church is at eleven on Sunday; the book club meets at two, the third Thursday each month. The activity promoted by the institution is regulated by the clock, and the schedule of one institution, unless it is definitely raiding the time and clientele of the other, must be fitted to the schedule of others within an inevitably tight competition for time. The family is evidently given less consideration, and "extra-curricular" activities often leave little time for the child to spend with his parents.

The special tempo that builds up in the non-familial institutions is noteworthy. The rigid schedule which service-club luncheons follow is well known: so many minutes for lunch—the late-comers must hurry, or sing with their pudding; so many minutes for singing and announcements; and a strict twenty minutes for the speaker. The same emphasis on precision, overshadowed by a general atmosphere of haste, may be noted in the fashionable congregations of the churches which circle Crestwood Heights.

The moment the last prayer was said, every one stood up and seemed in a great hurry to leave the church, and as the lady sitting beside me seemed particularly anxious to get by me I had little time to look around. Outside again, I noticed there was little loitering or conversation, and every one seemed instead to head straight for his car and drive away.

So that the service should not last longer than usual (in spite of the special ceremony and the delay in starting) at two points in the service the minister announced that the singing, first of the *Venite* and then of the *Benedictus*, would be omitted.

Another report from an independent observer revealed:

The hymns, readings, in fact the whole service, were conducted quickly and seemed to be rigidly limited to one hour. No one said "Good morning" on the way out. Ushers along with everyone else seemed to be in a hurry to get their coats on and be away.

The school is even more precisely geared to the clock in the administration of its curriculum; this aspect will be treated later in its place. We may observe here, however, that within the structure of the school, carefully graded by age, the child's achievement is measured by performance in each class, each day, each term, each year, and his progress through the school is marked off in a series of shorter and longer time spans.

In some ways, too, the school seems to anticipate the "piece-work" motif which dominates the existence of the adult; the student's timetable does not differ substantially from that of the dentist or executive who may be his father. For each, work consists of a series of short, relatively discrete and unique activities with separate persons or groups —in one case, successive unrelated clients or customers; in the other, a series of teachers.

TIME'S FRAME OF REFERENCE: THE CAREER

While the swing between the packed program and the idle vacation is a noticeable feature of the temporal life of Crestwood Heights, it is the career which creates the dominant perspective on time. The career, the most important imprint which the individual through his own efforts can make on his environment, will receive detailed attention in a following chapter; we wish to see here how it affects the ordering of time.

A prime requisite of the career is a seemingly effortless mobility, and the result, in terms of time, is, as it were, a foreshortening of perspective, a focusing on the present and on the immediate future with a consequent blurring of the past and the long-term future. Invention and change tend to sever links with the past; personal movement in physical and social space, even in the present, tends to distance the individual from his kin and from places and associations that maintain family solidarity. The rapidity of technological change, the pace of the succession of fashions and fads, contribute to the discarding of the old and the traditional. As for future time, while the Crestwood person is quite aware of geological and cosmological time perspectives, his involvement in them seems to be casual or academic unless they are related to the business of life or the life of business. The "facts" do not bind him to the past as much as the literal interpretation of the Garden of Eden story does those who believe that the earth was created in 4004 B.C.

As might be expected, there is in Crestwood Heights, with a few conspicuous exceptions, little evidence of pride in name and ancestry. Very few of those who were interviewed were able to go back in family history more than two or three generations, and even when this was possible the person who was questioned found it necessary to consult an older member of the family "who was really interested in such things." Life history documents were even more revealing. The child's or young adult's chief interest and pride referred to his own father and mother. If a grandfather had been famous or had performed some unusual exploit, or if a grandmother had unusual charm or talent, this would be recounted. If these ancestors had come from Scotland, or Poland, or Alsace, this might be mentioned, with the additional information that great-grandfather was a scholar or a landowner; but rarely was more than this known or recorded.

Thus kinship organization, social change, and personal mobility tend to minimize traditional values and a sense of history. It is therefore almost inevitable that sensate experiences and personal well-being in the present are emphasized. Health, happiness, security, the ability to cope with immediate situations are seen as the outstanding values. Other more universalistic considerations, which imply a lasting and valuable contribution to society, are almost wholly lacking. Few Crestwooders look hopefully to a life of contemplation and thought lived out in the light of eternity.

As a consequence of this perspective on time, the career of the individual in Crestwood Heights has a special character. It is seldom a long steady pull, but rather a steep climb, a relatively short period of recognized pre-eminence, then a sharp descent. The Crestwood male is desirous of reaching the plateau of recognition as early in life as possible, and of remaining there as long as possible. His achievement of it is above all a personal one; the requirements for a successful career cannot be inherited. The burden and the laurels rest largely upon the person who makes of it his opus within the narrow span of what are known as "his productive years."

The slow, difficult climb and the swift descent of the career suggest analogy with a roller-coaster. The roller-coaster ride also consists of a slow start; a long, dull, laborious ascent; a brief pause at the top during which there is scarcely time to enjoy the exhilarating view because the balance is precarious; then a sickening fall. The bottom offers no security; there is no gradual and reassuring deceleration, for the momentum of the descent is absorbed immediately in another steep climb. It is true that each descent facilitates the next ascent, that the last loop is small, and that finally the speed, which has never been as great as the person paying for the ride has sensed, diminishes. The halt is at the same point and level as the beginning.

The roller-coaster may serve to illustrate the tempo and perspective of the social experience through which the growing human organism passes, the life cycle for Crestwood Heights. Life's full term there consists of a slow start, a long tedious haul, a peak, a climactic fall, and a finish. And within this grand loop there are a series of small loops of varying sharpness, each with its own set of goals and rewards and its own finale; each is an independent cycle, yet each is integral, in some degree, to the grand design of the total pattern as prescribed by the culture and by the individual characteristics of the person involved. Each loop is "a little life" within a life. The Crestwooder does not live one serene, unbroken existence; he does not have nine lives, but ninety-nine.

If each loop constitutes "a little life," the normal attributes of a life cycle should be contained within it. One need not expect an absolute correspondence, but with surprising frequency one finds at the beginning of each loop a ritual acceptance into a new status, at which time the goals prescribed by the group or the situation are impressed upon the newcomer in an initiation ceremony of some sort, followed by the arduous acquisition of skills and accompanied by the establishment of personal relationships with others similarly involved. Briefly, skills are mastered and relationships are in balance; this momentary balance is shortly followed by a ritual "death" or descent into a new low status as the "rider" moves into a new group and a new situation. In this final phase, in the "graduation exercises," the individual is allowed to display his laurels or his skills, but he is inexorably pushed from the security and joy of the climax into the descent. Spectators of these ceremonies come to praise *and* to bury the graduate, for there are few figures more pathetic in this culture than the boy scout or the old boy who has won all his badges and prizes but who will not lay them aside to take up "a new and more challenging life."

Life in Crestwood would be relatively simple if the major loops were in sequence and in order: grade school, high school, college, occupation—each one a preparation for the next. Needless to say, such simplicity is absent. Within the school to job span there are myriad sub-systems of struggle and achievement: the music club, fraternities, the hockey team, the drama club, the school magazine. Outside school, there are summer camp, scouting, church activities, ballet, figure skating, music lessons, as well as personal hobbies. Into each of these the child must enter in a state of innocence and ignorance, and climb thence "to the top," only to find again that he must abandon the pinnacle. In the next chapter the functions of these patterns will be examined much more closely in relation to the career; they are introduced here merely to demonstrate the basic tempo of life in Crestwood Heights, where there is no simple set of loops such as may be found in pre-industrial societies in the Western world.[3] On the contrary the loops overlap somewhat, and are independent of one another, though in the net result they may tend to distribute fairly evenly both the tensions and the satisfactions.

TIME AND THE LIFE CYCLE

The peculiarities of perspective, tempo, and rhythm in Crestwood Heights have interesting results in the growing-up pattern through which the child passes. For one thing, the tempo and the emphasis on the present result in a pervasive feeling that *time is running out*; and there is a tendency for the child to push experience forward in advance of physiological development. Field reports repeatedly underline this theme.

In many of our experiences in Crestwood Heights, expression has been given to fear and uncertainty respecting the future. This has taken various forms but the constant theme is the number of things to be done and the shortness of time remaining. For them, time appears to be "running out." How unlike the easygoing Irishman who told his prosperous but harassed neighbor, "Take it easy, you have all the time there is!"

In a group of eleven- and twelve-year-old students, discussion really waxed hot over kissing games. The girls say they are really not in favor of them, but Guy said there was nothing bad about them and objected to the discussion. Some one countered that they were too young for such games. Then someone wanted to know if they should wait until they were thirty-five before having kissing games. Jerry argued that *now* was the time for them, since when you got older you didn't play them, and if "you don't do it now, when will you!" There is nothing unusual about the game, but the justification offered (that this is probably the last chance) does seem unusual. Indeed, if this trend were fully generalized it would entail the collapse toward youth of the entire life experience. Perhaps this is what happens, for if children are rushed to emancipation and adulthood there is little left for later years. Parents in Crestwood Heights frequently complain of this trend, but state that they are powerless to combat it since other children and other parents set the pace. This feeling is reciprocated by other parents, so that we have an example of an inflationary market system where normal controls are inoperative.

Mrs. A. has taken her four-year-old daughter to the hair-dresser for a permanent. . . .

. . . The B. family sent their little boy to camp this year. He is only three and one-half years old. The B.'s say this camp is taking children as young as two and one-half. . . .

. . . The Nursery School is taking two-year-olds now. . . .

. . . Ten-year-old children in our school have dates, go to movies in two-somes, and have evening dresses.

. . . Our twelve-year-old boy wants to buy a tuxedo. He says everyone else in his class is buying or renting one for the Prom.

. . . We were forced to buy evening clothes for C. [fifteen-year-old boy]. I felt sad about it. I thought "He is grown up now." There isn't much for him to look forward to. There are no thrills left for him.

. . . A group of parents are worried about lights-out parties which twelve- and thirteen-year-olds are having. Some of the parents [absent from the meeting] go to the show and leave the children unsupervised. The same group was unhappy about the introduction of corsages at the Prom.

. . . If there is an eagerness among children, and undoubtedly some parents, to taste experience earlier, one is left with the question: earlier than what?. . .

At one level the parent seems to say: "I want my child to have his child-hood, but my friends want him to get ahead. But perhaps I do the same for their children. . . ."

This rushing at experience has consequences for the child as he gradually forms a conception of himself as an "aging individual." The boy who rides a horse, wears long pants, and has a girl friend before puberty, has lost some of the means of validating his biological manhood at the moment in his physical and social maturation when such signs are most needed.[4] The boy's changing voice and the girl's first menstrual period are not accorded the public attention that one might expect from a culture where sexual matters are so often exposed to discussion. In contrast, there is, of course, no lack of ceremony in the areas where individual achievement and competition within the group are encouraged. These activities, which are often of a vigorous nature, and the rewards which attend them, together with opportunities for controlled eroticism (such as dances and mass behavior at football games), help to prolong adolescence and make it not simply tolerable, but "exciting."

The ceremonials just mentioned take place at the occasions in the "roller-coaster" ride when a new status that has been sought, is won, and the achievement is given social recognition and acclaim. It might have been expected that a progression of these numerous events would emphasize and add lustre to growing old. This expectation is only partially fulfilled. Up to a certain age, apparently, the passage of time is thought much too slow. Birthdays seem far apart, an impression which is fed by the other ceremonials of aging which occur during the year. After the crest of the golden ridge has been reached, the passage of time is viewed with regret; and birthdays, which are observed now with reluctance, seem too closely spaced. To those on the young side of this ridge, which is ascended so slowly, it is a compliment to say, "You are big for your age"; "You look more than sixteen." Once on the other side, the descent is all too swift; the compliment is rather, "You can't be that old"; "You don't look a day over twenty-four." The age of twenty-four, among women at least, seemed to be the "golden age"; for the male, the golden age is somewhat later, perhaps thirty-three. Up to that point, male youth seeks to be disguised behind a moustache or horn-rimmed glasses. Soon after, a man may find it difficult to alter his career line, or find a new practice or firm to work with, unless the move is clearly within the definition of career advancement.

For both sexes, despite these efforts to speed the clock, or, after a certain age, "to make time stand still," despite diets, cosmetics, and facial surgery, age creeps on. A critical period for the male, as it certainly is for the female, is the "change of life." Surrounded by more secrecy than is puberty, except when it is the subject of not too gentle joking, this period threatens, sobers, and frightens.

The crisis surrounding menopause is, however, more serious for the female, while the next general crisis, which comes at retirement, is almost exclusively a problem for the male. Since few unmarried professional women live in Crestwood Heights, and since few married ones are permitted the pursuit of a full-time occupation, retirement constitutes no threat to the female. One of her skills—housekeeping—remains with her in old age, to "give her something to do." The male, who has bent his energies entirely to the advancement of his career, finds, unless he is one of those few who can bask in the status of an elder statesman or seasoned consultant, that he has made his last descent but one. Retirement, more than menopause, is a sociological death. It is now fashionable for men to attempt to meet this problem by "pursuing a hobby."[5] The utility of such activity during and after retirement is evident, if it can absorb a man's energy and interest at the end of his work life.

The crises at menopause and retirement illustrate the delicate balance in male and female roles between work and leisure, between the capacity to create people and the capacity to produce things. The female senses her loss of creative capacity at menopause: if she can resume some of the work activities which she surrendered when she became a mother, she and her advisers feel that she can better adjust to the last phase of her life. The male at retirement has a similar hurdle to leap, but, in one sense, in the opposite direction. He is forced to surrender his work responsibilties; if he can pick up some of the avocational interests which he was forced to abandon progressively after kindergarten, after public school, after university graduation, after marriage and fatherhood, then it is thought that he can enjoy old age as much as the other phases of his life's span. If the woman can maintain a thread of "work" throughout her creative child-bearing years, old age is easier for her; if the man can continue some "creative" activities through his work years, old age is easier for him.

Retirement may be less severe in its impact for Crestwood men than for men at lower economic levels who must often rely on children for housing and financial support; at this class level the parent, it is assumed, is financially independent. If he is a man of considerable wealth, he can, moreover, even after he retires, wield a good deal of influence upon those who are dependent upon him. This group can include his wife and children as well as younger business associates. Even if he has given the children "a start," he can still maintain in them a state of apprehension about the ultimate disposal of his estate. This can hardly be called an affectionate bond, and the support which an old man can derive from it in his last days will not be great, but it is something. In any case, separation from the children cannot be linked entirely to questions of financial dependence and control. The children who were so skilfully launched upon careers while the parent was still wholly engrossed with his own, cannot often be expected to find a large place in their crowded programs for the aging parent. It is clear that independence is both bane and boon. Dependence, if humiliating, is still a bond.

Through all these details it is clear that the career, as a time system, imposes by its tempo thematic changes and dominates the time perspective. These factors become even clearer as we analyze the major units of time in Crestwood Heights.

TIME'S UNITS

A. THE DAY

The day, a universally recognized unit of time, is in Crestwood Heights tailored to fit the technological arrangements in which the community has a part. Factories, offices, and stores open and close by the clock. These organizations, as well as railways, radio broadcasts, schools, airlines, bus lines, and delivery services, work on schedule; all make certain demands, often in concert, upon the individual and family whose biological rhythms are considerably less mechanical than are those of the organizations from which these demands emanate. Such organizations—only a few are noted—are synchronized to the same time system and, with some notable exceptions, they commence the day between eight and nine o'clock in the morning. If the father works downtown, if the children go to school, the demands are imperious for action within the family to launch its various members in time to be on time for these daily, non-familial activities.

The work day[6] holds all but the youngest children away from the home until about three-thirty in the afternoon, when the school begins to release its charges. Precisely at the cessation of the work day, the "play" day begins to occupy the leisure of those who are released from productive activity; neighborhood theaters, special classes, take over as work and school leave off.

The daily routine displays both the synchronized time control that has been noticed in the school and the range of tempos manifested in the roller-coaster. A fascinating aspect of synchronization is the way routine events, moving in a wide series of orbits, converge upon one household, or one individual, and thus constitute for it or for him the particular daily round of events. The manner in which they converge is responsible, in fact, for changes in pace and tension.[7] The arrival of the morning paper, the eight o'clock newscast, the milk delivery, the deadline to place an order for groceries, the time for Kindergarten of the Air, the lunch for the kiddies at twelve-fifteen: these events are not controlled by the mother—they are controlled by outside schedules from among which she can, in a limited range at most, select. Therefore these discrete work units do not create a smooth flow (even disregarding the unscheduled but repetitive demands of the young child); rather they seem to bunch, providing the mother with crisis points in the day. The father in his office, even when the progression of events is regulated by a competent secretary, experiences the same pattern of serial explosion and flow. The phenomenon which the Crestwooder calls "pressure" is caused by this concentration of demands into limited units of time. A mother will say "I get so I can't cope with everything." No one is more admired than the person who is "never ruffled," who keeps the flow steady; and a primary work satisfaction comes from "having everything under control."

The ubiquitous desk calendar and appointment book facilitate this flow. The professional man and the executive are lost without them. The busy Crestwood woman makes appointments for herself and her family; where others are involved, she will wait until the dinner hour to synchronize the engagements. The appointment—and the control of time which it implies—enters into the regulation of the child's life at an early date. Soon after the pediatrician has succeeded the obstetrician, the child begins to visit the dentist; then the barber, and then the music and dancing class, at carefully spaced intervals. Thus begins a life in which time is segmented into measured units of work and play.

School and camp, for all their freedom, require a large element of control of time. Confronted by a vast mass of work to be done during the year, the curriculum arranges each task in sequence, though child or teacher may make minor decisions about order and emphasis.[8] The extra-curricular life of the school creates for the child situations which more nearly duplicate adult experience. Preparation for a meeting; choosing between two fraternities; deciding between glee club, orchestra, and camera club: these expose the child to adult pressures, especially if in the latter case the child, in his enthusiasm, decides to "compromise" by joining all three.[9] The successful and popular student is usually one who has learned to sort out the duties and discharge adequately the responsiblities that he has been encouraged to assume. If he succeeds here, he is thought to be "mature" and well on the way to adulthood.

The day does not, it is obvious, allow a simple or clear-cut division between work, relaxation, recuperation. The work day tends to be an orderly progression of appointments and separate tasks—interrupted, however, by the telephone and other uncharted stimuli. A second set of activities generally follows but partly cross-cuts these: the child's extra-curricular life; the father's quasi-social luncheon or business contact at the club; the mother's shopping and theater expeditions or her club work. These may not be "work," but they are much too seriously pursued, too near the heart of the career goals to be dismissed as "play," though they do change the tempo of the day. Still later, in some families, the father—if not exhausted by his "day"—comes home to preside over family affairs; in others, management problems are left to the mother while the father plays with the children. There is, briefly, a marked relinquishment of the father's downtown occupational role, and a similar marked shift of behavior in the child. The mother is less successful in reversing her role at this time of day, except in those families where the husband is willing to assume a goodly share of the household duties or competent domestic help is employed. Lastly, there is the recuperation which comes from intimate and relaxed family activity and attention to personal necessity, and from sleep.

B. THE WEEK

"The day" as we have described it, refers, of course, only to the five days Monday through Friday: Saturday and Sunday are not counted days in the ordinary sense. Thus the work week seems to end Friday afternoon. The "weekend" then commences, and extends to Sunday night. Production is the dominant motif of the work week, consumption of the weekend. The weekend must serve more functions than this, however. The work week produces fatigues and tensions from which recuperation (in addition to that provided daily) is required. During the weekend the swing away from work, away from the clock, is more pronounced than it is in the brief evenings of the work week. "Sleeping late" is permitted; meal hours are less rigidly observed. It is a time for fun and avocational activity.[10] Trips to the beach, the museum, or down to see the boats and trains are planned for the younger children. Sometimes the whole family will go to a football game or out for a picnic. However, these events are far from casual occurrences. They are planned in advance and must compete with the individual interests of each member of the family. A willing father must often defer to a Saturday movie; a willing child, to golf.

Crestwood people may at one time or another engage in many or all the activities described here, but it is still possible for some to "do nothing" for an extended period of time. Indeed the changes of tempo in the week may be extreme. A young man from a rural background who visited boarding school friends in Crestwood Heights made the following comment:

One of the most difficult things I had to get used to was not the food, or the soft beds, or even the pressure to get things done; it was the weekends when people did absolutely nothing. They would get up on Sunday and some-times on Saturday around noon. They would eat at any old time, lie around in their dressing gowns and their feet pushed into very dilapidated bedroom slippers. No one wanted to talk or do anything together. I can't help but feel that even the quiet times here are different. Back home we didn't talk a lot in our family; you did not feel that the others were somewhere else even if they did not talk. We never got as gay as they do here, and we never slowed down as slow as they do here.

The Crestwood weekend appears to be in transition. Closer analysis reveals that three ways of using time can be distinguished: one, traditional but disappearing; a second, representing a phase of transi-tion; a third, emerging seemingly as the norm.

For some, there is not a mere weekend, but rather a holy day, which is at once the finish of an old week, an occasion to prepare proper motivation for the trials and temptations ahead, and the beginning of a new week. For these people, the Sabbath (or the Sunday) is recupera-tive in the sense that the soul or inner heart of man which has been exposed six days to the world, is on the seventh "exposed to God," and thus sanctified and renewed.

For others, a not dissimilar content or intention receives a secular explanation and justification. Adherence to Sabbath or Sunday rite is less rigorous. Golf or fishing can be substituted for church or synagogue without unbearable guilt. Primary justification has now been found not in the recuperation of the soul but in the restoration of the body, in the maintenance of the health and happiness of the individual. Golf or a soothing religious service may be almost equally beneficial—depending, of course, on the weather.

For others again, justification is also secular and egocentric but they have moved on to consolidate further the logic of the assumptions which are implicit in the second form. For them, neither body nor soul is central. The career is now the end which is served by the well-spent weekend. Health and happiness must be sought, not simply as means of promoting personal well-being, but as means of refurbishing the career. The week now ends with a burst of calculated and calculating career manoeuvring. If there is still to be church, the "proper" church must be chosen to correspond with the status won by the career, and also to help advance that career. If there is to be golf, the partners in play must be potential clients or potential customers, or potential creditors or status-givers. If there is a cocktail party, it must be planned with the same single eye.

The families of Crestwood Heights adopt one or other of these patterns for the use of time—and there are some who, in subtle combinations, have caught and held all three. Within this wide range of norms and values, the one common determination is that there shall be no lost weekends!

C. THE YEAR

In the annual cycle of Crestwood Heights, we find greater complexity but, basically, a repetition of the pattern which has been identified in the daily and weekly cycle: a concentrated work period and a period of relief in relaxation and recuperation. The complexity of the year results from the fact that a series of sub-systems, each itself displaying the basic pattern, fits into the annual cycle. There is thus a simultaneous or overlapping series of "years": the solar year as determined by seasonal change; the year as identified by the birthdays of family members; the year as marked off by national or religious festivals; the fiscal year of the various organizations to which each member of the family belongs; and the fiscal year of the father's income—punctuated by such crises as the annual raise, the settling of the budget, and the filing of income tax returns. Each "year" is separate from, yet co-existent with, the others. Each, through its own set of associated expectations and rites, reinforces the sense of time. Each helps to establish the sensation that "time flies."

The Crestwood year, like the Crestwood day, does not, in spite of modern technical competence, treat time measured by natural phenomena as irrelevant. Night and day have been altered and redefined but not eliminated, even in an era of electrical illumination. The cycle of the four seasons with their extremes of heat and cold continues to give, as Canadians insist, spice and variety to life, despite the efforts of heating engineers.

These seasons, then, remain; but, sociologically speaking, there are really two seasons—a social-and-work season and a vacation—with two bridging transitional periods. If we borrowed names for these periods of transition from the natural seasons, we should have to reverse the conventional meaning to make them correspond to social fact. When winter is the period of activity and summer the period of lethargy, one "springs" into the winter season of fervid action, and "falls" into the rest and recuperation of summer. To avoid confusion, however, the words "spring" and "fall" will be used conventionally here. The social-and-work season absorbs the entire winter months as charted on the traditional calendar, and much of spring and fall. The latter two serve to facilitate the transition into and out of the winter season. Spring brings a renewal of outdoor activity and a progressive diminution in the number of social engagements; by the end of May it is virtually impossible to arrange for evening or afternoon meetings, even though school is still in progress and vacation time has not commenced.[11]

Vacation behavior seems to fall into two main types. One results in a partial separation of husband from wife, and a total separation of parent from child during at least part of the summer; the other results in a fairly complete restoration of family ties with an exclusion of competing secondary institutions. The second type may be observed in several manifestations. The family can remain in Crestwood Heights and ignore the absence of neighbors. To do this raises formidable difficulties, as one mother pointed out in an interview. She had stated earlier that she "hated the cottage." To the question "Why don't you stay in the city?" she replied:

Well, there are a lot of reasons. The children are harder to look after in the city. Sometimes they have to go ten blocks to get someone to play with, and that isn't fun for the mother if you don't have a car. If you do have a car it is easier. You can go to the zoo, the local beach, or on picnics. If you depend on your husband picking you up, that is just the time someone will call him for an urgent appointment, just like I am holding you up now. [It was 5:40 P.M.] In the country you don't worry about when you get up, what you wear, when you eat, or the way the house gets knocked about. You should be able to get up an hour later in the city during the summer, but it doesn't work. The man is still on a nine-to-five schedule, and you have to keep things revolving around him, so the children have to be kept quiet. In the city there are the lawn, flowers, and the neighbors to worry about. This is all changed in the country. Then, the children see the same children if they stay in town, the same house, and the same street. There is nothing to refresh them, nothing to make them glad to get back home. At the cottage they make new friends, too, and although I don't see them much in the winter, we are glad to get together again.

Other families who own a cottage also exhibit behavior of this second type. (The pattern is less elaborate for those who rent one.) The cottage is opened and used in a succession of weekends during the warm spring months. The moment school closes, late in June, mother and children migrate to the cottage. The mother remains there until after or just before Labor Day (in Canada, the first Monday in September). The father becomes a "bachelor," living alone in the house or moving to the club; he drives out to the cottage Friday night and returns to the city Sunday night or Monday morning. Sometimes he "stretches" these weekends if he is not too busy. Later, he spends his vacation at the cottage. The children may not be sent to camp, but learn some of the skills derivable at camp from the mother and older children. This pattern reinforces the matriarchal tendency of the family organization. It depends for its success upon the energy and independence of the mother and upon the willingness of the father to accept a fairly strenuous and possibly inconvenient living arrangement. However, the father may reassert or regain the position of leadership and authority, or have it thrust upon him, during the long weekends and throughout his own vacation. Many spouses do not like the separation resulting from this arrangement; their reasons are various. An interview throws some light on such attitudes, revealing at the same time that life at a northern lake is not one of unmitigated enjoyment, that the habit of relaxed summer vacations has not yet been thoroughly learned, and that the husband's notion of a vacation is to be left alone in the city.

It's because the husband and wife do not want to be separated all summer. Some wives are pretty suspicious. They are up at the cottage all summer, and their husbands in town, except on weekends. Some of them phone every night around 10:30 p.m. to see if he is in. Then they get sore if there is a lot of wet, cold weather, and the roof leaks and the wood won't burn, and there is an out-door toilet, while he is in town with an oil burner and a nice warm dry house. The men don't like the cottage either. I've seen them, after a few days at the cottage, down at the drugstore phoning the office, arranging for a telegram to call them back to the city "on urgent business." It made me so darn mad!

There is yet another variant of this type of behavior. In this case the family remains relatively intact. The mother, with all or some of the children, remains in Crestwood until the father's vacation. Then they take a boat or a motor trip together, or even a cruise on the family launch. Such events are less frequently observed since few families spend the summer in this manner regularly, though a trip to the Pacific or the Gaspé may occur under special circumstances, often to coincide with a necessary business trip of the father.

By way of contrast, an opposite pattern frequently occurs in which the children are sent to camp for all or part of the summer. Camps operate from four to eight weeks, offering a series of terms to accommodate parents who wish, for financial or personal reasons, to send their children for a more limited period. While children are at camp, the parents are free to pursue one of several courses. They are left to renew a romantic relationship which was interrupted by child-rearing. Or, if their relationship is already fragile, the disappearance of the children removes the need to maintain a façade of amiability. Camp for the children allows the parents to separate more completely, either by maintaining separate residence or by plunging independently into vigorous programs of golf, tennis, boating, fishing, or travel. Sometimes, however, the absence of part of the family leaves the parents, especially the mother, free to devote more time to a "problem child." Many mothers, again, expressed a preference for the summer months as a time for child-bearing, particularly when there were other children old enough for camp.

Well-established families, who enjoy inherited wealth, are somewhat more likely to own cottages. Their pattern will, accordingly, display more solidarity than that of families coming into wealth. The latter will rent a cottage, or patronize a hotel. This yields a less repetitive pattern, and offers fewer associations of last year, or the last generation.[12]

With the opening of school in early September, the winter season begins to accelerate gradually. Club and group activity does not fully resume until October. The outdoors still offers attractions to encourage the continuation of spring and summer activity. Canadian football, both collegiate and professional, engages much interest until the end of November. Sometime in October or November the last lingering weekend at the cottage takes place in the golden and crimson light of a Canadian Indian summer; if the trip has been delayed too long, it becomes a brief perfunctory action to forestall the ravages of weather and rodents. The economic machinery downtown, never idle, but quiescent enough to operate with limited vacation staffs at the managerial level, now gathers momentum again. The work week resumes its full schedule. The professional man welcomes a full appointment book, since this is a measure of his income and his success. The accumulation of work weeks constitutes the winter's work season.

Work, as an economic activity, is linked to the social season of Crestwood Heights in an association so intimate that the boundaries separating the two cannot easily be fixed. Some Crestwood parents are involved in military balls, hunt club life, and the like, but less so than are the childless couples and families of greater wealth and prestige who live elsewhere in the metropolis. Nevertheless, rounds of cocktail parties, study groups, subscription concerts, church and charitable duties do claim time. Similarly the child, early in the school year, finds the tempo altering as the extra-curricular demands increase. The nature of these demands and the tendency of duties and responsibilities to accumulate

and overlap have already been described. Within the winter season
there are cycles of tension and relief which vary with the individual,
marked by Christmas examinations for one member of the family, a
figure-skating carnival for another. Many people and families seek release from the pressure of this season by indulging in a winter vacation.
It may be taken in Florida, or in New York where the delights of Broad-
way and Park Avenue beckon, or in the Northland at a popular skiing
resort.

Recurring annual events and celebrations in Crestwood Heights,
coming, as they do, every few weeks, tend to punctuate and accentuate
the passage of time. They separate the minutiae of life from the broad
trends of existence. They provide "time out," as the phrase goes in
sport, when the play stops, when the rules do not apply, or when they
can be broken or contested. In so doing they impose a sense of time
sharply contrasted with that imposed by daily work schedules. Near
Christmas, a school girl exclaims "You know the year is almost half
gone, and I am not half way through any of my books." The "year"
referred to is, of course, the school year. Even a child lives many
"years" simultaneously, and the undertone of haste and finality to be
heard in this reference sets the year's end apart from the routine of
passing days.

Seen differently, however, the progression of year's-end events sets
up yet another routine which suggests the swift passage of time. The
school girl just quoted felt the school year was half gone because Christmas was approaching. These recurring ritual occasions, such as St.
Valentine's Day, the Queen's Birthday, and Canada Day, are numerous.
Some of the holidays are, of course, ignored by all but a few people;
they are noted only in a metropolitan editorial, or special radio program, or tag day.[13] Many of the days belong to one ethnic or religious
group—all others are only marginally related to the events of such days
as St. Patrick's. For most, the progression of such days is part of the
general environment of change and movement characteristic of urban
life, as are the innumerable cinema and concert offerings; each "day"
furnishes one more activity that is accessible, but which one must so
often miss, simply because "there isn't time to take in everything."

For each person, however, there are a few special events in a year
which have high meaning for him as well as for his family, or his group:
a birthday, a wedding anniversary, the anniversary of the loss of a loved
one. Such an event may not receive elaborate commemoration, yet it
is—just because it is annual and is felt to mark another end and another
beginning—in effect another New Year's Day.

The grandest of all finales in Crestwood Heights, for nearly all Gentiles and many Jews, is, of course, Christmas and New Year's.[14] They deserve special attention because the year whose end and beginning they mark, is nothing less than a "moral year." Where so much emphasis is placed upon the individual, his separateness and his capacity to achieve, it is to be expected that there should be ritual occasions to provide an opportunity for testing individual achievement in relation to general expectations, and for examining the premises upon which these expectations rest. Whether the sensation of the year's ending is pleasurable, sad, nostalgic, or anticipatory depends largely upon the individual's evaluation of the year's performance and the prospects for the year ahead; these tend to reflect his age and the point reached in his career. But it is, in any case, at this time of year that one may ask oneself: "What was I like a year ago? I am a year older: what have I accomplished? What will happen to me next year?" Or the questions may include a wider circle: "Think of what happened to us this year: I wonder what the future has in store for us?"

Even though they are so close in time, there are fascinating differences between the two events that are so similar in meaning and purpose.[15] Christmas is familial; the claims of secondary association are largely neglected. Children occupy the foreground, but not to the exclusion of parents, for now children are expected to be "good" in the conventional sense and parents "indulgent" in the conventional sense. One of the delights of Christmas is the behavior of the very small children, who do not yet know "what to ask for"; when their parcels are opened, their surprise is genuine, in contrast with the charming but counterfeit surprise of older members of the family who may have "guessed" what was concealed by the elaborate wrappings. The survival of the Santa Claus myth provides a symbol for an economy of plenty.[16] For the rest of the year, one gets what one "needs," and tries to get some measure of delight from window-shopping—from seeing things so attractively exhibited that they become desirable, though only a small portion of the display may be possessed. At Christmas time, Santa Claus may be asked for almost anything, and (by some) for almost everything. But to avoid disappointment, prudent parents caution their children, and themselves, to give some items higher priority than others.

The presents under the Christmas tree have, for the most part, replaced the presents in stockings in Crestwood, since few of the massive gifts would fit a stocking. These gifts stacked under the tree remain the object of excited curiosity until Christmas morning. Then, when the parcels are opened, the corner occupied by the tree becomes the focus of the entire family. Here is the window shopper's dream come true: the floor is littered with opened boxes and wrapping paper; there is scarcely time to savor one delight before another is at hand. If surfeit awaits the family at the table, it has already visited them at the tree. The days and weeks of planning, secrecy, discovering what the other wants, evasively letting the other know what is wanted, have come to a climax in this giving and receiving of gifts. Here, indeed, is a rite for a culture where property values are supreme, for the goodwill, joy, and genuine pleasure that is felt and shared by all mark Christmas morning as a memorable occasion!

The gift-giving which renews and sustains family ties, as well as kinship and friendship connections, is carried on nevertheless in a context of display and competition. The rivalry is, no doubt, good-humored, but the exhibition of Christmas cards on the mantel is more impressive if a well-engraved card from a Cabinet Minister, business tycoon, or famous actress appears with the others. The children communicate with their friends by telephone or by visiting, to discover, as they report it themselves, "the nature and extent of the loot." The wife who receives an expensive gift from her husband, also receives, with him, the accolade of friends.

Gift-giving, which draws the family closer together, thus reaches out into the secondary relationships to help validate the status of the family. The exchanges of cards, gifts, and visits permit it to approximate briefly or to simulate primary relations with a wide range of acquaintances. They become a device to reaffirm old associations and to solidify new ones, and the general level of expenditure and taste revealed in the entire operation furnishes one more criterion by which the status of the family in the community may be established.

New Year's Eve observances,[17] in contrast with those of Christmas Day, are non-familial, and the relationships beneath the *camaraderie* are more reserved and calculating. On Christmas Day, kin with whom one has little association at other times of the year expect and are expected to claim hospitality and fellowship. By New Year's Eve, the blood ties have become attenuated once again, and association is based on congeniality or interest even though intimacy may be lacking. Christmas is *fête* for children; on New Year's Eve, they are excluded. Christmas Day begins (lamentably, the adults think) with their early pre-dawn arousal by children in search of gifts; the festivities last throughout the day. New Year's Eve begins after the children are put to bed, and continues for many until daylight; it may end—anti-climactically—when the children begin to demand breakfast on the morning of the first day of the new year. Christmas Day is organized by the mother: preparation of food, planning of gifts, budgeting for the heavy expense. Preparation for and financing of the New Year's Eve celebration is much more likely to be the responsibility of the father. He is interested in having his own friends and clients included in the list of guests, and at the party itself he is expected to arrange and serve the drinks and to carve the fowl when the food is being served. Christmas emphasizes generosity, display, the exchange of property; and the inordinate consumption of food. New Year's has to do with the display of guests, or invitations to parties, or lavish spending; and the inordinate consumption of liquor. A religious façade remains before Christmas even though Santa Claus is now the central figure.[18] The religious motif in its conventional sense is almost totally absent from New Year's, and the symbolic figures of the bearded dying old man and the naked new-born child (both males, it should be noted) appear much less prominently in their season than does Santa Claus in his. The basic themes around which Christmas revolves are joy, liberality, peace on earth, and the birth of a child who represents goodness and righteousness. New Year's emphasizes an ending of things, and death: if there is a new-born babe who arises from the bier of the dead, he is innocently unaware of the tribulations ahead, unaware of his own death twelve months hence. Christmas is a time for intimacy and relaxation within "the inner circle" of home and kin; on New Year's Eve, people are encountered who have not been seen, or greatly missed, for a year, and new acquaintances are met who may eventually become friends or may never be seen again. In spite of their tenuity, however, these brief contacts are often made pleasurable by the interchange of news and banter, even though there is not an overwhelming desire to increase the frequency or intimacy of the contact.

On New Year's Eve, isolation is more to be avoided than on any other "occasion." One can remain at home to hear or see the festivity in Times Square or other points of celebration. A table may be reserved at a downtown hotel for a group of friends, or one can arrange to be invited to one or more house parties, for it is considered proper to accept more than a single invitation for that night. The more original and expensive manner of celebrating is to organize a party of one's own. To this are invited people who are certain to accept, plus a few really interesting persons who—if they accept—may be used to induce other interesting, but perhaps more discriminating, prospects to accept also. It is the ability to collect, and successfully intermingle, a provocative assortment of people, many of whom may be unknown to one another, but all of whom ought to be known by the host and hostess, which constitutes the recognized and applauded art of "putting on a good party."

The consumption of liquor is high on New Year's Eve; people who seldom or never drink at other times may do so at least moderately then; moderate drinking is less subject to censure on New Year's Eve than at any other time of year. It seems that gaiety and conviviality are compulsory at the year's end, but that these conditions cannot be attained without stimulants.

The New Year's Eve party of which we speak resembles, however, in some ways, the rural watch-night service of a generation ago. Then, the year was "watched out" in hymn singing and prayer, repenting the wrongs of the past, preparing for the renewed struggle against evil, each watcher standing spiritually naked and afraid before God. Then, even if it were not read, some of the melancholy poetry of the Book of Revelations would be felt:

. . . and behold, there was a great earthquake; and the sun became black as sackcloth, the full moon became like blood, and the stars of the sky fell to the earth as the fig tree sheds its winter fruit . . . the kings of the earth and the great men . . . hid in the caves and among the rocks . . . calling . . . "Fall on us and hide us from the face of him who is seated on the throne, and from the wrath of the Lamb; for the great day of their wrath has come, and who can stand before it?"

In Crestwood Heights such dark words are not spoken; what is felt, what is spoken, is:

Fill up your glass, it's five to twelve . . . my watch is stopped . . . see what they are doing on Times Square . . . Old Man '53 is just about finished . . . there goes the cheering . . . *and* it's '54 . . . where's my wife, I always kiss her first . . . another chapter's written, darling . . . I'm getting hungry. . . .

One year is over. Another, begun.

AGE is the child of time. Every society inescapably takes count of age in the distribution of rights and duties, in the attribution of characteristics and status. The distinctions that are made are various, but it seems safe to say that in no society are the distinctions carried further than in the one under study. Just as some societies have a dozen or more different terms for an arrow or a natural object that has unusual importance for them, so, in this society, one might say that terms for age grades—especially for children—are carried almost to the ultimate refinement. Not only is there, in effect, a sub-society of four-year-olds, as distinct from five-year-olds, for the children but there is very nearly a science of the four-year-olds as against a science of the three-year-olds for the adult. And not only a science, but a system of expectations and a system of obligations as well.

UP TO TWO: BIRTH AND EARLIEST DEPENDENCE

The planning which we have seen as characteristic of Crestwood Heights extends, of course, even to the advent of a child. Parents usually "arrange" to have children as they do to make a trip to Europe or to buy a new car; and this prior, deliberate choice is made possible and nearly sure by adequate contraceptive devices and knowledge. If, as often happens in other areas of Crestwood life, carefully laid plans miscarry, and a child is conceived without the element of forethought, the tendency is to regard the event as an accident which must be accepted with good grace. No Crestwood mother would admit ordinarily that her child was unwanted, since love and security norms now receive such emphasis.[1]

Birth in Crestwood Heights, and the pregnancy which precedes it, introduce a cultural situation which the child will continue to meet in his progress towards maturity. In our modern society with its intricate division of labor, it is not surprising that the advice of a medical specialist is sought to confirm the fact and supervise the process of the pregnancy. He is the first of a series of experts or specialists to whom the Crestwood couple will refer their problems connected with child-rearing. The link between the family and the non-familial institutions, with their attendant experts, begins to be elaborated at this early point.

The obstetrician cares for the woman throughout her pregnancy, prescribing in detail her diet, hours of rest, exercise, weight, attitudes, and expectations as to the development of the embryo. He is also responsible for the delivery of the child, in a downtown hospital, and for the care of the mother while in hospital.

The hospital birth, at a distance from home and family, provides another symbol: from the beginning, individualization is mapped out as a pattern of life in Crestwood Heights. As soon as he leaves his mother's body, the child is launched upon the first of a series of separations from her. He is cared for in the hospital nursery, and its staff regulates his first contacts with his mother. The scientific and antiseptic setting assures the physical survival of both mother and child, but it rarely takes into account the mother's anxieties and emotions, particularly lively at the birth of the first child. In the words of a Crestwood mother:

It all depends on how busy they are. If the nursery isn't too crowded and the nurses have more time, you see your baby oftener. But when Billy and Tom [her twins] were born, I was sure I didn't see Tom for days. They kept bringing in Billy for feeding. I knew the difference between them right away and I told them, but they were too busy to pay much attention. I got quite frantic about it.

It is evident that this mother's anxiety, ill or well founded, was not allayed.

Since independence is essential for the achievement-in-isolation which is highly valued by the culture, the significance of the hospital delivery for the later character of the adult can scarcely be over-emphasized. As has been pointed out by Margaret Mead,[2] the feeling-contact of child with mother in the first months and years of life is an important determinant of personality. The Crestwood Heights mother, in order to give birth to a child, is separated from her family. The infant is separated from his mother for most of the hours of his first days of life; his physical contacts are alternated between his mother and the efficient, crisply starched nurses. In the cluster of practices surrounding birth, the Crestwood mother and child would seem thus to be impressed immediately and deeply with the cultural concept that each has a separate and isolated identity: the mother at the conscious level, the infant at the deep feeling-nexus of existence, not yet touched by reason.[3] At the moment of birth, they take the first step in a long process of "psychic weaning" which will end finally in the breaking of all ties of dependency between them; this break will in turn enable the child, later, to repeat the same cycle with his own children.[4]

The relationship of the Crestwood child to his mother is of particular importance, especially in the earliest phases of his development, since the father may be absent for long periods, or at least for long working days. This relationship is also reinforced because the family is a separate unit, rather than an integral part of a larger family system as it would be in another culture or another era.

Yet the child must continue to learn, at this early stage, to accept substitutes for his mother, and she must learn to share the responsibility for her child with others. The nurse is but one of a series of women who now come and go within the family circle: the baby-sitter, the cleaning woman, the housekeeper who may come for a week or two after the mother's return from the hospital, the occasional friend or relative who may assume brief responsibility for the child.[5] Such substitution is inevitable in the Crestwood cultural pattern. The busy mother, who must run the house without the aid of a maid, entertain for husband and friends, attend meetings, and have "outside interests," is literally compelled to ration strictly her physical contacts with her child.[6] Thus in early infancy preparation continues for achievement-in-isolation, for the individual pursuit of materialistic goals in which human relationships must often be subordinated.

The two roles the mother is called on to play, which bring her now close to and now away from the child, are difficult to accept and practise, particularly in the child-centered culture of Crestwood Heights which emphasizes love and emotional security for the child. Her position is, of course, the more difficult because there is no universally agreed set of rules for child-rearing. In patriarchal family organization there were clearly defined rules, but in the more democratic family organization of Crestwood Heights there are many paths from which to choose.

Besides, there are no clear-cut norms as to what is expected, no absolute measuring sticks to serve as a guide. The child who is two this year is not expected to be exactly like the child who was two last year;

attitudes are required to be always flexible and "expectations" are constantly changing. What is constant is the expectation that expectations will change.

Because of the mother's uncertainty, her sense of responsibility towards the child increases. Because practices constantly change, she tends to seek advice and help from sources outside the family. A pediatrician will advise in matters of health. A vast amount of printed material is available to the highly literate Crestwood mother. In the women's magazines she is confronted with innumerable articles on child care written by convincing experts. These present opinions on topics ranging from the proper nutrition for her baby to the best means of "developing in a positive way the mental health of her child." Many of the articles are by professionals, but she is also bombarded by the statements of other persons, representing commercial and business interests: the toymakers,[7] the manufacturers of special foods and clothing for children. Each has a word of advice for the mother—or of censure. Each suggests something she should "buy," something which is calculated, if not guaranteed, to contribute to her child's welfare. There are also her friends, with whom she can exchange notes on the height, weight, walking ability and so on of her children and with whom she can search for solutions to the "problems" which confront her.

These innumerable recommendations do not, however, supply the mother with definite instructions. Their often contradictory directives only add to her uncertainty amid the changing patterns of her culture.[8]

The modern stress on physical, intellectual, and emotional growth, coexists, as Allison Davis has said,[9] with a necessity to teach respect for property. The Crestwood home, as has been pointed out, usually contains expensive decoration and household equipment, easily damaged or destroyed by small exploring fingers. From the moment he can toddle, the Crestwood child, not confined to a nursery or "picked up after" by a servant, encounters a series of instructions about the articles he may not touch, the flower he may not pick in his own or a neighboring garden, the dress or suit he must not dirty, the dangerous road on which he must not play.[10] Despite the prevalent view that too early and too severe toilet training may be "traumatic" for the child, many a Crestwood mother, given the setting of her immaculate home, is virtually compelled to focus attention upon this training. Broadloom is particularly incompatible with permissiveness in toilet training. To some considerable degree, therefore, the child is not free to explore and manipulate his material environment but is hampered by necessities growing out of the equally strong value placed upon the sacredness of property in this culture. The modified goals for this stage of the child's socialization seem to be the achievement of some independence and motor co-ordination within the narrow limits of the handling of gadgets and toys; property values and the very real dangers of traffic-crammed streets restrict his freedom to examine his immediate surroundings more fully.

In his first two years the child has become accustomed to his own crib and playpen, to the toys cannily designed to amuse and improve him; he has also become accustomed to an absence of long physical contact with his mother, and to prohibitions respecting many things which have a fascination for him at this period.

THREE, FOUR, FIVE: FIRST VENTURES BEYOND THE FAMILY

Around the age of three, the Crestwood Heights child may make his first direct and prolonged contact with a newly recognized child-rearing institution, the Nursery School. Even before this first important venture into the wider community, the child may have had many "experiences" outside the home (for example, intervals at the summer cottage and with relatives at a distance; meals eaten in restaurants; visits to the pediatrician and dentist; trips with the family by car or by airplane; or, more rarely, a period alone or with a brother or sister at a summer camp), but nursery school is likely to be the first place in which he has spent any length of time completely separated from his mother and from a familial environment.

The function of the nursery school, it is commonly thought, is to reinforce the child's emotional and physical independence of his mother, and to teach him social and physical skills under trained professional supervision and in contact with those of his own age. From the mother's viewpoint, the nursery school provides, in addition, responsible care for the child, and guides him along tested and therefore culturally approved lines of development.

Crestwood Heights has its own nursery school, supported on a voluntary basis by parents in the community. There are also many other, privately owned, nursery schools in adjacent Big City, a number of them on "The Crest" or at the outer edges of the Heights. Not by any means all parents wish or can find accommodation for their pre-schoolers, but for the busy, educated Crestwood mother, sending her child to nursery school seems to be emerging as a norm.

There is nevertheless frequently ambivalence in the mothers who send a child to nursery school. Some mothers relinquish their children re-

luctantly to nursery school, and do so only because they believe it will
be beneficial to them: it is thus common to hear a mother say that both
she and her child benefit from being apart for some of the day. Others,
under the conflicting pressures of the care of small children and their
other responsibilities, express relief—"I can hardly wait until Jackie is
ready for Nursery School"—though the admission is frequently made
with doubt or guilt.

Attendance at a private nursery school usually entails the assumption
of some responsibility by the parents; sometimes volunteer service is
expected or required; sometimes attendance at a parent education group
is made a condition of the child's admission; sometimes service on a
board of directors is requested. The privately administered nursery
school, therefore, tends to interpenetrate the child's home, and to influence considerably parental methods of child care.

Crestwood parents who support and patronize nursery schools expect
three returns for their time and money. First, they hope the child will
learn how to "get along with" other children of his own age group, for,
even at the age of three, four, or five, getting along amiably with peers
is considered of great importance. Second, they hope he will become
more independent of his parents, particularly of his mother, with whom
the closest ties have been forged. Third, they hope that the nursery
school personnel will give them "solutions" for the "problems" of child-
rearing which they have encountered. Parents who thoroughly believe in
the value of the nursery school hope to acquire up-to-date information
which will enable them "to become better parents."

Nursery school theory, which emphasizes the emotional and physical
development of the child in a permissive atmosphere, is implemented
in a setting of abundant play material and equipment. The child is presented with a wide choice of activity, which is carefully scaled to his
size and motor ability: chairs, for instance, are always small, and scis-
sors have blunt ends. The choices offered—between plasticene, poster
paint, jungle gym, record player, big blocks or toys—give him considerably more freedom[11] than he finds in his own home, whose furnishings and equipment are not adapted in the same way to his age level.

Evidence of the achievement of independent behavior in the nursery
school is sought not only in the child's initiative in the exploration and
use of his new environment, but also in his ability to adjust to the
absence of his mother (if he cannot easily renounce his claims on his
mother, *both* are likely to be regarded as "problems"), and to the
presence of other children. This adjustment is measured largely by his
capacity to "co-operate" with other children, and to accept the light

rein with which the supervisor presides over the children's purposeful play. In the name of co-operation he is expected to learn to control his aggressive impulses.[12] The nursery school is the first agency which impresses upon the child these cardinal middle-class demands. In his society, skills are also stressed, and they are similarily emphasized in the nursery school which is an ante-room to it: the child learns simple dances, and how to manipulate materials. The overriding concern, however, is with skills in human relations, and these will be exhibited in "co-operative" play under firm but amiable adult leadership.

The nursery school child learns in his contacts with the adult staff (if he has not previously done so) that adult time is strictly rationed where he is concerned. He must learn to share the teacher as well as the toys and play materials with his peers; again this necessity prepares for later expectations of his society. He must learn to terminate a project such as play at the sand tables when "it is time" in the routine for rest or song, or a trip to the toilet. As one would expect, the average attention-span for a three-year-old child, established by measurement or the supervisor's judgment, cannot coincide with the individual child's rhythm of attention and change. Nursery school helps him to take his cues from the group rather than from his own immediate predilections and inclinations.

Because of the situation in the Crestwood Heights family, this newer institution, the nursery school, is becoming more and more firmly established. It meets a definite need. In view of the varied roles played by adults in the culture, it is becoming essential that the child should, as soon as possible, learn to function in roles of his own. The mother, given the many activities which she is expected to carry on within the home and in the community, must be freed periodically from the care of her children. Failing a paid Nanny or a willing neighbor or relative, a substitute must be found. Through the nursery school experience, then, the mother takes another important step in the direction of delegating a responsibility which the circumstances of her life hinder her from retaining: the responsibility for her child's socialization. The nursery school teacher, who is thought to have none of the mother's emotional involvement with the child, is considered able to teach him to let go his emotional dependence on his mother, and to redirect this freed energy towards good relationships with children of his own age— who, in most cases, would not be available to the child in his own family circle, anyway. The cultural expectation is that the child will seem to be drawn into the society from the outside, rather than pushed out into it from the family nest. Individual differences determine how far this smooth and harmonious merging with peers under sympathetic and tolerant adult guidance will proceed.

SIX TO TWELVE: INSTITUTIONS SHARE THE CHILD

By the time the Crestwood child is five, the age for kindergarten, the basic pattern of his social behavior has been relatively set, chiefly by his experiences in the home, and at the nursery school if he has attended one. When the child graduates from nursery school,[13] he enters the state-supported school system, the most important, or second most important, institution for socialization in Crestwood Heights. The nursery school, which afforded a transition-stage for both child and parent, is now succeeded by an institution which will to a large extent regulate the life of the Crestwood child for the next thirteen or fourteen years.

Here, in the school, the long-sustained training of the child for his adult roles has its serious beginnings. Here, achievement-in-isolation gradually will take on real and earnest meaning for the child who must, year after year, increasingly adapt himself to the pace of the school program.

Probably the most marked feature of the Crestwood Heights school system to an outsider from another culture would be its division into grades by age, and even within the age grades, into "achievement levels." Despite its garden-like décor, Crestwood Heights reveals in the organization of the school strictly urban characteristics. It has a pattern markedly different from that of an Eskimo group teaching a boy the rudiments of hunting, or from that of the one-room rural school. Because of sheer pressure of numbers, the Crestwood school is compelled to sort the children into groups, on the basis of intelligence and performance, with a corresponding rough equivalence in chronological age. Thus the child at any one age level in the school may be conscious that there are other levels above him and perhaps below. In the one-room school, the set of requirements in other grades is part of each day's experience. In Crestwood Heights, the child is cut off from the other grades and the separation heightens a sense of mystery, difference, and, it seemed to at least one observer, anxiety. The "Grade" becomes an important means for the child's definition of self and others in his environment. An inescapable conclusion of the child's experience in the school system is his realization that the ladder leading to an adult career is exceedingly long.

For the child coming into the school system for the first time there may be many adjustments to make. Although the material environment of the nursery school and the kindergarten may appear similar—both have well-modulated light, space, movable furniture, toys—there are many differences.

Unlike the nursery school, which is often held in a home, a reconverted house, or a church hall, the kindergarten occupies one or two rooms in a building which also houses other school grades. One of the first facts the kindergarten child will assimilate in his new setting is that he belongs to the lowest group in the school hierarchy. Not infrequently, first-graders on the school playgrounds will yell at these newcomers: "Nyah! Nyah! Kindergarten babies!" This kind of expression is common, the peer opposition to the school's principle of "letting the child accept himself happily" at each stage of his school experience.

Thus the kindergarten child in his contact with older children in the school system recognizes early that there are innumerable stages ahead of him, in so long a vista that he can envisage neither the whole nor the end result towards which these stages are intended to move him. His horizons suddenly widen. He sees for himself that there are big boys and girls who are important in school affairs. Instead of a familiar group of adults, there is the loud-speaker system, relaying the voice of the Principal from his distant office to the kindergarten. Although the kindergarten child may have a warm relationship with his one, or perhaps two, teachers, he senses the larger world of the school, spreading out from his own classroom—a world from which his mother, his father, and his brothers and sisters are regularly excluded. Unlike nursery school, this school will bring him each year, as he advances through the grades, to another teacher, if not another peer group, and he realizes intuitively that continuous readjustment will be necessary. He listens to the conversation of older children. This teacher is "cross," that teacher is "nice" or "pretty" or "easy." Even very young children, as well as those in the higher grades, have all the teachers minutely classified. Fears and hopes are organized around these adult figures and the fictions or fact associated with them, and this complex is connected with incentives and strivings. "If you do good, you get into Miss T.'s class; all the other kids have to go to. . . ." Thus, if Miss T. is desired as a teacher, incentives are sharpened by anxiety.[14]

Whereas the nursery school child is encouraged to explore his environment, freedom of movement for the kindergarten child is necessarily more limited. The larger school building may at first seem overpowering. The child soon learns that there are certain areas he may not enter. He cannot, for instance, use the teachers' door. He must not play or linger in the halls. There is a certain manner of proceeding to the playground. No pupil goes in to the building before a certain time. In an astonishingly short space of time the newcomer has absorbed these taboos.[15] Indeed the rules stressed by the school may become more binding than those prevailing in the home. One mother, for example, ruefully told how the whole family had been forced to change its tooth-brushing habits at the insistence of a kindergarten child.

The kindergarten resembles nursery school in its atmosphere of per-missiveness, but there are certain subtle differences which are reflected to the child in the teacher's attitudes. The kindergarten and its teacher are related to the larger bureaucratic structure of the educational sys-tem. She must meet the standards of the Department of Education; her work is supervised by the Principal, and evaluated by visits from the Inspector of Schools. In addition, the public school teacher is strongly encouraged to improve her professional qualifications if she wishes to enjoy regular promotions or progress towards higher positions in the educational hierarchy. These are strains to which the nursery school teacher is not usually so subject.

The position of the public school teacher as a figure in the whole complex school system, affects her role as a parent-surrogate. Because of the self-contained program of the nursery school, the teacher and her volunteer helpers may be viewed by the small child more as he regards his own mother. Or, in the absence of close relatives beyond the parents and one or two other children, which is the case in the majority of families, it is not too difficult for the child to envisage the nursery school teacher as a kindly but firm aunt, interested in his play, or as a guide on many expeditions to new and fascinating experiences. In contrast, the elementary school teacher cannot be divorced in the child's mind from the more rigid structure of the public school, whose disciplinary methods reach, even though mediated by personal warmth and kindliness, to the kindergarten level. In the mind of the child in the early grades, the teacher is backed with all the authority of the system, no matter how gentle or permissive her demeanor.

At the elementary school level, the teacher, as the sole adult with direct responsibility for roughly thirty to forty children, must be shared by the class to a much greater extent than the nursery school supervisor, who, with her assistants, usually deals with fewer children.[16] Children at this age struggle—in reality or fantasy—for a disproportionate share of such attenuated attention as the teacher can give.

The public school teacher, too, enters the family orbit in a way quite unlike that of the nursery school supervisor. When the nursery school is a community venture like the one in Crestwood Heights, the teacher may be either a member of the community or an outside professional, but, in either case, the contact with the parent is close and informal. The nursery school teacher advises the parents on child-rearing problems, but it does not lie in her power to "pass" or to "fail" the child. Emotional and social development, together with evidence of certain motor skills, do count to a certain extent in reckoning achievement at nursery school, but chronological age remains the dominant criterion for passing out of it.

With the change to the public school, mental age and performance in school tasks tend to become the standards for advancement from one grade to the next, though emotional and social development also receive careful attention in the assessment of the child's "readiness" to progress through the school system. The child's "intelligence" is determined by scientific tests, administered under the school's jurisdiction (the results are the knowledge of the school alone), and this information controls to a large extent the rate of the child's advance. At the kindergarten level in Crestwood Heights schools, particular care is taken to give the parents a detailed and scientific profile of the child, and, in addition, informal sessions are held with the parents about the child's progress and development. The information is generally given a great deal of weight by the parents, even when they disagree with the conclusions, since it is backed by the authority of the educational system and presented by a recognized professional, one who has in her sphere of responsibility, moreover, the power to advance or to retard the child's progress up the educational ladder. Thus instead of being somewhat like a partner in responsibility, as was the case with the nursery school child, the parent assumes a far smaller role in the educational enterprise of the public school. With the increasing complexity of the school system and the increasing formality of the curriculum, however much the school may wish to involve the parent, the teacher's role becomes more professional, and the role of the parent becomes much more that of a "layman."

The elementary grades are composed of both boys and girls, and instruction is the same for both. The teacher is usually a single woman, although men and married women are welcomed to the teaching staff in Crestwood Heights. The teacher's professional role is in contrast with the approved feminine role for a woman: wife and mother within the family circle. But because of her professional status, the female teacher represents for many Crestwood mothers an ambition which has been extinguished.

The girl in the elementary school may experience some ambivalence about her projected female cultural role. She is, as she progresses in the school system, more and more cut off from smaller children unless she has younger brothers and sisters. Unlike the daughter in a lower-class family, she does not have charge of these younger siblings while the mother works, nor is she in a position to mix with or to help teach the children of an earlier grade, as she might be in the rural school. The Crestwood Heights girl, nevertheless, has a more prolonged and more intimate relationship with the mother than has the boy. Her difficulty in the home and in the elementary school is more to experience sufficient "maleness" in contact with male teachers and with her own father. She must depend upon her relationships with her brothers, or boys in her own age group, for much of her knowledge of masculinity in the culture.[17]

The boy is likewise largely deprived of a male model with which to identify himself in the elementary school setting and thus learn at first hand the masculine role in the culture. And he does not have the same opportunity as the girl for finding an image within the home, since the father plays his major masculine role outside it. Almost his only alternative, apart from male teachers and camp and Scout leaders, is afforded by his male school mates, who are in the same psychological position as himself. But the boy finds, as does the girl with female teachers, that his occasional male teachers and the Principal stand in partial or even marked contrast to the masculine values for the male role in his culture. The boy, even more than the girl, is therefore thrust into a dependency upon the peer group for his masculine models, and this group, in turn, has a tendency, in upper middle class culture, to select as its model the athletic hero or the currently popular movie or TV star.

Because of the complexity of the culture, there cannot be, for either boy or girl, one composite male or female image to serve as a guide in learning the expected cultural roles. The school, while it gives instruction in the *knowledge* essential for the main cultural roles, cannot, because of the very nature of its structure, offer at the elementary school level the emotional experience of close relationships between adults and children, which will lead to the identification by which adult cultural roles may be internalized. The school system has made attempts in this direction through its counselling services, but at this initial stage the whole complex matter of role-learning through emotional association rests primarily with the family.[18]

It is nevertheless largely the age-graded nature of the school, in concurrence with the existing social structure of the family, which determines the *means* by which the child learns his cultural roles. And this pattern is for the most part set in the early grades. The school experience, then, cuts across the socialization process initiated in the family. The parents, anxious for the child's "maturity" and "independence," relinquish much of their jurisdiction over him to this institution. The organization of the school, with large classes under one teacher,[19] throws the child into the beginning of long contact with his peer group, although he may orient himself in the general structure of the school to those above or below him.

The school, however, is not the only institution which, through age-graded activities, assists in the socializing of the child in this period of his life. The summer camp (which now accepts children of nursery school age as well as those up to and including the teens), is a supplement of the school in this respect. The age-graded structure of the school is somewhat relaxed in the more informal camp setting, but the division of the children according to chronology is generally closely adhered to. The influence of the camp social system is considerable in shaping the child's concept of cultural roles. The camp affords a communal existence, at some physical distance from the home, which allows for a closer emotional relationship between adult leaders and the children in their charge. Moreover, since the parents are, of course, not present except on visitors' days, the prevailing values of independence and maturity can be stressed by the counsellors.

Camp, unlike school, is not compulsory, but there is a widespread feeling that "camp is a good thing." Among the reasons most frequently given by parents for sending children is their desire for the child to have broader group experiences with a peer group and for him to develop social and physical skills; neither of these can be secured, it is felt, in the home situation.

The step from home to summer camp is a more difficult one for the child than the transition from home to school, since he lives entirely in the camp orbit. One of several letters written to her mother by a nine-year-old during her first summer at camp suggests the strain:

Camp Birch Bark,
August 15, 1951.

DEAR MOMMY,

I still want to go home but if you don't want me to come I'll stay here. If I'm staying here, I want some ink for my pen and some staishenairy and envolopes. But please may I come home on visitor's day. Today we went for a boat ride. I really want to come and if I don't I'll come back a reck. The food here tasts horrible. I really want to go hom. Please let me.

Love,
Linda.

Other institutional groupings lead the child of this age grade away from dependence exclusively on his own family. There are, for instance, church-sponsored groups for both Jewish and Gentile children. Many of the Jewish children enter the Hebrew school, where preparation is begun in the age level between five and twelve for a ceremony symbolizing adulthood: Bar-Mitzvah for the boy, and a corresponding, but more recently invented, ceremony for the girl. Although there is not the same religious uniformity among Gentiles, children still receive less formal, but nevertheless highly ritualized, preparation for Confirmation, for First Communion, or for joining the church.

Children between the ages of eight and twelve are eligible to enter the lowest ranks of such organizations as the Girl Guides or the Boy Scouts, and many children become Cubs and Brownies around the age of eight or nine. These groups too are graded by age, and a highly developed and internationally accepted series of symbols marks the child's passing from one age grade to the next, stressing as criteria for progress, factual knowledge, motor skills, and social qualities.

In addition to participating in the institutional activities enumerated above, the five- to twelve-year-old must learn many individual and social skills. This is the age at which adults consider it desirable to begin instruction in piano or some other musical instrument, in figure skating, swimming, eurhythmics, dramatics, art, and, for girls, in dress and general appearance. It is not uncommon for a five-year-old to have had her first "permanent," and for slightly older girls to "plan" their clothes with their mothers.[20]

What is noticeable in the life of the age group between five and twelve is not only the high degree of institutionalized activity at this level, but also the nature of the experiences to which children are introduced at this early age, despite the view, also part of the culture, that "the place for the small child is with his own mother in his own home."[21] There would seem to be an important relationship between these two emphases in this age period—the network of organized activity with the peer group, outside the home, and the tendency to push to an ever earlier period the beginning of activities formerly associated with an older age group. Dating and mixed parties and kissing games begin at the age of eleven or twelve, if not earlier. Such activities lead to fears on the part of parent and teachers alike (and these also express some of the values of the society) lest sex experience occur "too early" for the children.[22] (This pushing forward of experience has been mentioned in the chapter on "Time.") Adults are, however, committed to the notion that both sexes should learn to adjust to each other by boy-girl participation in extra-curricular activities; the school therefore attempts a careful regulation of those activities under its jurisdiction, and so also do the other related institutions in the community. The tightly filled time-schedule of the Crestwood Heights child thus serves also as a protective device, not only in adolescence, but as early as this five-to-twelve period.

A schedule of activities such as the Crestwood Heights child follows enables the parent to know where he is and what he is doing, and at the same time it offers preparation for the work habits of later life which enable the doctor, or lawyer, or business executive to put in long, arduous hours; these are essential if the material living standard of Crestwood Heights is to be maintained or improved. Punctuality and "responsibility" are the qualities which are highly emphasized in this context. Throughout the five-to-twelve period the "responsibilities" of the child are increasingly stressed as his skills develop: responsibility for doing his lessons, for helping around the home, for spending a small allowance of money which is gradually increased with his age. "Responsibility" in regard to a wide range of behavior is frequently the theme at Home and School meetings.

It is, thus, in the five-to-twelve year stage that serious formal steps are taken to develop in the child the qualities which are felt to be the prerequisites for success in adult occupational and social life. And it is the school, with its carefully graded system of education, its facilities for assessing the intellectual potentialities of the child, its authority to advance or to hold him back in his progress through the grades of the system, which is the most potent single institution in the society for teaching him the social roles which anticipate adult status. Compelled by law to attend school until the age of sixteen, the child is subject to its influences for the major portion of his time during the greater part of the year. Peripheral institutions support the school in its task of socialization, and one, the Home and School Association, attempts to include the parents in this process. And more and more, in Crestwood Heights, the child is institutionalized in his leisure hours as well, both through the school and otherwise.

Perhaps the most outstanding feature of the Crestwood Heights culture is becoming increasingly evident: the degree to which secondary groups are assuming responsibility for virtually the whole socialization process. As a result—or prerequisite—the Crestwood Heights child must learn very early how to function in secondary groups, which, as he grows older, will come to claim more and more of those areas of the personality once reserved for relationships with the primary group, and even those once thought private or open only to sacred scrutiny.

The family is still necessary to ensure the launching of the child into the society, as it were, but its traditional social function is widely shared with other institutions, in the endeavour to procure early and radical emancipation from the family of orientation. It is largely in the time span between five and twelve that the psychological and social groundwork is laid for this particular type of functioning in society. The child in Crestwood Heights does not "just grow up," loved and nurtured but unnoticed. As one might expect, in a society where time and the child are major preoccupations, where preparation for a career is emphasized, where health is seldom forgotten, an elaborate system to observe and evaluate the growth of the child has been perfected. The school offers the most obvious model for this system. Through its grades the child is made to pass, experiencing a succession of stages, each of which commences with ignorance and ends in a tested and classified level of competence and achievement. Other institutions follow this lead: summer camp, the special schools, the church and synagogue, Boy Scouts and Girl Guides, all practise a similar system of age grading. Within the home, in one respect, age grading is not so easily observed since each member is supposedly equal under the affectionate tutelage and watchfulness of the parents. But, in another respect, it is the family which mediates the age grading system through which the child is sent. Changes in dress and deportment, changes in obligation and privilege are supervised, and often initiated, by parents; they are frequently synchronized with the actual physical changes in the child and with his position in the extra-familial grades through which, as a normal growing child, he must pass.

It is important to note that this age grading creates a system of status which permits the recognition of physical growth and performance in the child. The "normal" child, so far as age grading is concerned, maintains a balance as he "grows in wisdom and stature." That child tends to become a problem who is too big for his age, or "too large for his hat." Each of the status levels is, as noted in discussion of the rollercoaster in the chapter on "Time," a "life" in itself. An entire book could be devoted to the genetic pattern of childhood development through these grades: each grade has its initiatory or birth phase, and passes thence through maturity and full competence to graduation and "death" rites, as a new status is won and a new initiation awaits. Perhaps in a rapidly changing society the norms of behavior and structure are too fluid to justify more detailed description, but the child's social development and physical growing in Crestwood Heights should be seen in relation to age grading.

THIRTEEN, FOURTEEN, FIFTEEN: EARLY ADOLESCENCE

It will already be clear that socialization in Crestwood Heights is by no means a steady, harmonious progression. It involves, as we anticipated in discussing "Time," many sharp breaks and new beginnings to which the child has been working since Grade I, and especially the new beginning which culminates with high school entrance. In many cultures, the physical transformation of puberty coincides with social recognition of adult status, but this is not the case in Crestwood Heights where children remain in prolonged economic dependence. Moreover, the temporal coincidence, for many children, between the onset of puberty and the sudden transfer from the top grade of the elementary school to the bottom grade of the Junior High School is often productive of heightened stress. This transition between childhood and what we might call "youthhood" is considered so difficult that the "Junior High School" has, indeed, been devised to help spread the adjustment over three years. The period in question is, however, marked by the child's growing consciousness of what his culture expects of him, a consciousness not evident to the same degree in preceding stages.

The preoccupations of the children in this age group (as revealed, for instance, in the free discussion of the Human Relations classes) indicate focal points in the socialization process. Concern centers around dating, summer work, choice of vocation, and sex roles; and considerable questioning of adult values may be discerned. The expectations of parents and teachers for academic achievement, for social skills, for "responsibility," are intensified at this age level. The child, in his turn, exerts a corresponding pressure upon himself since he has now more or less thoroughly internalized these cultural expectations.

In their new situation, the children have a number of behavior patterns to learn. The question of male-female sexual roles, and the difficulty of learning these roles, were again made evident in the Human Relations classes.

On one occasion a boy suggested a discussion on "whether or not the male sex is superior." Here the male role, emphasizing creativity in intellectual and technical spheres, physical strength, status in the social structure, and authority, was held up as the norm for superior and culturally approved behavior for both boys and girls alike. Girls were judged by some boys as inadequate in measuring up to these requirements—although they admitted that women might possibly compete with men even in physical strength (e.g., as truck drivers or women wrestlers); only two boys advanced the view that each sex had its own duties and responsibilities, and that, therefore, the whole argument was futile. One boy accused women of "remaining in the home" and "refusing to take chances," and yet another boy added the comment "housework isn't hard—I've tried it!" [laughter]— a direct devaluation of the traditional female role.

In this particular discussion, the girls were decidedly on the defensive. There was only the slightest hint that there might be a female role, differing from the male role in that it is biologically determined, when a girl commented that "women mature earlier than men." One girl, in refuting a boy's allegation that "housework is easy," did appear to resent this male view of the female role.

Girls were clearly weighing their own role against that of the male—and the female role, in its traditional sense of childbearer and homemaker, was found wanting by both boys and girls. From the children's conversations, it is evident that neither boy nor girl expects to be ready for the adult sex roles for many years—which lends a note of unreality and uncertainty to such discussions.

In the adult character of Crestwood Heights, as will be described later, there appears to be a growing convergence between types of social behavior once more clearly distinguished as male and female. Differences in social aspects of the male and female roles which were previously defined on the basis of biological difference alone, appear to be lessening in Crestwood Heights. This allows women to share more fully in the intellectual and rational orientation towards life, while the men are expected to participate in home and child-rearing functions formerly relegated to the mother. The conflicts raised in the Human Relations classes over the uncertain definition of the female role, in particular, are symptomatic of the shifts in social personality of both men and women.

No sustained effort is made by any Crestwood institution outside the family to teach the girl the arts of child care and homemaking. However, another ingredient in the female role is being strengthened; great emphasis is now being laid on physical attractiveness. At Junior High level, preoccupation with "glamor" begins to emerge, although girls of an earlier age are also concerned with appearance and dress. Both boys and girls esteem physical attractiveness highly, and recognize the importance of grooming and clothing. Although the boys expressed some hostility (based on the ultimate expense to the male) towards female competition in dress, the girls were almost unanimous that "glamor" was an integral part of the female role. Physical strength and intelligence, qualities which the girls also try to emulate, denote masculinity at this age.

Clothing, for both boys and girls of this age, becomes an important symbol of changing status. In one discussion the children branched off into talk of clothes and lipstick:

One girl said that in Grade VI and still a bit in Grade VII, their clothes were tunics and frilly sorts of thing, but that in Grade IX they got into longer skirts and smarter clothes—more grown up—and they started to use lipstick. The researcher asked about the boys. They gave a picturesque description of boys' graduation into drapes, key chains, loud shirts, and fancy shoes.

The children appear to follow the lead of the peer group rather than that of teacher or parent where dress and appearance are concerned, and the models seem to be TV and movie stars, or others provided by the mass communication media. That clothing and general appearance contribute largely to the adequate playing of the sex roles at this age is most evident.

Tied in with the learning of the sex roles at this stage is the dating pattern, which now definitely crystallizes after its first appearance at the previous age level.

In the twelve- to fifteen-year-old group, much concern is expressed over the choice of one partner. Although some children still voice a preference for group activities, there is an increasing trend towards what might be called "trial monogamy." The boys in Grade IX showed some uncertainty about assuming their masculine role in regard to dating, and questions arose about how far in advance an invitation should be given for a dance or a party. Though both boys and girls agreed that the choice of partner is the responsibility of the boy, some of the boys felt that the present system is financially unfair to them. It is evident that the economic dependence of children in the culture bears more heavily on the boys than on the girls, since the former feel that their prerogative of choosing a partner, an integral part of the male role in Crestwood Heights, is limited by this dependence.

A subtle distinction seems to exist between dating and friendship. As Caroline Tryon has demonstrated,[23] various criteria are used by adolescents to evaluate the *quality* of the relationship between girls and girls, between boys and boys, and between girls and boys. Within the wider term of friendship as it is understood in Crestwood Heights, the terms "boy friend" and "girl friend" underline the importance of the sex differential in relationships which imply some degree of permanency. The term "date" appears to highlight the qualities of physical attractiveness and glamor upon which the choice of sex partner is based in a culture permeated by the value of "romantic love." The "date" or "dates" symbolize the initial stage in the pattern of mate selection; with the prolongation of the adolescents' economic dependence on the parents, this stage later tapers off into "going steady" with a "girl friend" or "boy friend," without the expectation either of eventual marriage or even of relative permanency.

The report of a thirteen-year-old girl expresses the "friendship" pattern, which, she states, changes between Grades VII and VIII:

FRIENDS: What I do with them: Grade 7 went to movies, stag parties. Grade 8 go on dates—to movies—to parties—skating—skiing.

Then in a separate section, she adds:

How I pick boys: looks, personality, don't show off, sex appeal (good in sports). Girls: loyalty, uncattish, trustworthy, personality, kindness, etc.

In another discussion on "friendship," the question of money entered:

Peter indicated that "not all people have money, but all have friends." Another boy remarked that a wealthy person can have a television set and can always find friends who want to listen in. Johnny asked: "What is meant by a true friend? Some are parasites and do not wish to contribute anything to the friendship." Shirley felt that selfish people do not have friends, but if people use their money to help others, they will have more friends. Linda said that everyone wants to have friends and rich people buy friends if they do not get them any other way. Tom suggested that those who are friends only when you have money are not true friends. In reply to a question from one student as to how you could know which are true friends, Margie thought the best way was to lose your money and then see who stood by you. Johnny remarked "life is a mirror"; in your friends, you look for intellectual and social companionship, so choose your friend on your own level. Two or three boys now spoke of those friends who pretend to be loyal, but as soon as they find you have run out of money, they only grudgingly offer to help. The researcher threw a question, "What do you look for in a friend?" Moira replied, "People I can talk to seriously, have a good time with, share things with and get along well with."

"Dating" and "friendship," it would seem, are different, but the above discussion indicates uncertainty and shifting relationships in the area of friendship as well as in dating. In view of the many and subtle nuances of relationship between boy and girl in this group, and of friendships between members of the same sex, it is far from easy to learn sex roles, or to achieve the "maturity" expected of the pre-adolescent.

The choice of occupation presents another set of problems to the children in this age grade. During the years in Junior High, both boy and girl are expected to decide whether they wish to proceed to university, to take a business or commercial course, or to enter technical school. In practice, however, there is not much choice for the Crestwood Heights child, for there is a strong pressure on him from all sides to "elect" a university education. It is mostly those who cannot make the requisite academic grades, or those few who are going into business immediately upon leaving high school, who consider alternatives to university.

Although boys and girls in the school system are given almost identical academic training, future occupation is considered a more important question for the boy, since it is tacitly assumed that the girl will pursue a career only until she marries. Thus the boy, even in Junior High, fully realizes that he will ultimately become the breadwinner of a family, a role which demands intensive and prolonged training for a vocation. The hostility sometimes shown by boys of this age towards girls, ostensibly because of their competitive taste in clothes and their alleged tendency to coax a boy into spending more money than he actually possesses, may be a kind of protest against the demands of the male occupational role; it may also, of course, express restiveness under prolonged dependence upon the family.

The girl is "interested too" in an occupational role, but to a less degree than the boy, since she sees that women, for example, her mother and her mother's women friends, are not gainfully employed, although they may have been before marriage. The meaning of "occupation" for the girl is essentially different from what the boy understands by the term. For her, as for the boy, an occupation confers a sense of social worth; but in the case of the woman, the full stamp of cultural approval is given only if she later achieves husband and children. (The achievement of matrimonial and parental roles is of course important too for the male.) But the value for the girl of an occupation as a safeguard against the possible impermanency of marriage cannot be overlooked; its utility in this respect is alleged by the more outspoken women as a justification for it, over and above the mandate to self-fulfilment.

For both boy and girl, the question of future occupation is intertwined with the values of "responsibility" and "independence" stressed by parents and teachers alike. Summer jobs are viewed by the children both as chances to learn responsibility and independence, within or beyond the family circle, and as badges of impending adult status.

In the following discussion, all shades of feeling about work were expressed in a Human Relations class. There was obvious ambivalence. The Crestwood Heights culture, while it stresses the value of responsibility for its children, also expresses a strong collective feeling that the years of childhood should be as carefree as possible, and this view is mirrored in the children's conversation:

Kitty Taylor thought it was good for girls to go to C—— Inn and such places to work. It was good experience for girls to be on their own, to make their own decisions, learn how to get along with other people. Marilyn G. thought that two months' work made you somewhat independent in buying clothes and meeting people. A boy thought one might work to earn a hockey glove or some such things; otherwise he could go to camp. A boy thought that girls might work since they get married and someone else would support them anyway, but there was no point in boys working too soon! Bill said that most of the group spent the summer at cottages and they do not want to come home and go to work. Wilma S. said she wanted to work after five years of camp and four of boarding schools; she was "sick of it." She thought they'd get more experience in getting along with people if they worked. Milton C. said a boy might work into a good job through summer work; he might work in a department store and so work his way up to a good position in later life. Dave J. said some people worked through the summer to pay their way through college. It was pointed out that some kids couldn't afford to go to camp; camp and cottage depended on the financial status of the family. It would be up to the individual student to decide whether he should work. One boy said cynically that if the kids in the room got a job they'd not hold it for two weeks. Tom S. said it was all right just now to talk about jobs, but they'd not be so keen on working when the temperature was in the eighties. Cameron McN. said he was tired of camp last year, so he got a job, a tough job where he worked different hours. He'd like to get a job again this year, but he'd want a different job, such as trucking, where you'd see the countryside, have fun, and get paid for it. Linda B. said she liked to go to camp. She mentioned a canoe trip she'd made from camp to C—— Inn. She said the girls working there weren't too happy—they have small girls' sleeping quarters and aren't allowed in some parts of the establishment. Leonard H. said he'd like to hitchhike this summer; you couldn't get a better education than by hitchhiking. Sam said that if people wanted to go to camp, they could get a job right now and save enough money to pay for it. Meg M. thought it wasn't fair of parents to insist on their children going to the cottage, even though it was the only time when a good many fathers saw anything of their children.

Boris G. said some parents let their children eat whenever they wanted to, but when they went to camp they had to eat at mealtime or starve! One boy felt going to camp was good experience; if one were going into the Army, learning to obey rules would be valuable. Dan L. observed that two months away from girls didn't hurt anyone! Someone said that at school you were with your parents; if you got a job you'd be away from parents. The researcher inquired further, asking about dependency on parents. Alex D. said he tried to solve his own problems, even if his parents were in the next room. He felt that one needn't be dependent on parents, even if one lived with them. As for an easy life at the cottage, he'd learned that you couldn't sleep if you had younger brothers. Cameron McN. said he'd learned all the camp routine—canoeing, shooting with bow and arrow, etc., and now he'd rather meet adults. While working last year, he'd been sworn at, ordered about, worked from eleven to four A.M. and met all sorts of guys. Then he had stayed a week at a guy's cottage. This chap, he said, isn't out of diapers yet and doesn't go around with anyone and runs to his mother for everything. Marilyn said that not everyone had money to go to camp. She thought that if parents couldn't send their children to college, the children should work and pay their own way, as their brother, a dentist, had done. It wasn't necessary to go away to work; you could get a job in the city. Wilma S.

objected to Cameron's statement, saying not many were tied to their mother's apron strings. Said she, "We aren't exactly sick of parents but. . . ." In his speech, Cameron said he'd not take any job—only one that he liked. Boris inquired how he'd find such a job; he'd had jobs he disliked. Paul said if Boris didn't know what kind of a job he liked he couldn't very well go on looking for it. Leonard H. thought summer work was a good way to try out different jobs, e.g., law office, city newspaper. A boy spoke again of scouting, saying in response to Wilma's two hundred dollar estimate, that you needn't go to such a "ritzy," expensive camp. Other camps were better, for you were more on your own.

It is evident from the foregoing that in this age group some were discussing from actual experience, but many were projecting their ideas into a new area when talking about summer jobs. The boys seem particularly concerned about summer jobs in relation to adult status. Girls express some desire to work, but this seems chiefly a gesture towards independence from the family. A boy verbalized the cultural expectation that girls will work only up to the time of marriage.[24] Considerable ambivalence is expressed in the camp-cottage versus work argument. One boy shows interest in work as an opportunity to escape from limitations of social class; a girl reveals the contrary view, that summer work as a waitress puts one outside one's own class, a disadvantage which one does not find with camp.

It is interesting at this point to note that the children (like many of the women) may have only a hazy picture of the family's financial standing, and that, because of this, they cannot approach the job situation realistically. Throughout the children's debate, the element of choice in the decison to work or not to work is evident and striking. Such a choice does not confront the lower-class child who must begin to earn as soon as he is able.

With closer approximation to adulthood, in chronological if not always in social and emotional terms, the children of Crestwood Heights are found in the process of weighing and internalizing some of the adult values of the community. Norms of behavior as established by parent and school were frequently questioned in the Human Relations classes. Male reactions center around the status symbol of the car; smoking, another badge of adult status; parental controls, exemplified in expectations that the boy will be in by a certain hour; and the boy's financial dependence on the family.

The car is an item of great importance in Crestwood Heights. The boy, even before he reaches the age of fifteen, wants a driver's licence and access to the family car (or cars) since these are the accolade of adult male status; he commonly has not the economic ability to buy a car of his own. But although he desires freedom in the use of the car, he is also inclined to cast some blame on the parents if an accident occurs, and does not generally wish to assume responsibility either for the use of the car or for its financing. Girls do not appear to express the same concern about the use of the car, although a boy's ability to provide transportation will generally give him a higher rating as a date.[25]

Although the children seem to want freedom from parental controls, it is evident that in the case of a car this is a "difficult" demand. There are many variations of opinion among the parents as to the degree of freedom advisable at each age for the boy, to whom the car is such a vital symbol, when it is a question of sharing the car or cars between parents and children. Their problem is complicated by the fact that the car in North American culture generally, is recognized as a symbol of sexual freedom. It cannot be denied that the automobile has revolutionized sexual behavior on this continent. Freedom to drive the family car *alone* assumes even greater importance for the male adolescent since the privilege carries with it at least the possibility of sexual expression uncontrolled by direct adult supervision.

Since many Crestwood parents of both sexes smoke themselves, there does not seem to be as much conflict about this for either boys or girls; and smoking apparently does not carry the connotation it once did in regard to male adult status. A Human Relations discussion with a Grade VIII class in Junior High illustrates:

> They then started to talk about smoking. They admitted that boys smoke a bit from the time they are in Grade VI, but in Grade VIII they do it openly walking home from dances, etc. They said that boys do it to show off to the girls. The researcher then asked if they thought smoking was really a sign of growing up, and one boy said "No . . ." because boys that were really getting grown up didn't smoke, because they wanted to keep their wind for sports.
>
> Beryl S. said that if she were a mother, she'd want her children to smoke at home, not on the street corners; she thought girls might start to smoke at seventeen or eighteen, boys at fifteen or sixteen.

Girls appear to accept smoking as both a female and a male prerogative, but make some distinction on a sex basis about the age at which one may begin.[26] It is interesting to note that, though in a previous discussion the girls claim an earlier maturity than boys, they indicate a two-year difference here, and put themselves in the junior position. The school, it would seem, takes a stricter stand than do parents in the home: smoking by students on or near school property or during school hours is forbidden, ostensibly as a fire precaution or to avoid public criticism of the school.

The regular allowance of money given by parents is another topic for frequent discussions in the Junior High Human Relations classes. As in the case of the car, money to spend as one wishes is a sign of adult status, but the chances to earn it are limited. Boys and girls substantially agree that an allowance is necessary in this age group, but are quite divided as to how it should be obtained.

Sam began the discussion by saying that smaller boys don't need so much allowance because they can get to shows more cheaply. Another said that some boys are more mature in taste, and so need more allowance: a boy should get enough allowance to get practice in spending it. One girl felt an allowance should be big enough to include everything but clothes. Another girl said that they should get an allowance, and a job if the allowance isn't big enough, but they shouldn't take an allowance for granted. A girl objected to this, saying that the student's chief job was to get through school, not to hold down jobs, and if she did this, parents would be satisfied. A boy, Angus, and a girl, felt that allowances should be conditional upon doing work around home. Leonard said his parents gave him what he needed; he felt less money was wasted in this way than if he were receiving a regular allowance. A girl expressed the idea that an allowance should be considered from the viewpoint of training for later life; the student will learn the value of money through management of an allowance; if all the allowance is not spent, that part should be saved.

. . . A boy said that if you had to learn how to spend money, you may as well do it on your parents' money, so an allowance is a good thing. A girl felt money might be wasted through unwise choice; it was also suggested that parents could buy more cheaply as they might get things wholesale. A girl pointed out that parents aren't anxious for their children to be too independent. A boy felt it was necessary for boys to have an allowance so they could learn to budget their incomes. A girl felt it was necessary and important for girls to have a clothing allowance, but not for boys. This remark brought strong protests and many boys were anxious to speak on the question. It was felt that one couldn't generalize; it would depend on the parents' income. One boy felt an allowance helped develop a sense of responsibility; boys could save if they had a purpose in mind, such as a gift for Mother's Day. A girl pointed out that boys' styles change too, so they do need a clothing allowance. One boy, Angus, felt that boys needn't worry so much as girls about being in style. Said he, "Baldheaded fat men will get along all right, but a baldheaded fat woman won't get far!" He said if he were going to pick a girl, he'd pick a nice one, but of three nice girls, he'd pick the most stylish one . . . hence girls need a clothing allowance more than boys. A girl opposed the clothing allowance, saying they could get experience in handling money from their regular allowance, but they needed to know how to choose before being given a clothing allowance.

. . . As the class was going out, the boy who had suggested the topic came up to the researcher and said he hadn't a clothing allowance but he picked out the clothes he wanted, and then took his parents down to see them. "Dad didn't like these drapes," said he, glancing with obvious admiration at his trousers, "but I got them anyway."

Here again, it is obvious that the expectations of parents that the child become "responsible" and "independent" while at the same time he is financially dependent on them, create considerable confusion in the minds of many adolescents about the possession and spending of money. Money, a potent symbol of adult status, is usually given to the child in the form of an allowance, but there seems to be little uniformity in the amount or in the directives about how it should be spent. Few children appear to have money which they are completely free to spend without any adult supervision.

Although the children voice the opinion that money is of the utmost importance, and that the wise and responsible spending of it is both a sign of and a preparation for adult status, they also express some feeling about receiving money which they have not earned; this sentiment is shared by the parents.[27] As one researcher put it:

In connection with "spoiling," I got the impression that a majority of children would subscribe to the following views:
(a) Most Crestwood Heights children are spoiled.
(b) It is difficult to avoid being spoiled if you are wealthy.
(c) There is nothing the child can do to prevent being spoiled, if he is wealthy.
(d) The fault lies largely with the parents.
(e) It is a bad thing to be spoiled.[28]

This summary in its very succinctness reveals how the difficulties experienced by the child in living up to the expectations of both parents and the school for "responsibility" and "independence" amplify in an environment which largely eliminates necessity for striving in this direction.

The children in Junior High expressed certain clearly defined attitudes of this age period towards school, which for them is beginning to assume somewhat the same seriousness as the career for the adult. As one child expressed it (in the quotation below) "school isn't just preparation for life, it *is* life."[29] While the children seem to recognize that school connotes work, discipline, and a certain degree of impersonality (the "home-room" teacher has by now given way to subject-specialists), they also display regrets for the vanished freedom and emotional security of early childhood.

Sally C. pointed out that kindergarten and primary school children don't dislike school, but rather enjoy it. Norman F. thought that children liked school until they got to higher grades where they had to work. Fred O. felt that worry about examinations caused pupils to dislike school. Betty Joan G. thought some children were spoiled at home, and so they resented discipline at school. . . .

. . . Sally G. thought children naturally would dislike school since in pre-school days they had freedom and toys but in school they had to sit in classes and do as the teacher said.

. . . Morris S. felt that students should enjoy their school life because later on they had to assume great responsibilities and not enjoy life any more.[80] It was suggested by Sally G. that when adults talk about school days being the happiest days of their lives, they do so because they have forgotten the unhappy times and remember only the fun they had at school, dances, sports, etc. Fred O., in response to Sally's suggestion that the more education one had, the better equipped one was for life, pointed out that school isn't just preparation for life, it *is* life.

In the twelve-to-fifteen year level, therefore, the child himself, for the first time, becomes seriously aware of what the society demands of him, if he is to become adult. Both home and school impose high standards of performance. The child, at the same time, must adjust to the demands of his peer group, which frequently run counter to those of parents and of teachers. At this age, too, the child must form the heterosexual relationships which later lead to courtship and marriage. The achievement-in-isolation theme of the culture deepens and strengthens, as the child is expected to achieve more and more in the competitive academic life which leads to university entrance. Self-reliance must be developed through experience at the summer camp, or, more rarely, the part-time job. The girl, while expected to prepare for a career of her own, must also assimilate the idea of renouncing it for marriage; and the boy must, in the absence of close or clearly defined masculine models, learn what it means to play a man's role in the society. These are the difficult tasks of early adolescence.

SIXTEEN TO NINETEEN: DEPENDENT INDEPENDENCE

The emphasis for this particular age level in Crestwood Heights works to deepen and strengthen even further the trends noted for the previous stage. The period is characterized by a more intense experience with the peer group, experience which contributes to and is a manifestation of conflict between age group and parental standards.[81]

The arguments about fraternities and sororities in high school are but one manifestation of this conflict, and they may be selected for the purposes of illustration. Fraternities and sororities prove to be lingering thorns in the sides of both parents and teachers. They have been de-fended ably by the children when under adult attack. Fraternities and sororities, say the adolescents, give a sense of belonging and accept-ance, which they have been *taught* is important to their well-being.

And as for violating the principles of racial tolerance and equality, the children demonstrate that the same breach is present in many of the parents' clubs after which their own youth associations are patterned. Fraternities and sororities continue to exist despite criticism, providing for the children groups in which they are relatively free to formulate their own standards. These groupings are closed to adult supervision— which disturbs the parents and teachers, despite the stress they lay on responsible and independent action.

On the whole, though, the general pattern of this age group, as it is evident in the life history documents, seems to be one of acceptance of the adult values and way of life. Yet there are other evidences of a kind of rebellion somehow possible within the general frame of reference, set by adults, during this transitional period between childhood and adult life.

Contributions of senior students to the High School magazine reveal some criticisms of adult standards and behavior, as well as some comment on conventional values and current happenings at school and in the world about. Two issues, taken at random, for the years 1949–50 and 1950–51, were examined carefully. Fiction and articles were concerned with a variety of topics, often treated satirically. Four articles discussed general popularity and loss of it; two emphasized pleasant social manners as the criteria for successful human relationships; one definitely associated popularity with the possession of high social status and wealth. Three dealt with international understanding and the threat of war; three criticized the economic system; one was about racial prejudice towards a Negro business man. In one article, a boy penetratingly criticized life in the city, comparing it to that of a rat on a garbage dump.[32] In a story with a slight flavor of Somerset Maugham, the writer treated of the marital infidelity of a middle-aged woman. An essay satirized the high standards required in English classes. A final humorous article described a program of dieting, which was circumvented by a secret craving for chocolate (equated with alcoholism). The level of sophistication in these writings is high; the understanding of the "grown-up" world, acute and penetrating;[33] the tone, moralistic. Rebellion was expressed in the fantasy content of some of these contributions, but one might expect on the evidence of the foregoing to find "rebels" in this age group.

It is rare, however, to find Crestwood young people who act out the rebellion expressed in such fantasy. During the research, only a few such cases came to the attention of the observers. One was that of a young adult, who had continued to live at home, although receiving a salary from a downtown job. This young man went to visit relatives on one of the Channel Islands, and found life there so congenial that, after evaluating this experience in comparison with Crestwood Heights, he returned to the island to earn his living in a situation where it is extremely difficult to secure comparable monetary rewards.

The more general pattern is exemplified by a girl whose rebellion was within the framework of acceptance of the general patterns of the culture. Her rebellion-within-dependence took the form of graduate study, for which her father paid, in Europe. Despite her strong protestations that she wanted freedom from her family above all else, she returned to her Crestwood Heights home and continued her course of specialization, at the same time studiously avoiding all conformity with her family's wishes about social life.

Even these two persons were a little older than the high school group. Again we come back to the fact that the Crestwood Heights adolescent is still economically dependent upon his parents during this period of rebellion. It is true that from an early age he has been given an allowance, usually increased in direct proportion to his age, and that he may have earned money of his own from summer or part-time work. Yet he knows that he cannot approximate his father's income until long after he has completed high school and subsequent vocational preparation. So feelings of rebellion and desire for greater independence are generally subdued in favor of the path that leads to the career in the manner approved by the society.

Adult attitudes to the child's growing independence are also mixed. Father, in particular, would appear to expect the boy to undergo a period of "roughing it" on the way up, in imitation of his own initial struggles.[34] To "have it too easy" is definitely considered as a danger; but to encourage the child to make any real break with his family and its protections and comforts at this time would be considered a courting of even greater peril.

It is evident that adolescence in Crestwood Heights implies by no means a smooth and easy acceptance of adult values. The reports of Human Relations classes, the conduct of children meeting parent groups, and clinic records[35] all attest to a high degree of independent thought during this period. It appears that once again the pressure of cultural circumstances militates against the translation of this independence into deliberate rebellion. A cultural solution at this age level appears to be participation in fraternity or sorority, where the child achieves solidarity, where he has the support of his peers in evading some of the adult expectations, and where he may have a brief respite from the strenuous maturation process of which he is the object. Although the adolescent may seriously question race discrimination and exclusiveness, to the point of suggesting reform, he is by no means disposed, as we have noted, to give up exclusive fraternities and sororities, which are important and perhaps necessary social defences at his age.

While the peer group is assuming ever greater importance in the adolescent's environment, the world of school still bulks large, although it is soon to be discarded for university. The school in Crestwood Heights recognizes the fact that it must soon relinquish the child for higher education. Its concept of responsibility and maturity demands that he "reach autonomy in the direction of his own life, tolerance, individuality, knowledge, and judgment." In actual practice, however, the school does not delegate to the student at this stage anything like complete responsibility for his academic work or action. Marks and passing of examinations are too important in the achievement of academic or vocational success—one fundamental reason for the school's existence. Each school, too, is part of a competitive system and it measures *its* success in terms of the academic standing of its graduates.

The major solution of the Crestwood school to this well-recognized dilemma is the "Senior Plan" for Grade XIII. A general meeting of the Collegiate Home and School unit was devoted to an explanation and discussion of this plan. Mr. E. told the parents:

Grade XIII students had been consulted about this. They were asked how they thought the school could prepare them for life after high school. . . . They met in small groups to discuss "how they could accept responsibility and act more grown up." They approached their task with extreme caution. There was no feeling that "now we are free and can do what we like!" They asked themselves such questions as "Are we old enough to handle this freedom?" They made up a list of suggestions for Grade XIII teachers. These were gone over to see how far they would be practicable. One was that if a student were absent, there need be no note from school. Then they felt that study form was not a good place for Grade XIII. This meant that they were being treated as having no responsibility. A study room was set up for Grade XIII, a special room to which they could go or not, as they pleased. In this room there was no supervision. Then, detention was considered childish. Those who needed detention should have help or advice, not just punishment: they had not "outgrown childish tricks." When students were late, the real objection was that they disturbed twenty other students and the teacher. The penalty should be that the latecomer miss the class. "We," said Mr. E., "went on to consider safeguards." The plan was just a halfway step to the future.

1. No student was to be on the Senior Plan unless he wanted to be. If it is the wish of either the student or the parents, he may be excluded.

2. New students in the school are not included. They come without the

preparation or background of the other students and have not been in the school long enough to know what it is all about. This gives a chance to get a line on a new student. . . . The first report card, which comes at the end of October, usually gives this.

3. There is an advisory council to operate the plan. It is made up of two students from each of the four Grade XIII classes and the four home room teachers . . . the council will watch the progress of each Grade XIII student. The "failures" will be called before the council and asked why it happened. If necessary, help would be offered; but if improvement were not forthcoming, the council would notify the staff, who would take the student off the plan.[36]

This plan is a departure from the more stereotyped pupil-teacher relationship; it places a strong emphasis on the acceptance of responsibility for progress upon the students themselves. The weight of peer-group opinion is organized to safeguard its successful operation. At the same time, the teachers and the Principal, whose ultimate responsibility it is, are there in the background to ensure the maintenance of academic standards.

In the area of social adjustment, the school, as well as the peer group, expects the child to be a "joiner." A true criterion of belonging to the teen-age culture would appear to be membership in such an organization as the fraternity or sorority. The school, too, provides organizations for its extra-curricular program. To help the student in his general social adjustment, it appoints teacher-counsellors. As Mr. M. of the Collegiate explained:

The students in the schools needed to feel they had friends among the teachers, to whom they could go with any problems that bothered them. . . . Miss P. was doing this type of work with the girls and Mr. C., who was also responsible for sports, was working with the junior boys, as well as two others. Thus the schools had a complete team of people. Each student would find one of the four a helper and friend to whom he would naturally turn.

The school is here attempting, in the meeting of students' problems, to increase the number of face-to-face relationships which are difficult to maintain in an institution with such a large student body.

The school tries to maintain a balance between extra-curricular activities and school work, and to spread the executive responsibility as widely as possible among the students, but here again with large numbers there are difficulties.

It was explained that, at a meeting of teachers, the extra-curricular record of the student was checked against his results [academic]. They could deal only with extreme cases. At the June staff meeting, it was the job of the counsellors to get hold of the students who hadn't been doing enough in extra-curricular activities. It was done on a class and a personal basis. They had never been able to set a definite limit to the number of activities a student could participate in. They had been trying to spread out responsibility, and had had some success in having students with one position refuse others, if offered. . . . there was a "professional executive type" in the school. They could run things, but there were others with plenty of ability too.

Mr. Y. said that in the preparatory school especially, they were trying to develop club activities, an hour a week, where the student could join some club under the sponsorship of a teacher.

Mr. N. went on to elaborate on the extra-curricular activities. If the student failed in even one exam at Christmas, his extra-curricular activities were checked. If the case was an extreme one, the parents were notified. . . .

The promotion on the part of the school staff of extra-curricular activities indicates the importance assigned to them in this phase of social adjustment. However, when it is a question of priority, the school work essential for academic or vocational success comes first. Students who are members of the basketball team, for example, will be put off the team if they cannot pass all their term examinations.

On the one hand, therefore, the school expects mature students, responsible for the direction of their work and social activities. On the other hand, if the student fails to keep these demands in what is considered a proper balance, the teacher is still vested with sufficient authority to regulate them for him.

Thus the Crestwood child arrives on the threshold of adulthood extremely sophisticated in certain ways, such as intellectual ability and emotional independence. He is less adept, in all likelihood, at the actual tasks of adult life than is his rural counterpart, who if he is a farm boy has assumed different kinds of responsibilities as he encounters with his father situations which allow practical learning. The Crestwood child has been constantly urged by his parents and his teachers to become mature and responsible, but the culture has not provided many opportunities to become either in reality. Both boy and girl of this age understand more or less clearly what is required of them in the years ahead. The boy usually is more definite about his future plans than is the girl. She sees marriage as a goal, and her years at university are considered a useful interval and sometimes as a means of acquiring a husband.

Here, then, at a peak of the socialization process, as mediated by the family and the school, the Crestwood Heights boy and girl must be left. But ahead will be many new learnings and relearnings, for, sensitive to their changing culture as they are, they can only terminate such learning at death.

6. CAREER

TO THE PEOPLE of Crestwood Heights, the career is of all concerns the most momentous. It may be called "success," or "getting ahead," or "doing well." Whatever its name, it is thematic to the mythology of the Western world. Cinderella, Dick Whittington, Abraham Lincoln, or the Jack of numberless stories—Jack who killed the giant after taking his lyre and his gold, Jack who met and won the King's daughter[1]: these are stories that antedate capitalism and the expanding industrial technology of North America. Yet they have been so absorbed into the Western ethos that they continue to nourish the spirit and implant conceptions in the minds of children in Crestwood Heights.

THE SOCIAL SETTING

The Crestwood child's environment includes, as earlier chapters have described, the very criteria by which the success of the career is measured. The conditions which make for comfort are in themselves the hallmarks of success in the career: harmonious surroundings keyed to the latest conception of beauty and elegance; the opportunity to consume food which is rich, yet approved by nutritionists as nourishing; the house, and the privilege of living, in a select area; superior opportunities for travel, education, entertainment, and training in special skills. These are the rewards of the father's capacity to earn, which is thus a major measure of a successful career.

The connections between the career and the symbols of success and the attendant attitudes and values are obvious. The child, who in more static social situations might be permitted to take certain aspects of the common life for granted, is in Crestwood Heights made to "appreciate" the close connection between effort and achievement: where there has been rapid personal mobility (and will be more) one cannot take anything for granted. The past has been outmoded too recently. The present social and economic status of the parent is too precarious. The goals ahead, higher up the ladder of achievement, beckon too invitingly for complacency. It seems that personal mobility develops a momentum of its own, which, until it is spent, carries the individual and his family from status to status. Yet it is inevitable that the child for whom so much is being done should also tend to "take everything for granted," including the inevitability of his own success. At the same time there is much uncertainty in Crestwood Heights as to whether the person who does *not* receive such a good start (like many of the adults who voice these doubts) does not really have the advantage; is he not more strongly oriented towards struggle and competition—and therefore more likely to achieve?[2]

Various social interests have a stake in the development of career-oriented persons. We have said that the complex contemporary division of labor requires certain components at the professional and managerial level which become essential to the smooth operation of an industrial society. The maintenance of this group is, in turn, assured, it seems, by three conditions: mobility in space and in social class; occupational opportunity with commensurate rewards in material objects and class position; and finally, personal flexibility and adaptability within fairly well defined limits respecting attitude, behavior, and occupational techniques. These are the prerequisites of the successful career.

Mobility is, as we see it here, the highly developed pattern[3] of movement from one job to another, from one place of residence to another, from one city to another, from one class position to another. To the individual, therefore, moving must not only hold the promise of material reward and added prestige, but, in spite of cost and labor, it should itself be "exciting." The chance to meet new friends, the known but as yet untried amenities in the distant city, together with the exhilaration of leaving behind the frustrations and jealousies of office, clique, and neighborhood, help to make moving more than tolerable. The man and woman of the Heights have few bonds[4] that cannot be broken at the promise of a "promotion." They have been prepared for this from the cradle.[5]

Mobility must be matched by opportunity: opportunity for training, employment, and advancement. Training must be available if the mobile person, bent upon a career, is to acquire the expected and necessary technical skills and social graces. He must have, of course, at least a minimum standard of intelligence, energy, and poise; but, more importantly, he must be drawn towards the enterprise around which skill, grace, intelligence, energy, and poise will play, and out of which his own career will develop. He must *wish* to manage or cure—and be prepared to *learn* to cure or manage.

The web of occupational opportunity for executive and professional which extends outward from Crestwood Heights to other upper middle class communities is an essential part of the career orientation of the individual. There must be posts to fill. It is best if there are more opportunities than men, but even if the opposite is the case, the satisfactions which come from keen or even ruthless competition can be stressed. In either case, whether there is a buyers' market or a sellers', the experience is rationalized and justified.

The third prerequisite calls for a readiness in the professional and executive to abandon cherished usages and techniques as new ones arise. Of course the desire for change must not be so strong as to impair the individual's performance at the level presently occupied; the costs and risks of moving may help to bridle his ambition, but the job itself has its own satisfactions. Nevertheless, he must be willing to acquire new conceptions of life and organization, and to revise constantly in later life his procedures within his chosen field. The differences between the career of the person who has risen by his own effort and the person who has been placed in Crestwood Heights by the parent, have a relation to the flexibility which is so essential to the professional and executive person in a rapidly changing society, since the individual who "gets a good start" is more likely to accept current techniques and practices than the individual who is struggling upward. The latter must challenge the very arrangements which give advantage to the former. Personal flexibility is a valued characteristic, whereas rigidity is generally condemned. "Flexibility" allows the person to accept innovation, to manoeuvre in difficult situations where precedent gives little guidance, and to seek by his own efforts new solutions to social and technological problems.

Careers are made within a structure of relationships, some of the elements of which have already been mentioned: incentives, checks and limitations to ambition, compensation for failure, and a delicate balancing between opposites. These elements and others are caught up in the notion of competition as it is understood and played out in the daily rounds of work and play in Crestwood Heights.[6] In the Heights one encounters competition everywhere: in sport, in the classroom, at the dinner table ("Now let's see who will finish his vegetables first"), at the traffic light, in raising money for charity, in the mission work of the church.

Competition, it seems, like duelling or mating, requires the pairing of opposites, the pitting against one another for mutual gratification of (usually) two persons or groups, alike in all respects save one: the quality at issue.

Hockey and Canadian (Rugby) football, two typically male, typically North American games, seem to represent symbolically the structure of competition. More than any other game, football would appear to be the property of the upper middle class and is particularly associated with the university, where it is firmly established as an autumn cere-monial. By analogy, the structure of the relationships within which the person bent on a career plays out his roles may be illuminated by look-ing at the game.[7]

The game is played by two competing teams.[8] The teams are evenly matched in number, in ascribed roles and, if possible, in strength—for the odds for winning should be as even as possible. Equal strength depends on player ability, coaching and management skill, the eye appeal of the playing grounds, uniforms, equipment, and drum majorettes. The two teams are members of a league, and the league is tied in a series of relationships to other leagues devoted to the promotion of the game. In a single game, therefore, the issue at stake is not simply the final score of the game but actually the interlocking interests of all the teams in the league, of all the leagues, officials, players, coaches, and subsidiary parties to the game—of distributors of sporting equipment, news and radio commentators, and so on.

The teams play together in highly combative style. In essence, the play centers around a violent contention for possession of the ball. Possession gives the possessor nothing more than the right of initiative in the aggressive policy of gaining ground from the opposition. The play which ranges back and forth upon the territorial limits of the "field," is governed by a set of rules which are commonly accepted. These are administered by neutral officials whose prominent function it is to act as mobile judiciary as the game proceeds. The existence of a common body of codified usages em-phasizes that what appears as competition between two groups takes place *within* a large-scale cooperative effort of a single group, which besides those immediately engaged ultimately involves the public as represented by the spectators present and at home. Time, place, apparatus, rules and behavior, are largely agreed. What takes place is not so much competition as co-operation within a competitive setting.

Simultaneously, competition takes place within a cooperative setting. Like baseball (and unlike "soccer") the game is so structured that the "star" is prominent in the enterprise. To him the burden and glory of heroic be-havior are assigned. The possibilities of stardom are not equal for all members of the team, since the quarterback and back-field players are more visible, and are more often given the possession of the ball. For the men in the line, nevertheless, there are situations where any member of the team can win stardom. The game in its basic structure lies somewhere between a status or fixed arrangement, where only one member of the team, by virtue of his assigned role, is permitted a star's part, and a much more fluid situation where anyone might be the star—or none. The members of a team cooperate to defeat the opposition, but this is usually accomplished when one (or more) of the players on the team has outshone his comrades on the playing field. Their purpose, it seems, can best be accomplished when they are set against other members of their own team in a sharply competitive relation. However, the will to win usually keeps in check what might engender hostility between team-mates, revealing only the fighting spirit of each player bent on team victory.

A more detailed analysis of the game cannot be pursued, though a study of changes in it, of field rules, the foul, the fumble, and the stratagems of secrecy, suspense, and surprise are all relevant to the present argument and would illuminate more fully the basic competitive structure within which careers in Crestwood Heights are made and validated. The points of analogy are many. The career is also a device for permitting a degree of personal achievement and recognition for the individual. His "careerdom" is earned within a given context of action, partly with the help of colleagues and friends, and partly at their expense. The competitors oppose one another in pairs or groups; in either case, the classification that puts certain ones "in the same league" draws them together co-operatively against all others whether of higher or lower qualifications, and at the same time sets them against each other in earning the fruits of achievement. The context of action includes the prevailing legal and moral understandings in which the industrial system operates, as well as codes of professional or business ethics which regulate the activities of special groups.

Pairs are also counterposed in the game—passer and receiver, outfield peg and infield catch. So too we find in Crestwood Heights—in a setting where monogamy is the rule, where there is high mobility, and where an urban massing of the population creates a need for compensation—special emphasis upon the continual linking of pairs: in modern dancing, in the family where a third child is expected to create problems of adjustment, and in various work situations.[9]

The emergence of a dominant one in a pair, and the dissolution of the pair as its members move into solo efforts or into larger groupings, parallel the behavior of the star who is a *sine qua non* of sport and drama in North America. The career is the vehicle which permits the enactment of the star's role in a highly complex, hierarchical division of labor. In the characteristic breakdown into smaller groupings within the large corporation or the great hospital, individuals can excel in competition with others of like status. There is a place for a top sales-man, a proficient nurse, and an efficient foreman, within the larger grouping at a given place and level in the hierarchy. Rewards ap-propriate to the level give satisfaction, despite the knowledge that there are other and higher levels in the hierarchy or in the community.

There is an endless constraint, however, against "over-doing."[10] The star in Crestwood Heights must constantly practise "modesty," and pass the honor of victory on to the coach, his team-mates, or even his mother who has fed him so well. He must strive to establish the record, but once it is established he can be confident it will not be forgotten provided he properly disclaims credit for the victory. He can quickly submerge himself in the group, the team, or the firm.[11]

The fact that a star who excels too well puts himself out of his own league is a deterrent to over-performance; it helps a man to relate him-self more co-operatively to the team. In careers (as in baseball, hockey, and horse racing) if the performer is constantly superior to his fellows within the class or group, he is forced to compete in another class where his chances of starring are reduced. In the pursuit of the career, there is thus, as we shall see, a system of checks and balances where the good is blunted by the bad, incentive offset by deterrent, and ambition bridled by the fear of excess.

ORIENTATION TOWARDS THE CAREER

The career is set before the boy as a central life goal at an early age. He is encouraged jokingly almost as soon as he can talk to speculate upon what he is going to do when he grows up (not by his enlightened parents, but by their friends). His early responses give rise to gentle amusement for he does not discriminate too carefully between the practical and the romantic: he wants to be a cowboy, or a taxi driver, or a doctor, or a TV artist; or all these and more. In playful fantasy or in fanciful play he enacts, often in expensive costume, what he sup-poses are the roles that go with these designations. The boy is not likely to choose a girl's role. The girl, who discriminates less carefully, likes to fancy herself a nurse, or a doctor, or a nursery school teacher, or a singer or a mother. She nevertheless seems to sense very early that sex defines occupations for her, and to select only those congruent with it. The boy may wish to be a doctor like his father, but he will never say "I am going to be a father" though his sister may early regard parenthood as a career. The girl is more inclined to predict two careers for herself. Out of her girlish imagination, she will say that she plans to be an actress and a mother—without sensing the opposing demands such a combination implies. The continuing problem of this opposition will be discussed later at length.

Career considerations seem to "come from nowhere" in the environment of the young child. He senses them only at the deepest level and expresses them in those flashes of insight which surprise and amaze parents. Yet from the beginning these considerations shape his orientation towards adulthood.

The child's developing notion of the career derives in large part from his immediate social circumstances. The occupational roles filled by Crestwood adults contribute alike the information and misinformation which become incorporated into his conception of himself and his future. The high incomes and the high-status occupations which are enjoyed by the adults, the reputable houses, the automobiles, and other material manifestations of success, are, as we have had occasion to note before, not mere statistical data to the child.[12] He is constantly apprised of their meaning by parent, teacher, and especially peer. The true facts may well be exaggerated, but we do know that some version of the facts is constantly emphasized.[13]

The Crestwood child who is reared in an environment of prosperity and success, comes to feel that life's opportunities are limitless, that he can become anything he wishes to become. This environment, provided by the father as a result of successful prosecution of his career and by the other successful fathers who live in Crestwood Heights, sustains a feeling of well-being in, and is at the same time a source of pride to, the child, who easily learns to enjoy the comparative affluence and power enjoyed by his father and the fathers of his friends. Many advantages will be his: he will be sent to college and his father's "contacts" will be at his disposal when his career is formally launched. Yet the environment creates an excessively optimistic feeling as to opportunity —excessive not so much because the range of opportunity is limited, as because the fact that the father cannot transmit his own status to his son is largely concealed. The child's ignorance of conditions in which people live who are less successful than his father and his friends' fathers, furthers the illusion. But though the feeling of multiple opportunity helps the child to feel that life is easy, he is at the same time vaguely uneasy in knowing that this is so. He knows that he will be "given every opportunity" to get started, that his parents will not spare themselves to help him, but that he will also be called on to "exert himself." He knows that he is expected to excel, but he is afraid he is soft.[14]

Nevertheless his sense of well-being stems largely from his own experience, even if he has had to coax and wheedle for many of the things he got. His desires may not always have been satisfied—perhaps he did not get the cowboy suit or convertible he wanted—but he knows he will receive the necessary skills to earn his way and make his way when the time comes.

This combination of a sense of optimistic well-being and a vague malaise was a frequent observation in Crestwood Heights. Children of Grade VI would admit to one another, ruefully, in class discussions that they *were* spoiled. University students from the Heights, asked why they were attending, answered almost unanimously that they "just went," i.e., things happened in a certain way because everyone expected them to happen that way.

Yet the student finds the first year in college difficult, not knowing the important people on the campus, nor the best methods of taking lecture and reading notes. He often longs for the protection of the Crestwood school system. The student's difficulties in his first year in college reveal the basic relation between the child and the adult. The adult can start the child but he cannot establish him. He can pay the bills and assure bodily comfort, but the child at college, or on a new job, at camp or in the new fraternity, must make his way alone. The parent does not have the prestige or power, his name is not impressive enough, to secure and maintain a favored position for the child without the child's own most active intervention. The typical Crestwood Heights parent has a high income, but not a vast capital accumulation with which he can "set up" the child at the beginning of his adult life.[15] Even when the parent can provide completely for the child's economic well-being, it is done so as to give an appearance of self-support—by establishing a downtown office for him, and letting him assume the other trappings of a career. But even such aid the child might shun. He likes security; but he now wants to compete and to know the taste of struggle.

The child's behavior is, of course, a reflection of the ambivalence which is readily observable in the parent. The father's own motivation to succeed gains a large measure of its force from his desire to provide his children with comforts and opportunities which were denied him in his youth. Despite repeated expressions of belief in the "survival of the fittest," the father is reluctant to expose the child fully to the mercies of a competitive situation. Yet he is uneasy, and makes the child uneasy, if the child appears to take his advantages for granted.

The parent looks back upon his own struggle with some nostalgia: it was "fun" doing chores or working his way through college. If his child gets a job, the father will boast of this enterprise downtown; the child "does not need the money, but the experience will do him a world of good."

At a parents' meeting in the course of a discussion on "social responsibility," a mother asked why her child *should* wash dishes; she never did so herself, and the girl was too busy with her figure skating. She asked the question partly in self-defence, but also, it seemed, out of fear lest the child were being deprived of some valuable ingredient to her character formation. There was unanimous support for the view that children ought to wash dishes because "it is good for them to know how to work."

The Crestwood paper boy illustrates this point perfectly. The morning papers are delivered from door to door in the early hours, since a glance at the paper is thought to be as necessary to fortification for the day's work as shaving and coffee. It is a not uncommon sight to see a boy deliver papers in Crestwood Heights clad in a well-padded station-wagon coat and riding an expensive bicycle, which was donated by the father in tribute to the boy's spirit. On stormy days, the father or mother may be seen driving the paper boy from door to door. The father would admit laughingly that the family suffered a net loss on the paper route from a financial point of view, but contend that the gains for the boy's character were incalculable.

The insistence upon work as a moral value is, of course, not the only source of ambivalence. Nor does the insistence stem entirely from the knowledge that the child will have to make his own career. It has its roots, for many, in memories of the Depression (or other historic disasters) and in the foreboding that things will not always be as good as they are today.

Since the career is an integrating principle in Crestwood life, the process of choosing the career is well worth examination. A number of parents and their children were questioned about "aspirations": the aspirations of the parent for the child, the child's own aspirations and his conception of his parents' hopes. The parents' answers were general and philosophical. The children's were specific and concrete. The parent wished for such goods as health, happiness, a good marriage; the child named the specific occupation which he desired for himself, and the one he thought his parents desired for him. Both hoped for "prosperity, but not wealth"—or the equivalent. Behind the generality of the parents' hopes lay the belief that the parent ought not to choose for the child. The child must make the two most critical decisions of his life alone:

the choice of a career and the choice of a spouse. The child recognizes this parental reluctance.

"Both my parents feel," one boy writes, "that they must not influence me in a job for later life, because I may not be happy in the things they think best." Another grasped the subtlety of the relation more accurately: "I know this is what they want for me though they have never said. . . ."

Many children, however, are quite aware of the parents' paramount interest in the outcome of their efforts in child-rearing. Despite reticence, actual or alleged, there was direct intervention. One boy states:

As far back as I can remember, my parents have nagged me about my duties around the house. . . . I have come to the conclusion there must be something behind it all. They would not nag me just to be mean or because they like to squabble but to lead me in the right path to happiness in life.

Another boy, after stating his dislike of the assignment ("This idea does not impress me at all, but seeing that it must be done, here it is"), says (italics added):

I think my parents want for me a happy enjoyable life but not to be extravagant or do harm to our name, or be a crook or gangster. They have raised me from an infant, and after all their work and money that they have invested in me, I think that *they would want me to keep it up*, and show my thanks for all their efforts by being a worthy son, to do their family name no harm but to be a credit to it, *to be a success in life, not necessarily financially* because many wealthy men do not have a high character.

The parents face a solid dilemma. Their resolve not to intervene may be a common-sense recognition that in a changing world one cannot make specific plans, that arranged marriages and careers belong to other and bygone times. The romantic notion of the individual taking his own life in his hands and making good is still potent, and it too influences the parent to avoid making vocational choices for the child.

On the other hand, no one knows better than the parent in Crestwood Heights that there is "nothing left" for the child if his career goes awry. The father and mother might disagree on tactics: on the question of *how* to guide the child's decisions. The father who knows the rigors of downtown life would be more inclined to elbow the child out of the driver's seat if he thought this would avert disaster. The mother, who has heard more lectures on the theory of growth and who has watched the child learn to walk, is prepared to let the child make his own mistakes, and to drive, so to speak, from the back seat.

But regardless of how authoritarian the parent's direction becomes, he will find that he is balked in preparing the child for his career if he attempts to push to the limit the power which legal right, and control of the child's spending money, give. A show of parental strength can be met by rebellion, against which the parent seems to have little defence, or by acquiescence, which produces a placid, yielding, pleasantly ineffectual adult. Such an adult, if male, can manage effectively only under the vigorous tutelage of a parent or parent-substitute. A character of this type is considered undesirable; its possessor is handicapped in the projection of his own career, and may well face a severe crisis when the parent-figure is removed. He may submit to guidance, but be unable to measure up to parental expectation in college or even on jobs secured for him by the parent.

To assure the necessary independence of spirit and initiative, the parental role has to be one of careful management, in which protection of the child is delicately balanced against exposure to difficulty; and, since no formula is available, "each child must be treated as an individual case." Little wonder that desperation and resignation are expressed so often by the parents, as they seek the aid of experts and child-rearing institutions.

Parental resignation in the face of manifold complexities is tempered, however, not only by a blind faith in the expert, but by an inherent optimism (with an overlay of anxiety) which is founded on the belief that "everything will be all right in the end." This belief derives in part from the knowledge that young people *are* winning scholarships, making acceptable marriages, and finding lucrative posts every day. Even the victims of mésalliance *are* finding new partners; stomach ulcers *are* overcome, alcoholics *are* restored to their former earning capacities, and the victims of "nervous disorders" *have* found effective psychiatric treatment. It also derives, in part, from the ability of the adult to overlook his own uncertainty and anxiety, or to blame it on himself. Faith maintains that there is a way out of every difficulty.

To support that faith an extensive array of apparatus is now available to help launch the child on his career. There are instruments of diagnosis: the psychological test, the charts and records of the pediatrician, dentist, and school nurse. There is the armament of the nutritionist: the pills with which the child is bombarded even in prenatal existence, the prepared foods all recommended by some distant and willing authority and urged upon the family by unctuous personages through the mass media. There are the "health hints" from the insurance companies and the newspaper columnists; the educational toys to make play purposeful; the health shoes that compel the feet to "grow right." When the child is older, irregularities and imperfections can be erased or disguised by orthodontia, lipstick, speech therapy, brassières,[16] and flattering *tailleurs*. Behind each item and gadget there is a promise that the parent cannot resist, a promise that *this* will help the child. The child is no more impervious to salesmanship than the parent, and although he may demand one type of breakfast food because his friend likes it, or because they are giving away cowboy hats with it, the underlying message that he will be stronger, more attractive, and eventually more successful does not escape him.

Added to expert advice and useful gadget as a support for faith is "the skill," which will be discussed further in the next section. Skills provide a repertoire of abilities without which the child cannot face the future with confidence. It is part of his orientation for him to come to believe that he will be happier if, like his friends, he can do a jack-knife dive, or excel in down-hill skiing, or "pass" all his subjects on leaving high school. There is a peculiar, non-utilitarian view of these skills. It is more important to earn first-class honors in French than it is to be able to use the language in Quebec or to read Molière for private enjoyment. It is more important to *have been* able to play the violin, or to manage a three-gaited saddle pony, or to assemble an outstanding collection of coins, than it is to be able to do any or all of these things at some point in adult life. Yet the utmost importance is attached to these skills. Their purchase involves a considerable monetary expenditure. The conveying of children from one class to another after school and on weekends calls for adroit planning by the mother who must serve as chauffeur several hours each week during the winter season.[17] This teaching of skills that have so little pleasure- or use-value in adulthood seems planless and wasteful, when it is recalled that they are intended as aids to the career. The cult of "experience" demands that the skills be learned, and "rationality" extorts the hope that they may *somehow* be useful.

How successful are these preparations for adulthood? Do parental anxiety and the costly aids of school and expert "pay off"—to use a Crestwood phrase? From the point of view of specific training for adult jobs, the preparation appears to be excellent, especially for the boy who is to follow conventional middle-class occupations, since these occupations now require more skill in "man-management" and self-management than mastery of a technical field. As to preparation for more general adult roles, a clear-cut evaluation is difficult. The youth in high school or college evidences much ease and assurance of manner, but he is not sure of himself; and little trust or responsibility is placed in him. Ten years ago, boys of like age in military service were commanding men; these boys must wait several years before realizing the full confidence of manhood. Today, a boy whose parents cannot send him to college can enter the Air Force for a technical training, and to him may be entrusted a costly bomber; the Crestwood boy whose parents can, and do, send him to college, is considered by many parents (and some automobile insurance companies) as an unreliable driver and a poor risk. Somewhat like the Manus child, though for vastly different cultural reasons, the Crestwood youth who has concentrated on "carefree, wholesome enjoyment"[18] will find that he has many adjustments to make and a great deal more to learn after he starts his new job, after marriage, and when his own child arrives. That he does make these adjustments and assume these new roles indicates once again that the career, a major loop in the roller-coaster, has not been adversely affected by the smaller, earlier, simpler loops.[19]

THE BASES OF THE CAREER

Having looked at the social setting, and the orientation of the individual towards a career, the means and method of achieving it may be better understood: the choice of it, personal advancement in it, and realization of it.

Orientation to the career is general. Choice is specific and deliberate; but the actual designation of the vocation is most often delayed and vacillatory. The orientation is simply one aspect (and a result) of the child's environment. Undoubtedly there is many a Crestwood child who determines early in life to be a doctor, or a scientist, or a farmer, whether he can expect to be successful or not in the material sense. He may maintain this position fixedly and despite obstacles. The typical child, however, follows a somewhat less purposeful course: provided he can be "successful," he "would like" to choose a certain vocation.

This is remarkably different from the conception of a "calling" in terms of which a life-work was frequently chosen a generation or more ago. There was then in actuality, or by inference, a suggestion of Divine intervention or moral obligation in the choice of an occupation. In this choice there was undoubtedly a strong element of ambition: one might hope to be a great missionary, or surgeon, or inventor. It is unlikely that the desire for material reward was absent; in fact, in the unswerving optimism of the Victorian era this might even have been taken for granted. If a man felt impelled to choose a certain career, or to accept a certain duty, he expected material rewards in this world and

spiritual ones in the next as the normal consequences of proper sub-
mission to his call and industrious application in carrying out his vocation.

In listening to the children of Crestwood Heights speculating on
their future, one receives the impression that almost nothing is taken
for granted. The Crestwood child, being less certain of reward, seems
to be more than ever determined to ensure for himself a comfortable
material existence. There is no Divine calling: only the anxious and
often contradictory promptings of father and mother, the (to him)
ambiguous scores of "interest"-finding tests, and the non-directive techniques of guidance workers. It is from these the Crestwood child must
obtain a divination and lay the basis for concrete plans for his future.

In planning a career, the children seem generally to give first priority
to expected material reward; next to eminence; last, if at all, comes
some other and vaguely defined "good," not necessarily great, but
something somehow to be hoped for.[20]

There is extreme reticence about making serious claims in advance
about one's own destiny, as the statements of "expectation" in the High
School Yearbook illustrate. Beside each picture is given information
about the graduate. Two headings invariably appear: "Ambition" and
"Probable Destiny."[21] In Crestwood Heights, the future is faced with
wry humor, at least as far as the façade which it is permissible to
present to the peer group is concerned. In the Yearbook one finds the
ambition "to manufacture dolls," followed by the probable destiny,
"caretaker in the bank, and paper doll cutter for amusement." The ambition "to make a million dollars," is linked to the probable destiny "to
sell pencils;" when a boy wants "to own a TV and radio station," his
anticipated blossoms in the dust are "caretaker for the Canadian
Broadcasting Corporation (I'd shoot myself first)." The Crestwood
child seems to hope for a lot, but to have been disciplined not to expect
too much.[22]

It is essential at this point to distinguish between a career and a
vocation. The preparation for a vocation is clear-cut; it consists in
passing through a series of training situations of increasing refinement
and specialization, and it culminates in full recognition of a person's
readiness to pursue his chosen work. The preparation for a career is
nebulous; there are no formal criteria of doctrine, or indoctrination, or
training. Yet vocation and career are inseparably linked. The preparation for the career *includes* the vocational training. One might expect
a man whose training has been irreproachable would have laid a solid
foundation stone for a successful career, yet no one knows better than

the teacher that the gold medallist who has just finished one phase of his occupational training may not repeat his successes in business and professional life, for there are invariably great differences in career performance among those whose instruction and achievement in training situations have been equal.[23]

Preparation for the career, thus, includes more than vocational training, includes just about everything else that is considered "proper" in the child's experience: it is a composite of vocational training, plus the total life experience of the individual, plus luck, plus energy, plus what everyone but the psychologist refers to as "personality."

One may now see some explanation for the emphasis on skills, and comprehend why it is so important to meet, or know how to arrange to meet, the right people. Similarly it becomes understandable that parental aspiration should encompass only such very general attributes as happiness, health, "ability to appraise and meet life situations," tolerance, "self-control, resilience and perseverance." In the final analysis, almost everything the child needs, so far as the success of his career is concerned, and much of what he has learned, can be included in the techniques of personal advancement. These, the means by which a career is realized, now need to be examined.

They come into full play when the career is finally launched. Everything has been done that can be done for the child by parents, educational authorities, experts, and the institutions which they create or reshape; he has not only been submitted to but has entered wholeheartedly into the progression of activities which have characterized his childhood. Now he moves out into the realms of adulthood, undoubtedly with excitement and apprehension—the sensation "This is it!"—though there is little of Walt Whitman's sense of adventure:

> Afoot and light-hearted I take to the open road,
> Healthy, free, the world before me,
> The long brown path before me leading wherever I choose.

The future does indeed lie ahead, but good fortune is not sought by buying lottery tickets or by taking reckless chances or by disregarding the canons of appropriate behavior. On the contrary, the widely recommended techniques which are thought to assure good fortune and success are assiduously practised.

Beyond this point, our account cannot take the younger generation of Crestwood Heights since it is at this brink that they stand as this research project closes. But the careers of the fathers may prefigure those of the sons, and it may be worth while to continue the analysis by describing the former. (The woman's career will be the focus for the next section.)

The older men of Crestwood Heights are of two types. The one has succeeded by a careful observation of the techniques of personal advancement; the other has not needed these techniques. Members of the latter group have succeeded financially by sheer personal virtuosity. There is no way of knowing how many of the children now in Crestwood schools will achieve prominence by this means, but we do know that if they are influenced by their training, the path of prudence—or, perhaps more accurately, of prudent boldness—will appear more inviting.

The cycle of such a prudently bold career begins with a lengthy period of renunciation, followed by a relatively brief period of full realization, and a gradual decline shading into retirement. This gives the major loop in life's roller-coaster. If the career is launched at the age of twenty-five, the period of renunciation may continue for ten or fifteen years. The careerist who has not put himself in a strategic position to reap the benefits of the renunciation before he is forty, will invite melancholy speculation about his future. "Arrival," however, does not mean that he can relax, for it is known that one serious mistake (for example, by a business man or surgeon) can undo years of careful career planning. It simply means that a man is in a favored position to realize his ambitions by the judicious exploitation of the position he has secured. The first period, to use a financial analogy, is devoted to capital accumulation. The second is expected to be one of productivity and high earnings in anticipation of rapid obsolescence. There is a sense in which the entire period of renunciation, and, past this, the period of life's "practice," can be characterized as a preparation. However, graduation from college is usually thought to terminate the preparation and to be followed by the period of renunciation.

The career begins in this period as a long climb, a shrewd application of energy and charm and patience which is known as "hard work." There follows a series of promotions, or, if the business is a self-owned enterprise, expansions of the firm; and finally a man reaches the place where he will say "I have things arranged now the way I want them." He has not then finished his endeavor; he has actually "just started."[24] In this period, too, the man who is career-bent will provide himself with the "contacts," partners, trappings, and prerogatives of the career.

The contacts are an important part of his family endowment; his family should make it possible for him to meet the people who may some day be useful to him. This gives a man his "start"; these human beings are the material with which the foundations of a career are built. The contacts are ranged in ever widening circles of decreasing intimacy. Within the inner circles of friendship, the relation is more reciprocal and family-like; here, help is given and help is returned without immediate calculation of price or cost. In the outer circles, the relation becomes increasingly exploitative, particularly where colleagues are concerned. Customers and clients, still further out, stand in a highly formalized relationship in which the exchange of goods or services for money is taken as basic to the transaction. Somewhere within this series of circles, is the customer or client who brings in more customers and clients, receiving nothing tangible in return, although his contribution makes a career forge ahead.

Within the more intimate circle, and out of its personnel, the man chooses and forms his partners in personal advancement. The partners are those who succeed together with him: his wife and his closest friends. It will be necessary now to qualify a contention which was made earlier: that for the sake of social mobility and personal advancement, an individual must be prepared to leave his family, his neighborhood, his friends, and his colleagues behind as he moves on and up. The willingness to do this is essential, but the doing is not always necessary. A comment made on a lawyer's career illustrates just such a situation:

Robert had a long hard struggle establishing himself, but he was always a good fellow, always kidding around, and he was an ardent golfer and Service Club man. At first the trouble was he did not know the right people, and the people he did know had no business to give him, and could not swing any his way. Still he stuck to his friends and made the best of it. Finally, as his friends got older, they began to move into the money themselves. Then they began to have legal problems, and they swung everything they could to good old Robert; now he is in the money, too, or as they say, "He's doing very well for himself."

In this case a general movement swept a willing member of a group of executives and professional people onward and upward. What happened to Robert also suggests another necessity in the mobility which is such an important factor in the Crestwood style of life; it must be emphasized that travel[25] is deleterious to the career if it is horizontal, unless the move is one of evident opportunity. Much would have been lost to Robert's career if he had been forced to go to another city.

In the discussion of their careers with Crestwood Heights men, repeated reference was made to the "usefulness" of old friends in the establishment of a clientele or practice. One example could be cited of an unusually successful life insurance agent:

He had been sent at great sacrifice to a private school by his parents. They were unable to send him to University so he began selling, on the advice of an older man who pointed out that, lacking capital to start a business of his own, selling was the best way to begin, since energy and intelligence make up the only capital required. The old friend did not mention another important type of capital—friends. The young man had over two hundred names of persons he already "knew"; not all of these would buy but they would give him names of others; and so with these as assets his career began. To-day, after more than two decades of selling, some of these first prospects are still clients, and many, many more of those who have been added to his list since are now his "friends" also.[26]

Despite these qualifications, however, one should not conclude that such relationships are as durable as kinship ties in a rural community, for the friendship groups or cliques of the Crestwood men change as the occasion suits. Moreover, the friendships are often deliberately made to serve the career.

In our group in the club those who could not pull their weight moved in with other strangers; those who wanted to put on a show and spend too much were also made to feel unwanted. As it turned out, the people who stuck together came from different occupations. We had a big contractor in our gang, and he would not want another contractor horning into our group, and I doubt if he would want to come in. He would try to find a group where he would make good contacts and not have a competitor peering over his shoulder. Naturally, I felt the same way, for every member of our group are regular patients of mine, and I regard it as my game preserve.

Besides "friends," no partner is more important to the career than the wife; none can help more—and perhaps none can hinder more than she, though this is more difficult to establish. The choice of this partner is therefore extraordinarily important. The belief in Crestwood that love is blind and that romantic considerations are paramount when matches are in the making, renders isolation of the criteria of a "good marriage" unusually difficult. Yet when those discussing turn to other married couples, the relationship of the wife to the career is usually revealed.

A good match is of inestimable value to the man at the beginning of his career; indeed, it need only *appear* to be a good match to enable him to earn a certain measure of credit. It is preferable, of course, that in the long pull events should confirm the appearances. The question of "happiness" is, in one respect, irrelevant, provided the woman meets the standards; in other respects, happiness is assumed to be inseparable from other considerations, for it is thought that a man who is happy is more easily successful. Indeed happiness and success are often used as though interchangeable terms. However, it was stated in interviews that men who had unhappy homes to return to often spent extra time at the office and club—to their material advantage.

"Dowry" is never mentioned in Crestwood Heights, although the girl is expected to bring something more than herself to the marriage. The most important general contribution is her name, which she gives up at the altar, though it persists after marriage and becomes in a special sense a property of the husband's career. If the man has "married up," the girl's family name is a desirable addition; but even if her name is no special asset, she can in her own right bring the reputation of her skills. She need not practise them, but if she has been a tennis champion or a concert pianist (or "might have been one" if she had tried), this repute is part of her dowry. If she has personal wealth, delicate situations are created. Some wealth contributed to the marital enterprise appears to be acceptable; but too much of it or too blatant a display of it will hurt the husband's career, for his friends may be alienated: as one person said of a colleague, "We are beginning to feel that he has an unfair edge, that he is not in our league any more."

The numberless ways in which a wife can advance her husband's social and economic welfare, and therefore her own, have been frequently documented,[27] yet it was one of the few matters on which Crestwod adults were reticent in providing information about themselves. The wives take great care to emphasize that they have their own interests and activities, and that these have no connection with the husbands' success. Yet one heard frequent reference to the marriages of couples wherein the aid of the wife was both praised and condemned. She might be "a great little woman, the way she pitches in and helps"; but if her activities were "too aggressive," she would be discussed as a "busy-body" and the husband as "a weak sister." A wife of a salesman supplied a copy of the house organ of the Big City company which employs her husband. On the cover appeared a picture of four smartly dressed women at a bridge table; on the next page appeared this comment on the picture.

What are the girls talking about? No man could even approach a complete inventory of the topics that the average bridge foursome covers in two or three hours—but it is a safe guess that most of them concern life situations. As the bridge games goes on all the news of the week is reviewed and digested, neighbour by neighbour. Lucky the Life Underwriter whose wife has learned the value of her social contacts in developing her husband's business. If she is prospect conscious she makes a quick mental note of everything said—and once home, jots down the names, addresses and particulars of the good prospects she has sifted from the conversations. More than one highly successful Life Underwriting career has been aided tremendously by the prospecting aid that the wife has brought into the "family business."

Life situations are the raw material of Life Insurance selling. This is the first and most important lesson to be learned by an underwriter if he is to be successful—for the successful agent is the man who has a definite prospecting method and sticks to it. One important asset in building up a satisfactory prospecting method is to have a lot of people helping you—and who has more interest in giving help than the members of the underwriter's own family? . . .

Where can the well-trained wife look for prospects? The obvious sources are Church contacts, Parent-Teacher Associations, bridge and other social clubs, neighbourhood contacts—but a source that is often overlooked is her business contacts. "Who do I do business with?" is a basically sound question to consider periodically. Women, one expert estimates, spend 80¢ of every household dollar and in the course of her daily purchases the average housewife gets to know a substantial number of the small independent business men in the community. In addition to direct leads from these sources, they frequently can help keep her posted on the other neighbourhood news. Building these contacts may require long careful cultivation, but the experience of many underwriters has proved that the effort involved pays off handsomely in the end.

As the man's career enters upon a somewhat more mature or settled phase, its trappings, prerogatives, and duties become more readily visible. It has been noted that in the preparatory phases he must acquire certain essentials, such as adequate training, an appropriate manner, a range of skills, and useful friends and contacts, and that upon these initial resources he begins to build his career. A great deal of continuity between this preparation and realization is observable. It is not surprising then that some of these early interests and activities should promote attention and respect in later life. For instance, the Old Boys' and Alumni associations which are available to absorb the energies of those who retain nostalgic sentiments towards the *alma mater*, may become a vehicle of personal advancement. The athlete becomes in later years a "sports enthusiast." If his game in early years was tennis, he may join a fashionable tennis club which becomes a base for much of his social life. The interest may be boating, football, pure-bred livestock, stamps, welfare work, or even politics. Whatever it was that was one of the early prerequisites to launching the career may become an avocation in later life which is exceedingly important in giving the career substantiality.

These "continued interests," however, represent much more than an avocation. The tennis player who becomes the president of the tennis club has acquired a useful prerogative which may be one, but just one, of the crowning rewards of the career. These honorific prerogatives devolve upon the successful many, who tend often to think of them in many cases as "initiating duties." Somewhat earlier in life, the honor which he is receiving would have helped the man immeasurably to advance his career; now, when his success is "recognized," the coveted honor which earlier functioned as motivation is somewhat less satisfying as a reward, other and more glittering goals having become visible. Nevertheless, the prerogative and the honor do yield a measure of real satisfaction to the incumbent of a place on the Board of a philanthropic or welfare body, or the recipient of an invitation to address an assemblage or "sponsor" a worthy project.

At the peak of his career, a man begins to seek to generalize his success and to extend the field of his achievement. These excursions are not without their dangers. For instance, at a dinner where art had become the topic of conversation, a very successful lawyer began to offer his opinion on the subject in a spirited way. A business man replied jocularly, "Just because you charge $1,000 a minute for giving advice on a tricky piece of law, don't think your opinion is as valuable about everything else." The lawyer withdrew laughingly from the discussion. Yet it is into just such areas that the successful man is drawn; his success must also finally be validated outside his narrow special field, in other fields where he *is* a layman. In such areas, too, he is usually vulnerable to the art critic, the antique dealer, the horse trainer, in fact to any expert with whom he comes to associate. The jealous expert can lie in easy ambush for the man who has had to neglect many things to get as far as he has in his chosen field. At first, to be a success, he must specialize; to crown his success, he must despecialize—but it is usually too late. This is one reason why success is so often a bitter fruit.

Against this background of necessity, it is therefore not surprising to find the successful man, or writers describing him, stressing the *variety* of his achievements.

In referring to his hobby-painting, a successful businessman in an interview [for the Big City press] revealed his pride in it, and yet his need to emphasize that it was just a hobby not to be taken seriously, and that it actually helped him to do his work better. The reporter referred to his successful business career, linking it with "no mean success as an amateur painter," stating that here was a busy man who made a point of finding time for his hobbies, but indicating that he did better work because of his painting. The report concluded with this quotation: "I'll talk my painting down but not too much. I'm not a good painter, mind you. I have not taken lessons, but so far there have been no complaints."

A man's ability to authenticate his capacity in fields outside the one in which he has won his success is, in fact, a secondary means of embellishing his reputation as a successful person.

THE WOMAN'S CAREER

Nowhere is the transience of social norms and roles more evident than in the career of the woman in Crestwood Heights. Before marriage, the Crestwood girl usually has a job. She has realized one of the goals set before her, that of finding a useful place in society and of being able to look after her own financial needs. Matrimony and, more emphatically, motherhood, represent another set of goals, much more deeply rooted in society—and these are in conflict with the vocational goal. The few years between leaving school or college and motherhood, if set to music, would have little of the ominous or foreboding: there would be an exciting contrapuntal arrangement of the meticulous, metric, and neat sounds of a woman's work life interwoven and embroidered with romantic overtones of courting, mating, and marriage. There would be little suggestion of an impending conflict, and less that the conflicting elements would not be drawn into harmonious resolution.

The career of the woman in Crestwood Heights, compared with that of the man, contains many anomalies. Ideally, the man follows a continuous, if looping, spiral of development; the woman must pursue two goals and integrate them into one. The first goal has to do with a job, the second with matrimony and motherhood. The second, for the woman, is realized at the expense of the first; the man's two goals combine, since matrimony is expected to strengthen him for his work, and at it.

At about the time when the male is ready to launch his career, he seeks a life partner, a woman who will assume the traditional responsibilities of helpmate, *confidante*, companion, and mother of his children. He marries a girl who occupies about the same position in the class structure as himself. She is about as well educated as he is. Even when prosperous economic conditions make an early marriage a not too imprudent venture, the girl will be old enough and well enough educated to have a job, or be capable of securing one. However, marriages are more often prudently delayed until sufficient capital has been accumulated to make the establishment of a household a substantial venture, and a safe one for both contracting parties. Upon marriage, the woman takes charge of the home. When children come, they are her main responsibility. It was exceedingly difficult to find women in Crestwood Heights who had continued their vocations past motherhood. After marriage, the claims of the husband and, later, of the children on the woman's time and energy are so dominant that she must abandon her aspirations towards a career; often she may do this with reluctance, hoping to return to them later, only to find, in the fullness of time, that this is not to be. The role of wife and mother in these circumstances lacks many of the satisfactions commonly associated with it in a more stable rural type of society, even though the biological and emotional fulfilments it provides are still powerful.

Many a mother in Crestwood Heights stated somewhat ruefully that motherhood had "cut short" her career. She was unlikely to think of motherhood itself as a career, even though she felt that she was doing a good job as wife and mother. If questioned directly, she would aver that motherhood *was* a career, but she would omit mention of housekeeping, unless closely questioned as to her attitude towards it. Then, although she might not dismiss housekeeping as plain drudgery and lament the lack of domestic help, she would nevertheless qualify her acceptance of housekeeping by linking it to other ends: child-rearing, making her husband happy, or her interest in entertaining.

A field report of a cocktail party illustrates the uncertain and ill-defined conflict which characterizes the Crestwood woman:

Alice and Beatrice, old friends from the class of '38, are both married. Alice has children; Beatrice has none. Beatrice has a job; Alice has—well, as she says, "When my first child was born I quit working." As they met, directly in front of me, with squeals of delight, Beatrice drew her husband along with her. Alice's husband was nowhere in sight, so I made up the foursome.

As I looked at the two women, they both looked equally fragile, equally well-groomed; except that Alice's hands on close examination were a little redder and rougher than those of Beatrice. Beatrice's husband, after the gay greeting, asked Alice, "What are you doing now?"

It was a perfectly cordial question, and his tone clearly implied that she must have written an amusing story for the *New Yorker* about her suburban life, or that her Scotch collies must have taken several ribbons at the Royal Winter Fair. His wife who is a competent but unspectacular professional woman smilingly awaited an answer.

Alice responded to this friendly query very coyly. After sipping daintily at her cocktail, she replied, banteringly, "Oh, nothing." However, her tone was ever so slightly on the defensive, for it clearly implied that she considered that nothing was everything. Or perhaps she said, "Oh, nothing," with a slightly malicious intention of saying, "Nothing that you would understand or appreciate." Or perhaps, even more maliciously, "People who have no children have nothing."

Whatever her intention, Beatrice simply continued to smile charmingly while her husband fumbled for a reply; there was just enough edge in it that he could not say, "You're kidding." So rather lamely, he echoed, "Nothing?" then added: "But how many children have you had since we saw you last?"

"Just one," said Alice. "I have only two." Again her tone beneath the banter was still slightly on the defensive. It implied, "Two sounds like very little, but it is quite enough for me, thank you."

Beatrice and her husband stirred uneasily; what more was there to talk about? They asked about Alice's husband briefly, until they were diverted by someone else they had not seen for such a long time. Alice turned to me with a pretty shrug remarking: "They don't know what they are missing." Yet I knew, from previous conversations, she regretted very much that she had had to give up her career when her first child arrived. Later, I talked to Beatrice. She said she felt sorry for Alice. "She used to be such a good friend and so interesting. We visited together a lot, but after their children arrived, they moved to Crestwood Heights and when they asked us to their parties, the other women could not talk about anything but babies. They had not been to any of the plays we had been to. There was nothing to talk about, so we drifted apart. But I think it is such a shame she has lost all her outside interests."

It is interesting to notice that in spite of Beatrice's expressed attitude, she herself was very anxious to have children of her own and, after several miscarriages, is considering an adoption.

The question of whether the married woman of Crestwood Heights has an occupation will never, it seems, be settled satisfactorily. She will give the census-taker the response he expects; but when she says "housewife," she will do so with a wry smile. It is so much more than an occupation and so much less. The question of whether she has *had* a career will also be difficult to answer, though fortunately this question is asked less often in a direct way. A few Crestwood women do have a career downtown in the same sense that men do. For the rest, who receive some special recognition in community activities, whose marriage has been successful, whose children receive favorable notice, it is not quite certain whether these make up a career or not.

The female does not receive a preparation for adult roles categorically different from that of the male. Until she chooses a vocation, she apparently competes freely with males and other females. In some respects, it seems that sexual difference has been eliminated or that there is a genuine effort at elimination. The co-educational high school and college are thought to make for ease of relations between the sexes and to give the woman, so long excluded from occupations reserved for men, equality of opportunity. The majority of Crestwood girls do attend such institutions, but very few actually enter occupations still dominated by men: law, medicine, business. Yet they are exposed to much the same occupational stimuli as the boys who actually do enter such occupations.

In the classroom, the sex of the student is largely irrelevant. The girl who in ten years will be rinsing diapers, competes in the trigonometry class with the boy who will be an engineer—and often gets higher marks. Teacher and parent encourage the girl to excel quite as much as they do the boy, and the goal set in both cases is seldom knowledge for its own sake but preparation for the successful pursuit of a vocation.

In many instances, notably in the classroom, inter-sex relations are structured, as they are on the tennis court, with little regard for sex difference.[28] Outside school, in the daily affairs of the family, the sex roles are strongly enforced in certain respects; in others, they are minimized. Daintiness and cleanliness of clothing are encouraged for the girl; on occasion, she wears dresses and garments with frills and of delicate pattern; even when she wears a male form of dress, such as slacks, which are thought to minimize sexual difference, the garments are designedly different from the male garment. In other matters, most Crestwood parents choose to ignore traditional sex-required differences, for instance, in regard to "modesty."[29]

The effect of the studied ignoring of sex discrimination within the family circle is soon outweighed by other deeper feelings which are impressed on the child from without. In school and camp, boys and girls must use separate washrooms and toilets. The boy who loiters around the girls' washroom discovers that he is considered daring by his friends, and perhaps shocking by the adults,[30] who are expected by the parents to maintain high "moral" standards. Such standards of public decorum are expected not only by parents who by "modern" standards might be thought prudish, but also by those who consider prudery outmoded.

Shortly after they start to school, little girls learn that boys are rough and noisy; and little boys, if they are not already so, learn to become rough and noisy. Little girls then learn the delightful game of slamming doors, especially bedroom doors, in the faces of little boys; and little boys learn the anger this particular form of exclusion invariably produces, and the triumph which follows when, almost invariably, they break in or are allowed to do so. The girl knows she must flee with shrieks, the boy in pursuit with rowdy, raucous laughter. Six-year-old girls have been heard practising "the shriek"; boys of about the same age, "the laugh." And essential skills these are, for they belong to a series of learned behaviors which give significance to biological difference; they are areas of human conduct which have hardly been touched by increasing equality between the sexes.

Because of the measure of equality now prevailing, the girl passes through her early years in an environment which integrates her sufficiently into the male world to permit her, if circumstances and character so demand, to enter into the vocational world traditionally occupied by the male, to compete with men and other women in that world, and to pursue a career similar to, but not identical with, that of the male. She can do this without assuming male mannerisms or dress; she may even, though rarely, be a "wife and mother" as well. Although few women do pursue a career in this way, the environment, with what appears at first to be reckless liberality, provides this preparation for all women.

This provision is made in two ways. In one, the female is expected to mingle with the male on common ground. The girl who cannot do so is considered abnormal, diffident, and shy. The normal girl co-mingles with the boy in areas which are in a sense the exclusive property of neither sex, and the normal boy is likewise expected to accept this. There are, of course, areas that are exclusively male,[31] which the girl cannot occupy, but the environment also provides clothing and hair styles which in their severity approximate mannishness, and social situations in which a woman can associate with men in preference to women, and enjoy talking to men in their terms. Such alternatives are open to but not incumbent on the woman; if chosen, they do not preclude her from entering into matrimony and motherhood.

Femininity, on the other hand, seems to be suggested by other opportunities and ideals to which the girl is exposed. She has been expected to dress like a little girl, to play with dolls, and is perhaps more likely to have taken lessons in ballet and figure skating than the boy. Even before she reaches high school, she is eager to engage the attention and win the admiration and attendance of boys.

School, camp, and other institutions do not snuff out this interest in the opposite sex, but they do try to keep it within what are considered "wholesome limits." A girl who is shy and retiring from boys will be considered an incipient problem, but a girl who is "boy-crazy" is an "actual problem." A healthy attitude is thought to be one which includes devotion to school work and assignments; cordial relations in a circle of girls; a certain amount, but not too much, club or group activity; and a practice of dispersed dating with boys—almost in that order of importance. Having several boy friends is safer than having one; but a few is better than too many. Indeed a steady friend of the opposite sex is acceptable, and this is thought less abnormal than to have no dates whatever. About the prospect of matrimony the girl should have healthy optimism, devoid of impatience and hurry. She should apply herself in a workmanlike way to school studies, but she should not be over-ambitious. A girl who worked energetically in a biology class would be praised equally with a boy, but if she stated that she intended to become a surgeon she would be given much less encouragement than the boy. Here again one encounters the fact that the "middle" position of the Crestwood people in the class structure requires for successful performance of roles, the dexterity of a tight-rope walker. The position of the girl as she proceeds from puberty to motherhood demonstrates the need for a nice sense of balance.

A university student interviewed her own sister, who was in Grade XIII of an exclusive girls' school, on her ambitions and expectations. The older girl was perhaps more directive in her approach and the sister a little more belligerent in her responses than if a more experienced person had been in charge. But, in spite of this, and a typical sisterly finale, we have few documents that come so quickly to the heart of the dilemma of the middle-class woman where money, fame, marriage, and the chance to make a contribution are all aspirations. It is noteworthy that the younger girl does not dare to say she expects to realize any one of these ends without a greater effort than she is prepared to make and that, lacking the necessary drive, she is willing to be an average person:

ME: What do you want in life?
JANE: A million dollars.
ME: Is that all?
JANE: Oh, well, to be famous; to make a contribution.
ME: Anything else?
JANE: A home life—marriage.
ME: What would you like to be famous at?
JANE: In sports.
ME: Do you feel you would be making a contribution there?
JANE: No.
ME: Do you think you will ever be a famous sportswoman?
JANE: No.
ME: Why don't you work at it?
JANE: I'd have to give up too much. I'd have to make such a break—
ME: A break from what?
JANE: From society—my friends, everything I do now.

ME: You feel they are just as important?
JANE: Yes. They make you just as happy.
ME: Of course, you could make a million dollars at sports.
JANE: But it wouldn't be as good.
ME: As good as what?
JANE: As starting up in a business and making it that way.
ME: How about marrying a million dollars?
JANE: No, that wouldn't be as good.
ME: You'd like to make the million dollars yourself?
JANE: Yes.
ME: Do you think you'll ever make a million dollars?
JANE: No.
ME: What do you think you will get?
JANE: Oh—education.
ME: Do you want education?
JANE: Yes.
ME: Why?
JANE: Well, you don't want to be dumb around other people.
ME: Do you think it will get you any of the things you want—fame or money?
JANE: No.
ME: You don't think education helps you make a success of business?
JANE: No—not necessarily. Well—yes—it does help.
ME: What else do you think you will get?
JANE: Marriage—children—an average family—an average amount of money.
ME: Will you be satisfied with that? Will you feel you are making a contribution?
JANE: (Laughs) If I have children—yes.
ME: They will do what you couldn't?
JANE: Yes. They could be good athletes.
ME: You would want them to give up what you didn't to become good athletes?
JANE: I would start them at it younger.
ME: If you had started younger you think you might have been a famous sportswoman?
JANE: Yes—say, why are you asking me all this?
ME: I'm going to write down every word you said and mail it to the Crestwood Heights Project.
JANE: Well, I don't know where all this will get you!

The prospect which Jane foresees for herself is, her sister says, "very typical of Crestwood girls": she expects to get more education which will be of doubtful value in securing fame or money; she expects nothing more than an "average family and "average" income; her contribution will be her children who will succeed where she will fail, but only if they do things better than she and learn them earlier.[32] Some girls may be burdened as soon with this insight, but many others drift into school and into marriage taking things as a matter of course. One girl's account of herself reveals less ambition than Jane had, rather a certain indifference. Everything is very natural; there is no crisis, no bother, no difficulty. Yet, in spite of this "effortlessness," she is worried about examinations:

I never seriously questioned whether or not I would go to university. I always took it for granted that I would. In fact, I hardly even thought about a college education until I was in Grade XIII. I just knew that I would go and that was all, and there was no financial problem standing in the way.

Naturally a student has to have certain academic grades to qualify for admittance. . . . This fact was of little hindrance to me. I was always a very good student, although I had and still have the same pre-examination worries that everyone else has. However, I knew that with only the minimum of studying I could pass and even get first or second class honors. When I was in fifth form, I was asked to try for a scholarship but since I had no incentive to win one—financially I didn't need it, and I'm not a particularly ambitious person—I was more interested in who I was going out with on Saturday night.

She goes on to show that the school attempted to break up this indifference, but the result was only to encourage her to "go along with the crowd."

In Grade XIII I was called in for a vocational guidance interview. This was the first time I had even thought about going to college. We were asked to choose courses best suited to our future plans for education. Without much thought I chose the regular academic course most students choose. Since Crestwood Heights school caters mostly to those students going on to university, practically all the students took the same course as I did. The fact that the school I went to did not question very much whether students went on to college, is another reason why I accepted my fate so readily.

Another university student, though somewhat resentful, underlines the part the school plays in encouraging the girl to go to college, but in the end she admits there was little else for her to do; it was what her family expected, it was "natural and inevitable."

One of the reasons I went to college was that I was fitted for nothing else. I certainly was not trained for any particular job. The curriculum is so arranged as to be useless unless one goes on with one's education. High school prepares you for nothing except university; it has meaning only as a stepping stone to university. The chief incentive is the high school matriculation diploma. Bright students are urged to try for university scholarships in Grade XIII. For high schools are not judged on the number of fifth form students employed the following September, but on the number of scholarships awarded to their students. If I had not the economic means to go to college, the high school would have had no incentive to work hard to offer me. The high school uses certain means to make one want to play one's role, i.e., go to university. Certain cultural attitudes towards education are inculcated. The fight for free education and for the education of all is part of our history. Education is valued for itself in our culture. On the other hand, the small percentage of people who go to university make us want it as a privilege of the few. One teacher used to tell us that we were in the top 2% of the population if we went to college. He equated it with I.Q. rather than opportunity. Two other ideas that I had, tho' where I got them I don't know, are: first, that a college education in contrast to high school does fit one for a particular job or career; and secondly, that college graduates make more money and get better jobs than non-university people. Scores of self-made men without education are always the exception, i.e. "He made good *despite* the fact that he had little education."

Our high school had career forums to help students. The only careers discussed were those involving university degrees. Some graduates who were at university at the time were asked to come back to the school to tell us about their courses. Crestwood Heights is proud of its graduates. I remember teachers often referring to particular graduates by name and telling us about their successes at university. Despite the fact that high school tends to channel one to the university, many never go. Why I was more susceptible to this institutional shaping than others can be explained by my family and personal background. My father is a professional and a university graduate. He is also the most successful of his family. Education has been for him the means of social advancement and achievement. The economic means were available if I wanted to go to college. My family always assumed that I would go. For myself, I was sixteen at high school graduation. I was too young to marry. I was not fitted for any particular job. It was natural and inevitable that I continue my education. I also did well scholastically. I was obviously capable of doing university work. All these factors, the economic and I.Q. factor predominating, resulted in my going to college. I had always wanted to go to this university because it was my father's and also because it had a reputation as one of the best in the world.

As a girl approaches the end of the college course, she begins to examine her destiny somewhat more critically. The following statement reveals the choices which begin to press in upon her at this time:

In high school, I wanted three things—marriage to a "prince on a white horse," a career that would bring fame or at least help better mankind, and knowledge. College was the key to the last two and the first, I felt, would come in time.

Since that time aspirations have been somewhat levelled by expectations. College did not provide the answers to all one's questions but it has given a method of finding answers and altho' one can't ever expect to really know much about anything, it is a pleasant pastime to read and see the world for oneself. I want now to do a lot of travelling. I will never know as much as I aspire to, but will be satisfied with what I do learn because it will be the most I can achieve. The career has been modified—it must be interesting and satisfying. At Crestwood Heights, all school positions were open to women. I really believed that women had equal status with men. Many of my interests were those in which I competed with boys—I always felt equal with them. Now I realize that women have a different status than men in our society, that it is unbecoming for them to compete as aggressively as men. Women in politics and business seem to have to lose their femininity. I don't want to become a hard career woman and yet I want a career. At high school I never noticed that a life career conflicted with marriage. I had the male point of view: that the two could coexist. Now I want a career first and marriage later. But unless I am careful, the "career" will degenerate into sort of "messing around" until I get married.

Why I want to work—because I hope to express my personality through struggle and achievement. Why I want to get married—because my real role in society is that of wife and mother. If I don't get married, I will feel insecure—I will have no clearly defined role in society. I will probably sacrifice career to marriage if the opportunity comes because the rewards of marriage are obvious, those of a career uncertain. In a way I envy those girls who only want to get married. They don't have to equate two conflicting desires.

The girl who finishes her college course and secures a job is faced by considerations sufficient to cause her to look closely at her position. One has to do with her matrimonial prospects, as her friends about her drop out of school and college to be married. She will assess with increasing care her prospects and the value of the educational experience as well. A girl in her fourth year at college, popular with boys but with no "steady," who is in spite of high marks uncertain as to what employment her liberal arts degree has prepared her for, says about her education and that of her friends:

Here is what happened to my high school girl friends. One girl got married immediately after Grade XIII. Another quit high school in the middle of Grade XIII, modelled for two years and then got married. Another girl quit high school at the end of Grade XII, went to business school for a year, then went into Institutional Management (a university extension course) for two years, is now going to get married. Another is still at university. Other acquaintances fared the same way. Two girls went to a cram school to complete their Grade XIII. One got married after that. The other took one year of college and then got married. One girl went back to Crestwood Heights to complete her Grade XIII then went to Europe for a year, is now at college. One girl is at college with me. Only one high school friend is a university graduate. Only two other girls that I can think of in my year at Crestwood Heights are completing university courses. It makes one ponder on our high school educational system!

The college girl in many respects is unprepared for matrimony and motherhood. It is unlikely that her knowledge of children goes beyond baby-sitting and a course in child psychology in university, where she argued strenuously with the professor. The system of grades in the school and other institutions separated her from younger children. Indeed, if she played too much with younger children, this would be regarded as a mark of probable abnormality and would be a source of worry to her psychology-conscious teacher or parent.

This girl who has gone such a long way in preparing herself for a career and apparently such a short way in preparing herself for marriage and motherhood may be better prepared than one would suppose. Unquestionably she is attractive to men; if her perfume is Elizabeth Arden's *Blue Grass* rather than Lanvin's *My Sin* this is but one more indication that her relationships with men are subtle and varied. Her undoubted sexuality includes her wit, her intellectuality, and her practical sense of values, all of which make her an attractive prospect as a wife. Yet these are hardly in the tradition of *la femme fatale* and they are characteristics which she must reveal to the male with fine shadings of femininity so as not to challenge his masculine position. It cannot be over-emphasized that this type of femininity is new, precarious, and difficult to learn, and that the extended period of dating, which may begin at ten years and proceed for ten or fifteen years until matrimony, is a function of the complexity of the role.

Dating is of itself worth discussion. The long period of dating resembles the phase of renunciation in the male career, not least in the pattern of personal manoeuvring which is required.

The pattern of dating which girls in high school and college described begins with the general premise that a girl must be attractive; that she is attractive if she is dated; and that if she is not dated, she is not attractive. Her goal is to captivate as many boys as possible by her charms; she wants everyone to love her, but she wants to love one or no one— at least no one very deeply yet. This may appear as "psychological polyandry," except that she appears not to enter or be expected to enter these relationships with anything approaching reciprocity. She will "sell" to as many and "buy" from as few as possible. Said one girl:

It is not the actual dating that is important; it is the *appearance* of dating and popularity. Girls like to be "seen around." They like others to think they are popular. The reason for this is that popularity is imitative. She gets a status rating as datable—or not. Moreover some girl will become the rage and suddenly sink into obscurity. Girls feel insecure if they don't go out for a couple of weeks—they fear they will drop out of circulation. It is not a question of, "If I don't go to this school dance, I'll go to another." Instead she feels, "If I don't go this time, I will never go out again."

The need to appear to be everywhere, while also attending to the equally important obligations of school work and family responsibilities, calls for high strategy. The girl must not "fail her exams," or the surest basis for her association with her friends will be removed. She knows that "pursuit of dates is in conflict with school incentives," so she must attempt to balance the two. But the date means security, fun, and social life; school means working alone. If she "becomes the rage," there is a danger that she will appear to be too accessible. It is not the suggestion of promiscuity and the danger attending a bad reputation that she fears; it is rather that she must appear "hard to get," even if she feels (as one girl put it) that "getting and keeping popularity is never a sure thing— it takes a great deal of time." It is little wonder, when these demands are considered, that many children in high school "go steady."[33]

If we broaden the focus slightly, we see a girl whose interest is not simply in dating, but whose activities in school and out are directed towards the acquisition of skills. These skills are nevertheless related to dating for they help to make her attractive to the boy. Moreover she will meet the boy often in situations where skills are being acquired.

Skills, however, have a more serious purpose than simply contributing to a girl's popularity before she can seriously contemplate marriage. They reach to and beyond matrimony and motherhood. In making the analogy of the roller-coaster it was stressed that the child is constantly in preparation for the unknown, and that each new situation is screened from the individual until he approaches it; but that general preparation is made in the armament of skills and in the deepest attitudes which include the expectation of meeting the unknown. It is partly for this reason that the girl is given an education and a series of skills. These do help her to be popular and eventually to find a suitable man as husband. Should she, however, fail to find or be found, or should she prefer not to marry, or should the marriage collapse through death or incompatibility, she must be prepared to earn her own living and maintain a state of sexual and financial independence. Several fathers in Crestwood Heights stated that a good education was necessary in anticipation of such a contingency. High school and college and the subsidiary child-rearing institutions are intended as insurance against such eventualities.

Should marriage be consummated and children result from the union, the wife is singularly unprepared for the *details* of housekeeping and child-rearing. Indeed she has a hearty distrust of the advice of older people, which she dismisses as old wives' tales. Yet she is prepared in the sense that she has much more experience in coping with new situations. She can read books; she is not wholly cowed by the imposing appearance of a lecturer; and there are many books and lectures to tell her how to make her marital adjustment, how to bring up mature chil-

dren. One of the skills which she acquired in her college and high school
days had to do with group activity. We shall see later how the challenge
of parenthood is met by the proliferation of organizations, the activity
of acquiring new concepts and techniques, and how a woman can
achieve a certain sense of satisfaction, if not always as a parent, then as
a responsible adult. It must not be concluded, however, that the dual
orientation which the girl has held within the network of her aspirations
is brought into unity when the mother joins the Home and School Association and the other clubs which offer themselves for her instruction
and pleasure.

Like the boy, the girl of Crestwood Heights has followed the straight
line of academic progress. She has tasted some of the pleasures of
achievement and some of the bitterness of defeat. She knows something
about the competitive world of jobs and professions. This is what she
calls "work." On the other side is the world of romance, the knight on
horseback, the snug, not-so-little home. All the symbols of contentment,
peace, and sexual fulfilment beckon. If the job is dull or the future un-
promising, matrimony can look attractive and secure. Even when a
promising professional career lies ahead, a woman still feels it is the
"natural" course of events for her to marry and have children. She looks
forward to making a home, to becoming a hostess surrounded by her
own linens, silver, and crystal. She can see the silver tea service and the
lace tablecloth which she is almost certain to receive as wedding gifts;
but the problems and disappointments are more difficult to foresee.

An essay by an eight-year-old girl, written as a regular class assignment, might fitly provide an image of the woman's career. Indeed, the
symbolism is uncanny: the early promise of the career, the sickness
(could it be the first pregnancy?), the recovery (after menopause) of
her former interests and audience; her ripe productive matronhood;
and her death, in—of all times—the year Canada was established as a
federal nation.

Once there was a girl who wanted to learn to play the piano well. She started
to take lessons when she was six. She loved to practise all the time she could.
Her teacher's name was Miss Trout. The way Miss Trout liked to teach
Susan was to give her scales. For instance she gave Susan the scale C. Miss
Trout told her to keep her hand firm. Then her fingers would not bend. Her
fingers should be like a drum stick. You will see when Susan plays, her
finger tips touch the white keys. She has not been taught to use the black
keys yet. Then one day Susan's mother bought her a record. A musical
record. She listened to the record three or four times. Then she tried to play
the piece on the piano, and she did. She called the piece Hop Scotch. Then
lots of people heard her play. And she became a musician. She travelled all

around the world. Then she began to write more and more pieces. She came to be the best player in the world. One day she became sick. She was very sick for years and years. People began to wonder where she was. And then she got better. She could not play yet, because she was not strong enough. But then she got strong again and she could play better and better. More and more people came to hear her play. She went to towns and countries too. Then she got older and older. She could not play as well now. She did not play in public. One day she was seated at her piano. She thought about her childhood. And she began to play the first piece she composed which was Hop Scotch. She was very happy and she fell into a deep sleep never to awaken. Susan was dead but her music lived on. She was now 96 when she died in the year 1867.

CEILINGS FOR AMBITIONS : FLOORS FOR FAILURE

The career, goal and cultural instrument in Crestwood Heights, can now be seen in long range. In brief review of details, we can recall that the career is an important point of emphasis in child-rearing; that in the life cycle the career is the major phase; that a successful career is marked by concrete evidence of which a Crestwood house with all the material accessories is aim and symbol. Moreover, we know that the career is singularly linked to the temporal organization of life in Crestwood Heights. The tempo of hurry and strain is one manifestation. Another is the avidity for new experience—for experience that is not on the frontier of thought or adventure, but rather on "the crest" of style; for the new idea (or gadget, game, *modiste*, preacher, joke, fabric, psychologist, rabbi) which will be everyone's delight tomorrow; for the newest crest or wood on which or in which to build the newest home in the most acceptable style.

We have seen that the extreme emphasis on individuality and on personal achievement has two powerful checks: fear of the vulnerability which achievement gives; and apprehension, since achievement now can only be continued given the good opinion of the colleagues against whom one competes. One young man who had just entered a junior executive position described the delicacy of the manoeuvring for advancement.

We are all working in a very large room; an administrative section is simply a number of desks which are adjacent. I am not near the point where I will have a glass cubicle with a group of subordinates outside. So I carefully, week by week, effect small changes, to get an extra stenographer, to shift a file here, another there, to separate my section from the next. Everything is done in an atmosphere of extreme amiability. No one ever does anything to rock the boat, and everyone keeps smiling. Honest to God, my face was sore at the end of the first month, smiling at everyone. Smiling at the ones who were smilingly trying to thwart the little plans which I was trying to conceal. But there is never any open conflict, because the organization is greater than personal ambitions, and anyone who forgets that and rocks the boat to hasten his own advancement is putting himself right on the skids.

The panorama of opportunity is almost limitless, and the appetite for rewards is difficult to satiate, for ambition is carefully cultivated in the child who knows that the attractions which he learns to covet cannot be realized without money. At the same time he learns one must not be too brusque in the pursuit of money; the love of it is said to be the root of all evil; there are "the finer things," such as books, paintings, the symphony, and travel. These divert a man from sheer production, from making more money. On the other hand, consuming the finer things requires money, a great deal of it. Yet, if he consumes gracefully, and donates enough money to the symphony or buys enough paintings, he simply opens up new relationships which enhance the career and lead him to new contacts—and more money. Such an over-simplification of the mechanics of personal advancement, however, disguises the essential structure, which complicates advancement and yet places rewards and satisfactions at attainable levels without concealing the maximal goals.

The choices which face a man who is about to buy a car were described to us by an informant. They illustrate the structure admirably, although similar descriptions of choices of a house, or a neighborhood, or a church, or a boarding school, could have been selected for the same purpose.

A chap wants to go out and buy a car. He is prepared to expend a certain amount of money, and he has always driven a Chev. He could buy a new Chev., and have some money left over, or he could purchase one of the standard models of Oldsmobile or a '51 Cadillac. He has always wanted a Cadillac but he has never seriously thought of buying one. His friends might think he was putting on the dog if he bought an Olds. So what does he do, he buys the fanciest model Chev., goes out and loads it up with white wall tires, nylon slip covers, fog lights and anything else the salesman can think of.

The rejection of the accessible Cadillac and the "Olds" even though they are objects to dream about, can be elaborated. They are rejected because the buyer will be embarrassed. He fears the sanctions that will be imposed upon him by his friends; the chief basis of ridicule will be that he does not have a house or clothes or a job to go with a Cadillac. When he can acquire suitable examples of all these items of consumption, he will buy the big car, even if he becomes increasingly separated from his friends. The man in question, however, rationalizes his rejection of the bigger car in quite a different manner. He may select any one or several of a series of objections: that it costs too much to operate, that it is too hard to park, or that he does not like the design. Or he can marshal, from the folklore of the automobile, jokes, tales of disaster, experiences of someone's cousin which support his decision. If he is a mobile person socially, however, he will gradually revise his selections from the folklore to bolster his choice later of more expensive cars. The pattern which emerges from an extensive reference to the automobile indicates that the car which a man actually wants is the most expensive; but the one that he will buy if he has additional money, is the model just above his present one in cost and style.[34]

A similar set of considerations is operative in the management of the career. At the beginning, the fact of multiple opportunity and the ultimate goals of success are clearly in view. The child contemplates, if he is moving towards medicine, every field or specialty. The figures of Osler, Banting, and Penfield are held in mind as gods. In the long renunciatory climb, the goals become more limited and the view of them is sharpened. For the very few who break through to a unique position of eminence, there are a multitude who must realize they are not going to be world-beaters after all. This constitutes for many men a severe crisis, which they meet in mid-life. For many others, more faithful to their dreams, the dénouement comes when they are confronted with a severe break in health or with retirement. The man who can make his peace with his own capacities and skills as they relate to opportunity is considered to be mature, but such maturity should not come prematurely. The rather modest goals which many students claimed for themselves give some indication that the younger generation is rather sensitive to this critical aspect of career realization.

In the complex, changing society in which the life of Crestwood Heights is embedded, there are many opportunities for satisfaction at levels below the heights that have been pointed to or dreamt of. Such satisfactions become established as levels of aspiration, and actually operate as ceilings for ambition. They become encrusted, as does the avowed preference for a small car, with values of their own.

The central core of ambition impels in two directions: the first, production primarily for monetary rewards; the second, competence and achievement, according to generalized and universal criteria, within a given field of specialization. These two aims are not necessarily compatible. A man may have a high and profitable output, but make no significant contribution to his field. The failure to achieve the one can be softened by recognition with respect to the other; in fact a man can often and must sometimes pursue one goal at the expense of the other. Within each of these pursuits, there are a set of counter-claims on the individual which tend to divert him from the main goal, the achievement of which would crown his life's work; at the same time, they soften and ameliorate defeat. They are floors for failure.

Countering the orientation towards production and the exacting work schedules of life downtown is the world of leisure and affection uptown; the home and the fabric of family life may thus be seen also as a counter to disappointed ambitions. The community, too, may absorb the energy and divert the interest of the man who has gone as far as he can go in his chosen vocation. He counts for very little downtown, if the truth were known, but knowledge of this status—if he has faced the facts—is made tolerable by the support his family gives him, or by an important responsibility in a club, or by an office or political post he holds in the community. Substitutions of this kind can also be made within his career. Let us take the example of two industrial chemists in a large firm. The first has a very high rating among other chemists; he is asked to deliver papers at professional meetings, but within the firm he has never won the confidence of his superiors who are not chemists. His colleague is never taken very seriously by other chemists, but his boss always says "He is a damn good chemist." In each case an unstable career has been given substance and foundation by alternative types of recognition. The first chemist won his achievement by attacking universalistic problems, the latter by winning confidence within a circumscribed locality. The scientifically inclined chemist regarded his colleague as a "phony," but felt that his own devotion to science was exemplary. The chemist whom the boss liked, regarded his more academic colleague as an impractical dreamer, while he boasted of his own production record within the firm. In a sense both men had failed; neither one had been able to combine the ideals of production and of contributing something basic and universally significant; yet both had found a substantial measure of success. They were respected by others and had considerable confidence in themselves. If we could point to a third man who had been equally successful on both counts, his career would rate exceedingly high.

Each person in Crestwood Heights, no matter how mobile, finds a place in the social structure where he can work and live; even if he is oriented to go higher, he will, if fortunate, derive satisfactions from the level he occupies at the moment. That level represents a goal achieved. All his possessions, all his associations—formal and informal—help to make that position secure and tenable. He occupies a niche in the division of labor and in the social organization of his society; that niche, when compared with all others, affords a measure of the success of his career in the stratified, competitive world in which he lives.

Part Two

INSTITUTION AND FUNCTION

7. THE FAMILY

Primary Socialization

ONE GREAT DIFFICULTY in describing the family in Crestwood Heights[1] is created by the existence of a voluminous literature which makes it almost impossible to look freshly and directly at this family and to report with unspoiled objectivity what goes on in it. The description is further complicated by the obviousness of much of the material.

The upper middle class family is particularly well known, in its external features at least, through the happy, prosperous families portrayed by Hollywood, by innumerable radio and television programs, and by novels. "Ozzie and Harriet," "Father Knows Best," J. P. Marquand's less eccentric New England characters (where the middle-class dream sometimes rubs a little thin), Spencer Tracy's "Father of the Bride"— all have become as familiar as neighbors in the next street. These are the comfortable, delightful, middle-class families of fantasy. The Crestwood Heights family is not like these—and not unlike. How much like and unlike this chapter attempts to sketch.

ORIGIN AND CONTEXT

The family of Crestwood Heights approximates these fictitious representations at least in that it consists of father, mother, and two (rarely more) children. The children are healthy, physically well developed, attractively dressed, and poised as to outward behavior. The mother, assured in manner, is as like an illustration from *Vogue* or *Harper's Bazaar* as financial means and physical appearance will allow. The father, well tailored, more or less successful in radiating an impression of prosperity and power, rounds out the family group.

This small family is both lone and love-based. It is, more often than not, formed by the marriage of two persons from unrelated and often unacquainted families; persons perhaps differing in temperament and background, who are assumed to have chosen each other because they are "in love." Other reasons for the choice (perpetuation of property within one family, the linking of business or professional interests, an unadorned urge to upward social mobility and so on), even if influential, could not reputably be admitted as grounds for marriage. This family unit is not embedded in any extended kinship system. The newly formed family is frequently isolated geographically and often socially from the parental families. It is expected that the bride and groom will maintain a separate dwelling removed by varying degrees of distance from that of each set of parents—a physical separation which is often equalled psychologically by an upward movement in society of the younger couple, or by mutually antagonistic patterns of social behavior, resulting from differences in age or history between the generations. In a period of rapid social change, parents and children may no longer share attitudes or beliefs. The isolation of each family acts to decrease the ability of the family to transmit traditional patterns of behavior, which might otherwise be absorbed from close contact with, for instance, grandparents. The absence of kinship bonds also tends to concentrate the emotional life of the family upon a few individuals; institutions are now emerging expressly to supply the support once given by kinship ties. Where relationships with kin do, however, exist, neither set of relatives has marked precedence, although the existence of the time-honored mother-in-law jokes, related chiefly by men, may be indicative of a slightly deeper, if culturally unsanctioned, bond between the wife and her relatives. There are also other reasons for the existence of this tie: in Crestwood Heights it is the wife who performs the functions symbolic of family solidarity: letter-writing, sending gifts and cards, and keeping in touch by telephone.

One Crestwood Heights woman well depicts the general family attitude towards kin:

N. and G. have very little contact with their brothers and sisters. N. thinks that if it were not for a long background of family gatherings at Christmas, Easter, and birthdays, members of their families would never see each other. These festival occasions seem to evoke a feeling of duty to entertain one's family. Affectional ties seem very faint.

The larger kinship group in Crestwood Heights, as the above quotation suggests, usually meets only on ritual occasions. Otherwise, the relationship between the family unit and kin resembles friendship, in which individual preference rather than ties of blood determines association. Conversely, friends may take on functions resembling those of kin, as in the common instance of the unrelated "aunt."

In its narrowed size the Crestwood Family contrasts with the usual Victorian family. The contrast could be continued. The Crestwood family shows a change from a production to a consumption unit, with a high degree of reliance upon external impersonal services, both in a material and in a psychological sense. The upper middle class Victorian family also depended, it is true, upon a complex of services and possessions. The former, however, were more likely to be rendered by individuals within the home. There was more personal intimacy, if greater social distance, between members of the family and the nursemaid or governess who ruled the children's quarters, the dressmaker who came at intervals to stay and sew, the coachman and his family, the cook and housemaids who might be permanent additions to the household.

The Crestwood Heights family allows more individuality and freedom to its members than did earlier forms. Again, this fashion of family life has evolved within the life-time of persons who are now in their fifties.

A man and woman of this generation accompanied an architect on his inspection tour of an old house in Big City, which had been preserved intact from the late nineteenth century and which was being sold for the first time. It was about to be torn down and the two reminisced to the younger architect about their childhood in just such a house. The tales had an almost fictional quality, particularly the evening presentation to the father, in his study, of the children especially summoned from their nursery for the nightly ritual.

While the interaction within the home was undoubtedly more patterned and formal, the Victorian family, as a unit, tended to be self-contained in relation to the outside world. Men interacted with the community through business or profession, like the present-day Crestwood male, but the home and occupation were more strictly segregated. Women were not permitted the degree of activity in secondary groups open to men, but, on the other hand, had their own rigid and ritualized social round which has no counterpart in Crestwood Heights. Children, separated by a great psychological, and often spatial, distance from their parents and other adults, lived more completely in their own nursery and school sphere, to which adults penetrated only at intervals. The boundaries between childhood and adulthood were much more clearly demarcated psychologically than in contemporary Crestwood Heights.

The Victorian family, which included servants and kin within one house, formed a definite bulwark against unwarranted intrusion.[2] The Crestwood family is still considered a refuge from the world by its members, but it is far from being the impregnable fortress which the Victorian household represented; the walls have been breached in far too many places. Yet the contacts between family and the outside, while more numerous, are to a high degree impersonal, centering around things rather than persons, or, in the case of the mass communication media, even mechanical.

FUNCTIONS

The Crestwood Heights family, although it varies in organization, composition, and orientation from families in other cultures and from the family of other periods in the history of Western civilization, regulates, as the family always has, sexual and affectional expression in the patterns approved by the society. The life-long relationship between one man and one woman for the procreation of children is the basis of the family in Crestwood Heights. Given the highly mobile nature of the population, the relative lack of secondary institutions capable of absorbing unmarried individuals, and the absence of kin, the tie between husband and wife indeed becomes pre-eminently important, providing, as it does, the one enduring human relationship in the society. Even child-rearing, central as it is in Crestwood, is not so lasting a commitment, since, given the lengthened life-span of the individual, it now occupies relatively few years.

Child-rearing is still considered as essentially the responsibility of the family, and it is the father and mother who must legally assume the child's economic support. And no matter to what degree one parent or both may rely upon institutions and people outside the immediate family for guidance in the child-rearing process itself, it is the parents alone who must decide whether to accept or to reject the proffered services. Strong pressures will, of course, be brought to bear to ensure that they make the "right" decision, but technically it is they who decide.[3]

The family, too, remains the primary social unit in which individuals ideally relate to each other, first of all as human beings, free to express feelings of love and affection, anger or hostility. It is the family which ideally gives emotional security, enabling the individuals comprising it to play their cultural roles in the larger society, and which provides, if they are provided, the models for identification without which the psycho-sexual development of the child cannot be assured. Thus the family is both the biological and psychological nexus of the society.

Most Crestwooders value highly the privilege of functioning individually in the institutions of the culture. It is the economic and social status of the family which allows them so to function. Economic and social status is closely tied in with the ownership of property. The house, then, as has been already pointed out, in addition to being a powerful symbol of material prosperity, stands for family solidarity and strength; from this base of home and male career, which are almost inseparable, the family can articulate with the community. The family, together with the male career, provides the rationale and the validation of the man's role; and the family provides the chief content of the woman's role.

Finally, the family in Crestwood Heights, since it is ultimately responsible for child-rearing, must, in some sense, "transmit the culture." This transmission of the culture (or, rather, the cultures), as in the case of another important institution, the school, is no longer to any great degree a process of passing on fixed items of tradition; where the family is concerned, the process seems rather to result in the freeing to a considerable extent of individual members to create new cultural and family patterns, independent of those of the family of orientation, and often radically different. Parents and children alike must learn continually to accept forms of social behavior unlike those previously known and practised.

One highly intelligent and understanding Crestwood mother, when asked what were the professional or business aspirations of her teen-age sons, at first said she didn't know, and only remembered, under questioning, that the boys *had* expressed certain wishes. She took a day to consider the matter; then added further details after "checking" with her husband and sons. The family owns a business which could be inherited by the children. The father had entered the firm (owned by his family) during the Depression, renouncing the higher academic career for which he had been preparing.

This mother's ignorance of her children's ambitions and the lack of pressure on the children to enter the family business suggest the typical "freeing" of the children to develop new patterns of their own—"within limits, of course." Freedom for the children, as in this instance, can also mean freedom for the parents, who need not now feel constrained to keep the business after the father's retirement. Thus a relatively inexpensive investment in a university education for both sons would allow father and mother later to liquidate their assets for their own old age. New patterns of living would then be created for all family members.

The Crestwood family, as we have seen in other contexts, is definitely oriented to the future, which, apart from its likely disparity with the past, is felt as unknown and unpredictable. The past tends otherwise to be obliterated from the collective thinking of the family. Consciously, the future is optimistically viewed; and the task of the family is to equip the child as effectively as possible in the present with all available means for his later solitary climb to better and more prosperous worlds lying far ahead in time. This passionate optimism tends to be of an essentially catastrophic type—useless as belief and motive force unless *all* its conditions are realized. That the chances for a total realization are slight indeed, is a fact which many Crestwooders cannot easily accept. But the future nevertheless beckons with sufficient force that the parental generation, if it seriously hinders the child's "upward" progress, must be virtually abandoned; this is well understood by both parents and children. Only the promise of continuous upward social mobility (or, at the very least, continually validated status at the present level) can nerve the Crestwood Heights family to its obligations; and for its members to feel the full poignancy of the separation to which it, as a family, is dedicated, might well wreck the whole precarious structure. Such a family is peculiarly vulnerable to outside circumstance. A severe economic depression, for example, would have immediate and serious repercussions which the Crestwood family, given the primary functions outlined, has, it would seem, but few inner resources to meet.

IDEALS OF FAMILY LIFE

Since the community is made up of more than four thousand families,[4] each one differing from the other, and roughly divided between two ethnic groups, it is difficult to find a real family or construct an "ideal" one that embodies the prevailing regulating norms. There does, however, appear to be emerging an ideal pattern of family living to which both Jewish and Gentile families would subscribe, a pattern which has been considerably influenced by the developing social sciences and their representatives, near and far. What have been called elsewhere the "maturity values" form the core of this family ideology; and the means by which these values are inculcated are "democratic"—relatively free discussion, action only with the will of the majority, persuasion rather than force. The end of the process mediated by these democratic means is the child. To bring up a child, in Crestwood Heights, now is to create an adult, independent of the family of orientation, capable of making his own decisions as to career, and prepared vocationally and psychologically to found a family of his own. It will seem paradoxical to many to find in the complex economic and social structure of Crestwood Heights, dependent as it is on a technology which demands a high degree of mechanical skill and competitive activity, ideals which make the isolated individual and his good supreme; to others, the paradox will seem resolved by the statement that the kind of individual so produced is exactly what the system needs.

It may be surprising to discover—for those who lament the deterioration of traditional religion—that in a wealthy, supposedly materialistic community, sincere attempts; under circumstances of great difficulty, are made to use the great ethical teachings of the Judæo-Christian religion in the day-to-day process of family life and child-rearing.[5] It is true that the ultimate justification is different: harmony and co-operation within the family are now regarded as being essential to the child's welfare because he is a unique human being—rather than because he is a child of God. It is also true that many families respond to these new norms intellectually rather than emotionally. But, whatever the shortcomings of interpretation, and however much these norms may be misunderstood and thus wrongly applied, the ideal for family life in Crestwood Heights which is emerging bears much more resemblance to Christian ethics and to democratic practice than did the authoritarian pattern of those more traditionally religious families of Victorian days. It is also obvious that this ideology is sponsored first and foremost by the child-rearing experts active in Crestwood Heights.

Many families with a strong patriarchal bias, based on traditional religious norms, Jewish or Gentile, still persist but the case records of the Child Guidance Clinic strongly suggest that radical variation from now accepted and prevailing norms for effective functioning of the family defines such families for the clinician as problems requiring attention: this "malfunction" of the family is seen as frequently productive of "disturbance" in the child.[6]

The criteria of the Clinic are not only the criteria of the Clinic, but are now widely disseminated in the culture: they are new goals for approved family functioning. "Good" parents, thus defined, are emotionally secure, free from hyper-anxiety, and from covert or overt conflict with persons in their immediate environment. Sexual relations should be confined to the marriage partnership, free from tension and "anti-social tendencies."[7] Serious marital disagreement or conflict which may lead to dissolution of the marriage, while seen (perhaps strangely) as less serious than "disturbed behavior" involving extra-marital sex relations, is nevertheless viewed as damaging to the whole family constellation.

The good mother must not be over-solicitous or over-protective. She must be undisturbed by worries about the future, confident in her status and in her acceptance by the community, and sure of her adequacy in the fulfilment of her maternal role. She should not find it necessary to translate any anxieties she may have into specific worries about the child's health, safety, or ability to measure up to academic or social expectations, particularly in the school setting. The ideal mother is not "over-dominant"—an attitude manifested in nagging or "bossing" the child. She is neither over-permissive nor inconsistent in discipline; nor does she cater to the child's every whim.

The good father also exhibits these characteristics (although most discussion of parental behavior seems to refer to mothers). But in avoiding the Scylla of "authoritarianism," the good father must not run against the Charybdis of "indulgence." The Victorian father, patriarchal head of the family and owner of wife and progeny, is as frowned upon as the "over-dominant" and nagging mother. Severe discipline, a primary *differentium* of the authoritarian father, is defined —and disapproved of—as the "expectation of instant obedience, modelled on the military pattern." The good father should not leave complete or almost complete responsibility for the child's upbringing to the mother (even though he provides for the child's material needs) no matter how pressing are his business or professional duties.

Both father and mother are expected to feel a high degree of love for the child. Outright rejection of the child is, of course, a cardinal sin; and behavior which might *possibly* be interpreted by the child as a rejection (preoccupation with adult concerns, for example) is similarly condemned. "Unconditional" parental affection and acceptance, where the child is concerned, has now become the central ideal.

Conflict between mother and son, mother and daughter, father and son, father and daughter, is regarded as a symptom of family malfunction. Adolescent rebellion, likewise labelled as contributing to family disharmony, is a phase of family life with which the good parent must cope without allowing any open breaks in family solidarity to occur. On the other hand, family relationships must not become too binding, lest they shackle the child in his progress towards autonomy.

The relations between brothers and sisters must also be harmonious;

this harmony is expected as a direct result of the soundness of the husband-wife relationship. Jealousy, rivalry, or open conflict between siblings, usually attributed to faulty parental attitudes (favoritism, for instance) is not to be tolerated.

Finally, this ideal Crestwood family operates as a *separate* unit—it must not share living quarters or dependencies with other families; even the apartment building with its many divisions is not considered the proper material environment for family life. The detached house, which the family owns and inhabits in its entirety, is the only fully approved physical basis for a healthy, happy family. To share this house with kin is considered undesirable and, in many cases, a genuine hardship, since the presence of grandparents or other close relatives is viewed as inimical to smooth family functioning.

The ideal Crestwood family, is, therefore, greatly different from the ideal family of previous decades. If we might use an analogy, the Crestwood family now seems a little like a country which, having operated under an authoritarian form of government, has suddenly switched to a democratic form, without too much preparation for the change. The parents, who are still held legally responsible for the rearing of the children, are, at the same time, shorn of the moral sanction they once had for the exercise of absolute power over the subordinate children, an authority then thought to follow "naturally" from age and the dominant economic position of the parents (particularly the father), and further buttressed supernaturally by traditional religious norms. The father, it is true, still holds the economic power, but he is now culturally enjoined from exercising it in "despotic" ways. A central problem of the family now appears to be the allocation of power among its members so that each may participate, not in the earning of the family income, but in the emotional and social life of the family unit.

The extreme intricacy of the shift in family emphasis and relationships is well expressed in the somewhat ambiguous findings of the Clinic report referred to above.[8] The terminology used no longer conveys any exact meaning. Just what constitutes "over-severe" discipline or "over-permissiveness" cannot be stated in unequivocal theoretical terms, nor, frequently, agreed upon in practice. No longer are there any precise canons of behavior for children towards their parents or for parents towards their children. Parents who may tend to fall back upon patterns of behavior approved by traditional Judæo-Christian norms, in which the father played the role of dominating male, are seen as largely "bad" in the new light. As the Clinic report phrases it (italics added):

. . . academic problems occurred with the greatest frequency in children of authoritarian fathers (and oversolicitous mothers), or in the cases where the mother's prevailing relationship with the child was overdominant. Conduct discipline problems tended to occur more often when the mother was overdominant than when the father was authoritarian. The majority of "anti-social" problems, however, occurred in the children of authoritarian fathers. *All problems tended to be concentrated in children of authoritarian fathers and/or overdominant or oversolicitous mothers, relatively fewer problems occurring when parents were indulgent or over-permissive.*[9]

The report goes on to outline, in the case of the deviant children, the relation between types of deviancy and patterns of family behavior.

. . . 70% of the schizoid-schizophrenic types had authoritarian fathers (nearly all the mothers being over-solicitous as well). The cases of aggressive-impulsive and anxiety phobic reaction types, however, tended to occur more often where the mother was overdominant or oversolicitous regardless of the father's relationship with the child. The regressive reaction types were almost equally distributed between the authoritarian and non-authoritarian fathers.[10]

The clinician is clearly against the authoritarian pattern; the over-indulgent and over-permissive pattern is also condemned, but not as vehemently, since the effect upon the child is seen as less devastating in terms of the formation of those symptoms with which the Clinic is concerned.[11]

It is evident that a new ideal is now held up for the family—at least by the clinician who prepared this report. But it is also clear that many Crestwood Heights families are actively responding to these modern and expert-mediated patterns, just as they responded earlier to different deliverances of experts. The attendance at Home and School meetings and study groups, the numerous lectures on child-rearing, and the amount of printed matter referring to family relationships, bought or borrowed and consumed, are witness to the earnestness with which many Crestwooders try to live up to their democratic goals for family life. From one mother comes an extended picture of this endeavor:

Life in our house is pretty smooth. We hardly ever complain or grouch. The children have their responsibilities which they shoulder fairly well. . . . R. is very self-sufficient and able to get her own meals if necessary. She is very generous and will share all her possessions. She is brought up in an atmosphere where we praise effort and appreciate our own handiwork.

Everyone works in our house and our help [domestic] has been with us six years and is about to have a baby. We are all treated with the same respect and consideration. We always discuss the fact that each job in the world is very important, and if it is done well it is to be appreciated. R. knows that regardless of economic standing, she must be capable of earning her own living, and that at sixteen, camp will be over and that she will have to earn her own living during holidays. (She finds this thrilling, and is going to be a sales-girl in the scarf department at T.'s or R.'s.) R. is told only the truth as we know it, about everything, with a frank admission if we don't know. . . .

She has not as yet reached the stage of wanting to break away from her regular routine. She goes to a very wonderful and progressive camp . . . and she loves it and looks forward to it. She has a good sense of humor, and can take a lot of kidding from her Dad. She has been allowed to start a few things like tap dancing and dramatics and then drop them after finding she didn't like them. Piano is a must, . . . but she started 'cello a couple of years ago and is still taking.

R. had to make her first big choice between what she wanted to do and what she thought she ought to do, and what she felt was right to do. The second school dance at Junior High was being held the same evening as the staff dinner Christmas party that her Dad gives every year for all his employees. R. has been invited for the last five years and has always gone and loved it, and she has participated in the program. But the school dance sounded so exciting that she was very tempted to give her Dad's party the air. It was only when she sensed that he was very disappointed in her obvious preference that she came to her mother for help. This was at the dinner table with everyone participating in the conversation. Dad asked "How many school dances are there every year?" R.: "About four, Dad." "Well, there is only one staff party." R.: "I guess you think we should go to the staff party." Dad: "That is for you to decide." R.: "Mom, help me to make a decision." Mom: "I know what I would do if I were your age. I would go to the dance with my friends and then be sorry for it and wish I had done what I knew I should do." R.: "I really want to go to Dad's party but I would like to think about it. Could I tell you tomorrow Dad?" Dad: "Yes, but I'm sorry you have to think about it." R.: "Can B. do what he wants regardless of what I choose?" "Yes," Dad answered, but we all knew for the first time that the party meant a lot to Dad and that he would feel badly if the decision was in favor of the school dance. Next morning R. and B. came to me for help, but I said "This is your problem; think it through and call Dad this afternoon."

That evening Dad told me that R. had called him at lunch hour to tell him she was going to his party and that she was very glad to be going. B. had called him about five to ask if he could have another day to think it over. The next day he called to say that the school dance wasn't going to be so hot and it might be on another night and to make a reservation for him at the staff dinner. So all turned out well (so far).

In this account of family functioning, the first emphasis is upon respect for each member of the family as an individual (except for a great-aunt, mentioned at another point in the account, who lives in the house but who is not accepted as a fully participating member). The business of the family is largely carried on by "majority rule" after full discussion of the issue under consideration. There appears to be no authoritarian discipline from either parent, and no corporal punishment. When a clash arises between the children's desire to attend a peer group affair and their obligations to their parents, the final decision remains with the children, who are, however, left in no doubt as to the disappointment of the parents if the choice goes against them. In this case, rather than "hurt" father or mother, or both, the children decide to attend the staff party.[12]

Another controversial issue involving this family is described (but not included in the above excerpt): the twelve-year-old daughter, against her father's wishes, wants to accompany her classmates on a school-supervised overnight expedition. The mother adds this explanatory note:

Mother would like her to go for the educational value as well as the value of group living and being responsible for herself in all situations. R. knows that mother would like her to go and has only her Dad to conquer. She fought for her right to go very hard the first night that it was discussed, and her Dad told her to get all the information she could as to who was going, in regard to staff personnel and her friends. Since that time, a week ago, she has not mentioned it except to tell us that lots of girls and boys had registered their parents' permission. We have had no further discussions and I am waiting to see if she will try again for her fight for freedom from parental love and devotion. If she does she will win as her Dad is usually, in the end, guided by mother's judgment and he will willingly agree if he is convinced that it is best for R. He has faith in the fact that I will steer her in the right direction, even though it might mean a worrisome week for us.

Thus, as in all democracies, there can be within the family various alignments and pressures, but naked force is outlawed. The same mother expressed this ideal very well, when, in another connection, she speaks of the rivalry between her two children.

We had quite a time at first. . . . For a while B. would always push R. around—he doesn't like her to mother him. So I told him "B., we don't use our hands, we use our heads." Next time I came in he had his hands behind his back and was butting her around with his head.

The ideal of free discussion between parents and children is to a considerable extent, then, replacing corporal punishment or the parental "Do as I say, because I say it" of former years. In fact, the pendulum has swung so far in the opposite direction that small children, in particular, are sometimes bewildered by the multitudinous verbal choices of behavior presented to them. More often (as happens in other democratic ventures) the amount of talk about any given issue may obscure the fact that *no* decision or solution has been reached—or talk may be almost consciously used to prevent reaching one.

Closely linked with this respect for the individual, in the mother's account as quoted, is the emphasis on "responsible" behavior, towards oneself and others, for all members of the family (which, significantly, in the above report, extends also to the maid but not to the great-aunt). For the Crestwood children, such behavior is defined as the ability to handle money from an early age, to assume certain duties around the house, to care for and to select clothing.[13] The fiction is maintained that the daughter must be prepared to earn her own living (if only during holidays), an expectation which is taken for granted in the case of the boy, who may already have a paper route. The children are also required to achieve a degree of competence in certain skills, such as music, which they have some voice in choosing.

In a series of interviews this mother describes how she herself had had to learn responsibility, which is here clearly related to the proper spending of the husband's income:

WIFE: I was a pampered little darling and couldn't leave home . . . you know . . . Mother's pet! In a hysterical moment I promised her I would never leave. I don't know how my husband put up with me. We were so different. I was poetic, dreamy, and spoiled, and he was hard-working. I don't know how he put up with me. But he loved me and he had lots of patience. I can honestly say that now we're more in love than we ever were. . . .

When we were first married I certainly wasn't responsible. I had no idea of money. I thought it grew on trees. Honey, do you remember that dentist bill?

HUSBAND: Do I? Just after we were married I was making forty bucks a week and the first thing I get is a dentist's bill for one hundred and thirty-five dollars!

WIFE: And then there were the shoes. Just after we got back from the honeymoon I decided I needed some shoes. So I got them and had them sent up. He answered the door, and "Twelve ninety-five, please!" But I had no idea how much you were making. I should have known, I guess.[14]

"Responsible" behavior for the parents appears to be further defined in terms of community participation. Early married life for this couple revolved around having a good time with friends.

After we were married we went out seven nights a week—cards, talking, and so on. We were living with mother, and there wasn't much room. So we went out every night. We had a couple of bosom friends. It's funny, they weren't like us at all. She is quiet, serious—was a teacher. Then one night after a show we were having a soda and they came in. We invited them to join us and we found we liked each other and we have been bosom pals ever since.

Then we had another couple. They came from New York and were more flighty than us. She phoned my friend and said she didn't know anyone here and wanted to meet her. So we got together. She was wonderful and we loved her. Her husband was a playboy and we didn't like him but tolerated him because she was so wonderful. They lived in the —— Hotel and were more lavish than we were. We in turn were more lavish than our other friends, who had a baby by this time. This New York playboy never worked hard—two or three hours and then he'd play golf. He got my husband interested finally and we joined the Pleasant View Golf Club. We couldn't afford it but we both loved it, and we gave up our summer holidays. Now it's our main diversion.

With the advent of children and the move to Crestwood Heights, family behavior adjusted to new norms. Again the mother describes the present family pattern:

WIFE: I'm on the go all the time now. Busiest woman in the community. I'm in everything—Home and School, National Council of Women, Community Chest—oh, you couldn't list them all. For a long time I represented the N.C.W. at school board meetings. For years I went to every school board meeting. It is awfully important to have an active community spirit. So many people to-day aren't interested in anything. Do you know there are more sleeping pills sold to-day than you can imagine—and dope too! . . . Sometimes I have three or four, even five, meetings a day, all overlapping. Skip out of one to get to another.

HUSBAND: So we have dinner about six fifteen or six thirty. Mrs. K. and I are off to meetings or occasionally we stay at home. We prefer to stay home.

In contrast to this pattern of adult, "responsible" behavior, the great-aunt who lives with, but not in, the family group, is described as "irresponsible" and therefore inadequate.

HUSBAND: She has nothing to do with us, nor we with her. She comes and goes as she pleases.

WIFE: We don't know what to do with her. We tried getting her interested in some things. It worked for a couple of weeks and then—right back where we started.

HUSBAND: She's neurotic. She's been that way ever since Mrs. K.'s great-uncle died. She came from a large family and a family not well off. After she married, things came easily and she never had any responsibilities. Then, after her husband died, she went to pieces.

INTERVIEWER: Do you suppose that happens in tightly knit families? I know several very close families, where the husband's death leaves the wife disorganized.

HUSBAND: I don't think that's right. Some are like that but lots aren't. It all depends on the responsibilities they're used to. Her aunt never had any responsibilities so couldn't handle them if they were given to her. My mother was entirely different. When my father died, the youngest brother was five.

WIFE: Were any of you married?

HUSBAND: Yes, there was one married. But she carried on and raised the whole family. She'd always had responsibility and it was no strain when my father died.

Intimately associated with the "responsibility" theme is the emphasis on independent activities, minutely timed and scheduled, for each member of the family (with the exception of the great-aunt). This emphasis is in direct contrast to the stress, particularly by the mother, on the affection and love which is considered the outstanding characteristic of their family life.

WIFE: We're an amazingly close-knit family, considering we see so little of each other. The secret is we're routinized. Life is pretty much the same from Monday to Friday.

INTERVIEWER: Would you describe a typical day?

WIFE: I'm up first—about ten to eight—and start breakfast. Then I wake B. He's usually awake (he has an alarm clock which he sets) and is listening to the news. Then I poke my head in R.'s room. She's usually awake, maybe dressed or dressing. She nearly splits my head with her "Good morning, Mom."

Then we have breakfast. Four mornings a week hot cereal. R. loves it; B. hates it, but eats it anyway. On Friday morning he can have what he wants—cold cereal. Saturday and Sunday he gets his own breakfast so he gets what he wants. [The children usually bring coffee to the parents in bed on these mornings.] R. leaves at eight twenty and B. at eight thirty. They ride their bikes to school so get there fast. Both come home for lunch three days a week. The other days, they stay at school for orchestra or choir practice. B. plays a cornet and R. plays a cello and sings. . . .

HUSBAND: I get up last—about eight twenty—and come down after the kids are gone. I usually meet this [pointing to his wife] going up as I'm coming down. Then there's a phone call and she's off to a meeting at ten o'clock. . . . We spend our holidays together, not separately like most couples in the Heights. Only once did we have separate holidays. Remember that, dear?

WIFE: Yes, five years after we were married I took a week's holidays— New York by myself.

HUSBAND: The kids go to camp every summer. This will be R.'s seventh. She'll go this summer but next year we're going to take a trip together. That's our family project, a motor trip through the West.

INTERVIEWER: Other family projects?

HUSBAND: No, not really. We're great celebrators. We celebrate every birthday of aunts, cousins, everything.

WIFE: We usually celebrate by going to dinner—someplace where there's a show—a Big City night-club, if you can call them that.

Despite these separate rounds of activity, which intersect only occasionally (the husband states: "I am home so little, I only see the kids for
an hour in the evening, that is if I'm not going off to a meeting"), the
affection on the part of the children towards each other and their parents
is demonstrative and this behavior is given high approval. The mother's
accounts of the daily routine of her twelve-year-old daughter repeatedly
underline the child's happiness and display of affection. A typewritten
note attached to one document reads as follows:

TO MR. AND MRS. B. K.
IN THERE BED AT HOME SWEET HOME
                                                    Love, R.
Dear Mom and Dad, # # I love both of you. Do you love me as much
as i love you. Did you have a good sleep? I hope so. THE
WEATHER MAN ### SAY'S HIGH 40. I am going to come and visit you
now, so good-by, Love,

                                                    R. K.

A second pencilled note is addressed to the mother alone.

  Roses are Red   To a Mommy who is the most
  Violets are Blue   important person to me right now.
  Sugar is Sweet
  And so are you.   LOVE AND KISSES. R.

A third report states:

The other night at six fifteen they [R. and B.] came home together. . . .
I was listening to excerpts from famous operas on the recorder, and
knitting. The kids came in to tell me the doings of the day, as I hadn't seen
them since breakfast. R. was lying on the floor, still in her coat, and B. was
sitting beside her on the chair. R. said, "Oh Mom, you look so cute and I
love you so very much and I love Daddy so much and I love B." She then
threw her arms around his leg and kissed his pant leg." B. said "R., that is
unsanitary, my pants are not very clean." We all laughed and R. said, "Oh,
B.!" I said, "You know B., sometimes love is more important than even
cleanliness!" So saying, R. gave him another kiss on the pant leg.

 The norms for this particular family are, on the one hand, respect
for each individual member almost to the point of denying, at times,
the actual gap in age between parent and child; an attention to responsibility, the concept of which is related to age, with a strong emphasis
on community service for the adults and service to the family group for
the children; and family harmony, as judged by verbal and physical
acts of affection. The giving of presents in this family is a highly regarded token of love and esteem. An equally strong norm, on the other
hand, insists upon separate activities for each member of the family,
with less frequent events in the nature of holiday or anniversary cele-

brations involving the whole group (the summer holiday together must be planned for a year or more in advance). Only a high degree of efficiency (faintly reminiscent of that of a well-run club or office) in operating the household makes this individualistic pattern of outside activities workable at all. The actual help given by the children can be symbolic only; more helpful, and unusual, is the presence of the same maid with this family over a six-year period.

In assuring that these norms for family social behavior are met, the ostensible disciplinary means are, as has been said, those of free discussion and persuasion, rather than those of force, psychological or physical. The most obvious and drastic punishment, just as in nursery school, is exclusion from the group. The mother states:

If they [the children] break the rules, they get left out of the family fun, and believe me, that's a big threat in our family. There are always hockey tickets, wrestling, shows, dinners, and so on, especially on the weekends. We have a lot of fun, we're unique in that respect, and if you're left out of it, it's pretty dull.

While physical violence is, to a great extent, outlawed, and while explosive psychological pressure is disapproved, there are other factors working at a deeper level, as illustrated in the episodes of the staff party and the school expedition. Both father and mother do apply steady and sometimes relentless pressure. The most striking feature of this particular kind of control lies in the ability of the parents to use a minimum of violence and to economize psychological pressure in securing obedience. It is preferable to "win" or coax the child rather than to overwhelm it. Nor should the force exerted be patently disproportionate to the resistance against it. Nevertheless the pressure is acute, and, since it is ill-defined, many a child experiences great difficulty in running counter to it.

These, then, are the norms which are in the Crestwood air, as it were. Some families, like the one just quoted, accept them rather self-consciously, grafting them on to an earlier, now less congenial behavior pattern. Other families, although similarly exposed to the current ideology, remain relatively unaffected. Some families (probably a minority) may have long been operating in the new fashion; they use the present norms merely to corroborate a philosophy of family life, internalized and practised before such views became fashionable or widespread. Thus, at the very time when differences between Jew and Gentile tend to become reduced to points of superficial denominational variation, a new value-system is emerging, broad enough to contain both ethnic groups in Crestwood Heights.

ROLES WITHIN THE FAMILY

When the Crestwood family is viewed as a unit composed of a certain number of individuals related to each other and to the outside world, a complex pattern of behavior (or perhaps, behaviors) becomes apparent. Even though the patriarchal powers once associated with his role are largely dissipated, the father still stands as the symbolic head of the family. Under the new dispensation, he is expected to share his authority among all members of the family, in varying degrees; and, indeed, because of his frequent absence, his power to deal with situations and with persons within the family may largely pass to the woman. But, even more difficult, the man is at the same time now required to "participate" in the whole child-rearing process, and sometimes in the actual household routine as well. The Crestwood doctor who frequently puts his children to bed, staying at home for the evening while his wife goes out with friends or for a game of bridge, has few if any counterparts in Europe.[15] Yet the man's role in Crestwood Heights is more clearly defined than that of the woman, for whatever the cultural additions to it by way of demands for "companionship" and shared activities on a basis of equality with wife and children, he is viewed predominantly as the earner of the income upon which rests the whole structure of family life in Crestwood Heights. And, in return, the family, by its activities, often divorced entirely from those of the father, contributes indirectly to his career.

The father now seems to have more responsibility within the home, but without commensurate authority. Conversely, his position in the occupational world, *vis-à-vis* the family, is different from what it was in previous decades, when, for the urban dweller, occupation and home were more rigidly separated. There are now greater pressures in the pursuit of occupational success, and the man is held ultimately and personally responsible if, in this more hectic chase, the family, or any of its members, should "fail." If his wife cannot discharge the social obligations which facilitate his business or profession, it is he who is considered to have shown poor judgment in his choice, an error which is generalized with a potentially disastrous effect upon his career. If it is his child who cannot measure up to cultural expectations, the fault is attributable either to him or to his wife. If the fault is his, then he is held directly accountable; if it is his wife's, the man is still to blame, for he made the marital mistake in the first place. But since such a great part of his life is lived outside the home, the man has not the means, such as are available to him in his office, to supervise this particular department of his career.

The family has always contributed to the male career, but in the Victorian era it was still possible for the man, if he wished, to keep his home almost entirely apart from his business or professional life. This choice is increasingly impossible in Crestwood Heights. The male occupational role demands concentration upon rationalistic competition and efficiency, with progress gauged by profits or similar objective evidences. Personal relationships, even within the family, may be limited, impersonal, or pseudo-personal, directed towards specific ends. Thus the family may be used primarily to promote the career; and serious emotional involvements outside the family which might endanger the career are to be avoided on that ground, if no other. One Crestwood Heights husband expressed this attitude directly:

"No man who indulges in extra-marital relations is responsible." This he emphasized very strongly—that it was a sign that the man was weak or spoiled. However, he recognized occupational difficulty and suggested that brokers were more likely to deviate and, next to them, persons with inherited wealth, those persons who had never had to work. Professional men like doctors and lawyers he placed much lower on the list. When his wife discussed with him a very close relative and professional colleague who had deviated, he simply passed this off with the remark "X was spoiled."

Thus the family, for the man, represents a vital element in his occupational success, as well as the only approved source of emotional security. Difficulties in combining the two functions are often evident. One may predominate over the other, as in the case of the business man who said that when he shut the door of his home behind him in the morning, he felt as if he "were going out into the jungle." Other men, who also primarily wanted home as an emotionally safe refuge, for this very reason refused to become deeply involved with the members of their families. They needed protection against disturbance, and so chose a life of non-involvement. This was especially noticeable in some professional men, who spend their working hours in situations harassing psychologically.

Nevertheless though the man's individual emotional security largely depends on his roles as husband and father, these must necessarily become secondary to his primary role of breadwinner. And the occupational role differs widely from the roles of husband and father, in terms of ends, obligations, involvement, and emotional content. The man's life experience, primarily oriented as it is to the competitive world of business or profession, therefore does not prepare him to meet the new secondary cultural demands upon him as husband and father. Many men try to solve this conflict by carrying over into family life the standards and attitudes useful in building the career.[16] Needless to say, these are in direct opposition to the woman's values, and therefore a potent source of strain within the family. Indeed, many Crestwood Heights women express resentment at being regarded merely as decorative or useful adjuncts to their husbands' careers.[17]

The woman's role is again, like that of the man's, divided. She must not devote herself *wholly* to husband and children; yet they are still to be her first and most important responsibility—the woman must remain both for husband and for children the emotional hub of the family. One woman informant outlines the wife's role.

Food, sex, interesting activity must be provided by the wife to please and attract the husband. These activities the woman must enjoy equally with the man. She does not simply provide food, or sex, or parties; she must enter into them with equal ardor and gratification, or the husband will not be satisfied.

It was her opinion that some women did reach outside the family to a very large extent for affectional contacts, particularly with the opposite sex, but that these were usually kept within control because of fear of disrupting family ties. She underlined specifically the economic vulnerability of women, which tends to keep them from "going off." This phrase "going off" occurred over and over again in the interview. Her husband, presumably speaking more for the man, said that public pressure keeps the man in line, although the man has more freedom to deviate than the woman, and the woman's deviation is looked down on more than the man's. The informant agreed with him in this. The husband said it would not happen unless the man were unhappy at home. This statement had several ramifications. One was that the man's sexual needs were more overpowering than the woman's and therefore if the wife could not provide gratification, he had some justification for his actions. . . . In the case of a sister of the informant, who had marital difficulties, her husband said the man was justified because no one could possibly live with her.

The informant went on to underline her own feelings about this, agreeing that she had felt her sister had failed to measure up to her marital duties in spite of the fact that she had a very difficult husband. She felt at the time that the sister should have "developed the skill to take the jeers" because the man is working hard downtown and is carrying a heavy load. Therefore it is the woman who has the spare time to apply herself to her own job, which is to create an attractive home to which the husband wants to come back and to bring his friends. She should take pride in having a successful marriage and a happy home life.

As a mother, the Crestwood Heights woman is expected to provide an atmosphere of warmth, security, and unconditional love for her children. The education and pre-marital life experience of the Crestwood woman, however, have not usually prepared her particularly well to make this provision. Educationally, it is rare for a Crestwood woman, in her younger years, to have devoted much attention to the learning of housewifely skills or child care. And, psychologically, she herself, in all probability, has not had, as a child, the kind of gratification which would allow her to fulfil at all easily the cultural demands for unconditional love where her children are concerned. Her upbringing tends to drive her early to concentrate on those arts of glamor and physical attractiveness which will ultimately win and keep a husband able to maintain her in the style of Crestwood Heights. Then suddenly, after the excitement of romance and marriage, she may find herself alone in a Crestwood Heights home, well equipped mechanically, but intermittently empty of life until the arrival of her first baby. Moreover, while there is temporary relief for mothers of small children, none of the available resources provides the Crestwood woman with continuous companionship in her task, or relieves her in any way of the responsibility.[18]

Many a Crestwood mother, while "accepting" the culturally approved maternal role, reveals an underlying resentment. The demands made upon her as a wife and mother she may often find irksome in contrast to the communal, more lively world, of university, profession, or office. The ironical comments made by one mother about childish behavior at a birthday party are suggestive:

Mrs. T. [a guest] said she would have asked the researcher to *her* daughter's birthday party but couldn't imagine anyone enjoying it. The researcher assured her that he could enjoy almost anything. Mrs. T. said she had had thirty-two kids and fourteen adults. "By seven o'clock I was a tiny bit tired of children's voices. You should have seen those five year olds. They looked me over so, that I felt my slip was showing. They talked about clothing most of the time. They didn't play and enjoy themselves. . . . One had a dress from Miami, another shoes from New York. My daughter bawled me out for not getting her an organdy party dress. Honestly, I find it hard to take. I'm just the poor old work horse, and I take all the abuse."

This informant, as it happens, was a mother who devoted the major portion of her time to home and family, with no career ambitions as far as the interviewer knew. Other women may, but only with the greatest difficulty, allow the maternal role to take precedence over the work renounced at marriage. This conflict we have already observed in the chapter, "Career." The resulting ambivalence is illustrated again in the context of this chapter in the following interview with three young mothers:

Several statements were made by all of them, especially by Mrs. R. The researcher had remarked that, from their statement, he got the impression that some of their tensions in handling the children stemmed from the fact that their professional roles were in conflict with their maternal roles. They all agreed that this was the case. Mrs. S. left the impression that she "would never go back to work"; Mrs. T. that when her youngest was well into prep school she might; and Mrs. R. said that she had never really given up her job. She left for the birth of her first child "on a two months' leave." She said "I never got back, but I'm still going back. I've stayed close to the organization, and I want to go back." She said her first year as a mother was emotionally very disturbing. She loved the child, would not let anyone touch it, it was so precious. Yet she resented washing diapers since she had the ability to hold down a professional job.

In describing this situation, she reiterated several points. The desire to be a mother was prominent. . . . She also felt a repulsion from house-keeping, and her present efforts were her first serious attempt. She found the demands of motherhood both interesting and exacting, and for mixed reasons—she had a wonderful baby, she suffered from allergies, and she set up such high standards for herself. A desire to get back to work recurred frequently, although she had a feeling that no one else could look after the children properly. It was evident that a series of self-analyses had been in process (described by Mrs. T. and Mrs. R. as "guilt feelings") to the effect that what these informants felt to be behavior problems in the home were "all my fault."

Under such difficult circumstances it is understandable that many women, alone with their children and their labor-saving gadgets, long for the day when, the children in school, they may again go out to "join in the life of the community." At the opposite end of the pole are the women who continue to make home and children the center of existence. Some of these may be literally forced out unwillingly into the community when the children are grown and they suddenly find themselves emotionally bankrupt in an empty house.

Outside activities at the time of child-rearing, which are usually in the nature of philanthropic service or participation in associations such as Home and School, are highly approved of for the Crestwood mother. Many Crestwood Heights women, indeed, as a result of their education, feel that the actual work of homemaking is somewhat degrading unless it can be balanced by intellectual and aesthetic pursuits. Participation outside the home may therefore have as one function the reduction of strain within the family, especially if the woman is deeply antagonistic to her housewifely role. On the other hand, there is always the danger that the appeal of these activities may interfere with the welfare of husband and children, and they therefore can themselves be potential sources of strain within the family. These pursuits, however, cannot readily be escaped, even should the woman so desire, since they have strong status implications for the family. The requirement that the woman's extra-familial activities be "socially useful," but unpaid, may account largely for the amount of participation in the Home and School Association and in philanthropic work.[19]

Like the man in Crestwood Heights, the woman has one set of primary obligations. Hers are to husband, children, and home, just as his are to the career. In the case of the man, however, the responsibility is more definite, clear-cut, and compelling. It is obligatory that he spend the greater part of each day at the business of earning money, if he and his family wish to remain in Crestwood Heights. The woman, on the other hand, has a wider range of choice in her activities, especially since her preoccupations beyond the home are not concerned with money-making. The society, nevertheless, exerts indirect pressure upon her in regard to social behavior. As a mother, she is expected to be omniscient and omnicompetent. She must be patient, loving, and understanding with her children, intelligently informed at all times on child welfare. She must be prepared to become the object of her children's dependency, while concurrently working towards the diminution and final dissolution of this same dependency, at no matter what personal cost to her feelings.

Thus there is considerable ambivalence around both the major female roles, which each woman must try to resolve for herself. This task, for a woman with little or no preparation for child-rearing, and nevertheless expected to meet a particularly high standard of maternal behavior, is one of considerable magnitude. In attempting by "intellectual" activities to maintain some continuity with the self-image of premarital days, she may be tempted to relegate homemaking to the background, especially as her children grow older; but she is shut out from the business and professional world, the only one which, in her eyes, can reward her adequately in terms of her education and previous life-experience. Some types of unpaid institutional activity are open to her, but even in the field of welfare to which she gravitates naturally, the positions of real responsibility are held by single professional women, leaving only minor or marginal duties to the volunteer.

Compromise revolves about one basic fact which remains constant. The man's education and experience are geared more exclusively to the career, while the woman is not trained or encouraged by the society to regard her role as wife and mother as having an importance equal to that of the male career. Indeed, she has frequently been impelled towards a career of her own, if she has attended university and has accepted its standards for female success. In Crestwood Heights, it is still possible for the man to be a successful provider and a poor husband, father, and citizen; but the woman is required to be both an excellent mother and a socially conscious individual, striking some balance between the two roles, a type of compromise which is not demanded of the man to anything like the same degree.[20]

The child's time, particularly as he grows older, is also divided between home—where he or she is simultaneously son or daughter to the parents and also a brother or a sister—and peer group activities. The latter come to occupy more and more of his day, as he leaves the home for school and other institutions. Within the family circle, the child is the promise of the future, the family's main ostensible justification for existence, and the target of the whole elaborate socialization process of Crestwood Heights—which, in the end, as we have learned, will gradually dissolve all close ties between him and his parents, and often between him and his brothers and sisters as well.

The Crestwood child is viewed by the members of the community as an individual who is learning to become an adult capable of functioning independently. Yet the very term "child" denotes dependence, at first physical and emotional, later only economic and social. The democratic norms require that, whatever the training given by the home, the child must be treated as having rights and privileges *because he is a human being*.[21] As stated earlier, in the discussion of family norms, there may be much confusion both for parents and for children in this notion. Although the child is an individual, he differs in age and experience from the adults surrounding him, a situation which biologically and culturally necessitates a degree of subordination to parents. Yet both father and mother are commonly uncertain as to how much authority to exert, or as to the appropriate means of establishing their proper position, while still conforming to democratic norms. Children may react unfavorably in the face of parental insecurity, when no adult assumes the obligation to teach them with firmness and understanding the social behavior which will enable them, as adults, to be accepted by their society.[22]

Within the family, the child must establish relationships with brothers and sisters, older or younger than himself. Here again, although the ideals of individuality and equality may seem more easily attainable, each child cannot share identically in privileges and favors. A small child, to quote only one example, must submit or agree to an earlier bed-time than his older brother or sister, no matter what his own ideas on the subject may be. To determine and to put into practice these necessary limitations to the child's freedom—without recourse to "authoritarian" measures—may tax parental ingenuity to the limit.[23] Sex differences between siblings may also open up possibilities of strain within the family, since a girl cannot be treated in exactly the same manner as a boy by even the most permissive of parents. Indeed, extreme impartiality in this regard may make it difficult for the child to learn the approved sex role.

While the child is undergoing an intensive and strenuous socialization process in relation to father, mother, and siblings within the home itself, he is also required to learn adjustments to peers and to other adults outside the family altogether. In much the same way as the Crestwood man is divided betwen occupation and family, the child, particularly during adolescence, may be torn between the home and peer group, in which he spends more and more of his time as he grows older. In all societies, at some point, and in varying degree, a balance must be struck between allegiance to the family of orientation and the demands of adult life, with its primary responsibility to reproduce the race. But in Crestwood Heights this break is heralded earlier in the history of the family, and with unusual severity and finality. No Galsworthy or G. B. Stern, no Thomas Mann, no Mazo de la Roche could depict Forsythes, Rakonitzes, Buddenbrooks, Whiteoaks through several generations in the world of Crestwood Heights.

The family in Crestwood Heights is located, as it were, at but a *point* in time; it is a constellation of human beings, related to one another for a relatively short period by strong emotional bonds, which will again dissolve after the task of child-rearing is completed. Within this nexus, the psychosexual development of the child occurs; if successfully completed, it culminates in marriage and the founding of a new family unit. Also from the family, supplemented by increasing contacts with the personnel of outside institutions, the child acquires the patterns of social behavior which permit him to function in his society. As he grows older, the child returns less and less frequently to the island of emotional security which the Crestwood family represents; and finally he installs himself upon a similar psychological refuge, almost entirely isolated from the original base which launched him on his solitary voyage.

FAMILY ACTIVITIES

What occurs within the family during its relatively brief span of intense activity as a unit? What are its day-to-day concerns and what its major goals? How do its members co-operate to reach these ends, and how do they balance responsibility to the family with obligations to the world outside this circle? The answers to these questions will be grouped here under the categories in which the Crestwood family seems naturally to think: economic activities; household duties; child-rearing; and social and religious activities.

A. ECONOMIC ACTIVITIES

The Crestwood family, as has been said earlier, is essentially a consumption unit. Unlike, for instance, the Irish peasant family,[24] which is focused on production, the Crestwood Heights woman and her children do not usually contribute directly through their work to the economic enterprise of the family. The relatively few Crestwood Heights children who work and live at home while still unmarried,[25] are not required to contribute to the family income; or, should the rare exception occur, the contribution is nominal, a token only, for the sake of the child's "independence." The earning sphere is thus clear-cut, dominated by the male; the area of spending (which may, or may not, be male-dominated to some degree) is almost always shared with other members of the family. The most general pattern appears to be one in which the man decides, after consultation, on such major expenditures as a car or life insurance, and the woman decides, sometimes after discussion with her husband, upon the much larger aggregate of small things.

Although the democratic family norms dictate the co-operative spending of the income earned by the man, an air of secrecy often surrounds the actual amount of that income. Frequently, interviews with families reveal, the wife does not know, even roughly, how much her husband earns. One woman, who was seriously considering a separation from her husband, gave, as a major reason, his withholding of a substantial amount from the total income he had quoted to her, an omission which she discovered only by accident, while looking through his briefcase for something else altogether. Children are almost sure to have only the vaguest notions of the father's earnings. This secrecy in regard to income seems strangely inconsistent with the norms which require responsibility in the spending of money by all members of the family, a responsibility which can hardly be exercised intelligently without full knowledge of the economic facts.

This male attitude towards money may be closely associated with the "spoiling" of wife and children to which reference has been made. Women, viewed in this manner, must, like children, be protected from financial worries and problems, which the father accepts as his responsibility alone. In one joint interview with a Crestwood husband and wife, the latter was asked if she knew how much her husband earned. She replied, "As a matter of fact, I don't." Whereupon her husband added, "And that's right, you shouldn't know. Women should learn to live on a budget, but they shouldn't know what their husband's income is."

In the division of authority over spending, the wife more often makes the decisions in everything that pertains to the house: ordinary household purchases, food, interior decoration, equipment, and clothing for herself and her children. It is common for even young children to be consulted about such expenditures. One small boy of seven himself selected his bedroom furniture, chose a soft grey paint for the walls of the room, and added a note peculiarly his own—drapes featuring cowboys rampant on a bright red ground.

The methods of handling money jointly vary from family to family. Some families may decide together what items are to be bought, and the father then pays the bills. Some wives may have accounts of their own for certain expenditures, on which they themselves issue cheques. Again, the secretary of a professional man may look after some household bills.[26] Wives often quietly manipulate their household allowances to provide items for which their husbands are not willing to pay. One informant stated that

she had recently painted the playroom and a room upstairs in the house. The job, as a result, cost her twenty dollars for the paint instead of eighty dollars for a paint contract. She did this, not because the money for this kind of project comes out of her household budget, but because she wants to save the money (as she put it at first). On closer questioning, however, it turned out that she would, in fact, discuss such a project for improvement with her husband and if he did not feel enthusiastic about it, thinking that the room looked all right as it was, and preferring to spend his money on cars, clubs, and so on, the matter would be dropped and later she would get the paint. So whether or not she does the decoration job or has it done by contract is a matter of his judgment. He would be much more enthusiastic if the project had to do with clothes for her. He would sooner buy nice clothes for her than paint a room. Lately she had had to dissuade him from buying her a new fur coat.

Large, expensive items, such as cars, are frequently bought by the man. In a joint interview with husband and wife the researcher asked:

When you bought the house or the car, who did what?

HUSBAND: We both bought the house together. I bought the car myself. We talk it over if it's important. Nobody cares what kind of a car I buy. If I bought a black one, they'd want a grey one and vice versa. But generally, everybody knows what's happening before anything is done.

The cash income is all-important to the solidarity of the Crestwood Heights family, since upon it depends the social status of the family, which, in turn, determines the sense of belonging to the community—indeed the very possibility of staying in it. The self-image of each family member depends largely on the income, as we have had occasion to conclude before. Unlike the upper-class English family, which may preserve its feeling of worth almost intact in the face of dwindling wealth, the self-estimate of the Crestwood upper middle class family tends to rise and fall with income. In view of the central position which money occupies in the family, the preoccupation with teaching children to handle finances is completely understandable.

The earnings of young children may be insignificant in terms of the family income, but these attain great symbolic importance for the child's training. Earning is strongly encouraged, particularly for boys since it has a place in preparation for the career. This money is held to belong to the child, and not to the family as a whole; but it supplements rather than replaces the usual allowance, given by the parents and increased with increasing age. Although, in Crestwood Heights, opportunities are somewhat limited for boys and girls to earn money (baby-sitting is probably the most lucrative of possible employments) individual earnings of whatever amount receive a cultural stress as "teaching the child to know the value of money" and "giving him a sense of responsibility." "Earning" in this sense generally takes place outside the home. Performance of household duties is taken more or less for granted, although the allowance is frequently regarded as payment. Sometimes exceptional tasks performed by the child are rewarded with money. Earning is, of course, also closely tied in with the preparation of the child for eventual independence.

One mother reports in connection with her thirteen-year-old son's allowance and earnings:

ALLOWANCE—$1.35 a week, which covers streetcar transportation and haircuts. Out of this he contributes to Red Feather, etc., teacher's gift, and any gifts to friends. He occasionally augments his allowance by working in his father's store the odd Saturday, and by any cash birthday gifts he receives.

One twelve-year-old girl is described by her mother as being

on a dollar a week spending money allowance and she also receives a clothing allowance every September that takes care of everything except large items. She has been on this allowance since she was six. Each year she is given one more article of clothing to take care of. Once on this allowance, she does her own buying.

The same child is reported by her mother as purchasing a pair of shoes, which seems to have been obtained with money over and above her regular allowance.

R. asked if she could go downtown with a girl friend [same age, same class]. She wanted to buy a pair of shoes that she needed. She was granted permission with the understanding that she must make sure that the shoes fitted correctly and that they were comfortable. She was thrilled with her responsibility and was given ten dollars to buy her shoes. She phoned home at five o'clock to say (with great pride and excitement) that she had found a beautiful pair of navy suede, just what she wanted, and could she bring her friend for dinner? Mother said "Yes, of course" she could, and so they arrived home within the hour and R. put on her new shoes and they were a very wise choice, plain and comfortable. They cost nine ninety-five and R. apologized for spending so much but said she just couldn't do any better. Daddy came home then, and the shoes were admired once again.

Another family (consisting of father, mother, a seventeen-year-old daughter and a son of nineteen) handles children's allowances and general purchases somewhat differently.

Mrs. J. said the children were on an allowance, and got, in addition, earned money. They had a family conclave and decided how much labor around the house was worth. At first they had settled on thirty cents which was later increased to forty. Mrs. J. told me about how much this worked out to for B. It was enough to allow him to go downtown to a show twice a month. Out of this allowance, plus earned money, the children are expected to take care of their personal wants and pay their own way to shows. In addition, J. had a clothing allowance which was started last year. She is allowed twenty dollars a month which will be increased to thirty dollars next Fall. Out of this she first saved quite a bit of money, putting one hundred dollars in the bank. This is because she started out with a good wardrobe.

The researcher asked how they had decided on the twenty dollars.

Mrs. J. said that she had consulted with many mothers and arrived at the twenty dollars as an average figure. Some were higher and some were lower.

The child's education in spending may thus be more or less direct. His own earnings and his allowance are for his private purposes, and nominally he is free to spend as he pleases. In fact, however, strong and pervasive controls are exercised over the child's expenditure, until well into the teens. The final authority over the child's decisions in regard to spending is largely the mother. Control is more pronounced and extends over a longer period for girls than for boys, a fact which may presage the greater independence of the adult male in spending money.[27] Family status may serve as a check on the amount of money a child can earn for himself. Paper routes are approved for only the younger boys, and it is not usual for older boys to work in stores or businesses other than those owned or operated by the father. Baby-sitting is generally permitted to teen-age girls. Summer work in an office is also considered suitable for the girl, as well as table service in exclusive resort hotels. More lucrative factory work, as a summer job, would in all probability be outlawed entirely for girls and permitted only grudgingly to boys.

The mechanics of the control of spending are often very subtle. The child may be allowed to "buy on approval," i.e. he can "shop for himself," but purchases are then accepted or returned by the parent. A girl, for example, when she goes shopping for her clothes, even with her own allowance, may have several choices sent home, from which the mother may make the final selection. Supervision in spending the allowance may be exercised on the ground that the parent is "forming the child's taste" or "teaching him the value of money" or material objects. "What the Joneses do" is another powerful determinant of parental attitudes towards allowances. While some parents feel the child's allowance is too high, they nevertheless consider it necessary to follow the general practice, as in the case of the mother who consulted other mothers of her acquaintance about the correct amount for her daughter's clothing allowance. And finally, in the face of culturally approved methods of discipline, which rule out force and coercion, withholding of the allowance may be the only effective means of disciplining a Crestwood Heights teenager.

At the same time as the child is encouraged to earn and guided in his spending, he is also taught to save and to give. Many parents "help" the child to save a portion of earnings and allowance. Again, saving has symbolic rather than economic significance. The value of giving is stressed as an essential part of the family pattern, although "training in the art of giving" is now passing from the family to the school. Asked at a Home and School meeting for Grade XI parents, "What education does the school give the child in the art of giving?" a teacher gave the following answer, which illustrates very well the approved school (and family) attitude towards giving.

Children should learn how to give with an educated heart. Crestwood Heights schools had been the first to go into the agencies they were helping. This is a wealthy community, and it is important for the students to learn how to handle money and to give. She had been talking to Mr. N. and they were over the quota in the Community Chest drive—over the two hundred dollar mark. In the community at large, the children were giving better than the adults. Fourteen of the twenty-one classes in the school had already come to her for a family to help at Christmas time.

As the child advances in age, his allowance, and sometimes his earnings, increase in proportion to his responsibilities. Control over details of spending is not usually relaxed while the child remains at home, but there does appear to be a point around the mid-teens at which the mother's control of expenditures gives way to that of the father, where the boy is concerned. The significance of this realignment would appear to be great in establishing the typical adult orientations of Crestwood men and women towards spending.

Conflicts between parents and children over allowances occur most frequently in the teens, especially with boys, who begin to "need" what to parents may seem exorbitant amounts for their dates with popular girls. The battle may wage more furiously if the son proceeds through university on funds supplied by the father, as is usually the case.

Training in economic activities comes relatively late in the socialization of the Crestwood Heights child. The environment does not permit the child to earn much money even during his teens or early twenties. And before he is free to spend as an adult, he must first undergo a prolonged process of internalizing complicated values, centering around the sacredness of private property, the high symbolic importance accorded to material objects, and the necessity for postponing gratifications to the future. In other words, the Crestwood Heights adult must understand thoroughly the *expressive* qualities of money, the culturally approved ways of spending money on "appropriate" objects, material and non-material. Such highly complex patterns of social behavior are acquired only slowly and through much trial and error.

B. HOUSEHOLD DUTIES

Despite the reduced volume of work within the home itself, traditional divisions of labor are still discernible. The general administration of the household, the feeding and clothing of the children, are regarded as the wife's responsibility, although the woman who derives her maximum satisfaction in life from such activities is becoming increasingly rare, and the role of housewife tends to be devalued in the culture. Some Crestwood wives discharge their duties by supervising either full or part-time domestics; and many, by directing the services which enter the home from outside. But performance varies, and the Crestwood woman may do as much or as little of the housework herself as her inclination and means permit—provided only that the required neat and unlived-in appearance of the house is maintained.

Over and against this reduction, however, is an incredible increase in what must be done if the Crestwood home is to be a proper exhibition of status and thus an aid to the male career. No longer can the house be decorated once and for all time, or the furniture be placed finally, for the period of one's married life. Every month brings a wealth of opulently illustrated magazines which show the Crestwood woman new styles, materials, furniture, and arrangements for the home beautiful, the home efficient, the home livable, and, indeed, the home reputable. The woman must keep abreast of these constant changes for one of two reasons: so that she may defend her former arrangements successfully—even if only to herself—or be encouraged to sweep these aside in favor of new. She can accomplish neither defence nor attack unless she carefully follows the argument laid down in the decorating magazines, nor can she feel safe unless she is in a position to reject or to accept their dictates. As one woman informant commented:

I'm not as bad as X., I went right ahead and switched the whole living room over to modern. *She* actually kept a room in her house empty for two years before she could make up her mind what to put into it!

The Crestwood man is ritually responsible for those tasks requiring physical strength—gardening, window-cleaning, putting on storm windows, and so on. In practice, however, these duties are often delegated to commercial services, for which the husband usually, or the wife sometimes, makes the arrangements. The obligations of the career, for many men, make it just about literally impossible for them to assume much responsibility around the house. A surgeon who had recently moved to Crestwood Heights at first thought of stripping and repainting his house himself. He abandoned the idea because he could not spare the time, because other men in the neighborhood might criticize, and, most important of all, because he could not afford to risk injury to the skilled hands on which the family income entirely depended. His wife then arranged for the contractor who actually undertook the renovation.

Although the home is defined as the woman's world, Crestwood Heights husbands and children do "pitch in" to help the mother, particularly in emergencies. Where the man does share the woman's tasks, it is on a voluntary and flexible basis, seldom rising—without raising doubts about maleness—to the level of a regular and expected contribution. One husband, for example, washes dishes and does the laundry when his wife is pregnant; another always helps when his wife has had a hard day. A third professional man frequently stays at home in the evenings with the children to allow his wife some independent leisure activities of her own; as part of "his contribution," he bathes the children and puts them to bed, the sole opportunity in his busy day to play and to talk with them. Through such participation in the woman's mainly routine and instrumental tasks, the husband's assistance may take on particular emotional significance for the wife, since she cannot reciprocate by equivalent participation in the man's work. Many Crestwood wives try by all possible means to involve their husbands in responsibilities around the house. One woman whose husband's contribution consisted merely in *paying* the gardener, not in doing the task himself, stated with some satisfaction that she thus "had secured her husband's participation in the household routine."

Children's contributions to homemaking are viewed somewhat differently. Although there are few genuinely useful tasks which can be performed by children, the idea persists that household duties are an especially efficacious means of forming character. The child may be required to make his own bed from an early age, to dry the dishes, or to shovel the snow. Both boys and girls are encouraged to help, without too much sex discrimination—until the teens, when the boy may refuse such purely "womanly" operations as dish drying. A man or boy may cook, provided he does it as a hobby and confines his efforts to special dishes for the gourmet. The girl may, or may not, learn the housewifely skills from her mother; she is not under any particular obligation to become a skilful homemaker prior to marriage. Should a girl show unusual aptitude in homemaking, she often capitalizes on her talents through a career as dietician or home economist or interior decorator, outside the home altogether. Actually, higher prestige is likely to be accorded a dietician in an institution than to the "untrained" housewife creating a home for husband and children.

There are some dangers involved in the proffered help of husband and children, particularly if homemaking is the woman's chief preoccupation. The husband who aspires to be a good cook may be asked to restrict his efforts to the outdoor barbecue or to particular dishes. One father and his sons were forbidden to enter the kitchen when meals were being prepared. On the whole, however, with the woman's growing activity outside the home, the husband tends to be much more deeply involved in routine household tasks and child care than he was in Victorian days.

Family interviews reveal varied patterns of handling household activities, which seem to differ on a class basis. Generally, the lower the position of the family in the class structure, the more the members of the family can do for themselves. One marginal family (interviewed after it left Crestwood Heights) reported a high degree of co-operation in household tasks:

The researcher asked about responsibilties of household members. Mrs. H. immediately replied that they had great responsibilties, especially since her mother had been sick. Last night her husband had come home with a fever and had gone to bed, so that she was nurse, housemaid, and everything. The children [a girl of eighteen and a boy of sixteen] are a great help. They take turns helping her prepare the dinner. They often help her with the dishes, although she does not require this. When the grandmother was more active and able to be in the kitchen she [the grandmother] would not allow this. Mrs. H. said she was of the old school which didn't believe that children should work around the house. T. [the son] has the responsiblity for cutting the grass, a job he doesn't like. He also carries out the ashes. They have fixed up a small garden at the back of their house for which R. [the daughter] is mainly responsible. She likes working in the garden with flowers. The children usually get their own breakfast and may also get their own lunch if mother is not home. Mr. H.'s activities around the home are limited to being a handyman. He likes tinkering with all kinds of electrical and other gadgets. *This spring he had painted the whole house outside. He likes painting and at their home in Crestwood Heights had done all the inside painting.* [Italics added.]

This anecdote makes an interesting contrast with the behavior of the surgeon. The man who likes to paint, or wishes to economize by doing work himself, can do it openly, once away from Crestwood Heights—whether he goes "up" or "down" the social ladder.

In another family, longer established in Crestwood Heights and with somewhat higher social pretensions, a rather similar situation is described:

The children [a girl of seventeen and a boy of nineteen] have to make their own beds and tidy their own rooms. They also are expected to help with the dishes, setting the table, and preparing the dinner. This they do week about. J. [the son] looks after the lawns in summer and the snow in winter. L. [the daughter] shovels some of the snow if J. is busy shovelling other people's walks. For this work the children are paid. On Saturday morning each child is expected to do one hour's work. Both Mr. and Mrs. K. signified that this was quite a problem. Mr. K. said you needed a supervisor to make sure that the work got done. Mrs. K. admitted that it didn't always get done. Sometimes the children had other things they must do and Mrs. K. releases them from their hour's work, for instance when L. wants to go to a game at V. [a well-known boys' private school]. When the researcher asked about Mr. K.'s responsibilities, he said that working was enough for him. Although he only worked a seven and one-half hour day, he was away from home for ten hours, counting transportation. Mrs. K.'s responsibilities center around the home—buying and preparing the food.

Here, however, performance of household tasks appears to be more tied in with training for responsibility rather than with necessity. The father, too, by his own definition, remains aloof, which indicates that the family can afford to pay for the services he might have rendered.

It is significant to note here that as the male career becomes increasingly successful, this very success exerts a kind of cyclical effect upon the male role in the home. As the man spends more time away from his family, he must buy more services to replace the work he once did himself. As he buys more services, he also needs more income. And to make more money, he must spend more time away from home.

As children and parents live more and more outside the home, household activities are correspondingly lightened. The wife who has many community responsibilities tends to select food which can be quickly and easily prepared, rather than painstakingly plan dishes to build a reputation as an excellent cook. Her short-cut meals are facilitated by the refrigerator and, more recently, by the freezer and premixed foods. In the same way, the family which can afford a dishwashing machine need not place such emphasis upon children's help. Thus income, upon which position in the class structure largely depends, determines the number of mechanical gadgets and so to some extent the amount of leisure permitted to the family. Only the very well-to-do can secure full-time domestics, another factor that controls the free time available for family members to participate in activities outside the home. Where maids and equipment make it possible, there is less emphasis upon the actual performance of household tasks by any family members, although the feeling still persists that it is advantageous for the child to have some simple routine duties to train him in "responsible" adult behavior.[28]

C. CHILD CARE AND CONTROL

While these economic and domestic activities are important in Crestwood Heights, neither is seen as a sufficient reason for the family's existence. Both father and mother, within and without the home, perform their various roles largely, as we are now aware, "for the sake of the children." With only rare exceptions, Crestwood parents pretty well take for granted their responsibility for the physical care and social training of their children.[29] But beyond their fundamental and obvious legal responsibility, Crestwood Heights parents often wonder "what to do next" with their children, since they are given no support by traditionally sanctioned methods of child-rearing. There is great variation in the patterns of child care and control, and considerable parental uncertainty.

Nor are father and mother commonly agreed even in uncertainty as to how this function is to be discharged. Background for this division of opinion may be found in the career. It does not usually occur to the Crestwood Heights male to inquire deeply, if at all, into the emotional reactions of the subordinates who assist him in his occupation. Human beings, in this setting, exist to facilitate the flow of goods or services from which money is made. True, the Crestwood man may be well informed about personnel practices, but he usually views such innovations as "good for business" and only indirectly as good for people. If the experts in industrial relations can prove with figures that production is increased through their ministrations, the Crestwood Heights male will accept their advice, although he may still feel "diametrically opposed to the whole philosophy."

For such a man, the child-rearing theories which his wife espouses may seem arrant nonsense; and the male experts from whom she derives her information frequently appear to him, unless they are doctors, as inadequate men who have not been able to make the grade in the *really* masculine world. In the office, whatever his private reservations, the Crestwood man is prepared to go quite a distance along the personnel-directed path for the sake of production and industrial peace. At home, he is under no obligation to moderate his views; in the family he can give vent to his true feelings unopposed. Out of love for wife and children, he may, in time, be persuaded to take an interest in the new-fangled notions; rarely, however, will he come wholeheartedly to endorse the democratic and permissive norms now seeping into the family.[30] A father who does not pretend to understand the underlying psychological reasons for a child's failure to achieve in school is, nevertheless, deeply concerned over the immediate situation of the child's inability to meet the required standards. In such circumstances he often inclines first towards old-fashioned disciplinary measures as a remedy, only reluctantly and sometimes after exhausting all other possibilities accepting the methods of school, experts, and wife. Another type of father, as indicated below, moves in a rather uneasy but would-be helpful manner at the edge of the enterprise, feeling the uncertain willingness of the novice rather than the unwillingness of an opponent.

One observation report of Father's Day at a Crestwood Heights nursery school is particularly revealing as to paternal attitudes towards current child-rearing theories.[31] (The reader is referred to the notes for comments on the attitudes revealed as the report proceeds.)

When I [the researcher, a man] arrived at the Nursery School, Mr. X. [a father], whom I had met twice at meetings previously this week, was leading two children out to the playground, where there were already about a dozen children playing.

Mrs. N., the Nursery School supervisor, provided me with an observation form and sent me out to the playground. There a second father was trailing his daughter on the boardwalk. He followed her around solicitously three or four times, then left to come over to Mr. X. and me. Soon his daughter came running to him.

Both fathers tried periodically to participate with the children, but rather unsuccessfully. They very quickly got tired of the teeter and left. Very soon they were beginning to complain of the cold and to look at their watches.

Mrs. N. came out after a while and seemed compelled to keep the fathers informed and observing. At every free moment she would corner a father, telling him what was happening, psychologically, to the children here.

One father expressed concern about the children falling from the jungle gym. Mrs. N. said her theory was that they wouldn't climb farther than they safely could. "Other teachers [and presumably mothers] would agree with me on that."[32]

A third father, Mr. Y., arrived. He joined the ranks of the watching fathers, saying that things were different now. *His* father would never have come to school. He went on about the respect of children for aged parents. His father-in-law had always taken it out on his children because of his own inferiority complex. Now he was complaining that they didn't look after him. Mr. Y. himself said he wasn't going to rely on *his* children. He was buying a wheel chair and a coffin while he could.[33]

The other father, Mr. T., thought that it was silly for people to take vengeance on their children, or to be very strict simply for the sake of discipline.

Mr. X. commented that he didn't see how his son would be playing like this, when he had fallen at home several days previously and broken a collar bone.

Mrs. N. told Mr. Y. that the sandpile was a popular part of their equipment. "In the Fall, that's the first thing the disturbed children head for."

I asked Mr. X. how this compared with his childhood. He replied that nobody made all this fuss over *him*. "My mother had four children, and my old man was always out hustling, so I didn't get much attention." He didn't think it had done any harm, and that maybe they were making too much fuss.[34]

I asked how all this affected the children when they got home. Mr. X. said they were tired out and didn't want to play with kids in the block, but then that was unorganized play. He went on to tell me about his son [seven] playing space war. One tree was the bombs, another tree was a wing of the space ship and so on. He couldn't understand this, and his son became annoyed.

Back in the Nursery School, the fathers grouped themselves apart from the children. Mr. Y. commented that this was mother's stuff,[35] and the fathers were embarrassed. They were amazed that here the children were little adults, although at home they were just children; and he showed surprise when one child upset some blocks and spontaneously picked them up.

Mr. X. and I sneaked out for a smoke in the teacher's room. There he expanded his theories and ideas about modern youth. Their trouble was they had no initiative, no drive, no ambition. He saw that every day in his plant. All they wanted was a car. Single men were the worst. When they married and got some responsibilities their production tripled. His theory of character was that it was cyclical. One generation did well, gave their children everything. When they grew up, they saw that material goods weren't everything, and made their kids appreciate things and fend for themselves. He himself was spoiled but his kid was going to learn to earn.

When he was old enough, he would get him a paper route. Of course his son wouldn't lack material things, or love either, but he wouldn't get everything automatically.

The same father was later getting the names of all kinds of toys from the teachers for his son: tempera paints, blocks, easel for painting, etc. And all the time during indoor play, his son kept shouting "Hi, Dad!" Once the child broke away, ran over to his father, and kissed his well-manicured hand. Mr. X. said, "That makes it all worthwhile."[36]

He, too, during the rest period, made several comments to the effect that "they do these things in school but not at home. Why?"

Mr. H. came in and sat with his daughter who was rolling plasticene. She had a long, worm-like piece and asked her father what it was. He named many things, all of which she denied. Finally he gave up, but she wouldn't tell him what it was. He said, with annoyance, "Well, it *has* to be something. What's the sense if it's nothing?"[37]

About ten forty-five, another father came in. Later Mrs. N. said she was surprised to see Mr. D. His wife had phoned earlier in the week, asking how she could get her husband interested.[38] He just didn't want to be bothered with the children and refused to go to the school. Then when he turned up, Mrs. N. was surprised, but said with a knowing smile, "You can bet why he came!" Mr. D. left early and did not take his child home, saying he had to be back at the office.

As the children were prepared for leaving, Mr. X. got Mrs. N. aside, plying her with questions about discipline, how to get his children to do things, how many toys to buy them.[39]

After the fathers had left, and most of the children had been picked up by their mothers (five children had not come because their mothers didn't have time to bring them, and older brothers and sisters wouldn't be bothered), Mrs. N. commented "Fathers are less tied up with the children than mothers, but don't quote me on that. If we'd had the fathers earlier in the year, it might be different. When the mothers were here, they were much more involved with the children at play."[40]

The three teachers agreed that the fathers' visit had been a huge success, and that it did the fathers good to see what went on here.[41] The observer added the following pertinent analysis of paternal behavior in this session: It was particularly noticeable that fathers were uncomfortable when they tried to participate in the child's world. They admired and remarked about the teachers' patience, however. Their orientation to the world of reality prevented them from any genuine appreciation of the child's fantasy world, which definitely annoyed them because of its irrational nature. Some fathers markedly distrusted the material benefits which they freely give to their children, emphasizing that only hard work and individual effort would benefit the child in the long run. At the same time, some fathers appeared to pursue the very spoiling policies they deplored, asking the teachers for advice about toys to buy, wanting to give their children the most of the very best possible.

When fathers showed an interest, it was in their own child only. They paid no attention to other children, which may have been related to their embarrassment at finding themselves with women and children in the first place. While they were amazed at the difference between the behavior of children in school and at home, remarking on the "maturity" obvious in the school setting, they still manifested a strong under-current rejecting modern educational methods and "frills," clinging to a faith in their own early experience in the school of hard knocks.

And finally, fathers were most concerned about physical protection, tending to exhibit the solicitude traditionally associated with mothers. It is significant to note at this point that mothers are now being told by the child-rearing experts that over-solicitude is harmful to the child. Fathers, not being exposed to child-rearing theories to the same degree, may feel that mothers are becoming callous and may be attempting to take the mothers' place in the only area they now thoroughly understand, physical protection.

These generalized attitudes of paternal aloofness towards the child in nursery school are evident within the family, particularly where discipline is concerned; in many instances the fathers throw the full weight of responsibility for discipline as well as for child care upon the mother. One woman informant had assumed complete duty in this respect. (Italics added.)

Oh, he [her husband] was away a lot. Generally he left on Monday and came back Saturday, but there were times when he'd be away for three or four weeks at a time. Just when we were moving here, he had to go West for six weeks. I was a little worried; I didn't know how we would get moved but everything came out all right. *I was used to managing by myself by then. In fact, I preferred to manage by myself; Mr. C. was just a bother.* He's not much around the house. One time in Lea's Woods, he was alone and a fuse blew. He couldn't find the fuse box and had to call up an electrician. I could have fixed it in a jiffy and so could the kids. . . .

. . . However, Brown's [husband's firm] sent up a truck and a driver and the kids pitched in and we got moved. The furniture movers took the big things, of course. Brown's are very good that way. One time, Mr. B. was in the hospital all winter. He had an operation and nearly died. Those were terrible times. He was away all winter. Then Brown's sent him south for a couple of weeks' rest. I took the children down to the hospital once around Christmas. They say they remember it, but I don't know. *When their father came home, he was a complete stranger to them.*

I don't remember having any problems particularly in those days. I was busy all the time. There were anxious moments but we always got over them. The children weren't hard to manage. They'd be in bed by seven, so I had time to get things straightened up after that.

We lived in Lea's Woods and there was a playground right behind us so they were never far away. *They weren't hard to manage because they knew I was boss.* I would just have to speak to the older ones. The young ones, I would just slap lightly on the hand. That was as bad for them as a spanking. Even a little slap would break their hearts, but they soon got over it. I believed in letting them know who was the authority when they were young. Mr. C. would never discipline them when he came home. "I'm just home on weekends," he'd say, "and I don't want them to think I just came home to discipline them." He set my training back a little I guess, but that wasn't serious.

This family, in which the mother has assumed entirely the father's role as well as her own in regard to child care, represents an extreme—but not altogether unusual—case. The mother is completely absorbed in her maternal role and is critical of the more usual type of Crestwood Heights mother, who is interested in activities outside the home. Nor does she seem to have absorbed many of the current child-rearing preachments.

"In some families, nowadays," she continues, "even the small ones, children don't mean much to the mothers. The mothers are out all the time and when they do see the children, things are so intense there is often conflict. If they don't see them much they expect too much of them when they do. Children need a mother. When I chose my life as a mother, it was everything to me. My mother used to say 'You're burying yourself,' but that's what I wanted."

This family constellation well illustrates the effect of the absence of the father; but, while this is typical of almost all Crestwood families, the effect is not always so marked. The responsibility thus thrown upon the mother is not always accepted with the same willingness by other mothers who are not equally devoted to their maternal role, or who are perhaps more aware of current child-rearing recommendations than Mrs. C. appears to be.

At the other end of the scale is a family which believes in sharing responsibilities, where the wife is alert to current theories of child-rearing, and active in community affairs. The husband sets forth his views on discipline.

That sort of thing I don't know much about. I am home so little. I only see the kids for an hour in the evening, that is if I'm not going off to a meeting. *Really discipline is their mother's province.*

We have no trouble at all or practically none. That's partly because the kids [a girl of twelve and a boy slightly younger] are so busy. B. has to work a lot.

They know what they can do and can't. They know they can't look at TV or listen to the radio and they abide by it.

Just then Mrs. M. came in. The researcher explained that he and Mr. M. were discussing discipline and talking about TV and radio. Mrs. M. said:

We have a regular routine for that. None at all Monday through Friday, or I should say Monday through Thursday. They know that and govern themselves accordingly.

Mr. M. added that probably "they peek a little!" Mrs. M. continued,

They're both busy and have to spend time on their work. B. has a paper route and has to work so much he has no time. They know there's absolutely no TV in the week. If they finish their work they can read a book— B. likes reading—but they can't watch TV. I don't want them to rush through their work just to see a program they want. So when the work gets done, no TV.

The researcher asked how they got this system set up and the children adjusted to it. Mr. M. replied,

We just set down the rules and established a routine. Now everybody's happy. Our secret is routine. We have everything routinized. There's no trouble.

Mrs. M. added,

We're not an average family, you know. There's probably not another family like us in the Heights. We have everything on a schedule.

Again, in this family, which makes its own rules, we find the father designating discipline as the mother's province because he himself sees the children so little. The Crestwood father, when he is at home, appears to enjoy the children, but their care and control do not concern him directly; nevertheless, the father's participation in family activities and his emotional ties with wife and children, although largely symbolic, may be extremely important, as writers on the family with a psychoanalytic interest point out.[42] Psychosexual development in the child occurs by his identification of himself with emotionally charged adult models; this necessitates the presence of a father figure, actual or symbolic. Its presence is felt, together with its permissive or authoritarian aura, whether the father disciplines the children directly or abdicates in favor of the mother.

As his children advance beyond infancy and early childhood, the Crestwood Heights father "should" assume more responsibility for control. More serious disciplinary problems, particularly those calling for physical punishment, are widely held to be within the father's province. Although corporal punishment is, under the norms now governing family life, widely condemned, it nevertheless exists; and, if the children's assertions in the Clinic and in Human Relations classes are to be trusted, on a scale of considerable frequency and intensity. Where it does occur, it is usually the father who initiates the discipline and performs the act. One report states (italics added):

Both parents enter into the disciplining of the children. Whipping is done by Mr. J. This is done when necessary, about three times a year. Mr. J.

justifies this by saying that they need restraints in order to ensure respect and to "keep things operating." He said that this was a bit of a problem now since T. was over six feet tall and larger than he is. It was just a matter of who was going to get punished. T. would put his hand on his father's head and say, "Take it easy, Dad." *Mr. J. now thought the best means of punishment was the denial of certain things or putting children in their rooms.* Mrs. J. said that the children had all kinds of means of getting around the parents and had to be watched pretty closely—as, for instance, two boys would get on the phone and each would say that he couldn't go out because his parents wouldn't let him, speaking as if the other boy could, whereas in actual fact each parent had made it conditional upon the other one going. Decisions about the children are made jointly by Mr. and Mrs. J.

Few fathers, perhaps, go this far; but the number of children who mentioned spanking and strapping as most-feared experiences was rather large in view of the prevalent views in the community against these practices. Such punishment, as in the case of the school, may be "a last resort," but if this is true many fathers must reach this point early in the disciplinary process.

It is clear, therefore, that whatever the child-rearing theories held by Crestwood Heights parents, the father's actual participation is limited by his physical absence from the family and his psychological distance from the new ideas. Yet his symbolic importance remains great, regardless of how active or inactive his role as disciplinarian. It is also evident that the ideal of joint responsibility of father and mother in child care and control is particularly difficult to realize in Crestwood Heights, a situation which has serious implications for the husband-wife relationship. The mother, who has the time and the inclination to absorb the theories of the child-rearing experts, may find herself diametrically opposed to the paternally approved authoritarian discipline which she is yet expected to administer. She may, willingly or unwillingly, assume full responsibility for the child's control, or she may decline her disciplinary role altogether, with harmful consequences to the children. Most families arrive at some kind of compromise solution, illustrated by the allegedly "typically feminine" remark of one mother:

When Mr. R. gets home, he's tired and he likes to sit down and read. Oh, sometimes I ask his advice about discipline. I listen and he thinks I take it. I don't always, but I let him think I do.

In other areas of family life, much the same pattern prevails—the father acknowledges some responsibility, but delegates much of it to the mother, and assumes himself a minimal and peripheral role. In consequence, there is often a strong impression that Crestwood Heights is close to becoming a matriarchy.[48]

At certain points in the history of the family, however, the father becomes automatically involved. The mother's power to discipline children decreases sharply after they enter their teens, particularly where boys are concerned. Certain privileges, such as access to the family car, are customarily controlled by the father. The son may sometimes be felt acutely as a potential rival by the father; but, in general, disputes are avoided, and father and son tacitly by-pass any situations which call for direct paternal intervention and which might openly disrupt the cultural ideal of the "pal" relationship between father and son. The Crestwood Heights concept of time makes ageing and the looming prospect of the termination of the career a very real threat to the man; the prospect can be softened by playing down the actual gap in years between father and son. Greater age, connoting superior wisdom, is not a disciplinary weapon as readily available to the Crestwood Heights father as to his Victorian predecessor. As the son grows older, the father's last control over the son's behavior is likely to be only an economic one.

In times of family crisis or stress, the father also becomes directly and intimately involved as the active authority. Referral of the child to the Child Guidance Clinic is one such critical situation.[44] Although, in a few cases, such a referral reinforced the father's tendency to keep aloof from any responsibility in the child's care and control, the opposite was more often true. The father might even display a sudden and intense interest in the child, which was highly colored emotionally and quite at variance with his previous behavior. Again, should the child be expelled from school, or threatened with expulsion, the father may take time off from business to make a stormy and unexpected appearance in the Principal's office.

The mechanisms evolved to allow for and to control the access of parents to institutions such as the school are based on the tacit assumption (or conclusion) that it is the mother who is primarily concerned with problems of curriculum, homework, bed-time, and so forth. The very daytime nature of much school and clinic activity favors greater participation by the mother, although both institutions loudly proclaim the need to include fathers as well.[45] The Clinic, although it has encountered more difficulty in working with fathers, and complains of male antagonism to its work, recognizes the impossibility of adequately treating the child without the co-operation of both parents. But no serious attempt was made by Clinic personnel to give time in the evening, when fathers *were* available, nor was this move even discussed, to the knowledge of the research staff. It may well be that experts and teachers want the benefits of participation by the fathers without the draw-backs in obstruction and cross-examination it might involve. Fathers, in their turn, want the fruits of participation (respect, authority, friendship with their children) but without the costs which their own re-education and reorientation would entail. So Crestwood men ignore or inveigh against the experts, but do nothing until a crisis arises over the children, whereupon, from the experts' viewpoint, they may often do the wrong thing with a great deal of decisiveness and force.

In correction of an earlier statement it would, however, seem safer to say that Crestwood Heights, whatever the surface appearance may suggest, is quite far from being a matriarchy, since the paternal role does routinely have great symbolic significance and may become a highly active one in conditions of strain and uncertainty. The father's participation may tend to be peripheral and variable, dictated by personal choice rather than by custom, but non-participation does not negate his *potential* authority, which still "exists," even when it is not exercised. In this sense the father is, as it were, the president who, it is well understood by all, sits over the general manager even though he delegates much authority and responsibility and may often be absent or inaccessible. Thus the day-to-day situation within the family might suggest a father-controlled matriarchy, although in the ideal pattern dominance by the father is underlined.

The child's experience with, and training in, discipline is almost exclusively in the role of recipient. In Crestwood Heights culture, there is no recognized pattern of control over younger children by older brothers and sisters, since such supervision is not usually required. Indeed, looking after a younger brother or sister may be considered by the parents as a household task to be rewarded with money over and above the usual allowance.

Ideally, Crestwood Heights children are as nearly "equal" within the family as the differences in age will allow, which makes it difficult for one child to dominate directly another, even a younger sibling. Parents are generally concerned about treating all children alike. One mother, when asked what her children quarrelled about, replied:

Oh anything and everything. Mostly it's belongings. They have their own rooms but their belongings are not private. Whenever we bring them anything we have to be careful to get things equal. If one gets something better than the others, you hear about it. Even M. [the eldest] is like that.

Several children, however, were encountered who exercised a strong influence over the parents and who could, as a result, indirectly control brothers and sisters. One girl acted as the family go-between for favors, as the mother reported:

Whenever the boys want something from their father, they send N. to ask for it. They know she can get it when they can't. They always did that.[46]

Although there is no formal pattern of discipline over younger children by older siblings, there is undoubtedly a great deal of informal teaching, involving a certain amount of indirect supervision and control. The wider range of activities permitted in the culture to the teenager provides sufficient inducement for the younger child to grow up in the example of older and more privileged siblings, accepting their direction and relying on their advice in situations which may be new or strange to parents who have not lived all their lives in Crestwood Heights.

Despite the ideal of equality for all members of the family, recognizable differences occur in the degree and kind of care and control exerted by parents over boys as against girls. In general, parents display greater concern over girls' behavior and activities, although there is less physical punishment of girls. Boys, on the other hand, may be permitted much more freedom. They are even expected to get into occasional trouble, to fight, to demonstrate that they can take care of themselves, assert themselves, or stick up for themselves. A boy who hitch-hikes long distances or who takes on hard manual labor for a brief period is admired, especially by the father, whereas corresponding independence in a girl would be cause for deep disquiet. These family attitudes are, of course, an essential means of training children for the dominant sex roles they are to play as adults.

The whole area of child care and control is at present in a state of considerable flux in Crestwood Heights. Fathers may differ from mothers at almost every point in the complex socialization process. Families are divided between permissive and authoritarian ways of handling children, and so are individuals·at different times or—worse— the same time. Despite the general, over-all preoccupation with individual development and preparation for a future independent of the family of orientation, the Crestwood Heights child does not receive in the family the same consistent direction where discipline is concerned that he experiences in learning to earn and to spend money.

D. SOCIAL ACTIVITIES

"Social activities" involve the Crestwood Heights family more with individuals and institutions outside the home circle than with those inside it. The Crestwooder, when he thinks of such activities, does not envisage his family group gathered round the dining-room table playing games, or grouped in a sing-song near the living-room piano. Should he associate such activities with home at all, he would naturally think of the children entertaining their own "gang" in the recreation room, while he and his wife watched television in the living-room above or played a game of bridge with friends who might have crossed Big City in order to join them. "Social activities" in Crestwood Heights mean leisure spent with persons outside the family, sometimes including kin, mostly not. These activities are considered highly important for all members of the Crestwood Heights family. They may be pleasurable in themselves, but many use them (consciously or unconsciously) primarily as important means of maintaining or enhancing social status in the community.

In other families, however, where career ambitions are not perhaps as prominent, more time may be devoted to kin and to friends apart from the father's profession or business. A Jewish girl describes her family's friendship patterns:

My father is in business with two partners, one of whom is married to a Gentile girl, and whom my father rarely sees outside the business. The other is married to a Jewish girl and has two daughters, one a little older than myself, and the other my sister's age. My parents see this couple occasionally and they sometimes visit one another's homes, but my parents are not as close to them as to members of their own clique. The other business friends of my father are mostly clothing manufacturers, and they often get together for a game of cards. However, the wives of this group, although they know one another, are certainly not close friends and never get together as a group.

My father's kin group plays an important part in his life. He has two sisters and one brother, all of whom are extremely close to one another (much closer, in fact, than are my mother's family) and there is a great deal of visiting back and forth among themselves. It is usually on Friday night that they all get together at the home of my father's eldest sister. From what I gather (I have never been there on these occasions) they just sit around and talk; or if there is a good speaker at either of the Synagogues, they attend. They often get together on Sunday evenings also, each taking a turn at inviting the others to dinner, followed by a game of bridge. They don't see one another too often during the week, but nevertheless, speak to one another on the phone every few days. . . .

And then there is the clique to which my father and mother belong. There is a group of about seven couples, composed of very old friends of both my parents. (One of the men is a first cousin of my father's; and some of the women and my mother were friends long before they were married.) The group includes a lawyer, architect, engineer, insurance salesman, and three clothing manufacturers. They meet every Tuesday night (at a different member's home each Tuesday), the men playing gin rummy and the women playing Mah-Jong. Sometimes they see one another on Saturday nights also.

Coming now to my mother, I would be inclined to say that her closest friends would be female members of the clique just mentioned. In addition to the times when they get together with their husbands, the women of the clique sometimes see one another in the afternoons. Three of the couples belong to the same Synagogue as we do, and consequently, if there is a Sisterhood meeting at luncheon, these three women and my mother usually go together. She sometimes meets one or two of the female members of the clique for lunch downtown and then goes to a show or shopping with them. They phone one another frequently, talking about mutual friends, outstanding events, and their children. All the couples, with the exception of the insurance salesman and his wife, have children, and of these, five couples have daughters of about twenty-two (including my father and mother). Every one of the five daughters has either finished or is finishing University, and four of the five are either married or engaged. Hence, the women have many common interests, and are prone to voice these over the telephone for hours at a time.

My father's kin group plays an important part in my mother's life also. She is extremely close to his two sisters and sister-in-law, often going out with them in the afternoons (aside from the times that she gets together with them with my father). She often invites one of them to a Sisterhood luncheon, and, in turn, is often invited back by them to one of *their* Synagogue functions. My mother has two brothers, one of whom lives in the States (has no children) and with him my mother carries on a regular correspondence. The other is married to one of my father's first cousins, and has two children, a married son and a daughter of twenty-three who just became engaged. This brother also belongs to the same Synagogue as we do, and Mother and his wife sometimes go to Sisterhood meetings together. They phone each other quite often, but do not visit each other as much as do my father's sisters and my mother.

As has been mentioned before, my mother is a member of the women's organization of our Synagogue [i.e., the Sisterhood]. She goes to their meetings, attends their luncheons, supports their charity campaigns, sells raffle tickets for them, etc. She enjoys going to the Synagogue for Sabbath morning services, and attends frequently during the fall and spring (but not in the winter when the weather is bad, since she can't drive).

My mother is also a member of the Crestwood Heights Home and School Club. She still attends meetings, but was more active when I was at Crestwood Heights too (as well as my sister). She still takes a great interest in what is going on at the school, and my sister keeps her well informed on school activities. A few years ago, she was a Grade Mother, and worked with some of the Gentile women in the Club. This experience, together with her contacts with our non-Jewish neighbors, constitutes her only association with Gentile women.

She has no really close friends within our block. . . . The same could also be said about my father.[47]

In this account of family social activities, kinship ties, personal friendships, and religious affiliations appear to predominate over considerations of business or professional advancement, although these are not
entirely absent. It should be mentioned that this family is neither as
highly placed nor as mobile as most. The lack of strong neighborhood
friendships, brought out in this material, is, however, generally a feature
of social life in Crestwood Heights. Friends of the family are scattered
all through the metropolitan area and even beyond it. The Crestwooder
thinks little of driving thirty or fifty miles to spend an evening with
friends. Distance, while it can be obliterated to some extent by car and
telephone, nevertheless dictates a highly formalized pattern of interaction which is very different from the casual dropping in of neighbors
at unheralded times throughout the day.

In view of the importance of social activities for family status and
for the man's career, it is perhaps somewhat surprising to find that the
Crestwood Heights woman is usually the initiator of social activities.
A busy doctor, for instance, when asked to dinner by a friend during
office hours, referred the latter to his wife, remarking "Give A. a call—
she handles all that." Social activities, no matter how institutionalized,
or rationalized, or career-relevant, are still considered in Crestwood
Heights to be primarily related to expression and emotion, which may
account for their relegation to the woman's sphere. Whatever the reason, social activities, both within and without the family, are nearly
always thought up, planned, decided upon, and carried out by the wife.

In Crestwood Heights the amount of time which the family spends together is very restricted. Breakfast and lunch are almost universally eaten
separately or in small groups at the convenience of the individual members. Dinner is frequently a family occasion. Some families tend to keep
the evening meal a purely social affair, with only light talk exchanged.
Others make this meal a time for family discussions and decisions. In
a few, the presence of all members opens up so many conflicts that it
may be felt more convenient to have them eat separately.

Other family social activities may be institutionalized on a weekly
or an annual basis. Many Crestwood Heights families try to get together
on the weekends for Sabbath observance or Sunday dinner. Birthdays
and anniversaries are occasions for a family celebration. Often friends
and relatives are included, especially for children's birthday parties, if
these are not organized as separate entertainments for the peer group
alone. On other ritual occasions such as Christmas, Purim, Easter, or
a Bar-Mitzvah, the family is drawn together for a common observance

of the day, for reaffirmation of kinship ties, and for a revival of mutual obligations, symbolized by gift-giving. For some families, such occasions are the only ones on which relatives see each other. At all these celebrations, it is the mother who is the central figure. It is she who makes all the preparations, sends out the invitations, and creates a suitable atmosphere with decorations, flowers, table settings, and emotionally appropriate symbols.

Ritual occasions are not always celebrated in the home. Frequently they are used as opportunities for "a change" and the family goes out for a meal. In such cases, although the final decision may seem to be the mother's, other members are more likely to be drawn into the plans, since the whole idea may be "to give Mother a rest."

Other family social activities are not as formal. A trip to the country or opening or closing the summer cottage may involve the father, rather than the mother. With the boys particularly, the father plays the part of task leader, one occasion on which he can assume real authority in a family project, while still being a good "pal," as recommended.

When the child participates in social activities within the home, there is no clear-cut distinction between his status as a child and that of the adults around him. The old edict that a child should be seen and not heard, of course, no longer holds in Crestwood Heights. Young children join in the conversation of their elders at the dinner table and remain in the living-room, frequently interrupting the talk of the grown-ups, demanding attention for their play. More rarely, the child may be formally included in the social activity, perhaps helping to serve at a tea or cocktail party. A European boy of four who, when invited with his parents to afternoon tea, took the toys he had brought with him to a corner, and played quietly by himself without approaching the adults, was noteworthy to Crestwood Heights. There children are not led to believe that there are certain adult privileges which children cannot share. This constant inclusion of the children in adult concerns may deprive them of valuable help in the growing-up process, since they now are not required to listen in silence while the adults carry on a discussion of their own affairs, from which children might learn a great deal about adult behavior, ideas, and ideals.

As the child approaches his teens, participation in the family's social activities grows less and he joins more and more in the peer group fun, until finally his social life may be carried on in almost entire separation from that of his parents. The parents, indeed, may become bewildered by the child's independence, since current child-rearing theories, which stress separation, almost equally stress that parents should be the friends and companions of their children.

Often in the middle teens, a new relationship is established between mother and daughter, or father and son. Girls and their mothers more frequently build up strong friendship ties around common interests: shopping, luncheons, teas (sometimes the début), and finally the girl's engagement and marriage. Boys do not find it as easy to form such a relationship with the father, since they can rarely share as yet in the father's business or profession. A few fathers and sons do become "buddies," spending time together at baseball games, hunting or fishing, or in the family car.

The young Jewish girl who gave the excellent account of her father and mother's social life, goes on to describe that of herself and her teen-age sister (italics added):

Most of my sister's friendships can be traced to the school to which she goes. She participates in a wide range of school activities (modern dance group, choir, etc.) and hence has a wide range of friends. Her two closest friends are not as active as she, and both are in fifth form, while my sister is in fourth form. Both of them live very close to us and they all walk to school together every day. The boys that she goes out with are usually those in their fifth form at Crestwood Heights. They usually met her at fraternity parties when she was with a boy from Crestwood Heights. *Thus both her girl friends and boy friends can ultimately be traced to the school.*

Another group from which many of her friendships can be traced is the sorority to which she belongs. This group is composed of about twenty-three girls from different schools, of whom thirteen go to Crestwood Heights. The sorority helps to widen her sphere of friends both in terms of school affiliation and age (since the group is composed of girls from second to fifth forms, and even the "alums" maintain their interest in it, my sister tells me).

As for myself, my closest friends are those I've made at school. One of these I've known since second form High School, and we have gone right through high school and university together. The others I met when I first came to university. Most of them are in the same course as myself, though I have one very good friend in Psychology. I guess we more or less form a clique, sitting together in class, eating lunch together, borrowing notes from one another, etc. When I became engaged, these girls held a party for my fiancé and me, and similarly when another one of the clique became engaged, we held a sleigh-ride party for her. My two closest friends are engaged, and although I do not see as much of them in the evenings as I do of my fiancé's friends, nevertheless, I think I see more of them now than I did when each of us was unattached and going out with a different group of boys.

I find in my university course, not only my close friends (i.e. those that I see also when school is over) but also people whom I consider my friends, but whom I don't see outside of school. Among these are the Gentile girls in my class, whom I rarely see socially, unless they belong to a sorority, in which case we meet at inter-sorority affairs.

Another group to which I belong is the Hillel organization, a group embracing nearly all the Jewish students at the university, and offering a wide variety of religious and cultural activities. I used to write articles for the paper they put out, and still attend some of the lectures given by distinguished guest-speakers. I've also helped to canvass Fourth Year Honor Arts in Hillel's United Jewish Appeal, which brought me into touch with people from different courses, whom I had never known. However, although Hillel has provided many cultural activities which I could enjoy and participate in, I can't say that I have formed any lasting friendships through it. It is really too large an organization for this purpose, I feel. Nevertheless, I have met people through Hillel whom I would not otherwise have met, either in my course or in my sorority.

The sorority to which I belong has helped me to cement the friendships formed at school, for many of the latter are also sorority sisters, and hence we have the added bond of working together in a joint effort for a common purpose. Through the sorority, I have not only made friends among my peers, but have formed close relationships with the girls who have graduated, many of whom are now married and have children, and with the girls who have just entered Varsity and with those in their second and third years. The sorority has thus widened my sphere of friends, and by joining the alumni group next year, I intend to lend continuity to these friendships which I have gained as an undergraduate.

Another group that is becoming increasingly significant for me is the family and friendship group of my fiancé. Since he is an only son, I was afraid, at first, that his family might resent me. However, I've been extremely fortunate in that his parents have been wonderful to me and have always made me feel welcome. His mother likes to have me drop in on her some afternoon during the week, and, in fact, is quick to remind me if I skip a week or two. However, she is also quite understanding and takes an interest in my activities. I am usually at their home for dinner every Friday night, and feel very much at home there. With regard to the friends of my fiancé, two of them were friends even before I met my fiancé: one is the son of the family who used to live next door to us and who are still such close friends of my parents, and the other (who is now married) had gone to public school with me and had occasionally taken me out during high school and my first year of university. The other friends I got to know quite well simply from the process of double-dating with them whenever I was with my fiancé. Hence, these boys were not strangers to me when I became engaged, and I have come to look upon them more and more as my own friends.

This student goes on to interpret the material she has presented:

The fact that my father's business life and his life in the kin group may be represented by two separate spheres which never touch or overlap, is quite significant, I feel. . . . Furthermore, business and Synagogue membership have little inter-relationship, suggesting the further differentiation of sacred and secular functions in our society. . . . And even business and clique are only slightly related, suggesting that the common interests which bind the clique members together are not related to economic activity, nor even to their relationship to the means of production, nor are the members of the clique all in the same class position. . . .

The separation of my father's business life, not only from his other spheres of activity, but from the friendship groups of the other members of his family is also significant. This, together with the fact that his occupation demands that he be at business from 7:30 A.M. to 5:30 P.M. every weekday, means that we rarely get to see him for any length of time during the week, and that conditions are fostered which are certainly not conducive to promoting father-child relations. The situation in our home seems indicative of that existing in many other urban families today, where the father's business role takes him outside the home for long periods, and consequently his disciplinary role in the family is changed. That is, it is the *mother* who has the central role in integrating the family, and who now raises and disciplines the children. On the other hand, my father's occupation is such that he is in Big City all the time (except for a very brief business trip to New York every March), which means that we see him a good deal oftener than we would if he were doing his partner's job of trying to sell the clothing they manufacture, out West. It also means that our family has been able to build up a stable network of relationships radiating *out* into the city and community without having to disrupt these ties every so often by moving out of town.

One very significant pattern . . . seems to be the important role of the kin group (especially my father's kin group) in the friendship patterns of my sister and myself. . . . This may be due to the group's ethnicity. . . . Perhaps ties between Jewish kin are closer than those between Gentile kin. I am really not in a position to say, since I am not well enough acquainted with a Gentile family and kin group. However, I do know, that, as a rule, Jewish people place a high value on family life. Furthermore, many Jewish families in Canada today were born in the Old Country, and it was common practice for an older brother or sister to come over first, earn some money here, and then send for the younger sisters or brothers. It seems to me only natural that such conditions of mutual help would forge bonds of kinship which would be hard to break down. Then again, perhaps the inability of Jewish people to form as many warm and satisfying relationships in the larger society (which is usually predominantly Gentile) as Gentiles, leads them to turn inwards to their own family to meet their needs for companionship.

Another important pattern is the role of the Synagogue, especially in the lives of my father and mother. The fact that the Synagogue cuts across kin and friends is another indication of the proliferation of voluntary associations in our society. . . .

From the data given, I don't think it's possible to say that our block is a neighborhood or even a part of a neighborhood, if we mean by the above a group of people living near one another who have some kind of *Gemeinschaft* relation with one another. On our block, the relations are not of this sort. Instead they are limited, segmental, and superficial. Nor can I see that our block constitutes a primary group (which Cooley felt a neighborhood to be) for the face-to-face contacts are few and far between, and there are some faces in the block which I have never seen. The only possible exception to this lack of neighborhood feeling seems to be the relationship between my parents and the family next door. It seems to me that in a complex society like ours, the block or neighborhood is too narrow and confused a sphere to lend scope to all the varied interests of the complex, urban individual. His ties of friendship and loyalty are drawn towards the groups of people who share his interests, rather than towards the group of people near whom he lives (many of whom have different interests than he).

As the analysis continues, it points out that the mother is the only one of the family who has close ties in Crestwood Heights itself through Home and School affiliation, through neighborhood shopping, and through one or two intimate friends. This is understandable because of the mother's chief concern with the home itself. Father and two children have few ties in the community. The report goes on to record the climax towards which the writer's own pattern of friendship and social activities had moved from early childhood.

An interesting trend that emerges from the data I have given and one of which I have become increasingly aware these last few months, is the gradually changing pattern of relationship between my family and myself. Whereas, before I was engaged, I used to have dinner at home every Friday night (since this was a special night at my home i.e. Sabbath evening— with white tablecloth, candles, wine, etc.), I now spend every other Friday at the home of my fiancé and I know that some day I'll probably be spending the occasional Friday night at my *own* home (the others being spent alternately at mother's and mother-in-law's). Furthermore, I expect that, *ultimately*, I will spend every Friday evening in my own home and will probably hear my own daughter, one day, tell me to set one less place for Friday dinner.

Such is the pattern of social activities for one Crestwood Heights family. It differs chiefly in degree from others, where, in the highly complex associational society, ties to individuals and institutions outside the family may come to rival the primary group bonds between family members and the kinship system, and the creation of these ties by both individual members and family group is highly valued. Again and again, the complicated network of relationships forms and reforms, continuously shifting, constantly rent. Death, the one great threat to the solidarity of the primitive group, is here not the only wielder of shears. Social mobility demands, as we have seen in a number of contexts, that the people of Crestwood Heights experience, in the span from physical birth to physical death, a series of minor psychic deaths. Father, mother, brothers, sisters, kin, friends, and neighbors are all seen as necessarily expendable. But this necessity, in all its starkness, also holds out the promise of rebirth, not once, not twice, but many times during the course of one natural life.

E. RELIGIOUS ACTIVITIES

Crestwood Heights is a community with a constantly growing Jewish population, although Gentiles still retain an uneasy majority. It is perhaps symbolic of its mixed ethnic character that there are no large churches or synagogues within its boundaries. It is, rather, the school which dominates the community as an institution: officially neutral as to religion and politics, and dedicated to the maturity values which now regulate its progressive education as well as the democratic functioning of the family. It is against the background of this shift in population and this developing competing ideology that the religious activities of the family must be considered.

The very real strength of traditional religion in Crestwood Heights cannot be denied. Several Protestant churches and synagogues cluster around its edges, all with vigorous programs of worship and recreation; and to these many Crestwood Heights adults and children belong. Yet the religious observances of the family are now tending, like child-rearing, to be a matter of somewhat uncertainly feeling one's way among numerous directions instead of blindly following one set of traditions. Since the weight of tradition bears more heavily upon Jew than upon Gentile, the Jews perhaps find it more difficult to adjust to the new norms in the sphere of religious activity. But Jewish and Gentile parents alike may be confronted with many difficult choices of behavior where religious participation is concerned, choices which their parents could not even envisage. The Jewish family recently arrived from an area of first or second settlement must decide whether or not to send the children to the Orthodox synagogue, now away downtown. Or perhaps the father must renounce position in the Orthodox fold for mere participation in the "more liberal" Reformed synagogue, a step which can hardly be taken without a twist of the heart. Or it may be that the emancipated Jew, resident for some period in cosmopolitan Crestwood Heights, may suddenly feel that he wants his children to learn "what it means to be a Jew," heir of an ancient and a great tradition. Then back into the modern décor of a Crestwood Heights home come the Star of David and the candelabra, the Menorah and the quiet prayer of kerchiefed wife before the lighted candles, the full circle of the family around the table each Friday night. The break has been made by the parents only to be healed again by the children. And so the inexorable cycle continues—orthodoxy, complete renunciation, return to a revised

version of an ancient religion, one which can more readily be reconciled
with the over-all ideals of Crestwood Heights. The difficulties of pour-
ing old wine into new bottles are well expressed by one Jewish informant:

Mrs. L. said that she tried to keep a kosher kitchen and kosher dishes.
Both she and her husband had come from religious homes but had gotten
away from the synagogue. Now she is trying to keep the elements of their
religion for her family. Mrs. L. saw this as the woman's task mainly. Men
get away from the synagogue much more readily. Women maintain the
traditions; men hold to them less.[48] She said Mr. L. had never told her to
do anything or not do anything. He said that dietary laws were just a matter
of what you got used to anyway.

The L.'s belong to a synagogue downtown near to where they used to
live. They don't go every Sunday but do on High Holidays and special
occasions.

Friday nights they observe, but they don't have candles because, as Mrs.
L. said, "I'm afraid the children might get hurt or burn something." But she
didn't do any sewing or knitting on Friday night and tried to get S. [her son]
to do the same. It was harder for children to understand. And on Saturdays, S. had to go to art class and Mr. L. to work, so it wasn't easy to be
too rigid about the Sabbath.

It was hard to hold to the dietary laws with H. [another son]. If there
was milk or ice cream, he wanted it with his meal or right after and didn't
see why he should wait. S. understood this now. Mrs. L. said H. would too,
soon. For the rest of the family, she was kosher.

Other Jewish families break almost entirely with the dietary laws and
with orthodoxy.

Mrs. M. said that she was very busy on a big party they were having on the
coming weekend. R. had just turned thirteen and they were having a Bar-
Mitzvah at the church. Mr. M. explained that this was like a Confirmation
in other churches. They used to have it just for boys but they have started
it for girls now. They read from the Torah and so on. The researcher said
that he hadn't realized there was a ceremony for girls as well as for boys
and asked whether it was based on Jewish tradition. Mr. M. replied that it
wasn't. It was something new they had introduced at a seminary in the
United States and it was not strictly orthodox. Mrs. M. added that, for the
orthodox, women weren't allowed to touch the scrolls. Women were something less than human. Mr. M. added that they just started the ceremony at
the synagogue last year. It was a good idea because it bound the girls to the
church and that was important nowadays. Mrs. M. said it was connected
with the attempt to get girls to learn Hebrew too. Formerly they never
bothered, but since in the State of Israel Hebrew had become a living
language, they wanted to encourage it. The researcher inquired whether
it was just the M.'s synagogue which had introduced these innovations or
had other synagogues adopted them too. Mr. M. replied that these were
only in the conservative synagogue now, but would probably spread—

seemed to be catching on. The Orthodox would never accept these changes, but *"things are different now and you have to keep up with the times"* [italics added].

The same cycle is evident among Gentiles, although change from one phase to another may be accomplished without the same degree of pain. Nevertheless it is not uncommon for a Gentile family to leave the downtown fold of the Continuing Presbyterians for the Unitarian Church, or the ritual of the Church of England for the Quaker meeting. Such radical changes are the exception, rather than the rule, however. Where a Protestant denomination is adhered to, it is more a matter of habit than of deep conviction, a socially useful practice rather than a source of spiritual solace. And there are as many Gentiles as Jews who conform with no traditional religious practice.

Few mothers or fathers accept easily the role of religious director in the family. But there is a widespread feeling among Crestwood Heights parents (evident also in the school) that the child should be exposed in some form or other to *"some* religious training," from which the parents may, or may not, hold themselves entirely aloof. This theory holds that the child, when he reaches adulthood, may then "make his own choice": either to continue in his first religious tradition, to renounce it altogether, or to adopt some new and radically different faith. One Gentile mother remarked in a matter-of-fact way, "After Confirmation, church attendance is voluntary and G. chose not to go. It looks as if T. will go the same way." Another, a Jewish mother, in discussing the pressure brought to bear on her by her children to conform to Orthodox ritual, made the following remarks:

My husband's family were Orthodox and observed all the rituals. *My* family was free about religion. We only observed what seemed to us significant. . . . R. finds out about the rituals from her friends and at religious school. When she asks why we don't observe them, I just tell her the plain truth—that some people believe in them, but we don't. If she wants, she can grow up to have the other rituals if she likes them. B. is different; he doesn't say much about it at all. Maybe he associates it with the past he would like to forget.

The children go to religious school. R. goes all the time. They belong to the school of Goel Tzedec, no, it's Beth Tzedec now—they just amalgamated. It's way downtown in Big City but they're building a new synagogue (that's a church) on C. street. In the meantime, they have religious school in the Crestwood Heights school. The children go from three-thirty to four-thirty. It gives them a chance to get their homework done, if nothing else. . . . There are twelve in R.'s class and in B.'s there are only four. It's hard to make them go when they get to B.'s age.

Regardless of the religious activities of the parents, most children in

Crestwood Heights get some religious training. The school offers what it supposes to be strictly non-sectarian instruction and encourages mutual tolerance and respect between Jewish and Gentile children.[49] As in other areas of family life, the entry of the school into religious training reveals the degree to which the Crestwood Heights family has relinquished many once primary functions to the school.

If the father is involved at all in religious activities, he can scarcely avoid playing some role, since churches and synagogues are administered by men who occupy the positions of greatest power and responsibility. When the man does participate, it is usually as an individual rather than as the representative of a particular family. Attendance is frequently associated with the maintenance of status and with the wish to make good business contacts. One Jewish husband commented,

. . . I never go to Synagogue unless I have to . . . but I'm on the Board of Directors. . . . I don't know why. It's because I talk too much. Everytime you open your mouth you're put on a committee.

In the many religious associations sponsored by churches and synagogues, women are much more in evidence than men and more frequently represent the family, but such activities need not involve members other than the mother.

Synagogues and churches sponsor many activities for children, both religious and recreational: Mission Band, Young People's groups, Cubs, Guides, Scouts, Canadian Girls in Training. A large number of these are secular in character and parallel neatly the similar or identical activities of the school; the competition here is between auspices, not content. Educational directors or recreation leaders are appearing in the larger and more prosperous denominations. In the child's early years, his attendance at church or synagogue and at associations which they sponsor may or may not be encouraged by the mother. But as he grows older, strong peer group pressure may be brought to bear on the child, sufficiently powerful, in some cases, to ensure his presence even though his parents may be opposed to religious training of any kind.

Thus the religious activities of the Crestwood Heights family, like those of the school, serve to gird the child with the minimum of spiritual armor, which may be shed easily in favor of other defences, should it be experienced as obsolete or cumbersome. For the runner of the Crestwood race needs, first and foremost, to be *free* for the course he has to follow. He cannot afford to be held back by old-fashioned beliefs any more than he can allow himself to be tied to old-fashioned people or material objects. Like a new and finer house, a new and advanced religion can be a powerful source of reassurance to the Crestwooder that he has escaped his hampering past and can now grasp at a more alluring and dazzling future.

RECAPITULATION

After the foregoing description of the Crestwood Heights family, one might be tempted to pose the most embarrassing question which could be asked in this community of homes, "*Is* there such an institution as the family in Crestwood Heights?" Despite the high premium placed on individual development and achievement, the answer is very definitely in the affirmative.

Weighing the socialization demanded in the culture for both boys and girls against the resources of the family to bring it about, it must be admitted that the balance is light at the family end of the scale. Yet when so much of the socialization process is accomplished inevitably outside the family altogether, it is scarcely fair to blame it as an institution for any inadequacies, or to insist that it achieve the impossible.

The internal relationships of the family are deeply influenced by the outer trends of the culture. Should these be radically altered, the behavior of the family will also change profoundly. In any description of the contemporary family in Crestwood Heights, it is difficult to avoid comparisons implying value-judgments which might obscure the fact that the Crestwood Heights family *may* be exceptionally well adapted to perform the particular tasks required of it at present. But since no family is ever completely adjusted to its environment, strains are inevitable.

The roles now demanded of each member of the family may be contradictory, impossible of fulfilment by one person at one point in time, or not creative of sufficient satisfaction to ensure continuous performance of what is necessary. Furthermore, parenthood itself is very temporary. With fewer children to rear, parents are still young and vigorous when most of their duties to their children are at an end, a situation which bears more heavily on the mother.

A plurality of roles demands, in addition, a variety of behaviors, loyalties, and attitudes, all of which must be balanced one against another; this certainly makes individual integration a more difficult achievement than it would be in a simpler culture. Just as each member of the family must reach some subjective harmony by reconciling several roles, so the family, as a group, must reach some equilibrium in order to function adequately. The family is made up of interacting individuals, each with different capacities and temperaments, who must operate together intensively for some years. If the group is to act at all, direction or leadership is needed, with a corresponding delegation and definition of responsibility among the members. Sufficient stability and continuity of roles must be established to ensure more or less consistent care and nurture for the children. But persistence of the family group means much more than a mere staying together, which can, to some extent, be legally enforced. It also involves motivating family members to *want* to stay together, without too strong sanctions from outside. Indeed, the family which is kept together only by legal and possibly moral pressure, is now regarded as bad for the children, since it will be hampered, through lack of inner emotional cohesion, in performing what is seen to be its primary function of child-rearing.

And finally, serious problems can be engendered in the family by a lack of integration in the institutions closely associated with it, in the community, and in the larger society. In a complex, urban culture, where the division of labor has become intense and specialization is minute, there will commonly be some serious lack of integration. The spheres of action of institutions can never be fixed and final, so that conflict is often latent or actual. In the case of the school, for example, the community institution which in Crestwood Heights influences child and adult more deeply than any other, official policy and parental wishes do not always coincide.

Lack of integration in family and in institutions is obviously directly related to the rapidity of social change. Cultural lag in many areas of life (for example, in ethical beliefs) opens possibilities of internal division for the family, since parents and children may disagree on many issues.

Mobility in society, as a motivating drive, probably operates, like social change, to widen the gulf between generations, creating disharmony within the family, if not partial or complete disintegration. However oriented the family may have been originally towards the values of the social class into which it is moving, it seldom, if ever, feels completely at home when it finally arrives in Crestwood Heights.[50] Frequently there is confusion within the family because of the new social behavior to be learned.[51]

The majority of families in Crestwood Heights appear, however, to function fairly effectively, despite the strains to which they are subjected. Obviously, the Crestwood family fulfils its major function of regulating sexual expression, for a large proportion of Crestwood Heights adults are married and have children. That considerable dissatisfaction within marriage does exist cannot be denied. Perhaps the mutually opposed value-systems of husband and wife, together with their separate involvement in occupation and home, make it particularly difficult to achieve deeply felt emotional unity buttressed by a satisfactory sexual relationship, as now advocated by the family-life experts. Similarly, Crestwood Heights families do produce children who are usually "wanted," but again there may also be some degree of dissatisfaction, since the presence of children necessarily curtails the highly individualistic activities of both husband and wife. In other words, the confining of sexual expression to the marriage partnership and to the procreation of children, entails very real sacrifices for the persons involved. The "wish to have everything" which Karen Horney labels as a neurotic trend of our times,[52] seems to operate in the family as in other areas of Crestwood Heights life; and conscious recognition of the need to accept limits to individual freedom for the sake of a greater good in family life is often just that—merely conscious.

Indeed happiness for the individual is an important goal of family life in Crestwood Heights. "Happiness" is not too clearly defined: it appears to be a blend of material well-being, success, social status, good physical and mental health. And to achieve it marriage is considered essential.[53] It seems more important, in the Crestwood Heights view, for the individual rather than the group, to achieve happiness, although it is a debatable point whether such happiness *can* actually be achieved at the expense of the group.[54] The great majority of Crestwood Heights residents would, however, describe themselves as happy and ascribe their happiness largely to the family.

Closely related to happiness is individual security based on a "sense of belonging," which ideally is afforded by the family. In a society oriented towards the future and thus living in a short-term present, the feeling of security also tends to have a short-term reference. Yet even many socially mobile families are successful in producing relatively stable children. The security given by the family may take many forms, from a simple provision of food and shelter to an integrated and complicated system of emotional involvements. The latter is the type of security considered ideal by the society.

While the socialization of the child is not exclusively a function of the family in Crestwood Heights, sufficient of the cultural heritage is transmitted by parents to children to equip the latter for independent existence in the world outside the home. Not all these children turn out to be happy in the sense that the culture defines happiness. Nevertheless the family, in conjunction with schools and other institutions, does produce non-dependent, achievement-oriented adults in enough numbers to ensure the continuance of the culture.[55] The price which is paid may well be a new kind of acute dependence on the approval of a rather large, ill-defined, and possibly threatening "they," the peer group of the wider society, allegiance to which is replacing deep emotional ties to the family.[56]

Even successful family functioning has its costs. Many families, probably the majority of them, are able to balance these costs, whether they be emotional tension, or sacrifice of personal wishes in favor of family goals and needs, in ways which, on the whole, are satisfactory to the members of them. For some families, however, the costs are greater than they can bear. These families are the more crucial for this particular study, since they reveal the strains to which all families are subjected. It is still impossible to state exactly why some families are more susceptible to such strains than others. Yet even a cursory investigation of families which have succumbed to strains may throw some light on those cultural situations inimical to a healthy functioning.

Conflict between parents and teen-age children is one problem productive of intense strain within the family. In some instances, the problem can be solved by a simple redefinition of roles or the meaning of activities. One adolescent, for example, a Jewish girl, found herself in direct opposition to her mother over a Zionist youth organization outside Crestwood Heights, with which the child had become deeply involved emotionally. While the mother intellectually supported Zionism herself, she was greatly disturbed that her daughter wished to take an active part in the movement and was forming close friendships outside Crestwood Heights altogether.

While praising Zionism and her daughter's interest in it, Mrs. E. suggested that this was another "stage" which M. had to pass through and "get out of her system." Mrs. E. hoped to send her to Israel for three months after her first year at University to "get it out of her system."

This impasse was dissolved finally, when the mother realized that the child's organization was ultimately dedicated to the same ends as she herself, and that only the means were different. Parent and child thus were able to agree once more.

The differences in values, attitudes, and outlook between men and women in Crestwood Heights, which we have examined in this chapter, are also, in some families, the cause of considerable conflict. Communications may break down almost completely between husband and wife. They may continue in this tense, unhappy state or there may be a dissolution of the marriage. In one case, a professional man felt burdened by his uneducated wife, who could not speak good English and who was unacceptable to his colleagues and friends. He gradually assumed the dominant role in the home, unable to allow her any leeway in managing the household, and resentful of her and their disturbed children because they hindered his career. In another family, husband and wife continued living under the same roof only by an unstable, mutual avoidance scheme.

The problem of authority within the family is another frequent source of strain, as the chapter has shown. It is exceptional to find a family in which the parents have made conscious decisions as to the responsibility they will assume, and are also secure in the stand they have taken. This ambivalence of parents towards the wielding of authority has unfortunate consequences for family stability, since continuity and consistency in the child's relation to his parents are essential if the socialization process is to be effective.

In a highly individualistic culture such as Crestwood Heights, the family tends to become an aggregate of persons with little reason or motivation to stay together, although its primary function will then be affected adversely. The temptation to grow apart is much stronger for the parents than it is for children who are naturally, because of age, in a subordinate, dependent position. One, or both, parents can easily leave children in the charge of a maid or a baby-sitter while they take a winter vacation in Florida. But unlike the children of the South Seas, described by Margaret Mead,[57] Crestwood Heights children cannot pick up and visit kin if conditions at home are not to their liking! When family goals, as is frequently the case in Crestwood Heights, become secondary to individualistic goals, it is extremely difficult to provide the psychological atmosphere which will produce emotionally stable children, in the terms defined by the culture.

Physical proximity of family members does not necessarily mean relatedness in Crestwood Heights. One mother, for instance, complains that her husband rarely "sees" his daughter, although they spend a great deal of time "together."

Mrs. X. said that B. rarely sees her father. Mr. X. started to deny this, but didn't get far in advancing his opinon. He did say that they spent a lot of time in the same room, mainly after dinner when he wanted to turn on the TV, and B. wanted to practise the piano.

In another family which claimed a high degree of cohesion, it was obvious that the family was held together by a routine which regulated every minute of time for each member and even the occasion and display of affection. Where genuine solidarity is absent and must be artificially created, the results are obvious in insecure, disturbed persons, whatever the professed emotional climate of the family.

One final and particularly devastating strain upon the family occurs when the child is required by parents to meet certain culturally approved standards of behavior which are beyond his innate abilities. Whether or not such pressures arise from the parents' failure to achieve satisfactions either within the family or outside it, or are due to their high aspirations and social mobility, it is all too common to find in Crestwood Heights that many children are driven towards unrealistic goals. A child who is not academically inclined, or who is mentally dull, may be forced by extra tutoring and parental badgering into competing unsuccessfully for university entrance. Or a plain daughter may be pushed by an ambitious, pretty mother into social situations which she cannot handle. Such demands produce disturbance in the child, frustrate family hopes, and endanger status. It may well be that a child's failure to achieve is the greatest threat to family integration in Crestwood Heights. And beyond any doubt, cases in which a child has, for one reason or another, been unable to meet parental or school requirements in social behavior, predominate in the Child Guidance Clinic.

Since the family is a unit of the wider society, while it is affected by outside trends, it, in its turn, influences the society around it. Sometimes an imbalance within the family may, in the long run, benefit the society to some extent. Out of the value-differences and dissatisfactions of the family come various activities in which individuals attempt to find a meaning in life outside the home.[58] The woman who compulsively devotes ten hours a day to community, church, or charity enterprises, may make a very real contribution to society, if not always to her family. Perhaps, however, the very strains of family living, the value placed on independent achievement even within the home circle, may create the type of character most appropriate to the occupational world in which it must now function.[59]

Whether or not the gains outweigh the losses for the society as a whole we do not know, but we do know that there are some individuals in Crestwood Heights for whom family life holds no satisfactions, while their life outside the family similarly yields few compensations. The participation of such people in outside activities tends to be low, and through the few they undertake, they tend to spread their dissatisfaction. This process may be seen clearly in the schools, where it is frequently the unhappy, or even neurotic, parent who makes the most complaints —or is the most compliant. How far the present structure and functioning of the family influences such individual attitudes can only be suggested by this study.

But it does seem safe to state that family organization, as it exists at present, while it may supply the community with persons for positions of leadership, also creates persons who are problems. The families which produce children who are either highly motivated to achieve beyond their capabilities or who lack sufficient motivation to achieve at all, become a worry for the school and ultimately for the Child Guidance Clinic. The school, while it sponsors to some degree the high achievement goals favored by the parents, is sharply aware of the dispassionate results of its own psychological testing, and is therefore considerably more realistic in its assessment of over- and under-achievement (two of its perennial problems). Even for children who have the intellectual ability, the ambitious drive towards scholastic success is always tempered by the fear of failure, and this fear may be just as real for the child who dares not try at all. When the child's life both at home and at school is dominated by only two extremes, "failure" or "success," the chances of his becoming the autonomous, spontaneous individual envisaged by the maturity values are considerably lessened. And when the parents themselves are subject to the same fears, membership in the family will heighten rather than diminish tension and insecurity.

To some extent, the growing power and authority of the school have stepped into the vacuum created by the changes in the functions discharged in family life. Concentration of too much responsibility for the child's socialization under the school's jurisdiction may, in its turn, become a community problem. There is, perhaps, a danger in the concentration of too much power in any one institution. It may result in the recreation (after the Reformation interval) of a new, secular, but equally monolithic and all-pervasive "church" and a new society sharply bifurcated again into "clergy" and laity, distinguished by their unequal access to, and control over, the means of "salvation." The true threat is the emergence of a school monopoly in these goods—which are more important than the mere goods of economics.[60]

Highly individualistic, success-oriented persons, such as the Crestwood Heights family tends to produce, may be eminently suited to the business world but of limited usefulness beyond it. Although responsibility to the community is a value strongly stressed by home and school alike, there does not seem to be widespread participation in local affairs, particularly in the case of men. General apathy prevails towards municipal politics—and, we sense, politics in general—although there are notable exceptions, especially among women's groups. Clubs and associations are similarly used to reinforce status and prestige, with the public service aspect as a secondary consideration. To date, there have not appeared in Crestwood Heights any clear-cut definitions of individual or family obligations to the community, although "social consciousness" is widely held to be an important value. Families have not yet reached the point of solidarity and security which allowed the English upper-middle and upper classes to assume responsibility in community affairs as a matter of course, through long-established and sharply delineated patterns of social behavior.

What of the future, where the Crestwood Heights family is concerned? Will the emerging norms stressing democracy and the maturity values be sufficiently strong to buttress it against the strains placed upon it by the highly individualistic and diversified activities of its members, now that religious and even legal sanctions which once tended to preserve the family are obviously weakening? The needs for companionship and emotional security, which are seen by some sociologists[61] as possible foci for integration within the modern middle-class family, are, as we have seen, difficult to satisfy in Crestwood Heights.

Margaret Mead[62] suggests that North Americans cease to be nostalgic about the family of the past and that they accept their constantly changing society, with all the opportunities it offers for individual growth. If, she contends, the maturity values are emphasized, society must be so arranged that corresponding personality changes are not impeded by anachronistic laws. If divorce is recognized and applicable for such causes as one marriage partner outgrowing the other; or if the right is accorded each individual to shape his life as he himself wishes, then, says Margaret Mead, marriage will be undertaken with a more serious realization that husband and wife must work at the relationship between them, if they wish to preserve its value. Such an attitude, in her view, might subject marriage to greater dangers, but, at the same time, make it more meaningful.

The concern which is now evident in Crestwood Heights over human relations, uncertain, misdirected, and fumbling as it sometimes is, might well serve to further the kind of ideal marriage and family life which this social scientist envisages for North American society. With the marked trend towards individualism in family life, it does seem obvious that some such new values must emerge, if the tendency is to be halted at a point which will preserve some measure of family integration. Another social scientist, also a woman it is significant to note, adds a recent word on the subject of the contemporary, upper middle class family in North American culture. "If we are to produce achievement-minded, future-oriented and independent individuals, we must have the kind of family which permits individualistic expression and allows its members to go free of bonds that would tie them to particular people and places. . . . For all the strains which may be and are created by our having small and independent families between which bonds are few and tenuous it is a family type suited to our kind of society."[63]

Perhaps it is!

8. THE SCHOOL

Secondary Socialization

THE COMMUNITY of Crestwood Heights is, literally, built around its schools. It is the massive centrality of the schools that makes the most immediate physical impact on any outside observer coming into the Heights. In the absence of industrial development and of any large commercial center, the schools (and the houses) assert the community as a physically organized entity, as a psychological reality, and as a social fact. The churches, impressive though they are, remain marginal to the area spatially, since almost all are on the outskirts of Crestwood Heights proper, and perhaps also morally. It is true that giant apartment houses tower above one school at least. But these are, at present, only isolated intruders in a community of homes; and they dominate the area as impersonally as mountains, detracting little from the human interaction between home and school, which is carried on at eye level.

The school buildings, whether they stress the modern, clean lines of functional design, or the hominess of a Georgian country house set off by greensward and shrubbery, are thus an integral part of the landscape, a bridge between the homes, where the children are, and the wider community. The physical facts of school architecture mirror impressively the social facts. The school dominates the social scene; and in the structure of child-rearing, the major industry of Crestwood Heights, the school is all-important. The socializing function of its schools may be somewhat peculiar, in degree, to Crestwood Heights, but the development of the community can only be understood if the evolution of the School itself, as a social institution in Western culture, is comprehended.

THE HISTORICAL ROOTS[1]

A. EDUCATION IN THE WEST

The historic origins of the school in the Western world are inextricably interwoven with the development of the Holy Catholic Church, which, sometime after the collapse of the Roman Empire, began systematically to train a numerous personnel, lay as well as cleric, to administer its complex spiritual and temporal affairs. Education was confined to a chosen few, based upon the absolute authority of the church, and with a major emphasis on salvation for the life to come.

However, even during the Middle Ages, the church did not entirely dominate education. The institution of chivalry, intimately associated with feudalism, trained the second great social order of this period, the lords temporal, who ruled their respective realms, often under churchly tutelage. This type of education was aristocratic and secular in essence, differing in method and emphasis from the training given by the church, and directed more towards life "in the world."

As, later, the cities of the Middle Ages grew from small clusters of buildings around a castle or cathedral to busy trading centers, a third educational system arose: the craftsmen's gilds. Although not concerned with education in any formal sense, the gilds were structured institutions, which gave vocational and social training to their members, as well as a status in the society. The rise from apprentice, through journeyman, and finally to master, provided for social mobility and foreshadowed the future middle class of wealthy burghers. Many of the tasks which members of the gilds performed were in the service of the church, but the training they gave was of necessity largely practical and secular.

A fourth type of education appeared towards the end of the Middle Ages, when the counting houses of the Hanseatic League, Venice, and other rising cities demanded still a different kind of individual to carry on their growing business. The abstract knowledge of the theologian or the courtly training of the knight became useless in the new cultural context which demanded concentration, first on things, and later on people.

With the discovery of printing, education spread slowly to the bulk of the population, spurred on by Protestant doctrines of salvation which made it obligatory for each man to search the Scriptures on his own behalf. But printing could not be confined, even by the power of the church, Catholic or Protestant, to the Bible alone. Following the Renaissance and the Reformation came the centuries of scientific discovery; of widening geographical horizons; of revolution for the right of every man to determine his own political and religious destiny: a struggle during which print played an all-important part in the securing of free education for the many rather than for the few. The growing industrialization of the Western world began to demand skilled technicians in bewildering diversity, with the consequence that education largely forsook its aristocratic and philosophical orientation, heritage of the Middle Ages and the Renaissance, in favor of a secular, practical training.

Only slowly did the school differentiate itself as a separate institution from the churches, Catholic and Protestant, which had sponsored it originally.[2] Now, however, the word "school," to the average North American, symbolizes a unit in a publicly financed "educational system." He does not usually think of the school as being associated with any other institution, although he may be vaguely aware of the wider network of which it is a part. In countries such as the United States and Canada, public education has become one of the most important socializing agencies, as well as the most certain means for upward social mobility.[3]

The educational systems of present-day Western countries have become tightly knit, interlocking bureaucracies, staffed by administrators and specialists, providing more or less similar curricula, and aimed primarily at preparing pupils for a middle-class vocation in a highly industrialized culture.[4] With centralization, bureaucratic organization, and specialization, the actual teaching situation at the classroom level is undergoing changes. The career line, particularly for the more able teachers, points towards the acquisition of more and more qualifications which will permit movement upward in the educational hierarchy, leaving the teaching itself to less experienced, less ambitious, and often younger teachers.[5]

B. EDUCATION IN NORTH AMERICA

The goals of education in North America are, more and more, the preparation of individuals to fill roles in a highly specialized industrial society and the socialization of children in terms of the middle-class values which are the regulative ideology of North American culture. Education, under the direction of the national state, is secular, emphasizing vocational skills to be used in the present. The liberal, humanitarian, aristocratic tradition has been shifted from its central place: preoccupation with the content of the curriculum has yielded to concern with the general socializing function of the school.[6] The social personality of the upper middle class child in North America does not derive, as is (or was till recently) the case in England, from the internalization of the aristocratic and balanced wisdom of the classics, supplemented by a rigid program of physical exercise. North American education is, rather, split between vocational training and extra-curricular activities specifically aimed at socializing the child in terms of middle-class ethical and social values; it is based only in part (and at second hand) on the democratic, liberal, and humanitarian values of the past.[7] North American education now aims to prepare *all* children for secular functions in an urban, industrialized society. The liberal and humanitarian values have been blended with or confused among values that will best further the industrial development of the Western world, a development now reaching a new climax on the North American continent. The regulative ideology of the North American culture is now transmitted by way of the school more than by way of any religious or other institution.

C. EDUCATION IN THE PROVINCE

In the Province to which Crestwood Heights belongs, several social strands are deeply woven into the historical background of education.[8] Education and religion were the focal points around which centered the struggle for power between a small minority of England-oriented landed gentry and the great majority of small farmers and village storekeepers. A long-drawn-out struggle between a Church of England bishop and a Nonconformist preacher revolved around the freeing of popular education from the domination of the Church of England and the widening of the task of education to include the whole population rather than the wealthy few. Ironically, the victory of the Nonconformist forces, perhaps even more passionately religious than their Anglican opponents, opened the way to the virtually complete secularization of education in the Province. Yet this religious background has left behind a residue of habitual formal acts and accepted psychological attitudes in the teacher. The reciting of the Lord's Prayer and Bible reading may still continue in schools which are officially neutral towards denominationalism. And in many teachers a sense of religious mission is strong. "I couldn't teach if I did not feel I was bringing the children closer to religion," one Crestwood Heights teacher put it.

A second influence on educational development was and is the change from a rural to an urban, industrial economy. The cluster of small farms and crossroads villages on the fringe of the wilderness slowly evolved into cities built around growing industries. This progress of industrialization was accelerated by World War I; and it led to a shift in the basic Canadian economy, from agriculture and the production of raw materials to manufacturing, during World War II. Fortunate geographical location and dense population made the southern wedge of the Province in which Crestwood lies the industrial heart of the nation.

The pioneer society of the Province was relatively simple in its structure. The early ruling class had one definite educational program:

As guardians of the Simcoe tradition, Strachan and those who saw with him had sought to rear in Upper Canada a social system which like the constitution should be the "exact image and transcript" of that of England. In religion, all should defer to an Established Church, and contribute to its support; in education, a few well-placed Grammar Schools, and at the capital a preparatory College and a University, should produce the men to maintain the system. But already the people of Upper Canada were objecting to being pressed in any such mold.[9]

For the bulk of the population, the one-room rural school was considered sufficient. This institution gave children chiefly those facts needed to function *vocationally* in their culture. The home was held responsible for the social development of the child. The church was still the authority for ethical training; the parents were to act as its deputies in the family. The teacher was concerned about character formation only to the degree that the character so formed facilitated the acquisition of the facts the school was empowered to impart.

With the change from a rural to an urban culture, the division of labor became increasingly complex, and technical skills were called for far beyond the capacity of the one-room rural school to teach. With the move from country to city, the family, too, changed in character. No longer a patriarchal, tightly knit group, organized as a productive unit, the family itself became more specialized and diversified in its roles. These shifts have resulted in a greater reliance upon institutions other than the family to socialize the child, and it is the school which has now become the dominant socializing agency. Neither church nor family now possesses enough or suitable means to teach the child many of the necessary roles of adult life; they can be learned only in a prolonged, intensive, and specialized formal training.[10]

The one-room school, accordingly, has been transformed into the large, highly specialized educational plant which is the school of today. The training of teachers has also been intensified and diversified; and specialization within the profession has become the norm. The administration of such a complex institution as the school has become a profession in itself. The Principal of a large urban high school, for example, does not now usually teach classes himself. Directors of education, school inspectors, provincial administrators of education, all the members of the vast educational hierarchy, stand over against the local citizen boards of education, which still control the tax-supplied funds. Within the curriculum itself, there have been great shifts in emphasis. The early school had concentrated on "the three R's." Discipline, of course, had always been a feature of this educational system; but the attention devoted to character by the school was almost completely in the direction of breaking the child to a suitable point of docility, not so much for this virtue's sake, but because it was believed that only in this state would he be receptive to the learning offered.[11] Scant importance was attached otherwise to the child's *feelings* about the process in which he was involved. Nor was the school concerned particularly about the child's capacity for co-operation with his fellow students. Children were regarded by the teacher somewhat in the light of numerous passive receptacles to be filled with the milk of knowledge, which need not necessarily flow from one vessel to another, providing it brimmed to the top in each separate container.

A highly interdependent and complex urban society, however, demands a more flexible, "co-operative," and at the same time, individuated human being to function in it. Respect for individual personality, the necessity so to use the child as to assure a constant flow of suitable personnel for industry and business, and insight into the role of early experience in forming the personality structure of the child—all have played a part in directing the concern of the school towards the mental health of its pupils. The older idea that the efficacy of education came, to some degree, from its difficulty and unpleasantness, gave ground to the idea that "experience," gained in free exploration of the environment, is the true educative force.[12] A great paradox at this point confronts the school. The child must be free in accordance with democratic ideology; but he must, by no means, become free to the point of renouncing either the material success goals or the engineered co-operation integral to the adequate functioning of an industrial civilization.

To succeed in modern, urban society, the child must learn to maintain both competition and co-operation in a delicate balance of forces, and he must develop this balance through the learning situation itself. More exactly, he must learn a kind of covert competition, much more strenuous to keep up than open competition or abandonment of competition altogether: he must compete but he must not *seem* competitive.[13] The school deals with the dilemma by overtly "promoting" co-operation (for example, by adjusting the teaching program and methods so that group experiences replace "individualistic" learning) and by covertly "tolerating" competition (for example, by retaining the system of competitive examinations and marks, modified to some extent through the years).[14]

The social mobility of upper middle class families forces the school into a wide program of preparation, involving both social skills and technical training. In many cases these families have attained their status only recently; the parents have themselves not sufficiently absorbed the new folkways and hence cannot readily transmit their "own" culture patterns—not to mention the patterns of the lower upper and upper upper classes, into which there is a possibility that their children and grandchildren may eventually move.

Generally speaking, indeed, while the curriculum is organized around practical subjects, the social expectations of many parents are centered around their children's learning the behavior patterns of a superior class. Secular knowledge, in the sense of technical know-how, is of course a prerequisite for the occupations, which are the one avenue, in the absence of a long-established privileged class, towards a social status still to be achieved; social knowledge, *savoir faire*, an appropriate social character are equally indispensable.

These various necessities of today have created a type of school different even from that of several decades ago. The public schools which served the urban middle-class Canadian in the twenties were relatively uncomplicated in their organization. They existed to prepare children to earn a living within a somewhat limited and, it was believed, predictable range of occupations, and the emphasis at the elementary school level was upon the inculcation of "the basic skills"— reading, writing, and arithmetic—in an atmosphere which made but slight concession to comfort or to beauty. Some degree of specialization was recognized in the provision of simple woodworking for boys and domestic science for girls. This education was not noticeably different at the secondary school level.[15]

Children, in this urban school system, passed eight years in the elementary school, and four or five in high school or collegiate. Some attention at the elementary school level was paid to the physical health of the pupils and to their level of intelligence, but there were few attempts to help children who, for one reason or another, fell outside the normal range. Discipline was rigid, and corporal punishment common. The black rubber strap was made familiar to almost all children, by hearsay, or by strappings which took place before the class or in the Principal's office. The seating arrangements were as inflexible as the disciplinary measures; silence was a value for which to strive; and formal recitation, the approved method of learning. The left-handed child was forced to conform with his right-handed fellows; the tone-deaf child (stigmatized as a "listener") was prevented from singing with the class, and the "project method" was used sparingly, if at all. Entry to the school was stringently controlled, girls entering by one door and boys by another. Children filed into the school in a single line, with teachers at the top and bottom of the stairs to ensure with warning bell that no intrepid soul deviated from the allotted path. Boys and girls were segregated even at "recess." A not unusual disciplinary measure moved a fractious boy to the "girls' side" and vice versa. The appearance of the Principal, the school inspector, the music supervisor, the school doctor or nurse could throw a whole classroom into consternation, bordering on terror for the more timid, and indeed raise anxiety in the teacher—who passed it on to the children, directly, or by her increased severity or excitement.[16]

Competition was not veiled; even in the early grades appropriate conduct and academic progress were rewarded with gold and silver stars. In the higher grades, a report card unequivocally stated the child's academic standing, paying little attention to personal qualities other than by the ubiquitous "mark" for conduct, defined almost entirely in terms of conformity to school values, the chief among which was obedience. The school concert, generally a set of unrelated pieces, starred individuals, and gave only slight attention to group effort. (This star system is still in use in Crestwood schools, but within an atmosphere of good-humored camaraderie—"We can't all be stars, can we?" The child here is thus encouraged to strive and to enjoy the visible fruit of success, but he is also cushioned against failure, and protected, to a degree, from the antagonism of the vanquished, by an attenuation of the reward. This duality is carefully maintained so that there are always two frames of reference available to the child: one, gratifying if he succeeds; the other, comforting if he fails.[17]) Such physical education as there was consisted of drill and exercises, which emphasized individual rather than concerted action, under a direction reminiscent of the parade ground, sometimes indeed under former army men. Social learning was purely incidental and occurred chiefly in relatively unstructured play at "recess."

At the secondary school level, the early direct regimentation slackened somewhat, but the competitive pace was intensified. In the urban high schools and collegiates which specialized in academic studies leading to university, students were groomed for scholarships as carefully as athletes for track meets, with no attempt on the part of the school authorities to cloak these obvious facts. The efforts of teaching staff and such peripheral experts as existed were concentrated upon academic subjects and semi-professional sports, which left the social life of the school to the students, under some informal teacher supervision. The social distance between teacher and student was considerable, with little or no pressure upon the teacher to act in the capacity of counsellor or friend towards the student.

The parents did not usually impinge upon the school system at any point, except when the child was in some serious disciplinary difficulty with the school authorities. Fathers and mothers entered the school buildings only on certain occasions: for prize-givings, for the school concert, or the school play. The Home and School Association had not developed to any great extent; and, where it existed, the emphasis was less upon parent education and more upon independent social activities among the members, mostly aimed at fund-raising for supplementary school equipment. The school, for its part, felt little need to create "good public relations" with the parents, and the latter were not consulted at any point about school operation or policy. Indeed, Home and School activity was (and in many places still is) regarded in the light of an unwarranted and impertinent intrusion into the functioning of the school. The demands of education upon the tax structure were not sufficiently exorbitant to cause much more than a ripple of concern among the tax-paying adult population, and even this protest was part of the expected formal behavior culturally enjoined wherever any public expenditure was in question.

The primary focus of this type of school was upon the transmission of factual knowledge.[18] The discipline was engineered to facilitate rote learning, and it was bolstered by a complicated mechanism of frankly competitive rewards. This combination of strict discipline, in which corporal punishment was included, and reward for competitive effort was thought to provide the appropriate motivation for learning without which, it was held, learning could rarely take place.[19] Schooling was not considered in terms of current life experience; rather it was to provide convenient tools to be used at some future date when *real* life— earning a living—should begin. Both boys and girls were subjected to much the same kind of education, apart from minor concessions to sex difference.[20]

The prestige of the school has increased greatly since the era of the twenties. As a profession (if, indeed, it was so considered at that time) teaching in urban areas ranked then much lower socially than law, medicine, dentistry, the ministry, or almost any position in business or in industry above the rank of clerk or foreman. For the elementary level, "Normal School" (following "Junior Matriculation") was the standard preparation for the teacher. University degrees were not general, except sometimes for school principals, inspectors, and, of course, some secondary school teachers. Salaries were low, so that few able men were attracted to the schools.[21] Community attention to overseeing the "moral" behavior of teachers, both male and female, while it did not attain the degree of minute regulation characteristic of rural areas, was considerable, even in the larger cities.

World War II had serious repercussions on schools and teachers. The latter abandoned their positions in such numbers that grave consternation arose among parents who had unquestioningly accepted the service rendered their children by the educational system, without much consideration in any human sense for the people who supplied it. For the first time in Canadian educational history those teachers who remained in the schools found themselves in an exceedingly strong bargaining position. Instead of a somewhat despised minority service group, with supply exceeding demand, teachers discovered that the whole social system was disrupted when there were not enough of them to supervise the children assigned them by law for the major portion of the year. Salaries, in consequence, were increased, with the result that professionally minded educational administrators were able to insist upon higher standards in teacher training. Although many schools, particularly in the rural areas, were forced by shortages of teachers to lower qualifications, those teachers genuinely concerned about professional standing found it possible to advance their claims for recognition.

Further urbanization and technological development in these years also profoundly affected the schools. Canada was entering upon a period of rapid expansion, with a rising standard of living, particularly among the upper middle class income group. Under the prevailing ideology, positions of power and reward in the social structure were to be accorded to those best qualified, and each individual had a right to compete for social status by developing, if he could, those qualities which the status demanded. Since the strategic power positions, apart from those in government, were to be found first in the area of technology, and later in commerce (especially finance), education in terms of know-how and of the ability to manipulate personality within the new complex industrial and occupational structure became a paramount need. Because both government and technology had advanced with incredible rapidity, preparation for new skills and new behavior patterns was essential. The church and family, which had traditionally mediated the Christian ideology, also looked to the school to perform the task for which they were becoming decreasingly competent. The school thus began to assume responsibility for the simultaneous transmission of the humanitarian values, the technological knowledge, and the "co-operative skills" which alone could enable the increasingly complex social structure to maintain its equilibrium. The social need which the school was adapting itself to meet supported the move within the educational system itself towards professionalism and specialization.

THE SCHOOL UNFOLDS IN CRESTWOOD HEIGHTS

It is not by accident that Crestwood Heights has literally grown up around a school. This development has the same social logic as had the cathedral-centered communities of medieval Europe, or the chapel-governed towns of seventeenth-century New England. There could be no better indication than this central focus in the school that a great cultural shift has occurred towards a society most of whose dominant concerns are now secular.

A member of the Board of Education, in a speech to the community, stated that Crestwood Heights and the school are one and the same; that the Crestwoods Heights social and municipal organization virtually exists to make the school possible; that the school is the center of the community, and that everything revolves around and within it. He spoke a little as a Catholic priest in some French-Canadian parish might about his church. Summing up the relation of the school to Crestwood Heights, he said "The school is all we have."

This dominance—physical and psychological—of the school over "its" community has many causes, and a long history. The virtual co-emergence of school and community, the nature of local class structure and ambition, the relative weakness or weakening of other institutions; new sources of power in the school, and of influence and capacity and concern: all these combine to force the school towards a lone eminence, from which it can hardly be said to have actively fought shy.

In the first place, the school system of Crestwood Heights was co-existent with the establishment of the community itself, and has been largely responsible for the community's subsequent growth. School and neighborhood have evolved together. The reputation of the schools has been, and still remains, the magnet drawing residents to the area.[22] In turn, the increasing population has necessitated the expansion of the schools from one original plant to five units: three elementary schools, a junior high school, and finally a collegiate. Qualitative improvements, in turn, attracted still more people, who would demand still better education, to the community. At the present time, these units, in combination, form an educational system well known throughout Canada for its bold, progressive, and experimental orientation. The school meanwhile has by no means remained a static core for the community. It rather incorporates, and sometimes leads in, all the marked changes in educational theory and its application which have occurred throughout the North American continent. A constant stream of visitors from Canada and abroad passes through the schools of Crestwood Heights, to watch and absorb the latest and the best in Canadian educational methods.

The quantitative changes in the Crestwood Heights school system, since its beginnings in the early 1920's, are relatively easy to demonstrate since these depend on figures which are readily understood and impressive to the eye.[23] The qualitative changes are more difficult to assess, since these are contingent upon rapidly changing values which both play upon the school from the outer world and also directly and through the school mold the ideology of the community to which the school is central.

In a community such as Crestwood Heights, the social forces described in the last section play with peculiar force and tend perhaps more rapidly and more radically than elsewhere to force the school into the role of cultural *factotum*. In the Heights live many of the men who have attained positions of considerable influence in the social structure: the unusually successful doctors, lawyers, dentists; the owners of businesses; the senior executives of large enterprises; a Lieutenant-Governor of the Province. It is true that they are not all, even the majority of them, "at the top of the tree"; there is a strong feeling among them that there are many more fields to be conquered, if not by themselves, then by their children. There is already present an emerging managerial and professional class, which clearly wishes its children educated at least to assume the positions which must eventually be vacated by the parents, if not to do somewhat better. In this area of vocational preparation where the school has long held sway, its influence and power are unquestioned.

Had it needed additional sources of power to establish hegemony, instead of having power thrust upon it, new techniques in career selection and new and more stringent conditions for admission to a vocation, would have tipped the balance in its favor. The development and use of psychological tests have added unquestionably to the authority of the school, in this area, since these together with the results from competitive examinations go far towards determining the child's vocational future. Both are tools almost wholly in possession of the school—certainly they are not subject in any way to the parents' manipulation or control. Should the parental choice of occupation conflict with the abilities of the child as scientifically determined by the school, it is almost invariably the school which ultimately wins.[24] The coveted entrance to university cannot be achieved unless the child meets standards set jointly by the school and the provincial Department of Education. And since a university degree is the most important key to occupational and vocational success, the school is left in a position of considerable power and responsibility.

There can be, therefore, little competition for the school from other directions in the all-important area of academic-vocational achievement. It deals successfully with such distractions as may exist by incorporating a great many leisure-time activities within its actual program. The school, therefore, begins to parallel the career pattern of the adult, particularly that of the male, in that it now absorbs more and more of the personality of the child in a productive, workmanlike process, leaving fewer and fewer private areas and less and less opportunity for alternative institutions to exert an influence on character development in the direction of fun or enjoyment unsubordinated to the demands of the career.

Responsibility for the child's social development has not yet, however, been left entirely to the school. In Crestwood Heights, the various churches peripheral to the municipality and a Community Center are among those institutions (which also include private social clubs) actively competing for the children's leisure time. The competition is quite marked, and goes on in what seems from the viewpoint of the children to be a situation of surplus, but from the viewpoint of the adults a situation of shortage. In spite of the recreational programs of the churches, the community center, and the school, many Crestwood Heights adults think that the children (and particularly the teenagers) have not enough "constructive" activities. The preference among parents and teachers leans heavily in the direction of ready-made entertainment under adult supervision, with the children drawn in as consultants. The resulting apathy on the part of the children is met by the grown-ups with resentment at the youngsters' "ingratitude for all that is done for them." An official of the community center expressed a widely prevalent adult attitude:

He said he had met with the children and planned a Teen Town. The children's ideas of what they wanted were far removed from what the adults wanted. The adults thought of craft groups, interest groups, camera club, athletics, informal as well as highly organized. This wasn't the children's idea at all. Their idea of quitting time was different too. Finally he'd had a real showdown with the children. They said that if they were forced out at 10.30, they'd go around to a coke bar or someone's home and finish off there! They just wouldn't come out for the time between 7.30 and 10.30. The older students wouldn't come out for that, and if the older ones didn't come, the younger ones wouldn't either. They finally agreed on eleven and to go home right after. If there were any complaints, there'd be no Teen Town. The program had been dictated by the children. They wanted a radio in the lower gym, blaring away, and the lights dim. The children even flicked the safety lights on and off. They danced in the lower gym. He'd tried athletics in the upper gym. The kids would come up and bat a volley-ball around a bit and then drift away to the coke bar. "It all seemed fairly meaningless to me and the parents certainly weren't happy about it." The children weren't to blame. "It's the parents' fault *if they don't know when they're having fun. It's up to us to teach them.*" He'd like to see a Teen Town training course for leaders: how to conduct a Teen Town, how to open cokes at a bar, how to act as hostesses, and to lead in games—*a training program to teach the children how to have a good time.* As Mrs. T. had remarked to him, "You can't learn algebra without doing the exercises" —and you can't turn children loose in a Teen Town without training. [Italics added.]

A similar attitude is expressed by the school. In an address to parents one Principal began by saying that

he hoped he wasn't raising a tempest in a teapot, but at times, he was literally stampeded by parents. "We," he said, "have been concerned about parties for a long time." They [the parties] weren't giving students enough fun. And the students didn't care whether or not anyone else was having any fun. They were just standing around doing nothing, or wandering around the parts of the school that had been left open, looking glum! The staff met with the Student Council, but had had little success in "up-grading" parties. The students were hostile to the suggestions made. They got as far as letting some member of the staff introduce a game "just to humor us [the staff]." Mr. D. added "I felt, and the staff felt, that this had been going on quite long enough! So we put it up to them. Unless they wanted 'upgraded' parties and to take in those not having a good time, we'd stop the parties altogether." *Then* they were ready to listen to suggestions.

The solution had been to have Grade parties. When the whole school had been together, it meant five hundred and sixty children. In a Grade party, there were one hundred and seventy-five. They'd involved the staff more in the planning. The Grade VIII party was last Friday night. At the time, the students said they'd had a marvellous time. Then they went home and thought it over. *Then* they decided they had had a wretched time, when they realized how much the teachers had interfered. There had been resent-ment and hostility towards the teachers, but Mr. D. said he hoped sub-sequent meetings would "soften them" and they'd be more amenable to suggestions from the staff. It meant involving the staff more. *The students don't know when they are having a good time.* It would be a long time before there was a co-operative feeling between the staff and the students which would make the parties a success. [Italics added.]

The parental view in regard to the school and the community center was also made clear in the meeting referred to above.

Mrs. K. agreed that the parents were to blame. At the same time, parents shouldn't be unduly concerned. It was just a phase the children were passing through. *But she did think they should try to find a way to inveigle them* [the children] *"so they don't criticize us so much. We should try to win them over to cooperate with us,* to let us show them what is really fun. In this community we haven't demonstrated what a cultural group could really do. If they don't know what they want, it's our responsibility to show them." [Italics added.]

Mrs. K. asked Mr. E. [an official of the community center] if the Teen Town had been organized with a mayor and a council. Mr. E. replied that they didn't want it. They didn't want cards, or membership lists. They just wanted to come in. Mr. D. [a Principal] said they just wanted to transfer the coke bar or the drugstore into the school and just hang around. Mrs. K. said there had been three attempts at a Teen Town in Crestwood Heights. In the first one everything had been provided for them, even an orchestra. Although she might be an antiquarian, it was only six or seven years ago. It had been a fair success, but just a dance. In the second, they had been given a free hand to do what they liked. It didn't last. They couldn't assume any responsibility. They couldn't balance their books at the end of the year and they never had a quorum at meetings. In the fall, they'd had a wiener roast and they went into debt over that. The few who *had* been faithful had to pay to get them out of debt. "*They* aren't able to do it alone, and they aren't going to let us do it for them."

In the area of social development, the school, as is evident from the foregoing quotations, finds itself partly co-operating, partly competing with other institutions: the church and its sponsored recreation programs, the community center and the program under its jurisdiction, and the families and their wishes. Many of the children who are the intended beneficiaries of all these efforts by parents, teachers, and youth leaders are evidently either openly hostile to the entertainment provided, apathetic, or intent on the building up of their own sororities and fraternities which are anathema to parents and teachers alike. The school, while it seems to view its recreational program as necessary to its aims—the inculcation of loyalty has a bearing on learning—still feels it proper to confer with church, community center, and family in any plans for extra-curricular activities. The community center, while conducting an independent recreational program, both for adults and for children, co-operates informally, at intervals, with the school, and both institutions encounter much the same problems at the teen-age level.

The parents, imbued with the belief that it is their responsibility to provide recreational outlets for their children, and baffled as to the means for accomplishing their ends, turn, as usual, primarily to the school for help. Since the school, as a publicly supported institution, is in a more favorable financial and official position to initiate extra-curricular activities, it tends progressively to diminish the need for church and community center programs, which are supported more precariously by voluntary contributions and leadership. Even the summer camp tends to fall into the school orbit—not officially, of course—since many teachers direct or fill positions of leadership in such camps. Camp organization tends to take over some features of the school structure, while school becomes imbued with some of the features of camp. The school, willing or unwilling, ready or unready, appears also, then, to be moving steadily into a position of dominance where the social development of the child is concerned.

The sphere of ethical and religious training is still not clearly assigned territory: the school, the various religious denominations, and to a much less degree, the home divide the labor with no clear mandate or separation of function. In the presence of a steadily growing Jewish group, the school has from the beginning laid particular stress on inter-ethnic and inter-religious respect. But where religion proper is concerned, the school is in a somewhat anomalous position. As the institution invested with the major responsibility for transmitting the dominant cultural values, it is also expected to transmit a "religious heritage," without, however, espousing the position of any one of the competing "religions" or forms of religion. This necessity, together with the special care inevitably enjoined upon a school system encompassing two religious groups supposedly as widely divergent as Jew and Gentile, accounts for something of whatever may be peculiar in the religious instruction of the schools of Crestwood Heights.

As has already been indicated, religion in Crestwood Heights tends to be emotionally cool, with a central mandate to be "nice" (in the sense of being polite) to everyone; it is, therefore, rather a guide to a style of behavior than to any particular routine of conduct, not to mention ritual. It embodies vague recommendations against aggression, and in favor of love and sympathy; but these are so qualified and hedged about that they can scarcely be considered as behavioral guides, even at this level of abstraction. Admitted to the school curriculum, these and other attenuated recommendations from Judaism and Christianity occasion little disruption of those aspirations and ultimate values which the school is under major mandate to instil.

The methods by which such views are induced and fostered appear to consist almost exclusively in the translation of pleasant small-group or primary-group experiences into a weakened vocabulary of traditional religion—as, for example, in the kindergarten pause "to give thanks for a lovely day" to some not too clearly defined "source of good" in the universe. The setting in which reverent attitudes and theological propositions, even of this diluted sort, are conveyed, is notably social, "we-oriented," and mutually approving. The central theological figure is mildly parental, displaying the attitude of an all-comprehending adult who, while he may have certain vague general standards, will continue to understand, no matter what goes wrong. This gentle instruction, while disapproved of by the traditionally religious in any case, is less likely to bring the school under the criticism of those experts who hold that the old-fashioned religion was a potent source of fear and other potentialities for emotional disability. The school must tread a perilous line between those, few but vocal, who believe the school's central mandate is religious and the experts who do not wish the child to become too deeply involved with the darker aspects of traditional religion—Hell and the Devil, for example.[25]

In spite of the ensuing uncertain and divided attitudes, a great deal of religious activity takes place in the school, permitted but not enjoined by official policy.[26] The public school, here as elsewhere in the Province, must constantly protect itself from the charge, with all its dangers to the teaching profession, that it is "a godless school."[27] To counter any such attacks, the school has created a third "position," namely, that it is not a godless school, but neither is it a school with a specific theological dogma (such as that of the "Separate School"). This position has been recently reinforced in the present state of world affairs by a widespread belief in the efficacy of religion as an antidote to Communism.

The kind of religious activity found in Crestwood Heights schools, like that of the community, has little to do with a preoccupation with *ultimate* values.[28] The questions asked by teachers and parents alike indicate that they view religion as a *means* to other and much more important ends, for example, "happiness," peace of mind, or mental health. Parents asked again and again whether a given theological teaching was "bad for the child," that is, damaging to his personality or to the likelihood of his success, in any one of its innumerable meanings—*excluding* salvation.[29] The tone suggested clearly that, if the answer to the question were positive, religion would have to be reluctantly sacrificed in favor of health or success, as the case might be. One earnest, well-informed, and competent teacher, on two different occasions, inquired with a genuine air of worry and distress whether the researcher thought the short prayers she used at the conclusion of her kindergarten classes would really harm the children in the sense of making them over-dependent, or of risking authoritarian elements in their characters and thinking.[30] In Crestwood Heights, a negligible few were encountered who were concerned as to whether the teachings of religion are, or are not, true to fact, or good as to ethical content. The question was almost always an instrumental one, as to what religion is *good for*. Traditional religious values, formerly accepted as revealed norms for conduct and belief, seem widely to have been deposed in favor of another set of values: success, health, happiness. These now largely regulate action and belief. They are received not in revelation but in education; like the values they replace, they are rarely or never to be subjected to criticism in terms of their goodness or badness.

If the relationship of the school to the church is considered in this context, an interesting reversal may be observed. Formerly the views of the church dominated the parent who in turn dominated the child and the teacher directly—and the child again indirectly through the teacher. The existing configuration would suggest that the teacher now influences child and parent, who mutually influence each other, and these, in turn, unite to influence the church.[31] The school, supported by the human relations experts and their institutions, has largely replaced the church as an ideological source, as Figure 3 suggests.

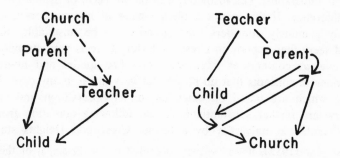

FIGURE 3. Pattern of dominance *circa* 1850 (left) and 1950 (right).

Little is known about the effects upon the child of this new attitude and configuration. It may actually obscure for him what the meaning of religion is (or might be) since those values which could become

CRESTWOOD HEIGHTS

central for him, and about which he might come to care passionately, can have no place in such a scheme of placid, well-modulated religious exercises. These do, on the other hand, appear to leave him satisfied that, whatever religion is or is not, he has about as much or as little of it as his neighbor—which may be a potent source of reassurance, from a social if not a religious point of view.

Added to these complications are others growing out of the ethnic composition of the community. In the religious activities of the school, a conscious, designed, and strenuous attempt is made to be fair to both Jew and Gentile. In spite of this, Jewish children are widely taught Christian hymns and other practices, by Gentile teachers[32] who simply know these better than any others, and have not been trained to the subtlety of picking out those hymns, readings, or prayers which might be "common" to the two cultures, in the minimal sense that nothing in them contradicts or contravenes the specific teaching of either. This is not only a matter of private classroom practice: even in such public performances as school concerts or musicales, with half Jewish, half Gentile audiences, the teachers will, seemingly without awareness of inconsistency, permit their children to sing or to recite specifically Christian material. The children, with the same equanimity, and with no sense of impropriety or uneasiness, will take part in these perform-ances. With respect to peculiarly religious connotations, it would ap-pear that, in a sophisticated, modern, urban community, the religious difference between Jew and Gentile has been reduced to the level of the difference between Presbyterian and United Church,[33] or United Church and Baptist, i.e., to the level of indifference, or distinction with-out difference. If this is not a phenomenon of non-resistance, and if nobody genuinely considers such practices to be unsuitable, then it would seem that nobody in Crestwood Heights feels very strongly that the *religious* contents at issue are more than quaint and interesting variations in concepts that do not matter very much in any case. These views, which are based on extended, direct observation and careful inquiry, are further substantiated in the following quotation from an essay written at university by a former Crestwood Heights student:

Last year [1952], it was secretly proposed to the Principal of the Col-legiate that the Jewish students be excused from singing and participating in Christmas carols and programs in the auditorium periods. The Principal, not wishing to take such a drastic step, passed around a bulletin saying that if Jewish students did not wish to attend the Christmas program they would be excused from doing so. It can honestly be said that not more than one or two Jewish students missed that program and that those who did are the ones who stay away from every auditorium assembly. Even to the Jewish students, the Christmas carols are something that they look forward to hearing.

Last year I had the opportunity to visit one of the three preparatory schools in Crestwood Heights. I sat in one of the kindergarten classes at the same time as the Jewish holiday of Chanukah is celebrated. The teacher placed on a table in front of the class the Jewish candlestick holders with the eight candles which commemorate the miracle of the burning of oil for eight days during the persecution of the Jews by the Greeks under Antiochus Epiphanes. This lighting of the candles represents the story of Chanukah to the Jews. Each day, for the length of the holiday (so the teacher explained to me) one Jewish student is called up to light a candle and to explain to the Jewish children the story of the Gentile Christmas. Thus even at an early age the children are encouraged to understand and to respect their neighbors' religion and beliefs.

It is evident that the school is more and more being entrusted with the task of developing in the child adherence to the emerging value-system of health, happiness, and success. It must pay some deference, however, to traditional values—without jeopardizing clear transmission of the new ideology. The resultant "toleration of religion" makes easier perhaps the desired and necessary inter-religious tolerance. Yet the teachers would be the first to oppose the view that traditional religion has no place in the public school, for it is the very situation described that allows teachers to express freely such religious beliefs as they may individually choose. And many are deeply religious.

Just as responsibility for the child's social and ethical and religious development is passing largely into school and other "official" hands, so also is considerable responsibility for his emotional well-being. This is almost inevitable since the emotional life cannot be divorced from the other aspects of the child's living, and the recognition of this fact has been increasingly forced on the school from within and without. From within, it has long been seen that the attempt to care for the child in so wide a sense is in practice defeated unless due attention is given to his complex inner life. From without, the experts have hammered at the inseparability of the emotional, intellectual, physical (indeed all forms of) development, and have sought to make the emotional criterion central. "You do not teach arithmetic—you teach children" is part of the modern teacher's indigenous wisdom.

The school attempts to adapt for the adequate discharge of this responsibility. The acceptance and use of the Child Guidance Clinic, the organization of "counselling teams," and its own teacher-operated counselling system bear witness to the school's extension of interest. Necessarily, the functioning of the child's family must and does become a matter of concern to the school, partly because the school is now in a quasi-parental or para-parental relation to the child, and partly because any disturbance in family life leads shortly to disturbance in school life. It is almost a foregone conclusion that the school must, if necessary, help "educate"—or sponsor or promote the re-education of —such parents as make the discharge of its responsibility difficult or impossible. If a child is "being forced too fast for his capacity" by the parents, who except school personnel can bring this to their attention, and, if necessary, point out to them underlying motives which cause them so to press upon their child? The school may do this on the basis of a particular case (remedially) or on the basis of lectures (pro-phylactically) in which this view is put by a teacher, the school psychologist, a principal, or an outside "expert": these are simply matters of tactics.

Not all teachers share these views, of course, and in the transition between one point of view and another, some confusion occurs. When the Child Guidance Clinic was first introduced into Crestwood Heights (and for a considerable time thereafter) many of the cases referred by teachers proved to be primarily disciplinary problems for the school.[34] But since the clinic, in accordance with modern practice, advocates treatment of the child in conjunction with at least one, but preferably both parents, the child's family was also involved, as home and school environments merged. The school, through the counselling sessions with clinic personnel, now became an active participant in the therapeutic process, with knowledge of areas in the private emotional lives of both children and adults equalled formerly only by that of the priest, rabbi, and minister, or latterly, the psychiatrist. School Principals (several of whom also function during the summer months as camp directors) are more and more oriented attitudinally towards the idea of the school being responsible for the whole child, which is also the prevailing school policy. However, the child's emotional life is by no means yet entirely within the grasp of the school, since the child does not live twenty-four hours a day under its jurisdiction and within its buildings.

In this time sense, the schools of Crestwood Heights do not parallel the English boarding schools. On the contrary, the school in Crest-wood Heights extends its influence over the lives of both children and adults in a *way* unknown to the traditional English schools, which are also devoted to the ideal of "character-building": they would, con-fronted with the increasingly permissive and psychiatrically oriented views of the Crestwood Heights school system, have displayed nothing but blank incomprehension. The English boarding school would have hesitated on moral and tactical grounds to breach the culturally accepted wall of privacy which allows the child to veil his innermost thoughts and feelings. Indeed, the child was encouraged to withhold these, by disapproval of too great intimacy with his peers as "soppy" and too great intimacy with adults as bordering on impropriety. And the parents were not at hand to be influenced, even had the school so desired. The difference in the social situation of the children affected is almost perfectly registered in the orientation of the school in each case.

Education, in Crestwood Heights, has thus evolved from the relatively simple transmission of factual knowledge, for the purpose of earning a living in a not very industrialized urban culture, against a material background of utilitarian ugliness, to the present-day schools, which more and more are concerned with the socialization of the whole child in an environment stressing aesthetic and humanitarian values and the direct experiencing of a highly complex outer reality, both human and non-human, as the true educative process. The focus of the school has shifted from curriculum to consumer.[35] The educational system of Crestwood Heights is becoming, to a greater and greater degree, responsible for the successful "adjustment" of the child, as a person, to the culture in which he lives. The school, as we have seen, can do little to investigate or to question the values which regulate social behavior in Crestwood Heights.[36] That it has been unable to do more is in no sense a proper criticism of the educational system. The school exists both as a creation of the society and as a perpetuating institution of that same society. Environmental forces, such as the particular tax structure of the community, help to mold the school, and impose the material limits for its operation. On the other hand, the ideological influences within the teaching profession itself are a reflection of the more comprehensive values shaping social living in the total culture, and these, in their turn, are neither logical nor consistent. There is the trend towards individual freedom and initiative, which is countered by the equally strong trend towards bureaucracy and regimentation. There is the respect for individual personality, but also the tendency to treat the person like a marketable commodity, and to encourage him, if not force him, so to manipulate himself. There is abhorrence of authoritarian tactics; and at the same time, reward and prestige for the captains of industry and finance, who maintain their power by these very practices. There is concern for both spiritual and physical health—offset by wars which can, from a distance which eliminates the human aspect of the enemy, destroy life on a scale unparalleled in history. In the face of this welter of conflicting values, it is too much to expect that the school, now the most important socializing institution in the culture, can remain unshaken by the general ideological turmoil. That it can accomplish what it does, in the face of the difficulties with which it is confronted, is one of the hopeful auguries for the future.

THE SCHOOL AS A PHYSICAL PLANT

The plant in which this cultural processing goes forward may well deserve some attention. Except for stores and offices, none of which are impressive, the Crestwood schools are the only large buildings in the community not devoted to residential use. These four school units represent the major municipal investment in education and the arts: there are no theaters, museums, or art galleries, and only one small commercial movie house. The schools are used, after hours, by the adult population for concerts, lectures, plays, and meetings. School grounds, edged by trees and shrubs and merging into streets of closely built homes, are the only open spaces of any size. But although the school grounds are ample, their wide expanses offer no accommodation for the general public, being devoted almost wholly to the play of children under the supervision of teachers. Discreet fences or clumps of shrubs succeed effectively in barring all but school children from their precincts. This physical separation of school grounds from community emphasizes the strictly age-graded function of the school.

The schools, in which, as we have seen, are provided the means of socializing the child in conformity with the community's norms, are all-important in maintaining the prestige of Crestwood Heights as an eminently desirable place in which to live. Less prosperous families moving to the district in large numbers would have an immediate and restricting effect upon the school, from the point of view of both building extension and maintenance, and of program. School and residents, therefore, have a common interest in maintaining the high income level of the community. Property values and the educational system are inextricably interwoven. They rise or fall together.

The actual physical properties of the school buildings and equipment are also closely linked to the social structure of the municipality. Crestwood Heights is a comparatively new community, and its schools were built well within the modern era of school architecture. With the exception of Birch Prep, which is in the traditional block style of architecture, they are widespread, low, brick buildings with ample window space. The design of the schools, both interior and exterior, mirrors similar developments in the houses of the community. In recent house-building there is the same tendency towards the one-floor plan with an increasing number of large windows. Inside, the schools parallel the interior decoration of Crestwood Heights houses. Gone from these schools are the gloomy walls, the floors dark and grimy from many coats of oil, the brown desks screwed with black clamps to the floor. Instead, there are movable desks in light wood, especially designed with size of occupant in mind; drapes in light shades; pictures of vivid Canadian landscapes; deep-colored walls, even "black-boards" which depart from the traditional black. Within the Crestwood Heights house, there has been a similar shift from dingy browns and buffs, heavy damask drapes, oriental rugs, dark oil paintings solidly framed in gold, and massive oak woodwork, to clear colors, light furniture, simple home-spuns, broadloom rugs in solid hues.

The school lies artistically as well as socially midway between the home and the occupational structure. While partaking of some characteristics of the house, the school manifests decorative touches suggestive of factory, office building, or department store. The Collegiate corridors with their glass-fronted, interior-lighted display cases are much like those of an exclusive shop or a luxury hotel. The combined Board Room and Office of the Director of Education has great resemblance to the topflight executive offices of a prosperous corporation, while the antiseptic school corridors, lined with lockers, are typical of a factory or a modern hospital. Where the old type of school was a monument to the efficacy of learning in a puritanically ugly environment, the new school stresses social learning in an atmosphere of lightness, color, and accepted and self-conscious modernity. The contrasting types of school building are eloquent reminders of the general cultural shift from production for acquisition and saving, to consumption for conspicuous display and spending,[37] a transition which has also manifested itself in house decoration and architecture, and which is backed by all the forces of present-day advertising.

While social change, in general, has been to a large measure responsible for the schools of Crestwood Heights, technological change, in particular, has made available many new materials and varieties of equipment. Steel construction, glass, cork flooring, fluorescent lighting, to mention only a few items, make possible the modern school building. Radio and inter-communication systems link the school with the outside world and together within its own confines. Long-playing records and pianos bring music within the range of all students. The tape-recorder and moving-picture projector add to the teaching situation a new dimension. Tennis courts, gymnasiums, outdoor hockey rinks are more easily provided (although perhaps more expensively) by present-day construction methods.[88]

The increased use of glass, both in windows and as interior divisions, is particularly striking. Glass, while it divides, does not ensure privacy. More and more, the tendency is to open up to scrutiny the social organization of school, factory, or office building, much as a scientist might construct an experimental beehive. The use of glass does not necessarily symbolize or parallel a more intimate type of social organization, as might at first appear, but may actually contribute to social disorganization by this destruction of privacy, which, as Simmel has emphasized, is essential for adequate social functioning.[89] In a similar way, such mechanical contrivances as the public address system do not always lead to solidarity.[40] Classroom doors frequently have glass panels, through which proceedings may be viewed by those passers-by who care to look in, but, while they may thus be more open to observation, they cannot be as readily surprised.[41] In this sense, the glass door may well perform a protective function. It may indeed symbolize perfectly the new type of interpersonal relations in the society—in one sense more open, in another merely quasi-open. This spatial arrangement within the school, moreover, corresponds to the decreasing areas of privacy within the modern one-floor house, where sleeping and bath rooms are in close proximity to living-room and recreational areas. In the newest schools, only those most important areas (inner administrative offices, maintenance, and toilet facilities) are completely blocked off from the casual view (i.e., glass is not used). In the older schools, administrative authority was securely buttressed behind several solid doors. In the recently completed Crestwood Heights High School, however, the general administrative offices are clearly visible behind glass, although the office of the Principal is not open to public scrutiny. In the Collegiate, cloudy glass marks off the office of the Director of Education. But where the body and its functions are concerned, the multiple protection of several solid doors is preserved without modification. Change has gone far but has affected, to only the slightest degree, the areas of most guarded privacy, those surrounding the body and the innermost administrative authority.[42]

In the interior layout of the school buildings, the center of authority, the Principal's office, is in close proximity to, but shielded from, the entrance. An outer office and a secretary, as in a business organization, separate students and adult callers from the Principal's sanctum. Corridors and classrooms radiate from near this central point.

The school, itself, is largely a material arrangement of various types of classroom. Each classroom is a physical entity, the site on which the principal social activity, education, is carried on. Each classroom is self-contained within four walls. The longest dimension usually runs parallel to the outside wall, which is invariably on the left side of the students, in conformity with the belief that the light should fall from the left. The wall opposite the windows separates the classroom from the corridor. This corridor, in general, runs between and connects a series of classrooms which are schematically similar in that their cubic footage, area of floor, window space, heat intake, etc., are about the same.

The students generally sit in movable desks facing in one direction, which is known as "the front of the room." Although the invidious, old-time platform has vanished from the front, the teacher usually has a desk in this position, where he or she may be seen and heard by the students. This desk, resembling in its flat-topped design the desk in a modern office, is equipped with drawers and provided with a swivel chair. The students each have a plain chair and a small table, or seat and desk unit with a drawer for books under the seat. The superior status and differential function of the teacher are clearly defined by these physical arrangements, even though some teachers may move their desks to the back of the classroom.[43]

Classrooms, it has been pointed out, are equipped either with telephones or with an inter-communication system which permits the Principal to talk with the teacher. These conversations are expected to be brief, and to occur only when some important matter arises which cannot be delayed. The telephone is used regularly for intrusions which the Principal would otherwise have to make in person. There is also a "P.A." system, which gives an opportunity to present a general announcement from the Principal to the whole school; to play records; or in similar ways to communicate with the entire school population simultaneously.[44] These occasions, however, are structured, and they occur, except in unusual circumstances, when announcements are expected and during the period allotted for them in the time-table. The new technical equipment offers the advantages and dangers of mass communication media, which can appear here as anywhere else: the possibility of tightening too loose social bonds—and the possibility of their being drawn uncomfortably close.

There appear to be two types of classroom: the classroom intended for specialized instruction—the chemistry laboratory, library, gymnasium, singing room, remedial reading room, conference room—and the classroom intended for general teaching. In the lower grades of the school system less of this specialization is to be noted in the planning of the classroom (with the exception of the kindergarten room) as also in the teaching assignments, the instruction, the disposal of teaching personnel.

What specialization there is in the lower grades is linked particularly to age-determined differences and competences officially recognized by the school system and by the Department of Education. Consequently the kindergarten and Grade I room are equipped to permit greater physical expression, both in bodily movement (open spaces are left for play grouping) and in the manipulation of materials (blocks, movable objects, large sheets of drawing paper, etc.). As we advance from grade to grade, from kindergarten up to Grade XIII, we can note perceptibly an increasing emphasis on subject material reflected in the wall displays and in the general rationale of the classroom construction. This finally culminates in the upper grade chemistry "lab," to which a chemistry teacher is attached, and into which flows, period by period, a fresh group of students from various classes and grades. Thus there is a linkage between first, what are recognized as the age-graded needs and capacities of the child; second, the competence of teachers to deal with these needs; and third, suitable classroom equipment to support the teachers in their instructional roles and the students in their learning roles.

The Crestwood Heights school impresses the visitor with its physical complexity, its aesthetic properties, its careful design to achieve its object and express its values. He cannot help being struck by the highly polished floors, the freshly painted and undefaced walls,[45] the vividly efficient indirect lighting, the careful control over heat, light, and ventilation (even the lockers in one Crestwood Heights school are ventilated). Why has the community felt obligated to provide an elaborate and increasingly expensive school plant? The answer is related directly to the family constellation in Crestwood Heights. The parents have been convinced that this material environment is essential for their children's present happiness and future development as mature and well-adjusted adults. On the school's side, since stress in education has shifted from concern about subject-matter to concern about the child, and since experience is held to be the true educative force (with personal interest as the motive) the rich environment comes close to being an absolute necessity.[46] Education, in this sense, is held to arise from the child's individual contacts with *outer* reality, and that reality must therefore actually exist in aesthetic complexity and variety. The emphasis upon decoration, color, and other items which impress *visually* is quite marked, and contrasts, for example, with a lesser emphasis upon books.[47]

The elaborate plant has another support from methods of teaching. Progressive education, as practised in Crestwood Heights, is connected with the new professionalism in teaching. Standards are in the process of being raised at all levels in the educational hierarchy. The increasing emphasis on advanced degrees in child training for kindergarten teachers, for example, is establishing the Dewey concepts and views firmly in the elementary school. The latter is also influenced strongly by currents from the nursery school, which, while it remains outside the state-supported school system has, nevertheless, profoundly modified kindergarten practices. Advanced training centers and postgraduate schools impress upon the teacher the necessity for considerable material equipment, if the modern educational ideas are to be "implemented." The teachers of Crestwood Heights are, with rare exceptions, well abreast of the latest educational theories, their very presence in this school system being indicative of their interest in advancing themselves professionally.[48] And increasing specialization in all school subjects, especially in science, makes expensive laboratory equipment an absolute necessity if the children are to be prepared for university, the focus of most parental hopes in Crestwood Heights. The mothers of the community are particularly concerned, in view of their high degree of literacy and sensitivity to child-rearing theories, about the young child who is entering the school system, and they are prepared to support to the hilt the teachers' professionally reinforced views as to the desirability of the best in equipment as well as in instruction. If some mothers are not at first enthusiastic supporters, they can be re-educated. Since the parents have relinquished to the school much of their responsibility for child-rearing in all areas of development, physical, social, and ethical, they are willing to support the purchase of the equipment the school considers essential if the job of socialization is to be adequately completed. This steadily increasing emphasis on the social adjustment of the child calls for an auditorium with a well-equipped stage and comfortable seating; for a gymnasium with provision for spectators as well as contestants; for space in which to hold parties and dances; and even for rooms in which to serve community groups, such as the Home and School Association.

At the present time, the level of income in Crestwood Heights, despite the taxes of World War II and following years, has been sufficiently high to sustain the educational demands upon it; and parental interests have dovetailed sufficiently with those of the school to ensure continuous public support. New schools, for example the Collegiate, have not, however, been obtained without concerted community effort (largely organized by the Home and School Association), against strong opposition. The political autonomy of Crestwood Heights has enabled the municipality to control its own educational system to date; but internal stresses arising from heavy and growing taxation on property, together with outside pressures resulting from the formation, within the last few years, of a Metropolitan Board of Education, will undoubtedly affect the support of education in the Crestwood Heights of the future.

The Crestwood school, as a physical plant, is a direct outgrowth of various configurations within the community: sensitivity to new currents in child-rearing and educational theory; the availability of modern materials and construction methods; the subtle reactions (fortified by advertising) to decorative trends, also evident in the homes of Crestwood Heights; the appeal, to parents and school officials, of expressive display; and, finally, the needs of a profession still concerned with consolidating its position in the occupational structure. Within an economic context capable of meeting these demands upon it, the educational system has taken material shape.

THE SOCIAL SYSTEM OF THE SCHOOL

The human interaction which is the social system of the school is not by any means coextensive only with its physical properties—buildings, grounds, or equipment. It is rather the sum total of all the activities taking place under school auspices, within and frequently beyond its own buildings. Indeed, the social system of the school is a network of relationships spreading throughout the whole community, and far beyond it.

Various groups within and without Crestwood Heights center their activities around the school: "experts"; the whole range of personnel associated with the teaching process itself; pupils; parents; and community groups—voluntary, for instance the Home and School Association, or elected, as in the case of the Board of Education. Each group interacts within itself and outwardly with all others, in varying degrees of intensity.

The first group, that of the experts (their function will be more fully treated in chapter 11), is, in itself, divided hierarchically. At the top stand the more eminent experts who invariably belong to the larger society beyond the borders of Crestwood Heights. It would almost be true to state that the eminence of an expert is in direct proportion to his physical remoteness from the Heights, but such an assertion would scarcely do justice to those experts from Big City whose steady presence has had perhaps an even greater cumulative influence upon the community than the meteoric appearance of more distant—often American —opposite numbers.

The eminent expert need not be directly concerned with education. In the past few years, a famous educator, two prominent social psychologists, and the public relations director for a Canadian university have been brought in as the expert attraction during the current season; each appearance was made, most significantly, at the graduation exercises of the Collegiate and under the sponsorship of the Home and School Association. The distant expert here makes a direct contact with the parents of the community, and with certain of the students and teachers, through the administrative group of the school. The Director of Education or the Chairman of the Board of Education usually introduces the speaker. On these occasions, the primary ideological target is the community.

The same expert, however, also deals on occasion with particular groups, for example, the annual conference of Crestwood Heights teachers at the beginning of each school year. Here again it is the Director of Education who makes the contact with the expert, and who usually conducts a concentrated series of meetings which are closed to outsiders. (Restrictions, however, have been relaxed recently to include representatives of the Home and School Association.) These meetings are so organized that the teaching rank and file has some controlled, direct access to the expert in the sessions for small groups held in accordance with the prevailing human dynamics technique, although a formal address by the expert has usually been an integral part of the proceedings.[49]

The metropolitan "high-level" expert might be represented by those who have had much the same type of contact with the teaching and administrative staff and with the parents as the more distant experts, but one more frequent, more prolonged, and more intensified. Here the interaction is chiefly with the Director of Education, who through his links with teachers and with the Home and School Association can open the appropriate channels for the expert's operations, or introduce him to one of the school specialists. The Director is, of course, also closely associated with the educational experts proper, in the provincial government, in the voluntary associations, and in the provincial teacher-training institutions. The importance of this aspect of the Director's role cannot be over-emphasized, since it is largely through him that the ideological influences of the expert group literally "percolate" the school and thence run on out to the community of Crestwood Heights.

A second level of the expert hierarchy ties in more directly with Crestwood Heights itself. There are, in this highly literate community, a number of local, "amateur" experts (amateur in the sense that they do not make their living from expertness as such). Some of these, with higher degrees in relevant fields, serve the school or the Home and School Association in various ways; their major contribution is made within Crestwood Heights itself since, unlike the Director of Education and the peripheral experts from the larger society, they are not on constant consultative call to other and more distant centers.

A third level of expert is now beginning to emerge within the central organization of the school proper. It may perhaps be typified in the Director of Education, who has to incorporate with other aspects of his role not only a high degree of expertness in his own field of education but also expertness in his function as the key to the interaction of the total group of experts with administrators, teachers, children, and parents. At least one other professional role, that of the school psychologist, displays a very considerable flavor of the expert. His operations, like those of the local expert, are more strictly limited to the school setting, but he cannot be classified as an amateur expert, since he derives his livelihood largely from the use of his expert skills. He is also very definitely not a "specialist," the point at which the stream of expertness appears to trickle away into the sands of the teaching profession *per se*. Like the Director of Education, however, the school psychologist could not readily make good in the school his claim to expertness unless he himself had once been a rank and file teacher— a condition which is not imposed upon the "outside" expert.

The specialist differs from the expert in that he is primarily a "doer" of child education rather than an "explainer" or a "teller." His role may, however, contain a certain potentiality of expertness—in kindergarten teaching, remedial reading, vocational guidance, individual counselling of students, and in parent education—in so far as his "explanations" of his activities take on a quality, and an intent, of oblique instruction. Specialists in these fields also have a different relationship with their students from that of the more traditional specialists in curriculum, since their ability to exercise their special skills involves a more intense knowledge of psychology, child-rearing, and mental health—a knowledge which brings them to the border of the area dominated by the experts.[50]

Within the school itself, there are a number of groups officially linked together to form its hierarchical system. The Director of Education, the

Business Administrator, and the five school Principals compose the most powerful group in the school hierarchy, setting the official school policy in consultation with the Board of Education and within the broad limits imposed by the provincial educational administrators. Here again, the Director of Education is the crucial link between the administrative groups (the provincial Department of Education, the local Board of Education, the Business Administrator of the school, the Principals of the five school units in Crestwood Heights) and the teachers.

The teachers conduct the business of the school at the level of face-to-face contact with the pupils. The teaching group is divided within itself, both in ideology and in rank, with a rough correlation between modernity or progressiveness of ideology and professional standing.

Teachers tend to be divided in their loyalties, according to the kind and order of experts who originally formed their views and upon whom, for the most part, their professional ideologies continue to depend. This situation is largely a function of age, but by no means wholly, since teachers, like other people, have the capacity for correcting their attitudes and the right to change their minds. Apart from such differences, there seems to be a clear tendency for male teachers, like fathers, to be oriented slightly more in the direction of achievement than are the female teachers. Within both groups of teachers, however, age is probably a much more significant factor than sex, since age will most often determine the period at which the teacher took his basic training. Here he developed his loyalties to those groups of experts around which his intellectual integration later took form. The rising and waning dominance of these experts, if followed over a period of years, plots ideological peak and hollow in the higher academic world.

Teachers who "went through" when Watson[51] was the last word among educators (although by this time, he had long since ceased to be the last word among psychologists) will find themselves intellectually and emotionally at variance with those who took their training when the writings of Freud and Dewey were beginning to come into their own. The succession of such experts and of such views, is therefore a matter of past history, on the one side; but, on the other, they are still incorporated in the school as a set of living cultural and social conflicts, roughly paralleling the age groups of the teachers. The situation is further complicated by the fact that these varying ideologies do not dovetail with the power structure of the school, since continued attachment to outmoded views may be a handicap to promotion. Thus, for the teacher, there is a continuous effort to reconcile age, ideology, and position.

This particular cultural conflict is peculiarly damaging and especially difficult to manage since it penetrates to ultimate presuppositions and feelings about human nature, values, methods, and human relationships, and also occurs within a group, the teachers, who have a specific necessity to present a united front, because of the emerging professionalism in teaching and because of their minute-to-minute need to exert power over and to control children on the one side and parents on the other. Their situation might be compared to that of a band of people composed of sub-groups deeply divided by character, ideology, and habit and custom, yet under strong compulsion to fight an action together against outside assailants until such time as a firm victory would permit attention to its own internecine differences.

Teaching is now considered both by members of the educational system and by Crestwood Heights residents as "a profession." This attitude has been in evidence for only a relatively short period; and, for the most part, a teacher is not recognized as the social equal of, for example, a doctor. The teacher is only slowly emerging from the status ascribed to him by Guizot and quoted with approval by Egerton Ryerson:

A good master ought to be a man who knows much more than he is called upon to teach, that he may teach with intelligence and taste; who is to live in a humble sphere, and yet have a noble and elevated spirit; that he may preserve that dignity of mind and of deportment, without which he will never obtain the respect and confidence of families; who possesses a rare mixture of gentleness and firmness; for inferior though he be, in station, to many individuals in the *Communes*, he ought to be the obsequious servant of none; a man not ignorant of his rights, but thinking much more of his duties; shewing to all a good example and serving to all as a counsellor; not given to change his condition, but satisfied with his situation, because it gives him the power of doing good;. . . .[52]

Entrance to the educational hierarchy, generally, is by way of the university, the provincial "Normal Schools," or the provincial College of Education. Training is furthered by perennial summer exposure to universities in Canada and the United States, especially to their departments and "Colleges" of Education. The selection of teachers for Crestwood Heights, however, is a complex and somewhat subtle process which does not depend entirely upon academic qualifications, although the Crestwood system has a healthy respect for professional training.[53] The process brings together a group with its own distinctive spirit, part of which is pride in membership.

. . . the method by which Crestwood Heights teachers are selected and the basis upon which they are selected, has resulted in a teaching staff which has a common outlook. Not only is their way of looking at things similar—but also many of the teachers were friends before coming to Crestwood Heights, all which tends to make of the staff a tightly knit group. They view themselves, and are viewed, as different from other school teachers. They think themselves different in terms of personal characteristics, and also in terms of teaching in a system unlike other school systems. But the differences extend further than personal characteristics and pedagogical uniqueness in the eyes of the teachers themselves. They think they are oriented in a slightly different direction than most other school teachers . . . there is an attempt on the part of the Crestwood Heights authorities to have their teachers at least moving with the times, if not before the times. All the teachers said during interviews that the Crestwood Heights school system was "progressive"; however the teachers who identified themselves as "old school," . . . hint that they find such "progressiveness" a bit strenuous, and perhaps even a bit faddish.[54]

This "common outlook" arises, it would seem, not from ideological accord, but rather from being a member of a select group. At the level of fun and social intercourse, Crestwood teachers *do*, mostly, like to be together. The divisions lie deeper at the point of doctrinal differences, which the teachers would prefer to regard as minor, when they can bring themselves to think of them at all.

Within the educational system, a necessarily bureaucratic, institutionalized social structure, the teacher is subordinate both to authority in the structure itself and to the citizen board of parents, which obviously controls the allocation of educational funds. The teacher, in contrast to the successful lawyer, dentist, doctor, or architect, is decidedly not his own boss. He has, on the other hand, a security of tenure and a financial protection which the independent professional practitioner does not have.

In any analysis of the school as a social system, and of the teacher's role within it, it is important to note the declining rewards in the actual teaching situation. The "natural-born teacher" can no longer use his or her art without having learned "techniques" from the expert.[55] And the teacher who is content to devote the whole of his or her attention to teaching tends to be regarded by his colleagues as old-fashioned. Some of these teachers may be markedly oriented towards subject-matter, bent on strict discipline, and somewhat apart from the prevailing staff *camaraderie*.[56] Should these tendencies go too far, the teachers in whom they are unduly obvious may not be considered good material for promotion.

The teacher, at the beginning of his career, must strike a delicate balance *vis-à-vis* the power structure. He must please his Principal, the Director of Education, the provincial government inspectors, and finally the more peripheral yet potent Board of Education. He has to accomplish his end without antagonizing any of the numerous specialists encompassing his path, both within and marginal to the school system. More difficult still, he must attempt to please, without appearing to do so. Like his opposite number, the budding junior executive, if he tries too hard, he runs counter to the prevailing tabu on competition and also to the society's maturity values which call for a high degree of independence and individuality. Yet if he does not try at all, he runs the risk of being thought apathetic, "unco-operative," or lacking in professional interest.

Once oriented in the structure, the teacher must, if possible, discover some way of excelling: of developing for immediate or future use some trait or talent of his own. He must, in other words, become a specialist. His road is made doubly rough by the climate in which he treads it. Although he cannot doubt the rigid nature of the structure in which he works, he is told that he is engaged in a democratic process, that the atmosphere is exceedingly tolerant and permissive. He constantly hears that all members of the hierarchy are equal, although he qualifies this statement by what he knows about the salary schedule.[57] These assurances, however, fail to lull him to a sense of false security; and he prudently devotes his summers or evenings (or both) to the acquisition of higher degrees, the open sesame to a field of specialization and subsequent promotion; such efforts indicate that the teacher is well aware of the hierarchical aspect of the institution in which he works.[58]

One speaker, during a conference of Crestwood Heights teachers, touched on this point of an opposition between democracy and hierarchy.

"We have placed a lot of emphasis on democracy in the classroom, but how can we get democracy in the school as well?" He went on to state this problem not in political terms, but in terms of almost primitive communism. He said "How can we equalize the busy and the lazy, the progressive and the conservative?" (The only contribution the researcher made was, at this point, to indicate that it was in our democratic tradition that the governed should elect their governors, but the teachers did not elect their Principals, and the students did not elect their teacher. . . . This contribution was not made in the tone of a full participant and they [the teachers] were able, as a result, to smile or laugh in a kindly way at the thought that this idea could be considered.)

This is a paradox that lies at the very center of the concept of teaching as a profession. The lawyer or the doctor, while subject to strict control in the exercising of his professional role, does possess some power of sharing in the election of the professional association which regulates the practice of law or medicine. Within certain limits, which the doctor or lawyer participates more directly in setting, each is afforded a wider freedom of action than the teacher is allowed within the social system of the school. This basic difference in the concept of profession as applied to teaching and to the longer established and less bureaucratic fields of law and medicine, is a most important factor in determining the external and internal patterns of the social process in which the teacher is engaged.

It may, at this point, appear too obvious to underline again the *reason* for the existence of the elaborate educational system of Crestwood Heights, but only in its context can the structure be appreciated. The schools of the community exist to prepare its children, socially and vocationally, to take their places as functioning adults in the society. The total educational structure is involved in the socialization process, but the focal point is the teacher-pupil relationship. His share in the process demands of the teacher that, within his professional frame of reference, he maintain a precarious balance in a hierarchically organized, bureaucratic power structure and advance through its ranks by acquiring specialized skills; that he sustain, with his pupils, an intensive personal contact; and that, somewhat outside the institution of the school, he develop a series of relationships with parents, admitted to certain fringe areas of school activity. Teaching, as a profession, thus entails client relationships with pupils and parents (paralleling somewhat the relationships between expert and client in other professions); but, at the same time, the teacher is granted neither the freedom nor the status inherent in the professions of law or medicine, for example. In this respect, the teacher is more akin to the social worker than to the lawyer or doctor, who, in Western society, are in the front ranks of those who set the professional norms. And, in addition, the parents, who are the indirect clients of the teacher in the school situation, are, also and at the same time, the tax-payers from whom the teacher ultimately derives his salary—and not a fee! In this situation neither teacher nor parent is allowed the freedom and choice which accompanies the doctor-patient or the lawyer-client relationship, either of which *does* depend upon direct fees for services given and received on a "voluntary" basis.

Such professionalism as the Crestwood Heights teacher does possess is guarded for him in the school hierarchy, formally by a teachers' council, with its own constitution, and informally through a liaison committee linking teachers, administration, and board. In the larger society, the teaching profession is protected by the Canadian Teachers' Federation, which, through its local branches, can bargain for better salaries, protest unjust dismissals, and, to a certain degree, influence education policy. But even this Federation is by no means the omnipotent and self-regulating equivalent of the Canadian Bar Association or the Canadian Medical Association. By the very nature of the publicly owned educational system, it is impossible for teaching to compare as a profession with the "pure" professions, such as law or medicine, in these respects. The Crestwood Heights teacher, therefore, as a professional stands in a peculiarly vulnerable position between two social groupings: the formally organized, hierarchical educational system and the aggregate of informal primary groups, comprising the families of his pupils. While the teacher, in the school, may be the professional who sets approval on the cultural progress of the child, he is also, outside this context, the servant of these same families, in their capacities as citizens and tax-payers. Under such conditions, the teacher must make some attempt at least to satisfy both God and Mammon, which at best allows him only an insecure status in the ranks of true professionalism.

In the school hierarchy, specialists rate more highly than do classroom teachers, the rank and file. Aspirations are definitely for an upward movement—through specialist to administrator, with a somewhat more remote possibility of eventual expert status. As mentioned earlier, actual teaching experience is a prerequisite for later advancement. Since specialization, based on high academic qualifications, is the main condition for the teacher's advancement, and is an index of the success towards which the majority of teachers aspire, a more detailed description of the process seems in order.

Specialization, within the educational system of Crestwood Heights, is closely associated with the new social functions of the school in the wider context of North American and Western culture generally. These new functions and their background were described in the introduction to the chapter, but certain points need a different emphasis here to explain the nature of specific specializations of today. In Europe the period of Enlightenment during the eighteenth century introduced two great trends which today strongly influence both North American and European culture. Education, as seen by Rousseau and his disciples, the prophets of the new age (see, for instance, *Emile*), was to be the means of perfecting each individual for a future humanist millennium. The development of each child's idiosyncratic personality was thus included within the scope of education. At the same time, the needs of the Industrial Revolution dictated that increasing numbers of men (and women) must acquire at least a rudimentary knowledge of reading, writing, figuring as well as simple technical skills if they were to be used in the tending of machines in the swiftly multiplying factories. Here the emphasis was less upon the personal growth of the individual, and much more upon the transmission of technical knowledge to men in the mass, i.e. to men viewed, not as "the noblest achievement of an evolutionary creation," but rather as an inexhaustible mechanical force to be manipulated, with slight regard for human dignity, in the service of the machines and the administrative processes surrounding them, and the interests of those who derived substantial livelihoods from these productions and managements.

These two ideological trends and the corresponding social acts were not always clearly distinguished from one another. In the nineteenth century, for example, Robert Owen attempted to "blend" the two in his kindergartens for the small children, taken into his mills as workers at an early age. Later in the century, at a high peak of its industrial evolution, Freud propounded his theories based upon his observation of the unfolding of individual personality. In opposition to one current of an era which was to view man more and more as a thing or a commodity, Freud dared to place the individual at the center of his whole conceptual scheme. Marx, on the contrary, subordinated individual man to the social and economic forces which he saw as virtually creating him. This twosome of pressures, stemming from technology and humanism, has marked Western culture since the eighteenth century and it cannot help but be reflected in the formal educational processes which have assumed greater and greater importance in preparing children for the society in which they are to function. The school, as we have seen in an earlier context, must now attempt to cope with the transmission of both the liberal, humanistic tradition, which emphasizes the development of individual personality, and the implemental or "materialistic" tradition, which subordinates man to the scientific techniques upon which the economic and social well-being of Western society largely depend. These ideologies, within the school itself, differentiate the first broad categories of specialization: the teachers who see education in accordance with humanistic norms as against those who see their responsibility as merely the teaching of the "scientific facts," with little regard for their effect upon the student or the subsequent use he may make of such knowledge.

Another type of specialization is an end result of the fact that, as we have seen, Crestwood Heights is a community embedded in a complex industrial and commercial urban aggregate (the type of community rapidly becoming dominant in Western civilization), and that a minute division of labor and a high degree of specialization are inherent in such a form of organization. The profound changes which this development has meant for family and school, frequent objects of attention in this study, have perhaps been a gain for the family in emotional strength (with all the attendant difficulties of interpersonal relationships which this entails) but they have undeniably caused it to delegate most of its function as a socializing agency to the school. The school, having "accepted the challenge," and being now a more and more important repository for communal values, must take it as its duty to transmit these values. Because of the complex, and often inconsistent nature of these values, it is inevitable that the school, if it is to be able to work in accordance with community norms, must, itself, become highly specialized.[59]

Specialization within the school, until fairly recent years, has meant specialization with technical and humanistic *subject-matter* as its object of concern. The most recent brand of specialization now centers around the child as object, concentrating more heavily upon his psychological processing. Here the emphasis is less upon *what* is to be transmitted and more upon *how* it is to be transmitted, with much attention to the consequences of the learning process upon the formation of the child's character. The latter type of specialization entered the school system chiefly via the route of psychological testing. Since the turn of the century, the "intelligence test" has been used more and more widely as a convenient measure for grouping students according to academic potentialities, or for vocational guidance. An integral part of the testing, it has been stressed, is the use of a trained psychologist to administer the tests. Thus, with the increased use of such tests, "educational psychologists" have been added to school staffs. The growing interest of the school in the personality development of its pupils has widened the work of the educational psychologist to the point where he collaborates with peripheral experts in the system, such as the psychiatrist, the psychiatric social worker, and the clinical psychologist. Within the school system itself, the educational psychologist, through his interest in the social and emotional, as well as the academic development of children, may find himself allied with other specialists (the physical education teacher, for example) who are also concerned with the teaching of social rather than academic and vocational skills. As a final stage in his career, such a specialist may reach the peak of specialization: a position in which he approaches the level of the school administrator.

At the elementary school level, the widening knowledge of child-rearing practices, beginning with Pestalozzi and accelerated by Freud, has brought in its wake the kindergarten specialist. The modern kindergarten specialists, some with advanced degrees in child psychology, are a far cry from the amiable ladies of yesteryear, who boasted only a normal school diploma, if that, and a vague fondness for children. Kindergarten is now viewed as "a basic experience," perhaps essential for proper personality development in the young child, subsequent to and complementary for the nursery school, an institution with which many Crestwood Heights children are familiar by the time they enter kindergarten. Kindergarten is firmly anchored in the humanistic tradition; and its orientation is almost wholly in the direction of "lessons in living," rather than towards the acquiring of technical skills, such as reading or writing.[60]

The human relations expert, in the person of the kindergarten specialist, has a counterpart, even in the lower grades, in the subject-matter specialist, the remedial reading teacher. Reading, one of the three R's, which used to be taught and absorbed as a matter of course has now become the object of much research and concern, since reading disabilities are now linked with emotional causes or consequences. Unlike the kindergarten teacher, who may be associated in the minds of other teachers with "new-fangled ideas in child psychology," the remedial reading specialist is more likely to be regarded as a highly competent technician who may be called upon to iron out quirks in otherwise smoothly functioning mechanical processes, and who, as such, does not present as great a threat as does the kindergarten specialist to old, established behavior patterns.

Midway between specialist proper and teaching teacher, at the elementary level, is the "specialist in slow-learners." The increased use of psychological tests and the wide acceptance of recognized achievement standards have resulted in a careful grading of children according to academic ability. Those Crestwood Heights children who are in the slow-learning category receive special attention; their teacher, however, is a kind of marginal specialist in relation to the remedial reading teacher, who has no full-time class.

It is at the secondary school level, however, that the specialist comes into his own; and it is at this level that there are more men to be found. (In the high school, indeed, all teachers could be considered specialists in the sense of having intensified training in their subject fields.)

Underlying and supporting these purely professional groupings within the school is its service staff, consisting of one maintenance superintendent and the twenty caretakers who ensure the smooth functioning of the physical plant which largely contains the interacting social system of the school. This group is cut off sharply from the teaching staff on the

one hand and from the clerical staff on the other. The eight full-time
and two part-time secretaries, together with the Business Administrator
(a former teacher), identify with the teaching staff.

Standing over against all these groups are the 2753 students—the
direct consumers of the educational product fashioned with such care
and expense by the administrative and teaching groups. They are, con-
comitantly, the sons and daughters of the parents who have selected
themselves from many areas of Big City, the province, and the country,
as residents of Crestwood Heights. As such, these pupils have a close
relation to the career patterns and aspirations of their parents. Increasingly, as residence in Crestwood Heights is prolonged, these children
also become members of a peer group which articulates at few points,
if any, with either the various teaching groups or with the parents.[61]

Parents, however, form the major part of the population in Crestwood Heights. In their role as parents, they are linked to the school
by their reliance upon it to a large extent to produce a potentially
successful child—the central reason for which many of them moved into
Crestwood Heights. In their capacity as citizens, they have an effect on
the educational system through the Board of Education. In spite of the
growing influence of women, men still fill the majority of places in the
elected Board of Education, which has the task of obtaining and allocating educational funds. Crestwood Heights has a reservoir of community
talent from which to draw Board membership. With the support also of
the Home and School Association, a balance has been struck in favor
of the values upheld particularly by the teaching staff and by the
women.

The total social system of the school interacts with the larger society,
as has been stressed earlier, on one side through the peripheral "super
experts" who largely create the ideological climate in which the school
functions, and on the other through the children who are the con-
stituents of the larger society in the next generation. The experts now
largely determine the values which it is the school's responsibility to
transmit. What are these values and how are they passed on to the
pupils? The answer to this question is found only by observing the
social system of the school in motion, as it were.

The prevailing psychological climate of the community is experimental, progressive, and "democratic." It is understandable that the
Director of Education, by temperament and training, should exemplify
these communal values. Selected on this basis, he is then relatively free
to make his own contacts with like-minded experts from the larger
society and to build a staff within the school itself which is sympathetic

to the general tone of Crestwood Heights. One educational administrator who had occupied this post was continually described as the direct opposite in character, and perennially at odds with both the teaching staff and influential segments of Crestwood Heights. The difficulties this created within and without the school system apparently came from the administrator's lack of openness in his arrangements, his inability to get along with people, and his use of methods that encouraged fear and subordination in both teachers and pupils. It is significant that the Home and School Association, while always active, did not reach its present pinnacle of power in the community until this administrator had been replaced: this may indicate an increasing strength arising from growth in population, but it also appears to be directly connected with the school's carefully selected policy of good public relations with the parents. One fact is evident, however: that the present Director of Education was deliberately chosen for his expected ability, in addition to his other qualities, to repair the damage to human relationships in the school system which had been caused by a much more authoritarian regime.[62]

The educational administrator's role is not by any means an easy one. Like liberal administrators everywhere, the Crestwood Director finds himself attempting to pour the new wine of human relations into the old bottles of authoritarian bureaucracy. His position requires that above everything else, he must deal at first hand with people, rather than with subject-matter or procedure. It is the Director who largely regulates the contacts between the school system and the larger society,[63] facilitates communication between school and community, and is responsible for harmonious staff relations within the school, which are believed fundamental to good teaching. Although a professional educator, recognized throughout the Province and beyond it as in the vanguard of modern theory and practice, the Director is not expected to function primarily as a scholar. Like many university presidents, he must devote an increasing amount of time to public relations, over and above his routine administrative duties.

The Director is deeply committed, publicly and privately, to the proposition that teachers, pupils, and parents should share as fully as possible in shaping and understanding school policy. Since much of his time is spent in work at the personal level with the various groups comprising the school social system, a perhaps not unnatural result is his strong interest in the current "group dynamics" approach to group functioning.[64] This approach emphasizes communication through small group discussions, and the application of it is a marked feature of the school activities in Crestwood Heights.[65] To an unusual degree, the process is used consciously, with staff, with students, and with parents in the Home and School Association. Undoubtedly a greater measure of participation is secured than is customary in most school systems, a situation for which the educational administration is very largely responsible.

Within the school itself, the Director sees the whole child as the true object of education, just as he relates continuing individual growth to sound teaching. Sometimes the stress upon the human values which is encouraged runs counter to the equally strong, if not stronger, demand for academic success, where the children are concerned, but these contrary stresses tend generally to be represented by different persons.

The Director's role is thus a complicated blend of those of expert, administrator, and public and human relations engineer. He represents, as it were, the catalytic agent which transforms the dross of divergent attitudes, conflicting values, and their resultant tensions into the gold of a co-operatively functioning system.

The application of this core ideology, stressing democratic procedure, permissiveness, responsibility, and co-operation on the one hand, and, on the other, success through achievement in academic studies, social activities, and over-all personality development has varying results through the school system. As filtered through the understandings and characters of the five Principals, it creates a somewhat different atmosphere in each of the school units. There is, however, one common climate evident throughout the whole educational system, a general "light touch." While education is still regarded as a serious business, it should now be "fun" as well. Again and again in the interviews, informants came back to the fun of teaching and learning in the Crestwood Heights schools, contrasting this privilege with the regimentation prevailing in less favored areas. According to one teacher's statement, pupils enjoy school so much that the threat of suspension is enough to ensure conformity:

. . . he [the Collegiate Principal] isn't *too* strict but the kids know that if they do anything he will suspend them. Usually it is only for a couple of days, but if it happens too often he suspends them completely. They know that he is being fair about it, and co-operate with him. By suspending them, he throws it back to the source of all the trouble—the parents—and leaves it up to them to correct the situation. Really the atmosphere around the school here is so pleasant that none of the children want suspension. He [the Principal] wants them to enjoy the school situation and they do enjoy it. I know a couple of kids who transferred over here from Y. . . . . Over there, they weren't having any fun in the school and were always into trouble. The staff thought the students were just incorrigibles but here their behavior is just angelic compared to what it was at Y . . . and they don't want to get out of line . . . they are enjoying it too much.

The whole "light" aspect of the modern school, as typified by Crestwood Heights, is expressed physically and aesthetically in its buildings, and again, in a different sense, in the "light touch" of the new education itself. The operational homologue to the soft, shining, light woods and the tasteful colors of pictures, walls, and drapes, is the kindly smile of the ideal teacher, the well-trained kindergarten specialist, for example. The equivalent to the adjustable seat is her flexible rule, and her bendable knee as she accommodates her tall figure to the child's stature when she speaks to him. Matching the delicacy and thinness of veneer walls and partitions is the discipline as it is first mediated to the child in kindergarten, gently, lightly, almost gaily, "We don't do *that* in school, *do* we?"—a discipline which may become even more binding, though it is far less painful, than its old authoritarian counterpart.

Between school units, there are important variations in the general theme, as each Principal reflects to staff and students what he has absorbed of the common ideology. One Principal might be symbolized by a quite stern but evidently loving father. There is some conformity in his school with the values shared by the profession, but he manifests strong personal reservations. The atmosphere is more task-oriented, using emotional values as means. In the total social system of the school, this unit may be regarded as half-modernized. It also reflects perhaps the strongest loyalty to English traditions.

A second Principal is typified in the image of the older brother who knows the pitfalls of life (but won't tell all) and who exerts a strong scout-masterly influence with a moralistic emphasis. He makes a conscientious effort to accept in its entirety the permissive philosophy of the Director, and is willing to employ it as an approved method without either understanding it or sympathizing with its implications. The tone of this school might be summed up in one phrase, "We *do* play games, but they have a hidden usefulness." This attitude is consistent with that of the group served by the school, a sensibly lower social stratum, which is geared to utilitarian values in education and still in the process of "realizing the importance of the development of personality."

A third Principal fills the role of good physician and wise young father. Emotional values are central in this school's functioning, both as ends and as means. This Principal is probably much closer to agreement with the dominant ideology than are the first two men. His school is the epitome of the light touch in education, the child's pursuit of butterflies through sunny fields of learning, as it were. This atmosphere is maintained except for those rare occasions when the stern pressures for academic achievement or orderly behavior crush defences which can also be "light."

A fourth Principal is clearly most deeply dedicated of all to the views that the Director shares, yet in his particular position in the school hierarchy—where students are already beginning to think of university and career—he stands at the point of greatest difficulty in translating the current ideology into action. Here it is obligatory to pay real and serious attention to the aspects of achievement and competition in education, which must, at the same time, be played down considerably in deference to the concept that the child's own interest should be the main motivation for learning. The potential clash between the two competing philosophies is here at its actual sharpest and it requires the most extraordinary intelligence, sympathy, and astuteness to hold an uneasy compromise.

The fifth Principal appears very much more like a typical father of the community, a successful business man who "goes along with" the current ideology because and in so far as it is "practical" to do so. He "stands no nonsense," and is felt to be "firm but fair," by teachers and students alike. He accepts the "ideal" of freedom, but only after multiple consent, and at times uses the threat of a withdrawal of privileges to ensure conformity. At the level of his particular school, it is even more difficult to screen out the success values in favor of the "having fun" aspect of education. Here it is virtually impossible to reconcile the necessity for high marks in competitive examinations with the "catching of educational butterflies," and there is a markedly lessened emphasis in the latter direction.

Despite the many interactions comprising the social system of the school, in which individuals or groups may be resistant to or may modify the current ideology, there is one common theme throughout all the interview material. Every group unanimously supports the view that Crestwood Heights is the best place in which to teach or to go to school. And it is extremely rare to encounter private reservations in regard to these beliefs. Unswerving loyalty, which admits no defects, has been manifested on many occasions. A valedictorian of the Collegiate graduating class (a delicately pretty, rather fragile girl) expressed the widespread and often deep feeling of the student body about the school, as she closed her address with the following anecdote:

I have a little sister who just started kindergarten this Fall. I took her by the hand the first day and realized that she was feeling frightened. But once she arrived at the kindergarten and met the teachers and the other children, she knew that it was going to be all right. And as I said goodbye to her, I wished that I had that wonderful thirteen years of work and play and friendship ahead of me again in the most wonderful school system in the world.

This sentiment on the part of the pupils is echoed by the teachers and by the Home and School Association. A teacher said in an interview, after commenting less favorably on his experience in other schools:

A sort of *esprit de corps* has been fostered here in a democratic way, for example, when forming policy, etc. We haven't a dictator for a head. All opinions are respected and we are encouraged to contribute ideas. This feeling of an *esprit de corps* brings out the best in you. You don't feel as if you are just a cog in a machine, but an important member of a going concern. A teacher feels that if he falls down he is letting the school down. The students become aware of this. They are quick to sense and to react to staff friction. They are quite impressed by the friendly relationship between members of the staff. It is a wholesome atmosphere. . . . The harmony is real, it is not just a front and I think I have been here long enough to say that. It can be mainly attributed to the Principal and the Director of Education; the Director really has the knack of working with people.

It is evident that, whatever tensions may also exist underlying the social system of the school (some of these have just been suggested, others were mentioned in the analysis, earlier in the chapter, of the theories of education which teachers adopted in their training), there is a very real and consciously felt cohesion.

Just as the over-all ideology is mediated to the Director of Education by the peripheral experts and by him to staff, Board of Education, and parents, with modifications at each stage of transmission arising from personality differences and from the tendency of the bearers of each sub-culture to alter the message, the teacher passes on to the students his particular version of the current ideology in the classroom situation. The class is the most potent unit of interaction in the whole social system of the school. Here the teacher, relatively subordinate in the hierarchical organization of the school, becomes the superordinate individual, free, within the defined ideology of the school, to deal with the pupils in his own way and on his own terms. It is true that he must meet standards of academic achievement set by the provincial Department of Education, a task in which he is closely supervised by provincial inspectors and by his own Principal. No matter how close modern devices of communication may bring the voices of these authorities, however, the teaching function does not lie with them, but with the man or woman who meets the children face to face, hour after hour, every day of the school year. The teachers of Crestwood Heights are fully assured of the support of the administration in their work, but while performing it they are encouraged to rely upon their own abilities and judgment. The teacher is definitely in charge of the classroom while he occupies it.

The teacher, however, has a delicate role in the Crestwood Heights classroom. He is responsible for transmitting to the children the selected facts and approved behaviors and attitudes, though the latter are, as has been stressed, multiple and conflicting separates rather than elements in a relatively integrated whole. It is for this purpose that his authority is delegated to him. At the same time, without damaging the position from which he can perform these tasks, he must also be the friend and counsellor of his students.

This dual obligation is especially confusing because in the Crestwood Heights culture, the distinction between child and adult is by no means clear. The child is regarded as immature and the adult as mature, and the problem of the school is to bridge the gap between the two states. But since the cultural concept of maturity is ill defined and still in a constant state of flux, it is extremely difficult to know what this desirable state momentarily is and what are the visible signs of its achievement. The situation is further complicated because the outward symbols of maturity—clothes, hair styles, ornaments, possessions—manifest themselves at an early age for both boys and girls.[66] This sophistication of the students has been countered by a policy of hiring the younger, and physically more attractive, teachers at the high school level (academic qualifications being equal). Several of the Collegiate women teachers are almost indistinguishable from the students in dress and appearance.[67]

Given this situation, the teacher's problem of maintaining, without recourse to unmitigated authoritarian measures, an emotional climate in which pupils are receptive to learning is a real and thorny one. The increasing use of the more subtle symbols of maturity (as defined in the mental health text-books, for example) makes it exceedingly difficult to establish a positive and lasting correlation between age and the degree of these qualities to be expected. The child must now be encouraged to participate in making classroom decisions—but how far he may be included, and at what grade, and for which purposes, is far from agreed. Sociometric testing, for instance, which discovers the social relations of individuals, now allows the pupil some voice in the selection of his classmates, but slow or fast learners may be brought together by the administration or teacher into special groups or classes, independent of the children's desires for sorting by friendship.

In the establishment of authority, there is now in the school, as within the family, an increasing reaction against a primitive, stern, punitive role for the adult towards the child, in favor of a democratic *camaraderie* which plays down or even attempts to deny the gap in age and experience which does exist between teacher and pupil, or parents and children. At the lower levels of the school, the authority and wisdom still attributed to the adult by the young child make it easier to disguise the element of control, but the exercise of it at the higher grades requires great dexterity. Here, a teacher may consciously or unconsciously use friendship with the student as a control (a device which is ultimately backed by the Principal's authority) with exclusion from the "friendship group" of teachers and students as the penalty for "serious" nonconformity. The problem of authority at these higher grades may be less strenuous perhaps at the two transitional levels—entrance to high school and to junior high school. More accurately, the pattern of authority may be the obverse of the roller-coaster which was used to symbolize the career: high points for the teacher come at the points of the pupil's descent.

The pupil, in his turn, finds his relationship to his teacher equally subtle and elusive. On the one hand, he is expected to submit to the teacher's authority, whether it be traditionally autocratic or expressed in the current permissive terminology and technique. Whatever the teacher's concept of discipline, the pupil knows that this is the adult in whose charge he will remain for a considerable portion of the school year. This teacher—not he, nor his fellow pupils—is the one who will decide whether or not he "passes." Even his parents have not this most particular power to decide his fate. At the same time, and increasingly as he rises in the school, the pupil is encouraged to combine with this authoritarian adult image, the image of the teacher as a friend. It is as hard for the pupil to blend these images convincingly as it is for the teacher to believe that everyone is his equal in the hierarchical structure of the school. It is, moreover, hard for the school to recognize clearly the difficulties inherent in these conflicting definitions and to accept the concrete limitations imposed by the teaching situation. The strain engendered by proceeding as if these tensions did not exist is particularly evident in the classroom and markedly so in the higher grades. Yet the children who adjust well to this climate, as the majority appear to do, probably acquire by that very adjustment the training essential to enable them as adults to maintain quasi-intimate relations with people in impersonal situations—such as, for instance, the business man who feels he must treat all his customers as "friends" (and perhaps also his "friends" as customers).

It is obvious that there can be infinite variations of performance in the classroom, since each class represents a unique set of individuals who react in subtly different ways to the core ideology of the school. Among the teachers, as we have seen earlier, there is a vast range in interpretation of role, and this range will appear again here at the practical level we are now observing. At one pole may be a kindergarten teacher who sees it as her major task to understand each of her children as a psychic entity; with some individual pupils in her class, there will be a resulting feeling of almost excessive responsibility for their personality development, even in those areas of family relationships upon which the school is just beginning to impinge.[68] A similar trend is also strongly marked in the working relationships of a woman high school teacher who acts informally as counsellor to the girls:

I am the female on the staff who has been married and can therefore discuss various problems of sex with the girls. Many of the girls are very friendly towards me, and eight separate girls gave me individual Christmas presents this year. I am pretty proud of that. The other lady teachers resent me being on such good and intimate terms with the students, but they have never been married and really can't discuss things with the children as I can . . . many of the boys come for guidance too. I don't know whether they go to any of the male teachers or not but I haven't heard of any of it. They should really go to their P.T. teachers but Miss Y. is so young and can't really help them and I don't know whether the boys go to their P.T. teachers or not. Some of the boys may possibly go to Mr. D. but I really don't know. This has been going on for some years now. We often come down to one of these offices or to my room. Or down at the old school with the stagger system I often couldn't get my own room and we would have to meet in the lobby and discuss things with the other students milling around. They [the children] are quite frank about it and will discuss problems in front of one another. Often the boys will hold up the girls and sometimes they will disagree. They seem to be most concerned about saying "good-night." Every year before the Prom we have two periods of discussing boy-girl relationships and obligations—during the history classes.

At the other pole is the strict disciplinarian who still can operate within the framework of the school while obviously employing control methods which take no regard for the personality of the students. An observer reports on the particular type of classroom situation which this viewpoint produces:

The seats were very close together in this room, forty seats, thirty students, and a fairly wide passage on the door side of the room. There was barely room to walk between the lines of desks and the desks in each row were pushed close together. It gave a very crowded feeling. The project shelf was empty and there were no signs of projects in evidence except for a map on the side wall, which Mr. Y. said was a worthwhile project. The students got their information, he said, by writing letters to each country. On the back wall were pictures of the Four Freedoms with the Royal family in the middle. This was about the only decoration. The room was equipped with blackout curtains. The boys and girls were well dressed and clean. I had noted before that it seemed to be a matter of choice for the students whether or not they stood to answer a question. The one thing that seemed to irritate Mr. Y. was the quiet voice in which questions were answered. Because it irritated him, I felt this was one way in which the students expressed their hostility to the dictatorship system. At one time he asked a boy if he had heard an answer. I am sure he hadn't, because I was sitting opposite him and I had not heard, but he answered "Yes," as if to say "You are not going to bully the other students on account of me." Mr. Y. said, disappointed, "Well, you must be a better hearer than I am." Throughout the morning, he was constantly complaining about these quiet answers, but getting no support from the class, and, at one time, said, "Well, it must be just me, my ears."

The children also have an infinite number of patterns of response to the classroom situation. At the lower levels, each class is more generally in the charge of one teacher. It is perhaps easier for the child to adjust to the particular ideological climate as mediated by one teacher than it is for him to readjust his behavior to a number of changing teachers every day, each of whom brings with him into the classroom his own emotional atmosphere. One Human Relations session at the Junior High level, already studied in another context, brings out the pupils' various reactions to activity in the classroom (see pages 111–112). The children severally and sometimes within themselves exhibit strong mutually contrary views and desires. There is a pull between spontaneity (wanting to play out of doors on fine days) and regimentation; a regressive longing for the freedom and toys of pre-school days and a drive towards achievement and responsibility; finally there is the equating of school with "living"—the statement that the world of the classroom is not a preparation for life, but life itself. This child may have spoken more truly than he knew, for in the classroom, in microcosm, are situations like those which the child must meet as an adult in the larger society.

Fraternities and sororities, which are described in detail in the chapter on "The Club," begin to appear in the school system as early as Grade VI. Pupils as a group in the social system of the school are subject to varying pressures from teachers and parents, but the children manage, at the same time, to preserve this peer group (their own unique means of learning essential social behavior) against all adult efforts to control or to modify it. And, as Riesman and others have indicated,[69] the behavior patterns learned in the peer group, in turn, influence the behavior patterns of the adults, particularly the parents.

Auditorium sessions, dramatic presentations, "Commencements," are all occasions in which the interaction of groups within the social system of the school may be observed in detail. The auditorium sessions in Elm Prep are a sample of the general pattern.[70] A definite ritual is maintained, although the grades participating may change since separate sessions are held for three age levels. The ritual approximates an "order of service." The national anthem opens the proceedings. This is followed by a Scripture reading, chosen with the age level of the children in mind. Next comes a prayer (a children's prayer for the two lower levels, the Lord's Prayer for the older pupils); then a hymn, with words thrown on a screen for those who can read; followed by a short "sermon" in which the Principal emphasizes those matters of manners and morals or practical points of discipline which he feels the pupils should hear about. The main part of the auditorium program, which now follows, is purely entertainment, usually presented by the children themselves; it is concluded with a song (cowboy ditties are great favorites). A "benediction" (in which there may be incorporated additional moral admonitions) ends the auditorium session. The audience is composed of pupils, teachers, and occasionally parents, particularly those of children at the lower levels (mostly mothers, although fathers, too, have been present on rare occasions).

The expectations for behavior at each age level are clearly evident. The younger children are not expected to be able to read, so for them printed lantern slides are not used, but pictures may be shown. Because the small children are inclined towards restlessness they must be kept occupied; they are, for instance, required to assume an attitude of prayer with their hands. Nor are these little pupils expected to comprehend Biblical language, so that the Scripture readings are radically simplified for their benefit.

Great stress is placed upon the children's own ability to conduct the entertainment part of the program. Teachers may help beforehand in coaching, but it is obligatory for the children themselves to present the skit or other entertainment, which they carry out with pleasure and obviously without self-consciousness. The emphasis in this part of the program is about equally divided between co-operative efforts and star attractions, for instance, piano solos, which appear to cause slightly more strain for the small performer. The same exhibitionistic element carries over into more formal educational affairs, such as the "Open House" where the children's work is on display and an actual performance of some kind is always included. Evidence of the strong influence of the peer group and mass media is shown by the choice of entertainment—one little tap-dancer impersonates Betty Grable, for example; a group of boys puts on a "Bergen" show; and a current radio series— it might be "Our Miss Brooks"—provides one class with material.

The role played in these sessions by the Principal is paternal, if not priestly.[71] The talks on manners and morals are adjusted to suit age; children at the lower levels are rather coaxed and wheedled; at a slightly higher level the tone tends to be rather mysterious and dramatic; in the highest grades the strictly no-nonsense level is reached. At one auditorium session, the Principal put across the disciplinary point he wished to make in the following moralistically playful words:

Girls and boys, this morning we are going to be watched very carefully to see who are the *poor* little girls and *poor* little boys who have no shoes or slippers, or boots of any kind, and have to walk around at school with only their socks on, and if we find any of them, I'm afraid we'll just have to send them home and say we're very sorry we can't have them at school without any shoes or slippers at all, because our concrete floors here are very cold, and sometimes they are wet, too, and it is very easy for boys and girls to catch cold that way. I know, though, that when I have stopped some of you before and asked you about your shoes, I've found that you *have* had your slippers but were just too lazy to put them on! But to-day I've got some very special glasses on (smiling). They've got a special little place at the top for seeing long distances, and a special little place at the bottom for seeing short distances, and I have polished them well and pushed them far up on my nose, so no one need think that he or she can escape me, no matter how far away he runs, or how close up to me he comes. These are my *magic* glasses!

Here is paternalistic, magic authority, although it can become sternly autocratic if its behests, couched in gentle terminology, are violated. But autocracy, it is clear, will be used only as a last resort.

Such then, in action, is the social system of the school, the subtly balanced relationship of individuals and groups one with another: the Principal and teachers alternately authoritarian and permissive towards the children and internally, within their own group, co-operating with or rivalling each other; the children now in a position of subordination, now in a dominant place as they change their roles from pupil to entertainer; the parents, half-participants, half outsiders, but never disinterested spectators, in the world of the school to which their children belong.

This social system of many groups and individuals interacts within itself and with the community in a vast communication circle. It does not matter too much at what point one cuts into it. The experts educate the school, the school educates the children and their parents in the

Home and School Association, and in the process the experts, too, learn from their contacts with the community and with their clients. The experts also educate the public at large through the mass communication media, and the public, through its pressure groups, may in turn influence the tax-spending authorities, who support the school.

But it is upon the Crestwood child that all this activity centers. For him alone are all these psychological mountains moved, and for him these social hills made low, for he is the heir of the past and the promise of the future, the object of these devoted labors and the repository of so much hope.

9. PARENT EDUCATION

Re-socialization

THE MOST IMPORTANT voluntary association in Crestwood Heights is the Home and School Association, predominantly, in fact, a women's organization. This Association, increasingly active since the formation of the community, has progressed through various stages, from a more purely "social" (i.e., "sociable") type of organization centered around fund-raising, to the present one which puts its emphasis on parent education. Each school unit in the Heights has a Home and School group, and they are co-ordinated in a central council.

The conflict which has sometimes arisen in other communities between the school system and the Home and School Association has not occurred in Crestwood Heights. Indeed exceptionally good relations exist between the two, undoubtedly the result of co-operative effort in the past. Like the school system itself, the Home and School Association is well known throughout Canada for its progressive attitude, particularly towards parent education. The Association now prides itself upon the fact that its program is entirely devoted to education. Home and School includes both Jewish and Gentile women in its membership, which adds greatly to the influence which it wields in Crestwood Heights affairs. In a neighboring, slightly less affluent community, the strategic position in the social structure analogous to that of the Home and School Association in Crestwood Heights, is occupied by a men's service club. This difference between the two communities is not coincidental. The Home and School Association of Crestwood Heights is directly the outgrowth of a particular social configuration.

Important as parent education has become, it is by no means, how-

ever, the sole function of the Home and School Association. Another
is to offer certain possibilities to the women who are members. It is not,
of course, wholly a women's organization. A number of able women
hold executive positions, but many strategic roles have been and are
played by men: the Director of Education, the five school Principals,
the male teacher-experts, the director and the anthropologist of the
Crestwood Heights Project staff, and others. The high importance accorded the Association by the school hierarchy is obvious in the fact
that, over and over again, it lends its most significant authority figures,
also male, to sanction Home and School activities. This male participation—in the role of "expert"—is in striking contrast, however, to the
behavior of the men of the community. Some fathers are in evidence
at "open meetings" where general school policies are explained to parents, but with the exception of Maple Prep, which held its study groups
in the evening expressly to enable a few fathers to attend, there were no
fathers at any observed study groups or training sessions of Home and
School. The presence of a few fathers at the Maple Prep study groups
appears to be directly related to the class structure of the community.
The predominantly Gentile area around Maple Prep contains a larger
proportion of lower middle class people than does the upper middle
class district around Birch Prep or the neighborhood of Elm Prep with
its growing Jewish population. In contrast to other areas of Crestwood
Heights, some members of the Maple Prep Home and School unit appeared to be using it as an avenue for social mobility, with attendant
confusion about male and female cultural roles at the higher class level;
this may account for the slightly increased paternal participation in
Home and School affairs. The Home and School generally, however,
fulfils certain female rather than male social needs.

As has been pointed out by Talcott Parsons and Clara Thompson,[1]
women at this point in the social structure are under extreme psychological pressure. The fundamental status of a woman at this class level
is still determined by the marriage which she "makes," that is, by the
occupational status and social prestige of her husband. Yet, as Talcott
Parsons emphasizes, she lives in a culture which rates individual achievement highly. There is, therefore, an impetus towards activities which
would give the woman the satisfactions of an individual contribution
to society, over and above the biological contribution which is obligatory for her if she elects the fundamental role for a woman, that of wife
and mother.

The educated Crestwood Heights woman, tied close to her home
setting by the needs of her children, and thoroughly indoctrinated with

the cultural demand that she be both a good mother and a socially conscious individual, finds the Home and School Association an excellent stage on which to play these two major social roles. If her husband objects to her using her intellectual talents in Home and School activity, she can easily contend that she is only attentive to her children's welfare, as any good mother ought to be—an argument which she could not use with equal force about outside, paid employment. But she has also another satisfaction from Home and School. Through it she and her fellow members are able to exert considerable indirect influence on community affairs. Such community participation is largely denied to the men who play their major role well beyond their home community and who have, in consequence, little time or energy to devote to purely local affairs.

In terms of still another function, the Home and School Association in Crestwood Heights might be viewed as providing a kind of marketplace where ultimate responsibility for and functions in the transmission of those values governing the socialization process are traded back and forth between the family and the school. Certain aspects of this process seem to attract the attention of members particularly. Leaving aside the values rooted in the religious orientations of Jew and Gentile (which, as a matter of fact, introduce no cleavage in reference to educational matters) the community is largely agreed, as has already been emphasized, that two value systems are of supreme importance: first, the cluster of values around the concept of "maturity," and second, the "success" motif with all its component parts. As has been stressed in the discussion of the school, the means by which the success value-system is to be realized are highly competitive, although competition, outwardly at any rate, is generally emphatically disavowed in Crestwood Heights. For instance, the school, while supporting the system of competitive examinations, tends to deny that the child is competing with others; he is supposed to be competing "only with his own individual record of achievement." In Home and School meetings, however, parental and particularly paternal interest clearly centers around the child's performance in relation to that of others of the same age and grade; moreover, the students most honored in school functions for parents and the general public are those who have won either academic scholarships or awards in competitive sports, or, preferably, both.

Parental concern about the child's academic achievement was well exemplified during a Home and School meeting at which a teacher in an early grade attempted to explain to her pupils' parents the reasons for these students being grouped as "slow learners" in a special class.

Miss B. had told the parents that she did not consider the children "ready" to use the spelling book until Christmas time.

This speller was meant to be used by the child alone—each is supposed to be able to follow the exercises for himself. This is not a possibility for the slow learner [here Miss B. made a slip and said "poor" before she said "slow"], without the groundwork in spelling Miss B. had outlined on the board. Spelling ties right in with reading. The slow learner needs the basis of vowels and blends.

Here a father interrupted to ask if there were any class in the school which was taking the speller now. A mother followed him to ask how the slow child levels up in the end. At this point, there was a great racket upstairs, footsteps and chairs scraping. Miss B. said, with a resigned look, "We put up with that all day, and the piano too!" The mother replied, "No wonder it's a slow class with that noise going on overhead!"

Later in Miss B.'s remarks, a father spoke up, "Assuming our children are slow learners, *as for the moment we must*, what can we do as parents to help?" Another mother asked, "How often do we get a report of the student's progress?" A third parent wanted to know whether a poor learner lacked concentration and if so, whether concentration could be improved?

It came out very strongly in this Home and School session, and others, that concern *for* the *child* is often imbued with concern *about* the child's *performance* in relation to other children of the same age and in the same school. (The two are hard to separate and the distinction suggests more a primary orientation in the parent than an exclusive focus.) A larger representation of fathers was noticeable at this session; the men joined in the discussion more than usual and displayed particular interest in competitive standing. It was significant how quickly the parents seized on the fact that the room was noisy as a rationalization for their children's difficulties. Miss B. attempted to play down the competition theme, but was not very successful. Much of the parental participation at this meeting was primarily an attempt to discover how the slow learners measured up to other classes of the same grade in the school. Some resentment of the school's test results (proving "scientifically" that the children actually *were* slow learners) was evident as an undercurrent.

The success values, it would appear, determine, to a large degree, the interaction of school and Home and School Association. Since, as has been previously stated, the majority of Crestwood parents hope that their children will attend university, this expectation naturally exerts pressure upon the nature of the school curriculum, which is primarily directed towards preparing as many students as possible for university entrance. At the same time, the school is aware, through its vocational guidance techniques, that only a small proportion of the school population can be trained to compete for the highly esteemed professional occupations.[2] (Again the school appears as the child's protagonist, exerting a counter-influence to the general view, and if it is required championing the child's necessity to be different, should the parents demur.) The school must cushion the inevitable shock to the parents when many children cannot measure up to these training requirements. The existence of a Home and School Association gives the school an opportunity to carry out this difficult task.

At a Home and School meeting of Grade XII parents, a vocational guidance teacher in the Collegiate attempted to put across the fact that a technical, non-university vocation could be considered as "successful" as a career in medicine. Mr. D. used two examples from the school files: A, who was "university material" and who ended up in the Faculty of Medicine, and B, who was technical, "non-university material."

Mr. D. then had us turn our chairs around to face the screen. The lights were put out, and he had thrown on the screen the records of two cases, "A" and "B," which were so far back in the files that he didn't think anyone present could possibly identify them. He would show what their measured interests were and stress especially the individual difference between the two. He gave the figures for the current mathematics and physics course at the University of Big City to show that only a small percentage of those who started the course survived even the first year. Mr. D. appealed to the group, "Don't you thing it's time we stopped kidding ourselves and allowing our students to kid themselves that they can do work, when they haven't got what it takes?"

Of all the Home and School meetings attended by the researcher, this particular session was the most apathetic from the point of view of parent participation. A period was set aside for questions at the end of Mr. D.'s remarks. Parents were supplied with paper and pencils, so that they might remain anonymous in their questions if they wished. There were no questions, and no spontaneous show of interest came from the parents, in marked contrast to the other three meetings in this series for parents of collegiate students. The school's emphasis upon individual differences commonly falls on unresponsive ears, if the differences alluded to appear to threaten the career line, in this community which believes that all its children must be alike, at least with regard to successful academic-vocational achievement.[3]

The Crestwood Heights child, feeling the contradictory demands of his upper middle class culture, tends to accept the values of success. He may attempt to stave off any possibility of conflict by pretending that his competitive activities can be reconciled with co-operative behavior—if his preoccupation with competition allows him to consider co-operation at all. This ritual of antagonistic co-operation is not recognized by Crestwood Heights, whose members would tend to insist that inner freedom for the individual[4] is the communal norm and co-operation the means; they are inclined to deny or "play down" the existence of the success value-system, together with the competitive means by which it is realized. The child, who is the center of the socialization process in which both home and school are involved, is not usually misled, however. Despite all the talk about "maturity," "spontaneity," and "freedom," he knows beyond a doubt that his true interests inevitably must lie in one direction: graduating from the educational system of Crestwood Heights with as high marks as possible. If he has not internalized this aim, school and home have various methods of inducing him to conform, many of which are agreed upon in Home and School sessions. Children who reach the Child Guidance Clinic are in many instances only too well aware that they have been expected to achieve *beyond* their actual capacity. The majority of children, nevertheless, manage to arrive at some compromise which allows them to function more or less adequately, and to have something of both worlds.

The child, therefore, is confidently expected to realize *all* the contradictory features of Crestwood Heights culture: humanitarianism, material sucess, high social status, competition, co-operation—all the basic elements of the maturity- and success-systems. The elaborate family home, the complex activities of its members, the expensive school plant and organization, exist to train the child towards this end. The parents are convinced that the realization of these values can be achieved through education. If they themselves have fallen short at some points, it was through lack of sufficient training. Achievement, in the minds of the adult population, bears a direct relation to hard work and skill. Given the schools of Crestwood Heights and the background of material prosperity provided by the family, there should be no limits to what can be accomplished by the privileged children of the community. The Home and School Association exists to celebrate these beliefs, and to reinsure them.

The school, as already indicated, considers itself largely responsible for the child's development in academic-vocational success, social adjustment, and ethical development and emotional well-being; and it has its own definite ideas as to how the child is best handled to secure the maximum of each. Through Home and School meetings the school proposes to the parents the means of persuading the child to conform to both school and parental expectations. In a study group, a teacher expressed this point of view:

Mr. R. turned to the board and said we had some very good clues there. If we started with intellectual development, what kind of problems or things [correcting himself quickly] would we want to deal with here? Mrs. S. suggested: attention-span and concentration. Mr. R. asked if we wanted intellectual development in regard to what we expected the child to do in school. He wrote down "Mental ability in relation to performance, motives, and incentives," adding *"in other words, how to make the child like what we think he ought to do, but he doesn't."* [Italics added.]

The child remains in a peculiarly vulnerable position in the face of this particular socialization process. On the common meeting ground of Home and School, parents and school personnel reach agreement as to the communal values of maturity and success. A major problem consists in deciding which institution, the family or the school, shall assume which responsibility in achieving the desired ends, and what are the appropriate means to use in each context. The allocating of functions between family and school has not been agreed upon in any final sense, as Home and School activities clearly demonstrate, but the *means* are accepted by both the interested parties. The maturity values, as has been stated in other contexts, are inculcated through the agency of various brands of permissiveness. In other words, the child must be "free" to make his own "choice" as to what is the behavior pattern to follow. The success values, however, dictate equally stringently that the child must make choices which will lead most efficiently to academic-vocational achievement. The child is thus forced into the position of *having to choose* those competitive means which will assure his ultimate entrance into an appropriate adult occupational status. The further result is that he sees no authority figures against which to rebel, should he feel the desire to do so. It is one thing to kick against the pricks of a stern father or mother, or even a teacher in the role of parent surrogate, whose coercion is felt to be unfair; but it is quite another matter to defy the gentle, permissive figures who merely "want the best interests of the child" to be satisfied. The child has, therefore, only one recourse should a conflict arise between his own wishes and those of teachers and parents: to turn his attacks against himself. He is thus not as free in actuality to choose between alternative forms of behavior as he is led to believe he is. The burden of responsibility for choice of behavior is laid upon the child, while he is, at the same time, in effect virtually deprived of any alternative to the "choice" he is required to make. The confusion created in the child's mind should he become aware for some reason of the contradictions inherent in the adult expectations for him, is, understandably, great, particularly in view of his immaturity and his prolonged economic and emotional dependence upon the parents. This situation may cause extreme tension within the family which it cannot absorb and regulate unaided; but the Home and School Association does provide at least one arena where such problems may be aired, if not immediately solved.

It has become clear as we have studied the school that it is taking over more and more of the responsibility for the socialization of the child, and that it is more certain of its methods than the parents are of theirs. In Crestwood Heights, while the children are direct clients of the school, the parents have now become the indirect ones; in some cases they are equally dependent with their children on the school system. At Home and School meetings it was not uncommon for parents to ask teachers what the proper hour for bed should be, or how to prevent a child's telephone conversations during home-work. The parents of one kindergarten child were contemplating a move from Crestwood Heights which was not undertaken until the teacher had given it as her opinion that the change would not be detrimental to the child. In Home and School meetings, parents are *educated* by the school for their cultural obligation towards the child, which approaches, increasingly, the role of trusteeship for the school, which in turn is presumably trustee for "society." Just as in an earlier age, the parents were regarded as agents of the church, the institution which alone could prepare their children for heaven and immortality, they are now viewed by the school somewhat as junior partners in the business of preparing children for material success in temporal life. A favorite in-group joke of Crestwood Heights teachers states that "the ideal child is an orphan." The children are dealt with as clients in classes; the parents, as clients, in Home and School "groups."

In the light of the cultural complexity of life in Crestwood Heights, many reasons for the activity of Home and School become understandable. One has only to point to the preoccupation with the child and his training for adult life; the insecurity among some parents, especially among mothers, about their own relationship to their children; the enthusiasm for techniques and methods in interpersonal relations, as demonstrated by the current interest shown both by the Home and School Association and by the school system in the approach by way of human dynamics to the handling of groups. Yet even with these facts in mind, it is necessary to make a clear distinction between the formal and informal, conscious and unconscious aspects of the experience undergone by parents in the Home and School Association. The "trading" of child-rearing functions between the family and the school which occurs in the setting of the Home and School Association is not, on the whole, a conscious exchange. If, for example, a Home and School member were asked directly what she had learned about child-rearing practices in the parent education groups or in the open sessions, she would not, in all likelihood, describe the effects of this training in terms like those used above. She would be more inclined to relate a certain amount of factual knowledge which she had picked up from various experts with little or no integration of the material, which is itself frequently conflicting in content.

Crestwood Heights is a highly literate, socially mobile community which, for reasons explained earlier, is peculiarly open to new ideas in almost every aspect of its cultural life. This sensitivity to the new and different, so marked in the school system as well as in other institutions, has been an important factor in determining the special nature of the Crestwood Heights Home and School Association, since this orientation is most crucial for the propagation and absorption of current ideologies in education and child-rearing.[5]

While the school has always been alert to the possibilities of parent education and has conducted some study groups for Home and School members, it could not, from the very nature of its structure and function, link such discussions to the fundamental child-rearing problems created by the culture in which it is itself so deeply embedded. We might quote here a document which indicates the type of parent education that the Association *can* welcome and contain. It describes an activity of the Crestwood Heights Project, which through the Home and School Association formed seminar groups, limited at first to executive members of Home and School but later opened to all interested members.

Both Jewish and Gentile women joined the seminars; but at no time were there more than thirty women in these groups during any one year. Topics discussed included personality and culture theory; educational philosophy and the school; Jewish-Gentile values; a study of the family; reports by mothers on the day-to-day happenings in the home; reading of, and comments on, some of the research in progress. At least two women enrolled in university courses in sociology as a direct result of their seminar participation.

The seminars were not without strain for many members. Especially difficult was the realization that the "experts" in this case offered no panacea or even solution for the problems raised. Stereotypes and traditional habits of thought were challenged, particularly in the area of Jewish-Gentile relations. Women confessed frequently to members of the research staff that they were deeply disturbed by facts brought forward during the discussions. At other times, seminar members reported relief after clarification of a social reality bearing, for them, an intimate and profound connotation.

Some women, unable to stand the stress of these discussions, dropped out. Often a rationalization that they were "not intelligent enough" for such discussion was evident with some women, causing distress and a rejection of the seminars. Nevertheless, a core of a dozen or more Home and School members stayed with the seminars throughout the three years of this experiment.[6]

Such an experiment in parent education is of particular significance in the field of mental health. The most interesting feature of the seminars is the use of the individual members themselves as the subjects of study. These women have been encouraged to look, at first hand, at the culture in which they live, drawing their understanding of it from their own reactions to it, in an atmosphere of warmth and mutual support. To some extent, psychiatric action-principles have been applied to the analysis of a social situation and, most important, the mental health experts have offered their own concepts and values for *joint investigation and discussion*. Whether such knowledge will make it more or less difficult for these women to function effectively in their culture is still to be determined; and this area would appear to be one of the most important for future investigation.

The seminars meant many different things to different people. For some, participation meant intellectual contact with men who hold views divergent from those of the majority of Crestwood Heights males. This contact served as a reinforcement for the changing attitudes of the women— a reinforcement which the husbands, in most cases, could not give.[7]

If now the concept of socialization is widened and the spotlight removed from the web of cultural influences immediately surrounding the child, it is evident that the Home and School fulfils other important functions, in addition to its major function as regulating force in the socialization process to which the child is central.

At the community level, education, as the product of increasingly big business, is "sold" to parent-consumers and other tax-payers largely through the Home and School Association. As mentioned earlier, the Home and School acts, on occasion, as a powerful pressure group in local politics. It often initiates educational, welfare, philanthropic, or recreational projects, such as the Community Center and the community nursery school, which may later be taken over by official bodies. Its most important function, however, at the community level, concerns the relations between Jews and Gentiles. Here the Home and School Association serves as the central integrating point between the two ethnic groups in Crestwood Heights.

The Jews, who began to move into the area during the thirties, were business and professional people, with higher-than-average incomes, who had come to Crestwood Heights in the hope of escaping from a more purely Jewish community. Among them, there were able women with highly developed skills which they exercised through the Home and School Association, without, however, reaching positions of power within it. No Jewish woman, for example, has at the time of writing been President of the central Home and School organization; and this "balance," a joint effect of Gentile and Jewish wishes,[8] is carefully maintained, largely through the clique structure of the Association, which operates by telephone behind the official scenes. Many Jews have moved into the community during and after World War II. The liberal core of original Jewish inhabitants, many of whom have severed almost completely their ties with orthodox Judaism,[9] and who prize their half-acceptance by the Gentiles, symbolized by membership in Home and School, feel threatened, like the Gentiles, by the later Jewish influx, regarded by both liberal Jew and Gentile as vulgar, ostentatious, ignorant, and detrimental to the community.

Although it seems that Jews may, in time, become a majority group in Crestwood Heights, and although Jewish students are already in the majority in the upper grades of the school, their understandable tendency is still to regard themselves as a minority, since for many or most the reference-group is the world, not the community, and the reference-period, history, not the present. For the sake of acceptance by Gentiles, the Jews are prepared to support the *status quo* on the Board of Education, in the Home and School Association, and in the school system. But time may very well bring about a situation in the schools in which almost all the students will be Jewish, although the school staff and administration would remain Gentile. This time is not yet, however, and at present the Home and School Association acts as a mediator of existing Jewish-Gentile tensions, thus enabling the educational system administered and staffed[10] by Gentiles to function more or less smoothly. But there are signs that it is becoming increasingly difficult for many liberal Gentiles to maintain their value of "tolerance" in the face of an actual marked increase in the Jewish population.

Lastly, we may see Home and School in the community from the viewpoint of the school: in the Association it finds an excellent channel for exporting its interpretations of children's "needs" and its program for child development to the parents of Crestwood Heights, who must ultimately foot the educational bills. The Director of Education—the link between the community and the educational system, and in a strategic position as perpetual Honorary Vice-President of Home and School —is, as has been sufficiently indicated, sensitive to the rapidly changing trends in education; and, in addition, it is he who receives the requests for equipment and services from the teachers within the school system. These he must re-interpret to the parents, if he is to retain their support for the high educational standards enjoyed. In an interview, the Director of Education showed that he was very much aware of the importance of the Home and School in the organizational structure of the community.

He had first come into contact with the Home and School Association when he was teaching in one of the Collegiate Institutes of Big City. Their Home and School Association had been at the bottom of a conflict which split the community in two. He happened to think the Home and School had been right in bringing the issue before the public. When he got to Crestwood Heights the community was beginning to establish contact with the school through the teachers. Formerly there had not been much contact. The Home and School had been more a fashionable organization that concentrated on social functions and bringing "big names" to speak in the community. There was a centralized committee composed of ten teachers and ten members of the Home and School. They had met around at each other's homes. Then a committee had been set up by the Principals and the Director, carefully chosen to get the right people on it. For two years they had met frequently, threshing out objectives. The Director was especially impressed with the friendly spirit of these meetings.

The Director said that thirty per cent of his time was now spent on the Home and School work. He brought his engagement book over from his desk and showed the number of afternoon conferences he had had with Home and School during the last month of school. He said that when he came to this position there was no definite work outlined, and he had more or less to carve out his own program. At first, there hadn't been an understanding of the importance of the work he was doing with Home and School; but now there was no question of its value; and if he decided he wanted to spend even more time with the Home and School, there wouldn't be the slightest objection from the Board or anyone.

In its turn, the school lends the weight of its knowledge and authority in the area of child-rearing practices to the mothers, many of whom are eager to avail themselves of expert help.

In the Grade Mother organization of Home and School (the place at which parents first take up official positions), the school has a powerful means of regulating contact between parents and teachers. The official pronouncement of the school is that parents are welcome to visit the school at any time. In actual practice, however, the teachers' rigid time schedule cannot afford such interruptions in the classroom. The school solves this problem by setting aside one afternoon a month for consultations with parents, and by encouraging parents to make definite appointments with the school staff for more serious discussions. Parents, nevertheless, severally tend to "corner" teachers at social functions and general meetings in order to talk about their individual children, a practice which is resented by the teachers. On such occasions, it is the duty of the Grade Mother to "protect" the teacher from monopolization by any one parent, or exhaustion by all. At a meeting of kindergarten Grade Mothers to plan for the Birch Prep Open House:

the Grade Mother convener broke in to ask whether the parents would go
directly to their children's rooms to meet the teacher. If they did that, no
one was to talk to the teacher for more than two minutes. Incidentally,
that was one of the duties of a Grade Mother, to keep the teacher from being
overwhelmed. One mother asked if that could *really* be done, and Mrs. M.
replied that it could and quite easily—all the Grade Mother had to do was
to watch the teacher, and if one parent seemed to be monopolizing her time,
she could bring up another parent and introduce *her*, which would make
the monopolizer move on! Miss D. [a teacher] was so kind that she had to
be protected from the worst offenders. Mrs. M. remarked that new parents
might not know of the parent interview days and the Grade Mother could
emphasize this. It would take a load off Miss D. "She's too kind-hearted!"

In the general meeting for all the Birch Prep Grade Mothers, this convener again made essentially the same statement: "At Open House,
you will keep the parents from overwhelming the teachers."

The fact that the Grade Mothers are often chosen by the teachers
and the Principals[11] means that the school has a doubly powerful control where parental intervention is concerned. To this is added the unwritten understanding that no Home and School meeting should be held
without the presence of a teacher, whether it be held in the school
buildings (as is usually the case) or in a private home.

The school is now concentrating deliberately on the Grade Mother
organization as a means of disseminating information about the school.
The Grade Mother convener for all the Home and School units had this
to say on the subject:

> The Director of Education was awfully keen on the Grade Mother group.
> He was meeting the conveners of the five schools. More could be done with
> this group. The same ideas could be got across to them as the study groups
> discussed, only it would have to be done in a different way. There was to
> be a general meeting for Grade Mothers, with a panel of the five Principals,
> with the Director in the chair. This would make the Grade meetings more
> like a discussion group, only centering around their interests.

The Director of Education elaborated this theme:

> At present, he was working through the Grade Mothers. He encouraged
> meetings at the school. The mothers met to discuss all sorts of problems.
> He wanted them to get the idea that they could say whatever they wanted.
> Even criticize the school, if they felt like it. . . . He was genuinely and
> deeply interested in this phase of the work. He had a meeting of Grade
> Mothers, in which he broke them up into small groups. Then the small
> groups reconvened and brought their questions to the general meeting. Thus
> no parent was identified as the raiser of a question.
> Last year, there had been the question of a recreational program for after
> hours, which involved the early closing of the schools. The Director imme-
> diately got the Grade Mothers together, again using the buzz-session[12]
> technique. This, he realized, was an interpretive group. The Grade Mothers

soon got the other women on the telephone all over Crestwood Heights. At first he and the Principals had used the meetings to tell the Grade Mothers what was being done; but now he was beginning to realize that it was a two-way process—they had got a good many suggestions back from the Grade Mothers. The Director was convinced of the value of such two-way communication.

He went on to talk about the initial demonstration classes in Human Relations. He said that the research team [of the Crestwood Heights Project] had done an awfully poor job of putting them on. Everyone was confused and apprehensive over what was happening and the parents were up in arms. . . . He had gotten the Grade Mothers together . . . and explained just what was being done. Then everything quietened down and they realized what a good thing these classes were. He mentioned how much easier it was to effect changes when everyone understood what was going on.

The school, therefore, consciously utilizes the Grade Mother organization to regulate contacts between parents and teacher and to influence parental opinion in favor of school policy. With its network of telephone communications, the Home and School serves as a powerful auxiliary arm for the formal school system of Crestwood Heights. Conversely, the Home and School web of communications absorbs from the community at large subtle shadings of opinion and attitudes towards the school system, which it relays back to the latter institution at all administrative levels. The school is sensitive to these nuances of public feeling, since, like other institutions in the society, it is also dependent to a large extent upon the support and goodwill of its community, particularly when that community pays such a high proportion of its taxes for education.

Crestwood Heights (and comparable North American communities) is confronted by a prospect of increasingly expensive educational services, which some residents (not all, by any means) deem desirable, but which are more and more difficult to finance through the existing municipal tax structure. In Crestwood Heights, a high value is placed upon property as a symbol of social status, and the demands for rapid capital accumulations for this purpose are economically incompatible with the demand for a high rate of expenditure for school taxes. On the whole, Crestwooders understand and approve the necessity for larger, more beautiful, and more adequately equipped school buildings. They are not quite as alert, however, to the equally costly demands created by the specialization and growing professionalism within the educational system. A remedial reading teacher, a visiting psychiatrist, or some other radical addition to the traditional staff may not as readily be seen as essential by the whole community. The women within the Home and School Association are usually those most sympathetic to these more indirectly justifiable innovations and can lend substantial support to the educational administrator and to the enlightened Board member who is sensitive to both sets of community demands. Indeed, Home and School has already achieved sufficient power to ensure the election of approved candidates to the Board of Education, and has thus become a strong bulwark of progressive education in Crestwood Heights.

The Crestwood Heights Home and School Association answers important specific needs, both social and individual, as the preceding material has underlined. As its major social function, Home and School mitigates the tensions arising between the school and the family, institutions which, in Crestwood Heights, are embedded in a general culture with its own strains. The strains grow out of the struggle for social mobility, the intense competition entailed in earning enough money to remain in Crestwood Heights or to pass through it to a community of higher social status, the organized isolation of its inhabitants, and extremely important, the presence in the area of two ethnic groups, Jewish and Gentile. For its function in relation to individuals, the Home and School offers personal satisfactions, primarily to women: in companionship, in opportunity to use professional skills and abilities, in the possibility of an escape from a feeling of futility. In its relation to the school, the Home and School Association is effective in protecting and promoting its progressive policies in regard to the education which is not only vital to but comes close to being the core of the Crestwood way of life.

Sociality

"MY, aren't we a bunch of joiners!" commented a woman informant during an interview.[1] Clubs and associations are, indeed, marked features of life in Crestwood Heights, for both children and adults; here again is evidence of how human relationships in the Heights are, more and more, being channelled into impersonal, highly structured, institutionalized patterns. These particular human relationships, like others, serve a definite purpose. Just as it is becoming less common to take a trip of any length merely "for pleasure" (unless, of course, one is retired) and without some ulterior business or professional motive, it is also less usual for people to meet each other purely on a basis of affection or of liking to be together. Human contacts are now more generally organized around some activity or "cause," preferably one which will also advance or make plain the social standing of the participating individuals.

PURPOSES

Clubs and associations in Crestwood Heights exist to relate people to one another and to their culture: they are means directed to ends—ends which also enter into the functioning of more formal institutions.[2] For instance, a business man's association, devoted primarily to furthering the financial interests of its members, may produce intimacy as a by-product. Such a group might not be too different from a service club, which has intimacy as its aim but is also useful in promoting business or professional contacts. In the same way, the institution of the school, while organized for certain formal ends, does provide through its extra-curricular and peripheral activities a considerable degree of intimacy for its students and staff. Thus, in any Crestwood club or association, only the most careful scrutiny can determine the balance which may be struck through membership between intimacy and some less sentimental utility.

Though mixed with other attractions, the element of intimacy in clubs and associations is none the less significant. Together with occupation, they have become important auxiliaries in creating a solidarity which cannot now be achieved solely within the primary group. It is perhaps inevitable that there should be many such external ties for each individual in a society which stresses independent activity dissociated almost entirely from the kinship system or other habitual primary ties. A man's business or professional affiliations in Crestwood Heights may hold out to him more emotional security than his family circle, and they are most certainly essential to his earning power. Indeed, the club or association is in itself a form of psychological shelter, almost equivalent in potency to the protection afforded by the office or the home. As one male informant, the owner of an architect-planned home, said of his club, "That's where you can *really* feel at home!"

In their "purposes" clubs and associations in Crestwood Heights represent a blend of philanthropic, utilitarian, and aesthetic elements. The community has not reached upper-class freedom to enjoy leisure or perhaps to regard it with contempt or indifference, merely because it is there in abundance and is continuously at one's disposal. Just as a Crestwooder cannot usually waste money without some trace of guilt, he is also generally unable to waste time. He must always be "doing something," but it is equally mandatory that this something be "useful," either to himself or to others. Self-improvement, self-promotion, both important for the Crestwooder, are goals eminently suited for realization through associations. The desire to help others less fortunate than oneself is also most easily fulfilled by joining some philanthropic group since opportunities for mutual aid on a personal and individual basis are extremely limited, even among kin.

Closely allied with the practices associated with this utilitarian, "rational," and, perhaps, Puritan concept of leisure, is the use of the club, association, and, to a less degree, the intimate friendship group, for the furthering of business or profession or other ulterior aims. Many men, who might in their heart of hearts prefer to putter around a lathe in the basement during their rare free hours, join a golf club instead because "that's where the contacts are made, in the locker room." Or a doctor's wife may make dressings with a hospital auxiliary, even though she confesses to her close friends (who have no connection with the auxiliary in question) that she considers the activity to be a waste of time and useless in the over-all organization of the hospital.

Clubs and associations also provide an outlet for the professional and organizing skills of married Crestwood Heights women. Women on the governing board of a social agency or a women's organization or in some other role will often work as hard, as much, and as seriously, in their volunteer positions as they did in their professional capacities before marriage. For many of these women, the work satisfaction predominates over the social prestige accruing from the activity. Others, perhaps less able, seek executive positions in strategic associations simply for the status which these confer, primarily upon the family.[3]

The acquisition of valuable skills is also an enticement to membership. The school has, as already indicated, entered to a large extent into the teaching of the skills required to maintain or raise social status, but it is considered desirable by many that this instruction be reinforced or augmented in a somewhat more exclusive milieu or even in a private school.[4] There is more prestige in learning figure skating at one of the "better" clubs organized solely for this purpose than at the public school or the locally supported community center. Club membership for this sport automatically ensures excellent instruction, and, even more important, inclusion in competitions and social events restricted to the "in-group." If the club is a "good" one, its insignia may be proudly worn on other occasions, proclaiming to "all who know anything" that here is a selected individual who *belongs*—by financial right as well as by a hardly won competence in the sport itself. The necessity to acquire the skill thus legitimizes and sanctifies what would otherwise be a mere exhibition of buying power. Skills are required to make the exhibition of gains a reputable behavior, and hence a springboard for further gains.

The number of clubs and associations to which Crestwood Heighters belong is legion. For some purposes, the distinction between "formal" and "informal" associations does not seem too important. Whether the association is a formal one like the Home and School Association or an informal one like the intimate friendship group, the gains from membership appear to be much the same. The Crestwooder who understands his environment chooses his human contacts somewhat as a painter mixes colors—a membership here, a patronage there, all blending into an acceptable, harmonious design which will cast due luster on its creator and serve as an enduring symbol of his taste and skill.

These numerous associations to which Crestwooders belong, whether formal or informal, seem to fall naturally into three groups. First are the adult-centered, adult-controlled associations; second, the child-centered adult-controlled associations; third, the child-centered, child-controlled groups.

The adult-centered and adult-controlled associations will engage our attention first. These are oriented to the present and the future, but inevitably incorporate elements from past experience of the members in other communities and even countries. Included in this category are "service" clubs, social clubs, recreational clubs, philanthropic and professional organizations.[5]

One primary function of these groupings is to assign status to individuals, or, more often, to families, although many members may be not fully aware of the function. This function has already been suggested above and should perhaps receive fuller description.

STATUS AND STATUS-LENDERS

In a community which has had only a brief life history, family name can have but little weight, since almost all residents are strangers to one another or relatively new acquaintances. Prestige depends more on wealth than lineage, and it is still highly approved behavior in Crestwood Heights to have amassed that wealth oneself or at least to have had it amassed within living memory. Since profound secrecy must surround the actual amount of income, other sure ways must be found to proclaim one's financial potency and hence one's claim to social status. Membership in exclusive or expensive clubs is a convenient and effective means of proclamation. And if a Crestwooder is successful in ascending through the hierarchy of club membership, he ultimately touches the fringe of the upper class, where family and inherited wealth *do* cast over him a corner of their mantle. Among the initiated of Big City, the list of clubs and associations to which the Crestwooder belongs places him as quickly and irrevocably as his street address or his occupation: for this subtle indirection of non-conspicuous conspicuous consumption is itself financially and emotionally costly—and hence an evidence of "being able to afford it."

Occupation, also a highly important determinant of status, is not sufficient in itself to assure prestige. A brilliant lawyer, for example, who held himself apart from all associational activity, would, in Crestwood Heights, generally be regarded as eccentric, no matter what his bank account or his record in the courts. The demands of his career, which bear heavily upon the Crestwood man, make this activity, like participation in the family, difficult in many cases. Yet membership in the "right" clubs and associations, even though he may rarely appear there, is considered useful, if not essential, to validate the male career.

Status, in Crestwood Heights, is somewhat like a commodity—similar to money, but perhaps more enduring. The Crestwooder, faced by annual income tax and periodic death duties, rarely thinks of money in terms of inherited wealth; he acquires it by his own efforts. He may use this wealth to give his children every material advantage, but it is still assumed that the child, in his turn, will "earn his own way" as an adult as far as money is concerned. Status, however, is seen in a somewhat different light. It must be won, like money, but it can more readily be conferred. Family status, handed on to the children, is a real and fungible asset. True, even the Crestwood child may have to work for the money to maintain the status; but the status is already there to be maintained, secure and solid.[6] Status *can* be passed on to the child, although it increasingly becomes his own responsibility to protect and, if possible, to enhance his inheritance. And while the parent is consolidating the family status in adult-centered and adult-controlled associations, the child is being groomed to receive this inheritance in child-centered, adult-controlled associations and in the highly influential child-centered, child-controlled associations.

Status for the Crestwooder has largely lost its meaning as a clearly defined system of hierarchical positions. Because the dominating ideology proclaims that all individuals are of equal worth as human beings, he must deny with part of his mind at least that there is any such phenomenon as rank by status.[7] In day-to-day pursuits a major effort centers around maintaining or improving social position in the community, but a Crestwooder, if asked directly whether he occupies a position of high social status, will in all likelihood deny that he is "any better or worse than his neighbors." Forced into an estimate of his own status, or tricked into revealing ambitions for social mobility, he tends to be diffident, evasive, or frankly angry.[8] Yet he will readily refer to other persons as having a high or a low status.

The analogy with money may be stated at this point in a different way. Status for the Crestwooder means psychic and social capital. Memberships in clubs and associations which are widely recognized as being of high social status, are like negotiable securities (no less real for being psychological) which he may cash, transfer, or use as collateral in negotiating a wide variety of social investments in the course of his upward progress.

This "speculation" with status is strikingly similar to the actual manipulation in the market. Cash is indeed necessary (in most instances) to achieve the skills which are one important prerequisite for entrance to the exclusive associations. Once the money has been spent to acquire the skills, a series of complicated manoeuvres ensues, some of which have nothing further to do with money. The exclusive association, of course, is not like the corporation which brings out a new issue of stock or debenture bonds on the open market; it by no means "accepts the funds" of all those who wish to invest in it. The social standing of the association or club is first created by a few individuals, frequently from a social level above that of Crestwood Heights, who have status to "lend." Money, occupation, and family are essential to the "status-lender," and with these he "backs" the associations of his choice. He then bands together with his fellow "lenders" rigorously to screen a selected number of members, also on the basis of money, occupation, and, to a less degree, of family, although the applicant need not, and often *must* not, fully match the status-lenders' assets in these respects.

A woman informant, Mrs. E., having rated the various professional clubs and associations, described the status-lenders as follows:

> There are a lot of professional people in them, of course. I don't really know whether there would be a majority of any one profession, but there are a lot of doctors, lawyers, dentists, etc. I imagine there must be a lot of big business executives, particularly among the Jews. Then you have people like I., E., D., the M.'s and the D.'s who really are not active in Crestwood Heights affairs at all. They don't mix socially with Heights people, and move in their own little sphere above the Heights. They are all very wealthy. They have homes here but that is all. When we were arranging for the plebiscite about the new school, we were going over the voters' lists and when we came to a name like the M.'s or the D.'s, it was a form of humor to ask who could we get to go after their vote! Those people send their children to private schools, or are older people who have no interest in such things!

A stronghold of such status-lenders, the Loyalist Club, is described in the following interview:

> . . . The Loyalist Club is the only one of its kind that is really tough to get into. I don't know how they have managed to keep it so exclusive and keep up the financing. They have refused fabulous offers for the ground where they are, but somehow they have managed to refuse and keep the membership rigidly limited. They want now to keep too many doctors from joining. The doctors are anxious to join because of the convenience, just across from the Medical Center, but the majority of the members are big business men who are interested in keeping the contacts in the club for business purposes, and the doctors cannot help them much in that way. They also claim that the doctors get better service in the dining-room! I don't know whether the doctors demand it or not, but that is what they say. The doctors also get special food. There is one special kind of cake that is only served to the doctors. The members of each profession eat together and separate from each other. . . .

The Loyalist Club membership is made up of very powerful people and they are out to maintain that power. It is strictly a power club. The membership is mainly made up of the liquor families, old Progressive-Conservative families, doctors who run the hospitals, big merchants, brokers, life insurance heads, bond heads, the financial promoters, etc.

The wife and family are members automatically and the wife carries on her membership after the husband dies. This is one of the interesting features to me. Usually in such clubs, the membership dies with the husband. The son keeps his membership for life, and his wife and family are admitted when he marries, but the daughter loses her membership when she marries, unless her husband is already a member, or is someone who will be admitted to membership.

Wife and children of a member must live in the husband's home in order to be members. The wife loses her membership if she is divorced. There must be no discussion of politics in the Club, but I don't see how they can stick strictly to that rule now, as I would think that conversation would be impossible without bringing in politics to-day.

The status-lenders do not, as is widely thought, form associations of their peers into which outsiders try to break; they act rather as a syndicate of peers, to receive the not-quite-equal into a relationship of dependency and tutelage. This provides the status-lenders with a suitable field in which to exercise dominance, with a means to drain off tensions from the innermost group, and thus also with a *cordon sanitaire* protecting them from those of still lower status.

The type of club has not yet appeared in Big City, membership in which places the individual socially once and for all beyond dispute, and in which status may lie, as it were, dormant.[9] The Crestwooder, who can never be completely sure that he has arrived at the apex of the associational pyramid, tends rather to shop around, joining where he finds a soft spot, discarding earlier and more easily achieved affiliations as he breaches less pregnable walls. And in this socially mobile community, there is frequently no established, recognized correlation between the status conferred by the association and the social role it demands. Securing the privileges of membership may absorb the concentration of the aspiring members much more than the resulting obligations. Several informants related that they had achieved membership in certain coveted clubs, only to discover later that they could not meet the financial or other demands which such membership entailed, because of the cost of participation in club activities or of the outside entertaining associated with it. Eventually, these individuals were faced with the necessity of revising their social investment portfolio, since they had been buying too heavily on financial or social margin.

Status has been compared to a kind of security (fiscal, not psychological). But the analogy breaks down when it is recognized that, unlike the security, status cannot simply be "held" by an individual. The individual, it is true, owns shares as it were in the association; but while an actual security may be filed away in a bank vault, status can never be allowed to lie dormant. It must be continuously *recalled* that Mr. X. or Mrs. Y. is a member in good standing of such and such a club. These people may lend the prestige of occupation or family to a club or association in which they themselves may or may not participate. But *active* membership at the appropriate class level is essential to maintain or create the status, which may or may not be used to support prestige-borrowing associations. Others, in their turn, may join the latter associations to consolidate their individual status and, in time, build up social capital to a point where it also may be "lent." Status in Crestwood Heights, if it is to be recognized, must be in virtually continuous circulation through associational membership; and it is essentially cumulative.

The prestige of a given association appears to be in direct proportion to the number and position of the status-lenders who back it with their social capital. But, as has been pointed out, the process is circular: the status-lender also maintains and increases his capital by lending it, which, in turn, strengthens his power to impart status.[10]

The borrowing and lending of status in Crestwood Heights has not yet reached the highly regulated state of negotiations in a great metropolitan area, such as New York.[11] The process of joining associations has, however, a fairly consistent pattern. If a man wishes to become a member of a high-status golf club, for instance, he does need to be able to play a reasonably good game of golf. But even if the prospective member approximates professional excellence in the sport, he must also have the personal sponsorship of at least two present members of the club. Entrance is made considerably easier if the aspirant has already belonged or belongs to one or more clubs at this class level, and if his sponsors are also members of them. Indeed, when his application for membership comes up for consideration before the golf club's committee, all previous associational affiliations of the applicant are scrutinized closely in estimating his desirability. His "social assets," or lack of them, his social debts or errors, are thus as binding in the social market as are the results of good or bad investments in the financial market.

Those who are widely recognized as having status, who must safeguard and perpetuate their possession by exercising it constantly in club membership or in "backing" associational activities, may also validate their status by sponsoring selected neophytes. By so doing, they are investing a measure of their own status; and in order to protect their investment, or profit by it, they may be compelled to take upon themselves the responsibility for coaching the prospective member in appropriate behavior.[12]

Once accepted into membership in one or more recognized associations at a certain position in the social structure, the individual belongs to an "in-group" whose members "understand" each other. With this backing, he is well equipped to feel his way in Crestwood Heights. Two strangers may establish rapport by bringing into conversation the names of the associations to which each belongs. These are not usually spelled out in full, but subtle references are made with initials ("J. B.") or contractions ("Old Jeff"), by calling a prominent member by given name or even nickname, which establishes that the speaker is solidly a member of the group and even on familiar terms with a chief statuslender. If the strangers pick up each other's cues, firm ground is found for continuing the relationship.[13]

Status is thus the hub around which associational membership moves in Crestwood Heights. The adult-centered, adult-controlled associations operate largely to validate the present social status of the members and to open avenues to higher status in the future. In them it is possible for adults to learn new patterns of behavior under the sponsorship of other adults.[14] Hence belonging to the right associations is essential for successful career movement; at the same time it also provides a degree of human intimacy in the cliques which develop within the larger association.

THE PATTERN OF ACTIVITIES

The principal method of safeguarding the status capital of the adult club or association is the rigorous inclusion-exclusion mechanism which has already been mentioned.[15] A certain amount of skill and an adequate demonstration of suitable behavior are the prerequisites for inclusion; and the sense of worth and belongingness of those who are already members is further heightened by the fact of exclusion of the many. The process is continuously selective. If the lessons are well learned in an association of lower status, entrance to a higher-status association may be the reward for effort expended. The lessons to be learned within each association are numerous and complex. One woman informant gives a revealing account of the membership pattern of her husband over a period of some years. Their first important association was a golf club of high, but not the highest, status. She describes the clique structure of the first club, selective for higher status in the future.

The men's and women's locker rooms [in the Maple Leaf Club] were very important places. This was the period when clubs did not have liquor permits and were not allowed to have liquor on the premises. This law was completely ignored in the locker rooms. Most of the men either liked to drink or thought it was expected of them and drank because it was good for business. All those who could not fit into this pattern moved their lockers to remote parts of the room where their strangeness was not so apparent. This resulted in a centrally located neighborly group of good fellows who called themselves Scotch Block. Each man kept a bottle in his locker and at the end of a game the required amount was dispensed among the group. Spongers were not tolerated. Each man must have noticed how much he drank, himself, and how much each of the others drank because it seemed to end in a fair exchange. Those who could not pull their weight moved their lockers with the other "Strangers." Those who wanted to "put on a show" were also made to feel unwanted.

The women's lockers did not become organized in this way. Not until many years later were private bottles concealed in the lockers. This did not mean that the women did not drink. The men sent drinks to the women by the servants. Two drinks were the usual quota. When the women finished these, they went to the lounge to wait for their husbands. This wait often amounted to two hours or more. Women reacted to this in different ways. Some gave up coming to the Club; others got bottles of their own and went back to the locker room and poured themselves further refreshments; others docilely sat.

G. [the informant's husband, a professional man] did not consider it suitable for the promotion of his practice to drink to any extent during the week. One of G.'s contributions to the sociability of the Scotch Block group was his ability to tell jokes. G. expected that his moderate drinking would create the impression that he would allow nothing to interfere with the excellence of his work the next day.

Members of Scotch Block gradually began to think of themselves as the backbone of the Club and the cream of the crop. As N. [wife] did not have any companionship with wives or husbands outside of Scotch Block now, she had no idea what the outsiders thought.

There was no definite organization to include or exclude members. The location and ownership of the lockers did this. If a member wanted to bring in another, he invited him to share his locker. When a locker became vacant either through death or the owner moving away, this locker was taken over by the new member. Each Scotch Block member knows what kind of man will be acceptable in the group and rarely brings in anyone objectionable. If this happens, the newcomer is gradually frozen out; he is not notified or expected to attend the parties, or invited to join in drinks, jokes and songs.

Parties were the major development of Scotch Block activities. These always included the wives. Large dinners were arranged and an orchestra procured. There were favors, corsages, and drinks for the women. The supper hour was interspersed with speeches extolling the beauty, desirability, and good sportsmanship of the wives. Members performed according to their talents—songs, dancing, mimicry, and clowning. The parties were noisy, hilarious, and exhausting.

As the years went by, Scotch Block members took up curling. This change of sport eliminated many of the women. The women's curling section was small. Only one occasion for mixed curling was arranged during the year. This has since been changed. There is a large women's curling section now, and mixed games take place weekly. For numerous reasons N. refused to become a curler.

As prosperity increased, the Maple Leaf Club membership became larger. The club had to be enlarged. Scotch Block moved to new and roomier quarters, which meant that more lockers were available for membership in the inner group. G. had been the *only one* of his profession in Scotch Block for about twelve years. By this time almost all of Scotch Block were regular patients at G.'s office.

Someone brought into Scotch Block another man, X., in G.'s profession, who specialized in one area only. X. was never as popular as G. He was more skilful in sports and threatened the sporting prestige a number of the men had built up. However, professionally, he was considered well trained and a good operator. G. and X. were both interested in the same type of practice, namely, a wealthy one. They had different specialities. Each had a good word to say for the other.

Prosperity in the community was increasing and with it the membership in the Club. Amongst the numerous brokers, insurance agents, junior and senior executives, and salesmen admitted to membership, were from six to ten of X.'s and G.'s professional contemporaries. Some of them had their eyes on Scotch Block. However, X. and G. decided that this was their game preserve. Whenever a locker became vacant, X. and G. had a good fellow to fill it. Usually in order to get in, your locker had to be shared by the member you were bringing in, until there was a vacant one. G. told N. that H., F. and J. tried very hard to get in, but *unfortunately* there was *no room*. [Italics added.]

For a period of almost twenty years, G. was the only one of his profession (with the exception of X. for about the last eight years) in a group of around a hundred.

When clubs and hotels were allowed a liquor licence, the Maple Leaf Club built an attractive bar downstairs near the lounges. Drinking in the locker room lost much of its flavor and Scotch Block is gradually losing its character. A number of the leading lights have died or taken up different interests or businesses.

G. has been considering dropping his Maple Leaf Club membership. He is developing other interests. He is well satisfied with the contribution the Maple Leaf Club made to the kind of practice he wanted.

As this family's income increased, the Scotch Block pattern of its social activities changed correspondingly.

About thirteen years ago, G. and N. joined the Three Oaks Golf Club. They had belonged to two other golf clubs previously. Some of G.'s friends persuaded him that this was a suitable club. They were opening up their membership to entice a small number of *suitable* men between the ages of thirty-five and forty-five, as their membership seemed to be leaning a little on the old side.

The Three Oaks Golf Club is a much more exclusive club than the Maple

Leaf Club. G. was approached by members already in the Club. G.'s prosperity at this time had reached a very comfortable level. At the Maple Leaf Club and the other golf clubs, when a man becomes a member, his wife automatically has membership privileges, but not at the Three Oaks Club. The wife has to be sponsored independently by women and voted upon by a women's committee.

G. was not a member for long at the Three Oaks Club until he was invited to join Scotch Block there. The Three Oaks Club's Scotch Block has quite a different atmosphere from the one at the Maple Leaf Club. Before the licensing of the clubs, the bottle and the location of the lockers were factors drawing together the members of this group. The atmosphere, however, is much more dignified and quiet. There are no activities which include women. The men in this group arrange matches together. Once a year, a competition including all Scotch Block members is arranged and a banquet is given by two of its members. The hosts for this banquet vary from year to year. Each member is expected to take his turn. This is an expensive project.

Membership in the Three Oaks Club's Scotch Block was more carefully planned than at the Maple Leaf Club. They have a committee for this purpose. Names are brought up at the yearly meeting and anyone objecting to a new member disqualifies that person from Scotch Block. One of the Maple Leaf Club's presidents himself was not considered suitable.

There are a number of Maple Leaf Club members at the Three Oaks Club, but quite a number have been refused membership. The reasons given were, "He is a noisy show-off," "His friends are objectionable," "He would want to run everything."

These rounds of social activity, in which the man participates more than the woman, arrive in the end at something like an approximation of the decorous, traditional English club, with women excluded entirely. This report depicts extremely well the institutionalized social life of the Crestwood male, which has important implications for the career and provides companionship and emotional satisfaction only as a by-product. It is perhaps significant that liquor plays so important a part in creating intimacy, in what for many is an otherwise tense situation.

Associations concerned primarily with status seem to be either limited to men or partially open to women for whom some provision must be made, *because* they are wives of members. A Crestwood Heights woman, for instance, will join her husband's golf club and accept restricted participation rather than take extra membership in a ladies' golf club. If she wishes to enhance her own and her family's social prestige solely as a woman, she tends to join an association such as the I.O.D.E., the Jewish Council of Women, Hadassah, Red Cross, or any of a number of charitable boards or committees sponsoring the arts, where women may outnumber or replace men altogether. The number of associations where men and women may participate equally are few if any. This situation is often irksome to the woman who has earlier experienced the freedom of a co-educational university or of colleague-ship in business or profession.

ASSOCIATIONS FOR THE CHILDREN

The adult-centered, adult-controlled associations are undoubtedly of primary importance in the social life of Crestwood Heights, but it is the child-centered, adult-controlled associations which touch on child-rearing most directly. Crestwood parents, many of whom are deeply involved in ensuring status through associational membership, will also, given their desire to groom the child for an adult status which may surpass their own, create or endorse suitable associations for the child. In this they have the backing of those child-rearing experts who regard participation in such associations as an important condition of social-ization. With pressure on two fronts, the Crestwood child, almost from the cradle, is directed through a series of age-graded associations espe-cially devised for his physical, mental, and emotional needs at each stage of growth, until he finally joins his parents in their own adult associations. Here he may be required to meet further age-graded re-quirements, by progressing through junior and intermediate ranks until finally he emerges as an adult member in good standing.[16]

It is only in rare instances that the status of the parents as symbol-ized by associational membership is surpassed by that of the child dur-ing their lifetime. More frequently, further upward social mobility occurs after the parents' death. Should it take place earlier, it often indicates that the parents have been shaken off by a geographical move of the children.

Exclusion operates to a large degree in children's associations, but it is not quite as rigid as in adult associations, and considerably more indulgence is accorded the child since he is considered to be subject to trial and error learning. Parents and adults are, indeed, extremely sensi-tive to the open exclusion practised by child-controlled children's asso-ciations. The inconsistency of this parental attitude and adult practice is used with consummate skill by the children to deflect adult pres-sure from their own activities. This kind of manoeuvring is marked in teen-age sororities and fraternities.

Crestwood parents are as liberal in providing their children with associational activity as they are in giving toys, spending-money, or expensive clothing. Although this parental indulgence towards children's associations may appear a function of pure generosity, it may also serve as a cloak for a forceful driving of the child to organize his leisure as rigidly as the parents deal with theirs. By keeping children gainfully occupied in the search for an achievement of status at every age level, the parents can, to a considerable degree, prevent the wanton wasting of leisure which is generally viewed in Crestwood Heights with very grave suspicion. Often a private school is chosen by the parents primarily for its power to offer appropriate friendships and to teach the social skills needed for social participation at their own class level or beyond. Parents, in regard to their own children, are sponsors and status-lenders; however, the status-getting of the child also adds to the parental status by demonstrating that the parents have another skill (teaching their children to get status) and another power (deriving status from the children's success).

The means used in child-centered, adult-controlled groupings to ensure that the child learns their skills are strikingly similar to those employed by the school in its formal instruction. The child is encouraged to compete in excellence with his age mates, and rewards are given for outstanding performance. The symbolic trappings of a high-ranking Boy Scout, for instance, outrival the military decorations of any army in the Western world, but not by so much as to make them seem patently fantastic or juvenile. And while the child is urged towards competition, he is also taught that he must co-operate with and be accepted by his peers.

The adult-controlled children's groupings share a common orientation towards the future—they regard themselves as preparing the child for the life he is hopefully going to lead as an adult. But, as mentioned above, since these activities are directed by adults, they inevitably incorporate some elements of traditionalism from the child's present class level. Thus the adults provide the activity or the training in a skill on the basis of what is at present acceptable in the culture, but with the hope that these acquisitions will also be of some use to the child in an unknown future.[17] This orientation in turn has a connection with competition. In these associations the child is instructed in appropriate skills and behavior in a more individualized way than is possible within the formal curriculum of the school. Yet the child's acquisition must be utilized for group participation and social acceptance, and there is frequently an emphasis on exhibitionism. The skill is not learned first for individual satisfaction—indeed it may often be considered to have no value unless performed before others. The higher the prestige accruing to a given activity or skill, the more necessary it becomes to display it and thus demonstrate that one belongs to the corresponding status level. Family status allows the child to join or prevents him from so doing; and the skills acquired through membership, in their turn, must reflect favorably upon the family prestige. Parents see an advantage for the future also in the fact that, like the adult associations, these children's groupings provide opportunities for their children to make congenial friends in a much more highly selective segment than that afforded by the school.

Parents and adult leaders of children's associations expect the co-operation and gratitude of the child "for all that is being done for him." Such associations should, in adult eyes, satisfy all the child's recreational needs. Adult reaction to the child-centered, child-controlled associations which do develop outside the orbit of adult control is one of marked suspicion and some anger, the elders' direct response to a rejection of their well-meant efforts.

The child-centered, adult-controlled associations are exceedingly numerous, and are both formal and informal in nature. Some are patterned upon the associations of which the parents are members, and are often subsidiary units of these adult groupings. They are also ranked as to class, but differ from the parental associations in the increased emphasis on age grading, which is superimposed on the status system and is, to some degree, a factor in the determination of status, at least among peers.

These child-centered, adult-controlled associations include Boy Scouts, Girl Guides, church and synagogue groups, summer camps, camera clubs, community center groups, "Teen-Towns," and many others. The extra-curricular program of the school,[18] with teachers acting as leaders or supervisors, is particularly notable in this area. The school, too, has extended its influence into the holiday period, since several of the Crestwood teachers are deeply involved in the direction of camp programs, which they assume as summer work. While the school has no formal control over the summer camp program, it is obvious that his professional orientation cannot be completely abandoned by the teacher even in his alternative summer occupation.

A. THE PRIVATE SCHOOL

Private residential schools and summer camps are the only associations which actually remove the child from his home for an extended period of time. The majority of Crestwood Heights children go to summer camp; private residential schools are attended by relatively few. Many of the children who do go to private school are "day students," since three of Canada's most outstanding private residential schools are adjacent to the area. Attendance at private school, whether as a day student or as a boarder, however, entails a double financial burden for the Crestwood parent, who must continue to pay public school tax, in addition to tuition and perhaps boarding fees at the private school.[19] And the liberally supported public school system is at hand to educate the child, as well, or even better, in the fundamental vocational skills, if not, as yet, in all the social graces.

Although it is financially possible for a number of Crestwood children to attend private school as day students, general opinion seems to indicate that residence is essential if the child is to derive maximum benefits from the private school training (i.e., if he is to learn properly the vital social skills). The bi-ethnic character of the population is a further push for many in the direction of the private school, if the parents can afford it.

One woman informant summed up the situation very frankly, though not with factual restraint:

Most of the Christians who do send their children to private school do so because of the Jews. I think that all of them would be in private schools if the parents could afford it. Actually the teaching standards are much higher in the Crestwood schools. Many parents feel that the children should go to private school for a while at least and then at the high school level let them go to the Crestwood schools. Many, however, do the opposite, which I think is best—give the children a good academic grounding in the Crestwood schools and then let them finish at a private school to get the social graces. It is really important in Big City to say that you went to an acceptable school. It makes me mad, but it is true. I don't think that the Crestwoods Heights Collegiate would ever be considered a good school even after it has run a few more years. The mere fact of its being a collegiate is sufficient to rule it out as socially acceptable. I know that my own daughter is going to go to private school later, not because I think it is better for her, but *because it is necessary socially.* [Italics added.] Also the Jews are in the majority at the Collegiate and in the Elm Prep, particularly. I think that it is very bad for any child to be a member of a minority group whether they are Jewish or Christian. If the numbers were equal it would be all right, but not when there is such a Jewish majority.[20]

Douglas Towers probably gets more Crestwood girls than the others, partly because it is convenient and also because being Anglican,[20a] it has a certain amount of snob appeal. For the boys, United Empire Academy gets a lot because it is convenient (they charge $600 a year for day students) but St. James' (out of town) probably gets more because of snob appeal. The private schools are good in many ways too. The discipline is much better than in the Crestwood Schools. The kids are treated too permissively and never learn any sense of responsibility. Their parents were brought up differently and don't try to follow the school plan of treatment. The child is treated permissively at school and the parents are authoritarian, resulting in conflict and frustration on both sides. They are taught tolerance and understanding in the schools and then learn all about prejudice at home. They learn materialistic values in the schools, mainly because of the insecurity of the Jews which has driven them to make a materialistic display of their position and wealth.

Other informants, when asked what benefits the child acquires at private school which he could not obtain equally well in public school, are not as specific as the woman quoted above. Answers vaguely mentioned social skills, or "opportunities to meet the right people," which will "pay off" with the contacts necessary for a successful adult career. Some parents send a boy for toughening under male masters, and for authoritarian discipline and corporal punishment. Others make use of the residential school because they are considering a marital separation or because a divorce has been granted. In such cases, the parents are not always willing to reveal the true reason, but fall back upon the generalities referred to earlier. Decision in the private versus public school debate is, for many parents, a toss-up since they must determine which is the more important for the child's future: the solid academic and vocational training (including science) which the public school can supply; or the social skills and contacts which only the private school can offer—advantages which may well offset the lower professional qualifications of some private school teachers.

The girl who attends a private school embarks upon a rigid training designed to groom her for the upper ranks of her society. Like her English counterpart, she must wear a uniform which seems in some cases deliberately planned to diminish temporarily her feminine attractiveness. The contrast between these uniformed daughters and their smart, youthful mothers is strikingly obvious when the two are seen together. It is almost as if the girls were required to put in a period of menial apprenticeship before winning their femininity, and challenging their mothers. Sports are emphasized, again following British school traditions. In the private schools, girls appear to be kept, purposefully, subservient and "innocent," in marked opposition to the freedom of the co-educational elementary school and collegiate, where girls of eleven are beginning to date, to wear pretty clothes, to experiment with their mother's lipstick, and to take other prerogatives.

Heterosexual relationships are, however, by no means excluded from the private school; they are merely much more rigidly controlled than in the public schools, and more carefully regulated as to age and social standing of the partner. Like the fashionable dancing class, the private school prepares the girl for a début, instructing her in dancing and in other social arts. Escorts are not left to chance; the boys of acceptable private schools are frequently invited in a body to school functions, a courtesy which the boys' private school is expected to return. Thus the selection of eligible partners is narrowed almost exclusively to the social class and ethnic group represented by the private school, although certain outsiders may, on occasion, be admitted.[21] The strict protective rules of the girls' private school are occasionally, however, relaxed, for instance for the début. During the Christmas holidays, many débutantes attend a nightly whirl of parties, staying out unchaperoned until the early hours of the day following the dance, which often ends with a breakfast party.

Social skills and mate-selection are also the concern of the boys' private schools, but career considerations appear to bulk larger in importance. Each of these is, of course, in this setting, a means to the other. Graduation from a recognized private school is a valuable preparation for business or professional life, even though the "old school tie" does not yet bear in Canada quite the connotation which it holds or held in England. Education in a girls' private school is, in contrast, not a particularly highly regarded basis for a female career.[22]

The private school makes a richer and a somewhat more conscious (but also seemingly less "contrived") use of ritual than the public school. A child, having grown up in its obedience and with his sentiments sensibly organized by its rites and "traditions," is finally launched upon the community in a ceremony perhaps as impressive as Bar-Mitzvah or Confirmation. Much belated, but in some sense analogous to primitive puberty rites, these ceremonies signify the "putting away of childish things" and the assumption of adult, or near-adult, stance and role.

B. THE SUMMER CAMP

Unlike the private school, the summer camp embraces a large proportion of Crestwood Heights children; but it is not limited to these or exclusively to children from similar upper middle class areas. The camp, even though a relatively recent development, is now provided for all levels of North American society. Every year, one Big City newspaper endorses a campaign to send under-privileged children away from the sizzling city pavements for a week or two at camp. And just as regularly appear the expensive brochures featuring sail-boat or canoe as symbol of the great benefits to be gained from a northern summer at Camp Wongaka or Laughing Bear.

Canada is, of course, a country of vast distances, settled densely only in a narrow strip along the length of its southern border. Cities and farms are left behind as soon as one drives a few hundred miles to the north of Big City. Here the tangled expanse of rock and water, forest and swamp, fans out to meet the Precambrian Shield, melting finally into the barren lands on the Arctic's edge. Much of this territory, ancient as the world itself, has been mapped only from the air. While this solemn land supports a sparse, indigenous population of Indians, Eskimos, trappers, traders, and white technicians, it is open to the urban dweller only on its southern fringes, for one must know a different kind of life to sustain oneself within this wilderness—a knowledge which the Crestwooder has never had. Yet the city-dweller is drawn to the North. The steady pushing of highways through trees and rock has brought lakes and islands, pines, and sweeping, changing skies within the Crestwood orbit. The Crestwooder, it is true, must be protected from the bleaker aspects of the North; but armed with car, cottage, motor-boat, electric dynamo, and summer camp, he has penetrated its vacation edge. In this context, one purpose of the summer camp may be readily understood: children unsupervised at cottage or camp could easily be lost and die of exposure or exhaustion within a few miles of safety. In contrast to the traditional English holiday at the sea or in some Continental beauty spot, a Canadian vacation in the North includes real dangers, from which both adults and children must be shielded. Thus the summer camp makes it possible for children unaccompanied by parents to enjoy a contrast with their city life which they might not experience in any other way.

Summer camps, like clubs, are ranked by status. Those camps catering to wealthy children are generally some greater distance to the north, and are equipped with elaborate permanent buildings, cleared (or even landscaped) grounds, flotillas of canoes, row-boats, and sail-boats, and stables of riding horses. At the other end of the scale are the camps sponsored by urban welfare agencies which are apt to be much closer to the city, with fewer permanent buildings, tents for the campers, less elaborate recreational facilities, and a conspicuous policy of "back to nature"—though, even then, not too far.

Despite these variations, all camps have certain basic features in common. It is generally agreed by camp personnel and by parents that the camp should be at some distance from the child's home, not directly accessible to any urban center but not beyond the reach of telephone, electricity, and good roads. The camp should be situated on or near a sizable body of water, but not in close proximity to a populous and public resort area. Water is essential, since swimming, together with canoeing and sailing for the better-off, is a skill which the camp usually teaches. A heavily wooded area dotted with lakes is equally necessary for overnight camping trips, which remove the child completely from his customary world of brick and stone, paved roads, and concrete sidewalks. Space and isolation are important, for both allow behavior which would not be tolerated within Crestwood Heights itself. A camp director reported that he considered "the skinny dip" one of the most valuable and enjoyable experiences for the campers, and regretted that the location of the swimming beach at his camp (for both boys and girls) did not permit this.

Camping experts are divided in their views about the desirability of elaborate equipment. Since the summer camp is not a functional part of the culture of the North and campers do not really live like or perform the duties of forest ranger, prospector, or trapper, at least a minimum of city comforts is inevitably required as a screen between the campers and their environment. Those experts who uphold the back-to-nature goal frown upon too many softening influences, but since the camp exists to train children in certain skills which are not always those that might teach them to live off the country, they agree that it is impossible to rule out "frills" altogether. Also, since the wider the proffered range of skills, the higher are the fees which may be imposed, arguments for or against luxurious facilities depend, to a certain degree, upon the financial resources and policy of the camp. Where (in a "third stage") a really expensive camp strongly advocates a back-to-nature policy, it must be carried out in the grand manner; the children must endure the right hardships, such as sleeping out overnight, but only in a correct, carefully planned ritual, without actually undergoing any real austerity.[23] Senior boys at such camps have mentioned the traumatic effect of toilet paper having been forgotten on an overnight hike. And one mother, with marked concern, asked if paper serviettes were not usually taken along to shore suppers, after her child told her about washing her hands in the lake and drying them on her shorts. A dearth of paper cups can create a minor crisis, and sharing a cup may be regarded as impossible.[24]

Since both experienced, responsible adults and elaborate equipment are necessary to give the child this particular contact with nature, it is understandable that camps are owned and operated by specialists and that camping has become big business. There are now camping associations which attempt to regulate standards and to train counsellors. But since camping is seasonal and can be carried on only during the vacation when children are free and the North accessible, camp leadership is with rare exceptions solely a part-time vocation, supplementing handily the annual income of the camp personnel. This opens camping to the professional teacher, and many of these do operate or staff summer camps, thus extending their socializing function towards the child to a year-round basis.

It is significant that the entire camp movement in the Province (there are at present about six hundred camps) was initiated over fifty years ago by a master at a well-known boys' private school; he took seven of his pupils on a canoe trip through the North, which the boys found so enjoyable that he repeated it for a larger group. From these simple beginnings, the teacher in question evolved a highly successful camp of his own, "very beautiful, with buildings worth a fortune." Camping has spread throughout the Province, paralleling similar developments in the rest of Canada and the United States. In its expansion within the Province it has become so closely identified with the teaching profession that the Department of Education has made a small grant to the provincial Camping Association for the training of counsellors.

Although both school and camp show similarities in their high degree of organization, there are sharp differences. The camp is voluntary and, for Crestwood children, on a fee basis. No parent is compelled by law to send his child to camp, which automatically limits the power of the teacher when he finds himself a camp director rather than in his customary more bureaucratic role. On the other hand, the teacher in the camp setting is free of the supervisory hierarchy of the school and he has greater responsibility for the child during the twenty-four hours of the day, parents being rigidly excluded except on "Visitors' Day." School Principals who are also camp directors, and teachers who act as leaders or counsellors or owners and directors, are likely to be oriented in their educational philosophy towards "dealing with the whole child." Few teachers would deny that the financial reward is important to them, but several have stated that their summer camp work has yielded them more satisfaction as teachers than their regular occupation in the school system.

The relationship between teacher and child is also subtly different in the camp setting, which excludes not only home and parents, but most outside influences of an urban community, in particular the mass communication media. Radio and daily newspapers at one camp were for the sole use of the supervisory staff. Some children complained that they missed television. One mass communication tool, however, could not be screened out of any camp observed during the research—campers clung tenaciously to their comic books! Within this highly structured social setting, the child is still required to look up to the teacher-leader as an adult superior in wisdom. But at the same time, the simplified communal life against a background of nature encourages the campers to treat members of the staff as respected "buddies," a situation somewhat reminiscent of the home relationship now advocated for children and their parents.

Paid camp personnel range through a cross-section of professions, from teachers through social group workers to doctors and nurses. Even the volunteer counsellors must almost all now have some type of formal preparation for their work. The senior positions at camp are occupied by professionals, and the rank and file counsellors approximate an apprenticeship system for which a minimum of advance instruction is required. Although a camp counsellor receives little or no money for his services, adult Crestwooders consider such a summer job eminently suitable for young people, particularly for boys, since it gives them experience in "handling" human beings, experience which will later be useful in the managerial sphere towards which most Crestwood male careers are directed. Counsellors must be close enough in age to the campers to be regarded as friends but sufficiently older to assume responsibility, which may be considerable, since it involves the physical safety of a number of youngsters in an unfamiliar environment. As one boys' camp leader expressed it,

. . . He liked the senior counsellors to be from twenty to twenty-four years of age; for the juniors, from eighteen to twenty; and for the Bantams (the youngest age group) from seventeen to eighteen. The counsellors for the seniors need to be older than the boys but still not too old to play with them. The senior counsellors need to be very trustworthy because they take the boys on trips, and at camp trips are an awful worry to the people in charge. With swimming and water-front activities, it was a constant worry that they might have a drowning. . . . Camps have had drownings. . . . When he was a counsellor at Tree Tops, a canoe-load of boys went on a trip and they decided to shoot the rapids and the canoe upset and one boy struck his head on a rock and was drowned . . . he and another counsellor had to go with a Mr. B., an official dragger from Big City, and drag the place for two days before they got the body. It was a gruesome sight and when they got back to camp they were in the infirmary for two days, completely unnerved.

Thus the camp counsellors form an age-graded society among themselves, with certain patterns of behavior which are like those of the campers, but with others which differ, since counsellors are, like the higher echelons of the camp personnel, a privileged group. The same camp leader enlarged on the counsellors' role.

It was difficult to get counsellors at present as the boys can earn so much more money by working in the city. Of course there are the boys from rich families who do not have to worry about earning money. He didn't choose the counsellors at his camp but he wished that he did. They had been very fortunate in getting good counsellors, especially in the senior section. There is a splendid spirit in the senior section and often counsellors who have been to camp before, write and ask to be placed in the senior section.

The greatest difficulty with counsellors at camp is to keep them on the camp site after duties are over. The best remedy for this is to provide a suitable program in camp for them. They [camp personnel] think they do this very well in the senior section. They have what they call the Brothers' Club and only counsellors in the senior section can belong. They make it quite exclusive. They each put two dollars in the pot and the club treasurer buys food with this money. They go down to the seniors' lodge every night, listen to the radio, and eat. He said that he never got to bed before midnight but you could always get up the next morning and be ready to go. If the counsellors are not kept on the camp site, they go into town and do stupid things and then the town people get down on the camp.

They have very little trouble with their counsellors' not getting along with each other. They believe this is overcome by the wise choice of counsellors. You never choose a counsellor without asking someone what kind of a fellow he is. You always ask a prospective counsellor what he expects from camp and sort of put him on his best behavior. If a counsellor cannot get along they would send him home. You can't jeopardize a whole section's summer by having a disagreeable counsellor. . . . A counsellor does not go to camp for a good time. They just can't expect it to be fun. They get their reward by giving service to the camp. A counsellor can't fool the kids. They can fool the rest of the staff for a long time and get away without working, but children know.

Counsellors are also expected to be highly versed in some particular skill:

. . . The best program in the world would be no good if you didn't have a good staff. The kids found campcraft the most boring of all activities. A few years ago the camp had a counsellor who knew he was going to teach campcraft, so he did a little preparation, before coming to camp. The rest of the staff were simply amazed that the kids were going to this craft class without any protest. So he [the Director] went down and sat in for some of the sessions. This counsellor just made campcraft come alive for the kids.

Below the supervisory level of the senior personnel and counsellors (junior and senior) are the campers, graded almost as strictly by age as the pupils in the school. A school Principal, who is also a summer camp director, is quoted on the organization of the campers:

. . . the most important thing is getting the kids divided into the right tribes. He finds the book put out by Scott Foresman *These Are Your Children*,[25] most valuable for understanding kids and therefore helping you to place them in the proper tribe. This book told him that six-year-old kids were far-sighted and that it wasn't until they were nine or ten that they developed adult vision. So you don't have six-year-old kids threading fine needles in craft work. The interviewer asked how the director knew the kids well enough to place them in tribes the first day. He assured her that he knew all the ones who were coming to his camp. For instance, there was one in the ten-year-old group who wouldn't be able to work with her own age-group. But on the whole his groups will be perfect. When he was with Mrs. X. [another camp director who was not a school teacher] she had an April party for the kids going to her camp and at this party you were able to size the kids up. For example, the kid that stood on the top of the piano just didn't go to camp![26]

It is evident from the above quotation that the teacher who is also a camp director has a better opportunity to screen his campers than the director who has no such year-round contact with children, and that the stages of physical and emotional maturation are considered as carefully at camp as they are in school. There are camps which specialize in younger children. One such junior camp, under the supervision of a woman who directs a nursery school during the winter, accepts about fifty children ranging in age from four to twelve. Both boys and girls are included, but no boys older than nine. Boys appear to be sent to camp more often than girls, since the camp experience is seen as particularly important for them, and perhaps somewhat analogous to the toughening under male masters at the traditional boys' private school. As the age level increases, the sexes tend to separate into their own camps. Most of the older, established, and exclusive camps are of this type. At the upper end of the age scale are the camp seniors, many of whom graduate into the counsellor's section, as juniors. Senior campers, particularly boys, may become problems to the camp. The senior camp official quoted earlier expanded on this point:

The trouble with the seniors is boredom. This not only applies to the seniors who come from broken homes but to all seniors. If they have come up through the camp, they have done everything there is to do. They [the staff] suggest at his camp that these boys go to another camp for their last years of camping and he thinks it would be a good idea if other camps did the same. Their camp specializes in sailing and every boy learns to be a good sailor. Now if those seniors who have this skill would go to another camp that specializes in another skill, it would be better for everyone concerned. The only cure for this boredom in camp is to send the seniors on lots of trips. This keeps them occupied.

In addition to the hierarchy of camp supervisors and the campers there are usually other persons who might be described as maintenance personnel. The cook is one such functionary, as important in these days of full employment as the school building superintendent, and even more difficult to replace.[27] Frequently teacher-directors and senior camp personnel bring wives and children to camp who may or may not be included in its activities. The same informant enlarges on this practice:

. . . He has three girls and he doesn't think they would fit into camp life. His oldest girl is thirteen and the fellows would want to be dating her and then there would be trouble. He has them about five miles down the lake at a lodge. R. [another senior man] has his family there too. He goes down on his day off and if he wants to go at night, he just tells R. who is in the same section and he stays on duty. Then he does the same for him. The director has his wife and little child at camp, but then his child is a boy. Some of the rest of the staff have their wives at camp, but the wives work in the Tuck Shop or as Camp Mother for the Bantams.

Although even greater efforts are made to disguise the facts, the summer camp, like the school, is characterized by a clearly defined and recognized hierarchy of personnel. At the top is the director with his aides, followed by the program director, personnel director, section directors—the number of such persons varying with the size, the exclusiveness, and the expensiveness of the camp. There are also the instructors in special skills (campcraft, music, handicrafts, swimming, and so on) who rate almost as highly as the administrative personnel. The counsellors, junior and senior, rank next, along with the business staff. Below these groups is the main body of campers, divided by age. The larger the camp, the greater the number of such differentiated age grades. Lowest socially (although exceedingly important in the camp social system) are the maintenance personnel, the cook and his helpers, and the handyman (if the camp boasts such a luxury). Professionalism is rewarded with a higher position in the scale; peripheral experts are related through this professional echelon with the main body of camp personnel and with the parents who foot the bills. It is chiefly the setting in which the summer camp operates that gives it a radical difference from the school.

The activities of the camp, like those of the school, follow a somewhat rigid pattern. The camp program centers around the teaching of skills, with different camps specializing in different skills. Beyond this difference, the underlying organization is strikingly similar. One basic feature of all summer camps is the emphasis upon planning every minute of the child's time. Even leisure is allotted and closely supervised.[28] Only for the very young, in camp as in school, is there any slight modification of the intensive program. One camp does not attempt to teach skills to children below the age of eight. A woman interviewer received the following schedule of activities, which seems typical for the majority of camps, although one, which prides itself upon its leisurely approach, starts the day as late as eight-fifteen A.M.:

Next the director outlined a day in camp for me:

7:45 a.m. He goes through the camp calling "Everybody up!" This is wash-up time, etc.

8:15 a.m. Council Rock. They begin with the hymn, "Father, we thank Thee for the night" (the first verse). Then they have a story. This story contains a lesson, or is a Nature story, or a combination of the two. He told about Mrs. N.'s [a camp director] good talk for the first morning. She would say to the kids, "Whose camp is this?" Someone would answer, "Yours." She would say, "Yes, we own the land, but whose camp is it?" Someone would eventually say, "It's ours." Then she would go on to say, "Whose fault is it, if we do not have a good time?" They would reply, "Ours." Then Mrs. N. would say, "If you do not have a good time here, where there is everything to have a good time with, what are you going to tell your parents when you get home?" The kids would answer, "We'll tell them it's our own fault."

The Council Rock is closed by singing the second verse of the above-mentioned hymn, which is never changed all during the camp.[29]

8:30 a.m. Breakfast. I remarked "These kids must be awfully hungry." The Director replied, "Yes, that's why we give them lots of porridge to fill them up: it's cheap!"

9:00 a.m. Housekeeping. This consists of bed-making and fixing up the camp. The nurse makes the cabin inspection.

9:20 a.m. Activity Period. Crafts for one group. The director [a school Principal] described how they kept everyone busy in the camp and it reminded me of a Junior High time-table. While one group is having crafts, another is having boating, and so on. He explained that the senior boys always had boating last because then they wouldn't go far afield, because if they did, they would miss the swim period.

10:00 a.m. The above group would have boating.

10:40 a.m. Games. All the boys have games at the same period and then all the girls are put together for their game period.

11:20 a.m. Projects. These consist of practising games for better performance, or wading, or building a fort, or making improvements around the camp.

12:00 a.m. Swimming. Everyone goes in at the same time. At Mrs. N.'s camp everyone went in "skinny." He explained that this was in the nude. There was quite a bit of criticism of this, but her camp was ideal for such a purpose because the point separated the beach and the girls could go in on one side and the boys on the other. His camp was not like this, so they had to wear suits. He seemed to regret this.

12:45 a.m. Everyone out.

1:00 p.m. Lunch.

2:30 p.m. Choices. These offer some alternatives—crafts, hiking, etc. The director went on to tell me how clever he thought his own son had been at choosing last year.

4:00 p.m. Swimming.

4:45 p.m. Free Time. He didn't tell me how they spend this, but he gave the impression he has it all planned.

5:30 p.m. Supper.

6:00–6:45 p.m. Free games or boating.

6:45–7:30 p.m. Camp Fire on Tuesday, Thursday, and Saturday. On Monday, Wednesday, and Friday and on wet nights, it is story-time.
8:00 p.m. Lights Out.

Cutting across the daily routine are special events which supplement the day-to-day activities:

He explained next that his camp was divided into four weeks and then two weeks. The first week you don't have to worry about. They are all busy exploring, etc. The third week you have a Sports Day on Saturday. You talk it up all week. You have three teams of boys and three teams of girls. You choose the three top boys and the three top girls as leaders of the teams. You try to have the teams as evenly matched as possible even if you have to help in the choosing! Everybody in camp does something on Sports Day. The team leaders decide what each one of his team is to do. "The leaders?" I said. "Oh, each team has the help of a counsellor," he said. . . . All the events on Sports Day depend on group efforts. Some of the events are diving, boat races, and a special kind of race called a Zizzie Race. There were two boats . . . made from plywood about as big as the top of his desk and as flat. They had sides about a foot high. They would hold two counsellors each. He told about one race where two male counsellors with their female partners (ones they liked) got in the zizzies and they had to sit with their legs entwined and paddle with their hands from away out in the lake to the shore. One of the couples got the bright idea of splashing the other zizzie full of water and it sank. The kids just love this race.

The second week you go on picnics. The fourth week is Circus Week,[30] and on Sunday of this week you have a Water Day. He didn't elaborate on these weeks' activities. The fifth week you have something comparable to a Circus Week and on the sixth week you have another Sports Day. . . .

Sunday is different at camp from other days. *You get up fifteen minutes later.* You have chapel. The chapel is a special place. Mrs. N.'s camp had a wonderful outdoor chapel. His hadn't such a good place. You never go into the chapel except on Sundays. You wouldn't think of playing there. Anyway it isn't a very good place to play as it is on the side of a hill. At chapel they make their own psalms. They pattern them after the Psalms in the Bible. The Chief says to the kids, "What are some of the things you see that are beautiful?" Then they make a list, such as moon, sun, trees and water, grass and shadows, etc. Then you make the psalm. It must be a balanced one such as "Praise ye the Lord, for He is good; for He gives us the sun and the moon," and so on. They have some wonderful psalms that they have made. The children also make their own prayers. They use the litany as a pattern. The story told on Sunday morning is along the same lines as on weekdays. I asked how he managed his religious exercises when he had Jews and Gentiles. He replied, "Just the same as I do in the auditorium here. You have been to auditorium, haven't you?" "No," I said. "I talk about the Fatherhood of God," he said.

On Sundays they have no crafts, projects, boating, or choices. They do special things on Sunday. They all have to write a letter on Sunday and it is their ticket for lunch. He told about helping the six-year-olds to write their letters. *Among the special things they do on Sunday is to go to the country school house. They get in via the window and the rich kids see where their poor country cousins go to school.*[31] He says the school is pretty awful. [Italics added.]

Many of these activities obviously resemble those of school. For instance, the formal identity of Council Rock with morning school assembly might be remarked. Tone, purpose, content, are all the same. Even the attempt to get the children to take the blame in advance in case the enterprise should fail is characteristic.[32] The religious aspects of the camp program are again very similar to the practices in the school, where some religious instruction is also given, but where it must, at the same time, be sufficiently "broad" to include both Jew and Gentile.[33] The camp differs in making a direct connection between religious feeling and a love of and veneration for nature. Nearly all camps strongly emphasize Indian names and lore, which may sometimes bear a religious connotation at the primitive level of Canada's history. A camp which does not include morning "devotions" does, for instance, play up the Indian theme, with a curious borrowing of an Indian puberty rite.

Mr. C. said he liked the Indian motif at camp. He explained that at Tall Trees, you could get an Indian name for yourself. You have to go out at sundown by yourself. You shoot a flaming arrow at the sun. You are about half a mile down the lake from the camp and you light a fire and you only have three matches. You must keep the fire burning all night and you are not to go to sleep. You do not take any food with you except a handful of raisins. The interviewer asked if the raisins had any significance, but the counsellor said that they didn't. You are supposed to sit there by your fire and meditate about what makes the world go round. He [the Counsellor, when he had gone] put his raisins on the canoe and tried to gauge the time by throwing a raisin away every fifteen minutes, as you are not allowed to have a watch. Soon he was joined by two field mice and every fifteen minutes or thereabouts he threw the raisin and they were right there to get it. You go back to camp when the sun comes up. At the next council ring, you either tell a story (an Indian one, of course) or teach the camp a new Indian game. You are then given your Indian name. His means "player of games." He felt that this was a wonderful experience.

This rite has but little of the fasting, or even torture, of the Indian ceremonials, although being alone for so great a length of time *without a watch* might well be felt as an ordeal by many Crestwood Heights youths. It is notable that the totem is not "revealed" to the waiting individual, but is conferred by the group on his return. The experience he receives is confined to the camp circle and does not spill over to the whole of life, serving only to integrate the boy into the temporary group.

The carefully structured camp activities, therefore, afford to Crestwood Heights children a limited contact with the Northland of their country. Such a period is very different from the childhood pictured by one prominent Englishman who told a class of students about his early life as a missionary's son in the islands of the South Pacific. His mother taught the children in the mornings. In the afternoons they were free to roam wherever they wished through their tropical heaven, hours of delight which had colored all his later life.[34] The urban child of Crestwood Heights is denied such freedom. The program of the summer camp is the closest approximation which he has, in many cases, to an unfettered exploration of any environment.

The activities of summer camp also present a special opportunity to the child who is not academically inclined. Here he may indulge in more exclusively physical skills. Here he can shine as an athletic hero, or even display outstanding ability in craft work, without being required to maintain at the same time the high academic standing expected from almost every child in Crestwood Heights.

The methods used to induce the child to conform to the camp program are, on the word of those in authority, different from the disciplinary measures of the school. To an outsider, however, whatever the means, the ends of the process are identical. The child must learn to act with the group, regardless of his private inclinations. At swim time, the child is expected to swim; at rest time, he rests. All this is, of course, useful training for adult life in Crestwood Heights, where one is expected to do many things simply because these *are* done, at certain times, under certain conditions. The same mechanism applies to skills. The discipline, quite as much as the skill content, is the relevant factor. The child learns the correct way to start a fire without matches, to fell trees, to calculate time by the sun, because these *are* the activities with which the camp program is concerned, although it is obvious that few of these skills will be practised when the child returns to his customary world of brick, stone, concrete, steel, and glass. Indeed, fire is used in Crestwood Heights very rarely, to light pipe or cigarette or in the fireplace on ritual occasions. And chopping of trees on private property would not be tolerated; on municipal property, it would be punished by law.

If the child does not take kindly to the organized life of the camp, the pressure of the peer group is evoked; spurred on by the camp leaders who prefer to use these means rather than the direct authoritarianism which the teacher-pupil relationship still allows to some extent within the bureaucratic structure of the school. Should this pressure prove inadequate, the camp leaders will intervene with the option of conformity or punishment, usually exclusion from the group by being sent to bed. That this is approved discipline is supported by the following comments from a veteran camp director:

"What about discipline at camp?" the interviewer asked.

"It is about the same as at school," he said. "There are all the different personalities; everyone is different from the other. Camp used to be run under the old sergeant-major type of discipline where everything was planned for the kids for the whole day. This has changed tremendously. Now they relax as many controls as possible. They reduce rules to a minimum. They adjust the rules to the level of ability of the kids. The juniors are more organized and supervised. They get more freedom as they get older and learn how to live together. They operate under two themes. The first is that they must live together, therefore cabins must be clean, etc. The second theme is that of safety.[35] You must not be on the dock after dark or you might fall in—and who would find you? At camp, everything is so vivid. The rules grow out of the situations.

If they find a kid not adjusting in his cabin (maybe he is untidy) he is given another chance. If he doesn't smarten up, they shift him to another cabin with another counsellor. If this doesn't work, he is put in isolation.[36] Some camps have a tent on purpose for this. Counsellors sometimes give a boy punishment such as cleaning up the section. X. thought this was bad, comparing it to a teacher giving a child arithmetic as a punishment. The least objectionable punishment in his opinion was to send the kid to bed. He feels that if a counsellor gives a punishment that he should stay with it until the time is up. He has found kids that have been in bed all afternoon just because the counsellor has told someone else to look after the boy and they had forgotten. He doesn't believe in the counsellor sending the boy to the section head for punishment. He compared this to sending a kid to the Principal for detention at school. He has seen corporal punishment used at camp and he says that there is a great deal of name calling which he does not approve. He talks to his counsellors about this all the time. . . . Discipline is not the same problem as in school. Everyone is doing the same thing. There is a great deal of social pressure at work.

To peer group pressure is sometimes added a system of rewards for performance. One camp director (also a teacher) stated:

Their only system of rewards is the winning of bars. When each child comes to camp he is given a wooden shield. As he acquires his skills, he gets a transfer for his wooden shield. When he has thirty-five transfers, he gets a metal shield which costs seven dollars. When he gets the metal shield and wins points he gets metal bars for his shield. No boy can win a metal shield in his first year at camp. He, himself, felt that this is a very good system, as the kid is working against himself and not in competition with others.[37]

The parallel with school report cards and prizes is too evident to need further comment.

As in the school, the child at camp is carefully induced to "want" what his elders deem is good for him. Guidance of children by adults is essential in any culture,[38] yet that of Crestwood Heights goes to considerable lengths to impress upon the child that *he* makes his own choices and decisions. This will, of course, be increasingly the case as the child grows older, but while he remains in camp or in school, a superior-subordinate relationship is almost inescapable.

Parental expectations in regard to camp are varied and complex, but in the main, parents hope that by handing their children over to the camp, they will receive them back in due course more mature, responsible, and fully equipped with social skills. These expectations are substantially the same as those directed towards the school during the remainder of the year. Some parents and many camp leaders, however, frankly state the children are packed off to camp to give the parents a respite. One senior camp leader summed up the reasons for parents sending their children as he, a professional, saw them.

The parents want them to learn the skills they can't teach them, such as swimming, boating, tying of knots, archery, etc. Parents also send them because they want them to become more mature. He said that they called it "becoming more socialized." He shook his head over this and explained again how the parents undid what they [the staff] did at camp. The third reason he gave for parents sending their kids to camp was so that the boy would learn to get along with others, "to be one of the boys." The fourth reason was so that the parents would get a holiday from their kids for a while. He always plays up the positive side of this. He doesn't say that the parents send their kids to camp just to get rid of them. The interviewer asked, "But some of them do, don't they?" "Yes," he replied, "but we don't say that. We must always have the positive approach! Kids are often sent to camp because their father was at the same camp. We get a lot of second generation kids at our camp."

Like the private school, the summer camp gets a small proportion of children from broken homes. Another counsellor elaborated this point:

When the interviewer asked him why parents sent their children to camp he said he felt that seventy per cent of them sent them to get rid of them. They have a large number from broken homes, and these frequently present quite a problem. Sometimes the kids from these homes form a real attachment for the counsellor and maybe it is the first time in their lives that any one person has taken an interest in them. The chief difficulty with the Bantams [youngest age group] who come from broken homes, is to get them to rest. The Juniors get homesick. They [staff] don't know why they get homesick, because some of them have no home. They are all right after two or three days, especially if they make friends.

Besides these, there are parents who afford the child experience at camp because to them it represents a golden pleasure they missed in their own childhood. On the other hand, there are a very few parents who choose camp because they feel that their child should learn how less fortunate children live. One wealthy, socially conscious couple deliberately sent their small son to a camp for under-privileged children, where the child was acutely miserable. In such cases, the child may virtually be a pawn to compensate the parent for happiness he may have missed or to assuage parental guilt for a too-comfortable existence.

Camp leaders themselves see the camp as fulfilling a definite social purpose. As one leader put it:

> Objectives . . . vary from camp to camp. The director and the owner of his camp shape the policy. At Tree Tops, the owner is not always there but he and the director [a school Principal] do not always agree on policy. The owner wants a lot of religion in the camp, but the director wants to play up character-building and not religion.
>
> His own objectives are: (1) Education, that is the learning of skills and knowledge of the great Northland. The skills are swimming, sailing, etc. Then there is so much to learn about the North and Nature. (2) Socialization, which is learning to live together. (3) Growth, which means emotional and social maturity. (4) Character development which is accomplished by living close to God through Nature.
>
> The old idea of camp being a place where the children are sent just to be looked after for the summer is gone and these new ideas are taking over.

These objectives may not, however, be in the minds of parents when the children return to the city. Camp personnel at the highest level frequently express themselves in regard to parents very much as teachers speak about parents in the school. One interviewer reports:

> Then he [camp leader] started to tell me about the problems with parents. At his camp, founded in the early nineteen-hundreds, they try to teach kids self-discipline and self-control. Often they get kids who have no sense of responsibility and they teach them this at camp. Then when the kids come home, the mothers treat the kids just the same as they did before they went to camp. The kids have grown all summer but the parents haven't. The kids have learned to meet frustration by saying "Oh, darn it," etc. but when they come home they regress to meeting it with tears or temper tantrums. He told how they teach kids to make their beds and not to lose things and how to keep the cabin tidy, but when they come home they are not allowed to do this, as these parents have servants in their homes. He told about one boy who had been taught how to make his bed, and a month or so after the kid was home from camp he met the mother in the street and asked her how Bill liked camp and she said, "Just fine." Then he asked if the boy was still making his own bed and she replied, "Oh, we have a maid to do those things and we had to ask him not to do it!" He thought this was a bad mistake. He said of course this wouldn't happen in every section of the city, but that was what happened in Crestwood Heights.

Camp experience, for the child, appears to facilitate certain developmental phases which are considered extremely important, if not crucial, in the Crestwood Heights culture. It is at the summer camp that girls are expected to have their crushes on other girls, and boys to go through the homosexual phase of their development. At camp, many children receive their informal sex education and learn the sexual mores, sometimes from their peers, but also to some extent from their counsellors who are most often only a few years older than the campers themselves. While this function of the camp is never overtly discussed, it seems to be accepted by parents who, while holding or professing a "progressive" attitude towards sex, still prefer or feel compelled to delegate the responsibility for the sex education of their children to some outside institution.

For many children, perhaps the majority, camp is the first environment which gives them an opportunity to expose their bodies to their peers of the same sex, despite the great freedom now prevalent within the Crestwood Heights home where small children of opposite sex are frequently bathed together in the same tub. It was observed during the camp study that many children displayed extreme modesty, even in the intimacy of the sleeping cabin or tent; this is always shared with other children of the same sex and age, in contrast to the private room the child may occupy at home. Some were reluctant to undress completely; several children reported that they "always wore their underwear with pajamas," even when at home. Here again, there is a conflict in child-rearing. Modesty, taught consciously or unconsciously in the home by parental precept or example, must be unlearned, sometimes at considerable expense, in the camp. The child, as a result, must make the fine discrimination between excessive modesty and exhibitionism, and it is not surprising that mistakes are made.

One camp policy on this point was explicit. The campers were required to undress completely before putting on pajamas, and at first enforcement of the rule required considerable persuasion by leaders and counsellors. Some instances of juvenile exhibitionism occurred, which were discouraged either by the counsellor in charge or by taunts or ridicule and teasing from other cabin mates. It is interesting to note that both "modesty" and "immodesty" were more frequently expressed at bed-time than was the case before swimming.[39]

The lines between what was to be regarded as "excessive modesty," "naturalness," and outright "exhibitionism" were not too precise, although the existence of such limits was beyond doubt. A boy, for example, who objected in the intimacy of the cabin group to removing his underwear was reproved by the counsellor and teased by his cabin mates. At the opposite extreme, another boy who stood naked in his upper bunk, calling attention to his body, particularly his genitals, was similarly rebuked and ridiculed. From these episodes, one might infer that "naturalness" seems to consist of an awareness of sex, with the ability to expose or to cover one's body as the appropriate occasions dictate, without behavior or comment which will call attention either to the exposure or to the covering.

In one mixed camp studied (which included age groups from five to eleven), several instances of homosexual crushes between both boys and boys, and girls and girls were noted, and also a few cases of heterosexual attachments, the friendship between a five-year-old girl and a five-and-a-half-year-old boy being the most exceptional. Such relationships, however, seemed to be free of sexual experimentation.

Curiosity about sex was indulged through looking, peeping, and listening, accompanied by giggling and teasing. "Looking" is confined to cabin mates of the same sex; "peeping" is directed towards the opposite sex; and "listening" was indulged in principally by girls. The looking took place in the intimacy of the sleeping cabin or in the "kybo." The peeping was carried on outside cabins, tents, or the kybo, girls attempting to peep at the boys, running away and shrieking if discovered; the boys behaved in similar fashion if found peeping at the girls. Listening, through the board wall dividing the kybo, was quite possibly a unique feature at one mixed camp. Counsellors would frequently disperse these groups, but no threat of punishment was made for these slightly sex-oriented activities. Camp leaders accept sexual curiosity, with its potential for experimentation, as a normal behavior pattern, to be tolerated, to be kept wherever possible from leading to actual sex-experience, but to be discouraged with the least possible display of emotion on the side of the adults.

In the more natural setting of the camp, the Crestwood child finds some faint approximation to the environment of the rural child, who learns his facts about sex by first-hand observation of animals. Although farm parents may be much more reticent in discussing sex with their children than are Crestwood Heights parents, they may also be exceedingly frank in their conversations about the breeding of animals. And even if his parents do not speak openly about it, the rural child can readily see for himself the mating of animals. The effect upon the sexual symbolism of the city child of the gradual disappearance of animals within urban society has not been assessed; perhaps the presence of domestic pets may compensate to some degree for the missing contact with the seasonal cycles of birth on the farm.

Children are expected to form friendships at camp, but these relationships do not often carry over to the home setting. Sometimes, of course, friendship predates the camp experience and has been a factor, though perhaps a minor one, in the parental decision about the particular camp to which the child is to be sent. No camps studied were restricted to Crestwood Heights children; several drew more than half their clientele from that area. Within this extended group, parents have no control over the child's informal associations, which may be in part responsible for the dissolution of camp friendships after the return home. Some instances are on record of parents encouraging camp friendships which they considered desirable by inviting these friends to parties or to spend a weekend, or by allowing their own children to accept such invitations.

The summer camp experience, for the child who does not attend private school as a boarder, is something of an equivalent in so far as it teaches him to get along without his parents and the comforts of home. One might expect that, in Canada, a new country, children would be given this experience by contact with their North through some kind of communal service, such as fire-ranging, timber-cutting, or reforestation,[40] but Canadians, like Americans, do not take kindly to government-regulated work experience for youth. Camp fulfils largely educational, recreational, and to some extent status-conferring functions. Also, like school and university, the camp helps to fill the lengthening period between childhood and full maturity, the stretched-out period before the adult is finally permitted to become a contributing member of his society.

C. THE TEEN-AGE CULTURE : FRATERNITIES AND SORORITIES

While it may appear from the foregoing descriptions of highly organized leisure during childhood and youth, that time is rigidly controlled, there are other activities which are relatively free, although still supervised by adults. Much informal home entertaining falls into this category—the celebration of birthdays and special occasions such as Christmas or Chanukah. Plays, formal dances, and other activities are held outside the home, frequently in the school, and adult control is patterned and inevitable. But in the Crestwood house, the child's own bedroom and the family rumpus room are areas of comparative freedom, where he may entertain his friends with a minimum of grown-up supervision.

The rumpus room may occupy half or more of the basement in a Crestwood Heights house. It is usually sound-proofed, decorated with an eye to utility, accessible by either side or rear door, so that there is no need to disturb those in the living-room. Frequently the television set is put in the recreation room and, in the wealthier homes, this room may be equipped as well with refrigerator, stove, and bar, so that refreshments may be served without going to the kitchen on the ground floor.

When the children of teen-age, or even younger, begin to entertain at home, the rumpus room tends to become their exclusive domain. Usually mother, father, or another adult is expected to be elsewhere in the house while such entertaining is going on. Sometimes one or both parents will wait until all guests have arrived, make their appearance for introductions, and only then size up the situation to determine how close their supervision should be. After this inspection, they can decide on periodic visits downstairs or a few rubbers of bridge next door.

Free from adult company, the youngsters may lounge on furniture which need not be treated as respectfully as that in the living-room above: last year's chesterfield, or sturdily upholstered chairs and sofa bought with foresight to withstand hard usage. Here they can dance to the latest name-band records, play games, or occasionally study in a group. Unless it is a special event, a birthday party or a gathering including outsiders as well as the intimate peer group, dress is stylishly informal: jeans and pullovers with moccasins or loafers. Frequently shoes are discarded for the special ease of socked or bare feet. Freezer or refrigerator must be stocked adequately with ice-cream and soft drinks; and sandwiches, cakes, and cookies must be in abundant supply if the evening has been planned beforehand. Should the parents neglect these details many children will quickly complain of their absence. The opportunity to help oneself indefinitely and at will is the criterion of liberality.

Formal parties are arranged by parents to celebrate birthdays or for other special occasions, such as a supper-party before a big dance. These are always carefully supervised, although teenagers are encouraged "to assume some responsibility" in "planning" their own parties. Parents, however, scan the guest lists closely. Teen-age parties have been of special concern to parents in Crestwood Heights. Indeed, several sessions of a Home and School study group were devoted to a discussion about the organization of such parties.

Towards the mid-teens, children are increasingly introduced to adult parties, in their own home, at clubs, and at the houses of their parents' friends. This early participation[41] in adult social activities provides training for the child, and fulfils the additional function of restricting his friendships mainly to those of the parental circle.[42]

Although Crestwood Heights adults would properly deny the exist-

ence of arranged marriages, such social gatherings do afford an opportunity for young people to meet others of their own age who are
"acceptable" to their parents, contacts which may blossom into long-
term friendship or even courtship. At the same time, by furthering such
social participation, the parents are actually filling the child's leisure
time, to an extent which protects him from undesirable peer-group
associations and dating patterns which could conceivably lead to marriage outside his class or ethnic group. It is *tacitly* accepted that Jewish
boys must not "date" Gentile girls and that Gentile boys should not
"date" Jewish girls. Free association across these ethnic lines is permitted to pre-adolescents and to young children, but as adolescence is
approached, with its ritualized dating patterns, the child is expected to
conform to the communal norms. If he does not spontaneously act
according to the "right" usage, he is guided or directed either subtly or
under parental, grandparental, or peer control towards those social
situations which allow him little opportunity for unacceptable behavior.
His freedom to choose a mate is in reality narrowed to a highly select
group, approved by his parents, although he himself may believe in the
cultural myth that marriage is based upon romantic love for *any* individual at *any* class level of society.[43]

All does not move as smoothly as the above description might
suggest. Children frequently manipulate or exploit the parents, in some
cases displaying almost complete defiance of them or rejection of their
values. In one Home and School study group, a mother described with
considerable feeling how she and her husband had given a rumpus
room party for her son and his friends, planned in advance to the last
detail. The children refused to watch the movie provided, preferring to
dance with each other or to play the suspect "spin the bottle."[44] In
spite of the requirement that parents should trust their children, mothers
—and more frequently fathers—voiced extreme uneasiness over the
late home-comings of their children. This concern was typically more
marked in reference to girls, with the mothers acting as intermediaries
to soften paternal wrath if the daughter stayed to a party's end.[45] Many
parents appeared to subscribe to the hours of teen-age parties only for
the sake of their child's popularity. The peer group seemed sufficiently
well organized to withstand any adult attempts on the part of either
parents or teachers to regulate the hours of parties, even those for pre-
adolescents.

In the interview and observation material there is but little evidence
of outright rebellion on the part of teenagers or young adults against
the social activities of Crestwood Heights. The children do, however,

form certain social groupings of their own, which are not controlled by adults. In the face of the economic dependence of these children, and the intensive adult control which is attempted during the total social-ization process, the strength and cohesion of these groupings must be enormous to permit their survival. Most important among them are the fraternities and sororities, which have reached down from university to high school, and, more recently, permeated junior high and the later grades of the elementary school. Fraternities and sororities differ from the gang and friendship groups (which may also have secret rituals) in that they are more formal and are commonly "Chapters" of an international organization, frequently with headquarters in the United States. Parents and teachers often express their dislike of fraternities and sororities on the basis of this "remote and irresponsible control" by officers who are "too young to know what they are doing."

The age for membership ranges roughly from ten to sixteen. The largest proportion of members is drawn from around the Grade XI level (fifteen, sixteen, and seventeen years of age); the membership includes about 75 per cent of all Crestwood Heights children in this age group.[46] Belonging to fraternities and sororities bestows high prestige on Crestwood Heights children, because of the exclusive nature of these groupings. "Rushing" is a feature, which means that many may be called but few chosen. Popularity, as understood in Crestwood Heights, is the criterion for selection: ease in social situations for both sexes, glamorous appearance for the girl and athletic prowess for the boy. Family standing, the type of house, the freedom to drive a car (the family car or preferably a car of one's own), membership in other status-conferring associations, are all important considerations. It is usually these aspects of the fraternities and sororities which become the overt target of parental objections. The members themselves present a somewhat different picture of fraternity and sorority activities. At a joint meeting of parents and collegiate students to discuss "the problem of fraternities and sororities," a male member defended methods of selection:

I think I should tell you something about how the choosing is done. The prospective pledge comes down for the evening [the phrase "comes down for the evening" was used several times but whether it meant a meeting place outside Crestwood Heights itself was not specified] and I admit that it is hard to pick or to refuse a person just from seeing him for one evening, but he is a friend of someone in the frat. We have a questionnaire that we use to find out as much about him as we possibly can. We often sit up talking a candidate over until two or three in the morning [shock registered by the parents] trying to give him fair consideration and treatment. On the questionnaire we have his name, grade in school, age, other organizations that he belongs to, etc. We then try to decide how many members the frat can hold and limit the number of pledges accordingly. The size of living-room in the houses of the members is a limiting factor! [Later it was emphasized that it was the living-room of present not prospective members that was considered.] . . . Not all of the people who are rejected by a frat are turned down for a specific reason. Often it is just the workable size of the organization that forces the restriction and closing of membership. Originally the pledge period was meant to test the prospect and to see whether he could live up to the standards of the frat, but now pledging has just become a formality and the razzing, baiting period has lost all its original meaning.

Parents, especially Jewish ones, took very marked exception in this meeting to the discrimination practised in selection. (Not that the discrimination was primarily anti-Jewish. Jewish parents were equally "concerned" about the discrimination in wholly Jewish fraternities.) A second boy, in an effort to placate the enraged adults, said:

I have a suggestion for a solution. It isn't all my own idea. I was talking to a man down in the corner after the last meeting—I've forgotten his name. He was telling me that the Elks and some other adult groups never ask a person to join, but the person must come to them. Then if he *is* refused, he doesn't feel so bad because he knows before he applies that he may be refused and still he applies of his own accord. If all the frats would have their members sign a pledge that they would not ask others to join, but let them show interest and come forward on their own, it would help the situation a lot.

The first student returned to the attack, sensing the tender area beneath the adult protests:

It was mentioned at the last meeting and earlier this evening that we meet disappointments all through life and that we have to expect this and to go on living anyway. I feel that the hard part of it is that they [the prospective pledges] are refused in front of others and are humiliated by the experience. If the frats were more discreet and secret about whom they rejected, the effect upon the rejected individual would not be so strong as when they are publicly refused. Then word spreads all through the school that so-and-so was refused by such-and-such. That sort of thing can harm a person for life, especially some of the younger ones. They get the feeling that they are not wanted by anyone and it harms them permanently.

No more painful probe could be made into the ambivalent parental feelings: yearning for social acceptance on the one hand, and fear of rejection on the other.

The Jewish mother who chaired the meeting attempted to consolidate the adult position:

We have discussed quite a bit now. Can I sum up to this point by saying that it appears that there *is* a form of discrimination in the method of selection for fraternities and sororities and that we all consider this to be one of the faults of these groups.

Another mother, a Gentile (the Citizenship Convener of Home and School) backed up the chairman:

I would like to know whether these students feel that the fraternities and sororities are democratic organizations. We have the United Nations working for democracy and world citizenship and other things like this. Are fraternities and sororities and their methods of selection democratic?

Thereupon, the children carried the battle right into the enemy camp, using the adults' own weapons against them.

STUDENT (Male): You have organizations like the Masons with Presidents belonging, and nearly all the Kings of England have belonged for centuries. They are selective organizations, and yet they are thought of highly by Kings and Presidents.

STUDENT (Male): You are talking about democracy and yet you try to deny us the freedom of choice of the group that we choose to belong to. That is not democracy either. Did you say that the United Nations was democratic? They refuse nations membership.

PARENT (Citizenship Convener): I didn't say they were democratic. I said they were working for democracy.

STUDENT (Male): I belong to the Hi-Y [a school association] and feel they are democratic. Any person who belongs to a club or any kind of organization is going to learn something about democratic procedure in the elections and discussions held by the group. They [fraternities and sororities] are not democratic when it comes to choosing members and pledging, but they can learn of democracy in other ways.

STUDENT (Male): Going back in history to the founder of democracy, Thomas Jefferson, he defined it as the right of each person to pick and choose according to the pursuit of his individual happiness.

STUDENT (Male): You have talked about those being excluded from frats being hurt. The United Nations doesn't admit every country that applies for membership, and do you think there are no feelings hurt there?

STUDENT (Female): It is just the same for adults. How about people being refused membership in the Loyalist Club? You have to have sponsors who are well known in the club and be voted on and all that sort of thing. Don't you feel that many feelings are hurt about that sort of thing?

PARENTS [General confusion]: We are not talking about adult groups. Just because adult groups do it, it doesn't mean that children have to do it too.

The same adult attitude was evident when the question of Jewish-Gentile segregation in the fraternities and sororities was brought up by a prominent Gentile member of the Board of Education. Although they admitted that discrimination did exist, the teenagers again parried the attacks of the adults by confronting them with their own prejudices.

STUDENT (Male): I would like to ask a question, particularly of the parents. I am probably safe in saying that all of the parents here tonight want a non-sectarian group to replace the religiously segregated ones we now have, but would *all* other parents want a non-sectarian group? There are lots of parents that I know who wouldn't stand for it at all!

PARENTS [General confusion]: That *still* doesn't make it right. You, the coming generation, should advance and improve on the mistakes of your parents. (The last student speaker was shouted down and not permitted to finish what he wanted to say.)

The Collegiate Principal then entered the fray to put forward the school point of view:

It has always been the policy of the school and we try to teach the students that people should be judged for what they are and not for their race or religion. It seems that many of the fraternities and sororities reject people because of the homes they live in or because of their religion.

Again the children defended their associations:

STUDENT (Male): All fraternities and sororities have some members with small homes. They haven't the space to be able to have the meetings at their places, but they are welcome in our homes and the size or condition of their homes is not considered. Many live in apartments and can't have meetings at their places, but they are still welcome in our homes.

COLLEGIATE PRINCIPAL: Is that true of all fraternities and sororities?

GENERAL SHOUT: *Yes!*

STUDENT (Female): You say that the school has always been democratic and not shown discrimination. How about the segregation of the Jewish and Gentile classes that took place two years ago!

She was groaned down. Several teachers spoke at once, saying that the move had been taken in all good faith, that it was an error, and had been corrected; that the school was not infallible; that they tried to correct all such errors immediately, etc.[47]

It was a girl student who gave the harried parents the final turn of the screw.

This may seem shocking to the parents here and would shock other parents too, but I feel it is a vital matter and should be mentioned. Imagine what would happen if most of the students went home and said, "Look here, Mother and Dad, I'm joining a non-sectarian group, and I'm going out with a non-Jewish or a non-Gentile boy or girl." It would lead to total disruption and much unhappiness in the home. Many parents, although they profess tolerance, would definitely be upset if their children were to start going out with those not of their religious or racial group. The same thing happens between Protestants and Catholics for the Gentiles. Just because they belong to the same group and go out with each other doesn't mean that it is going to lead to marriage, but that would be the thought in all parents' minds. We don't need to go into the problems and difficulties of intermarriage now, but at the very least, it is bad because of all the . . . indecision . . . that results.

From this point in the meeting, the parents were in retreat. The chairman capitulated completely. After thanking the participants, she went on to say:

Now, it depends on the various [children's] organizations to do constructive thinking about the situation. *It is your problem not ours.* You are the people we are looking forward to as the future of our country, and *you must do something about it.* [Italics added.][48]

Again the maturity values and success values were in conflict. The parents who, at the meeting, overtly supported the maturity axis of ethnic tolerance, respect for the individual, disregard for material possessions in judging personality were virtually "unmasked" by their children, who won by exposing what underlay the mask: the anxious drive for acceptance, the symbolism of money to connote social worth, the fear of rejection, the equation of status (as demonstrated by associational membership) with success. The unconscious guilt which the parents hoped might be expiated by their children was accepted and defended by them, in their turn. Later, perhaps, these same children as adults in other versions of Crestwood Heights may reprove their children for the same shortcomings which are also their own and which they, unwittingly, in the manner of *their* parents, have transmitted to another generation.[49]

Students who do not join fraternities and sororities display predominantly two attitudes. One type does not, openly at least, aspire to belong, and condemns the discriminatory policies of these groups. Frequently such students are active in school-sponsored societies, strengthened by the approval of the teaching staff and of some parents. They may, however, sacrifice a feeling of solidarity with the peer group, since they do not band together against adult pressures but rather cooperate with them. A second type, having dared to seek membership and been rejected, reacts with feelings of frustration and inferiority. One student is reported to have left school because she was refused membership in a sorority. Another girl, who ran away from home, gave as the reason for her action, failure to achieve a particularly high mark in a school subject and rejection by a sorority. A clipping from a Big City paper states:

HURT BY SORORITY SNUB—MISSING STUDENT IS FOUND

[B.N.] 14, [Crestwood Heights] Collegiate student was found by police . . . two days after she had disappeared from her [Crestwood Heights] home. Police were told she had been depressed because she had not been asked to join a high-school sorority that had accepted her best girl friend [H. J.], and because she thought her piano marks of 63 had not been satisfactory, although her teacher had considered her a good player for her age and the mark satisfactory.

Since fraternities and sororities are secret organizations, and since their members are extremely protective of this area of privacy, no detailed account of activities has been secured, either by observation or through interviews. As in adult fraternities and sororities, the expressed aim of these groups is intimate brotherhood and fellowship, which reaches its peak in the local chapter. This bond is heightened by the selection methods, which stress an in-group and out-group relationship. It is almost inevitable, given the realities rather than the verbalizations of this community's life, that children of similar religious denomination, with resultant common interests and like fates, should band together.[50] This situation is particularly complicated in Crestwood Heights, however, since a high social value is placed upon friendly relations between the two ethnic groups. Yet sororities and fraternities here recruit the majority of their membership from the Jewish group. This group still remains a minority in the total population, but Jewish children are nevertheless in the majority in at least one school, with the result that fraternity and sorority activities are doubly suspect and open to adult criticism, because, in addition to screening out adult control, they also appear to the Gentile to strengthen Jewishness, and, to many Jews, to jeopardize "acceptance."[51]

Parents and teachers fear the unfettered freedom to practise adult and sophisticated behavior which the fraternities and sororities afford. Some adults condemn these teen-age associations because, it is rumored, they foster immoral and undesirable activities—gambling and drinking, and petting which could or may cross the line into actual sex experimentation. School personnel object on the grounds that pledging and initiation disrupt discipline, and keep the child out late at night so that he is too tired to cope with school work during the day. In addition, these groups interfere with the smooth functioning of the extracurricular activities under the school's jurisdiction, subverting the wider democracy of the school system. One teacher cited instances of fraternities and sororities "railroading" school elections and a school beauty contest.

The children themselves are sensitive to adult criticism and misunderstanding of fraternity and sorority activities, but display no willingness to allow adults to clean house for them. If socially worthwhile goals are to be added to the program, the children themselves intend to incorporate the changes, as one boy flatly told the parent-teacher meeting previously quoted. This student had been in charge of a Friday night gathering in a local synagogue, sponsored by Jewish fraternities and sororities.

The main object of the affair was to attempt to organize fraternities and sororities and to "bring them around to a more cultural angle." "We hope to organize all fraternities and sororities in the city to talk over ways in which they can be benefited and to hope for improvement that will give them a better name. I know that fraternities and sororities are looked down upon now and have a bad name. I know that we are interested and anxious to deal with the problem through organization. All of the presidents of the fraternities and sororities have agreed that the method of selection is poor, that the exclusive membership and religious segregation is poor, and we hope to improve these things." Someone from the audience interrupted to ask if the Presidents of Gentile fraternities and sororities were represented. "No, they weren't. We wanted to have them but I was busy looking after all the Jewish groups, and had to keep up with my homework and didn't have time to call the Gentiles, but we do hope to have them come into the inter-frat council."

It is thus that the members of the fraternities and sororities guard the right to direct their own activities themselves. That Crestwood children should wish to defend these groupings and do so ardently is completely understandable, in view of the adult-controlled activities which fill the major portion of their time. Under the protective cover of the fraternity or sorority, they band together against adult pressures to conform with the self-contradictory value-systems of the community. Here they may try out patterns of behavior which are permitted to adults in the culture, but denied to youth. Supported by the strength of the peer group, they may respond to the cultural norms disseminated through the mass communication media, which are by no means those upheld by parents and teachers. For a few years they may escape without guilt into sheer irresponsibility and high spirits, enjoying each other (once the rigid selection process has been effected) as human beings, exchanging intimacies, having crushes, trying out heterosexual relationships, learning the social ropes. But, as we have seen, adult standards for mature behavior, as interpreted by the society, penetrate these groupings in the end, and the children must leave the shelter of fraternities and sororities for the associations characteristic of adult life.

Activity in fraternities and sororities for the most part precedes puberty, i.e., coincides with the period of pubescence. By sixteen or eighteen, major adolescent crises are past. Dating patterns have been consolidated and appropriate behavior has been learned. Frequently during the last year of high school, many students drop their active membership. Some children expressed the view that these fraternity and sorority activities were childish, once this age level had been reached. Others explained that they were now "going steady," which took up the time previously devoted to fraternity or sorority (it, however, had afforded them the opportunity to select from among many the one steady date). Others, again, gave as a reason for severing their ties the importance and extra academic work of the final collegiate year.

Fraternities and sororities function, then, to allow Crestwood Heights children some expression of the independence for which the socialization process has prepared them, and in which it is supposedly already giving them practice. Adult opposition to these groups strongly suggests how effective they are in creating a genuine, if temporary, freedom of action for teenagers, an independence which it is especially difficult for them to win since they are still economically dependent upon their parents and will remain so for some time. In other words, fraternities and sororities provide ritualized, but not adult-accepted, ways for the child to screen out as far as possible for a time the influence of parents and all experts concerned with socialization. In these groups, Crestwood teenagers develop a feeling of worth through intimate association with their peers. Membership also provides an opportunity to practise *directing* an association, which is a serious upper middle class preoccupation in business, the professions, and in community life. Fraternities and sororities may also be crucial in establishing courtship patterns. Girls learn from each other the approved approach to boys in the culture and they, in their turn, derive support in their approach to girls. Considerable cross-dating between sororities and fraternities occurs, similar to that encouraged between girls' and boys' private schools, but with the important difference in the fraternities and sororities that such activities are controlled largely by the teenagers themselves.

The independence gained through membership in these associations paves the way for many Crestwood children to participate in the internationally recognized and long-established university fraternities and sororities. Ultimately, of course, the young adult must leave the protection of even these groups, although he may, in some instances, maintain his contact through active participation in alumni projects.[52] If he becomes a successful professional or business man in Crestwood Heights, he may owe both wife and clients to his membership in a fraternity, either during high school or at university.

It is difficult to understand why more children in Crestwood Heights do not use the period of free association with their peers to evolve goals and values which are different from those of the adult generation. This may be due in large measure to the potent influence of the mass communication media, to which these teen-age groups are particularly open. Another cause may be the relative lack of alternative institutions advocating any radically divergent system of values. Neither the Protestant churches nor the Jewish synagogues, to one or other of which the majority of Crestwood residents "belong," preach a fundamental cleavage between the way of the world and the way of the spirit, as the Roman Catholic church still does, for instance, in at least one other province of Canada. In the whole of Crestwood Heights and, indeed throughout the metropolitan area, it would be quite possible to pass a lifetime without once seeing the habit of a religious order, symbolizing a strictly differing scale of values on the part of the wearer. Gone, too, is the bearded rabbi in his skull cap; and the not too obvious clerical collar of the clergyman, if worn, passes unnoticed as he drives in his car from one appointment to another. Unlike the slum child, the Crestwood Heights teenager does not know the teeming life of the city streets, or the tenements harboring immigrants from all countries of the world. Here, far from the sea, no foreign ships disgorge their sailors for a few hours ashore, before steaming back to home ports on the far side of the earth. A selected group from high school may, of course, be taken to visit the United Nations Headquarters in New York. Other children may travel with their parents. But within Crestwood Heights itself, few, if any, alternative cultural patterns present themselves. Unless he is extremely fortunate in being sent abroad to school or university, or less so in being caught in the maelstrom of a major war, the Crestwood boy has virtually no choice but to enter the business or professional life of Big City, and to live subsequently in Crestwood Heights or other suburbs like it. Some Jewish children may visualize Israel as the Promised Land, but they must have unusual perseverance and initiative to get there.[53]

That children do, however, develop ideals and goals of their own, which they may not have the strength to translate into reality, is readily evident in cases coming to the Child Guidance Clinic. The progressive and democratic complex of socialization techniques leaves the child scant opportunity to indulge such individual desires as he may acknowledge to himself. The majority of children give up the battle after a relatively brief period of rebellion between childhood and adulthood. As adulthood approaches, they gradually assume the adult expectations for appropriate behavior at their particular age level. They must grapple, as their parents have done in *their* past, with a reconciliation of the maturity–success value-systems underlying the cultural life of Crestwood Heights.

An attempt has been made, in a necessarily telescoped form, to describe some of the associational activities of the Crestwood Heights child. He is encouraged, directed, or subtly pressured into a variety of situations where he meets both peers and adults during the leisure hours which are left him after school and other institutionalized pursuits. Members for these associations are closely screened to ensure that only those from the child's present status level (or above) are included. Within this range, he is given a free choice of intimates, but the chances are virtually non-existent that he will be exposed to any behavior patterns radically different from his own. Even in the fraternities and sororities from which adults are excluded, there are few possibilities of escape from the Crestwood way of life.

For the most part, the associational activities of the Crestwood Heights child have been and are competitive in essence. In varying degrees, a rigid inclusion-exclusion process governs membership in adult- or child-controlled associations. All demand a high degree of skill and performance. Thus membership provides the child with valuable experience of the situations he will meet in adult life. In these groupings, he may try his wings, make mistakes which, if they are not too serious, time will still allow him to rectify. Here he acquires friends, "contacts"; these, though still at the juvenile level, cement the firm foundations on which alone the career of the future may be built. Parents support the child's participation in associations in the hope that he will gain advantages now and, for his subsequent adjustment, a social armor, which the parents themselves may have lacked or acquired only after much conscious and perhaps painful striving.

Some experiences (for example, summer camp) are designed on balance perhaps to impress upon the child the superiority of urban life over even highly vaunted Nature. The stark contrast between a few weeks of "roughing it" in the wilds and the normal, inexhaustible material comforts of home are brought unforgettably to his attention. Camp organization and apparatus may be highly artificial in terms of the real culture of the North, but both, once again, effectively protect the Crestwood child from any direct experience which might lure him away from the behavior approved in Crestwood Heights. As in the case of religious training, the child is inoculated with just enough freedom to make him immune to any disrupting attacks in adult life. In much the same way, experiences at another class level, whether undergone at summer camp or through the school-sponsored activities with less privileged members of society, bar the child from any genuine identification with these groups. An inevitable by-product is his deepened appreciation of what his true goals should be in the light of family values, goals which he must at all costs maintain and, if possible, advance.

Here may be seen one reason why the success of the children in child-centered and child-controlled associations is not always to the liking of the parents; the values of these groups do not, and in fact cannot, exactly coincide with those of the adults, given the rapid technological and social change which has driven the age-gap between the generations. Yet fraternities and sororities have become so important and so integral a part of the total socialization process in Crestwood Heights that parents and school together have been unable either to eradicate or to control their activities. Fraternities and sororities appear to function primarily as a protected area where children may consolidate certain new behavior patterns which they sense may be of more importance to them as adults than norms currently held up by parents and teachers. Once this phase has been completed, the child is able to blend his new cultural learning with the old and to proceed upon his adult way.

The adult-planned curriculum for the child's associational education is almost as rigidly laid down as the program of the school, although no printed curricula exist. Nevertheless, the unwritten law is sometimes equally binding with the written, and sometimes it may constrict more—a fact which the children well appreciate. Not only is a child expected to achieve in the academic work of the school. He is also required to win and to maintain exceedingly "high marks" in social activities. At the same time, the child *must*, according to Crestwood values, enjoy his childhood. Nowhere are these contradictory demands more evident than in typical conversations between mothers. "Shall I let Sally go to that party? Should she wear lipstick? Will she come home in good time? Should I let Fred call for her? If I don't, will he be furious? Will they play 'Spin the bottle'?" The poignancy of these self-examinations will be exceeded only by the maternal (and sometimes paternal) anguish, should Sally be excluded from the party altogether. Perhaps there should be time for a child to be a child, but in Crestwood Heights both parents and children are acutely aware that it becomes each year more limited and precious. To all private doubts, all public questionings, for grown-ups and for children, where associational activity is concerned, there is only the one answer and one refrain: "It's better to get into the swim early than not at all."

Part Three

INTEGRATION

11. LAYMAN AND EXPERT

The Belief Market

IN THE FIRST PART of this book attention was focused on the dimensions of and the ways of organizing life in Crestwood Heights: space and time; shelter; the age-grading system and the career. In the second part we looked at the institutions that function within those dimensions and contribute to or express those ways of organizing life. We wish now to examine the beliefs that accompany, grow out of, justify, and alter these institutions and life-ways.

The most striking aspect of belief in Crestwood Heights, as will presently appear, is its relative lack of fixity, its flux and flow, the rapidity with which views and opinions are born, matured, and, in effect, killed off or abandoned. For this reason—because belief-making as a process is more striking than belief as a state—it has seemed wise to describe the process first, leaving the product, the consequent beliefs, for another chapter.

But, unfortunately for simplicity, this process by which beliefs are produced and, as it were, consumed—or, in any case, used up or destroyed—cannot be understood by attending narrowly to Crestwood Heights itself. Just as the Crestwood family is primarily a consumption unit for material goods which are produced in specialized units elsewhere, so also it seems is Crestwood Heights itself a consumption unit for ideas, views, theories, opinions that are produced elsewhere, also by a core of persons specialized for such production. And just as the families (taken together with other families) affect by their purchases what is and will be produced for the commodity market, so does Crestwood Heights (together with communities like it) affect what is produced for the idea or belief or opinion or attitude market. The transactions are perhaps less obvious than purchases of commodities, but the elements of a market would seem to be there: producers and consumers, exchange, supply and demand, and even currency of a sort.[1]

Moreover, this transaction system—which we have called, in analogy, a belief market—cannot be understood in terms of Crestwood Heights alone because the situation of the "producers," the belief-makers, is as relevant to what they "supply" as the situation of the Crestwood Heighters, the "consumers," is to what they "demand." The happy fit of the one to the other is what makes the market possible.

But who are these producers? In one sense, the producers are the whole of what in Europe is freely called "the intelligentsia": the authors, editors, ideologists, preachers, politicians, makers of and dealers in ideas and opinions. But, partly because of the preoccupation of this volume, partly because of the preoccupation of the people of Crestwood Heights, we shall be concerned with only some small segment of that intelligentsia: the specialists in the theories and practices of "human relations," those whom earlier, and here again, we have referred to as "the experts." These people, "expert" by local definition and their own consent, find themselves in so intimate an involvement with Crestwood Heights (and communities like it) that together they may almost be viewed as a single social or interaction system. Indeed, in sketching the Crestwood Heights school we were hardly able to avoid being drawn into detailed description of the expert system if we were to make the

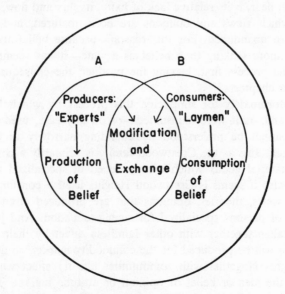

FIGURE 4. The interaction of expert and layman.

school intelligible. The relations are something like those of Figure 4—and whether this is to be described as one system or two is a matter of choice. For the sake of clarity, however, we have chosen to describe the "sub-systems" (A and B) separately, before trying to describe the whole. We shall accordingly treat serially Supply and Demand, Production and Consumption, turning from A to B, and then back again.

SUPPLY

It is of particular importance at the outset to establish wherein the "expert" is like and wherein he is unlike the Crestwood Heights "layman," for the fit of what he has to supply to what Crestwooders demand turns as well on the identity as on the difference.

The expert is characteristically a child of Western history; most frequently a product of North American culture; almost invariably middle class in his primary orientations, if not by birth, then by adoption or conviction; and, like the citizen of Crestwood Heights, mobile, deracinated, and living in a world he may have made, but to which he is not by first nature accustomed.

What differentiates him principally from the Crestwood layman is the process of selection through which he has been recruited, the training he has received, and his operating conditions—the social system to which, apart from Crestwood Heights, he belongs.

A. SELECTION AND RESELECTION

The expert, like any other specialist, is the end-product of a process of selection and reselection which might be thought of in terms of Figure 5. The sketch represents one face of a pyramid[2] in which in successive periods the "learned" are selected from the general population; the human relations theorists from among the learned; those who will be closely related to the public from among these; and those who will sustain close relations with Crestwood Heights from among the last.

The selection of the learned from among the population is very largely shrouded in mystery. That those who have the first opportunity to qualify, in terms of chances to attend a university or college, are largely selected by social class and wealth, is well documented by several studies.[3] But of this relatively large group endowed with opportunity, a very much smaller number is withdrawn as the cadre for the next group: the learned.

Capacity, performance, and desire all enter as criteria. But, generally, here as elsewhere, capacity is a mere condition, and is, probably, in considerable over-supply. Given desire, performance, both technical

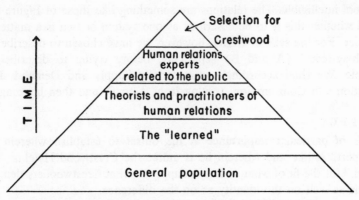

FIGURE 5. The selection and reselection of "experts."

and diplomatic or manipulative has, in the opinion of students and the observations of professors, a marked and often decisive effect. Because of the general Puritan orientation in the North American culture-area, and probably also because of the manner in which the present learned were themselves selected, there is a tendency, other things being equal, to select, on the basis of sympathy and promise, the student who is "working very hard." This is very often the student who is demonstrating ability to overcome to an unusual degree the obstacles of background and origin, and also (and by implication) to make unusual use of his native and acquired talents and capacities.[4] The student thus selected is quite likely, therefore, to be marginally middle class, mobile towards the middle middle class in terms of background and aspiration, and to a notable and sympathy-eliciting degree mining his talents with considerable intensity.[5]

Thus there well may be among the candidates for the learned occupations a not inconsiderable concentration of those whose basic orientation is neurotic or self-exploitative. Such concentration as there is will take place for the reasons alleged, and also because the learned who are now selecting, almost inevitably include a large number of those who over-estimate the power and importance of thought and verbal events in human affairs—a common characteristic of the neurotic, but one well supported by the folkways of the learned occupations.

The second selection, of those who will be candidates for the sciences of human behavior, represents a further sorting of a quite important kind. In the first place, in these occupations are disproportionately represented those who, despite high basic capacity and immense willingness to develop that capacity in a risky and ill-defined field, are also willing to sell these talents for relatively small and uncertain returns, material or other, as compared, say, with the returns from like capacity and self-development obtained by doctors (except probably medical missionaries and psychiatrists) or engineers.[6] Moreover, the basis of self-selection for candidacy is usually quite openly moralistic and unselfish: "This is what the world needs at the present hour," or "It is the most important field at the present time," i.e. most important not in terms of reward or recognition but in terms of social necessity.[7]

In the second place, the field, by virtue of its concern with the "problems" of people (i.e., human problems) will tend markedly to select out those who have sufficiently heightened awareness of these problems, and those who are motivated to labor against heavy odds for their solution. This kind of awareness of the problematic in human affairs may come by learning, but comes more generally out of experience and introspection. The willingness, likewise, derives for some from the expanded sense of a healthy ego, but for others from a necessity either to avoid one's own problems by working at those of others or to solve one's own problems by attacking them at a more general and much less anxiety-provoking level.

Beyond this selection for the fields of social science *expertise*, there is the selection for prominence, and then for public-relatedness. Little is known about selection for prominence as against selection, say, for productivity,[8] although obviously some positive relation between the two obtains.[9] Probably here, as elsewhere, all the factors that make for competitive success operate, and these will include factors that operate against the selection of the neurotic as well as those that operate to select him.

As to the selection for public-relatedness—the next-to-top level of the pyramid—the only generalization that seems warranted is that this selection excludes those whose primary mechanism for the resolution of conflict is flight. These are likely to be found working away in their ivory towers or laboratories, obsessively or otherwise, but certainly avoiding public contact by every personal and institutional defence available. What is left beyond this selection will be the non-neurotic and, from the contingent of the neurotic, only those who are capable of "acting out."[10]

The further selection of candidates for temporary domination in Crestwood Heights seems to depend less on personal characteristics (beyond the minima for social presentability) and more on the constantly shifting needs of the Crestwood Heights population.[11] As will be pointed out below, what is needed by that population is usually whatever is radically antithetic to what was last presented, in order that its experience may be of a clear, clean break and a fresh start rather than a minor differentiation in beliefs and practices now felt to be unsatisfactory.[12]

B. TRAINING[13]

The enormous and rapid accumulation of social-scientific knowledge in the last half-century, the incredible multiplication and proliferation of arts and techniques, has been accompanied (as cause and effect) by a minute division of labor and an immense increase in specialization in this, as in other, fields.[14] The upshot, so far as the training process is concerned, has been here, as elsewhere, a longer period of total training, a longer period of specialization. But the latter, having grown more rapidly than the former, has tended to increase at its expense so that narrowing and specialization take place earlier than formerly. This curtailment of general education and early narrowing of focus, combined with the opening of ever greater gaps in the corpus of knowledge and the increasing independence and separation between fields, tends to produce a specialist who, in the words of an old joke, is "a man who knows more and more about less and less." It is, at least, more difficult for him to see his body of special knowledge in relation to the whole of knowledge than it ever was before.

The seemingly necessary sacrifice in the area of general education has been nowhere more radical than in the field of philosophy out of which, historically, the several disciplines in question emerged. Partly out of necessity, partly to separate themselves clearly from their parent-discipline, and partly because of conditions internal to the field of philosophy itself, the new disciplines have been less and less inclined to encourage (let alone to require) in their trainees a firm foundation in philosophy before specialization. One result is that the new expert, who has great difficulty in relating his scientific field to those of others, has an even greater difficulty in relating his art to any general scheme of values or any over-all social or individual philosophy. The resultant empiricism in theory and disorientation in large-scale matters of practice, is a marked characteristic of the learned professions in America, as has been noted before by observers, American and other.

A third aspect of training in the human sciences, the importance of which for the resultant product can hardly be over-stressed, is its nearly pure intellectualism.[15] The effect of such teaching is largely to alienate the learner from the kind of insight into self and others that ought to be the core of it, or to lead him to discount such insight—it has no examination-value!—or at the best to leave integration to the accidents of the learner's initiative. What ought to be the heart of the training process for the prospective behavior-expert—a process enabling him to recognize, take into account, and partially disentangle himself from the skein of personal and cultural biases which are everyman's heritage— is thus commonly pushed to the periphery, talked about as an end while being neglected in the choice of means, or left to a hoped-for fall of chance apart from the process proper.

Even where such a statement requires qualification (i.e. where some attention *is* paid to the recognition of personal bias or cultural bias) it is rare indeed to find consideration of both types. The best that can commonly be achieved under these circumstances, then, is either an individual-centered expert—aware of and able to make allowances for his personal motivation, but blind to his cultural biases, prejudices, pre-conceptions, and selective inattentions—or a society-centered expert —aware of most of the cultural distortions, but unaware beyond the most naïve level of the structure of his own system of motives and the meaning and effect of his own acts in relation to his knowledge.[16]

A fourth aspect of the training of the experts which must be given recognition is that it embodies—just as does the Crestwood Heights school system, but perhaps with less critical awareness—a marked irresolution between what have been called the "success" and the "maturity" values. Competition is sharpened rather than diminished for the expert by the previous selective processes; the need for competition to be covert is increased by the co-operative norms of colleagueship; and the conflict of value-systems is heightened because the very nature of the subject-matter invites penetration of conventions while the social situation loads explicit recognition with potentially sizeable penalties.[17] The competitive realities, the co-operative forms, and the increasing need for covertness certainly cannot be said to furnish ideal circum-stances for the establishment of integration and integrity.

What has been argued so far is that the training process is such— and perhaps increasingly such—as to make for an alienation of the expert from other bodies of knowledge; from any general value-scheme; from insight either into his own motives or into the nature of his culture, or both; and from the understanding of the social situation in which his training takes place.

It is now necessary to consider the expert's operating conditions— the circumstances upon which he enters, once trained.

C. THE INNER SOCIAL SYSTEM OF THE EXPERTS

The expert in the course of his development moves generally into a social system which, in most respects, is not unlike the training situation in which he has been caught up. However, to his insecurities and difficulties as a student will now be added others.

In the first place, he is likely to be on the staff of an institution which is anywhere from somewhat to extremely insecure. It may be a social agency which is dependent for its support on the vagaries of public giving or on the distribution from a rather unpredictable Community Chest; it may be a national agency with extremely constricted and uncertain resources; it may be a university, dependent from moment to moment, in large part, on the gifts and goodwill of foundations, financially powerful individuals, and, latterly, of government.

Within this institution, itself insecure, he will—if it is a large institution or a university—be a member of a sizeable bureaucracy which resembles the Crestwood Heights school system in that to a notably greater degree than elsewhere, it is difficult to discover and define the conditions for graduation from rank to rank within it. Again, as in the Crestwood Heights school, there is the maintenance of something that cannot quite be called a fiction, to the effect that all members of the academic faculty or agency staff have equality, and the chief executive is simply a *primus inter pares*.[18]

In this ill-defined situation, in this insecure institution, the budding expert will, for a long time, hold uncertain tenure, because the insecurity of the institution cannot make his tenure more certain, because the Puritan orientation dictates that such uncertainty is good for him, and because the counsels of prudence dictate that the longer a final arrangement can be put off, the longer period there will be for administrators to cover possible errors in judging human material.

Uncertainly holding a post in an insecure institution, he will also have to cope with the lack of clear-cut definitions of the boundaries of his field of competence. He will find representatives of other fields of knowledge claiming jurisdiction in his own, and he will find himself making claims to competence which are resented by those who define their fields in such a way as to claim the area over which his statements extend.

He will also find that, in spite of the definition prevailing of scientific detachment, his field is divided up into orthodoxies and heresies, sects and followings, much as were the fields in the other sciences prior to their relatively modern structuring and their discovery of ways of proof and disproof which could command nearly universal assent.

It is indeed true—given the newness of these fields, and perhaps for intrinsic reasons as well—that at any one time with reference to any topic of any importance within them, a whole series of hypotheses are available of approximately equal plausibility from among which the expert can pick and choose. It is also true, for reasons which will be gone into in more detail later, that every few years brings a crop of new insights and new hypotheses, which come to dominate the field in a manner reminiscent of fashion rather than to take it on the basis of proof or disproof of contending and prior hypotheses.[19]

In this exceedingly fluid situation, the expert is himself confronted with what is, in effect, a vast projective system: what he selects and accepts, what he perceives and invents, what he communicates and how he communicates it, may shed more light on his inner necessities and social situation than it does on the hypotheses under the usual criteria for validity and reliability.

D. THE RESULTING SUPPLY FUNCTION

These conditions in selection, training, and operation constitute a matrix of pressure upon the emerging expert which tends to drive him in one or more of several possible directions.

The fluidity and uncertainty of knowledge in his field permit wide scope for any latent talents of invention or synthesis that he may possess. The large, unexplored territory is an invitation to pioneer— with the attendant risks of large rewards or disaster that pioneering entails. The relative isolation which is the product of covert competition makes for marked individuation and allows opportunity for difference. The uncertainty of status at any given moment, and the obscurity of the conditions for promotion, put a premium on efforts to achieve rapid differentiation and distinction.

Given these circumstances, the public (i.e., people generally outside whatever is defined as the colleagueship) appears in a quite special, and, as far as the scientist is concerned, somewhat novel light. It appears as capable of furnishing a number of compensatory gratifications which, under the circumstances depicted, are to many extraordinarily attractive. A relatively easy and safe dominance can be readily established with a public, which would to a degree offset the more precarious and anxious contacts with the colleagueship group. Mutual aid—affectual and even financial—might come to supplement the covert competition with colleagues. The prevailingly critical atmosphere might be exchanged for a prevailingly appreciative one. Hostilities, overt or covert, which could be discharged only with danger in the in-group, might find a target with relative safety on the outside. These and other inferrable conditions account for the appeal *of* the public.

Beyond this, and perhaps more serious, lies the appeal *to* the public in the sense in which in law an appeal may be taken to a higher, and hopefully more favorable, court. There is a constant potential temptation to secure recognition where it is available, and this may mean an attempt to seek a more sympathetic audience or even, more simply, a group which will allow greater latitude for experimentation or the testing-out of opinion. If it were wholly true that no real appeal could lie from the colleagueship to the laity, then all that might face the would-be expert would be a clear choice between audiences and roles: he could choose *either* scholarly recognition to be awarded or refused by the colleagueship *or* a different recognition to be awarded or refused by the public. But he knows that this simple alternative is not, in fact, what is presented. The appeal to the public may result in a climate of opinion outside the colleagueship to which few scholars and still fewer administrators of scholarly institutions can be wholly immune.[20] In this sense, a genuine appeal lies from the one court to the other, i.e. in the sense that a modification of verdict may be had in the first court as a result of pleas in appeal before the second.

The expert, so "supplied" or supplying himself to meet the existing "demand," will thus tend to combine in himself—as his middle-class clients will combine in themselves—a variety of entrepreneurial and exploitative needs, orientations, methods, and perhaps doctrines[21] with a contradictory, or at least, unreconciled set of humanistic, nurturing, supportive ones.

DEMAND

For the description and understanding of the "demand" for what the expert has to "supply," a summary and an expansion of what has already been sketched of Crestwood Heights are required. Perhaps what needs to be said can best be caught up in a series of gradually narrowing frames of reference: much of it would be true for the Western world generally; some for only the middle class; the least part of it for Crestwood Heights alone, or distinctively.

A. THE WESTERN WORLD

It is possible, as Mr. Toynbee's work amply demonstrates, to see the larger patterns of history in numberless ways. One way, fruitful perhaps from the viewpoint of this study, is to see it in terms of a succession of "revolutions."[22] The theological revolution that brought the church to dominance for many centuries, coincides with the dissolution of Rome. Two technological revolutions, the agricultural and the industrial, end the Middle Ages and bring us to the verge of modern history. An economic revolution (the emergence of finance as dominant over production) and a political one (the emergence of the state as dominant over all other forms of power-organization) fall in the early part of our period. It is, however, the insufficiently remarked social and psychological revolution we are now *in* that is of peculiar significance for Crestwood Heights. The revolutions mark the transition, in effect, from a god-centered society to a thing-centered society to a man-centered society; from the ideological dominance of theology (and philosophy) to the dominance of physics (and biology) to the emerging dominance of the social sciences,[23] spearheaded by psychology (and psychiatry). What is now to be rationalized is not the relation of man to God, or man to things, but man to man and man to himself.

Perhaps a restatement of these views, as one of the authors has put them elsewhere, may be helpful in indicating the direction and sweep of the change as well as its relevance to the community under study.

Virtually all societies, in all times and places, have set themselves the task of procuring certain rearrangements in the physical order, the biological order, the human order, and the supernatural order: they have tried to shelter themselves; they have tried to maintain health; they have sought power over men; and they have essayed to coerce, cajole, or otherwise control the gods. Each society at any given moment manifests in its ethos, its institutions, and the personalities of its members the consequences of a concentration on one or more of these tasks. . . .

. . . latter-day changes in Western society have secured a differential concentration of this kind on the human order; . . . the community we have studied, to a sensible and difference-making degree, embodies and perhaps epitomizes that change. Some of the changes that are relevant to this change might be here briefly touched upon. The correlated advance of natural science, technology, and economic organization of the last few centuries has permitted (although not made necessary) a relative abandonment of concentration upon the physical order: materials, in usable form, are now relatively easily come by. The secondary impact of natural science (through physics on metaphysics) and of technology on man's relative impotence and dependence in the universe, have combined, seemingly, with other causes to render peripheral earlier concern with the supernatural order. Lastly, the emergence of the social sciences, as changing bodies of knowledge about and a constant attitude towards human beings and human problems, has again made possible (though not necessary) a concentration on the human order. The concentration on the biological order which preceded it (and still, partly, overlaps it) was represented at its crest in diminishing rates of infant deaths and of infectious diseases, running roughly from the sixteenth century to yesterday's wonder-drug.

What has made *possible*, then, the concentration on the human order as against the alternatives is a combination of circumstances, foremost of which are the relatively complete conquest of the physical and biological orders, with a consequent attrition of the felt importance of the supernatural, and, correlative with these, the emergence of a body of knowledge about social and psychological matters, and widespread acquaintance with the attitudes that made that knowledge accrue.

What made *necessary* the concentration referred to was the survival in undiminished or heightened form of the Judæo-Protestant (with heavier emphasis on the latter) ethic, stripped now of its theological vocabulary and foundation, but, curiously, more pervasive and mandatory in its attitude. Perhaps the term is ill-chosen, since it does not distinguish fully or exclusively the Protestant ethic from some elements in Catholicism or even in non-Christian thought; but the existence of the complex of attitudes which are loosely referred to as "Puritan" is of fundamental consequence. Without it, the larger impact of psychology might have been the development of parlor games, instead of a tendency, by its aid, to make even parlor games deadly serious business. (Would you give even your baby anything but an "educational" or "sensible" toy?)

What emerges from this then is a shift in relative preoccupation with the various possible orders, the passing into the general culture of a mass of psychological and sociological "knowledge," the growth of technique in a radically new sense (i.e., as applied to human beings instead of non-human objects), the incorporation of these in existing institutions (if amenable) or new ones, a shift in the intermediate (if not in the ultimate) value-scheme, a redistribution of power, influence, and material and human resources between institutions, a redefinition of criteria for success and failure, and, one would suppose, a radical shift in the nature of social and psychological dynamics, and a corresponding alteration in the content, if not in the "form" of psychopathology.[24]

The succession and yet compresence of these revolutions summarizes, if it does not account for, many of the major problems of the Western world. The problems faced in Soviet Russia, or in Nazi Germany, or in Socialist England, or in middle-class Crestwood Heights of *what to do* in the face of the new knowledge and extended techniques that make the control of man by man possible in a radical sense in which it was never possible before, are products of this revolution, just as are the emergence of psychoanalysis, group dynamics, training laboratories, and short courses in winning friends and influencing people.

B. NORTH AMERICA

The impact of these revolutions has for various reasons a quite distinctive character in English-speaking North America.[25] It is common to refer to America as "the New World," and while this designation makes an historic point, it misses a contemporary one, namely that America is not merely the new world but is the "perennially new world." It is a world to which, by the working-out of the immigration policy, there has been brought virtually from its foundation to nearly the present day, a continuous flow of new ideas, new ways of doing things, new traditions, new questions, and new disturbances—economic, political, social, and ethical.[26] On the North American continent, probably to a greater degree than anywhere else in the Western world, the clash of cultures resulted not, as elsewhere, merely in a break-up and attrition of tradition, but more nearly in a pulverization, not to say atomization, of it. This pulverization of tradition left the way much clearer for new ideological crops, and provided a much more fertile field for their rapid growth and luxuriance than had any previously known situation.[27]

The breach with and fragmentation of tradition, which became almost a tradition in itself, extended to all but a handful of central values. These, however, no matter how transformed and disguised, still provide continuity between the America of the founding fathers and the America of the present day. Now translated into secular terms and applied to secular objects, these surviving values represent the core of what has been called the "Protestant ethic."[28] Among these Protestant values were certainly the emphasis on the individual and his conscience, as against the church and her voice earlier—or the group and its voice now; the emphasis on reason as a method *par excellence* for unravelling the mysteries of the universe; the responsibility for *working* out one's own salvation—individually, not collectively; and an orientation in which the chief glories are promised for the future—not only the heavenly one, but that of one's own mature years and the immediately succeeding generations.

The radical decline of the church as a dominant institution, and the sharp decline under the impact of science in the value for the integration of individual or society of the traditional religions, left not so much a clear field but rather one with continuing constellations of emotions, looking in effect for new objects: old bottles, as it were, looking for new wine.[29] Messianic hopes and orientations, disappointed of their previous fulfilment, went looking for new Messiahs, economic, political, medical, or other.[30] Old terms which disappeared from polite conversation, such as "sin" and "grace," tended to be replaced with new and secular terms, which embodied the same emotional overtones and supplied to a considerable degree the same psychological necessities: "immaturity," "irresponsibility," "failure"; "maturity," "responsibility," "success."

These orientations seeking expression in the secular world underlie the beliefs about and the value placed upon rationality, gadgets, gimmicks, techniques of human organization, rules for a happy life, and experts in every field, from nucleonics to marriage. In America, the dominant view is that for every problem there must be a rational solution, either available or capable of invention; that human problems can be largely solved by the discovery of rules or the passage of laws that would compel a solution; and that in this process, the expert is the virtually indispensable man.[31]

In general these orientations tended to produce in the new countries a relative absence of structure (or, to put it another way, an immense flexibility of structure), an incredible valuation of movement as against position or stability, a widespread feeling of limitless possibilities—"the sky is the limit"—and a kind of jackpot psychology, which holds out a permanent possibility of large rewards on the basis of small efforts, although the latter are not calculably related to the former.

What is true of America generally is true with special force for its middle class.

C. THE MIDDLE CLASS

Within this general context, the middle class in America by virtue of its history, its role or function in the society, the means available to it for the performance of that role, its status and general orientation, is in a quite peculiar position.

It is, in fact, and almost by definition, a class of high and recent mobility, both in a vertical and in a horizontal sense. It is, or has been until recently, a class which has been largely recruited, because of the rapidly expanding need in America for the roles and services it supplies, from the classes below it (and to some degree, from the failures in the class above it). It is not characteristically a class which has supplied itself from its own ranks for many generations, which accepts its own middle-class character, or which looks forward, over future generations, to its continuation in its present position. Psychologically, it is to many of its members a mere stepping-stone, a *pied-à-terre*, a precarious resting point, in a vertical movement, in which upward hopes and downward fears have, and are felt to have, a very high probability of realization. This vertical mobility, fluidity, or precariousness in social space, has necessitated in America a corresponding horizontal mobility in geographical space, so that no opportunity of upward movement might be lost and no risk of downward mobility go unprovided against.

The dominant specific role of the middle class in America has been, and increasingly is, the role of management.[32] Management carries with it quite specific necessities and orientations. It is of necessity a life of action rather than, say, a life of contemplation; it is a life that puts the highest possible premium on foresight and control, as against, say, retrospection and enjoyment; it is a life of prudent calculation rather than brilliant intuition; it is a life, chiefly, whose ends are given, and which requires primarily the organization of means towards the effectuation of those ends, without any incentive to—indeed, with a handicap on—the examination of the ends as such. It is a life in which, under modern conditions, human problems have replaced technical ones as major obstructions to the fulfilment of policy, and the knowledges, skills, and techniques of human organization and manipulation are those which bring rewards, financial, in prestige, and, what is far more important, in satisfaction of the need for accomplishment, for effective agency, which is the manager's *raison d'être* and his source of morale.[33]

A class with this history and this role and function, understandably relies heavily if not nearly exclusively on the manipulation of symbols. The almost boundless faith exhibited by the American middle class in the efficacy of literacy and learning, has been noted by virtually every student of American life, and amounts, at times, to an ascription of virtual omnipotence to these means for almost any conceivable end. Knowledge, thought, technique, rationalization, if not competent to restructure the entire universe, are felt as competent to restructure virtually every important element of it.

Given this faith, and also the evident fact that these means have, so far, failed notably to achieve those ends, a partial explanation of the orientation towards the future of the middle class is evident.

The "temporary" nature of the middle-class definition, and lack of access to lower-class resignation or upper-class safety,[34] result in a constant living in and discounting of, the future, extending beyond, but not too far beyond, the lifetime of the adult. Success for the child of the adult is needed as the seal and validation of adult status because the career of the adult spans, in foresight, more than his own life. It is understandable then if, at this class level, we find that the home is child-centered, quantity of children is sacrificed to quality of children, and the child (who carries so much of the parents' hopes and aspirations on his back) is conceived of as a problem to be solved, very like other problems encountered in the managerial world.

What is true of the middle class generally is perhaps more readily evident in such an upper middle class suburb as Crestwood Heights.

D. CRESTWOOD HEIGHTS

In order to understand the psychological situation of the laymen-adults in Crestwood Heights we shall need to look, serially, at the way in which they are selected for residence there, at the implications of this particular mobility, at the culture and the social system they encounter, and, finally, at the effects of concentration of relatively like-minded people of the kind selected.[35]

Selection. Earlier sections of this volume will already have made clear how Crestwood Heights became differentiated as a life-site, unique perhaps for this metropolitan area. Within a quarter-century, land that lay open to blade and plough was plotted, purchased, built over, and bid up to many times its previous value. Earlier chapters will doubtless also already have made clear how in a relatively short interval the community which had first little attraction except for its pleasantness and reputability, became noted for its schools.

As the fame of the school system justly grew, and simultaneously the control of immigration was left largely to the real-estate market, a second wave of residents was drawn into the community for whom the existence of this outstanding school system was the paramount consideration. These in turn acted in concert to make it possible for the school system to improve itself further at an accelerating pace, and thus to become more of a Mecca than ever for those who wanted their children raised under modern methods and with, presumably, maximum educational advantage.

The community as a life-site had by then substantially changed its character. It is true that it still had stiff minimum economic requirements, but from among those relatively many who could meet those requirements it tended to select a relative few: those to whom the education of their children in the new and differentially advantageous way was a consideration of sufficient weight to justify, in many cases, immense sacrifices in terms of economics or separation from those with whom they otherwise felt most comfortable.[36]

The people thus drawn in were, therefore, people whose hopes and fears, aspirations and self-estimates, were perhaps inordinately bound up with the fate of their children. Moreover, these were, selectively, people who on one ground or another looked with special confidence to the public school to do for them a job they could not do or could do less well for themselves.[37] They tended to be, further, people who had an extraordinarily high regard for schooling, learning, and, in general, the intellectual process. They tended, lastly, to be people for whom the most recent deliverances of science on human nature, and the consequent appropriate educational procedure, had an overwhelming appeal, based sometimes upon awe before the unknown, sometimes upon familiarity with the matters whereof the new experts spoke. This combination of requirements—sufficient worldly success to permit entry to Crestwood Heights together with sufficient devotion to the type of schooling for which Crestwood Heights is noted—makes, in general, for the selection of a quite particular type of individual.

Classwise, it of course excludes the upper and lower classes: the former on the basis both of their previous establishment in other areas and of the discrepancy between their educational aims and those embedded in the Crestwood Heights system; the latter on the basis of inability to afford the living standards of Crestwood Heights, and equally firm rejection of its educational views. This leaves the middle class, but the selection tends to exclude even the established upper portion of that class whose views border closely on those of the upper class into which it might move. The selection draws together, then, largely people of lower middle-class or lower origins, who are desirous of and capable of rapid transition to middle middle-class status or "better."

Ethnically, the selection tends to pick out members from among those groups who have for a variety of historical reasons—peculiar dangers, usually combined with deprivation of other means of effective defence—come to lay unusual stress on the importance of learning as a social and moral asset and on intellectual competence as a tool of control and protection.

Personality-wise, it tends to select from within these class-ethnic candidates those who sustain and embody the energy and ambition to give effect to the required mobility, and, further, those who, to an unusual degree, implicate their children both as means and as ends in the organization of their careers and ambitions. These are, for the most part, future-oriented, voluntaristic, individualistic, control-aspirant, rationalizing,[38] organizing people, who bring such orientations, and any anxieties which may underlie them and flow from them, to Crestwood Heights when they come. In Crestwood Heights, it will be argued, these orientations are given reinforcement and support, are translated into shared generalizations both as to facts and as to ideals, and institutionalized in such ways that they are finally seen not as personal characteristics (and, perhaps, defects) but as social necessities.

People moving rapidly upward economically and socially, specially devoted to the welfare of their children, highly valuing education (particularly some variation of progressive education), possessing the orientations mentioned above, are not necessarily or even *prima facie* self-exploitative or neurotic or anxiety-ridden. It is true, however, that many neurotic, self-exploitative, and anxiety-ridden people will share these orientations, and these are not likely to be under-represented in a population selected as is that of Crestwood Heights.[39]

Mobility.[40] Despite all that has already been said about mobility in the earlier chapters, some additional points seem worth making in the present context.

Movement into Crestwood Heights is, of course, meant to and does express moral or social as well as spatial difference and distance.[41] Moreover movement into Crestwood Heights is a mark of personal or family distinction, not part of a collective move, perceived as such. It is an isolation by achievement, a something that separates as it distinguishes the "me" from the "them." The rapidity with which the transition has to be accomplished, and the depth to which change must penetrate the personality are such as to call for the greatest flexibility of behavior and stability of personality. Ideology, speech sometimes, food habits, and preferences in décor must be made over with relative suddenness and in the absence of unmistakable clues as to the behavior to be adopted. Success is by leap rather than by glide; the kind of difference sought can be established *only* by a single dramatic gesture, not by a gradual accumulation of minor distinctions.

Because of the fineness of the Crestwood Heights mesh, because many may yearn but few arrive, those who do attain will not probably know one another. They arrive, scattered, bringing neither friends nor acquaintances with them. Indeed, were group movement possible, the shift would lose the greater part of its present meaning: its evidence to oneself and to others of superior personal or idiosyncratic worth and accomplishment. This individual basis from which the move derives its essential meaning, however, tends to establish a very abrupt distinction between "me" and what was once "us." The distinction, in turn, not only issues in sharply accentuated feelings of loneliness and isolation, but calls into play a rather elaborate system of explanation and justification of the difference between people like oneself and people like one's former friends, relations, and intimates.

The combination of minimal geographic distance with maximal moral distance adds its problems. It entails the spatial proximity of those people and institutions, rapid separation from whom is the *sine qua non* of entrée to the new world. What for the emigrant from a distance might ostensibly be the natural acts of a busy and inaccessible man building for himself a new life—spacing out letters, "forgetting" birthdays and connections, letting ritual lapse—are in this situation acts whose deliberate nature it is difficult to conceal from oneself and others, acts which call for much more elaborate rationalizations than "Isn't that the way things happen?" Positively, also, the proximity leaves intact and available all the associations which call the individual, particularly in moments of frustration and loneliness, back to earlier habits, familiar sensations, former loyalties. They constitute thus the equivalent of a vividly present system of temptations—a system whose remembered rewards and foreseen consequences for the newly established status make the present "adjustment" all the more precarious and knife-edge.[42]

Culture. To these difficulties must be added two more: one having to do with the "form" and one with the "content" of the culture which the newcomer to Crestwood Heights encounters.

The content of the culture—predominantly a mixture of beliefs, techniques, orientations, and customs associated with "success" and corresponding elements from a radically different set of assumptions and goals associated with "maturity"—has been so often encountered in the course of this book that detailed treatment here is not necessary.

The permissive and tolerant form of the culture—or perhaps one should say the manner of its mediation (which is intrinsic to it)—makes it unusually difficult for the newcomer to discover what are the essentials of the "new" culture and to adapt to them, and thus begin securing at least the secondary satisfactions of acceptance and adjustment. A culture which operates as a fairly plain system of rights and duties, or enjoinders and prescriptions, may be difficult to adjust to if one's habits have been otherwise fashioned, but it can be apprehended with relative ease and assimilation can be accepted or refused. A culture such as that of Crestwood Heights, on the other hand, whose principal ostensible values are toleration and permissiveness, gives little clue to the beginner as to what ought to be the content of his behavior. Within gross limits, of course, it is easy to learn that there are some things one must *not* do: appear in the garden in one's undershirt, show dirty nails, etc. But these are what might be called minor entry qualifications. In order to enter fully into the culture, as has been indicated, a system of word-ways, thought-ways, feeling-ways, even postures must be acquired and made natural; and this system can only be discovered by extended living in the culture or most acute penetration of its ostensible character. At its core this culture calls for an orientation almost the polar opposite of the one which draws people to Crestwood Heights in the first place or which permits them to maintain themselves there economically thereafter. But this basic contradiction will have to be left for later discussion.

E. THE CONSEQUENT DEMAND

Some of the reasons will now be readily appreciated for the degree of uncertainty and confusion about precisely those areas of life that are felt to have overwhelming practical and moral importance. Given, in addition, the belief that problems are rationally soluble, and the strong reliance on the use of money and human organization to secure solutions (wherever one does not have resources to procure them directly) the stage is set for the emergence of a demand, strongly backed emotionally and financially, for the advice of experts of all kinds.

The services of the experts are, as has been indicated, required to obtain or build a house, in the ordinary sense of a shelter or, more particularly, in the new sense of a "matrix for living."[43] The once relatively simple matter of feeding the family requires the services of domestic science specialists; consumers' guides; hygienists and health teachers in general; pediatricians; specialists who can advise on the meaning of food and food preparation in the maintenance of happy married relationships; and communications experts, journalistic and novelistic, who will give clues as to what "the best people" are *really* eating, regardless of all the foregoing considerations. Not only must the body be cared for in the ordinary sense, but cosmeticians are ready to advise on the style of hair-do which is appropriate to a personality (which its bearer does not herself recognize); newspaper columnists will advise on how to get fat or thin, with or without pain. And even within these specializations, further specializations by age levels may be detected: particularly relevant messages may be addressed to those entering their teens, to the adolescents, to the young married couples, and others.

The demand for aid from the experts, while quite forceful in general, is most urgent for the services of those in the behavioral sciences—the experts who deal with human relations and behavior, in their most intimate and vital aspects.

The "human experts," for whose help such a widespread and intense demand is thus created, are roughly of two kinds: experts in the solution of collective, organizational, social, or "inter-personal" problems on one side; and experts in the solution of "intra-personal" or individual problems on the other. They range through marriage counsellors to personal psychotherapists, and include experts on how to live, how to rear children, how to deal with the problems of the aged, and so on.

The facts heretofore cited established the character of the demand. Other facts were to establish in it a peculiar quality. It seemed, generally speaking, that the greater the uncertainty and confusion and the more important the area in which that uncertainty and confusion lay, the greater was the trust in rational solution in the abstract, combined with a sense of impotence in the finding of rational solution in the particular, and the greater the need for finality. What may at first have been merely excessive faith in simple solutions became in fact, under the pressure of cumulating uncertainty, an emotion-laden demand for such solutions, and moreover, solutions not only simple but short-order.

These necessities, somewhat desperately generalized, met what has been referred to earlier as the Protestant heritage, and the meeting led to a demand that had definite Messianic overtones. What emerged initially as a need for particular helps in particular crises became very nearly, and quite generally, a demand for a Savior-general whose pronouncements would be simple, definite, and so far-reaching as to contain within themselves at least the seeds of solution to all probable problems. At times this demand seemed to be not only for a species of omnicompetence, but for a Messianic orientation in the guide towards the subjects: an intention of "saving" all, and saving all in all respects. This is, of course, not only a matter of power and skill, but also a matter of love and character, and it is against this kind of demand—which he has perhaps also helped to create—that the operation of the expert must be seen. To this operation we must now turn.

PRODUCTION

A. LEADERSHIP

Experts, of course, share with any other leaders a basic mode of operation. Attempts have been made to explain leadership in at least two sets of terms. One line of explanation, a sociological one, is related to interaction: the leader is he who "originates action in the majority of [set] events"[44] (i.e., events in which more than two people participate). The other line of explanation is psychological, and the leader is here described as one who is able to represent to his followers whatever is common to their "superegos."[45] The first view needs correction before it can be brought into line with the second, at least in the context of Crestwood Heights.

Within any given set of events formally like, there are, particularly in a crisis-ridden society, a very small number, relatively, of *crucial* events. They may be crucial for a "subjective" reason, i.e., the participants merely *feel* that this event is of great importance, or an "objective" one in the sense that the effect of the given event is unusually large in determining the course of subsequent events.[46] The leader in the situation we are describing is *not* the person who originates in the majority of "set" events, but the person who exerts a decisive or disproportionate effect in the majority of those few events that are crucial. It is, here, the very rarity of the leader's interventions, combined with their obviously disproportionate effects, that tends to give him the magical and charismatic aura which is a necessity of his operation.

Opposed to the "set" events in the sociological explanation of leadership are "pair" events (i.e., events in which only two people participate); it is to the latter that the leader is said to "respond." However, any attempt by any leader in Crestwood Heights to originate in the majority of "set" events, while responding only in the majority of "pair" events, would be regarded as "hogging the limelight" or manifesting pushing or immature behavior. Moreover, the responding on the part of the leader need not be, and is by no means generally, to pairs alone: in any smaller subgroup than the total group he may be—indeed must to some degree be—respondent rather than originator. What is central in the definition for Crestwood Heights is the fact that in any group smaller than "the set" he will secure a kind of information which members will not be willing to communicate in the total group[47] and be able to establish a kind of influence which he also cannot establish in the total group.[48]

B. THE EXPERT'S AURA

This influence depends partly on the expert's differential access to books, to other experts, to people like the members of the group he is dealing with. For these reasons, plus the fact that he is the only one to have access to all the subgroups, there is often imputed to him the characteristic of "knowing us better than we do ourselves." It is not a far cry from this to casting him in a role where he is expected radically to effect changes in the ego-system (or reality-system) of members of the group, and to the degree that his intervention in crucial events *is* decisive he has already been given considerable power over the superego. His power thus rests less on any fundamental identity in superego between leader and led and far more on his felt capacity to shake or restructure personal and group views of reality and value.[49]

The process tends to be cyclical. At an early stage, on the basis largely of knowledge imputed to him, the expert is made the recipient of knowledge and confidences which are intended partly to "correct" any erroneous views he may be forming. As this communication with him cumulates, he is felt to know more about the situation than anyone in it and he becomes therefore a potential source of help, both individual and collective. Unless great care is taken, the process tends to move to a point of genuine and profound dependency on the part of the layman and of unusually far-reaching power and dominance on the part of the expert. Where the inner necessities and outer situation of either party or both are served by this relationship it becomes particularly difficult to avoid the drift towards it.

As far as the outer situation of the expert is concerned, the technicality and complexity of his field make it very difficult for him to communicate with the layman, under the circumstances usually prevailing, without radical over-simplification. In scientific discourse, his generalizations are sharply limited by a more exact jargon, by probability statements, by restrictions, qualifications, and a whole host of background understandings. In communication with laymen, these safeguards are necessarily largely dropped, and there is great likelihood, even where care is taken, of over-generalization in delivery and, even more, in reception or understanding by the layman. In so far as this over-simplification once more reduces a complex picture of life to a few large bold strokes, it contributes further to the quasi-magical aura of the expert from whom it stems or seems to stem. Even where the expert is driven by scrupulosity to put in evidence his reasoning sequence and his complex testing methods, this too heightens rather than diminishes the magical aspects of the person and the act. The sequence and methods are not understood, but they do represent evidence of competence in a new jargon or methodology, and this evidence simply adds to the wonder of the act as would the production of a rabbit out of an empty hat.[50]

C. EDUCATION FOR DEPENDENCY

These effects are necessary rather than accidental because of the relative infrequency and the short duration of any one exposure to each other of expert and layman. The nature of their contact, which is in turn a function of busy, time-pressed lives on both sides, means that any message must be collapsed into a very brief communiqué, and that there must not be too many of these before the communication is felt to be complete.

The process tends to become, therefore, because of initial expectation (sometimes inner need) and its own necessities, an education for dependency in which the likelihood of the layman's ever coming into possession of the tools which make the expert able to render the judgments he does, becomes ever more remote.

Sometimes, of course, this process and this outcome are a rather good fit to the inner needs of the expert, and to his necessities for survival in his own organization of experts. In some cases the patent enjoyment of what would otherwise be thought of as an uncomfortable situation, and the near-total unconsciousness of what is being done, hint that some deep-seated need of the expert is indeed being satisfied. The lack of distress in mining the gold of guilt in his audience and dredging advantage from its dependency, the uninhibited satisfaction of his own needs for exploit and for exploitation, suggest the building of bastions by the expert against some felt inner passive dependency.

Added to these difficulties of communication are those flowing out of the asymmetry of the relationship between layman and expert. The expert's need for "therapeutic anonymity" or "ambiguity of definition," which is met and matched by the desire on the part of the layman to see the expert as a being of a different sort, an image which too much intimacy might destroy, determines that the interaction between them proceeds in such a way that the life and behavior and inner feeling of the layman form the public subject-matter of discussion and the life and behavior and inner feeling of the expert are almost wholly outside the universe of discourse. The discussion process, or lecture and learning process, quite openly addresses itself to the difficulties, weaknesses, falsities, foibles, deeper motivations, and problems of the layman. The corresponding elements within the expert are rarely or never out on the table; if they were, he would cease to be the kind of expert we have been talking about.[51]

This concealment—whether deliberate on the part of the expert or growing out of the layman's needs or the conventions of communication—of the essential identity of layman and expert in most points except mere information serves to make impossible for both parties any meaningful analysis of the problems they are considering. If an expert talks about destructive tendencies, in a social situation in which his talk is a function of *his* destructive tendencies, without permitting or causing his audience to see what he says in the context of his own needs as well as theirs, his indirect teaching is of a first-order degree of falsity. If he talks about maturity and responsibility as though from an achieved mature and responsible viewpoint, when in actuality his point of view is, to say the least, undefined, and may not be at all as suggested, he is really attempting to secure mature and responsible behavior in others by an immature and irresponsible act on his part.[52] A quite specific social situation in which the inner needs of expert and layman are deeply enmeshed and engaged—the situation from which illumination is to be derived—is passed off implicitly as a situation in which the laymen are human and the experts have the quasi-divine characteristics of a measuring rod whose peculiarities do not need to be taken into account (at least as compared with the peculiarities of the populations under measurement or discussion).[53]

It is only with recognition of this necessity of the expert to feel above the battle or outside the conflict, and to appear so, that the concrete content of some of his teaching becomes at all intelligible. This teaching, or its assumptions, frequently contains contradictions of logic so obvious and immediate, that its capacity to evoke loyalty and to hold it for a decade or more must be a matter of marvel. What is commonly involved is nothing less than a radical split in the interpretation of reality.

On the assumption, for instance, that behavior is determined like other natural phenomena in a purely cause-and-effect sequence, parents will be led by experts to the view that they must not submit the behavior of their children to moral judgment. If Billy hits Mummy, his action is the natural consequence of what has gone before in Billy's life; it is not merely that he is "blameless": there can be no question of praise or blame in a sequence of cause-and-effect. If, however, the same mother, whose behavior is presumably also determined, responds with anger or strikes back or takes a more obscure revenge later, she is often encouraged to feel that her actions *are* justiciable and subject to moral evaluation, that she is an "inadequate" mother—with a clear implication that, as a largely free agent, she "ought to" do something about it.[54]

Similarly, the expert who will explain that capacity for loving depends on a commensurate experience of having been loved, will lead the parent to a deep concern with loving her child sufficiently in order that the child may ultimately be capable of this priceless experience of loving. The parent's incapacity to do so will tend, however, to be blamed or lamented or complained about, although (on the logic of the equation) it ought to be attributed to her lack of the experience of having been loved.[55]

One could multiply such instances almost indefinitely. Another example is the "family expert" who, having clearly recognized and indeed taught that the family is a system of interdependent roles and feelings and relations, proceeds to advise or teach as if his adult students were the independent variables on which the others were dependent. This applies not only to the adult-child relation, but to that of the spouses, depending largely only on which of them the expert has momentarily under tutelage.

Multiplication could, however, merely permit one generalization, namely that what is common to all these contradictions is their capacity to increase the guilt of the layman upon whom, by determinism, so much depends, and who must therefore, by indeterminism, make a great effort to do better in securing the important results. This is what was referred to earlier when the expert was described as "mining the gold of guilt."

If there is a major error in the foregoing description, it lies in making even the "worst" expert seem much more calculating and opportunistic than he actually is. It is true that by maximizing the guilt of laymen and increasing their dependency upon him, he thereby increases, simultaneously, his present power and prestige and the possibility of the security of an unthreatened position. But it would be misleading, we believe, to imply that these are the conscious grounds, or at least the primary grounds, for the conduct of the operation. To do so would make the expert seem much more clever and scheming than the layman, which is rarely the case. These are, rather, secondary rewards, which some experts discover to accrue in this kind of situation, from the outworking of their own inner needs to satisfy aggression in safe ways, i.e. without threatening their equal need for dependency. It is this direct and unapprehended (indeed, carefully concealed) mixture of aggression and dependency which, in the given situation, pays off so handsomely.[56]

D. THE SUCCESSION OF EXPERTS

For a variety of reasons which merit discussion, various kinds of experts, various schools of thought within a given class of expert, and various individuals within a given kind and school, tend to succeed one another: to come out of the wilds of effective anonymity, pass in orderly fashion up the gradient of power and popularity, stand out in a given social setting as they replace their predecessors at the peak, dominate briefly, and, under the impact of the next wave, pass on.

This succession has marked consequences on the laymen-adults and on the local specialists and semi-experts, and through both on the children.

One reason for this succession lies in science itself and the arts and technologies founded upon it. It is in the very nature of Western science —and indeed it is its chief virtue—that it is an activity which, taken as a whole, has built into it certain self-corrective tendencies. Dogma has relative permanence only at one level of abstraction: its method. The productivity of science may almost be measured by the rapidity with which it renders older propositions untrue, in whole or in part, by demonstrating these propositions to be erroneous, partial, or qualified, or mere special cases of more general and important classes of cases.[57] This mode of development necessitates a succession of theories in every scientific field, and this succession of theories is a necessary but not a sufficient condition for the succession of experts alluded to above.

It is not a sufficient condition because it would be abstractly possible for the expert to change his view with the changing deliverances of his science, and, accordingly, for the succession of theories to leave the personnel largely unaffected. Indeed a rough approximation to this state of affairs holds in those sciences that are relatively remote from the public eye and interest, and almost in direct proportion as they are so. No mathematician need suffer social difficulties, in addition to any inherent intellectual difficulties, by adopting in the middle of his career the view that Euclidean geometry is only a special case, and that propositions which he formerly believed to hold under all conditions now demonstrably hold only under some. No biologist would have to give much consideration to the effect on his status of some new discovery that might seriously qualify current views of evolution. A physician who had publicly stood out against a remedy that had later proved to be economical and efficacious is in an intermediate position, and might expect serious repercussions on his inter- and extra-professional interests.[58] An educator who takes a stand against "the coming thing" or a stand that turns out later to be incompatible with the succeeding view is, however, in a very precarious position.

A succession of theorists, rather than merely a succession of theories held by the same theorists, or a succession of practitioners, rather than merely of practices, is, then, a function of more than changing theories; it depends on the sociology of the relevant professions, and on the sociology of the system in which the expert and the layman interact.

The professions that provide experts of the kind we have been discussing are based upon relatively new fields of knowledge. In an old field, changes are generally likely to be minor, and of little public interest since they touch general orientations little or not visibly; where they are major (e.g., Einstein's reformulation) the field is so well integrated that the change is rapidly adopted or refused by all, and rarely becomes the basis for the formation of a school or faction or identifiable *avant-garde* group. A new field is necessarily one in which the theorists or practitioners are marginal in a number of senses. They are likely to be marginal to their colleagues in the wider science within which they are seeking to establish a sub-field; for example, the coming child psychologist, when the sub-field is new, is likely to be looked on askance by his colleagues in general psychology and its established sub-fields who "doubt if there really is such a field." They are likely to be marginal in reference to the administrations of their institutions and to sources of funds, since it is almost inevitably felt that they have to prove themselves before the institutions can make firm commitments or justify the ploughing in of large sums of money. In the fields in which we are here interested, the social sciences, they are particularly likely to be marginal to their publics, since what they are defining as their specialty is widely believed at first to be within the competence of laymen; for example, everyman, who has long since ceased to be his own lawyer, is still in his own mind his own economist.

For these reasons, and others having to do with selection for such enterprises, the relations between colleagues even within the new sub-discipline are likely to be relatively strained and anxiety-laden. The newness of the field permits its experts to make radical explorations in different directions; the necessity to explore it rapidly encourages such diversity; the uncertainty of the collective security makes every man concerned about what the rest are doing; the uncertainty of the individual expert's fate increases the desirability of doing something distinctive; the unstructured character of the emerging hierarchy encourages the expert to centralize in his behavior, if not in his awareness, considerations of power and competition.

This situation in turn tends to make for increasingly rapid differentiation of ideas—differentiation at a rate far higher than the general knowledge would ordinarily indicate as desirable or supportable in the sub-field. Differentiation, once achieved, must be justified, and the justification would be a rapid increase in the reward—the number and particularly the importance of new discoveries in the differentiated field. The number of discoveries follows naturally enough; the importance not so surely.

There is a marked tendency to fill the gap thus left by means of over-rapid and over-wide generalization. A finding, interesting enough perhaps as a point of departure for further more detailed research, or as a datum of intrinsic usefulness, is speedily ripped from its limited context and made to do defence-duty for the whole specialty in which it was discovered. Thus, for example, the phenomenon in visual perception which is identified as "closure" expands rapidly into a school of Gestalt Psychology, thence into a general outlook or philosophy, and finally into a cosmology. With such expansion, the originally marginal discoverers and their students and disciples move rapidly into the public eye, into demand as mentors, and into power, security, and control of resources for the sake of their field, which is in this sense "established."

Yet, even given the nature of the scientific process and the pressures on the theorist or practitioner in the new field, the outcome referred to as succession might not eventuate were it not for the corresponding nature of public demand.

The public—or at least the literate, middle-class portion of it that is most relevant for the expert's career—meets the scientific product with an insatiable demand. But much of the demand, as we have already made clear, is itself pre-scientific and quasi-magical. It expresses the hope that science—the magic-killer—will magically supply answers of so transforming a quality as to remove from human life all its inherent uncertainties and contingencies, particularly the unhappy ones. Science, which made the discoveries which permitted technology to supply cheap machines to "take the drudgery out of housework," is in these areas expected to make discoveries to take the difficulties out of living. More than that, these discoveries are to require little or no effort for their employment. A few simple rules for the bringing-up of tension-free but successful children, for securing one's neurosis-dictated ends without the associated pains, for managing one's self or a group are all that is required.

Given this orientation in the public, it is difficult for the most secure scientist, even one who can afford to be meticulously accurate about what he communicates, to prevent his followers and popularizers from generalizing his most careful statements to a point for which there is no scientific warrant. He will, without intent, be cast in a role for which he realizes there is no justification in the knowledge or skill that he has; but even his disclaimers will be reinterpreted by the public out of its own inner and outer needs as manifesting scientific modesty and as further evidence for the stature ascribed to him. If the scientist, for reasons internal to him or intrinsic to his sub-field and its internal and external relations in the scientific world, cannot afford the mighty effort required to stem the distortion of what he can say with justification, there ensues a process that is not—except, perhaps, in terms of crudity —unlike the process by which a Hollywood star is born. Perhaps it would be kinder to say that it is very like the process by which a new "prophet" is recognized.[59]

The public demand for "commitment" on the side of the expert is decisive for the fact of succession. Without this demand it would be possible for established experts to change their teaching, even radically, without losing their position as experts: perhaps, indeed, change would confirm it. But given the expectation of commitment—and, indeed, the view that any change in the teaching is a desertion of the disciples who have adopted it, a sign of uncertainty in the leader, and therefore a symptom of incapacity for leadership—the power and influence of the expert are almost purely a function of the position of the theory he invented, discovered, or espoused, in the succession of theories. *It* is doomed to obsolescence in the scientific process; and, with it, *he*, in the social.

The consequences of this succession for laymen-adults and intermediary experts need to be assessed separately.

On the laymen-adults it has commonly one short-run positive effect and one long-run negative one: the first is exhilaration; the second confusion. The sequence is not unlike that following consumption of alcohol.[60]

The short-run effect—to be more exact, the progression of short-run effects—is very like a periodic new lease on life. It takes some time to become acquainted with a new theory or a new viewpoint, and, for most, this carries with it the excitement of novelty and an upsurge of optimism. As acquaintance proceeds, there is the delight of exploring a well-elaborated system and finding how beautifully it "hangs together." Then follows application, usually in reference to outside reality, but sometimes only in restructuring inner beliefs and attitudes, really or again in imagination. At this point some checks may be met, if reality in any of its aspects proves refractory. These checks can be minimized in their emotional effect by a period of proselytizing for the new view. This is a period of intense missionary effort with all its satisfactions; and of attempts to cope with reality in terms of the new directives expressed or implied. The period begins with solid satisfaction and ends with disappointment: disappointment because the new view never provides the solution looked for, life is still difficult, and the reality that was to be overwhelmed is still refractory. Disappointment is increased since by this time a new theory, with obviously better possibilities, is waxing and needs a new novitiate.

This rather neat fit between disappointment with the practical and theoretical rewards of the theory on the lay side, and the emergence of a new theory to fill what would otherwise be a vacuum in ideology and loyalty, is something more than the happy coincidence of two parallel and independent developments. There is sufficient feedback between the experts, as a group, and the laymen, that the knowledge of growing dissatisfaction on the lay side serves to raise genuine intellectual doubts among the younger and uncommitted and as yet unestablished experts. These doubts lead properly to further scientific examination by the expert and, shortly, to restatement, redefinition, and new theory by a new emergent expert at precisely the point where, on the consumption side, the market for a new theory and a new theorist is at its point of greatest demand.

The series of short-run effects through a sequence of enthusiasms, exhilarations, and exaltations (largely remembered) and disappointments and relative depressions (largely forgotten) is, however, often paralleled, at a deeper level, by a more general and mounting feeling of futility, disillusionment, and frustration. This deeper feeling, for reasons which may by now be obvious, does not become effective in the sense that it gives rise to self-examination or to an examination of the system of adopting and rejecting experts.

The existence of the feeling requires for its explanation the recognition of one more aspect of the succession of theories that underlies it. If the theories followed one another in such a way that each new one could be interpreted as being merely a refinement or expansion of an older one—if there were, in other words, a sort of straight-line ideological evolution—the succession of theories and theorists might have quite other psychological effects. But the very necessities of the competitive struggle among the experts, on one side, and the psychological necessities of clean breaks and fresh starts for the laymen, on the other, combine to ensure that succeeding theories are not so much expansive as contradictory of one another. Thus child-training theories founded on Watsonian behaviorism are succeeded, not by a modification of these views, but by a radically different set founded on the social theories of John Dewey, and these, in turn, not by a refinement of Dewey, but by the critically different individual-centered theories of "unconditional love." The succession may have a haphazard form or may be at bottom dialectical; it is certainly not a straight-line evolution.

In any case, there tends to be among the laymen a series of attachments and exhilarations followed by detachments and disappointments, accompanied by a cumulative sense of disorientation and impotence, since each layman presumes that his inability to make intellectual sense and emotional satisfaction of "all this" is a function of his personal shortcomings. This may be the primary reason why the system itself never comes in for examination.

At its worst, the growing sense of impotence and uncertainty seems to make more desperate the search *by the same methods* for a definitive answer. The greater effort tends only to increase both the amplitude of the acceptance-rejection wave and its frequency, so that the turnover of experts is speeded up. With respect to the distribution of roles between institutions, it tends to increase the rate at which family responsibilities are relinquished to other institutions (for example, the "accepted" school, and, curiously, the "rejected" church or synagogue). With respect to the personality of the parent, it leads for some to a radical increase in anxiety via a diminishing self-esteem and a simultaneous increase in the need for self-glorification.

E. THE SPECIALIST

For the local specialists and sub-specialists this succession has important and interesting consequences. The specialists are, of course, differently situated from the experts in a number of vital respects: time,

space, dominance, relation to practice (as against theory), and opportunities and necessities.

With respect to time, they expect to endure longer in their present
roles or others very like them; with respect to space, their field of concern and operation is very much more restricted to Crestwood Heights
or Big City; with respect to dominance, their influence is both less as
to degree and more limited as to the numbers over whom it is exerted;
with respect to the theory-practice polarity, they must, to maintain
themselves, stick very closely to the practical problems of other laymen-adults. Each of these conditions, and all of them together, has
consequences for what is transmitted, how it is transmitted, and the
relations in which the transmission occurs.

The paramount requirement for endurance through time is very like
the requirement upon a senior civil servant in the British tradition who
wishes to continue serving through a rapid and radical succession of
changing political policies. He must be able, in effect, to enter enthusiastically into the thinking and plans and outlook of each new Minister
(or, in the United States, Department Head) but not so enthusiastically
as to label himself irrevocably a partisan or devotee.[61] The analogy is
not exact, since, in fact, the situation of the specialist is more difficult.
The civil servant in question is supported by the expectation that he
will as far as possible be above the battle (actually below it) and that
this is his proper function. The specialist or sub-specialist in Crestwood
Heights is confronted, however, with the religious-prophetic orientation
previously alluded to, and the expectation, therefore, that he will show
"real commitment" and the enthusiasm that flows out of it.

Since it is essential that the local expert enter into each new hierarchy of influence, and that he be able to extricate himself therefrom
without damage, he must sustain a peculiar relation to the outside
expert, to the lay public, and to himself. With the lay public, his role
is a leadership role, and it is mandatory that he show himself committed, confident, and clear. On the other hand, he must not permit
himself to be pushed so far by this public demand that his recorded
utterances and the practices he has caused to be institutionalized would
make his subsequent shift to a new allegiance a sign of apostasy, vacil-
lation, or error. This is most difficult, but the alternative would be a
succession of local experts as well as of outside experts; and, in fact,
though rarely, this does occur.

His double necessity leads the specialist to make a limited commit-
ment-for-a-trial. As the developing situation demands, then, either the
commitment or the experimental element can be stressed. Early enthusiasm can be fully justified on the basis of giving the new system or

theory a *fair* trial; later rejection can be equally justified by re-emphasis of the fair *trial*.[62]

The position of the specialist would seem at first sight like an ideal balance-wheel or governor to the otherwise relatively unrestrained flights of enthusiasm among the laymen, but it is less than that. Nevertheless, there is some tendency towards suspended judgment, limited trial, the watering-down of the by-now exaggerated claims to generality or certainty of the new theories. Indeed, it can hardly be doubted that, but for these tendencies, the swings in institutional practices would be wider than they are.

F. SUMMARY

In summarizing "production" we may say that we have, therefore, a set of circumstances which conspire to create a type-performance. The type-performance is limited in duration, since the expert is aware that in succeeding he has succeeded someone, and that he in his turn will be succeeded. He may, then, either mine the terrain rapidly for whatever material or psychological profit lies in it, or himself seek to build out of his following an institution (e.g., a "school" or an "institute") so that institutional lag will protect him against a too rapid attenuation of his investment. He will already have had to choose to speak to a large and heterogeneous audience rather than a small and homogeneous one, even though for the benefit of his work he might prefer the latter. The latter, however, cannot give him the rewards he is driven to seek. With every increment in the magnitude of the audience he addresses he will have to accept an increment in their heterogeneity, and also a decrease in his exactitude and an increase in his triviality. To cover these costs he will find himself under the necessity either of being continually first in the field with new inventions or of clothing what he says with unusual dramatic skill—or both. He will be decreasingly able to afford directness and simplicity, and still less will he be able—much as he may admire such care—to allow time for new ideas to be tested and retested in the scientific crucible before they are offered to the public as honest ware. The patent market is no place for indecision or lengthy consideration.

The same dictates of time will also to a degree determine one aspect of the expert-layman relation. Essentially this is the relation of the permanent "stranger,"[63] the one who socially is simultaneously near and far, in whom confidences of the most intimate kind can be reposed precisely because with him one can never be really intimate.[64]

It is now time to turn our attention from the producer back to the consumer.

CONSUMPTION

A picture of the fully developed situation, and the time or stage sequence in which it occurs, may be gathered from an examination of Figure 6 which depicts roughly the temporal relations and the relations of dominance or influence among expert, specialist, adult, child, and mass communication media.[65]

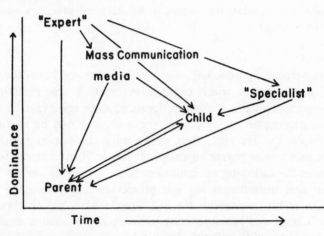

FIGURE 6. The social system of parent, child, specialist, expert, and mass communication media.

As seen from the perspective of the emerging family, in the beginning is the expert and the parent. The prospective parent is already affected directly by the expert in the course of his education and by the mass communication media through which the expert speaks, even before the advent of the central character of the drama, the child. Following upon that dramatic event, or shortly after, the child himself is brought under the expert's influence; and the parent, under the influence of the child. In the last stage, as already described—actually with the child's entry into nursery school or kindergarten—the specialist, himself in the expert's tutelage, has in fee a primary consumer, the child, and a secondary consumer in the parent.[66]

It would perhaps be an exaggeration to say that this situation in full intensity obtains for all parents in Crestwood Heights. It would be nearer the truth to say that with great frequency and over relatively long periods the actual situation comes sufficiently close to the situation depicted, and that it steadily moves towards such a point of equilibrium.

Here the amount of dependency established threatens—though the threat is rarely fully actualized—the possibility of a much greater dependency. For many, this threat even without actualization is sufficient to arouse considerable anxiety and uncertainty of behavior within parents and between them, and this anxiety and uncertainty tend in turn to make the role of the expert in belief-making more decisive as time runs on.

THE BELIEFS of men both relate them to objects, to one another, and to themselves and express the relations in which they actually find themselves. Beliefs influence behavior—albeit, frequently, in devious and obscure ways—and are also themselves an attempt to give form and expression to behavior existing temporally in advance of beliefs.

In any Western belief system at any given moment one can descry, whether or not the believers are conscious of it, an exhibition of elements deriving from almost every recorded historical period, and perhaps from some that antedate recorded history. One can observe that "compresent with twentieth century technology will commonly be nineteenth century political beliefs, eighteenth century economic ones, seventeenth century ethics, and medieval philosophy intertwined with the theology of 2000–3000 B.C. The atom bomb, national sovereignty, free enterprise theory, the ethics of exploit are simultaneously present for pattern and guide to the production of personal and collective behavior."[1] What is missing in this implied description is the recognition that *each* of the categories of thought cited co-exists with incompatible elements from different epochs. These elements are compresent, but not usually either co-evident or co-accessible: age, unconsciousness, inaccessibility, and intractability seem ordinarily in some rough relationship to one another, although a serious qualification of this view will have to be introduced later in the chapter.[2] Just such a collection of unrelated beliefs can be remarked in Crestwood Heights.

BELIEF IN CRESTWOOD HEIGHTS

The first impression made by the expressed beliefs of the population of Crestwood Heights upon any observer-listener might well be that pure chaos reigns within and between persons. A man who is a good and devoted, not to say passionate, Calvinist, an enthusiastic proponent of original sin and predestination, also believes in, and practises as far as he is able, a psychotherapy which can only be rationalized on the basis of utterly contrary premises. One informant is with equal fervor a devotee of Marxist dogma (and the program of those who presently call themselves Marxists), of Zionist nationalism, and of the detached and objective viewpoints of the cautious, sober social scientist. A religious leader can at one and the same time believe, and urge others to believe, that his parishioners are "in no way different from anybody else," *and* that they have a special history and a particular ethical and religious mission; that what is needed for his parish is much greater intimacy between his followers and those outside the fold, *and* that what is needed is "cultural pluralism," a situation of sufficient mutual isolation to allow each group to develop its own culture and its difference within a merely political or politico-economic framework. Instance could be piled upon instance. A great and good friend of children, who understands most of them intuitively and most of the rest out of his psychological learning, has concluded that corporal punishment is no aid to learning, indeed that it militates against the kind of learning which he wishes to secure. So he uses it, as a policy, "only as a last resort"— that is, precisely in those cases where his knowledge should have led him to conclude that something was seriously amiss and the most gentle, careful treatment was required, and precisely at those points where violence would have the greatest (i.e., from his own viewpoint, worst) effect.

The internal contradiction which was true for the same person was found to be *a fortiori* true between people who thought themselves like-minded—and in the respects in which they thought themselves like-minded. Verbal agreement as to the desirability of "discipline," "maturity," "responsibility," "democracy," "freedom," "autonomy," etc., joined together those who, on even slight probing or on the evidence of their behavior, differed about as much as conflicting ideologists in global war, hot or cold.

So marked were these internal contradictions that the possibility of writing a chapter on the system of beliefs of Crestwood Heights seemed virtually to be nil. The search for some system or order in the beliefs found was rendered doubly difficult by the false clues offered: particularly the clues that people would differ categorically in their beliefs principally according to class, ethnic, religious, and professional classifications. There were indeed such differences, but they can be disposed of in a few paragraphs. The only important discoverable difference in beliefs lay precisely in that area in which "informed people" informed us no real differences lay: there *was* a difference in the belief systems of the two sexes.

A. CLASS DIFFERENCES

As the remainder of the book may have sufficiently made clear, this community—and even more, our set of informants in it—constitutes a group relatively homogeneous as to class. Certainly it is all middle class—lower-middle, perhaps, middle-middle and upper-middle, if a collection of such awkward terms may be allowed.

Within that range, it was exceedingly difficult to discover anything that approximated systematic differences in the content of belief[3] although some differences in the manner of holding belief seemed evident. At the lower margin could be remarked great uncertainty of belief, visible either in confessed or stated uncertainty, or in a long-sustained wavering between alternatives. In the middle there is also uncertainty, covered by a great deal of hard inter- and intrapersonal work in sorting and sifting belief, but also, contrastingly, by over-passionate assertion of positions that turn out to be passing and ephemeral. At the higher margin, uncertainty is wedded to indifference, permitted by the luxury of social safety, so that a too-intense concern with resolving the inevitable confusion is almost, from this point on, class-stigmatic.

B. ETHNIC DIFFERENCES

No reasonably consistent differences—with one exception—between the two ethnic groups into which Crestwood Heights divided itself, emerged or stood up under careful analysis.[4] The sole exception has rather more to do with a generalized orientation and a preference for one mode or order of analysis over another than with a difference in the content of belief systems. Apart from this there was only the defining difference between Jew and Gentile, put locally in religious terms (i.e., the place assigned in religion and history to Jesus); and this difference, except in the case of one informant, made no other evident difference.

The difference in orientation, discovered again and again—in informal conversation, in discussion, in the interviews of an anthropologist in no other way related to the Project, and in some of the psychological test data—appeared to distinguish the two groups in terms of their approach to part and whole. The tendency—a marked tendency, but only a tendency—was for Jewish intellectual analysis and feeling to run from whole to part; for Gentile, to run from part to whole: for

Jew to try to settle first the general and then to derive the particular; for Gentile to try to settle, first, particulars and then scan for pattern or generalization: for a preference for deduction on the Jewish side as against induction on the Gentile. This appeared perhaps most noticeably in the interviews referred to above with reference to the aspirations held by mothers for their children. Mothers in the one group could not discuss these until they had declared and settled the general nature of the world in which their aspirations would be relevant and possible; mothers in the other group could discuss the aspirations for their children in particular, and sometimes for their family as a unit, but rarely reached in discussion the immediate community or the world beyond which was to be the context of those aspirations.[5]

C. LAY-PROFESSIONAL DIFFERENCES

The profoundest difference in Crestwood Heights might at first seem to be between layman and professional, the basis of discrimination having to do with *expertise* in psychological, educational, or child-rearing knowledge. It would appear thus at first glance that the community is bifurcated less on class or ethnic lines, which are much spoken of, and more on a different line: one which puts the children of tradition on one side, and the children of Freud, Dewey, the group dynamics school, and other modernisms on the other. This impression indeed endures and is expanded and confirmed. The fundamental division *is* between those in the rear and the van of what might be called the "post-Freudian revolution." At its clearest, the division is between those who look at human nature and human behavior from a viewpoint primarily rule-oriented and moralistic, and those whose views are primarily cause-oriented and naturalistic or scientific.[6] But the distinction is never so clear. The person who feels naturalistic about children's misbehavior, feels moralistic about any inability on her own part to see the behavior of her children always in this light. The person who thinks moralistically has actually so altered his feeling in the light of experience that he is no longer able, given his knowledge of cause-effect relationships, to feel as morally indignant as he feels he ought to feel. Nevertheless, the primary difference in belief system in Crestwood Heights, despite complication, confusion, and uncertainty, does lie just here. And it does, by and large, mark off the "professional" from the "layman," although there are enough naturalistic laymen and moralistic professionals to preclude neat distinctions.

What makes it difficult to treat this primary bifurcation as a lay-professional distinction—in spite of the fact that proximity to the expert *is* the distinguishing criterion—is its actual, historic involvement with a more fundamental distinction, that between the sexes.

D. SEX DIFFERENCES

In Crestwood Heights it is obviously the women who have taken up and are the banner-bearers and *avant-garde* element for the new movement; thus the distinction between traditional and new has become virtually identified to the layman with the distinction between man and woman. Moreover, elements from both sets of criteria are intertwined into a new constellation which is still indeed predominantly feminine, since it combines many of the primary orientations of mothering and other traditionally female orientations with the new naturalistic outlook to give a now indivisible whole.[7]

The authors have chosen to treat the basic distinction under the head of a sex difference, not merely because it is so seen by the majority,[8] but because it *is* now so bound up with the role and fate of women that its history and development will very largely be affected, if not determined, by theirs. Here, in this class setting, in America, at this point in time, as the women emerge to ideological dominance, they carry with them, like any other self-emancipating minority,[9] a banner for general liberation and a program for its implementation.

MEN AND WOMEN, AND BELIEF

The deepest cleavage[10] in the belief system of Crestwood Heights—more basic and deeper (we feel) than differences in age, ethnic group, or status—is created by the striking divergence in the belief systems of men and of women.[11] The differences, the polarities, the selective, unlike, and emphatic emphases exist not merely at the level of detail, but, more important, at the very core of belief.

This cleavage, which seems on the basis of our experience to appear in connection with virtually every important conviction, is obscured and covered over by another difference between men and women: as to whether, indeed, such important differences between them exist. Perhaps as a function of the conflict involved in the progressive emancipation of women in the last century or half-century, perhaps for other reasons,[12] the ideology of the women tends to minimize the differences between the sexes. The "without regard to race, creed or color" pronouncement, the "people are people" view, the individualistic approach which tends to regard any categorization of people as wicked: these are used with perhaps even greater warmth and emphasis to play down or deny differences between men and women, other than those unblinkably given by anatomy.[13] The women are thus—and here again they are in league with the experts—the promoters of an ideology of identity at the ideological level: men and women should (they feel) and would, except for irrational accidents of history, share a single value-system: the "maturity," individual-oriented values for which they themselves stand.

The men, on the contrary, tend to exaggerate the cleavage, and even, ideologically, to regard it as an impassable gulf to be accepted with good-humored tolerance. "Weaker sex," "inferior species" is now forbidden terminology, but the classification of "women and children" is more than a separation of convenience. Women are alleged to be unalterably sentimental, non-logical, and incapable of the heroic efforts needed for substantial accomplishment. This is supposed to be so much the case that the case cannot—in spite of all the evidence—be demonstrated to women. They must be "handled," like children, with careful concealment of the definition by which they are defined.

That the differences in ideology exist would be denied by one side (the women); that they ought to be examined as having validity, as possessing equal biological and social importance, as being complementary and mutually necessary in the division of labor, social and evolutionary, would be denied by the other side (the men).

An exhaustive treatment is not possible here, but some illustrations of such differences may be useful.

A. IDEOLOGY AND ACTION

1. *Individual and group.* One such striking difference, perhaps the most important in its effects on the formation of character and on human relations, is found in the estimate of the moral value and operational importance of "the individual" and "the group." For the women (and their allies among the experts, male and female) the supreme value is the happiness and well-being of the individual, which taken in its immediacy determines day-to-day policy. Does a general rule press heavily on a given child? Then the child ought to have special support, or an exception to the rule should be made, or the rule should be amended or abolished. The particular, the unique, the special, the case, the individual is both the focus of concern and the touchstone of policy. The institutional regularities are seen rather as obstacles than as aids to the achievement of the good life. Mores, folkways, laws, norms are considered to function as obstructions to the development of those unique characteristics, configurations, and activities which are the height of value, if not its very meaning. Individuals so reared and freed will,

it is felt, produce the minimum of order which may be required—if any is—for concerted action where that is necessary.

The men have a firm hold on the other horn of what is cast by both sides as a dilemma. For them generally, the organization, the business, the institution, the activity, the group, the club, the rules, the law are the focus of loyalty. True, they have a supplementary or supporting belief, that the stability and persistence of the group accrue to the good of the individual; but the "army" comes clearly before "the soldier" and indeed without it there will be no soldier. If the individual will learn to fit into the going institutions he will find therein whatever field of expression and achievement it is proper and permissible for him to have.

This polarity implies other polarities, reaching perhaps even deeper. For the man (say, a father) a given act (say, his child's) is one of a series of acts classified, according to its formal, quasi-legal properties, with other acts having similar external consequences—particularly, naturally, for government, authority, and the maintenance of norms and practices. For the woman (say, a mother) the same act is seen chiefly as embedded in its immediate context of meaning and emotion, with roots reaching back to previous, perhaps formally dissimilar acts, in that particular child's emotional history. The man's first step in the analysis of a problem is analytic and categorical; the woman's is synthetic and contextual. The man has the "play" as the frame of reference for the act; the woman has the "actor." The "universe of acts" of which the given act is a sample is, for the man, the universe of acts (regardless of agent) that have similar effects; for the woman, the universe of acts of which this is a sample is the universe of that particular actor's acts.[14] For the man, effect and achievement are the paramount dimensions of classification; for the woman, motive, intent, and feeling.[15]

These primary orientations which lie at the level of thought and feeling and expression, are, curiously, contradicted by each sex in its role as "operator." The men, who allege the supremacy of the organization, the collective, are the practitioners of skills which rest, consciously or not, upon contrary beliefs. They bring to rare perfection and are secretly (within or between themselves) proud of those arts of interpersonal manipulation that are intended to make the organization work to the benefit of a particular individual. They have the "know-how": they know "who's who" and "what's what."[16] Business is thus chiefly an interpersonal operation in which the ostensibly worshipped collective and its norms are *felt* to function (as the women *say* they do) as obstacles to be dealt with or circumvented as far as prudence will permit.

The appeal is taken by the individual to the individual for the sake of the individual, although the best cover for action is reference back to the welfare of the organization as the apparent ground.

The women, on the contrary, who allege the supremacy of the individual notably act in groups to persuade or coerce individuals into making changes in the conditions of group life, for example, a change in a norm system or activity. It is they who, instead of taking direct individual-to-individual action, organize, work in concert, know and use the techniques of group pressure, and so secure alteration in the circumstances of the group.

It should perhaps be re-emphasized that these contradictions within the sex-groups and oppositions of orientations between them are genuine, and not, as might be supposed, mere fronts or deceptive devices. For the women, the preoccupation with the good of the individual in all its immediacy is indeed paramount; it organizes thought and feeling and perception. No less genuine is the male attachment to the welfare of the organization. It is only that each sex, in action, moves as it would logically be expected to move if it held the ideology of the other.[17] What might be said, summarily, after due allowance for exceptional individuals or for ordinary individuals acting under exceptional circumstances, is that men tend to use a psychology of individual differences in the name of the institutions, quite commonly for an individual, competitive object; the women tend to use a social psychology in the name of individual autonomy, quite frequently to secure collective and cooperative alteration in the ways of groups.

2. *Voluntarism and determinism.* Logically subordinate, perhaps, but psychologically prior to the individual-group polarity is a polarity that, for want of a better name, might perhaps be called "voluntaristic–deterministic."

Ideologically, the women are great determinists of various schools of determinism, particularly, but not exclusively, psychological.[18] For them, the school psychologist's reiterated statement that "we should remember that behavior is caused" has the ring of the self-evident as well as sufficient statement. They, together with the majority of the experts, are concerned with the discovery of just those regularities in human behavior which will permit an expanding science of known laws or determinacies in reference to it.

The men, ideologically, find themselves very nearly at the opposite pole. They tend towards a Great Man theory of history, both ancient and everyday. They see and feel an active agency; the underlying theory of the free will is dominant; they are great voluntarists and, therefore, moralists. What a man can do depends largely on the strength of his desire or his will to do it, and the success-stories which they admire demonstrate the soundness of this view very nearly as well as the success-stories which they *are*.

What is true for each sex as a routine of thought and feeling is again contradicted for each, at the level of both goal and activity. The men believe that sufficient effort on their part as free agents will so order the world, human and non-human, that good results human and non-human will thenceforward and thereby be determined. The women believe that a sufficient exploration of and recognition of and adaptation to the determinacies in human and non-human affairs will lead towards an increase in autonomy, in freedom, in objective, effective agency.[19]

3. *Immutability and perfectibility*. The same kind of double contradiction between the sexes, and on the levels of both ideology and action, obtains with respect to attitudes towards human perfectibility.

The women incline ideologically towards the view of human perfectibility, taking their point of departure in the known plasticities of human nature, the established variations (throughout history and across contemporary cultures) in the culturally sanctioned ways of doing things. If this variety is possible, it is argued, so presumably is any amount of variation, which includes ever-better constellations. This bare possibility is further supported, as a matter of morale, by a rather vague inheritance from religious or evolutionary ideology or both, which is given the interpretation that, since things *may* get better, the universal process ensures that they *will* do so.

The men incline more to the recognition of invariances in human behavior, to a definition either that human nature is unchanging or, with more sophistication, *plus ça change, plus c'est la même chose*. Elevated or exalted views of human nature as it exists are dismissed as naïve; similar views about potentialities, as "utopian," in a pejorative sense.

Both sexes reverse themselves in action. It is the women who, by and large, in action take count of the intractabilities and unchangeableness in human beings, as given, and who "realistically" adapt themselves to these facts and operate quietly in their context. It is the men who demand a process of continuous perfecting in their operations, and who rail loudly against anyone sufficiently implastic to be incapable of constant improvement.

It is this differing attitude to perfectibility generally that in the first place underlies and in the second is a consequence of differing involvement with the psychological, human relations, or social science expert.[20]

The feeling among women is widespread that since human nature and social life both *are* perfectible and *ought* rapidly to be perfected, the answer to any given human problem from how to be happy in marriage to how to age gracefully either is or ought to be readily available and can be learned from the right expert, and, having been learned, will be put into practice either automatically or with a modicum of effort.[21] The men, who have long employed and subordinated the expert-in-reference-to-things, confront the expert-in-reference-to-people with, first, a deep and sometimes inveterate scepticism, and even where this is weakened, with a demand for his aid in the achievement of ends which they (the men) have already defined. Where this can be done, they can employ such experts also, but in a subordinate capacity as facilitators, i.e. they can use the "intelligence-testers" in the Selective Service system in wartime. Where the orientation of the expert raises questions about the ends, however—as, at the moment, in most cases it must—the tendency is to return to scepticism if not to move on to irritation or anger.[22]

4. *Emotionalism and rationalism*. Not unrelated to, but not wholly included logically or psychologically in, the voluntarism–determinism polarity is another which may be called "rationality–emotionality" or "thought–feeling."

The orientations for the two sexes are again dissimilar both as to fact and as to ideal: as to what is and what ought to be supreme, ultimate, decisive, or determinative. Again, the women, at the ideological level, give greatest weight to the feeling or emotional process, and indeed take the view that this both is and ought to be the final determinant of behavior. Rationality is to be at the service of emotion, and first place must be given to emotional considerations. It is an easy step from "the child cannot learn unless he is happy" (happiness is a necessary condition) to "the child will learn if he is happy" (happiness is a sufficient condition) and, while the two positions are rarely clearly separated, the women tend towards the second. Typically, however, in action and especially for themselves, they adopt practices that would be thought logical consequences of the ideological position of the men: "one cannot be happy unless one learns" (a necessary condition) or "by learning one will be made happy" (a sufficient condition).

The position of the men ideologically and their actions, are, as might now be expected, the point-for-point opposite. They cleave ideologically to the view that feeling is or ought to be subordinate to thought; they act on the assumption that feeling, or the distillate of experience which is intuition, is sufficient for their practices. There is very nearly the acting out of a conviction as to the "Divine Right of Men"; they act on the assumption that, without the study and thought so necessary to the women, they will know decisively at any given point what is right, or at least best or most suitable. It is to women that they attribute intuitive powers; but it is to themselves that they arrogate exclusive right of intuition-based action.[23]

What has been said so far might be represented in a table, in which it may be observed that the ideological tendency of each sex is "counterbalanced" by its own habits of action and by the prevailing ideology of the opposite sex: there is thus an inner and an outer check.[24]

DIFFERENCES IN IDEOLOGY AND ACTION ACCORDING TO SEX

SEX	SPHERE OF IDEOLOGY	SPHERE OF ACTION
Male	Collectivist	Individualist
	Voluntarist	Determinist
	Immutabilist	Perfectibilist
	Rationalist	Emotionalist
Female	Individualist	Collectivist
	Determinist	Voluntarist
	Perfectionist	Immutabilist
	Emotionalist	Rationalist

B. HABITS OF THOUGHT AND ACTION

Not quite identical with the ideology-action distinction between the sexes, is a similar distinction between characteristic habits or modes of thought and action.[24]

1. *Span of matter.* It is most notable that in the realm of thought itself it is the women who are the great system-builders and system-seekers; and the men who notably invent or accept innumerable little islands of unconnected—indeed often incompatible—belief. The urge to "philosophize,"[25] to integrate experience in an intellectually consistent, comprehensive fashion is quite markedly a female characteristic; the urge to leave experience as an enjoyable muddle, or, at most, to organize small areas of it intellectually *ad hoc* by crude rule-of-thumb, is quite definitely male.

In contrast, it is the women who are in action the great improvisers, inventors, and demonstrators and devotees of the value of spontaneity. It is they, and those influenced by them, who in an endless flow of minute-to-minute adaptations and improvisations fit action to unforeseen possibility or opportunity—to the point where men feel that directed movement is lost in the confusions of "tacking." For the man, any sense of direction in action, lies in habit, system, routine, rule, and institution to the point where, for the woman, his constancy of direction under shifting circumstance is a permanent or recurrent threat to arrival at the goal originally intended.

2. *Span of time.* Similar in its effects,[26] and perhaps necessary to the maintenance of the foregoing difference, is a difference with respect to the time-span habitually taken for granted in thought or action. The women predominantly think in the long range, almost *sub specie aeternitatis*, in terms of ultimate effects, just as they do in terms of logical conclusions. Their thinking attaches less to the immediacies of time and place, and tends to take into imaginative consideration not only the here and now, but the new generation, the "children yet unborn," altered circumstance, and perhaps even a new society as yet only vaguely envisioned. The men, on the contrary, much more earthbound and datum-driven, take into consideration an evanescent present or, at most, a very short-run future, in which things will be much as they are now and have always been. It is perhaps not a contradiction— on the assumption of changelessness—that the men, in action, are the makers of long-term plans and the builders of persistent material and social edifices. They, predominantly, are the authors of enduring buildings, indestructible dams, business and social organizations that are intended to and do have an immortality transcending their own lives. The women, again, adapt old buildings to new uses—homes as adult-education centers, schools as community recreation centers—and create the multiplicity of cliques, alignments, groups, temporary committees which they intend to be as short-lived as the purposes for which they were brought into being.

3. *Optimism and pessimism.* Perhaps just because of these different concentrations on a few large or many small expanses of time and subject- or thought-matter, there is a corresponding differential distribution of optimisms and pessimisms between the two sexes. First recognizable is a primary distinction similar to those already encountered: on the male side, an optimism in action and with reference to the consequences of action, accompanied by a pessimism as to the validity, utility, or indeed, possibility of thought when at all removed from the immediacies and urgencies of act; on the female side, a want of optimism (perhaps not a true pessimism) with reference to action and in action, but in thought and dream a radical, not to say utopian optimism.[27] In another dimension—which, psychologically, is not wholly independent of the

foregoing—the men seem incredibly optimistic with reference to things; the women with reference to human beings, values, and ideas.[28]

We shall have to touch, below, on a similar dichotomy of optimism and pessimism in the relation of means and ends, to which we may now turn.

C. MEANS AND ENDS

The relation of ends and means is, of course, not given in nature, but only in the nature of man. There are no things that are "naturally" means and others that are "naturally" ends. Objects are given an ends-means relation by the place they occupy in the schemes of a purposing and conscious being. Needless to say, such relations, then, tell us about purposes—and not about the natural order independent of human purpose.[29]

The differences between men and women as to ends and means seem again to run through nearly every important category or modality of experience, and only some of the most striking will be touched on here.[30]

1. *Basic location.* More fundamental perhaps than any following distinction is a difference between men and women as difficult to define in a single term as it is psychologically impressive and significant. We have called it one of "basic location" because it has to do with a fundamental feeling which each sex expresses as to where it is most comfortable, most secure, most "at home": the women among ends and ultimate or long-term purposes (about the means to which they are relatively uncertain and unclear); the men among a proliferation and elaboration of means (as to the ends or purposes which these are to serve, they are less sure, more uneasy, and less interested). It is to this difference that each sex points when it reports the difficulty of getting the other into "serious" discussion: for the men, this represents an accusation that the women's discussion of ends is irresponsible, relatively divorced as it is from the close consideration of means; for the women, the men's interminable discussion of mere means has, in the absence of clarified purposes, a futility so potent as to disbar any possible claim to seriousness.[31]

2. *Point and duration.* The fundamental orientation of the two sexes towards two aspects of time seems to provide the ground for a whole series of related distinctions in valuation.[32] Both sexes, needless to say, experience time in all its modalities or significances especially both as a series of discrete points (a sum of evanescent presents) and as a continuum, an unbroken (in one sense, timeless) flow or duration. For

the men, quite dominantly, duration has to be accepted for the sake of point, the spaces between for the sake of the crises that punctuate and enliven them, the states of being for the sake of the events that may be counted upon to follow and render them meaningful. For the women, with equal clarity, events are engineered for the sake of the states that are to follow, the points accepted for the sake of the durations they seem to prelude or promise. It is as though in a system that flows while it pulses and pulses while it flows, the men felt the pulse of experience and valued it, while the women felt and valued the flow.[33]

This differentiation tends to distinguish the preference for and the reaction to virtually all other experience. To use present happiness as a take-off point for future excitements; to see life as a sum of episodes or exploits, interleaved by preparations;[34] to see sharp boundaries around experiences and over-potent definitions: these are all male (or masculine) characteristics. Perhaps no deeper distinction can be reached, although there is reason to think something deeper does underlie it: the preoccupation of the women with the ego (and other egos), of the men with the non-ego; of the women with the reality of the subjective world, of the men with the objective world. Each, of course, in ascribing inferior reality to that which to the other seems most real, evidences radical objectivism or radical subjectivism.[35]

3. *Things and personalities.* It is probably only on the basis of this underlying distinction that the dominant preoccupation of men with the use of persons as a means to the production of things can be fully appreciated and understood in contrast with the women's unequivocal view that mere things are for the sake of their effect on the production and refinement of personality. This is not to say—here or anywhere else—that men never see things as means to the formation or alteration of personality. Of course, like others, they induce loyalty in their employees (by incentive pay and other schemes) and they buy their children toys to make them good or happy or well-adjusted children. But here as elsewhere the question is which is the psychologically ultimate term. For the women, the ultimate term is here at the personality level; a personality characteristic is a sufficient good. For the man, it is merely or chiefly a necessary good: an ingredient necessary to the thing-producing process. A good child is good because or if he is effective; his happiness is good because happy people work better; his adjustment is a good because adjustment makes for a smooth-running team, i.e. a team that makes a good game by counted goals of concrete achievement.[36]

4. *Order and freedom.* Almost inescapable in terms of the system

of beliefs and preferences so far described is it that women should regard order less as a good in itself and more as a grudgingly recognized means to freedom; and that men, primarily oriented to order, admit freedom as a safety-valve without which order would be in danger of an eruptive breach. This view seems consistently applied with reference to their own lives, with regard to ideals of personality for children, and in their aspiration for the good society. The women discipline themselves that the children and, if strength remains, they themselves may have room for impulse and spontaneity; the men indulge them, and occasionally themselves,[37] so that routine and order may be returned to with fresh spirit and be preserved with a more permanent and closer fit.

5. *Happiness and achievement.* Here for the first time, in the analysis of the written and spoken material, we seem to run into a psychological inconsistency.[38] Men seem to be telling one another and their children and such others as their propaganda may reach: "To be happy you must achieve." Women say: "To achieve, you must be happy." The first proclamation seems to look upon happiness as the end, achievement as the means; the second, to look the other way. Surely this is on both sides "out of character."

Indeed it is, for what has here been intercepted in the propaganda war of the sexes is a "message to the enemy" couched by each side in the vocabulary of the other in order to get inside his psychological defences. What the men are saying really is: "Even if you believe (mistakenly) that happiness is the end of life, it makes no difference; you can only get there by putting our first value, achievement, first. Then you may get happiness and not otherwise; and, if you don't, you will have achieved and that is what matters." Similarly the women are saying "Even the (mistakenly) achievement-oriented must know that happiness is indispensable to their aim, so they had better seek it first in the first place."

D. MISCELLANEOUS

One could perhaps continue indefinitely, or at least as long as the patience of readers would allow. Other contrasting words which the data show to be operationally significant for male and female come to mind: hard and soft; outward-oriented, inward-oriented; thought-reliant, feeling-reliant; fact-led towards a realism which discounts potentiality, wish-led towards a romanticism which discounts reality; rule-oriented, role-oriented; game-centered, player-centered; literal, symbolic—and so on. But since the object is to evoke a sufficient image of a primary orientation rather than to exhaust a definition, perhaps these examples will serve.

E. SUMMARY

An attempt to summarize the difference in the belief systems of men and women in Crestwood Heights, without judging between or evaluating the issues, might justly conclude that the fundamental difference is in their basic orientation to two complementary aspects of living.

The men seem primarily concerned about the preservation of life against destruction, and they feel and believe accordingly. The women seem concerned about the creative and elaborative processes, and they believe and feel accordingly. The men attend to the *necessary* conditions for living; the women to the conditions that would make life *sufficing*. The men are oriented to the biological and social substratum, to minima; the women to the social and psychological superstratum, to maxima. The men are concerned with the prevention of positive "evils"; the women with the procurement of positive "goods." The men live psychologically in an emotional climate of scarcity requiring the close and calculated adaptation of means to ends; the women, correspondingly, live in a climate of abundance requiring the wise selection and utilization of the riches available. The men are for prevision—and provision accordingly; the women for vision—and enjoyment as of now. The men are sensitized to necessity: the women to choice. Compulsion, the *vis a tergo*, the drive from the past press with more weight on the men and order their behavior; yearning, "final cause," the pull of the future, lure or govern the women. Rousseau speaks more nearly for the women; Hobbes for the men.

The disappearance of the patriarchal family from practice as impossible and from ideology as immoral has, seemingly, left untouched in the men the more general orientations which it bespoke, and to which under the then-existing conditions of life it was probably the best answer.

The functional utility of this strong representation by male and female of the defence and the elaboration of life, respectively, is evident. In terms of material goods, it is not unlikely that we are now in North America at a transition point between the stages where a logic of scarcity was, and a logic of abundance is, an appropriate adaptation.[39] What is true of material goods is probably no less true of the new knowledge, of emerging art forms, of new modes of human relating, of developing possibilities in the formation of character and the structure of personality. Perhaps this transition is—or seems to be—eternal, or at least coextensive in time with human life. In such situations there appears invariably to be a party that would outrun the possibilities of change, go "too fast," and a party that would outwait these possibilities, go "too slow." These parties usually see one another as enemies, frequently as mortal ones. Where the parties are, as in the present instance, divided largely on sex lines, and where the life-conserving or life-defending and the life-enriching or life-developing impulses are pitted against one another in the area of greatest intimacy and co-operation, it might seem that the possibility of fruitful juncture had been sacrificed to the necessity of adequate representation.

This would indeed appear to be the case. To the degree that the picture represented is a true one, every child is assured of the experience of being pulled in two different directions with respect to all important matters. He must not only achieve an integration that will permit him to function adequately at each stage in the presence of two such opposed parent-figures, but he must further "choose" to make dominant the orientation appropriate to his sex unless he is to become or feel a social and occupational misfit. This he is quite generally able to do, but the task is rendered no easier by the playing down of social and psychological sex-differences that has accompanied the twentieth century's recognition and rewarding of anatomical and physiological ones.

DISORDER AND OPERABILITY

If the picture of confusion, internal contradiction, and incompatibility in belief within persons and between them has any veracity, it may well be asked how it is possible in Crestwood Heights for individual human beings to operate as personalities at all, for families to remain visibly intact as families, or, more generally, for action to be concerted in any social act. On the basis of the situation described, one might expect very high rates of psychopathology and social disorganization—much higher than any actually found or even suggested.[40] What countervails against the production of the expected results?

It is probably not sufficient to say, in awe and wonder, that man can sustain an incredible degree of confusion, pain, and disorganization without becoming radically disorganized. Nor is it sufficient to point to the fact that—short of pathologically recognizable disorganization—a great deal of distress is borne, felt, and talked about as opportunity occurs by Crestwood Heights folk.[41] Even the widespread nature of this distress, recognized as such by its victims or not,[42] is lower, one senses, than the situation would lead one to expect.

In striving to account for the *relative* lack of disorganization, personal and social, one is driven to observe more closely the effects of habit and inertia, the viability of specific solutions in the face of disappearing general supports, the protective nature of the social structure as a guard against the full impact of confused beliefs.

A. A CULTURE OF SPECIFIC SOLUTIONS

In contrast with the confusion, uncertainty, and turmoil, chronic for many if not most in the realm of general beliefs, there is a marked sense of predictability for any one person or institution at the level of response to specific acts. No matter how wide the swing may be in the realm of belief from Watsonian "conditioning" of the child to "unconditional love," the Crestwood child who consistently brings mud into the broad-loomed house *will* be met by fairly consistent disapproval. He may at one time be shouted at—"conditioned" by startle. He may at another be made to clean it up—the unnaturally "natural consequence of his own act." He may be offered material reward or approval or love on a conditional basis—"seduction." He may be invited to consider the inner meaning to himself of his act—"insight therapy." He may be urged to consider its objective consequences—"reality orientation." He may be made competitive or ashamed, or given positive incentive. The act may be ignored as being a "stage"—and such evident, studious ignoring is a pressure that the child knows about. But, however done, and however varied, the teaching that mud in unreasonable amounts is not to be brought into the house will be effected, and mud in diminishing amounts will be brought in. The psychological theory will change, the feelings on both sides permitted release and expression will change, the rationalizations will change, the talk will change in volume and content, but finally, in view of the persistent realities of the mother's increasing work-load and diminishing access to sources of domestic aid, the volume of mud will diminish. Necessary tasks, close to brute compulsion, natural or social, will be carried out. Necessity is perhaps the mother of invariance rather than invention!

What is true for the perhaps objectively trifling problem of mud is true for such germane areas as personal cleanliness and sexual patterns and control. The meaning of mudpie-making or "messing" with finger-paints or other substitutes may at one period not be evident and at another quite evident to the latter-day parent. But necessity will drive her in both cases equally to find ways of reducing the child's messing to acceptable forms in acceptable places within the range of time she thinks public opinion, or the opinion of the figures significant to her, will tolerate. The action-lesson learned by the child of the former and latter-day parent will not differ too much; *how* it is learned and what it means psychodynamically to child and parent may vary a great deal.[43] Similarly, in psychosexual matters, children of homes that express the maximum degree of sexual permissiveness[44] will enter upon a period of sexual latency, and in steadiness and duration it will not differ from the similar period in a less progressive or permissive home.[45]

What might be called "behavioral lag" (since the behavior continues long after the support in belief or justification for it is gone)[46] thus introduces or maintains in conduct that would otherwise be chaotic, a sensible degree of order, indeed of behavior which is markedly similar to what it would have been if the belief system still stood intact. The props furnished by belief are gone, but *mirabile dictu*, the building made in action stands not visibly affected. The analogy perhaps fails, since there may be not only a behavioral invariance under changing belief; there may well be, as the foregoing material suggests, a compensating movement of behavior in opposition to belief or, to use the terms introduced above, of beliefs "action-expressed" in opposition to beliefs "ideology-expressed." If this is the case, the discrepancy constantly found between ideology and action would be accounted for, and its utility in providing a measure of stability in an unstable world would be manifest. Perhaps if anything is to be inveighed against or deplored, it is less this inconsistency than the demand for consistency—individual consistency—where the price of it may be stability—social stability.

A second countervailing mechanism to the swings in behavior that might otherwise be produced by the swings of belief lies in the relatively stable socio-economic structure, which local opinion cannot hope in the short run to affect.

It is possible, for instance, for the belief in the "dignity of the individual" and the "sacredness of personality," in the valuation of people "for what they are instead of what they have," to be widespread and genuinely and passionately held without untoward consequences for social arrangements that actually separate men largely according to what they have. In Crestwood Heights, particularly but not exclusively among the women, such views are indeed so held, and they come to their ultimate expression and test in the "romantic" view of how marriages of their children ought to be founded: on "love," sympathy, compatibility, and personality characteristics, "without regard to race, creed or color" or, above all—ugly word!—money. Despite these deeply held and pervasive views, the marriages that do occur are not notably different from those that might have been arranged in a caste system based on race, creed, color, and—above all—money. Marriages between Jew and Gentile, Protestant and Catholic, rich and poor,[47] are almost as rare as "marriages out" in any group that punishes them by formal expulsion (for example, the Quakers until recently).

These beliefs and these practices (which would be the objective outcome of the contradictory beliefs) can coexist without sensible strain at the crudest level simply because the socio-economic structure has already separated out all or most of the persons from the circle of interaction who could possibly put the beliefs to the test of action. A Crestwooder does not meet in his club people from a lower class-level;[48] or, if he does, he changes the club for a "better."[49] Crestwooders do not meet, at the summer resort, people from what is felt to be a different religious faith—or, if they do, when the children are small, they do so on the basis of a conscious tolerance which is about as firm a basis for exclusion from intimacy as law would be. Private schools are notably unmixed, and not only or primarily in reference to sex.[50] The sheer statistical probability of meeting "unsuitable" candidates for marriage or other intimacy is thus notably small, and the further probability of such meetings ripening into a commitment to further intimacy is still smaller.[51] Even in such large, public institutions as the university where the religious and economic range is much greater and the period of ostensible mutual exposure much longer, and where a transcendent basis for intimacy in a common dedication to scholarship is provided for, a whole set of countervailing institutions exists to re-separate the improper mixtures.[52] The long and careful indoctrination of the child in favor of personality alone as the basis for intimacy may be seen very largely as careful provision for a contingency which is rarely or never allowed to arise. Sometimes, however, it does arise, and how it is then, nevertheless, "favorably" solved will be discussed below.

Several more mechanisms in addition to those already mentioned above (behavioral lag, unconscious communication, and socio-economic rigidity) serve to restore to the social system a measure of stability. Four of these have to do with a division of labor in which someone other than the progressive parent teaches the child the reactionary views which the parent cannot on moral and ideological grounds pass on to him. These divisions of labor take place (1) within the family informally, (2) in a kind of barter of the function between similarly situated adults (friends of the family), and (3) in a trading of function either up to a special group of specialists or (4) down to the child's peers and age mates.

The division of labor within the Crestwood family has already unavoidably been described to some degree in the chapter on "The

Family" and in the description earlier in this chapter of the belief structure itself. In this division of labor, broadly speaking, the father supplies more than a touch of short-run realism, as he sees it, to offset the mother's long-term idealism. There can be—and in a few families is—a feeling that these views need to be joined, that they complement one another, that both report valid conclusions about real experiences which the child needs to understand in order to orient himself adequately in his world. In a few other families also, these are the grounds for and provide the weapons of an open struggle, in which now one side now the other dominates, and in which the child's emerging picture of reality is alternately built up and fractured while he is simultaneously buffeted in his relationships and torn in his loyalties. Mostly, however, what goes on is neither alliance and peace nor enmity and war, but a kind of antagonistic co-operation in which, without ever coming to a clear struggle, a kind of gentle, guerilla-like action is carried on, intermittently and for limited gains—indeed without total victory even as an objective. The parents appear to show each other and each other's views a great deal of respect and tolerance,[53] and the commentary on each other's views is carried on very largely at the level of gesture—set lip, raised eyebrow, flared or narrowed nostril, caught breath, fleeting smile, or short laugh. This division of labor within the family is only possible where father and mother can and do take opposite views, and where, moreover, they are not so strongly attached to these views that the difference becomes the ground for open war.

In most cases where both parents share in progressive views, the services of third parties must necessarily be employed if the child is not to take these views too seriously. Such third parties offer themselves in the shape of friends and relatives, specialists, and peers.

The commonest use of the third-party intervention occurs in what is virtually a straight barter deal. Parents who cannot bring themselves to describe to their own children the somewhat harsh facts of life— whether these facts are more obvious, as in the necessarily competitive character of many present social relationships, or less obvious, as in the mixed motivation of even the "best" acts—will be found somewhat if not considerably more free to tell these facts to other children. They will with fair freeness communicate not only hidden fact, but ideologically disapproved attitude and even forbidden action, for example, the offering of bribes for "good" conduct. That these things would happen almost anywhere, and that in the bygone days of the large family, grandparents largely performed this function is true. What is perhaps remarkable here is a substitution for the grandparental brake on parental acceleration in the production of social change, of a situation in which the same parent acts as accelerator in reference to his or her own children and brake to those of her friends. (More rarely, but nevertheless not infrequently, is the opposite effect seen: provision of progressive ideas to the children of conservative or reactionary parents.) This is striking enough, but what is most illuminating is what occurs when these corrective influences are exerted by friends in the presence of the original parents. A smile of genuine pleasure (with a little of the air of a secret, hugely enjoyed) is visible from the original parent and not the expected strained smile of tolerance—indicating that, ideology or no, a substantial and needed gratification is being had. In contrast with the situation within the family, where a covert gentle war is being carried on under cover of a nominal alliance, here a covert co-operation is being carried on under the guise of a seeming gentle war. Indeed, when all the parents in the friendship-group are seen as a system, it is clear that for each pair, the others are taking in the psychological washing that that pair cannot itself perform; and so for each pair in turn. What is nonsensical economics may be necessary psychology and sociology.

In spheres so tabu that no friend and neighbor can be found to take on the unpleasant task—for example, when the use of large doses of calculated ("dispassionate") violence is required—an outside, paid expert in the shape of the private schoolmaster may have to be employed.[54] Many children, for whom the Crestwood Heights culture proved to be too subtle (in the sense that they took its permissive mandates seriously and began to fail academically or behave anti-socially otherwise), were moved by their parents into the much more clearly defined and rigidly structured life of the private boarding-school. They were put there by families in which the dominant parent (or both parents) believed in the virtues of the new methods, and who were so committed to non-violence that they had neither employed it themselves nor fully countenanced even its limited use in the public school. These same parents, without changing their views or indeed losing an ideological step, would refer with pleasure bordering on glee to the fact that the child would now have to work "or else . . . [be corporally punished]." They could make the same straddle between a retained belief in "unconditional love" and "now he'll perhaps appreciate his home . . . [in terms of its luxuries and lack of violence]." Unpaid volunteers[55] such as Scoutmasters and "Brown Owls" may laud obedience to a level which the parental philosophy ought bluntly to deny or abhor, to be consistent, and may nevertheless be felt to perform a valuable if not indispensable function.

Similarly in areas which the foregoing arrangements either fail or refuse to cover, the peer group, also unpaid,[56] may be invoked as a compensator or regulator. Crestwood parents who would deem it morally wrong and psychologically destructive to regulate the expression of their children's tastes, after self-examination realized and stated that they were able to afford these views because and only because in these areas the peer group performed a satisfactory policing function for them. Happily, *they* didn't have to enjoin against scarlet nail-polish, violet eye-shadow, purple lipstick, orange tie, or over sharply cut suit because the peer group would control for them any marked deviations from accepted canons of good taste. In these matters, then, the parents could safely feel that they had given the children "freedom," that acceptable canons went safely inviolated, *and* that tyranny by the peer group over the tastes of individual children was most undesirable. If the peer group should not so regulate . . .? That would be a difficult situation; the parents agreed they would probably have to intervene.

Two other corrective operations have been noted that in turn tend to protect against the testing of belief by action. One has to do with the content of the belief itself; the second with the style of its expression.

Where the content of the belief is of the romantic, liberal kind described—"all men are basically good," or "intimacy should be based only on compatibility of personality"—the very basis for compatibility and intimacy comes to be, at a minimum, the sharing of this liberal belief. Without changing the belief to "some men are bad" or "money is an important consideration for mate-selection" a Crestwooder will automatically (i.e., on the basis of the belief itself) be repelled by people who are so mistaken, warped, or wrong-headed as to think the contrary. But people who think along these lines *are* predominantly middle-class people, and the contrary views (on different ground) of the lower and upper classes tend to render their possessors repugnant or less attractive as possible partners for intimacy or marriage. The very belief, therefore, that "class is of no consequence" (which is on one side a middle-class view exclusively) becomes a token of compatibility and a basis for intimacy, and in so far as it determines friendship, membership in a clique, and marriage, a potent factor in the maintenance of the class boundaries which "do not exist," "do not matter," or "ought not to be considered."

What is true for content is *a fortiori* true for style, in action and particularly in expression of belief. The "politeness" which the lower classes cannot afford and the upper classes no longer need,[57] is again taken as a most important expression of the personality, again becomes a basis for sifting and sorting, and again brings together and keeps together only those who believe that other things are overwhelmingly more important—but who express that belief in polite terminology, manner, and action.

The last to be discussed of the countervailing mechanisms that, intentionally or not, stabilize behavior in the face of unstable belief, are the ideologies and action-patterns of the people themselves in reference to the relative place and importance of ideology and action. Those who believe that ideology is quite decisive for behavior (or, even, semi-sacredly, of intrinsic importance) will tend to spend the greater part of their action in attempting to secure changed beliefs. Whether or not, then, they are in fact right in their belief, they tend in the short run to secure the contradiction of their beliefs by leaving the whole field of direct activity to those who think ideology unimportant. (By "direct" activity is meant here activity directed to changing external behavior and objective arrangements, regardless of what ideological grounds underlie consent.) Those who believe that action is more important, by contrast, do not set themselves to convince others of the rightness of this view directly, but to order action in a field left free by the ideologists. The resulting rearrangements tend to confirm their views; while, in contrast, the succession of contradictions of the views of the ideologists tends to give further ideological support to those who believe that ideology is relatively trivial.

The tendency of this mechanism is to disjoin still further the relation between belief and action in human conduct, and indeed to render them so disjunct that special arrangements have to be made to correct the growing child's naïve assumption that there ought to be some orderly relation between them. This task of teaching the children how to believe in one thing while acting as if on the contrary belief without betraying distress falls partly on the home, but even more upon the school and, most especially, the religious organization. The latter must, in effect, teach the child religious truths that patently call for a moral and social order different from the one he knows, and for a personal behavior necessitating a radically different character in himself—without sensibly affecting the moral order, the social arrangements, or the personal character upon which they depend for tolerance and support.

By these various mechanisms (and perhaps others unnoted) relative invariance in action can be maintained despite tremendous variation in ideology, and immense constancy in concrete or proximate ends with extreme variety of means.

B. COSTS

In spite of these stabilizing mechanisms which do tend to reduce the unpredictability of action, it should not be assumed too readily that the creation of effects in one sphere (belief) and their defeat or cancellation in another (action) is a "cost-free" process socially or psychologically.

Where the countervailing mechanism set up to abort aspiration or protect from the consequences of belief, depends on an interpersonal division of labor, as described, the sense of dependency for achievement, personal integration, and social safety on a host of others, ideologically defined as "opponents," creates a situation of markedly heightened tension. Perhaps quite generally, but certainly in a culture highly valuing self-sufficiency and independence, dependency is felt as "bad enough." But when the dependency must be upon those who are by definition and by the situation ideologically and emotionally distant and opposed, the capacity of the relation to produce anxiety and hostility is sensibly magnified.

Some of the statements about the expert and his Messianic role might now be better appreciated. There can hardly help but be, in people so situated, a continuous latent hope, impervious to all experience, that someone somewhere has sufficient knowledge and goodwill to resolve these intolerable relations of hostile dependency. That someone must be "someone who understands these things"—social relations and human affections. If he would but come, and render those dependencies unnecessary, the prospective dependency on him might be relatively tolerable—even where foreseen.

Where, in contrast, the countervailing mechanism depends not on a division of labor between people, but on one within them; where their action systematically negates their ideology, or their unconscious communication contradicts their conscious speech, it will seem that circumstances defeat honest intentions. Such continuous frustration, apparently coming from the outside, might be expected to lead eventually to an adjustment on the basis of a philosophy of resignation. That it rarely does so,[58] depends on two considerations, one cultural and one psychological. Culturally, resignation and acknowledgment of defeat are heavily disvalued; they belong with the complex of characteristics identified with the hated and feared old age, indeed are taken as symptoms of termination of the career, and are hence hardly emotionally possible solutions. Psychologically, the real source of the difficulty, in the self, and the real attitude to the defeat, partial gratification, cannot easily be held out of awareness. The threat that they might break into awareness can be counteracted in part by stepping up the rate of activity oriented towards others, and this in turn may raise sufficient resistance and hostility on their part to give ground—for the time being—to the belief that the difficulty is really outside.

Where, therefore, the countervailing mechanism is social—the interpersonal division of labor—the consequences are likely to be felt psychologically: an unexplained feeling of hostile dependency. Where the mechanism is psychological—self-counteraction in either of the forms described—the consequences are likely to be felt socially: an unexplained hostility in many human relationships.

The implications of these costs will need examination in the last chapter.

Part Four

IMPLICATION

13. IMPLICATION

THE IMPLICATIONS of this study are many: some of them are un-expected, and few are as clear or certain as we would wish.

It will be recalled that the Project of which this study is a part had many objects: to experiment with a technique of free discussion with children; to see what could be added to the armament of a good school system that would make its contribution to the mental health of its pupils greater or better; to provide a picture of the growing-up process in one more community, and to evaluate the consequences for mental health of that process.

The most unequivocal results were reached perhaps in the experimental discussion with children, reported on elsewhere.[1] These showed, with great probability, that children participating in such classes made varying psychological and social gains over children, otherwise matched, who did not. Even here, however, we have no evidence that these gains lasted beyond the three-year experimental period, or that they do not represent a *hastening* in the maturation of the experimental students rather than a differential gain that would remain differentiating. Even should the gains be permanent and differentiating, we are not certain what element in the bundle of circumstances presented by the classes was responsible or most responsible for the gains: the basic attitude of the class leader, the free selection of topics by the children, the warmth, the non-judgmental set? We do not know. We only know that something in that bundle evidently had its intended effects.

About the other objects we are less clear; and about one outcome of study—the problems of mental health education itself—which we had not set out to study, we are perhaps clearest of all.

We have no assured indication, from the experience in Crestwood Heights, as to what would improve the mental health facilities of a good school. In Crestwood Heights we added a Child Guidance Clinic, we helped organize "counselling teams," we aided in adult education, and we assisted in the in-service training of teachers. Common local opinion, both within the school and outside it, asserts that these things are or were "good" or "helpful," but demonstrative evidence in the form of diminished incidence for psychological distresses, we do not have. We cannot refuse our own clear impressions of aid, reinforced by numerous assertions by the aided as to the aid received; but we are not able to measure or adequately to assess this aid, or to assert with confidence that it was not offset or overshadowed by the disturbance we caused. There seems to be evidence that the people we trained and sent elsewhere added something in resource to their own local and frequently good schools or school systems.[2] At least, judgment independent of ours has it so. But even here, though we have no evidence of high costs for these gains, we have no evidence to the contrary.

As to the picture of the growing-up process in Crestwood Heights, we believe we have made as faithful a portrayal as the resources at our command would admit.[3] One might hope that, at a minimum, this would serve as a contribution to the description of the background of the upper middle class child, and hence as a bench-mark in the evaluation of what, for this class, is "normal" experience and behavior.

But to trace within this process the vicissitudes to mental health and to evaluate the outcome in mental health terms is, despite our hopes, beyond our capacity—or not possible by our methods. Here and there, throughout the book, we have pointed to threats to integration where they seemed obvious. We had clear impressions that incredible complexity, delicacy of balance, subtlety, and effort were required of the child in his assimilation into the culture described and the integration of his personality within it. At least one of the authors strongly felt both systems—the social and the personal—to be exceedingly labile, not to say fragile, dependent on a concatenation of circumstances difficult to guarantee in the modern world. But this is impression, and what could be added to it would be more impression.

The only objective evidence on this point would seem to point towards no better mental health, or perhaps worse, among children in this community compared with some others elsewhere. The California Personality Inventory was, for instance, applied: compared with the heterogeneous Californian child population upon whom the test was standardized, Crestwood Heights children of teen-age did notably worse on four of the twelve sub-tests; they did insignificantly worse on four more, and insignificantly better on four more.[4] On an Inventory of Physical Health, Crestwood Heights students claimed many times the number of complaints or symptoms claimed by Cincinnati children of the same age level.[5] But this evidence is suggestive, not conclusive: it suggests strongly, however, no unequivocal gain from all the differentially advantageous resources of this community—or some set of unidentified countervailing forces.

The evidence from the operation of the clinic for a four-year period yielded only what might be called "informed estimates." Militating against anything more exact is the very nature of clinical judgment itself, which is a result and expression of a communicated art rather than a mode of relatively precise measurement. Militating also against exactitude of estimate, even on this basis, was the fact that the single clinical team available was never able to plumb to the bottom the caseload available: at no time could it take any but the most urgent cases. The combined judgment of the clinic and local school personnel was that at any one time perhaps 5 per cent of the child population stood in need of clinical aid. Beyond this, an earlier estimate had it that four times this number could profit by the attention to individual cases of the counselling teams. These figures are rather higher than the estimates for Miami County, Ohio: 5 per cent of the children in need of aid, half of these needing full clinical attention.[6]

All this refers to children: the primary object of the study as originally defined. But it was impossible to keep our eye wholly on the children; we could hardly escape asking, though we could not readily answer, how their parents differed from parents we had known elsewhere, particularly again in Miami County. Estimates of relative anxiety are hard come by; evidences of concern are hard to evaluate and measure. Certainly here in Crestwood Heights, as compared with there in Miami County, expressions of concern, not to say perturbation, about the psychological problems or states of individual children were more easily elicited, more frequently voiced, more persistent, and more emotionally clothed. Parents in the Heights seemed, widely, more perturbed by their children's perturbations, as, quite generally, they were more concerned with their children's concerns.

But we get here into difficult territory. For even if the raw observations are correct, it is difficult to say how much of this focusing of concern, this new grammar of anxieties, was due to characteristics of the parents or their situation, and how much was due to the ministrations and educations of the experts who preceded and accompanied the Crestwood Heights Project. Certainly our sense is that the efforts of the latter did nothing to deflect anxiety from channelling itself into the anxiety, rapidly becoming reputable, about the child's anxiety, actual or potential, manifest or latent.

CRESTWOOD HEIGHTS AND MENTAL HEALTH EDUCATION

If the conclusions of other aspects of the study seem uncertain or in-definite (in relation, at least, to the hopes the study had raised) those conclusions that bear on mental health education[7] seem much clearer, unequivocal, and urgent. They would probably have been borne in on the researchers in any case, given the nature of the community and its occupations and preoccupations. But since these same researchers or some of them, in their alternative roles, were actively engaged in or involved with mental health education, they had access to their own experiences, and thus what they saw of the work of others struck them with redoubled effect as it set off echoes of their own doubts, reserva-tions, questions, and anxieties.

The rather unexpected and perhaps extraordinary spectacle presented by a community such as the one studied calls for a radical reconsidera-tion of the whole enterprise of mental health education. As the body of the study will have abundantly made clear, this community is rich in all the means ordinarily thought of as contributory to mental health. Life here is *not* nasty, short, or brutish. The setting is physically spacious. Time is purchasable in plenty, at least in the sense that reprieve from menial tasks and labor, seemingly pointless in a direct address to insti-tuting the good life, can be bought with relative ease. Institutions, gen-erously endowed, intelligently managed, adequately staffed with men and women of knowledge and goodwill, are not only present or avail-able, but consciously dedicated to those ends and procedures that the mental hygienist recommends. All those means, circumstances, and life-ways in terms of whose absence we habitually account for "patho-logy," personal or social, are there; and yet, as already indicated, no forcing of the data, no optimism, no sympathy with aims can lead us to suggest that mental health in the community is sensibly better than elsewhere or that after all this effort it is being sensibly improved. Why not?

It may well be that the presence of all these means is a necessary but not a sufficient condition for the achievement of mental hygiene. Or it may be that some unidentified factors, as specific for an area like this as other identified factors are specific for the slum, militate against the benefits in mental health that would otherwise obtain. Perhaps; we do not know. But certainly the mental health movement is so obviously failing here of some of its intentions and, for others, securing results quite other than intended, that attention to the whole mental health operation seems, in our present state of ignorance, to be most likely to yield theoretical rewards and fruitful practical implications.

Some of the problems of mental health education at this time in an area like this—or perhaps, indeed, anywhere—have to do with the state of the sciences which furnish the content of mental health doctrine. Some of the difficulties are difficulties of transcultural communication; some, of social engineering; some, of the very social system in which the whole enterprise goes forward. These need to be considered severally and together.

A. SCIENTIFIC DIFFICULTIES

Whether or not there is or can ever be a science of human affairs, or whether the application of the word "science" to human affairs requires a radical alteration in its meaning, are subjects of continuing debate. Whatever may be the answers, it seems clear that in reference to human beings little exists that resembles in extent, certainty, connectedness, or agreement the body of physical or even biological science. This state of the social sciences need discourage neither hope nor inquiry; what it does make difficult and perhaps dangerous is the application of the knowledge there is to large and important human affairs, in many cases in reckless extension by analogy of what is known to what is not.

Perhaps the most serious difficulty in applying social scientific knowledge to these affairs has not even been mentioned. This difficulty, which may be natural at this stage of scientific development, is the difficulty of the "over-simple model." It is, of course, inevitable in any science that the "model" or set of conceptions employed should eliminate from theory many aspects of the concrete reality. Newtonian physics worked satisfactorily, for instance, with a theory that treated solid bodies as if they were "mass-points." It operated satisfactorily in application partly because connecting theories rapidly came to deal with those aspects of reality not covered by the simple model, and partly because the simplified model was not unsuited to the solution of those questions it was proposed to address.

But in the social sciences we have no assurance that we have such a model, and grave reason to doubt the adequacy of the ones we have. Indeed, the resistance that many social scientific formulations evoke in the layman may be well founded in a contradiction between them and the experience they purport to describe, rather than ill founded in ignorance and bias.

The most fundamental over-simplification in social science models that purport to deal with complex human reality is the dropping from the model of that which is characteristically and distinctively *human*:

the capacity of the object to be affected by the act of description itself. Science is communication. Social science is communication with human beings as subject-matter and, soon or late, as communicants. Communicants are, even in the perspective of an over-simplified social science, affected in and by communication. Of this the model takes no count.

The neglect in the social science model of the distinguishing human characteristic tends to imbue all doctrine that comes under it with a kind of determinism that is foreign to the subject-matter and that, if true, would make nonsense or irrelevance of the teacher's and learner's motivation. If we tell a class of children that under given circumstances children like them will cheat in exams with a given frequency we have reported as a law a sometime fact, and already, most likely, altered the probabilities with which the children addressed will cheat—either up or down, depending on previous experience, the relations of teacher and learner, and other circumstances. This is not the problem of human affairs being too complex in the usual sense, of too many variables for prediction. Nor is it the problem of separating fact-learning from value-learning or from indoctrination. We are asserting that the facts are in reference to human affairs, that communication about them alters them by "mere" communication—and that the model on which the teaching goes forward denies this as a premise.

At the worst, this development leads to a sort of passivism or fatalism; or, since most people are too sound to deny reality to their sense of agency, to a system of excuses that pleads "Nature" for explanation of defect but feels pride and agency in achievement, where it occurs, nevertheless. At the best, if one can call it that, it leads to a throwing out of the baby with the bath, a rejection *toto corda* of the expert and his doctrine: it is too laborious to extract the grain of temporary truth from its false setting of timeless determinism.

But, as the last phrase indicates, the model is not only defective in its determinism, but also in its timelessness. To the degree that it presents a scientific model in the usual sense, it is "ahistoric," it treats human affairs as existing in a flow of qualitatively identical instants. The whole school of thought that sets up age-norms for children, for instance, on the basis of observing a given crop of children, leaves out of account entirely or almost so, in its preoccupation with *time*, the nature of *the times* through which those children are passing. To believe that the children of the 1890's are essentially like those of the Depression or the Boom is to fly in the face of the very doctrine on which the school founds its scientific procedure. The tendency, unfortunately, if the resultant norms are taken seriously, is to fasten the norms of one historic period on the next, so that the adaptation of cases to circumstances is altered, probably for the worse. Perhaps, to the degree that children refuse such behavioral hand-me-downs, the outcome is only confusion or disappointed expectation in the adult, or heightened conflict between adult and child.

Added to the two defects in the scientific model just mentioned—its ahuman and its atemporal character—is a third, an asocial conception, surprisingly. It is evident that in any social scientific study or operation, the scientist is himself inside the system he is studying; he can only study a social system at first hand by making it "his," at least to a very large degree. As the society becomes "his," he is involved with it in a way that differs radically from the manner in which the physical scientist is involved with his data. This has all long been recognized. But no model has yet been developed for the social sciences that conceptualizes the description of a system from one point within it when the point can only be defined from a description of all the other points.

B. PROBLEMS FROM THE CLASH OF CULTURES

A whole set of problems connected with mental health education may perhaps best be conceived in terms of what social scientists call the "clash of cultures." By a "culture" a social scientist means the socially approved, patterned ways of behavior, thinking, feeling that are the possession of every group and that distinguish one group from another. The culture may be seen as a sort of pattern of patterns, and the very use of the term "pattern" suggests one of its principal characteristics, i.e. that it is difficult to alter any part or element of the culture without altering the whole, sometimes in obscure ways: the invention of controlled explosions of gasoline leads through horseless carriages, to the hard-surfaced road, to the far motel, to the breakdown of a supervision system, to altered relations between the sexes, to the facts behind the Kinsey report. . . .

The "bearers" of a culture (the members of a society) who express it in their accustomed relations with one another and whose personalities have been patterned in, and to fit into, that culture, naturally tend to resist alteration and repatterning of the culture, wherever such alteration hurts or inconveniences them. Cultures in isolation from one another tend to change slowly, almost insensibly, both for want of inventions to disturb them and because of strong inbuilt inertial principles. Cultures in contact on the other hand tend to be cultures in clash because each is a source of potential inventions or importations for the other.

One principal way in which a culture strives to maintain its integrity (if we may reify "culture" for the sake of economy of expression) is by transforming the meaning of an incorporated element so as to create the minimum disturbance to the basic pattern. The simple addition, for instance, of a Western god to the gallery of gods and spirits of a more primitive group is an example of such transformation and incorporation following contact with missionary-brought culture. So, in the other direction, is the adoption of the pagan Easter or Spring festival by the Christian church for its Resurrection pageant.

The mental health education process is patently one in which two radically conflicting cultures are brought into contact, if not clash. Which of the two cultures will in the long run prove the stronger is difficult to state, but what one sees to be prevalent at the present time is the assimilation of mental health terms or practices to the business, school, or family culture, where after suitable transformation they can be incorporated. "Suitable transformation" may variously mean the emptying of all meaning out of a term by attenuation; or the distortion of a term into its virtual opposite. Thus, by attenuation, the term "neurotic" becomes equivalent merely to imperfect; and the answer to "Aren't we all neurotic?" becomes patently "Yes"; no distinction is any longer possible where no difference can be defined. Or by way of reversal: "training for responsibility," which in the theory of one school is the essential element in a sound child-rearing process, means to the speaker progressive assumption by the child of self-regulatory mechanisms and practices; the same goal, heartily accepted by many parents encountered, and educators too, meant to them answerability and subordination to the parent or educator or, in some instances, the peer group. A term from a grammar of autonomy was insensibly transformed as it passed through the communication network into a term from the grammar of subordination or other-direction. Yet both sides thought they shared a common understanding.

Few examples in Crestwood Heights were, perhaps, so blatant.[8] Most transformations are, contrariwise, of so subtle a character as to defy any but the most skilful probing. They tend to escape observation again because of over-simplification of the model upon which description of human behavior is based. The simplest illustration may be drawn in terms of a paired set of values which have appeared and reappeared throughout this book: the "maturity" values and the "success" values. Generally, we have spoken as though these were neatly counterposed between people, or in conflict or uneasy blend within them. But in Crestwood Heights we frequently observed people—experts and laymen—who had espoused "maturity" values because they were able or believed able in a given situation to serve "success" values. At a most

obvious level, the business man who "strung along" with the new personnel policies because this added to his marketable repute is a case in
point; more subtle were the cases of people who attempted to make
over their core values, if not their personalities, because they believed
that only so could they achieve externally given goals. People who
genuinely strove to renounce narcissism for the sake of the narcissistic
satisfaction of being thought non-narcissistic were not unknown.

Complex as this may sound, it still represents an over-simplification:
the renunciation of A because renunciation contributes to B which contributes even more to A. A most commonplace example in the urban
area beyond Crestwood was the espousal of a complex "simple life"
which required even more care for what was reputably disreputable
than the complex, reputable life of Crestwood. It is still too simple a
model because behavior is not limited to such double reversals: they
may be treble, quadruple or even more complex. The person who tries
to humble himself in his pride about his humility is such a more involved instance. The problem is one in discovering the ultimate term,
not the presenting one, in such a series, for the meaning of the behavior
is determined by that term. Terminology for describing such behavior
is almost too unwieldy for effective communication, and techniques for
discovering such complexities, short of mass psychoanalysis, do not
easily suggest themselves. But without such terminology and such techniques, it is difficult to say whether or how an element of one culture
is being transformed for incorporation into an alien culture. And without knowledge of such transformation-in-depth, communication takes
place at a level of seeming understanding but is actually vitiated in a
fog of confusion.

There is not only a lack of awareness of these transformations-in-
depth but, closely related to it, very little feel, among would-be educators
and would-be learners alike, for the wholeness or integration of a culture. Few of the advocates of a deterministic view of behavior (as being
the proper everyday way to think about it) had worked out for themselves or communicated to their audience the theology (if any), the
ethics (if any), or the calculus of expediency or appropriateness that
would be implied in so radical a shift of perspective. Indeed few behaved, or even taught, on the basis of the views they propounded. And
the audiences, no less, that adopted these views, hoped to adopt them
without renouncing important, related culture-items which depended
on expressly contradictory assumptions. It is obvious that, given the
nature of culture, any attempt to alter it raises a problem of the simultaneous alteration of a sufficiently large number of elements unless a
great deal of confusion and distress is to ensue in the short run, and per-

haps an unanticipated result in the long. The problem is formally similar to the engineering of an armistice: the simultaneity and the scale of the cease-fire are central. A consequence of not facing this problem squarely in the field of mental health education is that what is sound on the scientific side is watered down or distorted to conform to lay preconceptions, and what is sound in the sureties of everyday experience is paled over in scientific uncertainty. The amalgam that results frequently fails scientific warrant just as it defies the test of experience. A good example is the schedule-bound infant crying in its crib because someone so inferred from Watson.

C. PROBLEMS OF THE SOCIAL SYSTEM

Another set of problems largely not looked at, let alone solved, has to do with the social system upon which or in which the mental health education is supposed to operate.

At its most elementary level it is important to distinguish whether it is the individual or the family or the community or the nation or the world that is the object of primary concern. We have already pointed to one consequence of failing to make such distinctions: "family relations" experts communicating their knowledge, their techniques, and their heightened concern to one member of each family (the wife and mother) and, in the process, disturbing the balance of power, the stability, and the ideological unity of the family. We have no evidence that this is the prelude to a better adjustment or higher synthesis in the near or far future. Nor will it do to say that "we cannot make omelets without breaking eggs." A family-life education that took itself seriously would surely treat the family as a unit or system rather than as a *congeries* of individuals to be won to one view or another. What is true for the family is true for larger systems. They are all constantly dealt with as though they were mere sums of individuals, although the organization of knowledge in each field is based precisely on the denial of this view.

The other problem of the intermeshing social systems of the scientific and lay communities has already, perhaps, been treated at sufficient length—though, perhaps, also not with sufficient depth. We referred earlier to the fact that the experts in the new fields of "human relations" tend to be marginal in their own social systems, if only because of the very newness and uncertainty of their theories. They are or tend to be correspondingly central in the lay community they are instructing. We pointed out that this sometimes constituted for the experts an appeal from their peers to their public.

But the very fact of this actual or potential appeal itself plays cyclically into both systems. It tends to get for the expert within the circle of his peers an increasingly marginal definition: the word "quack" may not be used, but indulgent smiles greet news of his activities and anticipations of his (self-chosen) fate. Increasing marginality in the peer group leads towards increasing dependency on and involvement with the public. The outcome turns largely upon whether or not a sufficiently notable and numerous following can be built on this side before the weakened relations with colleagues collapse on the other. It should be specially noted, perhaps, that the "public-related" expert, by the fact of public-relatedness itself, is alienated as readily from his colleagues if he comes from a "practical" field as if he comes from a "theoretical" one. In the first case, he ceases to be a "good practitioner"; in the second, he cannot be a "true scholar." The psychoanalyst who interests himself as a professional in community affairs raises questions about his likely competence as a therapist; the social theorist who does the like raises questions as to his scholarship. These questions, of course, are the questions of his colleagues. Ironically, conduct which *raises* questions among them, *settles* questions for the public: with equal irrelevance, therapeutic and scholarly competence are likely to be assessed or imputed by the public on the basis of a performance of quite different nature—imputed so strongly indeed that direct disclaimers have almost no effect. Ironically too, nothing but very great success with the public will lay the ghost of non-recognition by peers for the practitioners or scholars; and, last irony, by this time the public has begun to lose interest in its search for a newer Messianic voice.

The first problem, practically, for mental health education is not so much concerned with altering this complex social structure and dynamism, as with recognizing that it *is* the context in which mental health education goes forward, and that the context makes a great deal of difference to the psychological nature and to the content of the educational process.

ETHICAL PROBLEMS

Beyond or behind these technical problems are problems of ethics which have hitherto barely been looked at, let alone seriously attacked.

The fundamental problem is a problem for all education, but applies with special force in the fields we have been discussing. Knowledge is not power (as the proverb alleges) but it may readily be made use of to establish differences of power or to increase or perpetuate existing differences. In the psychological fields it is not unlikely that the knowledge of how to heal may also lead readily into knowledge of how to destroy. In any case, the question arises of what knowledge is to be transmitted in what order to whom in order to secure what effect. We *may* do little harm in passing on knowledge which can readily be turned to manipulation and control of children, if we are right in assuming good sense and goodwill in parents and if the new knowledge does not, of itself, make the blandishments of power irresistible. But is the same true if we should give differential access over such knowledge to, say, school administrators as against teachers, or employers as against employees, or clergy as against laity or—already touched upon—mothers as against fathers? It is difficult to refuse the view that the same problems arise here concerning the distribution of power, and hence the possibility of democracy, as arise from the new nature of armaments in the field of physical force.[9]

It is perhaps not sufficient to leave this problem to "the operation of the market," any more than it would be sufficient to leave to the market the distribution of machine-guns in the civil population. The result in both cases must, roughly, be that existing differences in power would be raised to new levels in a disorderly process of no visible ethical value. Distribution by the market in the case of mental health or psychological knowledge may well give the bulk of it to the insecure who are thereby rendered more insecure rather than less, and to the powerful who are interested in it in one sense with a view to manipulation of others and in another, with a view to manipulation of self.

The question as to who is to be served by the would-be mental health educator is thus unavoidable—and, as yet, unconfronted. He commonly does not know what he is doing to the power structure, though this want of knowledge could presumably be remedied by research. But, what is more serious, he commonly does not know what he *wants* to do to the structure, and it is this lack of a clear aim that is most promising of disaster. Even where, here and there, a lone mental health educator is clear as to what he wishes and even, a little, as to what he effects, it is obvious that between him and his colleagues there is no necessary agreement about intention or result. Indeed, this brings us to what is perhaps the most fundamental problem of all.

This problem is that the mental health practitioners—both therapists and educators—are, in effect, discharging priestly functions without the social structure of a church or the ideological support of a dogma.[10] Indeed, if mental hygienists are united in one thing it is in their desire to avoid either of these latter: so that the situation involved appears to be of long-term duration rather than short.

The priestly functions which the mental hygienist now discharges, either in competition with older priesthoods or in supersession of them, include the definition of the ultimate nature of man, of good and bad ("mature" and "immature"; "sick" or "well"), of what is proper or "rational," and, by implication, what is really "real" (a criterion of psychosis is "loss of touch with reality"). Even where some attempt has been made to come to terms with an older priestcraft by defining "irrational guilt" as the psychiatrist's province, leaving "rational guilt" to the priest, it is obvious that the definition of what *is* irrational guilt must be made on clinical grounds, and that therefore the clinician's is the last word. As one of the authors has put it in another context, "The protagonists and practitioners of mental health are increasingly called upon to pronounce on what used to be called moral questions, in the small and in the large, in general and in particular."[11] The pronouncements cover matters of both substance and method:

Breast feeding of infants, for instance, is currently "good," not under divine dispensation or because it is "natural," but because the mental hygienists say—probably quite rightly—it will help to produce a "good" child from the viewpoint of mental hygiene. The production of "good" children in another sense—what used to be called well-behaved children— by bad means such as fear or conditioning or seduction is held to be bad because it militates against integration, which is close to the mental hygienist's *summum bonum.*

Divorce is good or bad, not in and of itself, but in so far as it increases or decreases the mental health of the parties thereto; or, in a rare, wider view, all the parties concerned, including nonparticipants.

What is being said, in effect, is that of necessity it [the mental health movement] has the form and flavor of a church: organization, a message or mission, a set of central values, committed servants—lay and professional— activities, orthodoxies and heresies, celebrations and observances, excommunications at need, and the felt power in moral matters to bind and loose.

The emergence of a new priesthood is always peculiarly distressing: it arises in the first place because an older priesthood fails to alleviate existing discomforts, but in its emergence it inevitably creates new discomforts for those who cannot readily endure the pains of ideological and emotional transition. These inevitable pains of passing are perhaps complicated thrice over in the case of the mental health movement by three of its permanent characteristics.

The first characteristic is that, unlike most previous sects, it is itself a response to an excess of change rather than a deficit: it is not like a Methodist movement responding to the felt over-stable tradition of a Church of England, but rather a movement called out largely by the disturbances of those for whom the irregularity or aimlessness of modern life, produced by change, has created intolerable emotional problems. The second characteristic is that, as already pointed out, because it is in such close touch with the changing deliverances of science and because these are by no means yet cumulative, it is itself not only no island of stability, but a solvent of tradition and a promoter of further and perhaps endless change. Thus it can only meet the demand for stability by asking its followers to cope with unchanging change: a demand not easily met by the type of person most readily drawn into its orbit.

The third characteristic is that not only from time to time but at any given moment the movement is shot through with conflicting views that are not made explicit or, frequently, regarded as important. These differences have to do with what are precisely the most important matters, virtually ultimate considerations. Practically every view of man and his fate (from Existentialist to traditional Christian positions); of the place, value, and use of love and hostility; of man's potentiality and promise (from radical pessimism to radical optimism) finds its protagonists, has its practitioners, and spills forth its literature. Even the central question of whether mental health is a mere means to the good life or the touchstone of all other goods has not received an agreed answer. It is hard to see, perhaps, what unites these varying views; but the sense and reality of the unity are sufficient to mark a recognizable movement and even to call out for it "friends" and "enemies."

Given the nature of the movement as described and given the existence of such communities as the one we have pictured there seems to be an inevitable tendency for each to seek out the other with a view to an enduring symbiotic relationship. The community virtually offers itself as a laboratory, a proving-ground, or a recruitment body. The movement requires room for experiment, a following, and a support, psychological and social.

Such junctures seem unavoidable, but the situation of the mental health movement and the mental hygienist inevitably presents the temptation to exploit as a beachhead what should be protected as a laboratory—a laboratory moreover in which, as in a hospital, there is an *extraordinary* responsibility to the subjects of experiment. The latter position is difficult to preserve outside a structure corresponding to that of the hospital in which the returns or rewards to the practitioner are almost wholly independent of the favor or approval of the subjects. Such a structure the mental health movement is, for intrinsic and extrinsic reasons, not likely soon to see. Intrinsically, because in one sense, what is generally accepted in the long run *is* what is relevant, i.e.

mental health truths are not operationally relevant if acceptance for them cannot be had. Extrinsically, because, for the foreseeable future, funds for mental health research, education, and indeed therapy will come largely from government, and timid statesmen will require the support or pressure of public opinion, i.e. of a following produced by the mental health movement in partial denial or contradiction of its central aims.

How these losses are to be avoided it is probably not the business of this book to say. To make both parties to the transactions more self-conscious, as this book has attempted to do, may be an aid. To ask that all mental health education go forward only in most intimate contact with long-term research upon its effects is to suggest making the process permanent. To ask statesmen to have an eye special to the security of the mental health practitioners, and to ask the latter to have an eye special to reducing the vulnerability of their clientele is perhaps to ask for Utopia.

Perhaps the most that can be asked for is that another and more extended effort than is represented by this book make a fresh attempt to take a new look from a new perspective at what we have been doing and pool afresh such wisdom as we have or as we might, in the sharing, find.

APPENDIXES

The Crestwood Heights Project

IT IS PROPOSED to give here the more detailed account of the origin of the Crestwood Heights Project which was promised the reader in chapter 1. This Project was, as already mentioned, one outcome of the larger "National Mental Health Project" launched by the National Committee for Mental Hygiene (Canada) of which one of the present authors was an officer. At the time the "National Project" was put forward, in the period following the Second World War, it was a perfectly general suggestion, addressed to the public, to the professional agencies concerned, and to the political and administrative bodies involved, as to what might and should be done "to improve the mental health of the people of Canada."[1]

The Canadian National Committee at that time had behind it nearly thirty years of history, in the course of which it had devoted the major part of its effort to a variety of attempts to secure improvement of the conditions in mental hospitals.[2] The Committee had, however, at no time restricted its interests entirely to the mental hospitals; rather it had defined itself as a body that initiated or, in its own vocabulary, "sparked" or "fathered" or "pioneered" a great many activities, either originally independent or eventually to become independent of the Committee, but thought to be closely related to mental health. Among such children or foster-children it proudly included an Institute for Child Study, now a part of the University of Big City.

At the time of conception of the "National Mental Health Project," however, owing to the war itself and to other circumstances, the National Committee had launched no new venture for some time. The activities of wartime had nevertheless forced it to confront more boldly a problem, and permitted it more easily to envision a possibility. The problem was brought to the center of attention by the gloomy psychiatric statistics that were provided by the recruitment and discharge activities of the armed forces, and the related findings stemming from the civilian war effort. These depressing figures served to dramatize, though they did not discover, a vast reservoir of human misery and mental ill-health and deficiency in all the Allied nations that shared the same orientation to mental health and sickness. Even stripped of some dramatic effect by explanation, and in some cases by rationalization, the figures were impressive and the facts that underlay them most difficult to blink. The possibility, a vision of which had emerged *pari passu* with the looming problem, was embodied, albeit vaguely, in a term that came to have an almost magical connotation—"interdisciplinary cooperation." Could not a variety of practitioners of different arts—psychiatrists, psychologists, social workers, educators, and many others—working together, find more effective ways of assistance in a major effort?[3]

Out of all this, after some study, came the plan embodied in the National Project. The study briefly reviewed the now well-known statistics on rates of mental hospitalization, rates of army rejection and discharge on psychiatric grounds, and rates of maladjustment among children;[4] it also examined actual or suggested methods of counteraction.

The question that the National Committee asked itself was essentially: What steps could be recommended that would have a reasonable likelihood of being taken, with a reasonable hope of affecting within a generation the "level of mental health" of the Canadian population? It was, of course, to be understood that these steps would supplement rather than replace existing activities whose intent lay in the same direction.

It was decided to focus planning on the child, and on the public school as the institution through which children would be most accessible.[5]

The National Project, as a part of its action-plan, proposed the extension and strengthening of one existing element, and the invention and use of two more. The rather obvious first suggestion was that the traditional psychiatric clinic for children and their families be many times multiplied, but placed in a much closer spatial and moral contiguity to the schools. Child guidance clinics should be made available on a stated scale and at a stated rate over the next decade, and these should be placed as close to the school as possible and specially adapted to its service in ways that were briefly outlined.

Observation of the operation of existing child clinics, however, seemed to indicate that many of these had been substantially impeded, not to say paralyzed, in their function by the volume both of intractable cases and of trivial cases that were referred to them. This observation suggested that some kind of person somewhere in the referring agency—in this situation, the school system—was needed who could do three things: (1) provide "psychological first aid," mostly by the handling of situations, for cases which, given the shortage of psychiatric personnel and resources, must be looked upon as relatively trivial; (2) "spot," and helpfully refer to clinic personnel, more serious cases early in their development; (3) translate for educational personnel the general prescriptions of clinical personnel as to how a certain child should be handled in such a way that his problem might be coped with, or at least not exacerbated. This requirement ultimately called for a new kind of professionally specialized person who was primarily an educator, but who had, in addition to the skills usual for this profession, acquired the knowledge and competence that would enable him to function in the ways suggested. It was, moreover, hoped that the existence of such newly specialized personnel would, in turn, induce in teachers generally a heightened awareness of emotional problems in children which would permit them, in effect, and with the aid of the specialized educator, to perform these functions to a greater degree themselves.[6]

Both elements of the plan, so far, represented attempts to cope with children who had already got into difficulty, and their effort lay in the direction of "therapy" rather than "prevention." As an initial cast in the latter direction, the plan suggested that specially trained people conduct, on a regular basis, free discussions with ordinary school children, permitting the children to talk about anything they wanted to talk about, in an atmosphere that was as emotionally warm and morally judgment-free as it could be made.[7] The presumption was—and it was later borne out—that the children would talk about common problems, and that, in the course of such discussion, they would gain both knowledge about the world in which they lived and insight into themselves and one another, and that these effects would cause or imply other gains in mental health.

It was hoped, further, that the same "professionally specialized person" referred to above might be able to conduct such "classes" in the schools, and that, if properly trained, he would safeguard the process against the perversion to sadistic uses of which it is clearly capable.

BIRTH

With the details of social engineering, by which consent in principle and, in some cases, enthusiastic assent to these plans were secured, we shall not deal in detail here. Negotiations were involved with the relevant professional bodies, the provincial political and administrative authorities concerned, the boards of education who might be willing to attempt and pay for the experiment, and even with the voluntary associations, whose financial aid would be required in its support. Suffice it to say that in a very short interval—about six months—such consents and supports were somewhat readily obtained.

The organization of consent which had rapidly been going forward had, however, brought into association with the planning process a larger group of people who added chiefly scientific caution to existing enthusiasm—without damping the latter. Under their moderative influence, it finally seemed wiser to all to attempt two "pilot projects"— smaller, trial embodiments in two Canadian communities of those procedures and changes that the National Project had wished to see bodied forth as rapidly as possible in as many communities as could be persuaded to make the trial and supply the means. For reasons political as well as scientific, it was decided that these pilot projects should be launched one each in the neighborhood of Canada's two largest universities. One of these pilot projects failed to mature, and accordingly only the other, near Big City, came into being.

The staff charged with responsibility for the latter had a number of considerations in mind, among them the following. The community should be (1) close to Big City, (2) autonomous with respect to its school system, (3) of a high degree of literacy and (4) economically well off. *Strategically*, if effects were to be shown in a fairly short time, it would need to be a community to whose citizens the commonplaces of educational, psychological, and psychiatric discourse would not be entirely foreign; still strategically, it had to be a community of relative economic well-being, since it was at that time hoped that the community would itself support a large share of the cost of the program proposed. *Scientifically*, it seemed desirable to operate in such a community in order to demonstrate what could be added to an already good school system, and not what could be added that would improve a very bad school system—the answer in the latter case would presumably have been "anything." It also seemed desirable to work in such a community because it might represent a more critical audience, and one from which would come, in disproportionate degree, the leaders of opinion and others responsible for the fate of institutions in the next generation.

These requirements had narrowed the possibility to a list of about six suburbs in the immediate environs of Big City. At this point, by a fortunate historical coincidence, the Director of Education of Crestwood Heights and other officials happened to seek the advice of the National Committee for Mental Hygiene on a number of problems confronting them. It speedily appeared not only that they had definitions of the situation of their children similar to those of the National Committee, but that, further, they had been experimenting with relatively unstructured discussion (at least at one grade level) with results which had raised their interest and curiosity. It was almost immediately evident that there was a marked convergence of interests and that on the side of the educational authorities of Crestwood Heights there was a marked hospitality to the general ideas embodied in the planning of the National Committee. In a relatively short, easy, and pleasant period of negotiation with the Board of Education of Crestwood Heights, permission was secured to use that school system for the stated purposes as a pilot plant for one year. The term was later extended for an indefinite period, which actually amounted to five years.

At about this time, when ends had been agreed upon, and means, particularly financial means, were wanting, by another "coincidence," the Government of Canada announced a Mental Health Program which made available very substantial grants for training, for research, and for other purposes. These grants were to be made available to the Provinces[8]; and most of the Provinces, in turn, made the research portions of their grants available, chiefly, to the universities.

Since the moral support of the University of Big City had been sought from the beginning by the National Committee, in any case, and since voluntary aid and co-operation had been asked for, the availability of the new grants seemed to make possible a basis for still closer co-operation. A committee from the Departments of Education, Psychiatry, Psychology, and Social Work of the University of Big City was formed, and it recommended to the University that the pilot project of the National Committee, essentially as it had been envisioned, be financed and operated under University auspices, in co-operation with the National Committee, provided that every effort were made to extract from the experience the maximum research information that it was capable of yielding. It was understood from the beginning that the National Committee would continue to hold responsibility for public relations, would maintain liaison with educational authorities to secure candidates for training, and would give some aid in their instruction while simultaneously exercising some hospitable functions, which indeed, would provide them with a meeting-place, physically, and a "home," socially.

The University, on the other hand, was to assume general responsibility for the finance and administration of the whole project, for the instruction of trainees, for services provided the experimental community, and, chiefly, for research.

MATURATION

The arrangements as finally concluded meant that research, which had been a subsidiary consideration, emerged as a co-ordinate, if not the paramount, consideration in the continuation of the Project while, at the same time, all the commitments for service and training had to be maintained, and, in some cases, extended. The Project was thus an operation in which research, training, and service had to be made to yield results for one another. This was not as difficult as it might at first seem, and the results turned out to be more rewarding than had initially been expected, but the necessity never ceased to confront the directors of the Project with a feeling of over-complication and over-extendedness. One could emphasize now the rewards from such an operation, and now the costs; but no one ever entirely freed himself from the frustrations consequent upon a complex definition of his role. It was obvious, for instance, that the clinic staff could be pressed to be sensitive in their observations of community life, and to report those observations, and that they could be further asked to report their clinical experience in sufficient detail that those interested in other aspects of the Project than the individual patient could get material from clinical data. It was equally obvious that the clinic staff could be used, and had to be used, to aid in training the "professionally specialized personnel" who came to be known as "Liaison Officers." What was perhaps not obvious at first was that both of these demands would simultaneously enrich the clinic staff's experience, but seriously complicate their public relations, and frustrate their demand for a clear and simple definition of their role.

What was true for the service staff (clinical and other) was equally true for the training or the research staff—who were, in some cases, the same persons employed in their alternative capacities.

Part of the training experience for the "Liaison Officers" was so structured that it was carried out in the community upon which research was being done, in order that training activities would yield their quota of service, and indirectly, a quota of research information, in that setting. Research itself was complicated by the desire to give every trainee experience of research, to give people in Crestwood Heights a similar experience as part of the service that was being rendered, and, as far as possible, and as generally as possible, to make the act of inquiry which is central to research, itself contributory to some essentially therapeutic end. At many points, this set limits—probably proper ones —both on the kinds of inquiries which could be pursued and on the methods by which they might be pursued.

At the point so far reached, then, the University of Big City had agreed to train a number of teachers, annually, in the ways suggested, had agreed to supply a specified set of services to a given community, and had agreed to do research in that community. Details of the service supplied will be found elsewhere.[9]

It remains to describe the research tasks attempted. It was hoped that five connected research volumes would emerge from the enterprise as a whole:

1. A "Psychological Survey" of Crestwood Heights which would show whether or not the supposed personality differences which are believed to characterize social groups would show up in personality tests of children—despite crudeness of tests and crudeness of social categories. We were curious as to whether children of different sexes, different cultures, and different social classes would manifest significant differences in their test-behavior.[10]

2. A book on the "Human Relations Classes" which would report upon that experiment and provide a test of the psychological effectiveness of the techniques used, and by its concrete material give some insight into the process of growing up in Crestwood Heights as it appears from "within" the process, i.e., to the child.[11]

3. A report upon the services supplied, particularly the clinical services.[12]

4. An account of the experience with the "Liaison Officers" and their effects on their own communities after they had returned to them.[13]

5. A volume which attempted to describe the social life of the community in which the whole experiment had been undertaken, with special reference to the child-rearing process and its implications for mental health.

This fifth study is represented by the present volume.

APPENDIX 2

The Children and the Culture

THE TWO STORIES contained in this Appendix have been referred to in the chapter on "Age," page 113. They are reprinted by generous permission of the authors, who contributed them to their High School magazine. This material is reprinted here, not because it is excellent— though it is that—nor because it is typical in the sense of very like all other contributions. The stories were selected because they seemed to catch at or embody so much of the flavor of the teen-age culture whose portrayal in more formal terms has been attempted here and there, throughout this book.

WHY I STICK TO THE CITY

"Why do I stick to the city?" You might as well ask a rat why he sticks to the garbage dump.

When I walk along a crowded city street, I give the same little snicker that a rat gives when he dives into a load of freshly dumped garbage. The city is an interesting place, an exciting place, a place to have fun in. On this point the rat and I completely agree.

I think every "kid" should have a chance to be brought up in the city. Even living in the city is an education in itself. The city has several advantages for a "kid" trying to grow up. In a city there are plenty of ice cream cones, comic books and Frankenstein movies. When a boy reaches his adolescence, he has a larger choice of women to go out with than has his contemporary on the farm! And also, being a "sharp character" with more experience, he can "hand" his "doll" a better "line" than the average farmer can.

You can't slow down a city. Things have got to go on, and, unless there is a power cut-off, things never stop. If you try to slow down in the city, you just get pushed down and run over. Have you ever watched an old lady cross a busy intersection? She moves or else. This all adds to the interest and excitement that a city can offer.

Moreover it is never quiet in the city. There's none of this oppressive, irritating silence that you find in the country. You wake up in the morning to the pleasant chatter of power drills breaking up pavement outside your flat, and the contented chug of the steam-shovel as it joyfully scoops up jawfuls of nice city mud. During the rest of the day your ear drum is caressed with the sounds of horns honking, whistles blowing, bells ringing, typewriters clicking and tickertape tickering. Then in the evening you may listen to Fred Allen on the radio or go to a night club and hear Hotlips Harrigan and his Seventeen Slobovians. If you can't afford a night club or a radio, you may play a juke box or watch a brawl on the corner. In short, city life is never dull.

The food in the city is delightfully varied at all times of the year. In the country you eat asparagus all spring, strawberries all summer, apples all fall and potatoes all winter. Every drug store in the city has a wealth of popcorn, potato chips, chocolate bars, gum and vitamin pills. At any season you can have your favorite dish, be it caviar and whipped cream or lobster and chocolate sauce.

The city is the best place to earn an easy dollar and the best place to spend that dollar. There are more people here and consequently more "suckers" from whom easy dollars may be extracted. With this money you may go to the movies and see beautiful scenes or go to the burlesque and see beautiful sights. There is no end to the fun you can have in the city.

I have only mentioned a few of the many advantages that city life can offer, and I am certain the rat would agree with every word I have said.

THE MAGIC OF A TOOTH

When Jane Blake heard the happy news from the doctor, she immediately went out and bought some knitting needles, a pair of low-heeled shoes, and a copy of Dr. Crain's book, "Modern Child Care." During the months that followed, Jane and her husband Ralph read and re-read Dr. Crain's book; and by the time Cynthia Blake arrived, they could both reel off chapters of the book by memory. Miss Blake weighed exactly six pounds on arrival, a chubby, dimpled bundle of accuracy. At feeding time, an assortment of measuring spoons and scales was always on hand, so that Cynthia would receive the correct amount of vitamins, calories, and minerals. Everything about Cynthia Blake was scientifically precise.

Naturally, Ralph and Jane took a lot of heckling from relatives and friends. In the end, though, even the most sceptical of them had to admit that there was something to this "modern" technique of child-raising. Dr. Crain's book became dilapidated and tattered, but Cynthia Blake grew smarter and sturdier.

At the age of three and a half she was entered in the Midtown Nursery School; at the end of the 1st term she was the top "student" at the school. Cynthia was five years and three and a half months old that the Blakes

Cynthia was five years, and three and a half months old that the Blakes felt themselves at a loss as to what procedure they should follow.

When Ralph Blake came home from work on this certain evening, he noticed that Cynthia was holding something tightly in her hand as she sat down at the dinner-table.

"What have you got there, honey?" he asked.

The little girl looked up, smiled, and shyly held out her hand. In the chubby palm was a tooth. "My tooth. The first one out."

Jane came in from the kitchen, and answered her husband's questioning glance. "She's three months ahead of the book; I don't understand it. She's been getting all the calcium she needs."

"Don't worry," said Cynthia, with an impish grin. "It wouldn't have come out for a while, but I pushed it back and forth till it did. Now I can get the ten cents."

"Ten cents?" asked Ralph.

"Oh yes! You see, if you put your tooth under your pillow at night, a fairy comes and leaves ten cents. Sandra Bowen got ten cents yesterday." Cynthia carefully put the tooth into the pocket of her pinafore.

"H'm, I see," said Ralph. "I think I'll get a glass of water."

"I'd better look at the chops," Jane announced, and followed him out to the kitchen.

"This is bad," said Ralph. "Dr. Crain warned about 'acceptance of an unreal fantasy concept.' You know, I'm really surprised that the teachers at the school allow such things."

"I don't suppose they know about it. It's most likely something among the children themselves," Jane said.

"If we gently disillusion her now, it'll be easier than having to do it later. You want to do it, dear?" asked Ralph.

"No," answered Jane, "I think it should be the father."

As they went back into the dining-room, Cynthia was fingering the tooth.

"Cynthia, darling," said Ralph. "You know, there really isn't such a thing as a tooth fairy."

"Oh, but there must be," said Cynthia. "Sandra Bowen got ten cents from the tooth fairy yesterday." '

"Dear, that's just a story made up for children," said Jane, "like Cinderella, and Santa Claus, and . . . , and. . . ."

"Cinderella," said Ralph.

Cynthia frowned for a moment, then she smiled and said, "Maybe this is something that mothers and fathers don't know about. I'll put the tooth under my pillow tonight, and then tomorrow we'll know for sure. Okay?

"Cynthia," her father said, "don't you believe your mother and father when they tell you that there is no such thing as this tooth fairy?"

The little girl looked quickly from her father's face to her mother's, then dropped her eyes. Without raising her head, she said in a soft voice, "It won't hurt to try, will it? It worked for Sandra Bowen."

Dinner was eaten in silence, and as soon as the meal was over, Cynthia slipped from her chair and said, "I think I'll go to bed now, please."

"I think you can stay up a little later to-night," said Jane.

"Sure," said Ralph. "I'll read you a story."

"I think I'll go to bed," said Cynthia.

Jane put Cynthia to bed and came back into the living-room. "The tooth is under her pillow," Jane said. "Tomorrow morning she'll find it still there; she'll be so disappointed, but it's a lesson she must learn."

"That's right," said Ralph. "These things aren't easy to do, but it's for her own good."

Jane and Ralph were in bed by ten thirty and there was silence in the Blake household until seven the next morning, when a small, wild Indian in pink pajamas came bounding into the master bed-room, and started jumping up and down on the bed. "Wait till I see that Sandra Bowen!"

Ralph and Jane sat up in bed.

"After all . . ." said Ralph, with a guilty look at Jane.

"You can carry these things only so far," said Jane to Ralph.

"Just wait till I see that dopey Sandra Bowen," said Cynthia. "I got two dimes."

For a moment, Cynthia forgot her excitement and stared at her parents who were both laughing very hard.

NOTES

1. THE STAGE

1. The authors and their associates had great difficulty in creating a pseudonym that would suitably denote the psychological and social overtones of the original name. The one selected very nearly catches these subtle nuances. Among the pseudonyms thought of were: Hillgrove, Interwalden, Uppertown, Maple Heights, Montsylvania, Hillbrow Heights, Richview Heights, Hilltop Heights, Woodmount, Newmount and Urban Heights.

2. See F. R. Kluckhohn, "Dominant and Variant Value Orientations," in *Personality in Nature, Society, and Culture,* ed. C. Kluckhohn and H. A. Murray (2nd ed.; New York: Alfred A. Knopf, 1953), p. 346. These concepts are further elaborated by C. Kluckhohn in "Universal Categories of Culture," *Anthropology Today: An Encyclopedic Inventory* (Chicago: University of Chicago Press, 1953), pp. 507–523.

Dr. Kluckhohn gives three range-points covering the variability in each dimension:

Innate disposition:	Good—neither good nor bad—bad
Relation to nature:	Man subjugated to—in—over nature
Significant time:	Past—present—future
Valued personality:	Being—being-in-becoming—doing
Relation to others:	Lineal—Collateral—Individualistic

To the possibilities offered by these range-points, she adds methods of further specification that permit a more subtle analysis than has been employed in the text.

3. This infinite variety of subtle transactions dwarfs in mass and scope the essentially similar, if more primitive, practices of peoples like the Kwakiutl. See R. F. Benedict, *Patterns of Culture* (Boston: Houghton Mifflin Company, 1934), pp. 173–222; D. Riesman (in collaboration with R. Denney and N. Glazer), *The Lonely Crowd: A Study of the Changing American Character* (New Haven: Yale University Press, 1950), pp. 271–282.

4. The official population in 1951 was 15,305 which is the figure used in demographic analysis. At the time of writing, the municipal office gave

17,000 as the estimated population of Crestwood Heights. The population of Big City in 1951 was 676,000; that of the total metropolitan area 1,117,000. SOURCE: Canada, Bureau of Statistics, *Ninth Census of Canada 1951* (Ottawa: Queen's Printer, 1953), vol. I, Tables 1, 9, 17, 18.

5. Of the male labor force of Crestwood Heights 14 years of age and over (1951), 50.4 per cent were engaged in proprietary and managerial occupations and 18.3 per cent in professions, as against 10.4 per cent and 8.0 per cent respectively for Big City. Of the professional people of Crestwood Heights (1951), 18.1 per cent were lawyers and notaries, 16 per cent accountants and auditors, 14.8 per cent physicians and surgeons, 6.3 per cent teachers; all others, 44.8 per cent. SOURCE: Canada, Bureau of Statistics, *Ninth Census of Canada 1951*, vol. IV, Table 6.

6. Crestwood Heights is not completely servantless. The proportion of wage-earning females 14 years of age and over listed as domestic workers diminished from 58.63 per cent in 1941 to 40.32 per cent in 1951. In 1941, female domestic workers made up 8.55 per cent of the total population of the Heights; in 1951, 5.07 per cent.

7. A perhaps amusing instance of this situation happened to a friend of one of the writers recently. In a questionnaire for young pre-adolescents, intended to secure information about their activities, the perfectly literal question was asked "Do you play house?" The investigator was amazed to discover that he had provoked a community uproar: to these children and their parents the question referred specifically to inter-child sex investigation and experimentation. Moreover, to ask about it in this matter-of-fact way had an air, to the adults, of improper suggestion. The inquiry was accordingly deleted from the questionnaire. Ordinarily, such incidents become matters for gossip among scientists, and it is the results of the corrected questionnaire which are published. Our point is only that this event from the history of the study is a legitimate and important part of the study, and ought so to be reported.

8. Considerations other than context operated to incline us towards this type of method in any case. See below.

9. But not too far. For qualification, see below, pp. 16 *et seq.*

10. At a level of still greater intimacy, many adults brought their problems to members of the research team who referred them to public and private therapeutic facilities, where appropriate. The handling of requests for personal help, and the listening to substantial detailed accounts of personal problems became for at least one researcher an unsought major additional duty.

11. For a more general argument, see J. R. Seeley, "Social Science in Social Action," *Canadian Journal of Economics and Political Science* (Toronto), vol. XVII (1951), pp. 84–89.

12. As a matter of fact, it is probable that many of the effects which were most markedly therapeutic socially, resulted not from operations therapeutically intended (e.g., the clinic) but from operations whose intentions were quite different.

13. For details, see T. J. Mallinson, "An Experimental Investigation of Group-Directed Discussion in the Classroom" (Ph.D. dissertation, Department of Psychology, University of Toronto, 1954); and J. R. Seeley and

T. J. Mallinson, "A Controlled Experiment in Group-Directed Discussion with Children" (unpublished paper, read at the 1951 meeting of the American Psychiatric Association).

14. One additional reason for the choice of our loose method may be given. It might have been easy to add to the sum of knowledge by repeating in essence and perhaps refining a type of study that had already been outstandingly well done, for example, in the Warner studies or those of the Lynds'. (See the "Yankee City Series" by W. L. Warner and Others, 4 volumes [New Haven: Yale University Press, 1941–1947]; R. S. Lynd and H. M. Lynd, *Middletown: A Study in Contemporary American Culture* [New York: Harcourt, Brace and Company, 1929]; R. S. Lynd and H. M. Lynd, *Middletown in Transition: A Study in Cultural Conflicts* [New York: Harcourt, Brace and Company, 1937].) But since we wished to see what would emerge on the basis of a less structured approach, we accepted cheerfully the risk that the data would seem to many to be less objective, the findings less secure, and the methods sufficiently old-fashioned to be reminiscent of earlier work in anthropology. We had weighed the risk of securing highly reliable data, by approved methods, on relatively narrow or already well explored problems, against the risk of making a wider, looser cast, and securing thereby materials which, if more dubious, might have more general interest and importance—and we had chosen the latter. Whether or not this was a wise decision can only be evaluated on the basis of the report.

15. One member of the research team has pointed to the fact that every interview is a social situation, as well as a mode of scientific investigation, and has made a preliminary analysis, applicable to his portion of the volume, of what were the expectations and rewards, on the part of researcher and subject, and how these would tend to affect the data secured. N. W. Bell, "Family Reactions to Strain: The Impact of the Genesis and Treatment of Social and Emotional Problems in Children" (Master's thesis, Department of Political Economy, University of Toronto, 1953).

16. J. R. Seeley, "Social Science in Social Action," *Canadian Journal of Economics and Political Science* (Toronto), vol. XVII (1951), pp. 84–89.

17. See Acknowledgments for list of contributory studies.

18. E. W. Loosley, "The Home and School Association as a Socializing Agency in an Upper-Middle-Class Canadian Community" (Master's thesis, Department of Education, Division of the Social Sciences, University of Chicago, 1952), pp. ii-iii.

19. Thus in addition to obtaining the obvious, hoped-for products of research—new knowledge for the researchers—the researchers are also psychologically and socially altered, sometimes quite radically, in the research experience. They also ". . . cannot step into the same river twice."

Even in studying an animal population, a sensitive researcher might not remain untouched, by virtue of his community of nature with the remaining animal world. A student studying a culture largely alien to his own is often touched, in a quite sensible degree, as the evidence, not to mention the behavior, of many anthropologists attests. When the student of human life moves on to the study of his own culture, in general; and from there to the study of the sub-culture of the social class which he shares; and from

there to that liberal-intellectual segment of the sub-culture which is nearest
his own in moral space, he comes perilously close to studying himself—with
all the explosive, and revelatory, risks of this kind of study.

It is just such a study that is here reported.

And it is, moreover, a critical study—perhaps a pitilessly critical study;
this means that it has been attended, for the researchers, with all the
pain that a rigorously critical study of the individual self of the researcher
and the shared life of all of them would have had. In fact, as various
chapters of the volume show, the study of those others, "the community,"
has entailed direct, painful attention to what these selves, both researchers
and teachers, were actually doing. Here as there, we have tried to maintain
the rigorously critical stance.

Part of the stress has turned on the dual relationship of the researchers
and the "researchees" in such a study. Here is not the traditional anthropological risk of "going native"; the researchers *were* in varying degree
native to the culture they were studying. The problem, psychologically, was
to sustain the stress involved in treating critically, as mere research objects,
fellow human beings, who, by virtue of their very nature and the nature
of the researchers, could hardly be felt as less than friends. It might be
thought that such friendships could have been avoided, and should have
been both for the sake of scientific accuracy and for the sake of peace of
mind. It is doubtful if they could have been avoided altogether, though they
might well have been minimized. In any case, even if it had been possible,
it is far from certain scientific accuracy would have benefited: much of the
material secured could only have been secured in a social relation that was
genuinely one of friendship on both sides. People do not—indeed, cannot—
tell some things except in a context of mutual warmth and support. As
for peace of mind, it would undoubtedly have increased in the absence of
such strains; but, having cast doubt upon its claim to the status of a primary
value for others, we could not ethically make it a prime value in action for
ourselves.

Within this dual and straining relationship, confronted with contradictory
demand from the scientific ethic and the humane imperative, we have again
and again questioned the legitimacy of our procedure, with a very real
alternative open of destroying the manuscript before it saw the light of day.

Such drastic solutions were considered at three kinds of points: where
we were not sure, or not sufficiently sure of the *accuracy* of our observations;
where, reasonably sure of our accuracy, we were sharply aware of our
critical bias, and therefore doubtful of the fairness or *justice* of our report;
and where, reasonably confident of both, we feared the effect on the community of the material revealed, and doubted, therefore, the *wisdom* of the
revelation.

Since we have published, it must be concluded that we have resolved our
doubts, but this is not wholly the case. Doubts about accuracy have been
handled by indicating as far as possible in the text where our uncertainties
lay. Doubts about justice cannot wholly be laid, and indeed it must be
emphasized that this is a *critical* study, and hence, if mistaken for a rounded
picture, by that *méprise*, unjust. Doubts about wisdom are not wholly
allayed, but we have taken a calculated risk, not under-sensitized but

rather over-sensitized by the knowledge that it was with other people's lives and relations, as well as our own, that we tampered. Since we were willing to run the risk for ourselves, we would have felt it arrogant to assume that others would be incapable of dealing with, or unwilling to face, the problems that thus arise.

Of one defect, greater than all others, we have been conscious. On the basis of our experience we have long felt, as indicated earlier, that research of this kind carries with it an implication of responsibility for social therapeutics. The "research" design—or rather the whole social action design which includes the research—should have made provision for a period of "working through" with the community the meaning, intellectual and emotional, of the report upon it. A very partial working-out was had in the course of the Project with a few people on a few points. Fully carried out, we are sure, accuracy would have been increased, the risk of serious injustice reduced, and the wisdom of revelation justified in the very act. That provision for such a process was lacking reflects upon our foresight and indicates how little consideration has so far been given to the place of scientific research in human affairs.

Whether or not the foregoing reasoning, which consoled us, will comfort others we do not know, but we would raise as a question what one of the authors set forth as a statement in another connection. Is it not true that if we ". . . should amputate our writing arms and seal our reluctant lips, the field would fall to the quack and the charlatan, and the principal difference would be that . . . self-consciousness would be worse-founded and more misleading"? If the answer is yes, then, despite error, bias, and folly, we may rest confident in having chosen at least the lesser of the two evils.

20. This is a source of distortion analytically separable from but not empirically independent of the biases discussed earlier.

2. SPACE

1. The area of Crestwood Heights is 1.48 square miles. The density of population for the municipality was 11,414.56 in 1941, and 10,341.22 in 1951.

2. L. J. Chapman and D. F. Putnam, *The Physiography of Southern Ontario* (Toronto: University of Toronto Press, 1951), p. 86.

3. E. C. Guillet, *Early Life in Upper Canada* (Toronto: Ontario Publishing Co., Limited, 1933), pp. 382–386.

4. S. D. Clark, *The Social Development of Canada* (Toronto: University of Toronto Press, 1942), pp. 204–307.

5. C. B. Sissons, *Egerton Ryerson: His Life and Letters* (Toronto: Clarke, Irwin & Company Limited, 1937), vol. I, pp. 17–18, 312–353.

6. Where no other sources are cited, information was derived from officials of the municipal office, older residents of the area, and metropolitan newspaper files.

7. The student of urban sociology might be interested in comparing the inverted T pattern of growth with the commonly accepted notion that the growth extends outward from the original center in concentric circles. Cf. R. E. Park, E. W. Burgess and R. D. McKenzie, *The City* (Chicago: University of Chicago Press, 1925), pp. 47–62.

8. M. H. Staples, *The Challenge of Agriculture: The Story of the United Farmers of Ontario* (Toronto: George N. Morang, 1921); W. L. Morton, *The Progressive Party in Canada*, in the series "Social Credit in Alberta: Its Background and Development" (Toronto: University of Toronto Press, 1950).

9. The teachers in Birch Prep are well aware of the southernmost enclave, since many of its children are conspicuous among the children of Crestwood's wealthiest families. The assessment departments in the Town Hall were quick to identify the two houses which were evaluated in the 1941 census at less than $500.

10. One of the issues around which the argument for a separate organization was waged had to do with snow-plowing the roads, and the municipal office still exhibits photographs of the roads prior to and after the municipal organization which demonstrate the superiority of the service the municipality was prepared to render the resident in this respect. These photographs, in a sense, symbolize the justification of the municipality since its inception.

11. If Crestwood Heights had been a zone in a larger municipality, the large assessments and consequent large contributions to municipal expenses which derive from heavy industry would have benefited the owner of the large home. But as long as Crestwood Heights was primarily occupied by large houses, and as long as the property owner absorbed many of his own costs (including the sending of his children to private schools), the absence of industrial assessments was not felt. And the exclusion of industry was, of course, necessary to protect residential property values. When, however, the municipality became more densely populated by persons of more modest financial means, the demand for services (schools, library, police protection, and the like) was greatly extended. The costs of these became staggering in the years following World War II, mounting to a point where Crestwood taxes were about as high as those of Big City.

12. For instance, in 1941 Crestwood Heights had a population 89.04 per cent non-Jewish and 10.96 Jewish in religion. In 1951 the percentages were, respectively, 60.32 and 39.68; in Big City for the same year the population was 93.35 per cent non-Jewish and 6.65 Jewish in religion. SOURCE: *Eighth Census of Canada 1941* (Ottawa: Queen's Printer, 1944) and *Ninth Census of Canada 1951* (Ottawa: Queen's Printer, 1953).

13. Persons from so-called ethnic groups, the largest of which was the Jewish, were neither excluded brusquely nor accepted warmly. They were sufficiently accepted, especially in school and Home and School affairs, to be criticized by Gentiles, and even by themselves, for having a separate religious and cultural existence. Yet in the outer world of the metropolis and nation, especially in the face of the policies of downtown clubs and golf clubs, they were impressed with the need for the comfort and protection that such separate organization affords.

14. The school system provides another example of duality. In it, an effort was made to duplicate all the advantages to be derived from attendance at a private school. The school was public and available to all—all, that is, who could buy property in Crestwood Heights. The exclusiveness thus afforded is thought to be praiseworthy, for it is recognized that children

should have congenial surroundings and "suitable" friends, but to go beyond this to the additional exclusiveness afforded by the private school is considered by many residents blameworthy.

3. SHELTER

1. We are indebted to Morgan for his pioneering interest in shelter, and to Malinowski for showing how an exploration of the meaning and function of artifacts can be helpful to the social investigator. Cf. L. H. Morgan, *Houses and House-Life of the American Aborigines*, "Contributions to North American Ethnology," vol. IV (United States, Department of the Interior, Geographical and Geological Survey of the Rocky Mountain Region; Washington: Government Printing Office, 1881); and B. Malinowski, *A Scientific Theory of Culture and Other Essays* (Chapel Hill: University of North Carolina Press, 1944).

2. The size of house is indicative of the importance placed upon domicile in the Crestwood system of values. A fifth of the houses owned in Crestwood Heights have ten rooms or more (as compared with 6.5 per cent in Big City). Only 7.1 per cent have less than six rooms (as compared with 16.2 per cent in Big City). More than 88 per cent of Crestwood Heights homeowners have oil heat. There is also a higher proportion of "living conveniences" (such as powered washing-machines, electric vacuum cleaners, telephones, radios, passenger automobiles) in Crestwood Heights than in Big City. SOURCE: *Ninth Census of Canada 1951* (Ottawa: Queen's Printer, 1953) vol. III, Tables 14, 24, 26, 40, 42, 85.

3. We have no data on the number of mortgage-free homes. The number of references we heard to the amount of family income required by the house, and to the extravagance of those (usually not the speakers) who had bought more expensive homes than they could afford, suggests that the proportion of houses with clear title is small.

4. The annual average temperature is 44.4° Fahrenheit, with a mean temperature of 23.4° for winter, 41.0° for spring, 64.8° for summer, and 45.5° for autumn. Temperature ranges from 103.2° to −26.5° F. Technically the climate is "temperate" perhaps, but it is rather rigorous.

5. One important exception to this rule is the fur coat; when not in use it is serviced and stored outside the home by a commercial furrier.

6. Cf. A. Bertram, *The House, a Machine for Living In: A Summary of the Art and Science of Homemaking Considered Functionally* (London: A. & C. Black Ltd., 1935).

7. Cf. A. I. Hallowell, "The Nature and Function of Property as a Social Institution," *Journal of Legal and Political Sociology* (New York), vol. I (1943), pp. 115–138; and R. F. Benedict, *Patterns of Culture* (Boston: Houghton Mifflin Company, 1934), pp. 181 *et seq.*

8. For a description of the potlatch as a primitive ceremonial, see R. F. Benedict, *Patterns of Culture*, pp. 184–211.

9. The house is not the only stage on which hospitality is enacted but techniques of entertaining are much the same whether the home, the club, or the exclusive restaurant is the chosen field of display. Moreover, decorative features of the one may carry over to the other. The bar, for instance, which

is an increasingly prominent feature of restaurant and club, is often repro-
duced, in miniature, as part of the rumpus room. In the club setting, however, it is the fact of membership which is brought into prominence; in the
case of the home, it is the amenities of the house.

10. There are certain situations of ungraded intimacy, for instance service
club meetings, office parties, and community rallies, but these are rare and of
a ceremonial nature. A man's work downtown, even though he may be
guarded by a secretary, does expose him to jostling in elevators and the
importunities of salesmen and colleagues.

11. These gradients of privacy are clearly recognized by all. The door
of the bathroom, to which the visitor has right of access, is locked, even
though the occupant may be innocently washing his hands. The bedroom
which the visitor has no right to enter is less tightly sealed, although the
body is more likely to be naked and interpersonal intimacies are more
likely to occur here than in the bathroom.

12. Even the stranger has easier access to some aspects of this private
area than another member of the family. For instance, the milkman may
know where the household money is kept, and be better aware than the
father how much is left in the "kitty" at the end of the month, precisely
because the information means very little to him.

13. The lack of "responsibility" in and towards the home on the part of
the teenager is a common topic for discussion among Crestwood parents.

14. A casual survey of the "better homes" type of magazine will reveal
that more than one or two children are seldom shown in the advertisements
or in the illustrated stories.

15. See C. Lewis, *Children of the Cumberland* (New York: Columbia
University Press, 1946).

4. TIME

1. See A. Korzybski, *Science and Sanity: An Introduction to Non-
Aristotelian Systems and General Semantics* (3rd ed., Lakeville, Conn.:
International Non-Aristotelian Library Publishing Co.; Institute of General
Semantics, 1948); E. E. Evans-Pritchard, *The Nuer: A Description of the
Modes of Livelihood and Political Institutions of a Nilotic People* (Oxford:
At the Clarendon Press, 1940), pp. 94–138; E. R. Leach, "Cronus and
Chronos," *Explorations: Studies in Culture and Communication* (Toronto),
no. 1 (December, 1953), pp. 15–23. The authors are also indebted to
Professor E. S. Carpenter of the University of Toronto for access to his as
yet unpublished study of time and the cosmological concepts of the Eskimo,
and for his help in connection with this chapter.

2. E. A. Evans-Pritchard in his description of the Nuer has this to say
of "time" in their world (*The Nuer*, p. 103):

Though I have spoken of time and units of time the Nuer have no expression
equivalent to "time" in our language, and they cannot, therefore, as we can,
speak of time as though it were something actual, which passes, can be wasted,
can be saved, and so forth. I do not think that they ever experienced the same
feeling of fighting against time or of having to coordinate activities with an
abstract passage of time, because their points of reference are mainly the activities
themselves, which are generally of a leisurely character. Events follow a logical

order, but they are not controlled by an abstract system, there being no autonomous points of reference to which activities have to conform with precision. Nuer are fortunate.

3. Cf. H. Miner, *St. Denis: A French-Canadian Parish* (Chicago: University of Chicago Press, 1939), pp. 141–232; C. M. Arensberg and S. T. Kimball, *Family and Community in Ireland* (Cambridge, Mass.: Harvard University Press, 1940).

4. The continued financial dependence upon the parent of the "child" until he is long past puberty, and the growing reluctance of parents and insurance companies to permit a young man or woman the use of the automobile, are but two examples of the absence of recognition of the significance of puberty as a life-stage. For further discussion, see the chapter on "Age."

5. There is one case on record of a man who collects and repairs clocks. Regardless of the obvious utility of the hobby in later life, and in spite of its value as a means of conspicuous display, men in Crestwood Heights have much difficulty in finding a suitable hobby. Even if a hobby is selected and pursued there is the problem of feeling right about it. One hears of men who shift restlessly from sailing boats to sport cars, from trotting horses to pedigreed cattle, or from fly casting to photography. In the pursuit of the hobby, which often calls for a reckless waste of time and money, there are serious psychological, and sometimes financial, obstacles. Indeed, it is difficult to see how it could be otherwise. These career-directed men have been formed in a process that grants a sense of peace only in the midst of strife, that permits the feeling of rest only when effort is being "fruitfully" expended. So formed, they must work at their leisure—without the compensation of being able to idle at their work.

6. This section refers only to the work day, not to the daily round on vacation or weekend.

7. This description is an extension of the notion put forward by E. C. Hughes of the University of Chicago, that one man's crisis is another man's routine. For instance, according to Hughes, a major operation is a personal and familial crisis, but it is part of a day's work for the surgeon and hospital staff. In Crestwood Heights the delivery man's routine is the housewife's crisis.

8. Sometimes these decisions are not so minor. The efforts the school makes to adapt to special needs, to preserve some freedom within order, are often heroic.

9. Again if he "goes too far" the school will attempt to protect him, if his parents do not.

10. There is, of course, much variation: some men return to the office regularly over the weekend, some bring work home with them at night and over the weekend. A difference between the sexes is evident, especially in maidless homes. Where there is adequate domestic help, the mother will follow the male pattern more closely. If there are young children, the father may assume somewhat more responsibility for their care.

11. Individual and family patterns vary markedly. There are some activities appropriate to this time of year which draw the family together and which may be repeated year after year: a picnic in the country, a weekend

up north, opening up the cottage, a Sunday drive to see the spring blossoms, and gardening—if the latter is not done by a professional gardener under contract.

12. Jewish families sometimes encounter an additional difficulty in establishing a regular summer activity, owing to restrictions in many hotels and summer colonies.

13. Even more attenuated and continuous is the series of proclaimed days, weeks, and months: "Education Week," "Restaurant Week," "Children's Day," etc.

14. There are special problems for the Jewish parent whose child demands full-scale and nearly simultaneous celebration of Christmas and a newly elaborated Chanukah.

15. There are many types of observance and celebration of the year's end in Crestwood Heights. Since the purpose here is merely to demonstrate the relation of these rites to the concept of time, the Jewish, fundamentalist Christian, and Roman Catholic ceremonial are, for lack of space, omitted.

16. Parents do not lie to their children about Santa Claus; after agreeing that he does not exist, they continue to refer to him as though he did.

17. We deal exclusively with secular New Year's Eve celebrations. For a *few*, New Year's Eve is still a time for reflection and prayer and New Year's Day an occasion for visiting and feasting, but the shift is rapidly towards noise-making.

18. Santa Claus appears to be an increasingly tawdry and pathetic figure in *New Yorker* cartoons, but it should be noted that a widespread outcry arose a few years ago when a prominent psychiatrist, then Canada's Deputy Minister of Health, was thought to have condemned the Santa Claus legend. Much of the excitement centered around the allegation that his sentiments were actually anti-religious. Cf. G. B. Chisholm, "Tell Them the Truth," as reported by B. Fraser, *Maclean's* (Montreal), January 15, 1946, pp. 9, 42–44; and G. B. Chisholm, "The Reestablishment of Peacetime Society," *Psychiatry* (Washington, D.C.), vol. IX (1946), pp. 3–20.

5. AGE

1. Clinic cases drew enough such reluctant admissions, however, to suggest that many children were unwanted—planned for or not.

2. M. Mead, *Male and Female: A Study of the Sexes in a Changing World* (New York: William Morrow & Co., 1949), pp. 51–160.

3. This situation is in marked contrast with that existing in many a primitive society, where the newborn infant is differentiated only slowly from the mother and the kinship group closely surrounding him.

4. In the Crestwood culture, ". . . the nuclear family is dependent for its (temporary) persistence and institutionally required dissolution on a process of socialization which allows children as well as parents to do without each other." K. D. Naegele, "Hostility and Aggression in Middle Class American Families" (Doctor's dissertation, Department of Social Relations, Harvard University, 1952), p. 142.

5. Even where a maid or housekeeper is employed full time, she seldom remains long, seldom assumes the supportive role of a "Nanny."

6. From the child-rearing experts she has learned the great importance attached to this physical contact, both for good and for ill. Too much may bind the child to her forever and restrict his psychosexual development; too little may make him insecure and "mentally ill" as an adult. Cf. J. R. Seeley, "Bali-like treatment of Children in Crestwood Heights" (listed among contributory studies in "Acknowledgments").

7. Advertisements for a well-known line of educational toys stress the value of "learning while playing."

8. See M. Mead, *And Keep Your Powder Dry: An Anthropologist Looks at America* (New York: William Morrow and Co., 1942).

9. W. A. Davis and R. J. Havighurst, *Father of the Man: How Your Child Gets His Personality* (Boston: Houghton Mifflin Company, 1947), pp. 171–172, 207.

10. Children at a later stage of growth, in the Project-sponsored Human Relations classes in the Crestwood schools, expressed resentment that there was "no place to play" in Crestwood Heights. The slum child, also an urban resident, would not make the same complaint, since he aggressively takes over the whole of his neighborhood as play space.

11. The freedom, of course, always entails careful supervision, and follows upon the selection by adults of what is considered workable and appropriate for the nursery school group.

12. The afore-mentioned "messy" materials—clay, plasticene, finger paint —as well as play-acting, may serve as outlets for the "sublimation" of aggression not allowed expression in other areas.

13. A photograph in a local newspaper bore the following caption: "Tots GRADUATE. Wearing caps and gowns are 27 five-year-olds in front of Marillac Social Center's school in Chicago for graduation from Tiny Tots Town into kindergarten. Children are prepared for kindergarten in Tiny Tots Town." *Globe and Mail* (Toronto), September 1, 1952, p. 8. In the nursery school, the child talks of "juniors" and "seniors," just as later in kindergarten he talks of the "older children," the "younger ones," or contemptuously of "babies," and even of "failing."

14. If she is desired as a teacher, but not as a person, conflict may be set up early in grade school between desires for "success" and desires for comfort. Desire for success bulks large for even the kindergarten child; pupils in the earliest grades fearfully discuss the possibility of "failure." (Father's comment on his child's behavior, while a pupil in Birch Prep.)

15. One mother reported that during his first months at kindergarten her small son fell into a puddle on his way to school. Since he had no other snowsuit, his mother drove him to school in his wet suit, with the intention of handing him over immediately to his teacher. The child worried all the way to school: "Mr. A. [the Principal] won't LET you in the school! I HAVE to stay outside and play until the bell rings!" His mother attempted to explain that rules did not matter in an emergency, but her remarks had no effect whatever. When she stopped the car in the school yard, the child tried to run away. A group of children gathered in consternation, asking "What's wrong, B.?" The mother felt most hard-hearted as she propelled B. into the school. His teacher happened to be passing. She took in the situation at once, and escorted B. into the classroom to take off his wet clothes. A

few months previously, this child (a nursery school product) would not have objected to entering the school at any hour, with or without an adult, as his mother emphasized.

16. Since adult approval is the most potent incentive towards learning acceptable patterns of social behavior, particularly at this age level, the size of classes, increased by the high post-war birth-rate, would appear to have some direct bearing on the socialization process.

17. That this happens early is witnessed by the comment of a little kindergarten girl to her teacher after being pushed by a male class-mate, "Miss X., some boys are just *born* babies!"

18. The description of a first-year Crestwood Heights university student (female) of student-teacher relationships at the collegiate level underlines the difference between the elementary and secondary schools:

It requires little or no effort on the part of the student to become a good friend of one of his teachers. He does not have to be a member of this particular teacher's class. The student need only be registered at the school. Of course, as in any relationship, he must have the desire to become friends with an individual. And if this desire is latent, more than likely the teacher or teachers will find it and do more than their share to initiate the friendship. Often a certain teacher can become a second mother or father to the pupil. This is a wonderful experience, so long as the teacher's importance to the boy or girl is secondary to that of his or her parents. A student feels free to discuss practically every aspect of his life with his teacher. He will learn to confide in his teacher and to consider him as one of his very close friends. I myself developed such a relationship with one of my teachers. After school was over, providing I had no meeting or game to attend, I would go into his classroom and talk to him for hours, as I would with a good friend. This friendship grew from my first year in high school until now. Although I no longer attend collegiate, I try to keep in touch with my teachers and I miss their companionship very much.

This would appear to be more an experience of adolescence (and even then somewhat uncommon) than of the age group five-to-twelve.

19. Contrast the situation in Birmingham, England, where there are four teachers to every thirty children in the nursery classes attached to Infants' Schools. *Globe and Mail* (Toronto), April 10, 1953, p. 6.

20. One researcher reported a conversation with a Crestwood Heights mother in which she described how her five-year-old daughter would lay out at bed-time the dress and accessories to be worn the next day. If a hair ribbon happened to be rumpled, the child would iron it. Cf., also, reference above (note 13) to news photography of pre-school children in caps and gowns at Marillac Social Center nursery school, Chicago.

21. It is important also to note the rapid tempo of the planned activities of the child in this age group. The time diaries, kept for research purposes on an hourly basis by children in grades throughout the school system, demonstrate a tightly packed series of organized activities; spontaneous play is minimal.

22. In a Human Relations class (Grade VI) this topic came up for discussion:

. . . there was more talk about the game and with much giggling. R. told that it was Spinning the Bottle. Evidently there is some kissing connected with it. They are only supposed to kiss on the hand, but some of the boys kissed right up the arm to the cheek! It was out! This was the game about which there were so many guilt feelings. Someone suggested that they should plan their parties and avoid this game.

23. C. M. Tryon, "Evaluations of Adolescent Personality by Adolescents," in *Child Behavior and Development: A Course of Representative Studies*, ed. R. G. Barker, J. S. Kounin, and H. F. Wright (New York: McGraw-Hill Book Company, Inc., 1943), pp. 545–566.

24. It should be noted, however, that women's work in the home, which may actually be more laborious, is not "work" to the boys and men. If the psychological criterion for work is used (i.e., effort or negatively toned tension) both boys and girls are destined to "work" nearly all their lives in both work and leisure portions of the day.

25. An interesting detail is that children themselves do not want parents to teach them to drive. This view was presented in a Human Relations class:

Most children don't want their parents to teach them to drive. Parents expect too much—they're too impatient. There was a chorus of "That's right!"

This attitude is evident not only about learning to drive, but about many other skills which children would prefer to acquire from someone other than the parents. Almost anyone else will do, even a person of less competence. It is also curious that women, by their own wish, would rather be taught to drive by someone other than a husband or male relative; they express first preference for a commercial service. The inner meaning of this disposition is conjectural. At least, it helps to open a profitable market to the male expert, even though it gives cause for understandable male jealousy in the husband.

26. Here again is the tendency, in the face of the universally accepted and perhaps unfounded belief that females mature earlier than males, to permit boys earlier access to adult privileges such as smoking and heterosexual experience. It was a girl who blandly put forward this view in the discussion quoted. The same girl will, in all likelihood, concurrently or later, fight a desperate ideological battle for equality of male and female.

27. In a discussion parents gave recognition to the favored position of these children:

Mrs. J. wondered if the parents weren't to blame for not giving the children enough responsibility. Everything was given to them—they didn't have to work for a thing. . . . Mrs. P. said: "They don't even want anything very badly." "Perhaps that's because they get things before they even know they want them," Mrs. J. replied.

28. The researcher might have asked what "spoiling" means since, of course, it is a more nebulous concept than the above ideas connote.

29. This is, of course, a third or fourth-hand parroting of one of the distinguishing views of "progressive" educators.

30. This statement is overwhelmingly significant, in view of the strenuous efforts made by family and school to ensure glad acceptance of responsibility as one important means to the good and the happy life.

31. Cf. T. Parsons, "Age and Sex in the Social Structure of the United States," in *Personality in Nature, Society and Culture*, ed. C. Kluckhohn and H. A. Murray (2nd ed., New York: Alfred A. Knopf, 1953), pp. 365–367; and M. Mead, "Administrative Contributions to Democratic Character Formation at the Adolescent Level," *ibid.*, pp. 665–666.

32. See Appendix 2, "Why I Stick to the City."

33. See Appendix 2, "The Magic of a Tooth."

34. "Imitation" is here used in its strictest sense. The boy must not repeat the father's *real* struggles with their real benefits, and losses. His efforts can have only symbolic reference to the earlier trials experienced by his father in much the same way as the candyless Lent is now but an attenuated shadow of the original forty-day fast. Indeed, this whole mechanism of imitation might be termed "participant magic."

35. Several children "ran away" in the course of the five-year Project, mostly girls! At least two "escaped" more realistically and permanently, one to Britain, the other to Palestine.

36. Note that "freedom" needs triple or quadruple consent: pupil, staff, peers, and parents.

6. CAREER

1. R. Chase (ed.), *The Jack Tales* (Boston: Houghton Mifflin Company, 1943).

2. Such an interpretation of the career could only be checked by watching one generation through all the stages of the career, rather than observing, as in this study, different generations in all the stages of the career.

3. Mobility has a somewhat different pattern among professional and executive people, but only in the sense that the executive is sent and the professional is "called." The executive operates within the orbit of "the firm"; his moves are in response to its needs. The professional senses in a new location an opportunity to serve or advance and seeks to establish himself in the new environment.

4. It should be noted that "bond" is the most popular term to describe meaningful social linkage, and this sociological terminology unconsciously reflects the contemporary notion that intimate social relationship implies constraint; so do such alternative words as "ties," "links," etc.

5. Emotionally, they are gypsies. It is perhaps a pity that their way of life calls for the accumulation of so much furniture. It is interesting to note that E. M. Forster, writing in 1910, made this comment in *Howard's End* about "moving":

The Age of Property holds bitter moments even for a proprietor. When a move is imminent, furniture becomes ridiculous. . . . It was absurd, if you came to think of it. . . . The feudal ownership of land did bring dignity, whereas the modern ownership of movables is reducing us again to a nomadic horde. We are reverting to the civilization of luggage, and historians of the future will note how the middle classes accreted possessions without taking root in the earth, and may find in this the secret of their imaginative poverty.

6. Competition as a form of behavior is found in all cultures, but in each it appears in a form peculiar to the group under observation.

7. Canadian Rugby football is derived from English Rugby football. Football was imported into the United States from McGill University by Harvard and Yale, the first game being played in 1874. Since this importation, an American game has developed with little resemblance to the original; from it Canadian Rugby football has recently adopted many rules

and play formations. For an early history of football see W. C. Camp and L. F. Deland, *Football* (Boston and New York: Houghton, Mifflin and Company, 1896); and for a suggestive treatment of football with the thought that it may yet be used as a means of acculturation as the world seeks the explanation of American military and financial successes on the playing fields of Notre Dame, see D. Riesman and R. Denney, "Football in America: A Study in Culture Diffusion," *American Quarterly* (University of Minnesota), vol. III (1951), pp. 309–325.

8. Note also the frequent identification of the moiety as one of two mutually exclusive divisions of a group which is made in the social organization of primitive societies. They are frequently concerned with ritual and games. Cf. E. D. Chapple and C. S. Coon, *Principles of Anthropology* (New York: Henry Holt and Company, 1942), pp. 321–322; and, for a discussion of symbols and techniques of competition, pp. 614–628.

9. The pair is, of course, a universal social form, for as Simmel says, "The fact that male and female strive after their mutual union is the foremost example or primordial image of a dualism which stamps our life-contents generally." *The Sociology of Georg Simmel,* trans. and ed. K. H. Wolff (Glencoe, Ill.: Free Press, 1950), p. 128.

10. Such restraint is found even in the vastly more expressive culture of the Kwakiutl. Cf. R. F. Benedict, *Patterns of Culture* (Boston and New York: Houghton Mifflin Company, 1934), pp. 173–222.

11. The boxer, on the other hand shakes hands with himself after the victory; but then boxing is not a Crestwood game.

12. The objective facts as they are contained in census reports are known.

13. Two voluminous files of items which bear out this contention were collected during the research. The files include obituaries of Crestwood residents, newspaper biographies, news items honoring some Crestwood person, and classroom projects such as that of a teacher who provided pupils with the names of nineteen residents, most of them successful business men, along with the question, "Why are these men important?" (The phrasing of the question reveals the unconscious indoctrination which often occurs in the classroom. The question is certainly tendentious; "Why are they prominent?" might have provoked some genuine social insight.)

14. His anxiety about his preferred position may also stem from the fact that parents are reluctant to give the child everything he wants, not because the money is lacking but because they are afraid of "spoiling" the child. The child "earns his way" by arguing lustily for what he wants, but in the process it is often his enjoyment of the thing won that is spoiled.

15. Capital distribution will come much later when the adult's own old age security has been assured.

16. A placard in a store window in Crestwood Heights announced, "All women will be made equal." The word "created" had been stroked out from the old manifesto and "made" substituted—a new type of brassière was for sale.

17. The parent who cannot refuse on the grounds of poverty often has little defence from the demands of the child; since the child's happiness is a chief parental aspiration, it is hard to refuse his demands, supported as they often are by authoritative recommendations from other parents, from experts

(in the name of character-building—another aspiration), and from still others who are selling skills with that blend of genteel indifference and bland enthusiasm which befits those whose clients are prosperous.

18. M. Mead, "Growing Up in New Guinea," *From the South Seas: Studies of Adolescence and Sex in Primitive Societies* (New York: William Morrow & Co., 1939), pp. 118–134.

19. The similarities and differences might be underlined. The Manus seem to have one major adjustment to make at the time of marriage and the establishment of a family. At the same time occupational adjustments are also made. In short, the individual passes from childhood to adulthood in one step without, it appears, preparation in one status for life in the next. The Crestwood child, in contrast, has many such experiences, as we saw when we examined the age-grading structure. The independence which parents encourage in the child tends, as in the Manus, to screen the new status from him. The screening appears not to be so effective nor adjustment to new roles as difficult as with the Manus except possibly in the case of parenthood; the Crestwood child becomes parent himself with little fore-warning and little preparation. *Ibid.*, pp. 204–210.

20. This type of thinking might be explained as a reflection of the shrinking frontier and the disappearance of the so-called self-made man. Not many boys in Crestwood Heights are likely to be able at career's end to consider themselves self-made successes. Whether or not they would welcome a destiny of prominence and greatness if they could be assured otherwise of financial security and physical comfort, must be an un-answered question.

21. It is noteworthy that the yearbook of a boys' boarding school, which many Crestwood boys attend, covers these entries neatly with a single heading: "Chosen Profession." In the select boarding school, it appears, the future should be and is settled before college entrance; and the choice, even if it is "stock-broker," is by definition a profession.

22. This careful balancing is closely linked to the contemporary notion of maturity which Crestwood teachers and parents hold as an ideal. Similar reticence is manifested earlier and later in "window shopping": the child who finds himself in front of a candy counter with his allowance in his pocket must learn, if he is to achieve "maturity," that it is not only bad for his health and ruinous to his allowance, but also "wrong," if he "buys everything in sight."

23. Indeed, a teacher frequently "encourages" backward or lazy students by telling them of the success in adult life of former students whose academic work was *not* above reproach.

24. For the professional man, this period includes the internship, the certification as specialist and the building of a practice. The terms apply best to a doctor or dentist, but the structure of the situation is similar for the other professions, such as teaching and social work.

25. We refer here to travel in a professional setting. The travel of the tourist except on an easily justified and well-planned holiday is for the younger man considered frivolous, even though such an experience can later be used for prestige-making conversational coin.

26. Interestingly, this successful salesman has no thought of his own son becoming a salesman. He has stated emphatically that his son is to enter one of the professions. The basis for this decision would seem to be partly the boy's personality. The boy's temperament, experience, and outlook on life seem at the moment in conflict with the behavior adjustments the father developed in order to achieve his business success. More important, though, the father thought a professional man had more prestige; and, moreover, he could provide the means (with a rueful look backwards at his own parents' financial limitations) which would permit a higher occupational status for his son. Whether the son was permitted to choose his own career, and if so, how, is not known.

27. Cf. W. H. Whyte Jr., "The Wives of Management," *Fortune* (New York), vol. XLIV (1951), pp. 86-88, 204-213, and W. H. Whyte Jr., "The Corporation and the Wife," *ibid.*, pp. 109-111, 150-158.

28. Outside the classroom, differences are often recognized. Some sports exhibit the two types of male-female relations manifest in Crestwood Heights. In football, the aggressive and muscular attributes of masculinity are on display: the male capacity to organize a group strategy against opponents, to seek victory within not too well defined moral limits by the exercise of cunning, surprise, and force, to establish impregnable defence, and marshal fierce, heroic attack—these are evident features of the game. Tennis, in contrast, offers a situation where both sexes interact on a basis approaching equality. There are few men today who can maintain an air of gallant chivalry with a member of the opposite sex on the tennis court, if this behavior requires that he give his fair opponent easy serves. Costumes, equipment, rules are identical or nearly so for the two sexes, and most men expect their partners, regardless of their sex, to give a good stiff match. The relation in tennis is typical of many situations where men and women interact on almost equal terms, or assume roles which are interchangeable. But there are many other situations, perhaps diminishing and therefore requiring ceremonial attention, where the roles are rigidly differentiated. That these differences are not recognized in school and college contributes to a dilemma in the woman's realization of a career.

29. They feel that the human body should be exposed in the privacy of the home without too much inhibition. Such exposure, of course, also helps to inform the child of biological *differences,* and therefore does in the end encourage differentiation rather than identification.

30. In the few cases observed, it was difficult to tell from the record whether the adult was really shocked, or merely affected to be so out of ritual necessity.

31. The girl can, before puberty, do boyish things without much censure; as she approaches puberty she will, if she continues, be labelled a tomboy and submitted increasingly to teasing and other measures of social control. After puberty, a number of alternatives are permitted. The girl can no longer play hockey on a boys' team, if she ever did. But she can play hockey with other girls, though the hilarity with which boys observe this activity indicates how jealously male territory is guarded.

32. This is a quite remarkable view, incidentally, in a community where

every year age-graded practices are encouraged in or yielded to younger
and younger children, i.e. everything from late bed-time to petting is
"started earlier."

33. "Going steady" is, nevertheless, another of the perennial sources of
wonder and "can't understand why . . ." among Crestwood parents and
teachers.

34. There is evidence also that the consumption of automobiles follows
a curve related to social status. Up to a certain point in the class structure,
the newest, shiniest, most costly car is desired and secured. Above this
level, the automobile is regarded with increasing indifference. A shabby big
car, or a cheap efficient small one, perhaps a British product, is then the
symbol of status at this higher level.

7. THE FAMILY

1. The material in this chapter is based largely on work done by Norman
W. Bell, in the Crestwood Heights Project, and adapted from a document
"The Social Structure of the Middle Class Family."

2. The living pattern of the ideal-typical Victorian family was relatively
clearly defined and at least on the surface was supposed to present a united
front. This cohesion was particularly symbolized by two areas of the house.
In place of the immaculate, somewhat empty food laboratory of Crestwood
Heights, there was the large, comfortable Victorian kitchen, boasting no
gay color scheme, but somehow close and familiar, with its wooden table
scrubbed to creamy white, its black, hooded range throwing out heat and
the savory smells of cooking, its countless gleaming pans and ladles, its bustle
of activity from early morning to late evening, as cook and housemaids
prepared and served all the food consumed by a family of perhaps ten
persons. In contrast to the breakfast nook of Crestwood Heights, shining
with chrome and plastic, or the dining alcove, where small table and chairs
blend into the furnishings of the living-room, the Victorian household made
the dining-room, with its long table draped in damask and solidly set three
times a day with heavy silver and English china, the very center and core
of family life. In such a setting, there could be no doubt that the Victorian
family was a cohesive group, with common interests, in which the members
interacted continuously with one another in a framework of stable routine
symbolized by food shared in common, among other things. What internal
divisions, hypocrisy, or double standards of behavior there were, were kept
carefully below the surface level of convention.

3. See J. R. Seeley, "Parents, the Last Proletariat" (unpublished, 1952).

4. In 1951 there were 4,130 families in the community, comprising
13,301 persons—87 per cent of the total population. In Big City, 79 per
cent of the population lived in family groups. Canada, Bureau of Statistics,
Ninth Census of Canada 1951 (Ottawa: Queen's Printer, 1953), Bulletin
3-1, Table 129.

5. A recent article in a well-known Canadian periodical emphasizes this
particular point. F. Bodsworth, "Christianity—Revival or Decline,"
Maclean's (Montreal), December 15, 1953, pp. 9-12, 57-65.

6. L. F. Maltby, "Report on Work of the Clinical Team, Crestwood Heights Schools' Child Guidance Services" (Typewritten report, submitted to the Department of Psychiatry, University of Big City), pp. 120–149.

7. Premarital continence or care is still the ideal, since illegitimacy, later legalized by marriage, is specifically mentioned as one important cause of family discord, particularly between husband and wife.

8. L. F. Maltby, "Report on Work of the Clinical Team, Crestwood Heights Schools' Child Guidance Services," pp. 120–149.

9. *Ibid.*, p. 142.

10. *Ibid.*, p. 146.

11. These clinical findings would appear to indicate the transitional state of the cultural norms regulating family behavior; professional interest is not focused on the strains produced by over-indulgence and permissiveness, which seem to be closer to the approved norms than is the authoritarian pattern, but this omission is not entirely in accord with the findings of at least one other Big City psychiatrist working on the same problems: cf. D. Cappon, "Some Psychodynamic and Sociodynamic Aspects of the Limits of Freedom in Modern Man and His Society," a paper read before the Journal Club (Toronto Psychiatric Hospital), Department of Psychiatry, University of Toronto, January 13, 1953 (Typewritten document, Library, Toronto Psychiatric Hospital).

12. But no open force or coercion is applied by either father or mother. Whether or not the guilt of the children at the rejection of parental wishes is a more powerful coercion than the old authoritarian methods is not the essential point in this context.

13. In quite a few cases also, it was by a curious inversion held to include also strict "obedience," in the sense of mere "willingness" to suffer punishment for disobeying.

14. Subsequent interview material reveals that this wife still remains in ignorance of the exact amount of her husband's income, although she is now presumably responsible for spending part of it at least.

15. This is in direct contrast to the European pattern, where the head of the family, as one Hungarian woman phrased it, "hardly knows where the kitchen is."

16. Cf. D. F. Aberle and K. D. Naegele, "Middle-Class Fathers' Occupational Role and Attitudes towards Children," *American Journal of Orthopsychiatry*, vol. XXII (1952), pp. 366–78.

17. It is the sharing of the spending of the income with wife and children which permits some approximation of the ideal companionship between husband, wife, and children. But this, like the joint parental responsibility in child-rearing and household activities, is again particularly difficult for the man to actualize because of occupational demands. Nor do the experts contribute much towards clarification of the issue of family and occupation, since many merely stridently proclaim that the man must work hard at being a companion to his wife and a "pal" to his children—an effort to be made somehow over and above the effort expended on the career proper.

18. The librarian in a community comparable to Crestwood Heights remarked on the number of mothers who came every afternoon to the

library with their pre-school children "just for someone to talk to"; in their homes or immediate vicinity there are usually no older women of the kinship system to whom they may turn for support or advice, or with whom they may gossip or pass time.

19. Activities of a purely "social" nature are secondary to institutional activities in Crestwood Heights. No woman in this community, for example, could become outstanding simply as a brilliant hostess, or as one of the ten best-dressed women of Big City.

20. Cf. T. Parsons, "Age and Sex in the Social Structure of the United States," in *Personality in Nature, Society and Culture*, ed. C. Kluckhohn and H. A. Murray (2nd ed., New York: Alfred A. Knopf, 1953), pp. 363–375, and C. Thompson, "Cultural Pressures in the Psychology of Women," and "The Rôle of Women in This Culture," in *A Study of Interpersonal Relations: New Contributions to Psychiatry*, ed. P. Mullahy (New York: Hermitage Press, Inc., 1949), pp. 130–146, 147–161, as well as F. R. Kluckhohn, "The American Family: Past and Present," in *Patterns for Modern Living* (Chicago: Delphian Society, 1952).

21. M. A. Ribble, *The Rights of Infants: Early Psychological Needs and Their Satisfaction* (New York: Columbia University Press, 1943).

22. It is only very recently that articles in popular magazines have begun urging parents not to be afraid to say "No" to their children. Cf. D. A. Bloch, "Don't Be Afraid of Don't," *Reader's Digest*, December, 1953, pp. 177–181; H. Eustis, "How to Handle the Young Male," *ibid.*, August, 1953, pp. 50–52. The implication here is that children "really" want this firmness, respond to it, and like it.

23. Much of the advice handed to parents might be applicable to one-child families, derived as it is from an individualistically oriented psychology. Parental frustration often stems from the conflict between such injunctions once accepted and the obvious necessities of maintaining the family *as a system*—which the admonitions calmly disregard!

24. C. M. Arensberg and S. T. Kimball, *Family and Community in Ireland* (Cambridge, Mass.: Harvard University Press, 1940).

25. There are no "boys" of forty or older, without a shilling to call their own, in Crestwood Heights.

26. A lawyer's wife airily remarked that her husband's secretary "wouldn't let her have" a pair of expensive lamps she wished to buy.

27. This control over the girl's spending applies later when she is a married woman, dependent economically upon her husband, no matter how much of his income is delegated to her. One woman is held to her wifely role largely by her economic dependence upon her husband. A wife in Crestwood Heights is forced to consider a divorce carefully, since her living standard would be considerably decreased once the decree became final. The same controls may also extend to the children, subduing adolescent impulses to break away from the family before the socialization process has been completed.

28. This is one of the attitudes that probably discriminates between upper middle class and lower upper. The latter would have marked reservations were their children to undertake "servants' jobs."

29. Desertions of the children by father, mother, or both are uncommon (though not unknown) and it is significant that the community boasts no child welfare or other social services, all of which are handled on a township rather than a municipal basis. Thus it is tacitly accepted that Crestwood Heights, as a prosperous middle-class suburb, has no need of such services, although these are regarded by Crestwooders as useful for other "less fortunate" families.

30. Repeated efforts by the Home and School Association to form study groups for fathers have been, on the whole, unsuccessful, although fathers will attend meetings concerned with the gross facts of competitive standing, vocational and professional training, and problems of student discipline.

31. It should not be forgotten at this point that the participation of both parents in the nursery school program is often an important prerequisite for the child's enrolment, which may account for the presence of these fathers.

32. Note the source of reassurance to the supervisor and the threat to the father. The lone father stands over and against a union of children, teachers, and mothers who are linked together by a common knowledge of children's behavior which may well seem incomprehensible to the man.

33. Fathers appear to have learned the cultural expectations for individual independence, although, as this account suggests, somewhat reluctantly.

34. This common paternal attitude may stem from the fact that many Crestwood men have had a more difficult childhood than their wives and thus display a more general jealousy of the child's new privileges. Whatever the cause, it is certain that if the child does not "produce" after all this pampering and psychological grooming, he will be up on the carpet as far as his father is concerned.

35. Attendance at a nursery school session is perhaps a little like buying lingerie—embarrassing, since it takes one into an unfamiliar and dangerous women's world.

36. The ambivalence of this father is marked. He is divided between a desire to toughen his son and the impulse to indulge him at the same time, for the sake of the emotional satisfaction he himself derives from spoiling the child. His reticence in expressing his deepest feelings for his son is typical for the Crestwood man, who does not expose his guiding theories for public discussion. In this respect Crestwood fathers are probably more private and inarticulate than any other group there.

37. A classic quotation for a Crestwood Heights male, the real meaning being "if it can't be related to the world of immediately useful and common-sense objects, it has *no* sense." No better illustration could be given of the typical orientation of the man's thinking in Crestwood Heights.

38. This knowing conspiracy of mother and teacher against father is a commonplace occurrence in Crestwood Heights. At one Home and School meeting, the mothers were discussing means of getting fathers out to sessions. The first stage, they agreed, was to elect men to the senior offices, then to give them strong women as subordinate officers who could do the work (so it would get done) and who could guide the men (so the work

would be done correctly). Their plans were more than a little reminiscent of adult-manoeuvred introductions of children to civics, by allowing the Boy Scouts to take over the City Hall offices for a (pretend) day.

39. Unlike the women, the men will not ask such pupil-like questions in a public meeting. There, before other men, and their own wives, they will argue, cross-question, criticize, suggest, but rarely or never abandon the male role of generalized leadership and dominance. If they do abandon it, they tend to get defined out of the group of *male* males.

40. Where the expert is concerned, the parent must somehow accept the fine distinction between "not being emotionally tied up" with the child (which is bad, if carried to the extreme) and "being emotionally involved" with the child (which is good, provided the link is not sufficiently deep to interfere with the expert's control of both parents and children in the situation).

41. Note the lack of real father-teacher communication. The teachers' "success" means: "We taught them something"—whether they learned anything or not.

42. J. C. Flügel, *The Psycho-Analytic Study of the Family* (London: International Psycho-Analytical Press, 1921), or T. Benedek, "The Emotional Structure of the Family," in *The Family: Its Function and Destiny*, ed. R. N. Anshen (New York: Harper & Brothers, 1949), pp. 202–225.

43. Cf. G. H. Caster, "Some Socio-Cultural Perspectives on the Behavior Patterns of Ten Jewish Children in [Crestwood Heights]" (M.S. thesis, New York School of Social Work, Columbia University, 1952). This study of highly mobile Jewish families in the Elm Prep area would tend to corroborate this view—except for crises and other special situations.

44. Cf. N. W. Bell, "Family Reactions to Strain: The Impact of the Genesis and Treatment of Social and Emotional Problems in Children" (Master's thesis, Department of Political Economy, University of Toronto, 1953).

45. Cf. E. W. Loosley, "The Home and School Association as a Socializing Agency in an Upper-Middle-Class Canadian Community" (Master's thesis, Department of Education, Division of the Social Sciences, University of Chicago, 1952), pp. 137–138.

46. The relationship between father and daughter is frequently of this type in Crestwood Heights, particularly if the child is the only girl in the family or the youngest child. The father may or may not extend his indulgence to the wife, but the daughter may often be the sole object of the father's deepest emotions which must be excluded from other areas of his life, notably occupation or profession.

47. Term Paper, Department of Sociology, University of Toronto, 1953. Handwritten document, Project Files.

48. Again this is a complete reversal of tradition; in the orthodox Jewish household the father in his role of priest carried the tradition and made the decisions which his wife merely carried out.

49. There are two important points in this connection. First, the school officially offers no religious instruction, the local Board of Education having been one of the very few to ask to be exempted, under statutory provision,

from the necessity to give religious training. The teachers, however, have not been equally content to let the matter rest here. Second, where teachers voluntarily offer instruction (and many do) they aim at non-sectarianism but mostly fail, because they themselves are uncertain as to where the sectarian lines are to be drawn. Thus we find Jewish children singing Christian hymns, including those which refer to Jesus as *our* Savior. Gentile and Jewish children repeat prayers or learn lessons which are distinctly Protestant in flavor. And further than this, Gentile children absorb only a minimum, and that minimum from the "middle range" of Protestantism, so that, for instance, the Catholicism of the Anglican or the Pietism of the Friend is not represented.

50. Cf. R. K. Merton and A. S. Kitt, "Contributions to the Theory of Reference Group Behavior," in *Continuities in Social Research: Studies in the Scope and Method of "The American Soldier,"* ed. R. K. Morton and P. F. Lazarsfeld (Glencoe, Ill.: Free Press, 1950), p. 92.

51. Several student essays in sociology have emphasized this point. While the advantages of the new environment of Crestwood Heights are stressed, there is an undercurrent of nostalgia for the old, familiar neighborhood and friends left behind there.

52. K. Horney, *Neurosis and Human Growth: The Struggle toward Self-Realization* (New York: W. W. Norton & Company, Inc., 1950), p. 59.

53. Cf. Letters from Women's Seminar, "What I Want for My Child," Project Files.

54. One visiting expert, however, aroused considerable ire in the community by frankly advocating that each family member pursue his own individualistic path, with the recognition and approval of the whole family group. Many Crestwooders, consciously dedicated to the co-operative functioning of the family, insisted that the expert's remarks had been "misinterpreted."

55. Allison Davis has termed the middle class the eyes and brains of the nation: "The 'small people' in the middle group are the backbone of our society; the 'upper middles' are the brain and the eyes of the society." "Socialization and Adolescent Personality," in *The Forty-Third Yearbook of the National Society for the Study of Education,* ed. N. B. Henry (Chicago: Department of Education, University of Chicago, 1944), Part I, p. 212.

56. Much material obtained in the teen-age Human Relations classes and from observations of behavior at school suggests just this. Cf. also David Riesman, *The Lonely Crowd* (New Haven: Yale University Press, 1950).

57. M. Mead, "Coming of Age in Samoa," *From the South Seas: Studies of Adolescence and Sex in Primitive Societies* (New York: William Morrow & Co., 1939), pp. 41–43.

58. It is significant to note that until fairly recent times religious orders, in most cases enforcing celibacy, were the approved social outlets for those individuals who, for one reason or another, decided against family life. This type of choice may well have permitted less anxious work but at a price, the "renunciation of this world." The Crestwooder faces unwillingly the necessity of renouncing even one minor good in favor of another, let alone the whole set of conventional goods.

59. Cf. the description of the market-oriented personality in E. Fromm, *Man for Himself: An Inquiry into the Psychology of Ethics* (New York: Rinehart & Company, 1947), pp. 67 ff. Also E. Fromm, *Escape from Freedom* (New York: Rinehart & Company, 1941), pp. 108 *et passim*.

60. See J. R. Seeley, "Social Values, the Mental Health Movement, and Mental Health," *Annals of the American Academy of Political and Social Science* (Philadelphia), vol. CCLXXXVI (1953), pp. 15-24.

61. E. W. Burgess and H. J. Locke, *The Family: From Institution to Companionship* (New York: American Book Company, 1945); W. F. Ogburn, "The Family's Loss of Functions," in K. Davis, H. C. Bredemeier, and M. J. Levy, Jr., *Modern American Society: Readings in the Problems of Order and Change* (New York: Rinehart, 1949), pp. 570-573.

62. M. Mead, *Male and Female: A Study of the Sexes in a Changing World* (New York: William Morrow & Co., 1949), pp. 342-366.

63. F. R. Kluckhohn, "The American Family, Past and Present," in *Patterns for Modern Living* (Chicago: Delphian Society, 1952), pp. 60, 63.

8. THE SCHOOL

1. The historical material on education is based in part on E. P. Cubberley, *The History of Education, Educational Practice and Progress Considered as a Phase of the Development and Spread of Western Civilization* (Boston: Houghton Mifflin Company, 1920).

2. Vestiges of the church school, for example, have remained in England to the present day; and the "Separate Schools" of the Roman Catholic and other churches continue to exist on the North American continent, in spite of the long-established official separation between Church and State in both Europe and North America. Various other ethnic and religious groups have been successful in maintaining their own schools to transmit the religious and cultural heritage of the group.

3. See W. L. Warner, R. J. Havighurst, and M. B. Loeb, *Who Shall Be Educated? The Challenge of Unequal Opportunities* (New York: Harper & Brothers, 1944).

4. Despite some tendencies in Canada and in the United States towards adapting curricula to the needs of specific geographic areas, or towards the progressive methods of Dewey and his disciples, the general trend is still in the direction of centralization. Such attempts appear to be only modifications of a core curriculum which remains relatively fixed for the whole country.

5. E. C. Hughes, "Mistakes at Work," *Canadian Journal of Economics and Political Science,* vol. XVII, (1951), pp. 320-327.

6. For evidence that in the transition immense confusion has been engendered among the schoolmen *and* their critics, see H. M. Neatby, *So Little for the Mind* (Toronto: Clarke, Irwin, 1953), and *A Temperate Dispute* (Toronto: Clarke, Irwin, 1954).

7. While the private school, the church, and the ethnic school exist alongside the publicly financed educational system, these institutions absorb only a small minority of the school-age population. The vast majority is

compelled by law to attend school; and by economics and sometimes by ideology to enter the public school.

8. J. M. McCutcheon, *Public Education in Ontario* (Toronto: T. H. Best Printing Company Ltd., 1941).

9. C. B. Sissons, *Egerton Ryerson: His Life and Letters* (Toronto: Clarke, Irwin & Company Limited, 1937), vol. I, pp. 80–81.

10. J. R. Seeley, "Education and Morals," *Yearbook of Education, 1951* (London: Evans Brothers, Ltd., 1952), pp. 386–395.

11. *Ibid.*

12. J. Dewey, *Interest and Effort in Education* (Boston: Houghton Mifflin Company, 1913); *Democracy and Education: An Introduction to the Philosophy of Education* (New York: The Macmillan Company, 1929); *Art as Experience* (New York: Minton, Balch & Company, 1934); *Experience and Education* (New York: The Macmillan Company, 1938); and other writings.

13. For a novelist's account, see J. P. Marquand, *Point of No Return* (Boston: Little, Brown, 1949). For a social scientist's, see D. Riesman (in collaboration with R. Denney and N. Glazer), *The Lonely Crowd: A Study of the Changing American Character* (New Haven: Yale University Press, 1950); and D. Riesman, *Individualism Reconsidered and Other Essays* (Glencoe, Ill.: Free Press, 1954).

14. The small, isolated, consumption-oriented family described earlier, obviously cannot teach the child much about the requisite delicate balance. The school alone affords the child a sufficient number of children among whom to learn the lessons of co-operation; and in any case rivalry among siblings in the family's highly charged emotional atmosphere makes such co-operation among peers difficult if not impossible.

15. There were, it is true, chemistry and physics laboratories equipped with the bare minimum of essentials; a domestic science room for girls, a manual training room for boys; and some provision for teaching simple commercial subjects, typing and bookkeeping in particular. The technical schools were slightly more fortunate as regards equipment, but here, again, there was little or no attempt to present education in an environment of taste or beauty.

16. For many teachers, but for fewer children, this orientation still prevails despite an attempt by the Province to redefine the inspector as a "helpful," rather than as a disciplinary figure.

17. The problems raised by this dual orientation have not been clearly confronted in this study, or in any other, to the authors' knowledge.

18. A secondary task was the backing up of church and home, by repeating with emphasis and piety their exhortations to be good in specified ways. See J. R. Seeley, "Education and Morals," *Yearbook of Education, 1951* (London: Evans Brothers Ltd., 1952), pp. 386–395.

19. Indeed, knowledge acquired without pain came close to losing its primary virtue—it was idle knowledge, as it were. The view that it does not much matter what is taught, so long as it be unpleasant, may seem a caricature of educational theory from the time of Duns Scotus, but it is, nevertheless, only a slight distortion.

20. With the introduction of compulsory education, the prolongation of

schooling (which effectively removed the child from the family for long periods of time), general attenuation of the readily visible differences between male and female roles (coinciding with the feminist moves towards emancipation which occurred before and after World War I) the urban child, who did not actually work in the family constellation alongside father and mother, as did the rural child, now had no adequate opportunity to learn at first hand the roles of man and woman in the culture. The school, now buttressed by all the authority of the law and truant officers, became supreme for the city child. No pull of seasonal work, distance, or family economic enterprise was sufficiently strong to depose education to secondary place, as happened frequently in the case of the rural family. This situation, as we have seen previously, contributed greatly to the present urban conception of male-female cultural roles.

21. Teaching was considered primarily a women's field and those men who filled even the administrative ranks were regarded, by other men, as partaking inevitably of the feminine nature of the profession.

22. The school is quite generally, but not universally, considered superior. However, a few parents, near the upper bound of the Crestwood Heights class system, said they would not send their children to Crestwood Heights schools just because these *are* progressive.

23. The number of pupils has, of course, continually increased. The Census returns, also, for instance, show that, in 1951, of the population 5 years of age and older, 20.5 per cent in Crestwood Heights were attending school and 12.2 per cent in Big City. SOURCE: Canada, Bureau of Statistics, *Ninth Census of Canada 1951* (Ottawa: Queen's Printer, 1953), Tables 61 and 62.

24. For reasons which may be obvious this is not nearly so often the case with children from other class-levels: with lower-class children, because their parents do not understand; with upper-class children, because their parents do.

25. See G. B. Chisholm, "Tell Them the Truth," as reported by B. Fraser, *Maclean's* (Montreal), January 15, 1946, pp. 9, 42–44; G. B. Chisholm, "The Reestablishment of Peacetime Society," *Psychiatry* (Washington, D.C.), vol. IX (1946), pp. 3–20; and S. Freud, *The Future of an Illusion*, trans. W. D. Robson–Scott (London: Hogarth Press and Institute of Psycho-Analysis, 1928).

26. The Crestwood Board of Education is one of the thirty-seven in the Province exempted (on petition) by the Minister of Education from the necessity to give regular religious instruction. Hence religious neutrality is an official school policy. Despite this position, there is a wide range of attitudes among the teachers—which may be shared more easily with their students because of the absence of any strong official policy.

27. For some appreciation of the resultant double-talk, see the "Hope Report": Ontario, Royal Commission on Education, 1950 (Chairman: J. A. Hope), *Report* (Toronto: King's Printer, 1951).

28. J. R. Seeley, "Social Values, the Mental Health Movement, and Mental Health," *Annals of the American Academy of Political and Social Science* (Philadelphia), vol. CCLXXXVI (1953), pp. 15–24.

29. It may be that some of these questions were asked because of the

known religious views of one of the authors, a Humanist. This would account for frequency. But it would not account for the sole concern being to defend the view that traditional religion and autonomy (or success or happiness) were compatible. A true traditionalist would regard these criteria as so secondary as to be irrelevant.

30. The question was posed after this researcher had emphasized, in a lecture, the statement of Fromm that a dominant trait of the authoritarian character was the search for the source of all good outside the self.

31. From what observation the research design permitted of the churches bordering Crestwood Heights, it would appear that clergymen of all denominations are even more sensitive than teachers in trying to find out what parents and children will accept in the way of beliefs and practices, in accordance with which public opinion they trim their ideological sails.

32. Approximately 95–98 per cent of the staff is non-Jewish.

33. In Canada, an amalgam or union of Methodist, Congregational, and non-continuing Presbyterian bodies.

34. See L. F. Maltby, "Report on Work of the Clinical Team, Crestwood Heights Schools' Child Guidance Services" (Typewritten report, submitted to the Department of Psychiatry, University of Big City, 1953).

35. The decline in teaching of the classics and of liberal arts subjects, such as German language and literature, is a case in point. Spanish, for example, may be encouraged, since it has immediate practical uses in trade with Latin America.

36. It should be added, in fairness, that it does do what it can, for example by encouraging outsiders to raise basic questions. But it is with the children and with the preconceptions it shares with the community that it can do least, where most is needed.

37. Cf. D. Riesman (in collaboration with R. Denney and N. Glazer), *The Lonely Crowd: A Study of the Changing American Character* (New Haven: Yale University Press, 1950), pp. 121–123.

38. Currently, however, the provincial Department of Education, faced with an alarming rise in cost of school buildings, has denounced these more expensive items as "frills," refusing grants-in-aid for these purposes. *Globe and Mail* (Toronto), February 18, 1953, p. 13.

39. *The Sociology of Georg Simmel*, trans. and ed. K. H. Wolff (Glencoe, Ill.: Free Press, 1950), pp. 330–344. A conversation with a young woman doctor on the staff of the Peckham Health Centre, London, England, may be quoted as a further amplification. She revealed that one cause of her dissatisfaction with a position which she subsequently left was the impossibility of finding any spot within that modern glass-filled building where one could go in and shut the door.

40. Where there is the knowledge that classroom procedure may be tuned in upon at any moment, without the consent of the teacher, the resulting anxiety may be disturbing for the whole teaching situation. Cf. S. Dewdney, *Wind without Rain* (Toronto: Copp Clark, 1936). There was no reason to think such anxiety at all prominent in Crestwood Heights; though the frequency with which it was stated that it was "unthinkable" that the P.A. system should be so used indicated an awareness of the possible threat, or its latent existence.

41. An observer walking along the school corridor can be seen approaching the room and, should he stop, this pause will occasion an interruption in the classroom activity of the moment.

42. Glass, again, may be symbolic of the separation without exclusion which comes close to the heart of one Crestwood Heights compromise. Glass, like the emphasis upon group activity in the psychological sense, promises an open access which may prove to be as illusory as the intimacy supposedly offered by the secondary group; in much the same way the picture window invites the stranger to enter the living-room, while he is denied an opportunity to knock on the door. The expectation is perhaps greater when the need for privacy is increasingly denied, and the shock is therefore greater when it is discovered that there *are* private areas which cannot finally be breached.

43. Some teachers are uncomfortable with the traditional physical arrangements of the classroom and attempt some modification. They may rearrange the children's desks in an open square, in a circle, or in some other formation.

44. It is also given a good deal of use by the students who by means of it announce the activities planned and carried out by their elected committees, with or without staff help.

45. Crestwood Heights students are encouraged to feel a "sense of proprietorship" in their school and pride in its beauty. No carving or mutilation of equipment is visible or acceptable. It is perhaps interesting that in the British public school where "our" school is also a focus of feeling, the opposite inference is drawn: that it is all right if not mandatory to make one's own mark—on the furniture!

46. J. Dewey, *Experience and Education* (New York: The Macmillan Company, 1938).

47. The picture of the intellectually alert child absorbing the classics, oblivious to drab surroundings, has little place in the Crestwood Heights educational vision. This is not to state that books hold no place in the school's system of values. Inevitably, however, some choice among values must be made; and books, the impetus to inner and individual enlightenment, are not accorded equal importance with the well-equipped auditorium, gymnasium, kindergarten, or science lab. A library at one elementary school was a project of the Home and School Association, which does not, as a general rule, concern itself with the provision of equipment for the schools—indicating that this was an area which the professionals considered unimportant enough to leave partly to the non-professional.

48. B. M. Harris, "The School-Teacher in an Upper-Middle-Class School" (Master's thesis, Department of Sociology, University of Chicago, 1952), pp. 23–30.

49. Two staff members of the Crestwood Heights school system pointed out, independently, that the most recent conferences (subequent to the collection of data for this report) had no such expert present.

50. It is the impression of school staff members themselves that the specialist does not rank higher than a "department head"; but the former does have the relatively free disposal of his time, which is regarded as an advantage.

51. J. B. Watson, *Behavior: An Introduction to Comparative Psychology* (New York: Henry Holt and Company, 1914); and *Psychology: From the*

Standpoint of a Behaviorist (3rd ed., Philadelphia: J. B. Lippincott Company, 1929).

52. E. Ryerson, *Report on a System of Public Elementary Instruction for Upper Canada* (Montreal: Lovell Gibson, 1847), pp. 156–157.

53. One of the key people concerned with selection said frequently and frankly that as far as female teachers were concerned, he paid a great deal of attention, within the competent group, to appearance and anatomy, since "the kids might as well look at a pretty teacher as an ugly one." This criterion will reappear at a later point in the chapter.

54. B. M. Harris, "The School-Teacher in an Upper-Middle-Class School" (Master's thesis, Department of Sociology, University of Chicago, 1952), pp. 29–30.

55. These techniques—billed as "methods"—form or have formed till recently a ponderous part of the content of teacher education.

56. Some, on the other hand, are at the opposite extreme, very nearly: oriented towards personality and interpersonal relations, "in love with teaching," intolerant of crude discipline—and also a little apart from the general staff *camaraderie*.

57. The school is only one of many institutions in North America where this particular atmosphere prevails. North Americans, in contrast to the British, tend to play down the facts of an hierarchical system and to be ambivalent about occupying power positions within it. The Englishman is more inclined to accept the situation. Concentration can then be centered upon the responsible exercise of the power which status confers, without dissipating energy in denying or disguising its existence in order to be accepted by colleagues. In this connection, it was pointed out by a school official that in Crestwood Heights and elsewhere, secondary school teachers are accorded higher status than primary school teachers although the salary scale is based on equal pay for equal qualifications at every level.

58. It has been pointed out by teachers that exceptionally good relations have existed between the staff, the present educational administrators, and the Board of Education in Crestwood Heights, which have made it possible to settle matters pertaining to status and salaries amicably. Summer courses are less generally used by Crestwood teachers to improve their status; but there is a voluntary and autonomous professional "improvement plan," made up of eight study groups, within the school system itself.

59. The changes within the teaching profession have also mirrored the growing complexity of the social environment: the one-room school is disappearing, even in the rural districts.

The trend towards specialization has not, of course, progressed at an even rate within the educational systems of the United States or Canada. For almost a hundred years, specialization at the university level has been the norm. From this point, specialization has gradually penetrated through the level of the secondary school system to the elementary level; and the trend shows promise of increase rather than decrease.

60. The appearance of the kindergarten specialist in the forefront of the elementary grades has upset somewhat the hierarchical distribution of specialists throughout the educational system. The kindergarten teachers, backed by the pronouncement of the child-rearing experts that the first years

of a child's life tend to determine his subsequent development, cannot now be treated in matters of status and salary on exactly the same terms as the young and recent Normal School graduates, who frequently teach the first grades. Nor can the kindergarten specialist achieve the rank of the specialist *par excellence*, who does not teach, since her particular art depends on intimate personal contact with children in a learning situation. In consequence, it may be possible to find highly trained persons operating at a level viewed ambivalently by parents and school administrator alike as vitally important in human terms, yet relatively unimportant in terms of salary, status, and professional recognition. Since high academic qualifications cannot go completely unrecognized, there may be some jealousy of the kindergarten specialist on the part of other teachers in the lower grades.

61. The function of the peer group has already been referred to in this study. It is specially noted by the following writers: T. Parsons, "Age and Sex in the Social Structure of the United States," in *Personality in Nature, Society and Culture*, ed. C. Kluckhohn and H. A. Murray (2nd ed., New York: Alfred A. Knopf, 1953), pp. 363–375; M. Mead, "Social Change and Cultural Surrogates," in *ibid.*, pp. 651–662; D. Riesman (in collaboration with R. Denney and N. Glazer), *The Lonely Crowd: A Study of the Changing American Character* (New Haven: Yale University Press, 1950), and *Individualism Reconsidered and Other Essays* (Glencoe, Ill.: Free Press, 1954).

62. In a telephone conversation the Director of Education said his job "depended on a set of relationships." He, the five Principals, and the Business Administrator "formed a work group." When he first took over the position, the chairman of the Board of Education had told him his job was "to keep the staff happy."

63. It is important to remember that the Director of Education was one of the first to accept members of the Project staff, who could not have carried on their work without his co-operation and support. Already sensitive to the particular research point of view, the Director was, and is, its most influential interpreter in Crestwood Heights.

64. The Director of Education, one school Principal, and a member of the Home and School Association have attended sessions of the National Training Laboratory on Group Development at Bethel, Maine. For a detailed description of the human dynamics process in school dealings with the Home and School Association, see E. W. Loosley, "The Home and School Association as a Socializing Agency in an Upper-Middle-Class Canadian Community" (Master's thesis, Department of Education, Division of the Social Sciences, University of Chicago, 1952), pp. 155–163.

65. The Human Relations classes which formed a part of the whole Crestwood Heights Project, as well as the views advanced by one or more of the authors, may have sensibly contributed to this emphasis. The tendency here is being noted—not attacked.

66. It is possible for a well-groomed high school girl far to outshine her woman teacher in dress and physical attractiveness. It may be no accident that many teachers stress the undesirability of too expensive clothes and possessions where their students are concerned.

Crestwood Heights children who travel with their parents may also have a knowledge of the world which some of their teachers lack.

67. It was not uncommon for students to give cardigans, or even station-wagon coats, to teachers as Christmas presents, which symbolizes the degree to which the difference between them has been minimized. The teachers themselves, recognizing the multiple "dangers" of this practice, organized informally to reduce student-to-teacher gifts closer to token level.

68. The feeling of "perhaps excessive responsibility" is a strain on this teacher, not a hindrance to the discharge of her function. Her perception, sensitivity, affection for successive groups of children and her skills, have not only made her nationally famous but have also made lasting happy impressions on the children, particularly the more "difficult" ones who have passed through her hands. The achievement is immense, but the cost to her is considerable: room for little else but the children is left in her life.

69. Cf. D. Riesman (in collaboration with R. Denney and N. Glazer), *The Lonely Crowd: A Study of the Changing American Character* (New Haven: Yale University Press, 1950), pp. 99–112; W. L. Warner (with the collaboration of W. C. Bailey and others), *Democracy in Jonesville: A Study in Quality and Inequality* (New York: Harper, 1949).

70. This description of an auditorium meeting is based on various reports in the Project files.

71. For other performances of the priestly role, but vested in the experts, cf. chapter 11, "Layman and Expert," and chapter 13, "Implication," pp. 418–20.

9. PARENT EDUCATION

1. T. Parsons, "Age and Sex in the Social Structure of the United States," in *Personality in Nature, Society and Culture*, ed. C. Kluckhohn and H. A. Murray (2nd ed., New York; Alfred A. Knopf, 1953), pp. 363–375; C. Thompson, "Cultural Pressures in the Psychology of Women," and "The Rôle of Women in This Culture," in *A Study of Interpersonal Relations: New Contributions to Psychiatry*, ed. P. Mullahy (New York: Hermitage Press, Inc., 1949), pp. 130–146, 147–161.

2. The "ideal" profession in Crestwood Heights seemed to be that of the doctor; his role combines the advantages of high social status, both academic and vocational success, and humanitarianism, and, most important of all, it can only be won through intense competition in which many individuals are eliminated, or prevented in the first place from competing. A doctor who might conceivably embrace the ideal of service to the extent of renouncing a lucrative practice for life and work in a remote outpost or city slum would, however, be incomprehensible to many, if not most, residents of Crestwood Heights. For in Crestwood the doctor's role derives its potency as a symbol from the very fact that the doctor can perform a service of great social value while being rewarded abundantly in a material sense.

3. E. W. Loosley, "The Home and School Association as a Socializing Agency in an Upper-Middle-Class Canadian Community" (Master's thesis,

Department of Education, Division of the Social Sciences, University of Chicago, 1952), pp. 74–76.

4. The special sense of this "autonomy" is defined in D. Riesman's *The Lonely Crowd: A Study of the Changing American Character* (New Haven: Yale University Press, 1950).

5. The attitude was also helpful to the researchers, since it aided whatever penetration in depth into the social system of Crestwood Heights was made.

6. Several of the women developed a sensitivity in reporting, which contributed insights of great value to the work of the Crestwood Heights Project.

7. The Home and School Association, as we have seen, is one of the most important means of facilitating social change in Crestwood Heights. It is an almost wholly female organization, yet much of its impetus towards change, it would seem, comes from men.

8. It cannot be over-emphasized that the "balance" achieved is acceptable to Jews as well as Gentiles. Given what they believe to be the situation—not merely locally, but in the world—many Jews were more anxious to keep out of positions of power or prominence than Gentiles were to keep them out. The politics of staying "out of power" were often clear, if complex.

9. Some of these later returned to even more orthodox positions than their parents occupied.

10. There were never at any one period in the time of the study more than two Jewish teachers on the staff. No conscious effort was made to select either for or against a teacher because he or she was Jewish.

11. A move is now under consideration to have more consultation with the Home and School people on this choice.

12. "Buzz session" is a technical term from group dynamics practice. It is a device for communication by which a large group is temporarily broken up into very small groups to discuss intensely and informally ("buzz") before general discussion or speaking is resumed.

10. THE CLUB

1. The material in this chapter is based largely on work done by D. F. Fleming, M.A., on the Crestwood Heights Project and adapted from a document "Clubs, Associations and Status in an Upper Middle Class Community"; and on M. Cook, "Interviews on Camps and Camping," Project Files.

2. These ends may be said to have both *Gemeinschaft* and *Gesellschaft* components. The terms "Gemeinschaft" and "Gesellschaft" to distinguish types of social organization stem from Ferdinand Tönnies. Redfield's "folk society," Cooley's "primary group," Durkheim's "mechanical solidarity" all point to aspects of the *Gemeinschaft* syndrome—the syndrome of intimacy, uniqueness, face-to-face relations. The basis of the distinction is probably that made by Kant and others in terms of the taking of others primarily as "ends" in themselves rather than as "means" to something else.

3. This particular attitude is clearly evident in certain high-status associa-

tions dedicated to public information in the field of health. It is quite possible for women, as well as men, to work tirelessly to promote for example, preventive theories which many doctors hold (often privately) to be unsound or even dangerous.

4. Conversely, parents ambitious to achieve upper middle class status may have their children taught most of the requisite skills and behavior in the public schools and then move them up into suitable clubs as the family income mounts, until they finally reach full acceptance at the upper middle class level.

5. Their headquarters with few exceptions (the Home and School is one) are not located in Crestwood Heights.

6. Status can also be lost—most readily if the child, when he is grown up, fails at money-making.

7. Cf. chapter 12, "Beliefs," pp. 396–397, for a description of some of the mechanisms by which such seeming contradictions can be maintained.

8. If a Crestwooder were openly to avow his preoccupation with status, he might be confronted with the necessity of accepting his present level or of modifying his strivings for a higher one. This would entail a recognition that his goal was won or blocked; his life-quest would, in either case, be ended and hence his motivations for being in Crestwood Heights at all would be seriously weakened or perhaps destroyed.

9. Represented in London, perhaps, by White's or Brooks'.

10. There thus seems to be no secure level of status (as exemplified for instance, by the British aristocracy) which can be reached or even approximated in Crestwood Heights.

11. There are no paid, professional "status-engineers," comparable to the social secretaries of Washington or New York, or status-lenders comparable with the titled ladies of Mayfair, discreetly rewarded for their services in many British Court presentations. The status market is, as it were, still fluid, and it is controlled by amateurs in Crestwood Heights, which gives the community socially somewhat of a frontier atmosphere. And status here has not yet been as far divorced from a "realistic" and materialistic concern with its usefulness to the career and in money-making.

12. In some respects, the function of the status-lenders may seem similar to that of "the experts"; but, unlike the experts, their skills are not for direct sale; and they are not professional experts *about* status, as the social secretary, for example, would be. They are independent amateurs, in a position to choose the associations upon which they will confer prestige, and hence they are able to guide and direct others who have not yet, or perhaps never will, accumulate the necessary social capital themselves to become status-lenders.

13. Indeed this mechanism is sometimes a skilful and effective form of flattery, when directed towards a member of the "out-group"; it assumes that he too must belong to the inner circle, or be at least worthy of inclusion at some date, since he is expected to understand the language. It may also be used to put the outsider in his place, by exposing his hopeless ignorance of the cues.

14. Children, too, learn this indirectly, by watching parental behavior in the process of changing through membership in associations.

15. Some exclusive clubs have deteriorated during and since World War II. Financially, these were forced to accept the money of most applicants for membership in order to remain solvent. Now these "laxities" are regretted.

16. "Junior" and "intermediate" are interesting terms applied to memberships in adult associations, since in most instances the age at which the new member must assume full adult responsibility, pay the highest fee, and receive free access to all privileges is considerably above both the legal age for adulthood and the age for marriage and even parenthood. Such junior and intermediate memberships are open only to sons and daughters of adult members; and the parents usually pay the fees until the "child" is accepted as an adult member. One family club permits intermediate membership until the individual is thirty years of age.

17. It is interesting to note that the adult directors and supervisors of these children's associations are most frequently not residents of Crestwood Heights; but they are, of course, acceptable to the community as amateur or professional specialists in this particular phase of the child's education. The headquarters of the most sought after associations are also not within the boundaries of Crestwood Heights; they belong rather to Big City.

18. One Crestwood Heights Principal reported forty-two extra-curricular activities in his school.

19. A private school education, however, may take precedence even over residence in Crestwood Heights itself. During the course of this study at least one family actually moved to a less expensive community so as to make it possible for a son to remain at an exclusive private residential school at some distance from Big City.

20. Actually because Jews constituted such a substantial minority, enough Gentiles sent their children to private school to change the proportions in the Crestwood collegiate to the point where Jewish students did constitute nearly half the population. This, in turn, became the grounds for further non-Jewish transfers, thus raising the Jews to majority status numerically.

20a. Anglican in Canada is equivalent to Episcopal in the United States.

21. Some Crestwood Heights boys who did not attend private schools complained that they had to wear their white gloves all evening at a girls' private school dance; the custom might well be taken to symbolize the inviolability of this select group.

22. In one large urban collegiate, girls preparing for university looked down on the few private school girls who were forced by the inadequacies of their private school curriculum to attend the collegiate, if they wished to secure Senior Matriculation to the universities.

23. At an earlier date, an interesting parallel to modern camp experience was the contrived expedition with the canoe brigades planned by the great fur-trading companies in the latter days of their glory, for distinguished visitors from England or the Continent. See Washington Irving, *Astoria; or, Anecdotes of an Enterprise beyond the Rocky Mountains.*

24. Here, once more, is the conflict between the desire to teach the child independence and self-reliance and "learning to do without when necessary," and, on the other hand, the strong desire that the child acquire a set of social skills which can only be taught in an environment liberally supplied with material objects.

25. G. G. Jenkins, H. Shacter, and W. W. Bauer, *These are Your Children: How They Develop and How to Guide Them* (Chicago: Scott, Foresman and Company, 1949), p. 40.

26. This child, in view of the camp's own philosophy, would however be the very child who most "needs" the experience.

27. This informant states "They have two cooks at their camp who do nothing but cook. There are four boys in the kitchen. The food is the most important thing at camp. *The program can be nothing as long as the food is good.* That is what the boys remember and come back for the next year."

28. Here the camp differs sharply from the summer cottage, which often connotes boredom for the child and a wanton "waste of time."

29. The theme of this hymn is direct, natural, and in the first verse, like the kindergarten prayers referred to earlier, one of gratitude for provision. The tune is simple—for fifth-grade (in age, not quality) singers. The words:

> Father, we thank Thee for the night,
> And for the pleasant morning light;
> For rest and food and loving care,
> And all that makes the day so fair.
>
> Help us to do the things we should,
> To be to others kind and good;
> In all we do, in work or play,
> To grow more loving every day.

The sequence of Council Rock thus seems to be: (1) Induce an expression of gratitude for prior gratification. (2) Shift responsibility for success wholly to the child, and buttress this with the prospect of guilt (" . . . what are you going to tell your parents . . . ?"). (3) Add "duty" as another motive to responsibility (" . . . do the things we should . . .) (4) Nevertheless, demand loving behavior and, presumably, feeling. Such an achievement must be by no means easy.

30. Note the similarity with the wider North American culture: Education Week, Mental Health Week, etc.

31. This symbolic linkage of school to Sabbath may faintly suggest again that the school is replacing the church as the dominant institution in Crestwood Heights. The unconscious inculcation of the implicit "Thank God I am not as other men" theme has been encountered before. (Perhaps poverty here replaces sin and damnation as a threat or object of abhorrence.)

32. This attempt has been described earlier in the chapter on "The School." The children are motivated to prevent failure (i.e., to "co-operate") but this is also a real hedge, just in case. When this attitude is taken by the adults, it amounts, virtually, to teaching responsibility by practising irresponsibility.

33. Defining the common core seems, however, to offer considerable difficulty in practice—more from the Gentile side than the Jewish because the former is less aware of precisely what it is that is, religiously, different. Cf. the chapter on "The School."

34. Dr. J. A. Hadfield in a lecture to overseas students, Institute of Education, University of London, session 1946–47.

35. Camp and school both carry heavy insurance against injury to

campers or students. In the case of the camp such insurance is obligatory if the camp is to be granted a licence to operate.

36. Note the similarity to nursery school discipline.

37. This contention, that in a situation where exploits are deliberately given recognition in symbols and publicized, the child is working against himself and not others, is characteristic of family, school, and camp.

38. Margaret Mead states " . . . in no situation where the greater knowledge and responsibility of an adult are needed can the child be made the sole arbiter of what it wants." M. Mead and F. C. Macgregor, *Growth and Culture: A Photographic Study of Balinese Children* (New York: G. P. Putnam's Sons, 1951), p. 11. Adult Crestwooders are, however, inclined to obscure this point in dealing with children—again a manifestation of their ambivalence towards power and its use.

39. See B. Bettelheim, *Love is Not Enough: The Treatment of Emotionally Disturbed Children* (Glencoe, Ill.: Free Press, 1950), pp. 115–132, 341–375, for a sensitive interpretation of what goes on at "in-between times" and bed-time.

40. The Junior High School in Crestwood Heights does provide annually one such exposure for some of its pupils (together with those of one private school) to the Reforestation Service.

41. This is not to deny that in the Victorian or even the contemporary European pattern the child was or is expected to participate early—but he participates as a child, well-mannered and unobtrusive. In Crestwood Heights, he is expected to take part early in a quasi-adult role.

42. While furthering his own social skills, the child may also reflect credit on the whole family by the way in which he passes refreshments at cocktail parties. At the same time, he may make a minor but genuine contribution to the family, by replacing or supplementing the none-too-plentiful and expensive domestic help.

43. The parents in one sense also "believe"—and deeply so—in the romantic tradition. Cf. chapter 12, "Beliefs," pp. 396–397. Crestwooders, who "believe" strongly in tolerance, find their human interaction limited in practice largely to those groups which exclude deviants who might upset the accepted belief patterns of Crestwood Heights itself.

44. A game in which the random selection of a "spun" bottle indicates a partner of the opposite sex for a kiss. See the chapter on "Age."

45. Cf. chapter 12, "Beliefs."

46. Figures are based on a verbatim report given at a meeting of the Home Education Committee of the Home and School Association to discuss fraternities and sororities (Typewritten report, Project Files). This statement was unfortunately not cross-checked against the membership lists of the organizations concerned, which were obtained (by a windfall) late in the life of the Project.

47. This reference is to an event not reported in this book because it and its repercussions would require a separate chapter. The school attempted to satisfy what it understood to be both Jewish and Gentile demands by so arranging classes that, at each grade, four of the classes were exactly the "ideal" half Jewish and half Gentile. By arithmetical necessity the remaining class would be predominantly or wholly Jewish. A provision was made that

no child would find himself in one of the residual classes more than once in his school career. This scheme was discussed with the staff, with two or more responsible Jewish leaders, with the children, and with the School Board. It was adopted and then, because of outside pressures, abandoned forever. To many who had thought of it as a local solution to a local problem, it seemed the most "rational" solution, given the existing opinions. To those who thought in global and historic terms, it seemed to open the gates to polite or not so polite recreation of the ghetto. The latter agree that *no* rational local solution is possible, i.e. conceivable. Why this view was not put to the administration before the adoption of the scheme is a fascinating chapter in the politics of staying out of power; cf. chapter on "Parent Education."

48. The overtones of "This is *your* camp . . . " from the preceding section are clearly audible.

49. Only one person (a girl) in one Human Relations class seemed to see this at all clearly when she said she thought these ethnocentric beliefs and practices wrong but saw no way to avoid in her life repeating the "mistakes" her parents had made.

50. It is the likeness of fates—or, in Max Weber's terminology, "life-chances"—that to our mind constitutes in a community like this the vital "ethnic" discriminant. The search for "objective" differences between Jew and Gentile which was periodically conducted was doomed partly because such differences, if they are there, are elusive, partly because it is the sensed future that makes the present difference—and makes the actual future when it comes. What *is* here in the present by way of difference is an expectation.

51. For others, who expected something less than "acceptance," the fear was present that dominant, exclusive Jewish fraternities laid Jews open to the charge of "anti-Gentilism"—and, of course, they did. This tended to heighten "anti-Semitism" or anti-Jewish social feeling. Yet it was out of this feeling that the felt need for religiously homogeneous fraternities had come. As is so often the case with social and psychological ills, the defence exacerbates the evil—and makes defence increasingly necessary. To conceive such problems in purely or predominantly psychological or individual terms is therefore to miss their essential character.

52. The secretary of a well-known lawyer complained that much of her time was spent in dealing with the "Snorties" and "Piggies" of camp and private school days, who were associated with her employer in plans to promote camp recruitment and in drives to secure financial support for their Alma Mater.

53. One girl who had taken the manifest message seriously and wanted to go and work in Israel was regarded as odd; she precipitated a family crisis and was a community concern.

11. LAYMAN AND EXPERT

1. The currency is social rather than fiscal—prestige rather than money —but it does function as a "medium of exchange."

2. "Pyramid" rather than "triangle," because several fields or disciplines

are involved. The figure must not be overinterpreted: it is not meant to suggest that the authors have actual knowledge of the relative magnitude of the several layers, nor indeed that there is a constant slope of the sides.

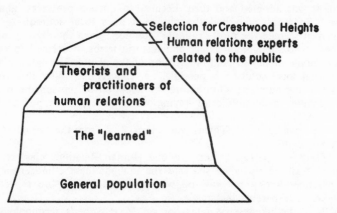

3. Cf. for instance W. L. Warner, R. J. Havighurst, and M. B. Loeb, *Who Shall Be Educated? The Challenge of Unequal Opportunities* (New York and London: Harper & Brothers, 1944), regarding class bias in educational opportunity. Cf. also the implications of the study here reported.

4. This tendency works against the student fortunately endowed in both respects who is likely to be felt as "sailing right through" and not in need of special sympathy, interest, and aid.

5. That there will be also many who are *realizing* their potentialities rather than mining them, goes without saying. Having consulted their real selves, these people are prepared to accept the limited rewards of the learned life as the price of self-realization. They, however, seem to be relatively more rare; they do not have the air of desperate striving which is what, other things being equal, would recommend them most obviously as candidates to those who themselves reached their status via that route, and who participate in a Puritan culture which considers easy virtue almost no virtue at all.

6. Again this is not to argue that these characteristics *cannot* be those of the autonomous or self-actualizing or self-realizing person. Given the norms of the culture, however, it is our impression that this is less frequently the case.

7. Again, there will be a minority for whom the need of self-realization is genuinely bound up with working in an intellectually exciting and socially critical field. For the majority, however, this is clearly a secularized version of the missionary drive. This statement is not contradicted by the firm, not to say desperate, efforts of the social scientists concerned to establish the essential freedom from values of their discipline. In the first place, this belief is itself an illusion; in the second, where the belief can be preserved, it shifts the ascetic, self-denying orientation to one higher level of abstraction, i.e. "I can serve man best by not being too directly preoccupied about his

direct service." In the third place the persistent over-protestation (in the face of clear contrary evidence) suggests a typical neurotic or neurotimorph defence.

8. See, for example, B. N. Meltzer, "Preprofessional Career and Early Publication as Factors in the Differential Productivity of Social Scientists" (Ph.D. dissertation, Department of Sociology, University of Chicago, 1948).

9. See Herbert A. Simon, "Productivity among American Psychologists: An Explanation," *American Psychologist*, vol. IX (1954), pp. 804–805.

10. This may be considered, properly, a "flight into activity," but the use of this term, while illuminating, ought not to be allowed to obscure the distinction between felt orientations and social consequences in each case. What may be, subjectively, flight is, objectively, attack. The acting out (which will need quite general attention later in connection with specialists and parents as well as experts) tends to take one of two opposite forms: a tendency to cope with the original trauma by repeating the behavior of its author or recreating the original situation, or a tendency to cope with the trauma by promoting behavior the direct emotional opposite of that related to the original traumatic experience.

11. There may be and probably is another concealed constant. An unconscious demand probably exists on the part of the consumers that the producers be very like them at the deepest (unconscious) level, at least in the one critical respect that the producers must also be mining the maturity values in the service of the success values, or, at least, trying to reconcile the two. All kinds of rebellion and pseudo-independence are permitted, but a really radical break with the success values and methods *as ends* would connote to the consumers mere "idealism"—to be smilingly indulged—or "impracticality"—to be reproached.

12. One might easily suppose that this "need" would give rise to a traceable dialectic process: the famous trio of "thesis," "antithesis," "synthesis." If so, it has escaped the authors who looked for it carefully. What is missing almost wholly is the vital link of anything that approximates synthesis. Nor is there a simple alternation among opposites, a "pendulum" effect, which would occur if the theories were unidimensional. An opposite theory—in another dimension—can always be found without a return to a prior, "used," theory or doctrine.

13. The subject of the training required to produce such experts is itself —in each branch of learning involved—a special field of study; and the field of operation, therefore, of another group of experts, experts in the production of experts. Nothing but a most cursory look can be given here to the general nature of such training, and then only in so far as it bears upon an understanding of Crestwood Heights and its belief-market.

14. It is only a few years ago that economics was a branch of "moral philosophy" (cf. Adam Smith, from 1752 to 1763); it is only yesterday that psychology was taught in the philosophy departments of many universities (and in some it still is); today sociology may still be a subsection of a department of political economy and be barely differentiated from history. As against this, see the multiplication of specialties over the last half-century: from psychology as a branch of philosophy to psychology as a

natural science, to, for example, a specialty in psychopathology, to a concentration on the psychopathology of the young, to a field of psychopathology of the young in relation to delinquency, etc.

15. Sciences whose discoveries run to the effect that emotion is an immensely important, if not an ultimately decisive aspect of life, that learning is an immensely complicated process in which the whole history of the learner is involved as well as the history of the teacher and the social situation in which the teaching goes forward, and which conclude that nothing much can be *taught* or learned by mere address to the intellect via ear and eye, are taught in precisely the contra-indicated way.

The rare exceptions are found in the teaching of two *arts*: social work, quite notably, and psychiatry, to a less degree. (In psychoanalysis, of course, this heightening of self-awareness is recognized as the greater part of the teaching process.) In social work, especially, the feelings aroused by new knowledge and insight are "handled" as part of the essential teaching process. But, be it noted, these are arts—and the "pure" scientist derives part of his disdain for these arts from the very fact that the involvement of feeling with knowledge is, in the teaching of these arts, given recognition.

16. It is difficult to say which of the two defects holds the greater potential for damage to the expert, to the sciences, or to the individuals or groups with which the scientist purports to deal.

Some slight efforts to remedy these defects are evident in many places where anthropology or sociology is being taught to clinicians, or depth-psychology to other social scientists. The exposures are so brief, however, and so intellectually oriented that they may function chiefly to add to ignorance a misleading sense of competence.

17. Again a partial exception should perhaps be made for social work.

18. This is not entirely fiction, of course, in the sense that it does actually govern politenesses and forms of behavior; it *is* a fiction, if it is taken to imply equal weight in the making of decisions, equal access to information, or equality of material or non-material reward. No guide can, of course, be given the novice as to those respects in which he is equal and those respects in which some are more equal than he.

19. Thus, for example, as Herbert Blumer has repeatedly pointed out, "instinct psychology became unfashionable, rather than refuted."

20. The weight of Freudian thought and practice, for instance, in the psychological and social disciplines and arts is by no means a function of Freud's ability to convince his medical colleagues on the basis of proof or even weight of argument. He convinced a "circle" and created a widespread public demand which made it difficult for many to pay the inattention to his claims that, as scholars, they thought these deserved. It is not intended to weigh these claims here, but, much more modestly, to assert that they were not and are not wholly weighed in the customary scientific balances. His following weighs much; and in creating that his own charismatic character weighed a great deal. See Ernest Jones, *The Life and Work of Sigmund Freud*, volume I, *The Formative Years and the Great Discoveries* (New York: Basic Books Inc., 1953).

21. The relation between the orientation of the expert and the doctrine he espouses or "stands for" is by no means simple. It is possible—indeed, it

has been observed in the course of the study—exploitatively to preach a doctrine of non-exploitation, punitively to tell «parents they should not be punitive, with authoritarian arrogance to warn them against authoritarian character-traits, arbitrarily to demand "democracy," or because of underlying hate insist on unvarying unconditional love in the layman as a condition of approval from the expert. Despite these observations, however, there does seem to be generally a loose positive correlation between the character-traits of the expert and the doctrine which he "puts out." Sometimes that correlation is negative; rarely or never is it zero.

22. A "revolution" occurs when in a given society one élite or power-group succeeds another, usually with relative suddenness.

23. The earliest social science that probably deserves the name consisted on one side of statistics (i.e., State-istics, or "political arithmetic") as exemplified in the writings of John Graunt, and on the other, earlier and later, of a kind of political analysis, as exemplified in Machiavelli's *Discourses,* or, more to the point here, in the German *Kameral-Wissenschaften.*

24. John R. Seeley, "The Social and Psychological Revolution of Our Time" (unpublished, 1952). See also Kenneth E. Boulding, *The Organizational Revolution* (New York: Harper, 1953).

25. North America in this respect is unlike Germany or France, where change seems to be characterized by relative periods of stability followed by major social and political explosions, and unlike England, where the change is almost lost in a nearly insensible flow of new institutional elements accompanied by the discarding of old. In America the only analogy that seems to fit the character of change is the continuous minor explosions of a string of firecrackers, each of which sets off the next so that a continuous series of small disruptive changes is going on without any evident period of stability.

26. The problem of assimilating the immigrant, which has been traditionally conceived of in terms of integrating him with a stable and existent culture, has actually been a problem which has called for and produced changes in the supposed host no less radical than those intended for the immigrant guest. The stable American culture against which that of the immigrant was to be viewed is largely, if not wholly, fictitious, and the real problem of assimilation has been the attempt to digest the varying philosophies and folkways imported with the immigrant in a situation where the original indigenous philosophy was only one competing element, and perhaps not the most powerful or important.

27. Except, perhaps, the situation of Greece in her declining years.

28. In America, even Catholicism is in this sense more Protestant than elsewhere. Judaism shares, if it does not epitomize, this orientation, most particularly in its Reform wing.

29. At this level of analysis, invariance in character remained in the face of immense variation in ideology.

30. For a picture of what happens when these orientations meet with a combination of new economics and politics with old religion, see W. E. Mann, *Sect, Cult, and Church in Alberta* (Toronto: University of Toronto Press, 1955). See also Jean Burnet, *Next-Year Country: A Study of Rural Social Organization in Alberta* (Toronto: University of Toronto Press,

1951); J. A. Irving, "Psychological Aspects of the Social Credit Movement in Alberta," *Canadian Journal of Psychology*, vol. I (1947), pp. 17–27, 75–86, 127–140; and S. M. Lipset, *Agrarian Socialism: The Co-operative Commonwealth Federation in Saskatchewan* (Berkeley and Los Angeles: University of California Press, 1950).

31. The emphasis on reason is thus European, but although in Europe, perhaps prematurely, some problems have been accepted as timeless and insoluble, the place of reason in human affairs had been judged very secondary (as against, say, the weight of habits and tradition); rules have been regarded as crutches to living rather than as providing solutions for all problems; experts have received a secure but not outstanding place.

32. It is true that a large element of entrepreneurial activity still survives, and in Crestwood Heights, for one of the ethnic groups, middle-class position rests largely on ownership, while, for the other ethnic group, it rests on management and professional functions. Even where, however, ownership is the ostensible base of middle-class position, it should be specifically noted that it is combined with the management function; indeed, ownership as such is almost peripheral to the tasks actually performed in private firms, which differ little from those performed by senior executives of public corporations.

33. See C. W. Mills, *White Collar* (New York: Oxford University Press, 1951).

34. These are, of course, shorthand symbols, and not too accurate ones, for complex orientations.

35. These factors are obviously interdependent, but they may be separately considered as a first approximation.

36. All the elements referred to—the importance of the child, the emphasis on education, the love for modernity or novelty—are, of course, quite general strands in the North American culture. What is probably different here is the concentration on these characteristics, and the degree to which they tend to override competing considerations.

37. The inability felt might be the result, for some, of feelings of personal inadequacy; for others, of a sense of the social distance to be traversed; but for many, of an ideal of the job to be done that puts it beyond the competence of any but the most expert. In many cases, these three factors operated together and reinforced one another.

38. "Rationalizing," not in the psychological sense of making something plausible (though that is widely done too) but in the sense of consciously adapting suitable means to ends.

39. Obviously, even where there are any underlying neurotic tendencies, they must not have reached the stage of break-through into consciousness or of a negative effect on economic productivity.

There is considerable warrant though no testable evidence, for believing in the actuality of the logically expected result: many direct confidences reposed in the researchers as to states of emotion; reasonable inferences from observed behavior; the impressions of others; the material secured in the Child Guidance Clinic, and more generally in Human Relations classes with children and in informal intercourse with them—all seem to support the view that this community does not manifest a notably low level of anxiety generally or any lack of individuals in whom the anxiety is sufficiently concentrated as to be discernible.

It should be especially pointed out, perhaps, that, if and in so far as there is selection for the anxious, this means selection not merely for a particular *level* of anxiety, but for a particular *focus* for its expression. Just as a noted spa might be expected to have its disproportionate quota of hypochondriacs, so, in virtue of its dominating institution and orientations, Crestwood Heights might first draw selectively those whose anxieties seek a particular object or form of expression—the welfare of the child—and then pattern those parallel anxieties so that, in effect, they form a *social* anxiety-system.

40. What is said in this section applies with special force to Jewish immigration, but by no means exclusively to it.

41. The distances are not, however, proportional. Downtown Big City is thousands of miles from Galicia or Posen in space, and only two leagues distance from Crestwood Heights. But socially—in philosophy, outlook, décor, life-ways—downtown is closer to Galicia.

42. Perhaps one or two accounts will give some insight into the tensions involved, and the manner of coping with them. One of these relates typical stages of decreasing involvement with earlier religious affiliations.

One not uncommon pattern after movement to Crestwood Heights consists in satisfying all needs except those of religious affiliation either in Crestwood Heights or some uptown area. The problem of religious affiliation cannot, however, be so solved, since adherence to an uptown congregation often involves a shift in denominational loyalty.

Stage one consists in leaving the small children at home, and maintaining attendance with the downtown congregation, but with decreasing frequency and, above all, with decreasing involvement, particularly in matters that might bring one's name and that of the institution into simultaneous publicity.

Stage two is entered when the children are old enough to go to "Sunday School," and for a variety of reasons they are encouraged to go to the uptown one. "Downtown is too far, one doesn't want to separate them from the others." "They're only kids; they don't understand all these differences." "Most of their friends are in . . . anyway, and it doesn't do to make them too different."

Stage three is reached when the parents feel they "have to help" the religious organization which is now helping their children. This is put to them as a moral obligation by the religious organization; as a wish (made almost mandatory by their rationalizations) by the children.

Stage four is reached when the parents become members of the uptown congregation because "It is silly to keep up these differences in the home," or "It's good for the child to know that his parents go there and know what's going on." Severance from downtown is now complete.

Another insight may be provided out of the attempts of two downtown institutions to move north in accordance with the foreseen and actual movement of their relevant populations. In both cases it was proposed to move the site of operation of the institution, but to continue the name, though perhaps modifying the practices, in the new climate. In both cases, the head of the institution claimed that by nefarious manoeuvres the move was being "fought" or "prevented" by those in the distinctive uptown institutions. Whether this was so or not, in fact, is unknown to the authors; that it was widely believed to be so, and "quite naturally," is a fact.

43. A "matrix for living," of course, requires the help of a sort of counsellor-psychologist-architect, who can translate vague aspirations into living plans and, then, into acceptably styled brick and concrete embodiments.

44. E. D. Chapple and C. S. Coon, *Principles of Anthropology* (New York: Henry Holt and Company, 1942), pp. 59–60. See also, for example, W. F. Whyte, *Street Corner Society: The Social Structure of an Italian Slum* (Chicago: University of Chicago Press, 1943), p. 24.

45. S. Freud, *Group Psychology and the Analysis of the Ego*, trans. J. Strachey (London: International Psycho-Analytical Press, 1922).

46. The terms "objective" and "subjective" are probably very ill-chosen. In the first place the mere "feeling" that something is of unusual importance is as much an objective datum as the consequences observed to flow from that event. Moreover, the two are not independent: in general but not invariably, the felt importance of the event will affect the probability of its having important other consequences, and the premonition of actual important consequences will tend to make the event "feel" important.

47. Information "too intimate" or "not of interest to the whole group."

48. In the subgroup he has the advantage of the feeling of preference and intimacy which, in the whole group, he has to distribute with relative equality.

49. A considerable range of operations and effects in leaders and led was noted all the way from relative independence to near-infantile dependency, for the latter, and, for the former, from attempts to strengthen to what looked like attempts to reinfantilize the led.

50. If a complex piece of machinery were used to extract the rabbit, this would make the act more wonderful, not less.

51. It does not much matter whether the expert carefully conceals what is common to him and the layman or expressly draws attention to it. If he does the latter, it is commonly taken as one more sign of superiority and difference, and ascribed to a modesty and honesty which the layman feels— and is allowed to feel—he does not possess. The expert, because of his own inner needs and outer necessities, frequently cannot use the emotional force that would be needed to destroy this illusion: it serves him too well. An extreme attempt was made by one expert who perennially claimed in his introductory remarks that he was simultaneously "moronic, neurotic, and psychotic"; he was assumed to be making a compassionate joke, to make people feel better, and he lost thereby none of the potentiality ascribed to him for discriminating levels of intelligence or degrees of disturbance, or indeed, for telling people quite generally how they should handle these and other problems. Indeed the extreme character of his statement ensured that it would be taken as a "joke."

Another expert, sensitive and experienced, had come close to sensing the phenomena to which this section points when he said of himself and his students: "We must not play God." But partly because of the asymmetry of the student-teacher relation, and partly because of his visible needs as played out in behavior, it was precisely on this ground that he appeared godlike to them, and fell into the trap of accepting their worship. He was cast as a god, who was above the necessity of godlike pretensions; this role, though even less fitting, he was driven to and could accept.

52. The judgment being made here is not moral but pragmatic. It may or may not be morally wrong to operate under these intended or unintended pretences; that is not the present point. The point is that what is ostensibly an operation to illuminate inevitably obscures; and what goes forward as liberating education is in reality an illusion-making which creates dependency.

53. The situation described might be partially corrected for if the expert could maintain a vivid and lively sense of the degree and nature of his own involvement, and could, even without bringing the process into the open, both make accurate estimates of his biases and act so as to offset or reduce them. The fact is that the biases that spring out of deep-seated needs are largely inaccessible to estimate, and even when accessible intellectually, indescribably difficult to offset in action—especially where the needs of others seem to offer an invitation to their exercise. In any case, such a covert palliation could only reduce and not eliminate the basic element of conscious or unconscious falsification.

54. Note that this form of analysis is rarely the perhaps tenable argument that while all behavior is conditioned, the adult by virtue of his greater knowledge and experience is freer to moderate his behavior than the child, and so perhaps ought to do so. It tends to be a black-white argument in which the child's behavior is viewed in a cause-and-effect frame of reference, and the parent's is viewed as morally evaluable—and morally evaluable, moreover, on an assumption of very great or nearly absolute freedom of action. The principal expert proponent of this view calls himself a "determinist"—and seeks to persuade others to "choose" his view!

55. Actually the expert frequently "withdraws love" from her (as she does from her child), or is felt so to do—thus (on his own theory) reducing the capacity for the lack of which she is being penalized.

56. It will be recalled that it has been stated that most of the experts are actually males, while most of the lay adults under tutelage are females. One must add that the few males drawn under tutelage by the system are felt by all parties to be inferentially feminized; here is one operating difficulty in drawing men into many of these activities: the threatened contempt of other men. One must also add that among the three women experts in the field during the period of observation at Crestwood Heights, two were felt as definitely mannish, one as essentially neuter (because of age), and one as incomprehensible because she did not seem to have mannish characteristics. The experts are seen or felt, no matter what their biological sex, as males; the laymen are felt, no matter what their sex, as female, by both parties to the transaction. By outsiders, however, the male experts are felt as having, in virtue of their support of womanly views and their participation in woman-organized activities, a feminoid role; but also, in view of their capacity to dominate and subdue these women, a markedly male role.

There was much joking about the relation between the male experts and the women among the "unconverted" males during the life of the Project, with reference both to Project experts and to the others, and directly and indirectly. Some of the joking was gentle, some resigned, some bitter: the common content was that the experts had more male power over the women than did their own husbands and male friends. The tone was the same in which a minor sexual irregularity, for example flirtation or petting, might have been discussed.

57. Thus phrenology proves to be unfounded and misleading; many propositions in psychology turn out to be true only for a given culture and not a part of "human nature"; and Newtonian mechanics turns out to be a special case whose conclusions hold only under special conditions not previously noticed.

58. At least what is said here is generally true in the West. In the "people's democracies," where the connections between biological theory and social practice are felt to be relatively immediate and important, the taking of one view about, for example, the inheritance of acquired characteristics, *does* have a life-and-death dimension, and does make for a succession of experts. This supports the general point: that change of view is rendered difficult not *per se*, but because of the interest and proximity of the public or other power-figures.

59. The word "prophet" is no accidental choice, since it carries with it almost exactly the connotations with which the public response to the expert is invested. What the expert says must be *new;* it must be a *higher* and more general truth; it must *deliver* them from their miseries by mere acceptance; and he himself must be *committed to* the views he expresses.

60. Of course, there are other alternative effects. Some laymen become indifferent; some become aware of their own strength and move in the direction of autonomy; some shop eclectically in the scientific cafeteria. But the mass effects described are difficult to resist.

61. This problem is avoided in political theory to the degree that a sharp distinction is made conceptually between policy and administration. In practice, however, senior administrative posts are inevitably points of political decision. In the U.S.S.R., the distinction is blinked with serious alterations in personal life-expectancies with each shift of the party line; in the United States, the distinction is exaggerated with a considerable amount of governmental deadlock as one alternative, and the return to political as against civil service category of "Schedule A" employees as the other.

62. It is not, however, and cannot be, an effective scepticism, since precisely the two things that would make scepticism effective are lacking. Theoretical competence, which is lacking, by definition, in the specialist as against the expert, would permit an effective scepticism to operate. Confidence in the practical knowledge and wisdom which the local expert actually has, could also be used as a base for scepticism, except for the fact, already pointed to, of the relationship of tutelage between the local experts and the institutions of higher learning. This relationship acts to weaken the confidence the local expert might otherwise have in his knowledge of his own local problems, at least, and the meaning of his own experience.

63. See *The Sociology of Georg Simmel*, trans. and ed. K. H. Wolff (Glencoe Ill.: Free Press, 1950), p. 404.

64. The strains thus set up in any expert, who is marginal and deracinated in other ways, must inevitably lead him to seek compensation for the dependency and intimacy denied him, in ways too oblique to be evident. These oblique methods of satisfaction are finally built into the very structure of the child-rearing industries.

65. Again the reader must be warned against over-interpretation. Equal distances on either axis do not represent exactly known or equal amounts of time or dominance; they represent, however, the writers' best sense of how what is happening may be presented pictorially.

66. See B. M. Harris, "The School-Teacher in an Upper-Middle-Class School" (Master's thesis, Dept. of Sociology, University of Chicago, 1952).

12. BELIEFS

1. John R. Seeley, "The Teacher and the Modern World," *Childhood Education* (Washington, D.C.), vol. XXVIII (1951), pp. 17–21.

2. See *infra*, pp. 36 *et seq*.

3. This statement requires qualification perhaps in the light of what is to follow. To the degree (and it was no insubstantial degree) that men dominated the scene at the two border zones—upper middle and lower middle—the content of belief was increasingly "male" (as detailed below) in these segments as compared with the middle zone, "the real middle class." In terms of mobility, this is the really crucial zone, and some of the matriarchal phenomena seemed as marked and are likely as passing as those described for Negro migration from South to North. Cf. E. F. Frazier, *The Negro Family in the United States* (Chicago: University of Chicago Press, 1939), pp. 89–163.

4. Since Crestwood Heights believed itself to be principally divided upon this line, and since the authors did an enormous amount of work in attempting themselves to discover or to help the members of the community discover such differences, the absence of results is not a function of the want of care or concentration on the topic.

5. For the difference in orientation as revealed in psychological test data see John R. Seeley, "Children Who Cease to Stutter" (unpublished paper presented in 1951 to the Ontario Neuropsychiatric Association). Its point was that in Crestwood Heights, Gentile children who ceased stuttering had made an intervening adjustment *to their family*; Jewish children, *to the community* and the world in which they lived.

6. This division is not the same as the distinction between those oriented to "success" values and those oriented to "maturity" values. It is true that the former are in the dominant Western tradition in the culture, and the latter prevalent among the "psychologically informed," but it is possible to find among the psychologically informed those who are oriented to traditional values (for example, a most religiously orthodox psychiatrist; the leading success-oriented, psychologically knowledgeable pediatrician, etc.) and among the not so informed, those who are oriented to maturity values as if by first nature rather than second intent.

7. This whole will be seen by the traditionally oriented, on the basis of a traditional distinction, as a female rather than a male outlook. It will be seen by the bearers of the new line as a traditional rather than an enlightened view. But these definitions are made on polemical and self-comforting grounds: in the one vocabulary "female" is a self-evidently invidious term; in the other, "traditional" is no less a word of censure.

8. The majority numerically; not, of course, in terms of influence.

9. On women as a "domestic minority" see D. Riesman, *Individualism Reconsidered* (Glencoe, Ill.: Free Press, 1954). The program of the scientifically oriented is currently directed to a minority—it is "for" the children —and borne by a minority—the women. It is suggestive again that in Crestwood Heights the ethnic minority is much more receptive to and enthusiastic about the new views.

10. The word "cleavage" may be ill chosen, since it implies that there ought to be (as perhaps there ought not) or that there was expected to be (as indeed there was) a substantial degree of unity, at least among adults, and at least with reference to basic beliefs.

11. There is evidence from Human Relations class material that these sex differences are established or emerge early, for example at age ten or eleven, and perhaps earlier.

12. The differences in orientation between the sexes must derive from a multiplicity of sources. The social history of men compared with that of women in the Western world must be of significance, as must the current differences in status, social definitions, and occupational tasks. Occupations have their preoccupations, and the basic division between child-rearing and family-tending, on one side, and all other occupations, on the other, cannot be excluded. Whether the Oedipal drama is regarded as a function in whole or in part of the foregoing or not, it is scarcely credible that the differences in role and mode of resolution between the sexes could fail to affect deep-lying feelings and modify basic attitudes accordingly. If behind all these and fundamental to them are biological differences both structural and functional at every level from the cell up, the existence of the radical differences which appear at the ideological level might be less an occasion for surprise than a confirmation of expectation. Cross-cultural studies give as yet no unambiguous answer as to what is (so far) culturally general and universally valid in the the distribution of attitudes between the sexes; we only know that the distribution by sex of tasks, status, and social definition differs over almost the whole range of possibility from society to society.

13. The extension of knowledge as to the role that difference in sex, as biologically given and socially defined, plays in every sphere of activity has been paralleled by the seeming denial that the difference makes any difference. The freedom to discuss sex freely, and the disappearance of the tabu against exchanging information on sexual activity (in its narrowest connotation), has been accompanied, for the women, by another tabu against discussing the proposition that men and women may have, on biogenic or sociogenic grounds or both, radically differing orientations towards critical issues and aspects of life.

14. A statistician might understand if it were said that women are "Q-oriented"; men, "R-oriented." Cf. W. Stephenson, *The Study of Behavior: Q-Technique and Its Methodology* (Chicago: University of Chicago Press, 1953) pp. 47–61.

15. It is perhaps more on this ground than on any other that the experts (and also some religious leaders) are felt by the men as "feminine"; the experts, like the women, stress the primacy of inner meanings over outer similarities.

16. Knowing "who's who" does not mean merely the memorizing of a table of organization, nor having for every person a knowledge of his

functional properties, i.e., the characteristics attributed to him because of the role he plays or the office he occupies. It means, on the contrary, knowing those psychological idiosyncrasies, those chinks in the armor which will permit him to be used in ways additional to or other than those which the mere discharge of his duty requires.

17. These polarities, which emerged as data of observation out of intimate intercourse with men and women individually, in the operation of a women's seminar (five years) and a men's group (much more briefly), and out of direct questions about aspiration, find strong suggestive support in material taken in a wholly different frame of reference. Cf. S. Ferenczi, *Sex in Psychoanalysis*, trans. E. Jones (New York: Basic Books, 1950), and E. Fromm, *The Forgotten Language: An Introduction to the Understanding of Dreams, Fairy Tales and Myths* (New York, Rinehart & Co., Inc., 1951), pp. 195–263.

18. This statement applies with one noteworthy exception—as to the role of biological heredity. The women lay much greater stress on the effects of environment, and the men proportionately greater stress on the effects of heredity. In actual mating behavior, however, the women pay careful attention to biological characteristics dispassionately considered; the men respond more impulsively to the immediate environment.

19. This may account, for example, for Lionel Trilling's observation that: "Educated people more and more accounted for human action by the influence of environment and the necessities and habits imposed by society. Yet innocence and guilt were more earnestly spoken of than ever before." L. Trilling, *The Middle of the Journey* (New York: Viking Press, 1947), p. 145.

20. See chapter 11.

21. Cf. R. de Roussy de Sales, "Love in America," *Atlantic Monthly*, May, 1938, pp. 645–651, where he observes this attitude in reference to love as "a national problem," but mistakenly, we think, attributes to the people generally what is a characteristic, dominantly middle-class and feminine. That he should do so, moving in intellectual circles of "experts," themselves representative of the "feminine" view, is understandable.

22. On the basis of this material on perfectibility and on attitude to the expert, which indicates a tendency for males to maintain ego and institution intact while strains mount unnoted, and for females to sacrifice ego and institution to the attempt to maintain continuous adjustment, one might expect, in the field of mental health phenomena: (1) continuous strain and gradualness of onset of trouble in the women; and (2) crisis (personal and institutional) and suddenness of onset in the men. Whether this expectation could be confirmed or not, we do not *know*. We have a strong impression (where there *is* pathology) of long-sustained harried tension in women and of eruptive phenomena (for example, sudden neurotic break-through, ulcers, etc.) in men; but it is no more than an impression.

23. Among the minor pieces of systematic evidence of general sex differences in hope or expectation or demand systems was some material cast up as a by-product of a Human Relations class in Grade XII. The topic selected by the students had been "popularity" and they had already recognized that their demand for this commodity was unlimited and that they had

no way of ever knowing when they had achieved it, or sufficient of it; it therefore presented an inescapable focus for continued concern and a permanent source of anxiety.

After about a month's discussion in which the character of their demand had been somewhat clarified, it occurred to the students to ask whether indeed such universal, unlimited popularity was within the realm of logical and psychological possibility. One avenue of exploration that suggested itself was for each student to secure from (a) peers of each sex, (b) teachers of each sex, and (c) their own two parents *separately*, lists of the three chief qualities "that would make a girl and a boy of my age rate tops with you." These "demands" on boys and girls were then tabulated by source and target. There was pooling to the maximum extent of qualities that might be similar, though called by different names, for example "grace" and "ladylikeness." Even after such pooling, however, the boys discovered that they would have to have 72 different (and many mutually incompatible) traits to "rate" with this small sample; and the girls would have to have at least 91.

What is of consequence, however, for this discussion is the distribution of most-demanded traits by parents according to the sex of the child. If a separation along general lines can be roughly made and the traits demanded grouped accordingly, the following picture emerges:

DOMINANT DEMANDS BY PARENTS ON GRADE XII STUDENTS

SEX OF CHILD	SEX OF PARENT	
	Male	Female
Male	Utilitarian	Decorative
	Active	Passive
	Differentiative	Conformative
	Aggressive	Controlled
Female	Decorative	Utilitarian
	Passive	Active
	Conformative	Differentiative
	Controlled	Aggressive

What was true for parents was also true, but less markedly, for teachers and peers.

Fathers wanted in their sons the "male" virtues which mothers wanted in their daughters; and fathers wanted in their daughters the "female" virtues that mothers wanted in their sons. This female support of *animus* in the daughter and *anima* in the son must be related to what has been said previously about the ideology of women in relation to impulse as against control. The suggestion can hardly be avoided that the women, themselves socially suppressed historically, are on the side of the psychologically suppressed (or repressed); the men on the side of suppression.

24. The ideology-action distinction presupposes a conscious argument, an ideology, logically and otherwise elaborated, pursued as a program of thought, and "recommended." What we subsequently call "thought-ways,"

are mere ways of thinking, which are mostly not conscious, do not constitute a "program," and would not be recommended by either party. How— if at all—they are related to ideology, it is difficult to say.

25. Note, in contrast, the coexisting male belief that women are "illogical," not only in general, but most particularly those known to any male speaker. The jokes, direct and indirect, on the topic are innumerable. Somewhat similar is the male allegation that they have "no organization," i.e. cannot organize their personal lives or concert action with others. The facts seem to run directly to the contrary.

26. Similar in the sense that philosophic "system" implies a large span of matter, and "long-range," a large span of events.

27. "Utopian" not now in its pejorative sense, but in the sense of a capacity to imagine a different and better state in the future, and to believe in its possibility without either flying in the face of established knowledge or leaning exclusively upon it. Cf. again Riesman on Utopias in *Individualism Reconsidered*, pp. 70–98.

28. In an older vocabulary, the men might be termed "material" optimists and "spiritual" pessimists; the women, the opposite.

29. It is, moreover, true—whatever philosophers may posit as ideal in the interests of neat systems—that, psychologically, ends do not fall into a stately hierarchy, nor is the distinction between ends and means categorical, clear, or constant. Variations occur in time and context so that X, a fellow human, may be now a means and later an end, or a means in this situation and an end in that, or even more characteristically, now and in this situation, a means in some respects and an end in others.

Having, however, paid this tribute to the necessary and perhaps not unprofitable disorder in any existent or perhaps possible means-ends schema, one can still make observations about recurrent or dominant patterns, about relative "ultimacy" of ends or "irreducibility" of preferences. Though these relative invariances do not correspond to the absolutes postulated by philosophers, it is no more necessary to abandon the terms than it is to abandon the concept of circularity because no circle is ever found in nature; indeed, we know the first to be foolish and the second (even conceptually) impossible. Thus the means-ends terminology is used here, though with due reservations as to exception and variation.

30. It is taken for granted that the reader will understand throughout that it is a relation of value, not of cause and effect, that is spoken of. The question is which is "for the sake of" what. Religion may or may not contribute to "peace of mind," but those who value it for the sake of peace make it, for themselves, a means to peace as an end. Whether or not it is an efficient means is a quite separate question, and one for psychology to determine; though one would suppose that here as elsewhere the perception of the behavior would also affect the effect of what is perceived.

31. Again, the ethnic minority follows the pattern of the domestic one; among them was noted a pronounced tendency to clear ultimate purposes first, indeed to proceed from whole to part, from generalization to particular. See *supra*, p. 383 *et seq.*

32. See chapter 4, "Time."

33. The possible basis for such a view, once recognized as having support in actuality, suggests itself all too obviously in the biology of the sexes; and such a possibility, the authors feel, can hardly be blinked. It must be recalled, however, that they came to their material with no preconception of this possibility, but indeed with the sociologists' professional bias against such biological explanation. The sociologist must still reserve judgment; he is not *driven* to a biological explanation, since the occupations and roles of the mother, as socially defined, would equally well account for the data. What is hard to resist is the conclusion that the socially ascribed roles are here a good fit to underlying biological tendency—or necessity!

34. See chapter 6, "Career."

35. They do not use the terms, but psychologically the women are at home with "phenomenology"; the men with "behaviorism."

36. A partial qualification must be entered here, and would be relevant also at many other points. Several men—some top executives—were ready to admit individually and under cross-examination that for them also the personal satisfactions were primary goods, and the production-bonus, if it occurred, a mere rationalization of or defence for their "humane" impulses. But a Puritan culture did not permit them to avow, nor in most cases to recognize, such gentle, "non-male" desires.

37. The defence by the men of the necessity for occasional vacations, poker parties, or holidays from fidelity is, in the writers' judgment, no mere rationalization. It is that; but it is also a valid claim, "out of whole nature."

38. Not to be confused with a logical inconsistency. By a psychological inconsistency is understood here what would be felt as emotionally (or aesthetically) inharmonious or clashing: something that prevents the formation of *Gestalt* in the personality. A logical inconsistency may do so—for logical people—but there is little, if any, necessary relation.

39. Cf. D. Riesman (in collaboration with R. Denney and N. Glazer), *The Lonely Crowd: A Study of the Changing American Character* (New Haven: Yale University Press, 1950) pp. 6–25.

40. We still have no way of estimating incidence or prevalence of various categories of psychological disturbance in Crestwood Heights. Even for the sub-population of school-age children actually in the Crestwood Heights public schools, where a psychiatric clinic was operated for five years for the benefit of these children, only a *minimum* rate can be estimated, since the clinic was always busy and could only accept a few of the cases proffered. On the basis of that experience, a least estimate of children needing and given aid would be 5 per cent of that population at any one time. Impression suggests that something more than twice this number were in need of expert aid; at any one time, probably 5 per cent or more of that child population acutely so. But these are low figures in the light of the situation as described. If *somehow* eighteen or more out of every twenty children can manage to get through childhood without direct psychiatric intervention, one would also have to regard the system as considerably less than wholly pathogenic. See also L. F. Maltby, "Report on Work of the Clinical Team, Crestwood Heights Schools' Child Guidance Services" (Typewritten report, submitted to the Department of Psychiatry, University of Big City, 1953). See also chapter 13, "Implication."

41. As has already been stated, at least one of the authors—and to some degree all of them—received throughout the period of the study a steady flow of direct requests for direct aid, or direct requests for help in securing aid (mostly psychiatric). This occurred despite the provision of the clinic for children already referred to, despite the authors' insistent disclaimers of therapeutic competence, and despite widespread knowledge that they were too busy to act as a referral agency. By a "steady flow" is meant a flow that involved, on the average, 5–10 per cent of a work-week—without any attempt to *treat* any case.

42. Manifest cases of disturbance, not defined as such by the victim, are those where marked signs or symptoms were put in evidence or claimed, without being referred by the claimant to any more general emotional problem.

43. Even here, however, variation will be much less than one might think, since the child learns more than the ostensible lessons mediated by the consciously chosen words and methods of his parents. He learns also, more importantly, from minimal cues which stem from the parents' unconscious mental processes, and which in turn give him the vital clues as to what they "really" want. These latter wants—for better or for worse—remain extremely persistent, forceful, and invariant despite enormous swings in belief.

44. The maximum permissiveness is not, of course, a permissiveness of commission but one of omission. In such a home, the child's infantile exhibitionisms, sexual "advances" or experiments will not be criticized, i.e. suppressive acts by the parents are *omitted*. In no case, will increased activity be encouraged, or the activity indulged in meet with its sought response from adult or sibling: there will be no *commission* of acts that would permit the child to secure the gratification he is seeking. (A few pathological stimulations of the child are found: pathological in the sense that they spring from the parent's repressions. But these are relatively rare.)

45. Parents permissive in this area are frequently amazed and sometimes (happily) surprised at the emergence of behavior which they could not help but be pleased by, though they would not openly demand it; for example, the spontaneous appearance of "modesty." There is no ground for invoking biological (instinctive) explanations, since such behavior obviously does not occur in all cultures. The learning is frequently from other adult relatives, teachers, Sunday school personnel, athletic coaches, friends, peers, or by reading, radio, TV or direct observation of how others behave. These sources furnish models, but their binding force and intensity of attraction are difficult to account for without the supposition that the child senses the relation of the models to the "real" and unconscious wishes of the parents.

46. Note how much of a contrast this description provides to accepted theories of "cultural lag," which maintain that technology changes first and most easily, institutional (e.g., family) patterns with some time-lag and greater resistance, beliefs with great difficulty and huge delay. Here, belief swings nearly free in the shifting winds from expert opinion; institutions (e.g., the school) are relatively adaptive; concrete personal habits, particularly at or near the technological level, change hardly and slowly, if at all.

As the Dean of a well-known medical school said: "Among doctors, there is no learning [of new techniques], only biological replacement." Cf., against this view, W. F. Ogburn, *Social Change, with Respect to Culture and Original Nature* (New York: Viking Press, 1938), pp. 200 *et seq.*

47. Marriages between Jew and Gentile are very rare, even in the synagogue of a liberal rabbi, who solemnizes reluctantly but "without making obstacles." Those between Protestant and Catholic are exceedingly rare, partly owing to the very small Roman Catholic population in Crestwood Heights (less than 5 per cent). Marriages between rich and poor are negligible; one such case came to attention in the five-year life of the Project.

48. They must be there in the shape of club managers and service personnel, but these are not so much "met" as people as "encountered" as furniture. The very American gestures of pseudo-intimacy—mostly in the form of badinage—function as a barrier, not a channel, to mutual awareness.

49. See chapter 10, "The Club."

50. Indeed, it seems that coeducation has only been sacrificed—like the mixture of religious and economic levels—so that the twin tasks of academic learning and social (i.e., class and ethnic and "religious") orientation may the more single-mindedly be pursued.

51. On the one side, no institution that would provide for such extended contact exists; on the other, the culture requires that the commitment be made only after extended contact. The last is rather curious, given the element in the romantic tradition that believes compatibility is recognized intuitively, recognition coming indeed at once in a moment of fulminating insight.

52. These countervailing institutions may be formal ones, administration-operated, such as the "Colleges" which not only largely separate Protestant from Catholic (and these from "the rest") but, within the former, one denomination from another; or formal ones, student-operated and administration-blessed, such as sororities and fraternities, clubs, and the like; or informal ones, wholly student-operated, such as friendship groups and cliques.

53. "Tolerance" here as elsewhere (for example, in inter-ethnic relations) takes the state of war as a premise and seeks merely to domesticate it in reality, or preferably, in appearance. It is a highly valued virtue in Crestwood Heights which simultaneously, however, values relationships in which tolerance is not merely unnecessary but offensive. It is not that one (tolerance) is, even mistakenly, viewed as a step to the other (peace); both are uncritically, simultaneously, and equally valued.

54. The cram-school teacher also performs a paid, unreputable function.

55. I.e., not paid in money. The pay in prestige, opportunities for association, and perhaps eventually cashable opportunities is, of course, pay.

56. Except in terms of privilege (such as access to the rumpus-room, kitchen, or house generally) or affection.

57. This is a most sensitive diagnostic. A certain stylized rudeness (of which graciousness is both a part and a counter-irritant) characterizes upper-class or status-giver behavior. Any premature assumption of such rudeness by a middle-class person is met with the same threats to status

as would attend his buying too large a house or trying to get into too exclusive a club.

58. Two such cases of adjustment turned up in the five-year period of intimacy with this community.

13. IMPLICATION

1. See T. J. Mallinson, "An Experimental Investigation of Group-Directed Discussion in the Classroom" (Ph.D. dissertation, Department of Psychology, University of Toronto, 1954).

2. A report by Isabel Laird and Harold Whitley is still in preparation.

3. Subject also to the possibilities, not to say likelihoods, of bias reported in chapter 1.

4. Significantly worse: Sense of Personal Freedom, Feeling of Belonging, Freedom from Withdrawing Tendencies, Community Relations. Insignificantly worse: Sense of Personal Worth, Social Standards, Social Skills, Family Relations. Insignificantly better: Self-Reliance, Freedom from Nervous Symptoms, Freedom from Anti-Social Tendencies, School Relations. It might be said that, with the exception of School Relations, this distribution is almost the mirror image (i.e., reversal) of the community's picture of itself.

5. See J. R. Hertzman, "High School Mental Hygiene Survey," *American Journal of Orthopsychiatry*, vol. XVIII (1948), pp. 238–256. Only some very small fraction of Crestwood Heights children were able to say that they did not suffer from so much examination anxiety that sleeping and eating were disturbed.

6. See A. R. Mangus and John R. Seeley, "Mental Health Needs in a Rural and Semi-Rural Area of Ohio," based on a study conducted jointly by the Division of Mental Hygiene of the Ohio State Department of Public Welfare, Ohio State University, Ohio Agricultural Experiment Station (Columbus, Ohio, 1950).

The only one of the authors who participated in this research and in the Crestwood Project had a marked impression for Miami County of fewer "cases" perhaps in total, but often more serious ones. This is not to say that child psychotics were not found in the schools in both places: they were.

Another marked contrast for one of the authors was the feeling that anxious children in Miami County tended to have sharp conflicts and clearly delineated or delineable sources for their anxiety: cruel fathers, "rejecting" mothers, intelligence handicaps at fairly gross levels. Crestwood Heights children who were anxious seemed to suffer from more pervasive, diffuse, chronic—and perhaps low-grade—anxiety, without a sharp focus or a clearly perceptible conflict. Much more subtle defects were sources of shame or guilt or grounds for inferiority than in Miami County.

7. "Mental health education" here means teaching about the facts of mental health, or teaching (of anything) consciously directed to the improvement of mental health as a primary aim, or discussion or any similar process with the same end in view. It does not include the training of mental health experts—"education for mental health education"—which must, however, be considered in its place.

8. The most blatant instance in our memory occurred where a child steadfastly and violently refused to remain at nursery school. After several abortive attempts, parent and teacher forced him to remain by restraint despite cries, kicks, screams. As we were told the story, they thus "helped him reach a decision!"

9. The "right of every man to bear weapons" had once a relation to the decent insubordination which is a condition for vital democracy. But that right has no meaning in an atom-bomb age. So with access via grade school and experience to traditional knowledge about how men may be manipulated or controlled, as against the new sciences of "man-management."

10. See John R. Seeley, "Social Values, the Mental Health Movement, and Mental Health," *Annals of the American Academy of Political and Social Science* (Philadelphia), vol. CCLXXXVI (1953), pp. 15–24.

11. *Ibid.*

APPENDIX 1:

THE CRESTWOOD HEIGHTS PROJECT

1. See "Blueprint for a National Mental Health Project" on file at the Canadian Mental Health Association (formerly the National Committee for Mental Hygiene, Canada).

2. In this it had followed the original impetus given to the movement by Clifford Beers. See C. W. Beers, *A Mind That Found Itself: An Autobiography* (7th ed., Garden City, N.Y.: Doubleday & Company, Inc., 1948).

3. One kind of "interdisciplinary co-operation" had been experienced in the armed services and elsewhere. Here a variety of "applied scientists" or practitioners of arts—psychiatrists, psychologists of many kinds, social workers, educators, recreation specialists, and even sociologists—had discovered that, working together, they could achieve more gratifying results than could any of them alone. Rehabilitation centers, indoctrination centers, induction centers, personnel selection activities: experience in all of them had given this kind of impression to many people, and with profound effect.

But more than this "combined operations" was meant by "interdisciplinary co-operation," and more had been experienced in actuality. Those who had first merely joined forces came to share views, and this was felt, subjectively, as a stimulating and rewarding experience, and regarded as contributing objectively to the better performance of the job in hand. What resulted—though few would have put the definition in these terms—was first what George Herbert Mead calls "taking the role of the other," and then what he calls "taking the role of the generalized other."

Also latent in the term lay an alluring hope. The hope was not merely that practitioners of different arts could come to understand and thus share in one another's viewpoint in a common activity, but that beyond this it might be possible to integrate the underlying, partial theories of behavior into one architectonic, grand and satisfying, scheme. It was further believed that this possibility would be advanced by more co-operation between those who now shared the same concern but brought to it such different frames of reference, or habits of analysis, or professional biases or specialized vocabularies.

4. On the latter, see A. R. Mangus and John R. Seeley, *Mental Health Needs in a Rural and Semi-Rural Area of Ohio,* based on a study conducted jointly by the Division of Mental Hygiene of the Ohio State Department of Public Welfare, Ohio State University, Ohio Agricultural Experiment Station (Columbus, Ohio, 1950).

5. In its initial thinking, the Committee had confronted three common dilemmas in this field of action, frequently thought of in terms of paired alternatives: concentration on children versus concentration on adults; concentration on the adjustment of the individual to the existing society versus concentration on the alteration of the existing society so as to make maladjustment of the individual less likely; concentration on "therapy" versus concentration on "prevention."

It is widely argued, for instance, that only children, and only young children at that, have sufficient plasticity to permit an economical expenditure of large-scale effort, directed towards either remedying existing weaknesses or inducing or educing new strengths; it is argued, on the other side, that since the child's strength or weakness in this regard is almost wholly a function of his parents' personalities and behaviors, no attack is likely to be effective unless it is first made upon them. The argument about "the individual" and "the society" is similar in form and effect. One half of it runs to the effect that the society is bad, or less good than it might be, with respect to mental health because the mental health of its constituent individuals is less good than it might be, and it is the latter that stands in need of improvement if the society itself is to be improved at all; the opposite half of the argument runs that no amount of individual therapy, or other effort directed towards individuals, stands any chance of success so long as a bad society is systematically producing maladjustment of various kinds. The "therapy" versus "prevention" argument is very nearly, though not wholly, a special case of the last one. It raises, however, other problems peculiar to it: the conflict between policy for the short term or the long run; the conflict between expending resources on the weak and damaged as against the strong and well, etc.

With respect to the supposed first dilemma, it was felt, in the context of the National Project, that given the cultural atmosphere of North America—or at least of middle-class North America—the only scheme which would have any chance of deeply involving parents, or adults generally, was a scheme which at least ostensibly addressed itself to children. A scheme addressed ostensibly to adults would, it was thought, arouse all the defensive anxieties organized to protect, for the adult individual, the extremely important value implied in such terms as "adequacy," "independence," "self-sufficiency." A scheme ostensibly addressed to children, on the other hand, would appeal precisely to this value, would permit direct dealing with the children, and would in the course of its unfolding inevitably involve the relevant adults, but with a minimum of initial resistance.

As to the second dilemma, it was argued that, since one major source of the individual's sense of inadequacy and impotence lies in his feeling that he can do little or nothing about a society which he does not understand, and since, *per contra,* his lack of understanding of and incompetence in dealing with social problems are in part a function of his personal inadequacy, a method must be devised which would be "therapeutic" or contrapathic in so far as it would strengthen the individual's feeling of personal strength and competence by putting him in possession of that information and those techniques which would enable him simultaneously to understand himself and the society in which he lives. If such a method could be devised, the line between social studies and therapy might turn out to be a pretty fine line!

As to the alternatives between therapy and prevention, a third kind of reconciliation—not either alternative but both, and both simultaneously and hand-in-hand—was made.

6. See V. Anderson, "For Their More Confident Tomorrows: The [Crestwood Heights] Project," *Food for Thought* (Toronto), vol. XI (1951) pp. 5–10; J. D. Griffin and J. R. Seeley, "Education for Mental Health: An Experiment," *Canadian Education* (Toronto), vol. VII (1952), pp. 15–25; and J. R. Seeley, "The Crestwood Heights Project," *Understanding the Child* (New York), vol. XXIII (1954), pp. 104–110.

7. It is hoped to publish soon a volume on these human relations classes, by J. R. Seeley and T. J. Mallinson. See also T. J. Mallinson, "An Experimental Investigation of Group-Directed Discussion in the Classroom" (Ph.D. dissertation, Department of Psychology, University of Toronto, 1954); and J. R. Seeley and T. J. Mallinson, "A Controlled Experiment in Group-Directed Discussion with Children" (unpublished paper, read at the 1951 meeting of the American Psychiatric Association).

8. Under the Canadian constitution, as embodied in the British North America Act and its interpretations, Education is exclusively a provincial responsibility; but both the government of Canada and those of the Provinces maintain Departments of Health (in the central government, conjoined with "Welfare").

9. See L. F. Maltby, "Report on Work of the Clinical Team, Crestwood Heights Schools' Child Guidance Services" (typewritten report, submitted to the Department of Psychiatry, University of Big City, 1953). See also note 6.

10. The psychological survey, probably too naïvely conceived, was abandoned. The experience with the data collected in this connection is such as to suggest that the more sophisticated the statistical analysis used upon the data the less likely is one to find stable, intelligible differences in pattern which are worth reporting, even though the analysis usually applied had produced "reliable" differences.

11. For the "Human Relations Classes" see note 7.

12. For the clinical services, see note 9.

13. A report on the Liaison Officers by Isabel Laird and Harold Whitley is still in preparation.

ACKNOWLEDGMENTS

ANY ATTEMPT to acknowledge adequately our obligations is fraught, in a work of this kind, with almost insuperable difficulties: we are indebted in so many ways to so many that space alone forbids even the bare listing of names.

We are indebted to the people of Crestwood Heights: first and foremost to the children and students who, with small hope of immediate gain, exposed their thoughts and feelings freely to us; second, only, to their parents and other adults who—much more difficult for them!—also allowed us access with almost equal freedom; third, to the school staff and administration who suffered us always with courtesy and generosity, and often with gladness.

We are obligated to our University, in general, most particularly to the co-operating Departments of Psychiatry and Psychology, the School of Social Work, and the College of Education. Among those on these faculties who aided us in special measure we must list, at least, the late Professor G. G. Brown (Anthropology), Professors E. S. Carpenter (Anthropology), D. Cappon (Psychiatry), E. Chinoy (Sociology), S. D. Clark (Sociology), C. E. Hendry (Social Work), J. D. Ketchum (Psychology), A. C. Lewis (Education), W. Line (Psychology), J. A. Long (Education), C. E. Phillips (Education), C. C. V. Pitt (Education), D. F. Putnam (Geography), M. G. Ross (Social Work), A. B. Stokes (Psychiatry) and F. C. Toombs (Business Administration). Professor Brown was most helpful in seminar participation and with advice; greatly interested himself, he also interested students in the anthropology of Crestwood Heights. We are also grateful to colleagues at other universities, particularly to Professors E. C. Hughes and David Riesman of the University of Chicago.

We are directly indebted, of course, to the Provincial Department of Health, and to the Department of National Health and Welfare of the Canadian Government, whose funds supported the enterprise.

We are also deeply grateful to the voluntary association in the field, the Canadian Mental Health Association, for its imaginative efforts and its active support and hospitality. Especially, we must thank Dr. C. M. Hincks (then, General Director), Dr. J. D. M. Griffin (then, Medical Director), Dr. W. Line, Dr. Reva Gerstein, and Miss Marjorie Keyes, R.N.

Direct contributors of documents which were integral to the study are listed in the section that follows—some of them, for obvious reasons, represented only by "pseudonymous" initials. Others who made sizable contributions by way of field reports or clerical aid included: Mr. Sydney Blum, Miss J. Cardwell, Mrs. Mary Currie, Mr. Kenneth Dawson, Miss Glenda Doherty (now Mrs. George Stoll), Mrs. E. Fogden, Miss Maude Gravestock, Miss A. Heikinheimo, Mr. Leonard Houzer, Miss Jean McGill, Miss Carman Parris, Mrs. J. Russell (now Mrs. Evans) and the Liaison Officers who, as already stated, were not only trainees but co-workers and producers.

Mr. Thomas Mallinson, who was primarily concerned, researchwise, with the analysis of the Human Relations Classes results, made several important and original contributions and was of great help with other aspects of the study.

Miss Francess G. Halpenny, Associate Editor of the University of Toronto Press, was of help too, far "beyond and above the call of duty." No one now knows better than the authors what a good editor can contribute.

If we may single out anyone for special gratitude, we should like to thank Miss Elisabeth Czeija who, adding unusual grace to talent and persistence, saw the manuscript through its various, sometimes painful, stages.

Beyond this, we are indebted to other members of our technical staff—and to one another.

None of these attributions of obligation implies responsibility for the content of the study. The study's shortcomings are those of the authors and editors, and, in some small degree perhaps, those of present scientific knowledge and techniques. One can only hope that growing knowledge and mastery will soon make studies such as this as obsolete as the earliest travellers' descriptions or anthropologists' field reports.

CONTRIBUTORY STUDIES

E. L. Abbot and L. F. Smith, "Some Notes on Impressions and Feelings Gained from a Three Months' Experience in Crestwood Heights Schools" (typewritten, 1949).

"D. B.," "Problems of My Community."

N. W. Bell, "Family Reactions to Strain: The Impact of the Genesis and Treatment of Social and Emotional Problems in Children" (unpublished Master's dissertation, Department of Political Economy, University of Toronto, 1953).

M. Blum, "The Effect of Nursery School Attendance upon the Later Personal and Social Adjustment of the Child Living in an Upper Middle-Class Community" (unpublished study, typewritten, 1953).

G. H. Caster, "Some Socio-Cultural Perspectives on the Behavior Patterns of Ten Jewish Children in [Crestwood Heights]" (unpublished M.S. thesis, New York School of Social Work, Columbia University, 1952).

K. J. Duncan, "The Teaching Profession and the Family: A Study of the Changing Role of the Teaching Profession in a Middle Class Urban Community" (unpublished M.A. dissertation in Sociology, Department of Political Economy, University of Toronto, 1951).

D. F. Fleming, Analysis of "My Life History" Documents. (As part of the requirements for a third-year Psychology course at the University of Big City the students were expected to complete an autobiographical sketch of themselves, with material on their families and early life experiences. With the permission of the department involved, and under agreement to protect the anonymity of the documents, a selection of these documents completed by Crestwood students was examined and analyzed for whatever light might be shed on the community.)

D. F. Fleming, Analysis of "My Summer Experiences" Documents. (It was the practice for certain teachers in the Preparatory schools to assign essays to their students shortly after the school term had commenced in September. One of our research personnel took the opportunity in September of 1951 to collect material specifically related to "My Experiences during the Summer Holidays." This material was partially viewed as an opportunity to amplify data gathered by this researcher while working in a summer camp.)

D. F. Fleming, "Summary and Analysis of a Study of Thirty Life History Documents of Upper-Middle-Class University Students."

D. F. Fleming, "Clubs, Associations and Status in an Upper Middle Class Community" (unpublished document in preparation for Ph.D. thesis, Department of Anthropology, University of Toronto, 1953).

D. F. Fleming and M. A. Cook, "Field Reports of Summer Camp Behavior" (typewritten, 1951).

B. M. Harris, "The School-Teacher in an Upper-Middle-Class School" (Master's dissertation, Department of Sociology, University of Chicago, 1952).

D. V. Hirtle, "A Study of Personality Characteristics of Children with Psychosomatic Disorders" (unpublished M.A. thesis, Department of Psychology, University of Toronto, 1950).

"G. J.," "The Sociology of the Classroom [in Crestwood Heights]."

"G. L.," "A Study of Community Spirit on Burnside Drive (1953)."

H. Libbey, "The Specialist: A Study of One Aspect of the Teaching Profession" (typewritten).

H. Lobb, "A Study Concerning Older-Younger Relationships [in Crestwood Heights]" (typewritten, 1950).

E. W. Loosley, "The Home and School Association as a Socializing Agency in an Upper-Middle-Class Canadian Community" (unpublished M.A. thesis, Department of Education, Division of the Social Sciences, University of Chicago, 1952).

"D. M.," "Analysis of a Women's Seminar [in Crestwood Heights]."

"G. M.," "My Family's Relations in Crestwood Heights compared with those in a Previous Place of Residence."

R. MacKenzie and J. Mahon, "Pertinent Historical and Social Data on Crestwood Heights" (typewritten, 1949).

T. J. Mallinson, "An Experimental Investigation of Group-Directed Discussion in the Classroom" (unpublished Ph.D. dissertation, Department of Psychology, University of Toronto, 1954).

L. F. Maltby, "Report on Work of the Clinical Team, Crestwood Heights Schools' Child Guidance Services" (typewritten report, submitted to the Department of Psychiatry, University of Big City, 1953).

M. A. Marshall and H. R. Matthews, "The Effect of Ordinal Position and Hebrew-Gentile Cultures on the Personality Traits of Children" (typewritten report, 1949).

L. Pettingell and J. P. Mayberry, "A History of the Jews in Big City" (typewritten, 1949).

C. Pitt, "A Study of School-leaving Patterns in Crestwood Heights" (typewritten).

V. Pullan, "A Longitudinal Study of Absenteeism among School Children and its Relation to Present Adjustment" (unpublished M.A. thesis, Department of Psychology, University of Toronto, 1950).

"F. S.," "A Sociological Study of Crestwood Heights Collegiate (1953)."

"R. S.," "Camp B'nai B'rith (1953)."

J. R. Seeley, "Bali-like Treatment of Children in Crestwood Heights" (Memorandum, Crestwood Heights Files).

J. R. Seeley, "Some Factors Involved in Securing Latin Marks at Crestwood Heights Collegiate Institute, 1947–49" (multigraphed report, 1948).

"R. T.," "Family and Friendship Patterns [in Crestwood Heights]."